Human Communication

THE BASIC COURSE

NINTH EDITION

Joseph A. DeVito

Hunter College of the City University of New York

Boston   New York   San Francisco
Mexico City   Montreal   Toronto   London   Madrid   Munich   Paris
Hong Kong   Singapore   Tokyo   Cape Town   Sydney

Vice President, Editor-in-Chief: Karen Hanson
Senior Editor: Karon Bowers
Editorial Assistant: Jennifer Trebby
Associate Development Editor: Alyssa Pratt
Marketing Manager: Mandee Eckersley
Editorial Production Administrator: Michael Granger
Editorial Production Service: Nesbitt Graphics, Inc.
Photo Researcher: Julie Tesser
Composition Buyer: Linda Cox
Manufacturing Buyer: Megan Cochran
Cover Administrator: Linda Knowles
Design and Electronic Composition: Nesbitt Graphics, Inc.

For related titles and support materials, visit our online catalog at www.ablongman.com.

Between the time Website information is gathered and then published, some sites may have closed. Also, the transcription of URLs can result in typographical errors. The publisher would appreciate notification where these occur so that they may be corrected in subsequent editions.

Many of the designations used by manufacturers and sellers to distinguish their products are claimed as trademarks. Where those designations appear in this book, and Allyn and Bacon was aware of a trademark claim, the designations have been printed in caps or initial caps.

ISBN 0-205-35390-8
CIP data not available at the time of publication.

Credits appear on page xxii, which constitutes a continuation of the copyright page.

Printed in the United States of America

10 9 8 7 6 5 4 RRD-OH 08 07 06 05 04 03

BRIEF CONTENTS

CONTENTS

CD-ROM Units

20. The Mass Media   415

21. Emotional Communication   426

22. Criticism in the Public
Speaking Classroom   441

23. Developing Special
Occasion Speeches   456

SPECIALIZED CONTENTS

Media Watch

Self-Tests

Communication @ Work

Reflections on Ethics in Human Communication

WELCOME TO *HUMAN COMMUNICATION: THE BASIC COURSE*

It's a pleasure to write a preface to a book that is now in its ninth edition. *Human Communication: The Basic Course* is designed for the introductory college course that surveys the broad field of communication. It covers classic approaches and new developments; it covers research and theory but gives coordinate attention to significant communication skills.

The book is addressed to students who have little or no prior background in communication. If this is your only communication course, *Human Communication* will provide you with a thorough foundation in the theory, research, and skills of this essential liberal art. For those of you who will take additional and advanced courses or who are beginning a major in communication, it will provide the essential foundation for more advanced and specialized study.

MAJOR FEATURES OF *HUMAN COMMUNICATION*

The ninth edition, revised in light of comments from a large number of instructors, builds on the successful features of previous editions but represents a major revision.

Website Integration

One of the most interesting developments in textbooks today is integration with the World Wide Web. This edition comes with an extensive website that complements the material presented in the text and in the typical introduction to communication course. As you'll see, the text website is extensive; it is not intended that every student read both the text and the entire website. Rather, the website is designed to offer extra avenues for pursuing topics raised in the text that will interest a wide variety of students and meet many course objectives. One student and one course might focus on the public speaking sections, another might focus more on the skill exercises, and still another on the self-tests. The textbook provides the essential foundation for all

students; the website provides an efficient means for learning more about specific areas that interest you.

Specifically, the website for this text—www. ablongman.com/devito—contains the following materials:

- **Self-Tests.** Twenty-one self-tests are offered on the website in addition to the 23 that appear in the text. These Test Yourself features include tests measuring openness in intercultural communication, shyness, directness, apprehension in conversations, the ethics of lying, politeness, satisfaction, leadership style, romanticism, assertiveness, and a variety of other traits and abilities.

- **Skill Building Exercises.** More than 30 skill exercises on the website complement those offered in the text's Building Communication Skills boxes. Among the areas covered are communication channels, contradictory messages, culture and gender, cultural beliefs, perception, listening, self-awareness and self-disclosure, conversational effectiveness, nonverbal messages, relationships, small group effectiveness, and public speaking.

- **Extensions and Elaborations.** Additional material on a variety of topics is included on the website. For example, there are additional approaches to friendship, love, and family, as well as elaborations of communication apprehension, assertiveness, and the influence of culture and gender on friendships and love. Similarly, the motivated sequence; questions of fact, value, and policy; and the speech of introduction are given more extended coverage on the website. Also included on the website are 13 skeletal outlines for a wide variety of speeches to help guide initial attempts at developing a public speech.

Additional Units

An accompanying CD-ROM offers four complete units, not available in the printed text:

- **Unit 20, Mass Media** discusses the functional and dysfunctional effects of the mass media and how you can become a more critical (and active) media consumer.

- **Unit 21, Emotional Communication** provides a concentrated focus on this one form of interpersonal communication. It covers emotions and emotional messages, obstacles in communicating emotions, and guidelines for communicating emotions effectively.

- **Unit 22, Criticism in the Public Speaking Classroom** addresses ways and means to criticize classroom speeches effectively and covers the nature and values of criticism, cultural differences, and standards and principles of criticism.

- **Unit 23, Developing Special Occasion Speeches** provides thorough coverage of a variety of special occasion speeches: speeches of introduction, presentation, and acceptance; speeches aimed at securing goodwill; and speeches of tribute. In addition, some cultural influences on the special occasion speech are considered.

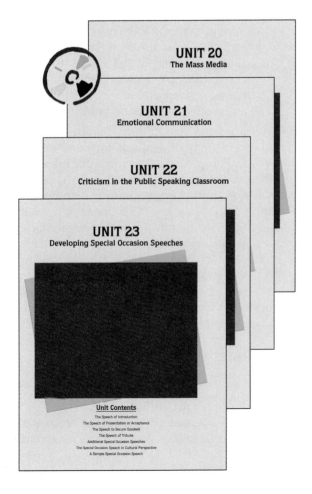

Comprehensive Coverage of Human Communication

The ninth edition of *Human Communication* offers comprehensive coverage of the fundamentals of human communication, including perception, listening, self, and verbal and nonverbal messages (Units 1–8); interpersonal communication (Units 9–11); small group communication, including interviewing (Units 12–14); and public speaking (Units 15–19). The discussion of culture, formerly Unit 6, is now Unit 3.

Balance of Theory/Research and Skills

The ninth edition gives coordinate emphasis to research and theory, on the one hand, and practical communication skills, on the other. To this end, 38 **Understanding Theory and Research** boxes appear throughout the text and highlight just a small sampling of the many theories and research findings in communication. These boxes provide an introductory explanation of how we know what we know about communication, how researchers go about expanding our knowledge of communication in all its forms, and some of the interesting theories and research findings. In addition, theories and research are discussed throughout the text. A complete list of these Understanding Theory and Research boxes appears in the Specialized Contents on page x.

Similarly, 38 **Building Communication Skills** boxes identify and provide practice in some of the more important skills in human communication. A complete list of these Building Communication Skills boxes appears in the Specialized Contents

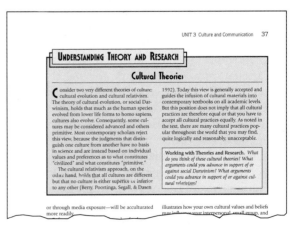

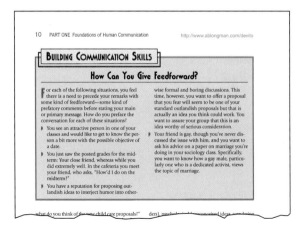

on pages x–xi. In addition, skills implications are discussed throughout the text.

Many of these boxes have been revised for this edition—tightened, focused, and updated. And a variety of new ones have been added. For example, cultural theories, the just world hypothesis, theories of gender differences, relationship commitment, relationship dialectics, conflict issues, group polarization, primacy and recency, speech rate, and signal-to-noise ratio are now featured as Understanding Theory and Research boxes. New Building Communication Skills box topics include giving feedforward; perceiving others; expressing empathy; empowering others; and constructing logical, motivational, and credibility appeals.

Thorough Coverage of Public Speaking

Five full text units are devoted to public speaking. The first three of these units cover the 10 essential steps for preparing and presenting a public speech.

Unit 15, "Public Speaking Topics, Audiences, and Research," introduces the study of public speaking, shows you how to manage your fear, and explains the first three steps for speech preparation: selecting the topic and purpose, analyzing the audience, and researching the topic.

Unit 16, "Supporting and Organizing Your Speech," covers four steps: formulating the thesis and major propositions; supporting the major propositions; organizing the speech; and constructing the conclusion, introduction, and transitions.

Unit 17, "Style and Delivery," covers the remaining three steps: wording the speech, rehearsing the speech, and presenting the speech.

The next two units (Unit 18, "The Informative Speech," and Unit 19, "The Persuasive Speech") cover informative and persuasive speeches in detail—the types of speeches and the strategies for informing and persuading an audience. In addition, two entire units on public speaking are available on the text's CD-ROM: "Criticism in the Public Speaking Classroom" and "Developing Special Occasion Speeches."

Inclusion of Cultural Issues

Like the previous edition, this edition reflects the growing importance of culture and intercultural interactions in all forms of human communication. There are few communications that are not influenced by culture in some way. Thus, a cultural consciousness is essential in any text in communication. In this ninth edition this cultural consciousness and coverage takes several forms.

First, an entire unit (Unit 3, "Culture and Communication") explains the nature of culture, some of the ways in which cultures differ from one another and the influences these differences have on communication, and some of the ways you can improve your own intercultural communication.

Cultural issues are also integrated throughout the text. Here are major examples:

- Unit 1 establishes the central role of the cultural context in all forms of communication.
- Unit 2 considers the role of culture and gender differences in the principles of communication.
- Unit 3 focuses entirely on culture.
- Unit 4 discusses the role of cultural scripts and of culture in implicit personality theory and in uncertainty.
- Unit 5 explores a variety of cultural and gender differences in listening.
- Unit 6 examines the role of culture in developing self-concept and its influence in self-disclosure.
- Unit 7 looks at cultural and gender rules in verbal messages (e.g., "rules" about directness and politeness); at sexist, heterosexist, and racist language; and the cultural identifiers people prefer.
- Unit 8 considers cultural influences on each of the major types of nonverbal communication.
- Unit 9 examines cultural influences on conversational rules, the nature of cultural sensitivity as a general conversational skill, and cultural differences in turn taking and in the qualities of conversational effectiveness.

- Unit 10 looks at cultural influences on the stages of interpersonal relationships and on relationship rules; the unit also addresses cultural bias in relationship research.
- Unit 11 discusses cultural and gender differences in interpersonal conflict and conflict resolution strategies as well as the importance of face-saving in different cultures.
- Unit 12 explores the cultural customs and differences in interviewing styles and preferences.
- Unit 13 examines the small group as a culture, the role of norms in small group communication, and the distinctions between high- and low-power-distance groups.
- Unit 14 looks at small group membership and leadership in cultural perspective.
- Unit 15 covers cultural sensitivity and speech topics, the role of culture and gender in audience analysis, and secular and sacred cultures.
- Unit 16 discusses cultural considerations in organization (high- and low-context cultures), cultural sensitivity in presentation aids, and culture shock (as illustrated by a PowerPoint speech).
- Unit 17 addresses the role of culture in emotional display and provides a sample speech outline on culture shock.
- Unit 18 discusses the cultural implications of the knowledge gap hypothesis.
- Unit 19 explains some of the cultural differences in the ways people use and respond to persuasive strategies.

In addition, much of the website material deals with cultural issues. For example, skill building exercises focus on the relationship of culture and gender, cultural beliefs as influences, and gift giving in different cultures. In the Extensions and Elaborations section there are discussions of culture, gender, and friendship; culture, gender, and love; and the role of culture in conflict. And self-tests deal with openness to intercultural communication, cultural awareness, and individualistic orientation.

Coverage of Workplace Communication

New to this edition is the application of the principles of human communication to the workplace.

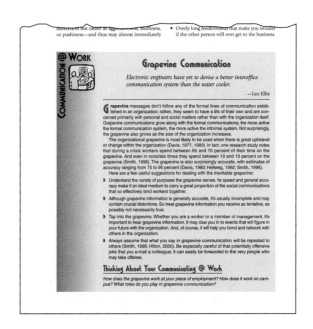

References to the workplace are integrated throughout the text. In addition, **Communication @ Work** boxes address specific workplace issues and apply the general skills of communication to the workplace context. Among the topics discussed in these boxes are communication networks, rules and norms of the workplace, power listening, grapevine communication, romance in the workplace, sexual harassment, confidence in the job interview, networking, mentoring, and information overload. Each of these boxes also contains a series of questions asking that you apply the substance and content of the box to your own communication at work. A list of these boxes appears in the Specialized Contents on page xi.

Coverage of Mass Media

The ninth edition gives new and added emphasis to mass media. First, each unit contains a **Media Watch** box that integrates mass media with the other areas of communication and sensitizes you to the ever present, ever influential media. These boxes also connect the concepts of interpersonal, small group, and public speaking with media concepts and theories. Media Watch boxes have been revised and updated for this edition and cover three major areas (discussions new to this edition appear in italics):

- **Media theories:** uses and gratifications theory (Unit 2); cultural imperialism (Unit 3), cultivation theory (Unit 4); spiral of silence (Unit 9);

UNIT 11 Interpersonal Conflict   207

MEDIA WATCH

VIOLENCE AND THE MEDIA

agenda-setting theory (Unit 14); *diffusion of innovations* (Unit 15); the knowledge gap hypothesis (Unit 18)

- **Central concepts:** media ethics (Unit 1); outing (Unit 6); *hate speech* (Unit 7); *violence and the media* (Unit 11); gatekeeping (Unit 13); media credibility (Unit 19)

- **Types and forms of media**: talk radio (Unit 5); legible clothing (Unit 8); parasocial relationships (Unit 10); television talk shows (Unit 12); *public relations* (Unit 16); *advertising* (Unit 17).

In addition, an entire unit on the mass media is available on the text's CD-ROM.

Integration of Technology

The integration of technology continues to be a special goal of *Human Communication*. The text addresses this goal in a variety of ways. First, numerous sections throughout the text cover communication via computer. For example:

- the ways in which online communication and face-to-face communication are similar and different (Units 1 and 2)

- the role of technology in easing intercultural communication (Unit 3)

- the ease of misperception in Internet interactions (Unit 4)

- self-disclosing on the Internet (Unit 6)

- politeness (netiquette) on the Net (Unit 7)

- emoticons as a form of nonverbal communication (Unit 8)

- e-mail as a form of conversation (Unit 9)

- the advantages and disadvantages of online relationships, how online and face-to-face relationships differ, and the role of online communication in relationship deterioration (Unit 10)

- online conflicts (Unit 11)

- the Web's value and how to use the Web in seeking employment and preparing for interviews (Unit 12)

- listservs and chat groups as small groups (Unit 13); leadership on the Internet (Unit 14)

- how to conduct research using e-mail, newsgroups, and the Web and how to evaluate Internet (and CD-ROM) material (Unit 15); Internet sources integrated alongside print sources throughout discussions of research materials

- a thorough discussion of computer-assisted presentations in public speaking, with suggestions for preparing slides and presenting them to an audience; illustrated by a complete slide show speech prepared in PowerPoint (Unit 16)

- the role of technology in widening the knowledge gap (Unit 18)

A second major way in which new technologies are integrated is in the **Going Online** boxes that appear throughout the text. These boxes introduce you to websites that can help you learn about and master the skills of human communication. Some of these websites are largely academic—for example, the websites of the National Communication Association and the International Listening Association—and help illustrate the breadth and depth of

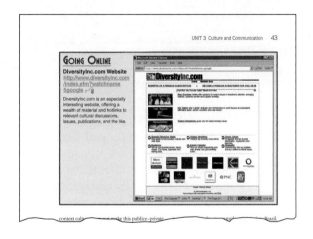

UNIT 3 Culture and Communication   43

GOING ONLINE

DiversityInc.com Website
http://www.diversityinc.com/index.efm?watchname§google

DiversityInc.com is an especially interesting website, offering a wealth of material and hotlinks to relevant cultural discussions, issues, publications, and the like.

the study of human communication. Others more playfully introduce a different perspective on human communication; for example, a website that writes love letters illustrates various theories of interpersonal relationships.

Third, this text integrates new technologies through a wide variety of ancillaries and supplements which are available with this text and focus on technology.

Coverage of Ethical Issues

New to this edition are **Reflections on Ethics in Human Communication** sections that appear at the end of each unit. These sections explore ethical principles and pose ethical dilemmas. The purpose of these sections is to connect ethical issues with the various topics of human communication and to encourage you to think about your own ethical system. Among the issues considered are censoring messages and interactions; making ethical choices; listening, speaking, and criticizing ethically; the ethics of self-monitoring, lying, interpersonal silence, gossip, and emotional appeals; ethics on the job; and the leader's ethical responsibility. A list of these Reflections on Ethics in Human Communication sections appears in the Specialized Contents on page xii.

Interactive Pedagogy

As in previous editions, *Human Communication* continues to emphasize new and useful pedagogical aids, especially those that are interactive, to help you better understand the theory and research and to enable you to effectively build and polish the skills of human communication.

- **Boxed interactives.** The Reflections on Ethics discussions, the Media Watch boxes, the Communication @ Work boxes, and the Understanding Theory and Research boxes that appear throughout the text contain interactive experiences designed to encourage you to interact with the concepts and relate these insights to your own everyday communication.

- **Self-tests.** Twenty-three popular interactive self-tests, called "Test Yourself," appear in this edition. These self-tests are designed to help personalize the material and appear throughout the text. Each self-test ends with a two-part discussion: *How did you do?* (which contains the scoring instructions and at times general norms) and *What will you do?* (which asks about the appropriate course of action that might be taken, given the insight the test provided). A list of these self-tests appears in the Specialized Contents on page xi.

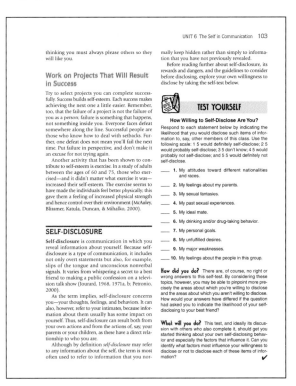

- **Critical thinking questions.** These questions, appearing at the end of each unit, now focus more clearly on the central concepts and skills of the unit. You can use these questions to expand on, evaluate, and apply the concepts, theories, and research findings discussed in the text.

- **Key terms and glossary.** A list of key terms is provided at the end of each unit to help you review the major terms and concepts discussed in the unit. In addition, a thorough glossary at the end of the book provides brief definitions of significant concepts and skills in the study of human communication.

- **Unit openers.** The major topics covered in the unit and the learning goals (both theory and skills) that you should be able to achieve are identified in the unit opener.

- **Summary statements.** At the end of each unit, a list of summary propositions review the essential concepts and principles covered in the unit.

ANCILLARIES/SUPPLEMENTARY MATERIALS

Instructor Supplements

Print Supplements

- **Instructor's Manual/Test Bank** by Richard Fiordo, North Dakota State University.

  This Instructor's Manual/Test Bank includes unit objectives, unit outlines, a wealth of thought-provoking discussion questions, and activities. The Test Bank contains hundreds of challenging multiple-choice, true–false, short answer, and essay questions along with an answer key. The questions closely follow the text units and are cross-referenced with corresponding page numbers.

- **Computerized Test Bank**

  The printed Test Bank is also available electronically through our computerized testing system, TestGen EQ. The fully networkable test generating software is now available on a multiplatform CD-ROM. The user-friendly interface enables instructors to view, edit, and add questions, transfer questions to tests, and print tests in a variety of fonts. Search and sort features allow instructors to locate questions quickly and arrange them in a preferred order.

- **A Guide for New Teachers of Introduction to Communication** by Susanna G. Porter, Kennesaw State University.

- This instructor's guide is designed to help new teachers effectively teach the introductory communication course.

- **The ESL Guide for Public Speaking** by Debra Gonsher Vinik, Bronx Community College of the City University of New York.

  This guide provides strategies and resources for instructors teaching in a bilingual or multilingual classroom. It also includes suggestions for further reading and a listing of related websites.

- **Allyn & Bacon Public Speaking Transparency Package**

  This set, produced using PowerPoint, includes 100 full-color transparencies.

- **The Blockbuster Approach: Teaching Interpersonal Communication with Video, 2/e,** by Thomas E. Jewell, Marymount College.

  This guide provides lists and descriptions of commercial videos that can be used in the classroom to illustrate interpersonal concepts and complex interpersonal relationships. Sample activities are included.

- **Great Ideas for Teaching Speech** by Raymond Zeuschner, California Polytechnic State University.

  This book provides descriptions of and guidelines for assignments successfully used by experienced public speaking instructors in their classrooms.

- **Interpersonal Challenge 3 Card Game**

  A classroom interactive exercise concerning self-perception, ethics, interpersonal relationships, and intercultural communication.

Electronic Supplements

- **Allyn & Bacon Digital Media Archive for Communication, Version 2.0**

  This CD-ROM offers still images, video clips, and assorted lecture resources that can be incorporated into multimedia presentations in the classroom.

- **PowerPoint Presentation Package for *Human Communication*, 9/e,** (available on the Web— www.ablongman.com/ppt) by Dan Cavanaugh.

  This text-specific package consists of a collection of lecture outlines and graphic images keyed to every chapter in the text.

- **Allyn & Bacon PowerPoint Presentation for Introduction to Communication** (available on the Web—www.ablongman.com/ppt).

This PowerPoint presentation includes approximately 50 slides that cover a range of communication topics: public speaking, interpersonal communication, group communication, mass media, and interviewing.

- **Allyn & Bacon PowerPoint Presentation for Public Speaking** (available on the Web—www.ablongman.com/ppt).

  This PowerPoint presentation includes 125 slides and a brief user's guide.

- **Allyn & Bacon Student Speeches Video Library**

  Instructors have their choice of one video from a collection of seven videos that includes three 2-hour American Forensic Association videos of award-winning student speeches and four videos with a range of student speeches delivered in the classroom. Some restrictions apply.

- **Allyn & Bacon Public Speaking Key Topics Video Library**

  This library contains three videos that address core topics covered in the classroom: Critiquing Student Speeches, Speaker Apprehension, and Addressing Your Audience. Some restrictions apply.

- **Allyn & Bacon Public Speaking Video**

  This video includes excerpts of classic and contemporary public speeches and student speeches to illustrate the public speaking process.

- **Video: Interpersonal Communication with Guidebook**

  Eight interpersonal scenarios examine a wide range of interpersonal issues. An extensive guide provides a script, class discussion questions, and exercises for each of the episodes.

- **Allyn & Bacon Interpersonal Communication Video**

  This interpersonal video contains three scenarios illustrating key concepts in interpersonal communication with a guide featuring transcripts and teaching activities. A separate video guide is available as well.

- **Allyn & Bacon Communication Video Library**

  A collection of communication videos produced by Films for the Humanities and Sciences. Contact your local Allyn & Bacon sales representative for ordering information. Some restrictions apply.

- **VideoWorkshop for Introduction to Communication Instructor's Teaching Guide,** by Edward Lee Lamoureux, Bradley University.

  This guide provides teaching suggestions and answers that will help instructors use the *VideoWorkshop for Introduction to Communication CD-ROM* in class. A correlation guide helps you relate the materials to your text. The complete CD-ROM and the pages from the Student Learning Guide are included. Go to www.ablongman.com/videoworkshop for more details.

- **CourseCompass**

  CourseCompass, powered by Blackboard, is the most flexible online course management system on the market today. By using this powerful suite of online tools in conjunction with Allyn & Bacon's preloaded textbook and testing content, you can create an online presence for your course in under 30 minutes. Log on at www.coursecompass.com and find out how you can get the most out of this dynamic teaching resource.

Student Supplements

Print Supplements

- **Preparing Visual Aids for Presentations, 3/e,** by Dan Cavanaugh.

  This 32-page booklet provides ideas to improve presentations, including suggestions for planning a presentation, guidelines for designing visual aids, storyboarding, and a PowerPoint presentation walk-through.

- **Public Speaking in the Multicultural Environment, 2/e,** by Devorah A. Lieberman, Portland State University.

  This booklet helps students learn to analyze cultural diversity within their audiences and adapt their presentations accordingly.

- **Speech Preparation Workbook** by Jennifer Dreyer and Gregory H. Patton, San Diego State University.

  This workbook takes students through the various stages of speech creation—from audience analysis to writing the speech—and provides supplementary assignments and tear-out forms.

- **Outlining Workbook** by Reeze L. Hanson and Sharon Condon, Haskell Indian Nations University.

This workbook includes activities, exercises, and answers to help students develop and master the critical skill of outlining.

- **Brainstorms** by Joseph A. DeVito.

  A guide to thinking more creatively about communication, or anything else. Students will find 19 practical, easy-to-use creative thinking techniques along with insights into the creative thinking process.

- **Studying Communication** by Joseph A. DeVito.

  An introduction to the study of any of the forms of communication. This guide helps students learn how to conduct research and get the most out of the communication classroom—whether attending a lecture, taking notes, reading a textbook, taking a test, or writing a research paper.

- **ContentSelect: A Student's Guide for Speech Communication**

  This guidebook includes information on how to access and use ContentSelect, a research database, as well as tips for conducting searches and citing research materials in a paper.

- **iSearch for Speech Communication**

  This resource guide for the Internet covers the basics of using the Internet, conducting Web searches, and critically evaluating and documenting Internet sources. It also contains Internet activities and URLs specific to the disipline of speech communication.

Electronic Supplements

- **DeVito** *Human Communication, 9/e,* **Student CD-ROM with Bonus Units**

  This CD-ROM contains four additional units that are not available anywhere else: Mass Media, Emotional Communication, Criticism in the Public Speaking Classroom, and Developing Special Occasion Speeches. Available on request in a special package with a new textbook. Ask your local representative for details.

- **Interactive Speechwriter Software, Version 1.1 (Windows and Macintosh)** by Martin R. Cox.

  This interactive software package for student purchase provides supplemental material, writing templates (for the informative, persuasive, and motivated sequence speeches, as well as for outlines), sample student speeches (text only), and

more! This program enhances students' understanding of key concepts discussed in the text and is available for Windows and Macintosh.

- **Speech Writer's Workshop CD-ROM 2.0**

  This interactive software will assist students with speech preparation and will enable them to write better speeches. The software includes four separate features: (1) a speech handbook with tips for researching and preparing speeches plus information about grammar, usage, and syntax; (2) a speech workshop that guides students through the speech-writing process and includes a series of questions at each stage; (3) a topics dictionary containing hundreds of speech ideas—all divided into subcategories to help students with outlining and organization; and (4) a citation database that formats bibliographic entries in MLA or APA style.

- **Companion Website Plus with Online Practice Tests** (http://www.ablongman.com/devito) by Joseph A. DeVito and Elizabeth Lindsey, New Mexico State University.

  This site includes self-tests, skill building exercises, and extensions and elaborations on the text. The website also includes an online study guide with practice tests and weblinks.

- **VideoWorkshop for Introduction to Communication Student Learning Guide,** by Edward Lee Lamoureux, Bradley University.

  This combination *VideoWorkshop Student Learning Guide* and CD-ROM package contains all the materials students need to get started: CD-ROM containing specially selected video clips and a tear-out page workbook with Learning Objectives, Web Links, Observation Questions, Next Step Questions, and a multiple choice quiz.

- **VideoWorkshop for Introduction to Communication CD-ROM,** by Edward Lee Lamoureux, Bradley University.

  This CD-ROM, available only in the Student Learning Guide or the Instructor's Teaching Guide for this VideoWorkshop, contains video clips that have been specially chosen to illustrate various communication concepts.

- **ContentSelect**

  Order access to ContentSelect for your students! This free research database, searchable by keyword, gives you immediate access to hundreds of scholarly journals and other popular publications. Ask your local representative for details.

- **CourseCompass Student PIN**

  This PIN code, available packaged with a new text, provides your students with access to your course set up in CourseCompass (see description under Instructor's Electronic Supplements).

ACKNOWLEDGMENTS

It's a real pleasure to thank the many people who contributed to this book. Karon Bowers served admirably as editor and supported the book with state of the art ancillaries. Her advice throughout the process was always helpful. It was a pleasure to work again with developmental editor, Nancy Crochiere, who offered a wealth of valuable suggestions throughout the process. I'm also grateful to Susan McIntyre, project manager at Nesbitt Graph-

ics, for guiding the process from manuscript to published book with extraordinary efficiency; Julie Tesser, photo researcher, for finding the great photos that appear here; and Jay Howland for her careful and insightful edits. Alyssa Pratt, Associate Development Editor, did a great job of assembling and coordinating the various ancillaries and, together with those who wrote various materials, made the supplements for this text truly outstanding.

I also owe a great debt to the reviewers who carefully read and commented upon this manuscript and who gave freely of their numerous and valuable insights: Holly Carolyn Baxter, University of Dayton; Robbin D. Crabtree, New Mexico State University; Quinton Davis, University of Texas at San Antonio; Randall Koper, University of the Pacific; Mitchell Perkins, Community College of Baltimore County; and Beth Richardson Mitchell, Mayland Community College. I incorporated many of their suggestions and the book is much improved for them.

CREDITS

Text and Illustrations

9: Used by permission of the National Communication Association, www.natcom.org.
25: Permission granted by the International Communication Association, www.icahdq.org.
43: Copyright © Diversity Inc.com, www.diversityinc.com. Reprinted by permission.
61: Courtesy of Dr. John Krantz. http://krantzj.hanover.edu.
84: International Listening Association, www.listen.org. Reprinted by permission.
99: Reprinted by permission of Selfgrowth.com, www.selfgrowth.com.
125: Web site by Homer J. Moore, Jr., www.general-semantics.org. Reprinted by permission.
138: Table 8.1: From Joseph A. DeVito, *Messages: Building Interpersonal Communication Skills*, Fifth Edition. Copyright © 2002. Reprinted by permission of Allyn & Bacon.
138: Courtesy of Peter Kruizinga, http://www.cs.rug.nl/~peterkr/FACE/face.html.
175: From Allyn & Bacon websites, www.abacon.com. Copyright © 1999. Reprinted by permission of Allyn & Bacon.
200: Copyright © Nando Media, http://www.nandomedia.com. Reprinted by permission.
215: Courtesy of Famvi.com, www.famvi.com.
234: Courtesy of Monster.com, www.monster.com.
251: From Allyn & Bacon websites, www.abacon.com. Copyright © 1999. Reprinted by permission of Allyn & Bacon.
272: Reprinted with permission of The Academy of Leadership, University of Maryland, www.academy.umd.edu.
292: From Allyn & Bacon websites, www.abacon.com. Copyright © 1997. Reprinted by permission of Allyn & Bacon.
320: Courtesy of Federal Statistics website, www.fedstats.gov/map.html.
359: Courtesy of Northwestern University's School of Speech, http://douglass.speech.nwu.edu.
379: Courtesy of Gifts of Speech, http://gos.sbc.edu.
394: Courtesy of Aaron Delwiche, http://carmen.artsci.washington.edu/propaganda.

Photos

1: Michael Doolittle/The Image Works; **7:** Bob Daemmrich/The Image Works; **13:** David R. Frazier; **19:** Sotographs/Liaison Agency/Getty Images; **24:** Kathy McLaughlin/The Image Works; **26:** Globe Photos, Inc.; **35:** Steve Niedorf/The Image Bank; **49:** John Riley/Stone/Getty Images; **55:** The Kobal Collection; **58:** Art Montes de Oca/FPG International/Getty Images; **65:** HBO/ MPTV; **77:** R. W. Jones/Corbis; **80:** Bob Daemmrich Photo, Inc.; **95:** Richard Lord/PhotoEdit, Inc.; **101:** AP/Wide World Photos; **105:** Bob Daemmrich/Stock Boston; **113:** Michael Newman/PhotoEdit, Inc.; **121:** Felicia Martinez/PhotoEdit, Inc.; **128:** Timothy Shonnard/Stone/Getty Images; **133:** Pictor Uniphoto; **146:** Walter Hodges/Corbis; **160:** © Stuart Cohen/The Image Works; **177:** Yellow Dog Productions/The Image Bank; **181:** Stone/Getty Images; **195:** Jim Whitmer; **198:** Andrew Lichtenstein/The Image Works; **205:** Bob Daemmrich Photo, Inc.; **211:** John Nordell/The Image Works; **216:** Jim Whitmer; **225:** AP/Wide World Photos; **241:** Bob Daemmrich/The Image Works; **245:** Chuck Savage/The Stock Market; **249:** Charles Gupton/Stock Boston; **266:** Globe Photos, Inc.; **274:** Dan Bosler/Stone/Getty Images; **285:** K. Shamsi-Basha/The Image Works; **299:** Michael Newman/PhotoEdit; **331:** Walter Hodges/Stone/Getty Images; **343:** Stone/Getty Images; **356:** Dratch/The Image Works; **371:** Richard Hutchings/PhotoEdit; **378:** Joe Gaffney/Retna Limited; **389:** Bob Daemmrich/Stock Boston; **404:** Pictor Uniphoto.

UNIT 1
Preliminaries to Human Communication

Unit Contents

Elements of Human Communication

Purposes of Human Communication

Types of Human Communication

Of all the knowledge and skills you have, those concerning communication will prove the most important and the most useful. They will always influence and play a crucial part in how effectively you live your personal and professional lives. And so it's vital to your success to learn how communication works and how you can master its most essential skills. In this first unit you'll learn:

▶ what communication is, the purposes it serves, and the forms it takes

▶ how understanding the way communication works can help you achieve a variety of personal and professional purposes

ELEMENTS OF HUMAN COMMUNICATION

Your communication knowledge and skills are among your most important assets. Your communication competence will prove useful in your personal, social, and professional life; in many cases, it may make the difference between failure and success. You use the knowledge and skills of communication in just about everything you do—asking for directions, discussing a movie with friends, interviewing for a job, persuading an audience to do something, watching television, or surfing the net. These communication abilities also play a significant part (perhaps the most significant part) in all your interactions—from making friends and lifelong partners, to resolving inevitable conflicts, to networking for professional advantage, to working on a team solving a problem, to informing and persuading large groups. Your communication knowledge and skills will prove of value whether you're speaking or listening.

More formally, **communication** occurs when one person (or more) sends and receives messages that are distorted by noise, occur within a context, have some effect, and provide some opportunity for feedback. This introductory unit explains the various parts of this definition and identifies the purposes and types of human communication. Throughout this explanation—and, in fact, throughout this book—the text makes reference to both face-to-face and electronic communication. No matter how sophisticated, electronic communication is still very similar to ordinary face-to-face interactions. For example, electronic communication allows for the same types of communication as does face-to-face interaction, whether interpersonal, small group, or public. In Internet communication you put your thoughts into words that you type on your keyboard and send via modem or cable; simi-

larly, in speech you put your thoughts into spoken words and send your sounds through the air.

Two-person, or interpersonal, communication can occur face-to-face or on the phone or through e-mail or snail mail. Similarly, you engage in interpersonal communication in chat groups when you "whisper" or single out just one person to receive your message instead of the entire group. In chat groups you can talk with a small group of others in ways similar to the way you'd talk around a table in the cafeteria or in a business organization or in a telephone or video conference. In newsgroups posting a message for members to read is in many ways similar to the way you express your thoughts in delivering a public speech to an audience. Of course, there are also differences between face-to-face and electronic communications, which we'll discuss as we consider the various forms of human communication throughout the text.

Before reading about these elements, think about your beliefs about communication by taking the self-test below.

 TEST YOURSELF

What Do You Believe about Communication?

Respond to each of the following statements with T (true) if you believe the statement is usually true and F (false) if you believe the statement is usually false.

_____ **1.** Good communicators are born, not made.

_____ **2.** The more a couple communicates, the better their relationship will be.

_____ **3.** Unlike effective speaking, effective listening can't be taught.

_____ **4.** Opening lines such as "How are you?" or "Fine weather today" or "Have you got a light?" serve no really useful communication purpose.

_____ 5. When two people are in a close relationship for a long period of time, one should not have to communicate his or her needs and wants; the other person should know what these are.

_____ 6. When verbal and nonverbal messages contradict each other, people believe the verbal message.

_____ 7. Complete openness should be the goal of any meaningful interpersonal relationship.

_____ 8. When there is interpersonal conflict, each person should aim to win even at the expense of the other person.

_____ 9. Like good communicators, leaders are born, not made.

_____ 10. Fear of speaking in public is detrimental and must be eliminated.

How did you do? As you may have figured out, all 10 statements are generally false. As you read this text, you'll discover not only why these beliefs are false but also the trouble you can get into when you assume they're true. Briefly, here are some of the reasons why each of the statements is generally false:

1. Effective communication is a learned skill; although some people are born brighter or more extroverted, all can improve their abilities and become more effective communicators.

2. If you practice bad habits, you're more likely to grow less effective than to become more effective; consequently, it's important to learn and follow the principles of effectiveness.

3. Like speaking, listening is a learned skill and can be improved, as you'll discover when you read Unit 5.

4. Actually, these "openers" serve an important social function; they literally open the channels of communication and pave the way for what is to follow (Unit 9).

5. This assumption is at the heart of many interpersonal difficulties—people aren't mind readers and to assume that they are merely sets up barriers to open and honest communication (Unit 10).

6. Whether you believe the verbal or the nonverbal messages depends on the total communication context, but generally research does find that people are more likely to believe the nonverbal messages (Units 7 and 8).

7. Although you may feel ethically obligated to be totally honest, this is generally not an effective strategy.

8. Interpersonal conflict does not have to involve a winner and a loser; both people can win, as demonstrated in Unit 11.

9. Leadership, like communication and listening, is a learned skill that you'll develop as you learn the principles of human communication in general and of group leadership in particular (Units 13 and 14).

10. Most speakers are nervous; managing, not eliminating, the fear will enable you to become effective regardless of your current level of fear (Unit 15).

What will you do? Consider how these beliefs about communication influence the way you communicate. Then, as you read this book and participate in class discussions and activities, reexamine your beliefs about communication and consider how new beliefs would influence the way you communicate. The theories and research discussed in this text will help you reconsider your own beliefs about communication, and the skill building activities will help you practice new ways of communicating. Two excellent websites containing a variety of self-tests on emotional intelligence, personality, knowledge, relationships, careers, and more are http://www.allthetests.com and www.queendom.com/tests. ✔

Figure 1.1 on page 4 illustrates the elements present in all communication acts, whether intrapersonal, interpersonal, small group, public speaking, or mass communication—or whether face-to-face, by telephone, or over the Internet.

Communication Context

All communication takes place in a **context** that has at least four dimensions: physical, social–psychological, temporal, and cultural. The *physical context* is the tangible or concrete environment in which communication takes place—the room or hallway or park. This physical context exerts some influence on the content of your messages (what you say) as well as on the form (how you say it).

The *social–psychological context* includes, for example, the status relationships among the participants, the roles and the games that people play, and the cultural rules of the society in which people are communicating. It also includes the friendliness or unfriendliness, formality or informality, and seriousness or humorousness of the situation. Communication that would be permitted at a graduation party might not be considered appropriate in a hospital.

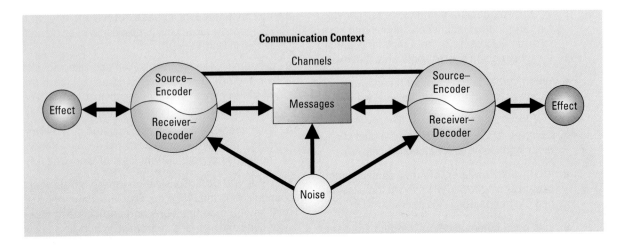

Figure 1.1
The Elements of Human Communication

This is a simplified view of the elements of human communication and their relationship to one another. Messages (including feedforward and feedback) are sent simultaneously through a variety of channels from one encoder–decoder to another. The communication process takes place in a context (physical, cultural, social–psychological, and temporal) and is subjected to interference by noise (physical, psychological, and semantic). The interaction of messages with the encoder–decoder leads to some effect.

The *temporal (or time) context* includes the time of day as well as the time in history in which the communication takes place. For many people, the morning is not a time for communication. For others, the morning is ideal. Historical context is no less important—because the appropriateness and impact of messages depend, in part, on the time in which they're uttered. Consider, for example, how messages on racial, sexual, or religious attitudes and values would be differently framed and responded to in different times in history.

Still another aspect of time is how a message fits into the sequence of communication events. For example, consider the varied meanings a "simple" compliment paid to a friend would have depending on whether you said it immediately after your friend paid you a compliment, immediately before you asked your friend for a favor, or during an argument.

The *cultural context* has to do with your (and others') **culture**: the beliefs, values, and ways of behaving that are shared by a group of people and passed down from one generation to the next. Cultural factors affect every interaction and influence what you say and how you say it. As you'll see throughout this book, the communication strategies and principles that work with members of

one culture may not work with members of other cultures. And this is why intercultural communication is so difficult and why culture is so crucial to communication.

These dimensions of context interact with one another. For example, arriving late for an appointment (temporal context) might violate a cultural rule, which might lead to changes in the social–psychological context, perhaps creating tension and unfriendliness, which in turn might lead to changes in the physical context—for example, choosing a less intimate restaurant for your lunch meeting.

Sources–Receivers

The compound term *sources–receivers* emphasizes that each person involved in communication is both a **source** (or speaker) and a **receiver** (or listener). You send messages when you speak, write, gesture, or smile. You receive messages in listening, reading, smelling, and so on. As you send messages, however, you're also receiving messages. You're receiving your own messages (you hear yourself, you feel your own movements, you see many of your own gestures), and you're receiving the messages of the other person—visually, aurally, or even through touch or smell. As you assign meaning to

UNDERSTANDING THEORY AND RESEARCH

Communication Theories

A **theory** is a generalization that explains how something works—for example, gravity, blood clotting, interpersonal attraction, or communication. In academic writing, the term *theory* is usually reserved for a well-established system of knowledge about how things work or how things are related.

The theories you'll encounter in this book try to explain how communication works; for example, how people accommodate their speaking style to their listeners, how communication works when relationships deteriorate, how friends self-disclose, how problem-solving groups communicate, how speakers influence audiences, and how the media affect people. As you can see from even these few examples, theories provide general principles that help you understand an enormous number of specific events—how and why these events occur and how they're related to each other.

Communication theories also help you predict future events. The theories summarize what's been found and can therefore offer reasonable predictions for events that you've never encountered. For example, theories of persuasion can enable you to predict whether strong, medium, or weak appeals to fear will be more effective in persuading an audience. Or theories of conflict resolution can help you predict what strategies will prove most effective in resolving differences.

Working with Theories and Research. *Try to develop your own communication theory about what verbal and nonverbal cues would lead you to assume someone was lying. (Then take a look at Understanding Theory and Research: Cues to Lying, p. 85.) Or try to develop your own theory as to the kinds of opening lines that work most effectively in beginning a relationship. (Then take a look at Understanding Theory and Research: Opening Lines, p. 161.)*

these verbal and nonverbal signals, you're performing receiving functions.

Source–Receiver Encoding–Decoding

The act of producing messages—for example, speaking or writing—is called **encoding**. By putting your ideas into sound waves or into a computer program you're putting these ideas into a **code**, hence encoding. The act of receiving messages—for example, listening or reading—is called **decoding**. By translating sound waves or words on a screen into ideas you take them out of code, hence decoding. Thus, speakers or writers are called **encoders**, and listeners or readers, **decoders**.

Like sources–receivers, the compound term *encoding–decoding* emphasizes that you perform these functions simultaneously, at least in face-to-face communication. As you speak (encoding), you're also deciphering the responses of the listener (decoding). In computer communication this simultaneous exchange of messages occurs only sometimes. In e-mail (as well as snail mail) and newsgroup communication, for example, the sending and receiving may be separated by several days or much longer. In chat groups and instant messaging, on the other hand, communication takes place in real time; the sending and receiving take place (almost) simultaneously.

Source–Receiver Communication Competence

The term **communication competence** refers to your knowledge of the social aspects of communication (Rubin, 1982, 1985; Spitzberg & Cupach, 1989). It includes knowledge of such factors as the role of context in influencing the content and form of communication messages—for example, the knowledge that in certain contexts and with certain listeners one topic is appropriate and another is not. Knowledge about the rules of nonverbal behavior—for example, the appropriateness of touching, vocal volume, and physical closeness—is also part of communication competence. The term *communication competence* is also taken to include your ability to apply this knowledge in communicating. So when you read about communication competence, realize that it includes both an understanding of how communication works and the ability to use this understanding in communicat-

ing effectively. Keep in mind, however, that communication competence is culture specific; the way communication works and the elements that make it effective differ from one culture to another.

Messages and Channels

Communication **messages** take many forms. You send and receive messages through any one or any

COMMUNICATION @ WORK

Communication in the Workplace

Organizations are almost entirely determined by communication techniques.

—Chester Barnard

Workplace communication consists of all the messages sent and received within an organization. As the organization becomes larger and more complex, so do the communications. In a three-person organization, communication is relatively simple, but in an organization of thousands it becomes highly complex. Workplace communication includes such varied activities as giving directions, counseling workers, interviewing new employees, evaluating personnel, motivating workers, analyzing problems, resolving conflicts, and establishing and monitoring work groups. These communications rely on the interpersonal, small group, and public communication skills discussed throughout this text—skills that are considered essential in just about every area of work (Morreale, Osborn, & Pearson, 2000).

Workplace communication may be either formal or informal. The formal communications are those that are sanctioned by the organization itself and are organizationally oriented. They deal with the workings of the organization, with productivity, and with the various jobs done throughout the organization; they include memos, policy statements, press releases, and employee newsletters. Another type of formal organizational communication is that which takes place between one organization and another and between the organization and the public; for example, advertising and public relations messages. The informal communications are socially sanctioned. These focus not on the organization itself but on the individual members and might concern celebrations of birthdays or anniversaries, discussions of family problems, feelings about the organization and the job, or plans for the future.

Because we all engage in workplace communication and because our communication effectiveness in the workplace has significant consequences—affecting our chances of getting a job, working comfortably and effectively with colleagues, and rising in the organization—workplace communication is given special prominence in this text. The skills of human communication, which form the basis for effectiveness in all communication, are covered throughout the text, but special Communication @ Work boxes are included in each unit to further emphasize the connection between the theories and skills discussed in the text and the very real world of the workplace.

Thinking about Your Communicating @ Work

What kinds of workplace communication will be most important to you in your professional life? What skills will you need to rise in the organizational hierarchy?

combination of sensory organs. Although you may customarily think of messages as being verbal (oral or written), you also communicate nonverbally. For example, the clothes you wear and the way you walk, shake hands, cock your head, comb your hair, sit, and smile all communicate messages. Everything about you communicates.

In face-to-face communication the actual message signals (the movements in the air) are evanescent; they fade almost as they're uttered. Some written messages, especially computer-mediated messages such as those sent via e-mail, are unerasable. E-mails that are sent among employees in a large corporation, for example, are often stored on disk or tape. Currently, much litigation is using as evidence racist or sexist e-mails that senders thought were erased, but weren't.

The communication **channel** is the medium through which the message passes. Communication rarely takes place over only one channel; you may use two, three, or four different channels simultaneously. For example, in face-to-face interactions you speak and listen (vocal channel), but you also gesture and receive signals visually (visual channel). In chat groups you type and read words and use various symbols and abbreviations to communicate the emotional tone of the message. If your computer system is especially sophisticated, you may communicate via the Internet through audio and visual means as well. In addition, in face-to-face communication you emit and detect odors (olfactory channel). Often you touch another person,

and this too communicates (tactile channel). An exercise designed to clarify the nature of channels, "How do you use communication channels?" may be found at **www.ablongman.com/devito**.

Two special types of messages need to be explained more fully; these are feedback (the messages you send that are reactions to other messages) and feedforward (the messages you send as preface to your "main" messages). Both feedback and feedforward are **metamessages**—messages that communicate about other messages. Such communication about communication, or **metacommunication**, may be verbal ("I agree with you" or "Wait until you hear this one") or nonverbal (a smile or a prolonged pause). Or, as is most often the case, it's some combination of verbal and nonverbal signals.

Feedback Messages

Throughout the listening process, a listener gives a speaker **feedback**—messages sent back to the speaker reacting to what is said. Feedback tells the speaker what effect he or she is having on the listener(s). This can take many forms; a frown or a smile, a yea or a nay, a pat on the back or a punch in the mouth are all types of feedback. On the basis of this feedback, the speaker may adjust the messages by strengthening, deemphasizing, or changing the content or form of the messages. These adjustments then serve as feedback to the receiver—who, in response, readjusts his or her feedback messages. The process is a circular one, with one person's feedback serving as the stimulus for the other person's

In what ways do you speak and listen differently when communicating face-to-face versus in e-mail, Internet chat groups, or newsgroups?

feedback, just as any message serves as the stimulus for another person's message.

Another type of feedback is the feedback you get from listening to yourself; you hear what you say, you feel the way you move, you see what you write. On the basis of this self-feedback you adjust your messages; for example, you may correct a mispronunciation, shorten your story, or increase your volume.

You can view feedback in terms of five important dimensions: positive–negative, person-focused–message-focused, immediate–delayed, low-monitored–high-monitored, and supportive–critical.

Positive–Negative. Positive feedback (applause, smiles, and head nods signifying approval) tells the speaker that the message is being well received and that he or she should continue speaking in the same general mode. Negative feedback (boos, frowns, puzzled looks, gestures signifying disapproval) tells the speaker that something is wrong and that some adjustment needs to be made.

Person-Focused–Message-Focused. Feedback may center on the person ("You're sweet," "You've a great smile") or on the message ("Can you repeat that phone number?" "Your argument is a good one").

Immediate–Delayed. In interpersonal situations feedback is most often conveyed immediately after the message is received. In other communication situations, however, the feedback may be delayed; in interview situations, for example, the feedback may come weeks after the interview. In media situations some feedback comes immediately—for example, through Nielsen ratings; other feedback comes much later, through viewing and buying patterns.

Low-Monitored–High-Monitored. Feedback varies from the spontaneous and totally honest reaction (low-monitored feedback) to the carefully constructed response designed to serve a specific purpose (high-monitored feedback). In most interpersonal situations you probably give feedback spontaneously; you allow your responses to show without any monitoring. At other times, however, you may be more guarded, as when your boss asks you how you like your job or when your grandmother asks what you think of her holiday fruitcake.

Supportive–Critical. Supportive feedback confirms the worth of the person and what that person says; it occurs when, for example, you console another or when you encourage the other to talk; it often involves affirmation of the person's self-definition. Critical feedback, on the other hand, is evaluative. When you give critical feedback you judge another's performance—as in, for example, evaluating a speech or coaching someone learning a new skill.

Each feedback opportunity, then, presents you with choices along at least these five dimensions. To use feedback effectively you need to make educated choices along these dimensions. Realize that

BUILDING COMMUNICATION SKILLS

How Can You Give Feedback?

How would you give feedback (positive or negative? person-focused or message-focused? immediate or delayed? low-monitored or high-monitored? supportive or critical?) in these varied situations? Write one or two sentences of feedback for each situation:

▶ A friend—someone you like but don't have romantic feelings for—asks you for a date.

▶ Your instructor asks you to evaluate the course.

▶ An interviewer asks if you want a credit card.

▶ A homeless person smiles at you on the street.

▶ A colleague at work tells a homophobic joke.

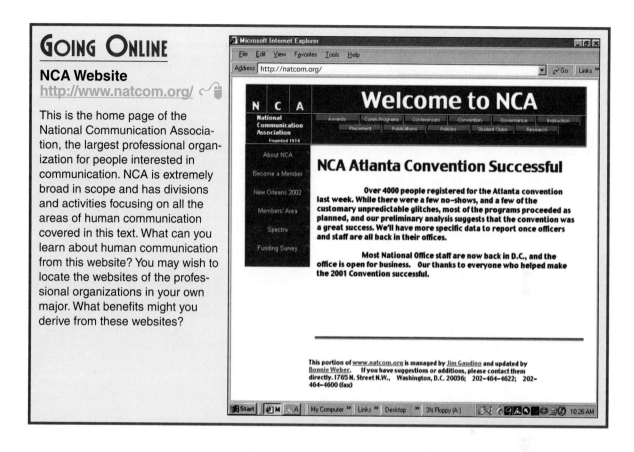

GOING ONLINE

NCA Website
http://www.natcom.org/

This is the home page of the National Communication Association, the largest professional organization for people interested in communication. NCA is extremely broad in scope and has divisions and activities focusing on all the areas of human communication covered in this text. What can you learn about human communication from this website? You may wish to locate the websites of the professional organizations in your own major. What benefits might you derive from these websites?

these categories are not exclusive. Feedback does not have to be either critical or supportive; it can be both. Thus, in teaching someone how to become a more effective interviewer, you might critically evaluate a specific interview but you might also express support for the effort. Similarly, you might respond to a friend's question immediately and then after a day or two elaborate on your response.

Feedforward Messages

Feedforward is information you provide before sending your primary messages; it reveals something about the messages to come (Richards, 1951). Feedforward includes such diverse examples as the preface or the table of contents in a book, the opening paragraph of a chapter, movie previews, magazine covers, and introductions in public speeches. Feedforward has four major functions: (1) to open the channels of communication, (2) to preview the message, (3) to altercast, and (4) to disclaim.

To Open the Channels of Communication.
Often we preface our messages with comments whose only function is to open the channels of

communication (Malinowski, 1923; Lu, 1998). The infamous "opening line" ("Do you come here often?" or "Haven't we met before?") is a clear example of this type of feedforward. In fact, when such feedforward messages don't precede an initial interaction, you sense that something is wrong and may conclude that the speaker lacks the basic skills of communication.

To Preview Future Messages. Feedforward messages frequently preview other messages. Feedforward may, for example, preview the content ("I have news for you"), the importance ("Listen to this before you make a move"), the form or style ("I'll be brief"), or the positive or negative quality of subsequent messages ("You're not going to like this, but here's what I heard").

To Altercast. The type of feedforward known as **altercasting** asks the receiver to approach your message from a particular role or even as someone else (McLaughlin, 1984; Weinstein & Deutschberger, 1963; Johnson, 1993; Pratkanis, 2000). For example, you might ask a friend, "As a single mother,

BUILDING COMMUNICATION SKILLS

How Can You Give Feedforward?

For each of the following situations, you feel there is a need to precede your remarks with some kind of feedforward—some kind of prefatory comments—before stating your main or primary message. How do you preface the conversation for each of these situations?

▶ You see an attractive person in one of your classes and would like to get to know the person a bit more with the possible objective of a date.

▶ You just saw the posted grades for the midterm: Your close friend failed, whereas you did extremely well. In the cafeteria you meet your friend, who asks, "How'd I do on the midterm?"

▶ You have a reputation for proposing outlandish ideas to interject humor into other-

wise formal and boring discussions. This time, however, you want to offer a proposal that you fear will seem to be one of your standard outlandish proposals but that is actually an idea you think could work. You want to assure your group that this is an idea worthy of serious consideration.

▶ Your friend is gay, though you've never discussed the issue with him, and you want to ask his advice on a paper on marriage you're doing in your sociology class. Specifically, you want to know how a gay male, particularly one who is a dedicated activist, views the topic of marriage.

what do you think of the new child care proposals?" This question casts your friend into the role of single mother (rather than that of teacher, Democrat, or Baptist, for example). It asks your friend to assume a particular perspective.

To Disclaim. The *disclaimer* is a statement that aims to ensure that your message will not reflect negatively on you. Disclaimers entice the listener to hear your message as you wish it to be heard rather than through some assumption that might reflect negatively on you (Hewitt & Stokes, 1975). For example, to ensure that people listen to you fairly, you might disclaim any thought that you're biased against one gender: "I'm no sexist, but . . . ." The disclaimer is discussed in greater detail in Unit 9.

Noise

Noise prevents a receiver from getting the message a source is sending. Noise may be physical (others talking loudly, cars honking, illegible handwriting, "garbage" on your computer screen), physiological (hearing or visual impairment, articulation

disorders), psychological (preconceived ideas, wandering thoughts), or semantic (misunderstood meanings). Technically, noise is any **barrier to communication**—anything that distorts the message, anything that prevents the receiver from receiving the message.

Because messages may be visual as well as spoken, noise too may be visual. Thus, sunglasses that prevent someone from seeing the nonverbal messages from your eyes would be considered noise, as would blurred type on a printed page. Table 1.1 identifies these four types of noise in more detail.

All communications contain noise. Noise cannot be totally eliminated, but its effects can be reduced. Making your language more precise, sharpening your skills for sending and receiving nonverbal messages, and improving your listening and feedback skills are some ways to combat the influence of noise.

Communication Effects

Communication always has some **effect** on one or more persons involved in the communication act. For every communication act, there is some conse-

TABLE 1.1   Four Types of Noise

One of the most important skills in communication is an ability to recognize the types of noise and to develop ways to combat them. Consider, for example, what kinds of noise occur in the classroom. What kinds of noise occur in your family communications? What kinds occur at work? What can you do to combat these kinds of noise?

Types of Noise	Definition	Example
Physical	Interference that is external to both speaker and listener; interferes with the physical transmission of the signal or message	Screeching of passing cars, hum of computer, sunglasses
Physiological	Physical barriers within the speaker or listener	Visual impairments, hearing loss, articulation problems, memory loss
Psychological	Cognitive or mental interference	Biases and prejudices in senders and receivers, closed-mindedness, inaccurate expectations, extreme emotionalism (anger, hate, love, grief)
Semantic	Assignment of different meanings by speaker and listener	People speaking different languages, use of jargon or overly complex terms not understood by listener, dialectical differences in meaning

quence. For example, you may gain knowledge or learn how to analyze, synthesize, or evaluate something. These are intellectual or cognitive effects. Or you may acquire or change your attitudes, beliefs, emotions, or feelings. These are affective effects. You may even learn new bodily movements, such as throwing a ball or painting a picture, as well as appropriate verbal and nonverbal behaviors. These are psychomotor effects.

Ethics

Because communication has consequences, it also involves questions of **ethics,** of right and wrong (Bok, 1978; Jaksa & Pritchard, 1994). For example, while it might be (temporarily) effective to exaggerate or even lie in order to sell a product or get elected, it would not be ethical to do so.

The ethical dimension of communication is complicated, because ethics is so interwoven with your personal philosophy of life and the culture in which you were raised that it's difficult to propose general guidelines for specific individuals. Nevertheless, ethical responsibilities need to be considered as integral to any communication act. The decisions you make concerning communication must be guided

by what you consider right as well as by what you consider effective. To emphasize this important dimension of communication, each unit of this text concludes with a Reflections on Ethics discussion designed to highlight the relevance of ethics, to raise ethical issues, and to ask you to consider how you'd respond to specific ethical dilemmas.

PURPOSES OF HUMAN COMMUNICATION

The purposes of human communication may be conscious or unconscious, recognizable or unrecognizable. And, although communication technologies are changing rapidly and drastically—we send electronic mail, work at computer terminals, and telecommute, for example—the purposes of communication are likely to remain essentially the same throughout the computer revolution and whatever revolutions follow. Five general purposes of communication can be identified: to discover, to relate, to help, to persuade, and to play (see Figure 1.2 on page 12). Purposes of the media—following this same fivefold classification—are presented in Chapter 20 on the accompanying CD-ROM.

Figure 1.2

The Multipurposeful Nature of Human Communication

The purposes of communication can also be looked at from at least two other perspectives. First, purposes may be seen as motives for engaging in communication. That is, you engage in communication to satisfy your need for knowledge or to form relationships. Second, these purposes may be viewed in terms of the results you want to achieve. That is, you engage in interpersonal communication to increase your knowledge of yourself and others or to exert influence or power over others. Any communication act serves a unique combination of purposes, is motivated by a unique combination of factors, and can produce a unique combination of results. A similar typology of purposes comes from research on motives for communicating. In a series of studies, Rubin and her colleagues (Rubin & Martin, 1998; Rubin, Fernandez-Collado, & Hernandez-Sampieri, 1992; Rubin & Martin, 1994; Rubin, Perse, & Barbato, 1988; Rubin & Rubin, 1992; Graham, 1994; Graham, Barbato, & Perse, 1993) have identified six primary motives for communication: pleasure, affection, inclusion, escape, relaxation, and control. How do these compare to the five purposes discussed here?

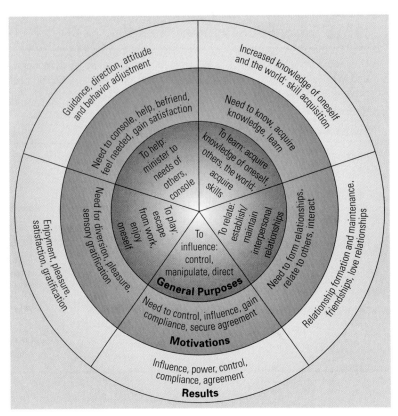

To Discover

One of the major purposes of communication concerns personal discovery. When you communicate with another person, you learn about yourself as well as about the other person. In fact, your self-perceptions result largely from what you've learned about yourself from others during communications, especially your interpersonal encounters.

Much as communication gives you a better understanding of yourself and of the person with whom you're communicating, it also helps you discover the external world—the world of objects, events, and other people. Today, you rely heavily on the various communications media for information about entertainment, sports, war, economic developments, health and dietary concerns, and new products to buy. Much of what you acquire from the media interacts with what you learn from your interpersonal interactions. You get information from the media, discuss it with other people, and ultimately learn or internalize the material as a result of the interaction between these two sources.

To Relate

One of our strongest motivations is to establish and maintain close relationships with others. The vast majority of people want to feel loved and liked, and in turn want to love and like others. You probably spend much of your communication time and energy establishing and maintaining social relationships. You communicate with your close friends in school, at work, and probably on the phone. You talk with your parents, children, and brothers and sisters. You interact with your relational partner. All told, this takes a great deal of your time and attests to the importance of this purpose of communication.

Of course, you may also use communication to distance yourself from others, to argue and fight with friends or romantic partners, and even to dissolve relationships.

To Help

Therapists, counselors, teachers, parents, and friends are just a few categories of those who often—though not always—communicate in order to help. As is the case with therapists and counselors, entire professions are built around this communication function. But there are few professions that don't make at least some significant use of this helping function. You also use this function when you constructively criticize, express empathy, work with a group to solve a problem, or listen attentively and supportively to a public speaker. Not surprisingly, obtaining and giving help are among the major functions of Internet communication and among the major reasons people use it (Meier, 2000).

To Persuade

People spend a great deal of their time in persuasion, both as sources and as receivers. In your everyday interpersonal and group encounters, you try to

What seems to be the primary purpose of the communication in this photo? Can you imagine additional purposes that might also be served?

UNDERSTANDING THEORY AND RESEARCH

Theories and Truth

Despite their many uses, theories don't reveal truth in any absolute sense. Rather, theories offer some degree of accuracy, some degree of truth. In the natural sciences, such as physics and chemistry, theories are extremely high in accuracy. If you mix two parts of hydrogen to one part of oxygen, you'll get water—every time you do it. In the social and behavioral sciences, such as communication, sociology, and psychology, the theories are far less accurate in describing the way things work and in predicting how things will work.

This failure to reveal truth, however, does not mean that theories are useless. In increasing your understanding and ability to predict, theories are extremely helpful. Also, theories often have practical implications for your own study of communication skills. For example, theories of interpersonal attraction offer practical insight into how to make yourself more attractive to others; theories of leadership offer practical advice on how you can lead more effectively. This interrelationship between theories and skills is a theme you'll find throughout this book; the more you know about how communication works (that is, understand theories and research), the more likely you'll be able to use it effectively (that is, build your communication skills).

Working with Theories and Research. *Can you identify one theory or basic assumption that you hold about good listening or about the best way to resolve interpersonal conflict? How does this theory or assumption influence your own communication behavior?*

change the attitudes and behaviors of others. You try to get them to vote a particular way, try a new diet, buy a particular item, see a movie, read a book, take a specific course, believe that something is true or false, value or devalue some idea, and so on. In interviews you may try to persuade a company to hire you, or in public speaking to persuade your audience that you should be elected. The list is endless. Few of your communications, in fact, don't seek to change attitudes or behaviors.

To Play

You probably also spend a great deal of your communication behavior on play. Communication as play includes motives of pleasure, escape, and relaxation (Barbato & Perse, 1992; Rubin, Perse, & Barbato, 1988). For example, you often listen to comedians—as well as friends—largely because

it's fun, enjoyable, and exciting. You tell jokes, say clever things, and relate interesting stories largely for the pleasure it gives to you and your listeners. Similarly, you may communicate because it relaxes you, allowing you to get away from pressures and responsibilities.

TYPES OF HUMAN COMMUNICATION

Human communication is a vast field and ranges from talking to yourself, to talking with one person or a small group, to speaking in public to an audience of hundreds, to mass communication in which you talk to millions (see Table 1.2).

In **intrapersonal communication** you talk with yourself. You learn about and evaluate yourself, persuade yourself of this or that, reason about pos-

MEDIA WATCH

USES AND GRATIFICATIONS THEORY

In much the same way that you communicate or enter relationships to serve some specific purpose, generally to gain some kind of reward, you also use the media to serve specific purposes and to gain rewards.

Rewards can be both immediate and delayed. So, for example, you may watch a particular television program because it satisfies your immediate need for information or entertainment. Or you may read a book because it contributes to satisfying a long-range dream of becoming a writer.

But using the media also requires effort. The amount of effort you'll have to expend to make use of the media will depend on the availability of different media and the ease with which you may use them as well as on the expense involved. For example, there's less effort required—less expense, less time lost—in watching television than in going to a movie. There's less effort in going to a movie than in going to a play. There's less effort in buying a book from the Internet than in driving to the nearest bookstore.

Media researchers propose that you're most likely to select those media that provide great rewards while requiring little effort and are less likely to select media that promise small rewards and require great effort. This idea is called the uses and gratifications

theory. According to this theory, the media are seen as competing with other sources (largely interpersonal) to serve the needs of the audience.

Research indicates that you derive four general gratifications from media (Dominick, 2000):

▶ learning something—for example, finding out what the new tax laws will involve or how movie reviewers rate the new film you want to see

▶ diversion—enjoying stimulation or perhaps the release of emotional energy (say, while watching a football game)

▶ affiliation—going to the movies with friends, talking about the developments on *Days of Our Lives,* or developing parasocial relationships (see Media Watch box in Unit 10)

▶ withdrawal—escaping from responsibilities and other people

Follow-Up. *Can you draw on the theory of uses and gratifications to explain your own media behavior? Can you use this theory to explain the changes that Internet service providers, search engines, and websites, generally, have made in recent years? If you need a hint, see Ruggiero (2000).*

TABLE 1.2   Human Communication

This table identifies and arranges the forms of communication in terms of the number of persons involved, from one (in intrapersonal communication) to thousands and millions (in mass communication). It also previews (in general) the progression of topics in this book.

Areas of Human Communication	Some Common Purposes	Some Theory-Related Concerns	Some Skills-Related Concerns
Intrapersonal: communication with oneself	To think, reason, analyze, reflect	How does one's self-concept develop? How does one's self-concept influence communication? How can problem-solving and analyzing abilities be improved and taught? What is the relationship between personality and communication?	Enhancing self-esteem, increasing self-awareness, improving problem-solving and analyzing abilities, increasing self-control, reducing stress, managing interpersonal conflict
Interpersonal: communication between two persons	To discover, relate, influence, play, help	What is interpersonal effectiveness? Why do people develop relationships? What holds friends, lovers, and families together? What tears them apart? How can relationships be repaired?	Increasing effectiveness in one-to-one communication, developing and maintaining effective relationships (friendship, love, family), improving conflict resolution abilities
Small group: communication within a small group of persons	To share information, generate ideas, solve problems, help	What makes a leader? What type of leadership works best? What roles do members play in groups? What do groups do well and what do they fail to do well? How can groups be made more effective?	Increasing effectiveness as a group member, improving leadership abilities, using groups to achieve specific purposes (for example, solving problems, generating ideas)
Public: communication of speaker with audience	To inform, persuade, entertain	What kinds of organizational structure work best in informative and persuasive speaking? How can audiences be most effectively analyzed and adapted to? How can ideas be best developed for communication to an audience?	Communicating information more effectively; increasing persuasive abilities; developing, organizing, styling, and delivering messages with greater effectiveness
Mass: communication addressed to an extremely large audience, mediated by audio and/or visual means	To entertain, persuade, and inform	What functions do the media serve? How do the media influence us? How can we influence the media? In what ways is information censored by the media for the public? How does advertising work?	Improving our ability to use the media to greater effectiveness, increasing our ability to control the media, avoiding being taken in by advertisements and tabloid journalism

sible decisions to make, and rehearse messages you intend to send to others.

Through **interpersonal communication** you interact with others, learn about them and about yourself, and reveal yourself to others. Whether with new acquaintances, old friends, lovers, or family members, it's through interpersonal communication that you establish, maintain, and sometimes destroy (and sometimes repair) your personal relationships.

In **small group communication** you interact with others, solving problems, developing new ideas, and sharing knowledge and experiences. From the employment interview to the executive board meeting, from the informal social group having coffee to the formal meeting discussing issues of international concern, your work life and social life are lived largely in small groups.

Through **public communication**, others inform and persuade you. And you in turn inform and persuade others—to do, to buy, or to think in a particular way, or to change an attitude, opinion, or value.

Through **mass communication** you are entertained, informed, and persuaded by the media—movies, television, radio, newspapers, and books. Also, through your viewing habits and buying patterns, you in turn influence the media's form and content.

All forms of communication except intrapersonal communication may be **intercultural communication,** in which you communicate with members of other cultures; that is, people who follow different customs, roles, and rules. Through intercultural communication you come to understand new ways of thinking and new ways of behaving and begin to see the tremendous variety in human thought and experience.

This book, then, is about these types of communication and about your personal communication. Its major goal is to explain the concepts and principles, the theory and research central to these varied areas of human communication. Another goal is to give you the foundation and direction for learning the skills of human communication and for increasing your own communication competency. The relevance of these skills is seen throughout the communication spectrum; such skills make the difference between

- the self-confident and the self-conscious speaker
- the person who is hired and the person who is passed over
- the couple who argue constructively and the couple who argue by hurting each other and eventually destroy their relationship
- the group member who is too self-focused to listen openly and contribute to the group's goals and the member who helps accomplish the group's task *and* satisfy the interpersonal needs of the members
- the public speaker who lacks credibility and persuasive appeal and the speaker whom audiences believe and follow
- the uncritical consumer of media who is influenced without awareness and the critical, watchful consumer who uses media constructively

REFLECTIONS ON ETHICS IN HUMAN COMMUNICATION

Approaching Ethics

In thinking about the ethics of communication, you can take the position that ethics is objective or that it's subjective. In an *objective view* you'd claim that the morality of an act—say, a communication message—is absolute and exists apart from the values or beliefs of any individual or culture. This objective view holds that there are standards that apply to all people in all situations at all times. If lying, advertising falsely, using illegally obtained evidence, or revealing secrets, for example, are considered unethical, then they'd be considered unethical regardless of the circumstances surrounding them or of the values and beliefs of the culture in which they occur.

In a *subjective view* you'd claim that the ethics of communication depends on the culture's values and beliefs as well as on the particular circumstances. Thus, from a subjective position you might claim that lying to win votes or sell cigarettes is wrong, but that lying is ethical if the end result is positive—as when we try to make people feel better by telling them they look great or that they'll get well soon.

What would you do? *At work you see a colleague repeatedly take toner cartridges home; so far,*

he's taken at least nine of them. When you confront him, he says that because he's so underpaid and was recently denied promotion on account of prejudice, he feels justified in taking this additional compensation. You agree that he is underpaid and that he was probably denied a well-earned promotion because of prejudice. He asks you if you think his behavior is unethical. What would you say if you took an objective view of ethics? What would you say if you took a subjective view? What would you say if your manager asked why so many toner cartridges were missing?

 SUMMARY

This unit explained the elements, purposes, and types of human communication that we'll focus on throughout the rest of this book.

1. Communication is the act, by one or more persons, of sending and receiving messages that are distorted by noise, occur within a context, have some effect (and some ethical dimension), and provide some opportunity for feedback.

2. The universals of communication—the elements present in every communication act—are context, culture, source–receiver, message, channel, noise, sending or encoding processes, receiving or decoding processes, feedback and feedforward, effect, and ethics.

3. The communication context has at least four dimensions: physical, social–psychological, temporal, and cultural.

4. Culture consists of the collection of beliefs, attitudes, values, and ways of behavior shared by a group of people and passed down from one generation to the next.

5. Communication competence is knowledge of the elements and rules of communication, which vary from one culture to another.

6. Communication messages may be of varied forms and may be sent and received through any combination of sensory organs. The communication channel is the medium through which the messages are sent.

7. Feedback is information or messages that are sent back to the source. It may come from the source itself or from the receiver and may be characterized along such dimensions as positive and negative, person-focused and message-focused, immediate and delayed, low-monitored and high-monitored, and supportive and critical.

8. Feedforward messages preface other messages and may be used to open the channels of communication, to preview future messages, to disclaim, and to altercast.

9. Noise is anything that distorts a message; it's present to some degree in every communication transaction and may be physical, physiological, psychological, or semantic in origin.

10. Communication always has an effect. Effects may be cognitive, affective, or psychomotor.

11. Ethics in communication consists of the rightness or wrongness—the morality—of a communication transaction. Ethics is integral to every communication transaction.

12. Communication is multipurposeful; we use communication to discover, relate, help, persuade, and play.

13. The major types of human communication are intrapersonal, interpersonal, small group, public, mass, and intercultural communication.

KEY TERMS

communication context	channel	ethics
culture	feedback	intrapersonal communication
sources–receivers	feedforward	interpersonal communication
encoders–decoders	altercasting	small group communication
encoding–decoding	disclaimer	public communication
communication competence	noise	mass communication
message	communication effects	intercultural communication

THINKING CRITICALLY ABOUT

Preliminaries to Human Communication

1. How would you describe the physical, sociopsychological, temporal, and cultural context of your communication classroom? How would you describe the context of a typical family dinner?

2. What kinds of feedforward can you find in this textbook? What specific functions do these feedforwards serve?

3. Do you agree that using e-mail and whispering in chat groups are similar to interpersonal conversation, that chat group communication is similar to small group communication, and that newsgroup messages are similar to public speeches? What other similarities can you identify? What differences?

4. What noted personality would you nominate for the "Communication Competence Hall of Fame"?

5. Some researchers (e.g., Beier, 1974) argue that the impulse to communicate two different feelings (such as "I love you" and "I don't love you") creates messages in which the nonverbal contradicts the verbal message. Do you think this idea has validity? What other explanations might you offer to account for contradictory messages?

6. **Researching Preliminaries to Human Communication.** How would you go about finding answers to such questions as these?
   - Are instructors who accurately read student feedback liked better than instructors who can't read feedback as accurately? Is there a relationship between the ability to read feedback and the ability to communicate information or to motivate or persuade an audience?
   - Is knowledge about communication related to the ability to communicate effectively? That is, are those who know more about communication more effective communicators than those who know less?
   - Do people who watch more television feel less positive about themselves than do those who watch less television?
   - Do sunglasses influence the effectiveness of a speaker's interpersonal, small group, and public communication?

UNIT 2
Principles of Communication

UNIT CONTENTS

Communication is a lot more complex than you probably think. But the more you understand this complex process, the more proficient you'll become in controlling the communication process to achieve your goals more effectively. In this unit you'll learn

▶ some of the complexities of communication and how communication works

▶ how you can use this understanding to communicate more effectively and more meaningfully

COMMUNICATION IS A PACKAGE OF SIGNALS

Communication behaviors, whether they involve verbal messages, gestures, or some combination thereof, usually occur in "packages" (Pittenger, Hockett, & Danehy, 1960). Usually, verbal and nonverbal behaviors reinforce or support each other. All parts of a message system normally work together to communicate a particular meaning. You don't express fear with words while the rest of your body is relaxed. You don't express anger through your posture while your face smiles. Your entire body works together—verbally and nonverbally—to express your thoughts and feelings.

In any form of communication, whether interpersonal, small group, public speaking, or mass media, you probably pay little attention to this "packaging." It goes unnoticed. But when there's an incongruity— when the weak handshake belies the verbal greeting, when the nervous posture belies the focused stare, when the constant preening belies the expres-

sions of being comfortable and at ease—you take notice. Invariably you begin to question the credibility, the sincerity, and the honesty of the individual.

Often contradictory messages are sent over a period of time. Note, for example, that in the following interaction the employee is being given two directives—use initiative and don't use initiative. These **mixed messages** place the employee in a "double bind": Regardless of what he or she does, rejection will follow.

Employer: You've got to learn to take more initiative. You never seem to take charge, to take control.

Employee: [Takes the initiative, makes decisions.]

Employer: You've got to learn to follow the chain of command and not do things just because you want to.

Employee: [Goes back to old ways, not taking any initiative.]

Employer: Well, I told you. We expect more initiative from you.

BUILDING COMMUNICATION SKILLS

How Can You Respond to Contradictory Messages?

Let's assume that each of these statements seems contradictory or somehow doesn't ring true on the basis of what you know about the person. Compose a response to each comment:

▶ Even if I do fail the course, so what? I don't need it for graduation.

▶ I called three people. They all have something to do on Saturday night. I guess I'll just curl up with a good book or a good movie. It'll be better than a lousy date anyway.

▶ My parents are getting divorced after 20 years of marriage. My mother and father are both dating other people now so everything is going okay.

▶ My youngest child is going to need special treatments if he's going to walk again. The doctors are deciding today on what kind of treatment. But all will end well in this, the best of all possible worlds.

These contradictory messages may be the result of the desire to communicate two different emotions or feelings. For example, you may like a person and want to communicate a positive feeling, but you may also feel resentment toward this person and want to communicate a negative feeling as well. The result is that you communicate both feelings; for example, you say that you're happy to see the person but your facial expression and body posture communicate your negative feelings (Beier, 1974). In this example, and in many similar cases, the socially acceptable message is usually communicated verbally while the less socially acceptable message is communicated nonverbally.

COMMUNICATION IS TRANSACTIONAL

Communication is **transactional** (Barnlund, 1970; Watzlawick, 1977, 1978; Watzlawick, Beavin, & Jackson, 1967; Wilmot 1987). One implication of viewing communication as transactional is that each person is seen as both speaker and listener, as simultaneously sending and receiving messages. Figure 2.1 illustrates this transactional view and compares it with earlier views—linear or **stimulus–response models of communication** that may still influence the way you see communication.

Its "transactional" nature also means that communication is an ever changing **process**. It's an ongoing activity; all the elements of communication are in a state of constant change. You're constantly changing, the people with whom you're communicating are changing, and your environment is changing. Nothing in communication ever remains static.

In any transactional process, each element relates integrally to every other element. The elements of communication are interdependent (never independent). Each exists in relation to the others. For example, there can be no source without a receiver. There can be no message without a source. There can be no feedback without a receiver. Because of this interdependence, a change in any one element of the process produces changes in the other elements. For example, you're talking with a group of your friends when your mother enters the group. This change in "audience" will lead to other changes. Perhaps you or your friends will adjust what you're

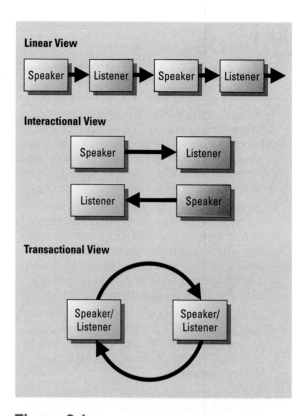

Figure 2.1

The Transactional View of Communication

The top figure represents a linear view of communication, in which the speaker speaks and the listener listens. The middle figure represents an interactional view, in which speaker and listener take turns speaking and listening; A speaks while B listens, then B speaks while A listens. The bottom figure represents a transactional view, in which each person serves simultaneously as speaker and listener; at the same time that you send messages, you're also receiving messages from your own communications and also from the messages of the other person(s).

saying or how you say it. The new situation may also influence how often certain people talk, and so on. Regardless of what change is introduced, other changes will be produced as a result.

Each person in a communication transaction acts and reacts on the basis of the present situation. But this present situation, your immediate context, is influenced by your history, past experiences, attitudes, cultural beliefs, self-image, future expectations, emotions, and a host of related issues. One implication of this is that actions and reactions in communication are determined not only by what is said, but also by the way each person interprets what is said. Your responses to a movie, for exam-

MEDIA WATCH

MEDIA ETHICS

Because of the media's tremendous influence, media ethics is important to everyone who listens to the radio, watches television, goes to the movies, reads a newspaper, or surfs the Net. To encourage you to watch more closely, here are just a few questions that raise ethical issues relevant to the media:

▶ What do you think of checkbook journalism? Is it ethical for a news organization to pay someone for a story? For example, is it ethical to pay, say, a juror from a high-profile case to reveal what went on at the trial or hearing? Can such payments lead people to distort the accuracy with which they present the events?

▶ At what point, if any, does hate speech fall outside protection by the first amendment? Does a person have the right to say anything? And, if not, what, specifically, should people be prevented from saying?

▶ Should anonymous speech (for example, writing and distributing social action pamphlets without any name attached) be granted the same protection as speech that identifies the author?

▶ What about depictions of sex, nudity, and violence? Should the media be allowed greater freedom? Should the regulations governing such portrayals be made more stringent? And what standard should be used in making decisions about what is "too sexual," involves "too much nudity," or is "too violent"?

▶ What do you think of shield laws—laws protecting reporters from revealing sources to whom they've promised anonymity?

▶ What do you think of gag rules—rules prohibiting reporters from revealing certain information? What types of information, if any, should be covered by gag rules?

Follow-Up. *Advertising campaigns for the Italian clothing conglomerate Benetton feature scenes evoking extremely strong feelings. Some of the scenes depicted in Benetton ads included a human body with "H.I.V. Positive" stamped on it, small Latin American children working in a stone quarry, and prisoners awaiting execution. A decision by a German court ruled some of these ads illegal. A French court fined Benetton $32,000 for the H.I.V. ad, claiming that the ads exploited human suffering. Do you think court decisions such as these violate Benetton's (or any person's or company's) freedom of expression?*

---

ple, don't depend solely on the words and pictures in the film but also on your previous experiences, present emotions, knowledge, physical well-being, and other factors.

Another implication is that two people listening to the same message will often derive two very different meanings. Although the words and symbols are the same, each person interprets them differently.

COMMUNICATION IS A PROCESS OF ADJUSTMENT

Communication can take place only to the extent that the communicators use the same system of signals (Pittenger, Hockett, & Danehy, 1960). You will not be able to communicate with another person to the extent that your language systems differ. In reality, however, no two persons use identical signal systems, so this principle of **adjustment** is relevant to all forms of communication. Parents and children, for example, not only have largely different vocabularies but also have different meanings for the terms they do share. Different cultures, even when they use a common language, often have greatly different nonverbal communication systems. To the extent that these systems differ, meaningful and effective communication will not take place.

Part of the art of communication is identifying the other person's signals, learning how they're used, and understanding what they mean. Those in close relationships will realize that learning the

UNDERSTANDING THEORY AND RESEARCH

Communication Research

Usually research is conducted on the basis of some theory and its predictions—though sometimes from a simple desire to answer a question. Communication research is a systematic search for information about communication, the very information that is discussed throughout this text—information about perception and listening, verbal and nonverbal messages, interpersonal interactions, small group encounters, and public speaking situations.

Some research is designed to explore what exists; for example, What do people say after getting caught in a lie? Other research is designed to describe the properties of some communication behavior; for example, What are the types of excuses? Still other research aims to predict what will happen in different situations; for

example, What types of excuses will work best in a business relationship?

Research findings bearing on these questions give you useful generalizations about communication and help clarify how communication works and how you might use it more effectively.

Working with Theories and Research. *What question about communication would you like answered? Survey the available research on your question in such popular databases as ERIC, PsycINFO, or Sociological Abstracts. Has research already answered your question? If not, how might you go about conducting your own research to secure the answer?*

---

other person's signals takes a great deal of time and often a great deal of patience. If you want to understand what another person means (by smiling, by saying "I love you," by arguing about trivia, by making self-deprecating comments), rather than simply acknowledging what the other person says or does, you have to learn that person's system of signals.

The principle of adjustment is especially important in intercultural communication, largely because people from different cultures use different signals—and sometimes also use the same signals to signify quite different things. Focused eye contact means honesty and openness in much of the United States. But in Japan and in many Hispanic cultures, that same behavior may signify arrogance or disrespect if, say, engaged in by a youngster with someone significantly older.

Communication Accommodation

Generally, you're more likely to view someone who is similar to you more positively and see that per-

son as more attractive than someone who is dissimilar. For example, in one study roommates who had similar communication attitudes (both were high in their willingness to communicate and low in their verbal aggressiveness) liked each other better and were more satisfied with their status as roommates than those with dissimilar attitudes (Martin & Anderson, 1995). Similarly, you're likely to judge a speaker as more believable when his or her language intensity is similar to your own (Aune & Kikuchi, 1993). And you're likely to see those whose speech rate is similar to yours as more sociable and intimate than those who speak much more slowly or more rapidly than you do (Buller, LePoire, Aune, & Eloy, 1992). These findings, and many more like them, support **communication accommodation theory,** the theory that you adjust to or accommodate to the speaking style of your listeners in order to gain a variety of benefits—not only believability and likeability, as already noted, but also general social approval and even communication efficiency (Giles, Mulac, Bradac, & Johnson, 1987).

How does the principle of adjustment relate to communication between parents and children? Communication between students and teachers? Communication between members of different races or religions?

COMMUNICATION INVOLVES CONTENT AND RELATIONSHIP DIMENSIONS

Communications, to a certain extent at least, refer to the real world, to something external to both speaker and listener. At the same time, however, communications also refer to the relationships between the parties (Watzlawick, Beavin, & Jackson, 1967). In other words, communication has both **content and relationship dimensions.**

For example, an employer may say to a worker, "See me after the meeting." This simple message has a content aspect and a relational aspect. The content aspect refers to the behavioral responses expected—namely, that the worker see the employer after the meeting. The **relationship message** tells how the communication is to be dealt with. For example, the use of the simple command says that there's a status difference between the two parties: The employer can command the worker. This aspect is perhaps seen most clearly if you imagine the worker giving this command to the employer; to do so would be awkward and out of place, because it would violate the expected communications between employer and worker.

In any communication situation the content dimension may stay the same but the relationship

aspect may vary. Or the relationship aspect may be the same while the content is different. For example, the employer could say to the worker either "You had better see me after the meeting" or "May I please see you after the meeting?" In each case the content is essentially the same; that is, the message being communicated about the behaviors expected is the same. But the relationship dimension is very different. The first example signifies a definite superior–inferior relationship and even a put-down of the worker. In the second, the employer signals a more equal relationship and shows respect for the worker.

Similarly, at times the content may be different but the relationship essentially the same. For example, a teenager might say to his or her parents, "May I go away this weekend?" and "May I use the car tonight?" The content of the two messages is clearly very different. The relationship dimension, however, is essentially the same. It clearly denotes a superior–inferior relationship in which permission to do certain things must be secured.

Ignoring Relationship Dimensions

Problems may arise when the distinction between the content and relationship levels of communication is ignored. Consider a couple arguing over the fact that Pat made plans to study with friends during the weekend without first asking Chris if that would be all right. Probably both would have agreed that to study over the weekend was the right choice to make. Thus the argument is not at all related to the content level. The argument centers on the relationship level. Chris expected to be consulted about plans for the weekend. Pat, in not doing so, rejected this definition of the relationship.

Let me give you a personal example. My mother came to stay for a week at a summer place I had. On the first day she swept the kitchen floor six times, though I had repeatedly told her that it did not need sweeping: I would be tracking in dirt and mud from outside, so all her effort would be wasted. But she persisted in sweeping, saying that the floor was dirty and should be swept. On the content level, we were talking about the value of sweeping the kitchen floor. But on the relationship level we were talking about something quite different. We were each saying, "This is my house." When we realized this (though only after considerable argument), I stopped complaining about the relative usefulness of sweeping a floor that did not need

sweeping and she stopped sweeping it. Consider the following interchange:

Paul: I'm going bowling tomorrow. The guys at the plant are starting a team. [He focuses on the content and ignores any relational implications of the message.]

Judy: Why can't we ever do anything together? [She responds primarily on a relational level, ignoring the content implications of the message and expressing her displeasure at being ignored in his decision.]

Paul: We can do something together anytime; tomorrow's the day they're organizing the team. [Again, he focuses almost exclusively on the content.]

This example reflects research findings that show that men tend to focus more on content messages, whereas women focus more on relationship messages (Pearson, West, & Turner, 1995). Once we recognize this gender difference, we may be able to develop increased sensitivity to the opposite sex.

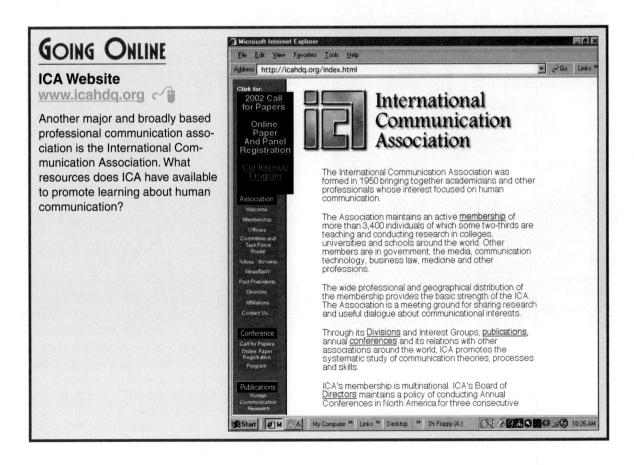

GOING ONLINE

ICA Website
www.icahdq.org

Another major and broadly based professional communication association is the International Communication Association. What resources does ICA have available to promote learning about human communication?

Recognizing Relationship Dimensions

Here's essentially the same situation but with added sensitivity to relationship messages:

Paul: The guys at the plant are organizing a bowling team. I'd sure like to be on the team. Do you mind if I go to the organizational meeting tomorrow? [Although he focuses on content, he shows awareness of the relational dimensions by asking if this would be a problem. He also shows this in expressing his desire rather than his decision to attend this meeting.]

Judy: That sounds great, but I'd really like to do something together tomorrow. [She focuses on the relational dimension but also ac-

How would you describe the relationships in popular television sitcoms in terms of symmetrical and complementary patterns? For example, what type of relationship exists between Frasier and Roz (in *Frasier*), Raymond and his brother (in *Everybody Loves Raymond*), or Ally and John (in *Ally McBeal*)?

knowledges his content message. Note too that she does not respond as if she has to defend herself or her emphasis on relational aspects.]

Paul: How about your meeting me at Luigi's for dinner after the organizational meeting? [He responds to the relational aspect without abandoning his desire to join the bowling team—and seeks to incorporate it into his communications. He attempts to negotiate a solution that will meet both Judy's and his needs and desires.]

Judy: That sounds great. I'm dying for spaghetti and meatballs. [She responds to both messages, approving of both his joining the team and their dinner date.]

Arguments over content are relatively easy to resolve. You can look something up in a book or ask someone what actually took place. Arguments on the relationship level, however, are much more difficult to resolve, in part because you (like me in the example with my mother) may not recognize that the argument is in fact a relationship one.

COMMUNICATION SEQUENCES ARE PUNCTUATED

Communication events are continuous transactions. There's no clear-cut beginning or ending. As a participant in or an observer of the communication act, you divide up this continuous, circular process into causes and effects, or **stimuli** and **responses.** That is, you segment this continuous stream of communication into smaller pieces. You label some of these pieces causes or stimuli and others effects or responses.

Consider an example: The students are apathetic; the teacher does not prepare for classes. Figure 2.2(a) illustrates the sequence of events, in which there's no absolute beginning and no absolute end. Each action (the students' apathy and the teacher's lack of preparation) stimulates the other. But there's no initial stimulus. Each of the events may be regarded as a stimulus and each as a response, but there's no way to determine which is which.

Consider how the teacher might divide up this continuous transaction. Figure 2.2(b) illustrates the teacher's perception of this situation. From this

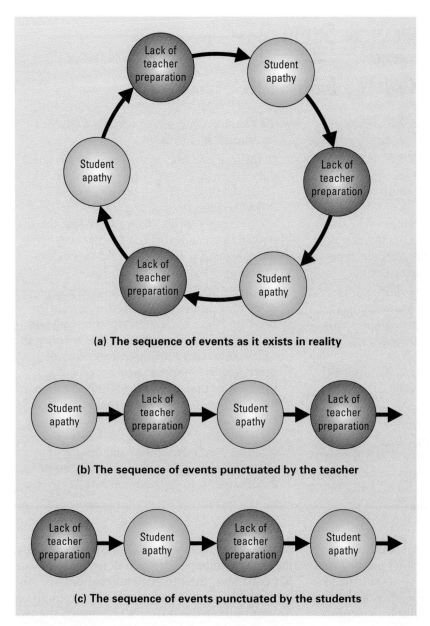

Figure 2.2
The Sequence of Events
Try using this three-part figure, discussed in the text, to explain what might go on when Pat complains about Chris's nagging and Chris complains about Pat's avoidance and silence.

(a) The sequence of events as it exists in reality

(b) The sequence of events punctuated by the teacher

(c) The sequence of events punctuated by the students

point of view, the teacher sees the students' apathy as the stimulus for his or her lack of preparation, and the lack of preparation as the response to the students' apathy. In Figure2.2(c) we see how the students might divide up the transaction. The students might see this "same" sequence of events as beginning with the teacher's lack of preparation as the stimulus (or cause) and their own apathy as the response (or effect).

This tendency to divide up the various communication transactions in sequences of stimuli and responses is referred to as **punctuation of communication** (Watzlawick, Beavin, & Jackson, 1967). People punctuate the continuous sequences of events into stimuli and responses for ease of understanding and remembering. And, as the example of the students and teacher illustrates, people punctuate communication in ways that allow them to look good and that are consistent with their own self-image.

If communication is to be effective, if you're to understand what another person means from his or

BUILDING COMMUNICATION SKILLS

How Can You Describe Relationships?

How would you use the principles discussed in this unit to describe (not to solve) what is happening in each of the following situations?

▶ A couple, together for 20 years, argue constantly about the seemingly most insignificant things—who takes the dog out, who does the shopping, who decides where to go to dinner, and so on. It's gotten to the point where they rarely have a day without argument; both are considering separating.

▶ In teaching communication skills, Professor Jones frequently asks students to role-play effective and ineffective communication patterns and offers criticism after each session. Although most students respond well to this instructional technique, Mariz has difficulty and has frequently left the class in tears.

▶ Pat has sought the assistance of a family therapist. The problem is simple: Whatever Pat says, Chris says the opposite. If Pat wants to eat Chinese, Chris wants to eat Italian; if Pat wants Italian, Chris wants Chinese. And on and on. The problem is made worse by

the fact that Chris has to win; Pat's wishes are invariably dismissed.

▶ In the heat of a big argument, Harry said he didn't want to ever see Peggy's family again: "They don't like me and I don't like them." Peggy reciprocated and said she felt the same way about his family. Now, weeks later, there remains a great deal of tension between them, especially when they find themselves with one or both families.

▶ Grace and Tom, senior executives at a large advertising agency, are engaged to be married. Recently, Grace made a presentation that was not received positively by the other members of the team. Grace feels that Tom—in not defending her proposal—conveyed a negative attitude and actually encouraged others to reject her ideas. Tom says that he felt he could not defend her proposal because others would have felt his defense was motivated by their relationship and not by an objective evaluation of her proposal. So he felt it was best to say nothing.

her point of view, then you have to see the sequence of events as punctuated by the other person. Further, you have to recognize that your punctuation does not reflect what exists in reality. Rather, it reflects your own unique but fallible perception.

COMMUNICATION INVOLVES SYMMETRICAL AND COMPLEMENTARY TRANSACTIONS

Relationships can be described as either symmetrical or complementary (Watzlawick, Beavin, & Jackson, 1967). In a **symmetrical relationship** the two individuals mirror each other's behavior. The behavior of one person is reflected in the behavior of the other. If one member nags, the other member

responds in kind. If one member expresses jealousy, the other member expresses jealousy. If one member is passive, the other member is passive. The relationship is one of equality, with the emphasis on minimizing the differences between the two individuals.

Note, however, the problems that can arise in this type of relationship. Consider the situation of a husband and wife, both of whom are aggressive. The aggressiveness of the husband fosters aggressiveness in the wife; the anger of the wife arouses anger in the husband. As this escalates, the aggressiveness can no longer be contained, and the relationship is consumed by aggression.

In a **complementary relationship** the two individuals engage in different behaviors. The behavior of one serves as the stimulus for the complementary behavior of the other. In complementary

Communication Networks

If an organization is to work effectively, the communication should be through the most effective channel regardless of the organization chart.

—David Packard

Organizations use a variety of different **communication networks,** configurations of channels through which messages pass from one person to another. The following five networks are among the most commonly used organizational communication patterns (Figure 2.3).

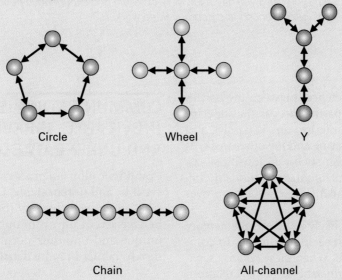

Circle   Wheel   Y

Chain   All-channel

Figure 2.3
Five Network Structures

These networks are defined by the exchange of messages. Such messages may be transmitted in any number of ways: face-to-face or via telephone, e-mail, intranet, teleconferencing, informal memos, or formal reports, to name a few.

▸ The *circle* has no leader. There is total equality; all members of the circle have exactly the same authority or power to influence the group. Each member may communicate with the two members on either side.

▸ The *all-channel* or *star* pattern is like the circle in that all members are equal and all have exactly the same amount of power to influence others. In the all-channel network, however, each member may communicate with any other member. This pattern allows for the greatest member participation.

▸ The *wheel* has a clear leader (at the hub or central position) who is the only person who can send and receive messages from all members. If one member wishes to communicate with another member, the message must go through this leader.

▸ The *Y* pattern is less centralized than the wheel but more centralized than the circle or the all-channel. In the Y the leader is the third person from the bottom and the second per-

continued

Communication @ Work continued

son from the bottom plays a secondary leadership role, because these two can communicate with more people than the others. The remaining three members can communicate with only one other person.

▶ The *chain* is similar to the circle except that the members on the ends may communicate with only one person each. There is some centrality here. The middle position has more leadership possibilities than any of the other positions.

Thinking about Your Communicating @ Work

If you were the manager of an organization, what pattern of communication would you establish if you had to get simple repetitive tasks done quickly and efficiently? What pattern would you use if you wanted to increase the morale of the workers? What pattern would you use if you had a few very excellent and experienced people and a vast majority of inexperienced and poorly trained workers?

---

relationships the differences between the parties are maximized. One partner acts as the superior and the other as the inferior, one is passive and the other active, one strong and the other weak. At times cultures establish such relationships—as, for example, the complementary relationship between teacher and student or between employer and employee.

Early marriages are likely to be complementary relationships in which each person tries to complete himself or herself. When these couples separate and form new partnerships, the new relationships are likely to be symmetrical and to involve a kind of reconfirmation of each partner's own identity (Prosky, 1992). Generally, research finds that complementary couples have a lower marital adjustment level than do symmetrical couples (Main & Oliver, 1988; Holden, 1991; McCall & Green, 1991).

A problem in complementary relationships—familiar to many college students—is the situation created by extreme rigidity. Whereas the complementary relationship between a nurturing and protective mother and a dependent child is at one stage vital and essential to the life of the child, a **rigid complementarity** when the child is older can become a handicap to further development, if the change so essential to growth is not allowed to occur.

For further discussion of these concepts see "Symmetrical and Complementary Relationships" at **www.ablongman.com/devito**.

COMMUNICATION IS INEVITABLE, IRREVERSIBLE, AND UNREPEATABLE

Communication is a process that is inevitable, irreversible, and unrepeatable. Communication messages are always being sent (or almost always), can't be reversed or uncommunicated, and are always unique and one-time occurrences. Let's look at these qualities in more detail.

Inevitability

In many instances communication takes place even though one of the individuals does not think he or she is communicating or does not want to communicate. Consider, for example, the student sitting in the back of the classroom with an expressionless face, perhaps staring out the window. Although the student might claim not to be communicating with the teacher, the teacher may derive any of a variety of messages from this behavior; for example, that the student lacks interest, is bored, or is worried about something. In any event, the teacher is receiving messages even though the student may not intend to communicate. In an interactional situation, you can't avoid communicating (Watzlawick, Beavin, & Jackson, 1967); communication is inevitable. This principle of **inevitability** does not mean, of course, that all behavior is communication. For example, if the student looked out the window and the teacher failed to notice this, no communication would have taken place.

Further, when you're in an interactional situation you can't avoid responding to the messages of others. For example, if you notice someone winking at you, you must respond in some way. Even if you don't respond actively or openly, that lack of response is itself a response, and it communicates. Again, if you don't notice the winking, then obviously communication has not occurred.

Irreversibility

Notice that you can reverse the processes of only some systems. For example, you can turn water into ice and then the ice back into water. And you can repeat this reversal process as many times as you wish. Other systems, however, are irreversible. You can turn grapes into wine, but you can't turn the wine back into grapes—the process can go in only one direction. Communication is such an irreversible process. Once you say something, once you press the send key on your e-mail, you can't uncommunicate it. You can of course try to reduce the effects of your message by saying, for example, "I really didn't mean what I said" or "I was so angry I couldn't think straight." But regardless of how you try to negate or reduce the effects of a message, the message itself, once it has been sent and received, can't be reversed.

Because of **irreversibility** (and unerasability), be careful not to say things you may be sorry for later. Especially in conflict situations, when tempers run high, avoid saying things you may later wish to withdraw. Commitment messages—the "I love you" messages and their variants—also need to be monitored. Similarly, online messages that

UNDERSTANDING THEORY AND RESEARCH

Evaluating Research

Just as you need to evaluate the proposed solutions to a problem, you also need to evaluate the methods and conclusions of research. I'll introduce this topic here and will return to it in Unit 15, where I discuss how to evaluate information generally and especially material from the Internet. After all, not all research is good research. Evaluate research by asking the following questions:

Are the results reliable? Reliability, a measure of the extent to which research findings are consistent, is always important to consider when you evaluate research findings. In investigating reliability, you ask if another researcher, using the same essential tools, would find the same results. Would the same people respond in the same way at other times? If the answer to such questions is yes, then the results are reliable. If the answer is no, then the results may be unreliable.

Are the results valid? Validity is a measure of the extent to which a measuring instrument measures what it claims to measure. For example, does your score on an intelligence test really measure what we think of as intelligence? Does your score on a test of communication apprehension measure what most people think of as constituting apprehension?

Do the results justify the conclusion? Results and conclusions are two different things. Results are objective findings, such as "Men scored higher than women on this test of romanticism." Conclusions are the researcher's (or reader's) interpretation of the results; for example, "Men are more romantic than women."

Working with Theories and Research. *Go online and read one of the research reports from one of the many Internet sites that popularize academic and scientific research. Do you find the research reliable? Is it valid? Does it justify the conclusion drawn?*

could be interpreted as sexist, racist, or homophobic, which you thought were private or erased from your computer, may later be recalled and retrieved by others, creating all sorts of problems for you and your organization. In group and public communication situations, when messages are received by many people, it's especially crucial to recognize their irreversibility.

Unrepeatability

The reason communication is unrepeatable is simple: everyone and everything is constantly changing. As a result, you can never recapture the exact same situation, frame of mind, or relationship dynamics that defined a previous communication act. For example, you can never repeat meeting someone for the first time, making a first impression in an interview, or resolving a specific group problem.

You can, of course, try again, as when you say, "I'm sorry I came off so forward, can we try again?" But even after you say this, you have not erased the initial impression. Instead you try to counteract this initial and perhaps negative impression by going through the motions again.

REFLECTIONS ON ETHICS IN HUMAN COMMUNICATION

Censoring Messages and Interactions

In all aspects of human communication, censors may intervene and regulate both the content and the relationship messages you receive. For example, television programmers censor the programs you see. Teachers, authors, and newsgroup moderators censor the information you receive in the classroom, in books, and online.

Similarly, censors regulate relationship messages, encouraging certain relationships and discouraging or even preventing other relationships. Parents, for example, often encourage their children to play with and become friends with children from the same racial or national group and religion and discourage friendship with children from different cultures. Your friends may also exert subtle pressure on you to date one person and not another, to associate with some people but not others.

What would you do? *Jennifer and Colleen have been friends all through college. Recently, John has been interested in Colleen and so approaches Jennifer to ask what his chances are, whether Jennifer likes him, and so on. John has been charged with physically abusing a former girlfriend, and rumor has it that he's still married. Colleen, on the other hand, is extremely vulnerable and would probably be tempted by John's fast talk. Jennifer is convinced that John would be bad for Colleen and so tells John that Colleen is not interested in him. Jennifer also decides not to tell Colleen anything about John's interest. Was Jennifer ethical in lying to John? Was she ethical in concealing John's expression of interest from Colleen? If you were Colleen's best friend, what would you do in this situation?*

 ## SUMMARY

In this unit we looked at some of the principles of human communication, principles that explain what communication is and how it works in a wide variety of situations and contexts.

1. Communication is normally a package of signals, each reinforcing the other. Opposing communication signals from the same source result in contradictory messages.

2. The double bind, a special kind of contradictory message, may be created when contradictory messages are sent simultaneously.

3. Communication is a transactional process in which each person simultaneously sends and receives messages.

4. Communication is a process of adjustment and takes place only to the extent that the communicators use the same system of signals.

5. Communication involves both content dimensions and relationship dimensions.

6. Communication sequences are punctuated for processing. Different people divide up the communication sequence into stimuli and responses differently.

7. Communication involves symmetrical and complementary transactions.

8. In any interactional situation, communication is inevitable; you can't avoid communicating, nor can you not respond to communication.

9. Communication is irreversible. You can't uncommunicate.

10. Communication is unrepeatable. You can't duplicate a previous communication act.

KEY TERMS

packaging	relationship messages	inevitability
transaction	punctuation of communication	irreversibility
adjustment	symmetrical relationship	unrepeatability
content messages	complementary relationship	

THINKING CRITICALLY ABOUT

The Principles of Human Communication

1. A good illustration of contradictory (sometimes called double-bind) messages is that which often takes place between a therapist and a client with disabilities; each person seems to send contradictory messages that create double binds for each other (Esten & Willmott, 1993). The client communicates not only the desire to focus on the disability but also the desire to disregard it. What does the therapist do? If the therapist focuses on the disability, he or she violates the client's desire to ignore it; and if the therapist ignores the disability, this violates the client's desire to concentrate on it. Regardless of how the therapist responds, the response will violate one of the client's preferences. What guidelines would you offer the therapist or the client, based on your understanding of contradictory messages?

2. Do you accommodate to the communication styles of those with whom you interact? Do teachers and students or lawyers and witnesses or doctors and patients accommodate to each other's communication style? In what direction is there likely to be greater accommodation? For example, is the teacher or the student more likely to accommodate to the other?

3. Some researchers (e.g., Beier, 1974) argue that the impulse to communicate two different feelings (for example, "I love you" and "I don't love you") creates messages in which the verbal and nonverbal signals contradict each other. Do you think this idea has validity? What other explanations might you offer to account for contradictory messages?

4. Will the new communication technologies (for example, electronic mail, working at computer terminals, and telecommuting) change the basic principles of communication identified here?

5. In the aftermath of the catastrophic attacks on the World Trade Center and the Pentagon on September 11, 2001, in which some 3,000 people were killed, the Reverend Jerry Falwell on Pat Robertson's "700 Club" said: "God continues to lift the curtain and allow the enemies of America to give us probably what we deserve." He added: "I really

believe that the pagans, and the abortionists, and the feminists, and the gays and lesbians who are actively trying to make that an alternative lifestyle, the ACLU, People For the American Way, all of them who have tried to secularize America. I point the finger in their face and say, 'You helped this happen'" (CNN.com, September 14, 2001). Later, after considerable criticism—even from the White House—was voiced, Falwell then said "I would never blame any human being except the terrorists, and if I left that impression with gays or lesbians or anyone else, I apologize." How effectively or ineffectively did Falwell manage to reverse his prior messages in your mind?

6. **Researching the Principles of Communication.** How would you go about finding answers to questions such as these?

- Is there a gender difference in the ability to appreciate the punctuation of another person?
- Does relative status influence who accommodates to whom?
- Does the higher marital adjustment evidenced by symmetrical couples (over complementary couples) hold for all age groups? Does it hold for homosexual as it seems to hold for heterosexual relationships?
- What is the most effective way to "take back" an unkind or culturally insensitive remark?
- Do men and women accommodate in the same way and to the same extent, or do they accommodate differently?

UNIT 3
Culture and Communication

Unit Contents

When you speak or listen, you're doing so as a member of a particular and unique culture—you're greatly influenced by the teachings of your religion, racial and national history, the social expectations for your gender, and a host of other factors. In this unit you'll learn

▶ how culture influences communication

▶ how you can communicate more effectively in a world that's becoming increasingly multicultural

CULTURE AND COMMUNICATION

Culture (introduced briefly in Unit 1) consists of the relatively specialized lifestyle of a group of people: their values, beliefs, artifacts, ways of behaving, and ways of communicating. Included in a social group's "culture" is everything that members of that group have produced and developed— their language; ways of thinking; art; laws; religion; and, of course, communication theories, styles, and attitudes.

Culture is passed on from one generation to the next through communication, not through genes. Thus, the term *culture* does not refer to color of skin or shape of eyes, as these are passed on through genes, not communication. Because members of a particular race or country are often taught similar beliefs, attitudes, and values, this similarity makes it possible to speak of "Hispanic culture" or "African American culture." But it's important to realize that within any large culture—especially a culture based on race or nationality—there will be enormous differences. The Kansas farmer and the Wall Street executive may both be, say, German American, but may differ widely in their attitudes, beliefs, and lifestyles. In some ways the Kansas farmer may be closer in attitudes and values to a Chinese farmer than to the New York financier.

Gender—although transmitted genetically and not by communication—is considered a cultural variable largely because cultures teach boys and girls different attitudes, beliefs, values, and ways of communicating and relating to one another. Thus, you act like a man or a woman in part because of what your culture has taught you about how men and women should act. This does not, of course, deny that biological differences also play a role in the differences between male and female behavior. In fact, research continues to uncover biological roots of male/female differences

we once thought were entirely learned (McCroskey, 1997). An exercise, "How Can You Get from Culture to Gender?" further explores this topic; visit **www.ablongman.com/devito**.

Culture is transmitted from one generation to another through **enculturation,** the process by which you learn the culture into which you're born (your native culture). Parents, peer groups, schools, religious institutions, and government agencies are the main teachers of culture.

A different process of learning culture is **acculturation,** the process by which you learn the rules and norms of a culture different from your native culture. In acculturation your original or native culture is modified through direct contact with or exposure to a new and different culture. For example, when immigrants settle in the United States (the host culture), their own culture becomes influenced by the host culture. Gradually, the values, ways of behaving, and beliefs of the host culture become more and more a part of the immigrants' culture. At the same time, of course, the host culture changes too as it interacts with the immigrants' culture. Generally, however, the culture of the immigrant changes more. The reasons for this are that the host country's members far outnumber the immigrant group and that the media are largely dominated by and reflect the values and customs of the host culture (Kim, 1988).

New citizens' acceptance of the new culture depends on many factors (Kim, 1988). Immigrants who come from cultures similar to the host culture will become acculturated more easily. Similarly, those who are younger and better educated become acculturated more quickly than do older and less well educated people. Personality factors also play a part. Persons who are risk takers and open-minded, for example, have greater acculturation potential. Also, persons who are familiar with the host culture before immigration—through interpersonal contact

UNDERSTANDING THEORY AND RESEARCH

Cultural Theories

Consider two very different theories of culture: cultural evolution and cultural relativism. The theory of cultural evolution, or social Darwinism, holds that much as the human species evolved from lower life forms to Homo sapiens, cultures also evolve. Consequently, some cultures may be considered advanced and others primitive. Most contemporary scholars reject this view, because the judgments that distinguish one culture from another have no basis in science and are instead based on individual values and preferences as to what constitutes "civilized" and what constitutes "primitive."

The cultural relativism approach, on the other hand, holds that all cultures are different but that no culture is either superior or inferior to any other (Berry, Poortinga, Segall, & Dasen, 1992). Today this view is generally accepted and guides the infusion of cultural materials into contemporary textbooks on all academic levels. But this position does not imply that all cultural practices are therefore equal or that you have to accept all cultural practices equally. As noted in the text, there are many cultural practices popular throughout the world that you may find, quite logically and reasonably, unacceptable.

> **Working with Theories and Research.** *What do you think of these cultural theories? What arguments could you advance in support of or against social Darwinism? What arguments could you advance in support of or against cultural relativism?*

or through media exposure—will be acculturated more readily.

Before exploring further the role of culture in communication, consider your own cultural values and beliefs by taking the self-test below. This test illustrates how your own cultural values and beliefs may influence your interpersonal, small group, and public communications—both the messages you send and the messages you listen to.

TEST YOURSELF

What Are Your Cultural Beliefs and Values?

Here the extremes of 10 cultural differences are identified. For each characteristic indicate your own values:

a. If you feel your values are very similar to the extremes, then select 1 or 7.

b. If you feel your values are quite similar to the extremes, then select 2 or 6.
c. If you feel your values are fairly similar to the extremes, then select 3 or 5.
d. If you feel you're in the middle, then select 4.

Men and women are equal and are entitled to equality in all areas.	**Gender Equality** 1 2 3 4 5 6 7	Men and women are very different and should stick to the specific roles assigned to them by their culture.
"Success" is measured by your contribution to the group.	**Group and Individual Orientation** 1 2 3 4 5 6 7	"Success" is measured by how far you outperform others.
You should enjoy yourself as much as possible.	**Hedonism** 1 2 3 4 5 6 7	You should work as much as possible.

Religion is the final arbiter of what is right and wrong; your first obligation is to abide by the rules and customs of your religion.	**Religion** 1 2 3 4 5 6 7	Religion is like any other social institution; it's not inherently moral or right just because it's a religion.
Your first obligation is to your family; each person is responsible for the welfare of his or her family.	**Family** 1 2 3 4 5 6 7	Your first obligation is to yourself; each person is responsible for himself or herself.
Work hard now for a better future.	**Time Orientation** 1 2 3 4 5 6 7	Live in the present; the future may never come.
Romantic relationships, once made, are forever.	**Relationship Permanency** 1 2 3 4 5 6 7	Romantic relationships should be maintained as long as they're more rewarding than punishing and dissolved when they're more punishing than rewarding.
People should express their emotions openly and freely.	**Emotional Expression** 1 2 3 4 5 6 7	People should not reveal their emotions, especially those that may reflect negatively on them or others or make others feel uncomfortable.
Money is extremely important and should be a major consideration in just about any decision you make.	**Money** 1 2 3 4 5 6 7	Money is relatively unimportant and should not enter into life's really important decisions, such as what relationship to enter or what career to pursue.
The world is a just place; bad things happen to bad people and good things happen to good people; what goes around comes around.	**Belief in a Just World** 1 2 3 4 5 6 7	The world is random; bad and good things happen to people without any reference to whether they're good or bad people.

How did you do? This test was designed to help you explore the possible influence of your cultural beliefs and values on communication. If you visualize communication as involving choices, as discussed in the ethics box at the end of this unit, then your beliefs will influence the choices you make and thus how you communicate and how you listen and respond to the communications of others. For example, your beliefs and values about gender equality will influence the way in which you communicate with and about the opposite sex. Your group and individual orientation will influence how you perform in work teams and how you deal with your peers at school and at work. Your degree of hedonism will influence the kinds of communications you engage in, the books you read, and the television programs you watch. Your religious beliefs will influence the ethical system you follow in communicating. Review the entire list of 10 characteristics and try to identify one specific way in which each characteristic influences your communication.

What will you do? Are you satisfied with your responses? If not, how might you get rid of your unproductive or unrealistic beliefs? What beliefs would you ideally like to substitute for these? You may wish to continue this cultural awareness experience by taking another self-test, "What's Your Cultural Awareness?" at www.ablongman.com/devito. ✔

The Relevance of Culture

There are lots of reasons for the current cultural emphasis in the field of communication. Most obvious, perhaps, are the vast demographic changes taking place throughout the United States. Whereas at one time the United States was largely a country populated by northern Europeans, it's now a country greatly influenced by the enormous number of new citizens from Central and South America, Africa, and Asia. And the same is true to an even greater extent on college and university campuses throughout the United States. With these changes have come different customs and the need to understand and adapt to new ways of looking at communication.

As a people we've become increasingly sensitive to cultural differences. American society has moved from an assimilationist perspective (which holds that people should leave their native culture behind and adapt to their new culture) to a perspective that values cultural diversity (which holds that people

BUILDING COMMUNICATION SKILLS

How Can Culture Influence the Way People Talk?

Below are presented four communication situations. For each one, indicate how two typical representatives of the cultural extremes indicated would talk. What are some of the communication problems that might reasonably occur when people from these two extremes talk with each other?

▶ A supervisor criticizes the poorly written report of a subordinate and says that it must be redone. (high- and low-power-distance cultures)

▶ A worker tells a colleague that she may have chronic fatigue syndrome and is awaiting results of her blood tests. (masculine and feminine cultures)

▶ A group of six new advertising executives prepare to interact for the first time on a new project. (high- and low-context cultures)

▶ A passerby sees two preteen neighborhood children fighting in the street; no other adults are around, and the passerby worries that they may get hurt. (individualistic and collectivist cultures)

should retain their native cultural ways). And, with some notable exceptions—hate speech, racism, sexism, homophobia, and classism come quickly to mind—we're more concerned with communicating respectfully and ultimately with developing a society where all cultures can coexist and enrich each other. At the same time, the ability to interact effectively with members of other cultures often translates into financial gain and increased employment opportunities and advancement prospects.

Today most countries are economically dependent on each other. Our economic lives depend on our ability to communicate effectively across different cultures. Similarly, our political well-being depends in great part on that of other cultures. Political unrest in any part of the world—South Africa, eastern Europe, or the Middle East, to take a few examples—affects our security in the United States. Following the World Trade Center and Pentagon attacks, it became especially clear that intercultural communication and understanding are now more crucial than ever.

The rapid spread of communication technology has brought foreign and sometimes very different cultures right into our living rooms. News from foreign countries is commonplace. You see nightly—in vivid color—what is going on in remote countries. Technology has made intercultural communica-tion easy, practical, and inevitable. Daily the media bombard you with evidence of racial tensions, religious disagreements, sexual bias, and all the other problems caused when intercultural communication fails. And, of course, the Internet has made intercultural communication as easy as writing a note on your computer. You can now communicate by e-mail just as easily with someone in Europe or Asia, for example, as with someone in another city or state.

Still another reason is that communication competence is specific to a given culture; what proves effective in one culture may be ineffective in another. For example, in the United States corporate executives get down to business during the first several minutes of a meeting. In Japan, however, business executives interact socially for an extended period and try to find out something about one another. Thus, the communication principle influenced by U.S. culture would advise participants to get down to the meeting's agenda during the first five minutes. The principle influenced by Japanese culture would advise participants to avoid dealing with business until everyone has socialized sufficiently and feels well enough acquainted to begin negotiations. Each principle seems effective within its own culture and ineffective outside its own culture.

COMMUNICATION @ WORK

Rules and Norms in the Workplace

If you're going to play the game properly, you'd better know every rule.

—Barbara Jordan

Each organization, much like a larger culture, has its own rituals, norms, and rules for communicating. These rules—whether in the interview situation or in friendly conversation—delineate appropriate and inappropriate behavior, prescribe rewards and punishments for violating norms, and tell you what will help you get the job (or succeed in your job) and what won't. For example, the general advice given throughout this text is to emphasize your positive qualities, to highlight your abilities, and to minimize any negative characteristics or failings. But in some cultures—especially collectivist cultures such as those of China, Korea, and Japan—workers are expected to show modesty (Copeland & Griggs, 1985). If you stress your own competencies too much, you may be seen as arrogant, brash, and unfit to work in an organization that emphasizes teamwork and cooperation.

In collectivist cultures, great deference is to be shown to managers who represent the company. If you don't treat managers with respect, you may appear to be disrespecting the entire company. On the other hand, in individualistic cultures, such as that of the United States, too much deference may make you appear unassertive, unsure of yourself, and unable to assume a position of authority.

Thinking about Your Communicating @ Work

Can you identify at least one rule or norm that operated in a place in which you worked? How did you learn this rule or norm? What happened when it was violated?

The Aim of a Cultural Perspective

Because culture permeates all forms of communication, it is necessary to understand its influences if you are to understand how communication works and master its skills. As illustrated throughout this text, culture influences communications of all types (Moon, 1996). It influences what you say to yourself and how you talk with friends, lovers, and family in everyday conversation. It influences how you interact in groups and how much importance you place on the group versus the individual. It influences the topics you talk about and the strategies you use in communicating information or in persuading. And it influences how you use the media and the credibility you attribute to them.

A cultural emphasis helps distinguish what is universal (true for all people) from what is relative (true for people in one culture but not for people in other cultures) (Matsumoto, 1994). The principles for communicating information and for changing listeners' attitudes, for example, will vary from one culture to another. If you are to understand communication, then you need to know how its principles vary and how the principles must be qualified and adjusted on the basis of cultural differences.

And of course this cultural understanding is needed to communicate effectively in a wide variety of intercultural situations. Success in communication—on your job and in your social life—will depend on your ability to communicate effectively with persons who are culturally different from yourself.

As demonstrated throughout this text, cultural differences exist across the communication spectrum—from the way you use eye contact to the way you develop or dissolve a relationship (Chang & Holt, 1996). But these should not blind you to the great number of similarities that also exist among even the most widely separated cultures.

Close interpersonal relationships, for example, are common in all cultures, though they may be entered into for very different reasons by members of different cultures. Further, when reading about cultural differences, remember that these are usually matters of degree. Thus, most cultures value honesty, but not all value it to the same degree. Also, advances in media and technology and the widespread use of the Internet are influencing cultures and cultural change and are perhaps homogenizing cultures to some extent, lessening the differences and increasing the similarities. They are also tending to Americanize different cultures, because the dominant values and customs evidenced in the media and on the Internet are in large part American, a product of current U. S. dominance in both media and technology.

An emphasis on cultural awareness does not imply that you should accept all cultural practices or that all cultural practices are equal (Hatfield & Rapson,1996). For example, cockfighting, foxhunting, and bullfighting are parts of the culture of some Latin American countries, England, and Spain, but you need not find these activities acceptable or equal to cultural practices in which animals are treated kindly. Further, a cultural emphasis does not imply that you have to accept or follow even the practices of your own culture. For example, even if the majority in your culture finds cockfighting acceptable, you need not agree with or follow the practice. Similarly, you can reject your culture's values and beliefs; its religion or political system; or its attitudes toward the homeless, the handicapped, or the culturally different. Of course, going against your culture's traditions and values is often very difficult. But it is important to realize that although culture influences you, it does not determine your values or behavior. Often, for example, personality factors (such as your degree of assertiveness, extroversion, or optimism) will prove more influential than culture (Hatfield & Rapson, 1996). You may, at this point, want to examine your own cultural beliefs by looking at "How Can Cultural Beliefs Influence You?" at www.ablongman.com/devito.

HOW CULTURES DIFFER

There are at least four major ways in which cultures differ that are especially important for communica-

tion. Following Hofstede (1997) and Hall and Hall (1987), we'll consider collectivism and individualism, high and low context, power distances, and masculine and feminine cultures.

Individual and Collective Orientation

Cultures differ in the extent to which they promote individual values (for example, power, achievement, hedonism, and stimulation) versus collectivist values (for example, benevolence, tradition, and conformity). Americans generally have a preference for the individual values (Kapoor, Wolfe, & Blue, 1995).

One of the major differences between these two orientations is the extent to which an individual's goals or the group's goals are given precedence. Individual and collective tendencies are, of course, not mutually exclusive; this is not an all-or-none dimension but rather one of emphasis. You probably have both tendencies. For example, you may compete with other members of your basketball team for the most baskets or most valuable player award (and thus emphasize individual goals). At the same time, however, you will—in a game—act in a way that will benefit the entire team (and thus emphasize group goals). In actual practice both individual and collective tendencies will help you and your team each achieve your goals. Yet most people and most cultures have a dominant orientation; they're more individually oriented or more collectively oriented in most situations, most of the time.

In some instances, these tendencies may come into conflict. For example, do you shoot for the basket and try to raise your own individual score, or do you pass the ball to another player who is better positioned to score and thus benefit your team? You make this distinction in popular talk when you call someone a team player (collectivist orientation) or an individual player (individualistic orientation). In an **individualistic culture** members are responsible for themselves and perhaps their immediate family. In a **collectivist culture** members are responsible for the entire group.

Success, in an individualistic culture, is measured by the extent to which you surpass other members of your group; you take pride in standing out from the crowd. And your heroes—in the media, for example—are likely to be those who are unique and who stand apart. In a collectivist culture success is measured by your contribution to the achievements of the group as a whole; you take pride in your similarity to other members of your group. Your heroes are more likely to be team players who don't stand out from the rest of the group's members.

In an individualistic culture you're responsible to your own conscience, and responsibility is largely an individual matter; in a collectivist culture you're responsible to the rules of the social group, and responsibility for an accomplishment or a failure is shared by all members. Competition is fostered in individualistic cultures, whereas cooperation is promoted in collectivist cultures. In small group settings in an individualistic culture, you may compete for leadership; there will likely be a very clear distinction between leaders and members. In a collectivist culture leadership will often be shared and rotated; there will likely be little distinction between leader and members. These orientations also influence the kinds of communication members consider appropriate in an organizational context. For example, individualistic organization members favor clarity and directness; in contrast, collectivists favor "face-saving" and the avoidance of hurting others or arousing negative evaluations (Kim & Sharkey, 1995).

Distinctions between in-group members and out-group members are extremely important in collectivist cultures. In individualistic cultures, which prize each person's individuality, the distinction is likely to be less important.

High- and Low-Context Cultures

Cultures also differ in the extent to which information is made explicit, on the one hand, or is assumed to be in the context or in the persons communicating, on the other. A **high-context culture** is one in which much of the information in communication is in the context or in the person—for example, information that was shared through previous communications, through assumptions about each other, and through shared experiences. The information is thus known by all participants but it is not explicitly stated in the verbal message. A **low-context culture** is one in which most of the information is explicitly stated in the verbal

message. In formal transactions it will be stated in written (or contract) form.

To appreciate the distinction between high and low context, consider giving directions ("Where's the voter registration center?") to someone who knows the neighborhood and to a newcomer to your city. With someone who knows the neighborhood (a high-context situation), you can assume that the person knows the local landmarks. So you can give directions such as "next to the laundromat on Main Street" or "the corner of Albany and Elm." With a newcomer (a low-context situation), you cannot assume that the person shares any information with you. So you have to use only those directions that even a stranger will understand; for example, "Make a left at the next stop sign" or "Go two blocks and then turn right."

High-context cultures are also collectivist cultures (Gudykunst, Ting-Toomey, & Chua, 1988; Gudykunst & Kim, 1992). These cultures (Japanese, Arabic, Latin American, Thai, Korean, Apache, and Mexican are examples) place great emphasis on personal relationships and oral agreements (Victor, 1992). Low-context cultures are also individualistic cultures. These cultures (German, Swedish, Norwegian, and American are examples) place less emphasis on personal relationships and more emphasis on verbalized, explicit explanation and, for example, on written contracts in business transactions.

Members of high-context cultures spend lots of time getting to know one another interpersonally and socially before any important transactions take place. Because of this prior personal knowledge, a great deal of information is shared by the members and therefore does not have to be explicitly stated. Members of low-context cultures spend a great deal less time getting to know one another and hence don't have that shared knowledge. As a result everything has to be stated explicitly.

A frequent source of intercultural misunderstanding that can be traced to the distinction between high- and low-context cultures can be seen in **face-saving** (Hall & Hall, 1987). People in high-context cultures place a great deal more emphasis on face-saving. For example, they're more likely to avoid argument for fear of causing others to lose face, whereas people in low-context cultures (with their individualistic orientation) will use argument to win a point. Similarly, in high-context cultures criticism should take place only in private. Low-

GOING ONLINE

DiversityInc.com Website
http://www.diversityinc.com/index.efm?watchname=google

DiversityInc.com is an especially interesting website, offering a wealth of material and hotlinks to relevant cultural discussions, issues, publications, and the like.

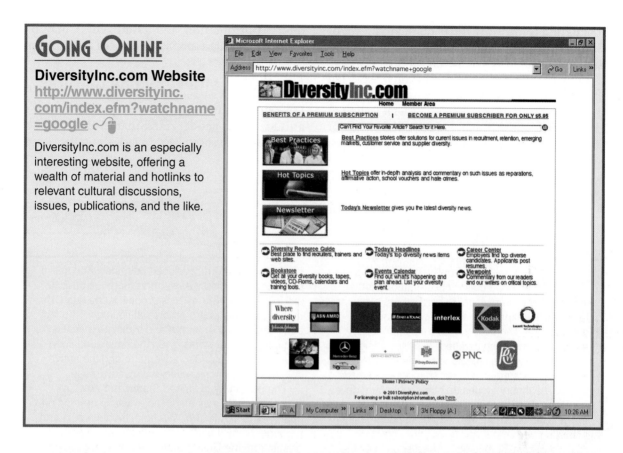

context cultures may not make this public–private distinction. Low-context managers who criticize high-context workers in public will find that their criticism causes interpersonal problems—and does little to resolve the original difficulty that led to the criticism in the first place (Victor, 1992).

Members of high-context cultures are reluctant to say *no* for fear of offending and causing the person to lose face. So, for example, it's necessary to understand when the Japanese executive's *yes* means yes and when it means no. The difference is not in the words used but in the way in which they're used. It's easy to see how the low-context individual may interpret this reluctance to be direct—to say no when you mean no—as a weakness or as an unwillingness to confront reality.

Power Distances

In some cultures power is concentrated in the hands of a few, and there's a great difference between the power held by these people and the power of the ordinary citizen. These are called *high-*power-distance cultures; examples are Mexico, Brazil, India, and the Philippines (Hofstede, 1997). In *low-power-distance cultures*, power is more evenly distributed throughout the citizenry; examples include Denmark, New Zealand, Sweden, and to a lesser extent the United States. These differences impact communication in numerous ways. For example, in high-power-distance cultures there's a great power distance between students and teachers; students are expected to be modest, polite, and totally respectful. In low-power-distance cultures (and you can see this clearly in U.S. college classrooms) students are expected to demonstrate their knowledge and command of the subject matter, participate in discussions with the teacher, and even challenge the teacher—something many high-power-distance culture members wouldn't even think of doing.

Friendship and dating relationships will also be influenced by the power distance between groups (Andersen, 1991). In India, for example, such relationships are expected to take place within your cultural class. In Sweden a person is expected to select friends and romantic partners on the basis not of class or culture but of individual factors such as personality, appearance, and the like.

In low-power-distance cultures you're expected to confront a friend, partner, or supervisor assertively; there is in these cultures a general feeling of equality that is consistent with assertive behavior (Borden, 1991). In high-power-distance cultures, direct confrontation and assertiveness may be viewed negatively, especially if directed at a superior.

Masculine and Feminine Cultures

Especially important for self-concept is the culture's attitude about gender roles; that is, about how a man or woman should act. In fact, a popular classi-

MEDIA WATCH

CULTURAL IMPERIALISM

Political imperialism is a policy of expanding the dominion of one country over that of another. The phrase *cultural imperialism* refers to a similar process: the expansion of dominion by one culture over another. The theory of cultural imperialism affords an interesting perspective on the influence of media, especially as media exert influence over and even dominate other cultures (Becker & Roberts, 1992). The theory argues that the media from developed countries such as the United States and western Europe dominate the cultures of countries importing such media.

This cultural dominance is also seen in online communication, in which the United States and the English language dominate. "And some countries," notes one journalist, "already unhappy with the encroachment of American culture—from jeans and Mickey Mouse to movies and TV programs—are worried that their cultures will be further eroded by an American dominance of cyberspace" (Pollack, 1995, p. D1).

Media products from the United States are likely to emphasize its dominant attitudes and values; for example, the preference for competition, the importance of individuality, the advantages of capitalism and democracy, safe sex and health consciousness, and the importance of money. Through cultural imperialism, it would be argued, the attitudes and values of the dominant U.S. media culture will become the attitudes and values of the rest of the world.

Television programs, films, and music from the United States and western Europe are so popular and so in demand in developing countries that they may actually inhibit the growth of native cultures' own talent. So, for example, instead of expressing their own vision in an original television drama or film, native writers in developing countries may find it easier and more secure to work as translators for products from more developed countries. And native promoters may find it easier and more lucrative to sell, say, United States rock groups' tapes and CDs than to cultivate and promote native talent. The fact that it is cheaper to import and translate than it is to create original works gives the developed country's products an added advantage and the native culture's productions a decided disadvantage.

The popularity of United States and Western Europe's media may also lead artists in developing countries to imitate. For example, media artists and producers may imitate films and television programs from the United States rather than develop their own styles, styles more consistent with their native culture.

Although the term *cultural imperialism* is a negative one, the actual process of media influence may be viewed as negative or positive, depending on your cultural perspective. Some people might argue that the media products from the United States are generally superior to those produced elsewhere and so serve as a kind of benchmark and standard for quality work throughout the world.

Also, it might be argued that such products introduce new trends and perspectives and hence enrich the native culture. Much as people in the United States profit from the influence of new cultural strains, the developing cultures profit when United States media introduce, for example, new perspectives on government and politics, foods, educational technologies, and health.

Follow-Up *What do you think of the influence the media from the United States and western Europe are having on native cultures throughout the world? How do you evaluate it? Do you see advantages? Disadvantages?*

fication of cultures is in terms of their masculinity and femininity (Hofstede, 1997, 1998). In a highly *masculine culture*, people value male aggressiveness, material success, and strength. Women, on the other hand, are valued for their modesty, focus on the quality of life, and tenderness. A highly *feminine culture* values modesty, concern for relationships and the quality of life, and tenderness in both men and women. On the basis of Hofstede's (1997, 1998) research, the 10 countries with the highest masculinity score are (beginning with the highest) Japan, Austria, Venezuela, Italy, Switzerland, Mexico, Ireland, Jamaica, Great Britain, and Germany. The 10 countries with the highest femininity score are (beginning with the highest) Sweden, Norway, Netherlands, Denmark, Costa Rica, Yugoslavia, Finland, Chile, Portugal, and Thailand. Of the 53 countries ranked, the United States ranks 15th most masculine.

Masculine cultures emphasize success and so socialize their members to be assertive, ambitious, and competitive. For example, members of masculine cultures are more likely to confront conflicts directly and to fight out any differences competitively; they're more likely to emphasize win–lose conflict strategies. Feminine cultures emphasize the quality of life and so socialize their members to be modest and to highlight close interpersonal relationships. Feminine cultures, for example, are more likely to utilize compromise and negotiation in resolving conflicts; they're more likely to seek win-win solutions.

Similarly, organizations can be viewed as masculine or feminine. Masculine organizations emphasize competitiveness and aggressiveness. They stress the bottom line and reward their workers on the basis of their contribution to the organization. Feminine organizations are less competitive and less aggressive. They emphasize worker satisfaction and reward their workers on the basis of need; those who have large families, for example, may get better raises than single people, even if they haven't contributed as much to the organization.

IMPROVING INTERCULTURAL COMMUNICATION

An understanding of the role of culture in communication is an essential foundation for understand-

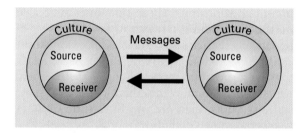

Figure 3.1
A Model of Intercultural Communication
This basic model of intercultural communication is designed to illustrate that culture is a part of every communication transaction. What other ways can you think of to illustrate the process of intercultural communication?

ing intercultural communication as it occurs interpersonally, in small groups, in public speaking, or in the media—and for appreciating the principles of effective intercultural communication. As discussed in Unit 1, the term *intercultural communication* refers to communication between persons who have different cultural beliefs, values, or ways of behaving. The model in Figure 3.1 illustrates this concept. The larger circles represent the culture of the individual communicator. The inner circles identify the communicators (the sources/receivers). In this model each communicator is a member of a different culture. In some instances the cultural differences are relatively slight—say, between persons from Toronto and New York. In other instances the cultural differences are great—say, between persons from Borneo and Germany, or between persons from rural Nigeria and industrialized England.

All messages originate from a specific and unique cultural context, and that context influences their content and form. You communicate as you do largely as a result of your culture. Culture (along with the processes of enculturation and acculturation) influences every aspect of your communication experience.

You receive messages through the filters imposed by your cultural context. That context influences what you receive and how you receive it. For example, people in some cultures rely heavily on television or newspapers and trust them implicitly. Others rely on face-to-face interpersonal interactions, distrusting many of the mass communication systems.

Here then are a variety of principles for increasing intercultural communication effectiveness—in conversation, on the job, and in friendly and romantic relationships. These guidelines are based on the intercultural research of a wide variety of researchers (Barna, 1985; Ruben, 1985; Gudykunst & Kim, 1992; Hofstede, 1997, 1998). As a preface to these suggestions, try examining your own openness to intercultural communication by taking the self-test "How open are you interculturally?" at www.ablongman.com/devito.

Recognize and Reduce Your Ethnocentrism

Ethnocentrism, one of the biggest obstacles to intercultural communication, is the tendency to see others and their behaviors through your own cultural filters, often as distortions of your own behaviors. It is the tendency to evaluate the values, beliefs, and behaviors of your own culture as superior—as more positive, logical, and natural than those of other cultures. To achieve effective interpersonal communication, you need to see yourself and others as different but as neither inferior nor superior—not an easily accomplished task.

Ethnocentrism exists on a continuum. People are not either ethnocentric or un-ethnocentric; rather, most are somewhere between these polar opposites (see Table 3.1). Note also that your degree of ethno-

centrism depends on the group on which you're focusing. For example, if you're a Greek American, you may have a low degree of ethnocentrism when dealing with Italian Americans but a high degree when dealing with Turkish Americans or Japanese Americans. Most important for our purposes is that your degree of ethnocentrism (and we are all ethnocentric to at least some degree) will influence your intercultural interpersonal communications.

Be Mindful

Being mindful rather than mindless (a distinction considered in Unit 9), is generally helpful in intercultural communication situations (Burgoon, Berger, & Waldron, 2000). When you're in a mindless state, you behave on the basis of assumptions that would not normally pass intellectual scrutiny. For example, you know that cancer is not contagious, and yet you may still avoid touching cancer patients. You know that people who are blind generally don't have hearing problems, yet you may use a louder voice when talking to persons without sight. Approximately one-third of the college students participating in one study said that they would not go swimming in a pool used by mental patients and that they would wash their hands after

---

TABLE 3.1   The Ethnocentrism Continuum

Drawing from several researchers (Lukens, 1978; Gudykunst & Kim, 1984; Gudykunst, 1991), this table summarizes some interconnections between ethnocentrism and communication. In this table five degrees of ethnocentrism are identified; in reality, of course, there are as many degrees as there are people. The "communication distances" are simply general terms that highlight the major communication attitude that dominates that level of ethnocentrism. Under "communications" are some ways a person might behave given his or her particular degree of ethnocentrism. How would you have rated yourself on this scale five years ago? How would you rate yourself today?

Degrees of Ethnocentrism	Communication Distance	Communications
Low	Equality	Treats others as equals; evaluates other ways of doing things as equal to own
	Sensitivity	Wants to decrease distance between self and others
	Indifference	Lacks concern for others but is not hostile
	Avoidance	Avoids and limits interpersonal interactions with others; prefers to be with own kind
High	Disparagement	Engages in hostile behavior; belittles others; views own culture as superior to other cultures

BUILDING COMMUNICATION SKILLS

How Can You Confront Intercultural Difficulties?

How might you deal with each of the following obstacles to intercultural communication? If you have the opportunity, share responses with others. You'll gain a wealth of practical insights.

▶ Your friend makes fun of Radha, who comes to class in her native African dress. You feel you want to object to this.

▶ Sarah is a close friend and is really an open-minded person. But she has the habit of referring to members of other racial and ethnic groups with the most derogatory language. You decide to tell her that you object to this way of talking.

▶ Tom, a good friend of yours, wants to ask Pat out for a date. Both you and Tom know that Pat is a lesbian and will refuse the date, yet Tom says he's going to have some fun and ask her anyway—just to give her a hard time. You think this is wrong and want to tell Tom you think so.

▶ Your parents persist in holding stereotypes about other religious, racial, and ethnic groups. These stereotypes come up in all sorts of conversations. You're really embarrassed by these attitudes and feel you must tell your parents how incorrect you think these stereotypes are.

▶ Lenny, a colleague at work, recently underwent a religious conversion. He now persists in trying to get everyone else—yourself included—to see the light. You decide to tell him that you find this behavior offensive.

touching a mental patient (Jones et al., 1984). When the discrepancies between behaviors and available evidence are pointed out and your mindful state is awakened, you quickly realize that these behaviors are not logical or realistic.

Face Fears

Another factor that stands in the way of effective intercultural communication is fear (Stephan & Stephan, 1985; Gudykunst, 1994). You may fear for your self-esteem. You may become anxious about your ability to control the intercultural situation, or you may worry about your own level of discomfort.

You may fear that you'll be taken advantage of by the member of the other culture. Depending on your own stereotypes, you may fear being lied to, financially duped, or made fun of. You may fear that members of this other group will react to you negatively. They may not like you or may disapprove of your attitudes or beliefs or may even reject you as a person. Conversely, you may fear negative reactions from members of your own group. They might, for example, disapprove of your socializing with people who are culturally different.

These fears—coupled with the greater effort that intercultural communication takes and the ease with which you communicate with those who are culturally similar—can easily create sufficient anxiety to make some people give up.

Recognize Differences

When you assume that all people are similar and ignore the differences between yourself and culturally different persons, your intercultural efforts are likely to fail. This is especially true in the area of values, attitudes, and beliefs. It's easy to see and accept different hairstyles, clothing, and foods. But when it comes to values and beliefs, it's easier to assume (mindlessly) that deep down we're all similar. We aren't. Henry may be a devout Baptist, Carol may be an atheist, and Jan may be a Muslim. Because of the differences in their religious views, each person sees his or her own life as having a very different meaning. When you assume similarities and ignore differences, you may implicitly communicate to others that you feel your ways are right and their ways are wrong. The result is confusion and misunderstanding on both sides.

Be especially alert to differences within cultural groups. Within every cultural group there are wide and important differences. Just as we know that all Americans are not alike (think of the various groups found in your city or even within your own school), so neither are all Jamaicans, Koreans, Mexicans, and so on. Within each culture there are many smaller cultures. These smaller cultures differ from one another and from the majority culture. Further, members of one smaller culture may share a great deal with members of that same smaller culture in another part of the world. Farmers in Indiana may have more in common with farmers in Borneo than with bankers in Indianapolis. For example, all will be concerned with weather conditions, crop rotation, and soil composition. Of course, these farmers, so similar when it comes to farming, may differ drastically on such issues as sales techniques, community governance, and the rights of women.

Avoid Overattribution

Overattribution is the tendency to attribute too much of a person's behavior or attitudes to one of that person's characteristics (she thinks that way because she's a woman; he believes that because he was raised as a Catholic). In intercultural communication situations, overattribution appears in two ways. First, it's the tendency to see too much of what a person believes or does as caused by the person's cultural identification. Second, it's the tendency to see a person as a spokesperson for his or her particular culture—to assume that because a person is, say, African American, he or she is therefore knowledgeable about the entire African American experience; or that the person's thoughts are always focused on African American issues. People's ways of thinking and ways of behaving are influenced by a wide variety of factors; culture is just one of them.

UNDERSTANDING THEORY AND RESEARCH

Language and Thought

The linguistic relativity hypothesis claims that because the language you speak influences the thoughts you have, people speaking widely differing languages will think differently and will see the world differently.

Theory and research, however, have not been able to find support for this claim. A more modified hypothesis currently seems supported: The language you speak helps you to talk about what you see and perhaps to highlight what you see. For example, if you speak a language that is rich in color terms (English is a good example), you will find it easier to talk about nuances of color than will someone from a culture that has fewer color terms; some cultures, for example, distinguish only two or three or four parts of the color spectrum. But this doesn't mean that people see the world differently, only that their language helps (or doesn't help) them to talk about certain variations in the world and may make it easier (or more difficult) for them to focus their thinking on such variations.

Nor does it mean that people speaking widely differing languages are doomed to misunderstand one another. Translation enables us to understand a great deal of the meaning in a foreign language message. And, of course, we have our communication skills; we can ask for clarification, additional examples, or restatement. We can give feedforward and feedback, use perception checking (Unit 4), and listen actively (Unit 5).

Language differences don't make for very important differences in perception or thought. Difficulties in intercultural understanding are more often due to ineffective communication than to differences in languages.

Working with Theories and Research. *Recall a few recent communication interactions in which misunderstandings occurred. What caused these misunderstandings? Can you recall any misunderstandings that might be attributed to a particular language's leading its speakers to see or interpret things differently?*

Recognize Differences in Meaning in Verbal and Nonverbal Messages

Meaning does not exist solely in the words we use. Rather, it exists mainly in the person using the words. This principle is especially important in intercultural communication. Consider the differences in meaning that might exist for the word *woman* to an American and an Iranian. What about *religion* to a Christian fundamentalist and to an atheist, or *lunch* to a Chinese rice farmer and a Wall Street executive? Or consider the meanings of the words *security, future,* and *family* when used by a New England prep school student and by a homeless teenager in Los Angeles.

When it comes to nonverbal messages, the potential differences are even greater. Thus, the over-the-head clasped hands that signify victory to an American may signify friendship to a Russian. To an American, holding up two fingers to make a V signifies victory. To certain South Americans, however, it's an obscene gesture that corresponds to our extended middle finger. Tapping the side of your nose will signify that you and the other person are in on a secret in England or Scotland, but that the other person is nosy in Wales. A friendly wave of the hand will prove insulting in Greece, where the wave of friendship must show the back rather than the front of the hand.

Avoid Violating Cultural Rules and Customs

Each culture has its own rules and customs for communicating. These **cultural rules** identify what is appropriate and what is inappropriate. Thus, for example, if you lived in a middle-class community in Connecticut, you would follow the rules of the culture and call the person you wished to date three or four days in advance. If you lived in a different culture, you might be expected to call the parents of your future date weeks or even months in advance. In this same Connecticut community, you might say, as a courteous remark to people you don't ever want to see again, "Come on over and pay us a visit." In other cultures, this comment would be sufficient to cause these people to visit at their convenience.

In some cultures, members show respect by avoiding direct eye contact with the person to whom they're speaking. In other cultures this same eye avoidance would signal lack of interest. In some Mediterranean cultures men walk arm in arm. Other cultures consider this inappropriate.

A good example of a series of rules for an extremely large and important culture that many people don't know appears in Table 3.2 on page 50. In looking over the list of "commandments" for communicating with people with disabilities, consider if you've seen any violations. Were you explicitly taught any of these principles?

Avoid Evaluating Differences Negatively

Be careful not to evaluate negatively the cultural differences you perceive. That is, avoid falling into the trap of ethnocentric thinking, evaluating your culture positively and other cultures negatively. For example, many Americans of northern European

Which suggestion for improving intercultural communication do you find most relevant? Can you identify the kinds of problems that might arise when such a suggestion is not followed?

TABLE 3.2   Ten Commandments for Communicating with People with Disabilities

1. Speak directly rather than through a companion or sign language interpreter who may be present.

2. Offer to shake hands when introduced. People with limited hand use or an artificial limb can usually shake hands, and offering the left hand is an acceptable greeting.

3. Always identify yourself and others who may be with you when meeting someone with a visual impairment. When conversing in a group, remember to identify the person to whom you're speaking.

4. If you offer assistance, wait until the offer is accepted. Then listen or ask for instructions.

5. Treat adults as adults. Address people who have disabilities by their first names only when extending that same familiarity to all others. Never patronize people in wheelchairs by patting them on the head or shoulder.

6. Don't lean against or hang on someone's wheelchair. Bear in mind that disabled people treat their chairs as extensions of their bodies.

7. Listen attentively when talking with people who have difficulty speaking and wait for them to finish. If necessary, ask short questions that require short answers, a nod, or shake of the head. Never pretend to understand if you're having difficulty doing so. Instead repeat what you've understood and allow the person to respond.

8. Place yourself at eye level when speaking with someone in a wheelchair or on crutches.

9. Tap a hearing impaired person on the shoulder or wave your hand to get his or her attention. Look directly at the person and speak clearly, slowly, and expressively to establish if the person can read your lips. If so, try to face the light source and keep hands, cigarettes, and food away from your mouth when speaking.

10. Relax. Don't be embarrassed if you happen to use common expressions such as "See you later," or "Did you hear about this?" that seem to relate to a person's ability.

Source: From the *New York Times*, June 7, 1993. Copyright © 1993 by the *New York Times*. Reprinted by permission.

---

descent evaluate negatively the tendency of many Hispanics and southern Europeans to use the street for a gathering place, for playing dominos, and for just sitting on a cool evening. Whether you like or dislike using the street in this way, recognize that neither attitude is logically correct or incorrect. This street behavior is simply adequate or inadequate for members of the culture.

Remember that you learned your behaviors from your culture. The behaviors are not natural or innate. Therefore, try viewing these variations nonevaluatively. See them as different but equal.

Recognize That Culture Shock Is Normal

The term **culture shock** refers to the psychological reaction you experience at being in a culture very different from your own (Furnham & Bochner, 1986). Culture shock is normal; most people expe-rience it when entering a new and different culture. Nevertheless, it can be unpleasant and frustrating and can sometimes lead to a permanently negative attitude toward this new culture. Understanding the normalcy of culture shock will help lessen any potential negative implications.

Part of culture shock results from your feelings of alienation, conspicuousness, and difference from everyone else. When you lack knowledge of the rules and customs of the new society, you can't communicate effectively. You're apt to blunder frequently and seriously. The person experiencing culture shock may not know some very basic things:

- how to ask someone for a favor or pay someone a compliment

- how to extend or accept an invitation for dinner

- how early or how late to arrive for an appointment or how long to stay

- how to distinguish seriousness from playfulness and politeness from indifference

- how to dress for an informal, formal, or business function
- how to order a meal in a restaurant or how to summon a server

Anthropologist Kalervo Oberg (1960), who first used the term *culture shock*, notes that it occurs in stages. These stages are useful for examining many encounters with the new and the different. Going away to college, getting married, or joining the military, for example, can all result in culture shock.

At the first stage, the *honeymoon*, there's fascination, even enchantment, with the new culture and its people. You finally have your own apartment. You're your own boss. Finally, on your own! Among people who are culturally different, the early (and superficial) relationships of this stage are characterized by cordiality and friendship. Many tourists remain at this stage because their stay in foreign countries is so brief.

At stage two, the *crisis* stage, the differences between your own culture and the new one create problems. In the new apartment example, no longer do you find dinner ready for you unless you do it yourself. Your clothes are not washed or ironed unless you do them yourself. Feelings of frustration and inadequacy come to the fore. This is the stage at which you experience the actual shock of the new culture. In one study of foreign students from more than 100 different countries studying in 11 different countries, it was found that 25 percent of the students experienced depression (Klineberg & Hull, 1979).

During the third period, *recovery*, you gain the skills necessary to function effectively. You learn how to shop, cook, and plan a meal. You find a local laundry and figure you'll learn how to iron later. You learn the language and ways of the new culture. Your feelings of inadequacy subside.

At the final stage, *adjustment*, you adjust to and come to enjoy the new culture and the new experiences. You may still experience periodic difficulties and strains, but on the whole the experience is pleasant. Actually, you're now a pretty decent cook. You're even coming to enjoy it. You're making a good salary, so why learn to iron?

Simply spending time in a foreign country is not sufficient for the development of positive attitudes; in fact, limited contact with nationals often leads to the development of negative attitudes. Rather, friendships with nationals are crucial for satisfaction with the new culture. Contacts only with other expatriates or sojourners are not sufficient (Torbiorn, 1982).

People may also experience culture shock when they return to their original culture after living in a foreign culture—a kind of reverse culture shock (Jandt, 2000). Consider, for example, Peace Corps volunteers who have been working in a rural and economically deprived area. Upon returning to Las Vegas or Beverly Hills, they too may experience culture shock. Sailors who serve long periods aboard ship and then return to an isolated farming community may also experience culture shock. In these cases, however, the recovery period is shorter and the sense of inadequacy and frustration is less.

REFLECTIONS ON ETHICS IN HUMAN COMMUNICATION

Culture and Ethics

Throughout history there have been numerous cultural practices that today would be judged unethical and even illegal. Sacrificing virgins to the gods and sending children to fight wars are obvious examples. But even today there are practices woven deep into the fabric of different cultures that many people would find unethical. Consider just a few of these:

1. Some cultures support bronco riding, a practice seen in numerous cowboy movies, in which the bull's testicles are tied to cause pain so that the animal will buck and throw off the rider.
2. Some cultures support cockfighting, in which chickens fight each other to the death, often with razor blades strapped onto their legs.

3. Some cultures support female circumcision, whereby part or all of a young girl's genitals are surgically altered so that she can never experience sexual intercourse without extreme pain, a practice designed to keep her a virgin until marriage.

4. Some cultures practice slavery, a system many people think has been erased from the globe.

5. Some cultures punish a woman for being raped—often to the extent of killing her.

6. Some cultures support the belief and practice that a woman must be subservient to her husband's will.

What would you do? *Imagine that you're on a television talk show dealing with the topic of cultural differences and diversity. During the discussion one or another panelist endorses each of the above practices, is arguing that each culture has a right to its own customs and beliefs and that no one has the right to object to cultural traditions. Given your own beliefs about these issues and about cultural diversity in general, what ethical obligations do you have as a member of this panel?*

 # SUMMARY

This unit introduced the study of culture and its relationship to communication and considered how cultures differ and some of the theories developed to explain how culture and communication affect each other. In addition, the unit introduced the study of intercultural communication and its nature and principles.

1. Culture consists of the relatively specialized lifestyle of a group of people—their values, beliefs, artifacts, ways of behaving, and ways of communicating—that is passed on from one generation to the next through communication rather than through genes.

2. Enculturation is the process by which culture is transmitted from one generation to the next.

3. Acculturation involves the processes by which one culture is modified through contact with or exposure to another culture.

4. Cultures differ in terms of individualistic or collectivist orientations, high and low context, high and low power distance, and masculinity and femininity.

5. Individualistic cultures emphasize individual values such as power and achievement, whereas collectivist cultures emphasize group values such as cooperation and responsibility to the group.

6. In high-context cultures much information is in the context or the person, whereas in low-context cultures information is expected to be made explicit.

7. In high-power-distance cultures there are large differences in power between people; in low-power-distance cultures power is more evenly distributed throughout the population.

8. Masculine cultures emphasize assertiveness, ambition, and competition; feminine cultures emphasize compromise and negotiation.

9. Intercultural communication is communication among people who have different cultural beliefs, values, or ways of behaving.

10. Among guidelines for more effective intercultural communication are: recognize and reduce your ethnocentrism, be mindful, face fears, recognize differences, avoid overattribution, recognize differences in meaning in verbal and nonverbal messages, avoid violating cultural rules and customs, avoid evaluating differences negatively, and recognize that culture shock is normal.

 # KEY TERMS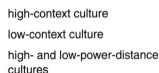

culture
enculturation
acculturation
collectivist and individualist cultures

high-context culture
low-context culture
high- and low-power-distance cultures

masculine culture
feminine culture
ethnocentrism
culture shock

THINKING CRITICALLY ABOUT

Culture and Communication

1. Theories of social Darwinism or cultural evolution hold that much as the human species evolved from lower life forms to Homo sapiens, cultures also evolve. Consequently, some cultures may be considered advanced and others primitive. Most contemporary scholars reject this view, because the judgments that distinguish one culture from another have no basis in science and are instead based on individual values and preferences as to what constitutes "civilized" and what constitutes "primitive." The cultural relativism approach, on the other hand, holds that all cultures are different but that no culture is either superior or inferior to any other (Berry, Poortinga, Segall, & Dasen, 1992). Today this view is generally accepted and guides the infusion of cultural materials into contemporary textbooks on all academic levels. What do you think of these positions?

2. Consider how cultural differences underlie some of the most hotly debated topics in the news today. The following, for example, is a brief list of some of these topics, here identified with specific questions. How would you answer these? How do your cultural attitudes, beliefs, and values influence your responses?

   - Should Christian Science parents be prosecuted for preventing their children from receiving life-saving treatment such as blood transfusions? Some states, such as Connecticut and Arizona, grant Christian Scientists special rights in this regard. Should this special treatment be adopted by all states? Should it be eliminated?
   - Should cockfighting be permitted or declared illegal in all states as "cruelty to animals"? Some Latin Americans have argued that this is a part of their culture and should be permitted. At present it's illegal in most of the United States but legal in five states and Puerto Rico.
   - Should same-sex marriages be legalized? Test cases of same-sex marriage and efforts to pass a Defense of Marriage Act (designed to prohibit such unions) are regularly in the news.
   - Should safe sex practices be taught in public schools? (Recall that President Clinton fired former U.S. Surgeon General Joycelyn Elders for suggesting that masturbation be discussed in the schools.)
   - Should those who commit hate or bias crimes be given harsher sentences?
   - Should doctor-assisted suicide be legalized?
   - Should the race of the child and that of the adopting parents be a relevant issue in adoption decisions?

3. The U.S. Department of Education has issued guidelines (recommendations that are not legally binding on school boards) covering the types of religious communications and activities public schools may permit (*New York Times*, August 26, 1995, Section A, pp. 1, 8). Among the permitted activities are student prayer, student-initiated discussions of religion, saying grace, proselytizing that would not be considered harassment, and the wearing of religious symbols and clothing. Among the forbidden activities: prayer endorsed by teachers or administrators, invitations to prayer that could constitute harassment, teaching a particular religion (rather than about religion), encouraging (officially or through teaching) either religious or antireligious activity, and denying school facilities to religious groups if these same facilities are provided to nonreligious groups. What do you think of these guidelines? If you were a member of a local school board, would you vote to adopt or reject these guidelines? How do your cultural beliefs influence your view of these guidelines?

4. In this age of multiculturalism, how do you feel about Article II, Section 1, of the U.S. Constitution? This section reads in part: "No person except a natural-born citizen, or citizen of the United States at the time of the adoption of this Constitution, shall be eligible to the office of President."

5. How do you feel about the Boy Scouts' being allowed to exclude gay men from serving as troop leaders? How do you feel about large corporations (Merrill Lynch, for example) that continue to support the Boy Scouts?

6. Recently, the Emma Lazarus poem on the Statue of Liberty was changed. The words "the wretched refuse of your teeming shore" were deleted and the poem now reads:

   > Give me your tired, your poor,
   > Your huddled masses yearning to breathe free, . . .
   > Send these, the homeless, tempest-tost to me:
   > I lift my lamp beside the golden door.

   Harvard zoologist Stephen Jay Gould, commenting on this change, notes that with the words omitted the poem no longer has balance or rhyme and, more important, no longer represents what Lazarus wrote (Gould, 1995). "The language police triumph," notes Gould, "and integrity bleeds." On the other hand, it can be argued that calling immigrants "wretched refuse" is insulting and degrading and that if Lazarus had been writing today, she would not have used that phrase. How do you feel about this? Would you have supported the deletion of this line?

7. With the growth of the Internet, the question of a universal language—that would be known by everyone around the world—has become a hot topic. In many ways, and largely because of the Internet, English is now the world's universal language. What do you think of English as a universal language? Would you propose a different language? What arguments for and against English as a universal language would you see as crucial in this debate (Kramarae, 1999)?

8. Do you agree with the assumption that everyone is ethnocentric to some degree? If so, where would you place yourself on the ethnocentric continuum when the "other" is a person of the opposite sex? A person of a different affectional orientation? A person of a different race? A person of a different religion?

9. Research shows that differences in power distance are significantly related to the style of leadership found in businesses and to the frequency of dis-agreements in the workplace (Offerman & Hellman, 1997; Smith, Dugan, Peterson, & Leung, 1998). What relationships do you think were found? For example, what type of leadership style would be more frequent in high-power-distance cultures? Which would be more frequent in low-power-distance cultures? In which cultural group would disagreements be more frequent?

10. **Researching Culture and Communication.** How would you go about finding answers to such questions as these?

    - Are relationships between persons of similar individualistic–collectivist orientations more or less likely to involve conflicts?
    - Are people living in high- and low-power-distance cultures different in terms of their perceived level of happiness?
    - Do men and women differ in their preference for explicit communications, despite their high- or low-context orientation?
    - Do men and women have different rules for politeness in conversation? In business?
    - Do couples with similar ratings on the cultural differences scale stay together longer than couples with dissimilar ratings? Do couples with similar ratings have fewer and less severe conflicts than couples with dissimilar ratings?
    - Are persons with greater education more likely to enter relationships with dissimilar others than persons with less education?

UNIT 4
Perception

Unit Contents

You speak or listen on the basis of the way you perceive yourself, other people, and the world in general. You don't, for example, communicate with friends and enemies in the same way; nor do you see yourself in the same way that others do. In this unit you'll learn

▶ how the processes of perception influence your communication

▶ how you can increase your perceptual accuracy and hence your communication efficiency and effectiveness

THE PERCEPTION PROCESS

Perception is the process by which you become aware of objects, events, and, especially, people through your senses: sight, smell, taste, touch, and hearing. Your perceptions result from what exists in the world *and* from your own experiences, desires, needs and wants, loves and hatreds. Among the reasons why perception is so important in communication is that it influences your communication choices. The messages you send and listen to will depend on how you see the world, on how you size up specific situations, on what you think of the people with whom you interact.

Perception is a continuous series of processes that blend into one another. *For convenience of discussion* we can separate these processes into five stages: (1) You sense some kind of stimulation; (2) you organize the stimuli in some way; (3) you interpret and evaluate what you perceive; (4) you store it in memory; and (5) you retrieve it when needed.

Stage 1: Stimulation

At this first stage, your sense organs are stimulated—you hear a new CD, you see a friend, you smell someone's perfume, you taste an orange, you feel another's sweaty palm. Naturally, you don't perceive everything; rather, you engage in *selective perception*, a general term that includes selective attention and selective exposure. In selective attention, you attend to those things that you anticipate will fulfill your needs or will prove enjoyable. For example, when daydreaming in class, you don't hear what the instructor is saying until your name is called. Your selective attention mechanism focuses your senses on your name.

Through *selective exposure* (see Unit 19) you expose yourself to people or messages that will confirm your existing beliefs, contribute to your objectives, or prove satisfying in some way. For example, after you buy a car, you're more apt to read and listen to advertisements for the car you just bought, because these messages tell you that you made the right decision. At the same time, you will tend to avoid advertisements for the cars that you considered but eventually rejected, because these messages would tell you that you made the wrong decision.

You're also more likely to perceive stimuli that are greater in intensity than surrounding stimuli and those that have novelty value. For example, television commercials normally play at a greater intensity than regular programming to ensure that you take special notice. You're also more likely to notice the coworker who dresses in a novel way than you are to notice the colleague who dresses like everyone else.

Stage 2: Organization

At the second stage, you organize the information your senses have picked up. You organize perceptions in three ways: by rules, by schemata, and by scripts.

Organization by Rules

Rules of perception lead you to see connections among elements that may or may not be present in reality. For example, following the rule of *physical closeness* or *proximity*, you'd perceive messages uttered in succession as a unit. Following a *temporal* rule, you'd perceive people who are often together as constituting a unit, such as "a couple" or "best friends."

Following the rule of *similarity*, you'd perceive things that are physically alike or have other similarities as belonging together and forming a unit. For example, you'd see people who dress alike as belonging together. Similarly, you might assume that people who work at the same jobs, who are of the same religion, who live in the same building, or who talk with the same accent belong together. The rule of *contrast* is the opposite of similarity: When items (people or messages, for example) are very different from one another, you conclude that they don't belong together; they're too different to be part of the same unit. If you're the only one who shows up at an informal gathering in a tuxedo, you'll be seen as not belonging to the group, because you contrast too much with other members.

Schemata

Another way you organize material is by creating schemata—mental templates or structures. Schemata help you organize the millions of items of information you come into contact with every day as well as those items you already have in memory. Schemata may thus be viewed as general ideas about people (about Pat and Chris, about Japanese people, about Baptists, about New Yorkers), yourself (your qualities, abilities, and even liabilities), or social roles (what's a police officer, professor, or multibillionaire CEO like). (The word *schemata* is the plural of *schema* and is preferred to the alternative plural *schemas*.)

You develop schemata from your experiences—from actual experiences as well as from television, reading, and hearsay. Thus, for example, you might have a schema for college athletes; it might include perceptions that athletes are strong, ambitious, academically weak, and egocentric. And, of course, you've probably developed schemata for different religious, racial, and national groups; for men and women; and for people of different affectional orientations. Each group with which you have some familiarity will be represented in your mind in some kind of schema. Schemata help you organize your perceptions by allowing you to classify millions of people into a manageable number of categories or classes.

Scripts

A script (a type of schema) is a general idea of how some event should play out or unfold; it's the rules governing events and their sequence. For example, you probably have a script for eating in a restaurant with the actions organized into a pattern something like this: Enter, take a seat, review the menu, order from the menu, eat your food, ask for the bill, leave a tip, pay the bill, exit the restaurant. Similarly, you probably have scripts for how you do laundry, how an interview is to be conducted, the stages you go through in introducing someone to someone else, and the way you ask for a date.

Stage 3: Interpretation–Evaluation

At this stage you give your perceptions meaning; you draw conclusions about what you're seeing or smelling, for example. This step is inevitably subjective and is greatly influenced by your experiences, needs, wants, values, beliefs about the way things are or should be, expectations, physical and emotional state, and so on. Your interpretation–evaluation will be influenced by your rules, schemata, and scripts as well as by your gender; for example, women have been found to view others more positively than men (Winquist, Mohr, & Kenny, 1998).

For example, on meeting Ben, who is introduced to you as a football player, you will apply your schema to Ben and view him as strong, ambitious, academically weak, and egocentric. You will, in other words, see this person through the filter of your schema and evaluate him according to your schema for athletes. Similarly, when viewing someone performing some series of actions (say, eating in a restaurant), you will apply your script to this event and view the event through the script. You'll then interpret the actions of the diner as appropriate or inappropriate depending on the script you had for this behavior and the ways in which the diner performed the sequence of actions.

Stage 4: Memory

Your perceptions and their interpretations–evaluations are put into memory; they're stored so that you may retrieve them at some later time. So, for example, you have in memory your schema for athletes and the fact that Ben Williams is a football player. Ben Williams is then stored in memory with "cognitive tags" that tell you that he's strong, ambitious, academically weak, and egocentric. Now, despite the fact that you've not witnessed Ben's strength or ambitions and have no idea of his academic record or his psychological profile, you still may store your memory of Ben along with the qualities that make up your scheme for "athletes."

Schemas act as filters or gatekeepers; they allow certain information to get stored in relatively objective form, much as you heard or read it, but may distort other information or prevent it from getting stored. Let's say, for example, that at different times you hear that Ben failed Spanish I (normally an A or B course at your school), that Ben got an A in chemistry (normally a tough course), and that Ben is transferring to Harvard as a theoretical physics major. Each of these three items of information about Ben is likely to get stored very differently in your memory.

For example, you might readily store the information that Ben failed Spanish, because it's consistent with your schema; it fits neatly into the template your have for college athletes. Information like this is consistent with your schema and so will strengthen your schema and make it more resistant to change (Aronson, Wilson, & Akert, 1999). Depending on the strength of your schema, you may also store in memory, even though you didn't hear it, a perception that Ben did poorly in other courses as well; this seems logical enough, given that he failed an extremely easy course. The information that Ben got an A in chemistry, because it contradicts your schema (it just doesn't seem right), may easily be distorted or lost. The information that Ben is transferring to Harvard, however, is a bit different. This information is so drastically inconsistent with your existing schema that you may begin to look at this mindfully and may even begin to question the logic of your schema. Or perhaps you'll view Ben as an exception to the general rule (and continue to entertain your original schema about athletes). In either case, you're going to etch Ben's transferring to Harvard very clearly in your mind.

Stage 5: Recall

At some later date, you may want to recall or access the information you have stored in memory. Let's say you want to retrieve your information about Ben because he's the topic of discussion among you and a few friends. You may, however, recall it with a variety of inaccuracies. For example, you're likely to

- recall information that is consistent with your schema; in fact, you may not even recall the specific information (about Ben) but may actually just recall your schema (which contains the information about college athletes and, because of this, also about Ben)

- fail to recall information that is inconsistent with your schema; you have no place to put that information, because it just doesn't fit into your existing schema, so you lose it or forget it

- recall information that drastically contradicts your schema, because it forces you to think (and perhaps rethink) about your schema and its accuracy; it may even force you to revise your schema for athletes in general

This five-stage model has several important implications for your own perceptions:

1. Everyone relies heavily on shortcuts; rules, schemata, and scripts, for example, are all useful shortcuts to simplify your understanding, remembering, and recalling information about

How do you feel about the people in this photo? Are your feelings generally positive or negative? Did you have to think before responding? Some research claims that immediately upon perceiving a person, idea, or thing, you attach a positive or negative value and that you make these evaluations automatically and without conscious thought (*New York Times*, August 8, 1995, pp. C1, C10). What do you think of this viewpoint? One bit of evidence against this position would be a person's ability to identify three or four things, ideas, or people about which he or she felt completely neutral. Can you do that?

people and events. If you didn't have these shortcuts, you'd have to treat every person, role, or action differently from each other person, role, or action. This would make every experience a new one, totally unrelated to anything you already know. If you didn't use these shortcuts, you'd be unable to generalize, draw connections, or otherwise profit from previously acquired knowledge.

2. Shortcuts, however, may mislead you; they may contribute to your remembering things that are consistent with your schemata (even if they didn't occur) and distorting or forgetting information that is inconsistent.

3. What you remember about a person or an event isn't an objective recollection but is more likely heavily influenced by your preconceptions or your schemata about what belongs and what doesn't belong, what fits into the templates in your brain and what doesn't fit. Your reconstruction of an event or person contains a lot of information that was not in the original sensory experience and may omit a lot that was in this experience.

4. Judgments about others are invariably ethnocentric. Your schemata and scripts are created on the basis of your own cultural experiences—and they can lead to inaccuracies when you apply these to members of other cultures who may follow different scripts. That is, you may feel that when members of other cultures do things that conform to your scripts, they're right, and when they do things that contradict your scripts, they're wrong—a classic example of ethnocentric thinking. As you can appreciate, this tendency can easily contribute to intercultural misunderstandings.

5. Memory is especially unreliable when the information can be interpreted in different ways, when it's ambiguous. Thus, for example, consider the statement that "Ben didn't do as well in his other courses as he would have liked." If your schema for Ben was "brilliant," then you may "remember" that Ben got Bs in those other courses. But if, as in our example, your schema was of the academically weak athlete, you may "remember" that Ben got Ds. Conveniently, but unreliably, schemata reduce ambiguity.

PROCESSES INFLUENCING PERCEPTION

Between the occurrence of the stimulus (the uttering of the message, the presence of the person, the smile or wink of the eye) and the evaluation or interpretation of that stimulus, perception is influenced by several significant psychological processes. Before reading about these processes, take the following self-test to analyze your own customary ways of perceiving others. Regardless of what form of communication you're engaged in—interpersonal, small group, public speaking, or mass communication—the ways in which you perceive the people involved will influence your communications and your communication effectiveness. The self-test below will give you an idea of the factors that make for accuracy in perception.

 TEST YOURSELF

How Accurate Are You at People Perception?

Respond to each of the following statements with T (true) if the statement is usually accurate in describing your behavior, F (false) if the statement is usually inaccurate. Resist the temptation to give the "preferred" or "desirable" answers; respond, instead, as you behave.

_____ 1. I base most of my impressions of people on the first few minutes of our meeting.

_____ 2. When I know some things about another person, I fill in what I don't know.

_____ 3. I make predictions about people's behaviors that generally prove to be true.

_____ 4. I have clear ideas of what people of different national, racial, and religious groups are really like.

_____ 5. I reserve making judgments about people until I learn a great deal about them and see them in a variety of situations.

_____ 6. On the basis of my observations of people, I formulate guesses (that I am willing to revise), rather than firmly held conclusions.

_____ 7. I pay special attention to people's behaviors that might contradict my initial impressions.

_____ 8. I delay formulating conclusions about people until I have lots of evidence.

_____ **9.** I avoid making assumptions about what is going on in someone else's head on the basis of their behaviors.

_____ **10.** I recognize that people are different and don't assume that everyone is like me.

How did you do? This brief perception test was designed to raise questions to be considered in this unit, not to provide you with a specific perception score. The first four items refer to tendencies to judge others on the basis of first impressions (item 1), implicit personality theories (2), prophecies (3), and stereotypes (4). Ideally you would have answered "false" to these four items, because they represent sources of distortion. Items 5 through 10 reflect specific guidelines for increasing accuracy in people perception: looking for a variety of cues (5), formulating hypotheses rather than conclusions (6), being especially alert to contradictory cues (7), delaying conclusions until more evidence is in (8), avoiding the tendency to mind read (9), and recognizing the diversity in people (10). Ideally you would have answered "true" to these six items, as they represent suggestions for increased accuracy in perception.

What will you do? As you read this unit, think about these guidelines and consider how you might use them for more accurate and reasonable people perception. At the same time, however, do recognize that situations vary widely. These suggestions will prove useful most of the time, but you may also want to identify situations in which you shouldn't follow these suggestions.   ✔

Here we discuss seven major processes that influence your perception of others (Cook, 1971; Rubin & McNeil, 1985): implicit personality theory, the self-fulfilling prophecy, perceptual accentuation, primacy–recency, consistency, stereotyping, and attribution. Each of these processes also contains potential barriers to accurate perception that can significantly distort your perceptions and your communication interactions.

Implicit Personality Theory

Each person has an **implicit personality theory,** a subconscious or implicit system of rules that says which characteristics of an individual go with other characteristics. The widely documented **halo effect** is a function of the implicit personality theory. If you believe an individual has certain positive qualities (for example, is kind, generous, and friendly), you make the inference that she or he also has other positive qualities (for example, is supportive or

empathic). The "reverse halo effect" operates in a similar way. If you know a person has certain negative qualities, you're likely to infer that the person also has other negative qualities.

As might be expected, the implicit personality theories that people hold differ from culture to culture, from group to group, and even from person to person. For example, the Chinese have a concept, *shi gu*, which refers to "someone who is worldly, devoted to his or her family, socially skillful, and somewhat reserved" (Aronson, Wilson, & Akert, 1999, p. 190). This concept is not easily encoded in English, as you can tell by trying to find a general concept that covers this type of person. In English, on the other hand, we have a concept of the "artistic type," a generalization that is absent in Chinese. Thus, although it's easy for speakers of English or Chinese to refer to specific descriptive concepts—such as "socially skilled" or "creative"— each language creates its own generalized categories. In Chinese the qualities that make up *shi gu* are more seen as going together easily than they might be for an English speaker; they're part of the implicit personality theory of more Chinese than English speakers.

Similarly, consider the different personality theories that graduate students and blue-collar high school dropouts might have for "college students." Likewise, one individual may have had great experiences with doctors and so may have a very positive personality theory of "doctors," whereas another person may have had negative experiences with doctors and may have developed a very negative personality theory.

Potential Barriers with Implicit Personality Theories

Two serious barriers to accurate perception can occur when you use implicit personality theories. First, your tendency to develop personality theories and to perceive individuals as confirming your theory can lead you to perceive qualities in an individual that your theory tells you should be present when they actually are not. For example, you may see "goodwill" in the "charitable" acts of a friend when a tax deduction may be the real motive. Conversely you may see "tax deduction" as the motive of the enemy when altruism may have been the motive. Because you remember information that is consistent with your implicit theories more easily than you recall inconsistent information, you're unlikely to revise or modify your theories even when you come upon contradictory evidence (Cohen, 1983). Second, implicit personality theories can also lead you to ignore or distort qualities or characteristics that don't conform to your theory. You may ignore (simply not see) negative qualities in your friends that you would easily see in your enemies.

Both of these perceptual inaccuracies are more likely to occur when you have few perceptual cues and know little of the other person. Thus, you're more likely to make these errors when interacting with someone on the Internet than when thinking about someone you've known a while and know a lot about.

The Self-Fulfilling Prophecy

A **self-fulfilling prophecy** occurs when you make a prediction or formulate a belief that comes true because you made the prediction and acted on it as if it were true (Insel & Jacobson, 1975; Merton, 1957; Darley & Oleson, 1993). There are four basic steps in the self-fulfilling prophecy:

1. You make a prediction or formulate a belief about a person or a situation. For example, you predict that Pat will be awkward in interpersonal situations.
2. You act toward that person or situation as if your prediction or belief were true. You act toward Pat as if Pat were awkward.
3. Because you act as if the belief were true, it becomes true. Because of the way you act toward Pat, Pat becomes tense and manifests awkwardness.
4. You observe your effect on the person or the resulting situation, and what you see strengthens your beliefs. You observe Pat's awkwardness, and this reinforces your belief that Pat is in fact awkward.

If you expect people to act in a certain way or if you make a prediction about the characteristics of a situation, your predictions will frequently come true because of the self-fulfilling prophecy. This has been demonstrated in widely different areas; for example, in leadership, athletic coaching, and effective stepfamilies (Eden, 1992; Solomon et al., 1996;

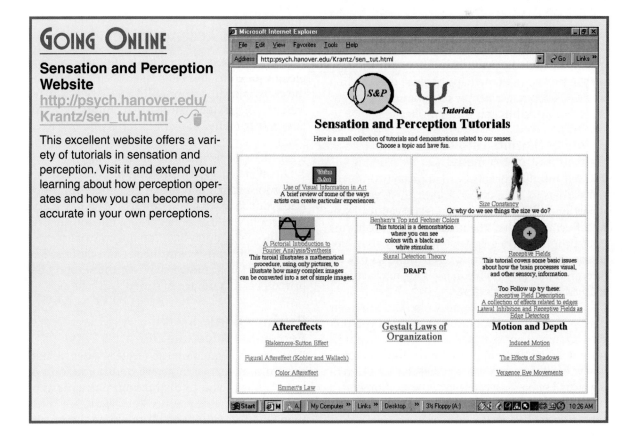

GOING ONLINE

Sensation and Perception Website

http://psych.hanover.edu/Krantz/sen_tut.html

This excellent website offers a variety of tutorials in sensation and perception. Visit it and extend your learning about how perception operates and how you can become more accurate in your own perceptions.

UNDERSTANDING THEORY AND RESEARCH

The Pygmalion Effect

A widely known example of the self-fulfilling prophecy is the Pygmalion effect (Rosenthal & Jacobson, 1992). The effect is named after Pygmalion, a sculptor in Greek mythology who created a statue of a beautiful woman and then fell in love with it. Venus, the goddess of love, rewarded Pygmalion by making the statue come to life as a real woman, Galatea. George Bernard Shaw used this idea for his play *Pygmalion*, the story of a poor and poorly educated London flower vendor who is taught "proper speech" and enters society's upper class. (The musical *My Fair Lady* was in turn based on Shaw's play.)

In one research study on this phenomenon, teachers were told that certain pupils were expected to do exceptionally well—that they were late bloomers. And although the experi-menters actually selected the "late bloomer" names at random, the students whose names were selected actually did perform at a higher level than their classmates. Like the beautiful statue, these students became what their teach-ers thought they were. The expectations of the teachers may have generated extra attention to the students and this perhaps positively affected their performance.

Working with Theories and Research. *Have you ever observed the Pygmalion effect at work on others or perhaps on yourself? What kind of additional evidence would you want before accepting this theory?*

Einstein, 1995). Consider, for example, people who enter a group situation convinced that the other members will dislike them. Almost invariably they're proved right, perhaps because they act in a way that encourages people to respond negatively. Such people fulfill their own prophecies.

Potential Barriers with the Self-Fulfilling Prophecy

The self-fulfilling prophecy may create two potential barriers to accurate perception. First, your tendency to fulfill your own prophecies can lead you to influence another's behavior so that it confirms your prophecy. Thus, if students believe that Professor Crawford is a boring teacher and so pay no attention and give no feedback, they may actually help create a boring lecturer.

The self-fulfilling prophecy also distorts your perception by influencing you to see what you predicted rather than what is really there. For example, it can lead you to see yourself as a failure because you've made this prediction rather than because of any actual setbacks. It can lead you to see someone's behavior as creative because you are expecting this person to act creatively.

Perceptual Accentuation

When researchers showed poor and rich children pictures of coins and later asked them to estimate the coins' size, the poor children's size estimates were much greater than the rich children's. Similarly, experiments show that hungry people need fewer visual cues to perceive food objects and food terms than do people who are not hungry (Wispé & Drambarean, 1953). These findings demonstrate the process called **perceptual accentuation**, which leads you to see what you expect or want to see. You see people you like as better looking and smarter than those you don't like. You magnify or accentu-ate what will satisfy your needs and desires: The thirsty person a mirage of water, the sexually de-prived person a mirage of sexual satisfaction.

Potential Barriers with Perceptual Accentuation

Perceptual accentuation can create a variety of barriers. Your tendency to perceive what you want or need can lead you to distort your perceptions of reality—to see what you need or want to see rather than what is really there. At the same time it can lead you to fail to perceive what you don't want to perceive. For example, people frequently perceive a salesperson's politeness and friendliness as demonstrating personal liking for them, not as a persuasive strategy. Similarly, you may not perceive that you're about to fail your chemistry course because you focus on what you want to perceive.

Accentuation can influence you to filter out or distort information that might damage or threaten your self image (for example, criticism of your writing or speaking) and thus can make self-improvement difficult. It can also lead you to perceive in others the negative characteristics or qualities you have yourself, a defense mechanism psychoanalysts refer to as **projection.**

In addition, accentuation can influence you to perceive and remember positive qualities more strongly than negative ones (the "Pollyanna effect") and thus can distort your perceptions of others. In one study, for example, students who liked and who disliked Madonna viewed her video "Open Your Heart." Those who liked Madonna saw the performance as the story of a dancer and her son. Those who disliked Madonna saw it as the story of sexual attraction between a young boy and an older woman (Brown & Schulze, 1990).

Misperception due to accentuation is something that is likely to occur frequently in Internet communication. Consider, for example, entering a chat room hoping to meet someone for a date. Because you expect and want to meet someone, you may read into another person's ambiguous cues a wonderful personality and a desire to meet you. The more you expect or want something to happen and the fewer the unambiguous cues you have to go on, the more likely you are to misperceive the cues you do have. So, for example, because of perceptual accentuation you might perceive relatively neutral comments from a chat room member to be a lot more positive and perhaps romantically slanted than the person intended. Or you might perceive a person who has expressed an interest in you to have a lot more positive qualities (and a lot fewer negative qualities) than you might have glimpsed if this person had not expressed this positive attitude toward you.

Primacy–Recency

Consider the following situation: You have been taking a course in which half the classes were ex-

tremely dull and half were extremely exciting. It's now the end of the semester, and you're reflecting on the course and the instructor. Will your evaluation be more favorable if the dull classes came during the first half of the semester and the exciting classes during the second half, or if the order is reversed? Similarly, would you evaluate a chat room member more favorably if your initial experiences were positive or if your most recent experiences were positive? If what comes first exerts the most influence on perception, the result is a **primacy effect.** If what comes last (or is the most recent) exerts the most influence, the result is a **recency effect.**

In an early study on the effects of **primacy–recency** in perception, a researcher read a list of adjectives describing a person to a group of students (Asch, 1946). Not surprisingly, the order in which the adjectives were read influenced the students' perceptions of the person. A person described as "intelligent, industrious, impulsive, critical, stubborn, and envious" was evaluated more positively than a person described as "envious, stubborn, critical, impulsive, industrious, and intelligent." This finding suggests that you use early information to provide yourself with a general idea of what a person is like. You use later information to make this general idea more specific. The obvious practical implication of primacy–recency is that the first impression you make—interpersonally, in small groups, or in public speaking—is likely to be the most important. Through this first impression, people will filter additional information to formulate a picture of who they perceive you to be.

Potential Barriers with Primacy–Recency

Primacy–recency may lead to two major types of barriers. Your tendency to give greater weight to early information and to interpret later information in light of these early impressions can lead you to form a "total" picture of an individual on the basis of initial impressions that may not be typical or accurate. For example, perhaps you form an image of someone as socially ill at ease. If this impression was based on watching the person at a stressful job interview, it's likely to be wrong. But because of primacy you may fail to see accurately the person's later comfortable behavior.

Primacy may even lead you to discount or distort later perceptions to avoid disrupting your initial impressions. For instance, you may fail to see signs

First Impressions

Manage every second of a first meeting. Do not delude yourself that a bad first impression can be easily corrected. Putting things right is a lot harder than getting them right the first time.

—David Lewis

Whether you are being interviewed for a job, getting started in a new job, or meeting new colleagues, first impressions are especially important—because they're so long lasting and so powerful in influencing future impressions and interactions (Parsons, Liden, & Bauer, 2001). Here are a few guidelines that will help you make a good first impression at work.

▶ Dress appropriately; any drastic deviation from the standard dress for your position is likely to be perceived negatively and may communicate that you somehow don't fit in.

▶ Verbally and nonverbally express positive attitudes toward the organization, the job, and your colleagues. Avoid negative talk and sarcasm (even in your humor); it's often perceived as an attack on others.

▶ Be open and friendly; be available and helpful as appropriate. Be cooperative and share rather than monopolize.

▶ Avoid stereotyping and comments that might be considered racist, sexist, or hetero-sexist. Otherwise, you're sure to offend someone.

▶ Be time conscious, and be respectful of other people's time.

▶ Discover what the organization's cultural rules and norms are and avoid violating them.

▶ Be a good listener; good listeners are invariably among the most popular people everywhere, and the workplace is no exception.

Thinking about Your Communicating @ Work

What type of first impressions do you usually make? Are you pleased with these first impressions? How might you go about improving the impressions you make?

of deceit in someone who made a good first impression because of the tendency to avoid disrupting or revising initial impressions.

Consistency

People have a strong tendency to maintain balance or consistency among perceptions. **Consistency** represents people's need to maintain balance among their attitudes. You expect certain things to go together and other things not to go together.

Consider your own attitudes in terms of consistency by responding to the following sentences;

note the word in parentheses that you feel best represents your attitudes.

1. I expect a person I like to (like, dislike) me.
2. I expect a person I dislike to (like, dislike) me.
3. I expect my friend to (like, dislike) my friend.
4. I expect my friend to (like, dislike) my enemy.
5. I expect my enemy to (like, dislike) my friend.
6. I expect my enemy to (like, dislike) my enemy.

According to most consistency theories, your expectations would be as follows: You would expect a person you liked to like you (1) and a person you disliked to dislike you (2). You would expect a friend to like a friend (3) and to dislike an enemy (4). You would expect your enemy to dislike your friend (5) and to like your other enemy (6). Further, you would expect someone you liked to have characteristics you liked or admired. And you'd expect your enemies not to possess characteristics you liked or admired. Conversely, you'd expect persons you liked to lack unpleasant characteristics and persons you disliked to have unpleasant characteristics. All these expectations seem intuitively right. But are they?

Potential Barriers with Consistency

Consistency can create two major barriers to accuracy in perception. Your tendency to see consistency in an individual can lead you to ignore or distort your perceptions of behaviors that are inconsistent with your picture of the whole person. For example, you may misinterpret Karla's unhappiness because your image of Karla is "happy, controlled, and contented."

Your desire for consistency may also lead you to perceive specific behaviors as emanating from positive qualities in the people you like and from negative qualities in the people you dislike. You therefore fail to see the positive qualities in the people you dislike and the negative qualities in the people you like.

Stereotyping

A frequently used shortcut in perception is stereotyping. Originally *stereotype* was a printing term that referred to a plate that printed the same image over and over. A sociological or psychological **stereotype** is a fixed impression of a group of people. Everyone has attitudinal stereotypes—images of national groups, religious groups, or racial groups, or perhaps of criminals, prostitutes, teachers, or plumbers. Consider, for example, if you have any stereotypes of, say, bodybuilders, the opposite sex, a racial group different from your own, members of a religion very different from your own, hard drug users, or college professors. Very likely you have stereotypes of several or perhaps all of these groups. Although we often think of stereotypes as negative ("They're lazy, dirty, and only interested in getting high"), they may also be positive ("They're smart, hardworking, and extremely loyal").

If you have these fixed impressions, you may, on meeting a member of a particular group, tend to see that person primarily as a member of that group. Initially this may provide you with some helpful orientation. But stereotyping creates problems when you apply to a person all the characteristics you assign to members of his or her group without examining the unique individual. If you meet a politician, for example, you may have a host of characteristics for politicians that you can readily apply to this person. To complicate matters further, you may perceive in this person's behavior the manifestation of various characteristics that you would not see if you did not know that the person was a politician.

Consider, however, another kind of stereotype: You're driving along a dark road and are stopped at a stop sign. A car pulls up beside you, and three

Some people feel that media portrayals of cultural groups often perpetuate stereotypes. Thus, for example, the HBO series *The Sopranos*, pictured here, has been accused of perpetuating the stereotype of Italian Americans as gangsters or of gangsters as Italian. How do you feel about the media's portrayals of your own cultural groups? For example, do the media create and perpetuate stereotypes of members of your own cultural groups? If so, are they basically positive or negative?

BUILDING COMMUNICATION SKILLS

How Can You Perceive Others' Perceptions?

Examine each of the following situations and indicate how each of the persons identified might view the situation. What one principle of perception can you derive from this brief experience? (Another exercise on perception helps identify your ability to take another's perspective: "How Can You Take Another's Perspective?" at www.ablongman.com/devito.)

▶ Pat, a single parent, has two children (ages 7 and 12) who often lack some of the important things children their age should have—such as school supplies, sneakers, and toys—because Pat can't afford them. Yet Pat smokes two packs of cigarettes a day.

Pat sees . . .

The 12-year-old daughter sees . . .

The children's teacher sees . . .

▶ Chris has extremely high standards, feels that getting all As in college is an absolute neces-

sity, and would be devastated with even one B. In fear of earning that first B (after three and a half years of college), Chris cheats on an examination in a course on family communication and gets caught by the instructor.

Chris sees . . .

The instructor sees . . .

The average B student sees . . .

▶ Pat, a supervisor in an automobile factory, has been ordered to increase production or be fired. In desperation Pat gives a really tough message to the workers—many of whom are greatly insulted and, as a result, slow down rather than increase their efforts.

Pat sees . . .

The average worker sees . . .

Pat's supervisor sees . . .

teenagers jump out and rap on your window. There may be a variety of potential reasons for this: They need help, they want to ask directions, they want to tell you that your trunk is open, or they are planning a carjacking. Your self-protective stereotype may lead you to decide on "carjacking" and may cause you to pull away and into the safety of a busy service station. In doing that, of course, you may have escaped being carjacked—or you may have failed to help people who reached out to you for assistance.

Potential Barriers with Stereotyping

Stereotyping can lead to two major barriers. The tendency to group people into classes and to respond to an individual primarily as a member of a class can lead you to perceive someone as having those qualities (usually negative) that you believe characterize the group to which he or she belongs. Then you will fail to appreciate the multifaceted nature of all people and all groups. For example,

consider your stereotype of people who spend a lot of time at their computers. Very likely it's quite different from the research findings—which show that such computer users are as often female as male and are as sociable, popular, and self-assured as their peers who are not into heavy computer use (Schott & Selwyn, 2000).

Stereotyping can also lead you to ignore the unique characteristics of an individual; therefore, you may fail to benefit from the special contributions each person can bring to an encounter.

Attribution

Attribution is the process through which you try to discover why people do what they do and even why you do what you do (Fiske & Taylor, 1984; Jones & Davis, 1965; Kelley, 1979). One way we try to answer this question (in part) is to ask if the person acts this way because of who the person is (personality) or because of the situation. That is, your task is to determine whether the cause of the behavior is internal (due to who the person really is) or external (due to extenuating circumstances).

Internal causes for behaviors involve the person's personality or some enduring trait. In this case you might hold the person responsible for his or her behaviors, and you would judge the behaviors and the person in light of this responsibility. External causes for behaviors, on the other hand, have to do with situational factors. In this case you might not hold the person responsible for his or her behaviors.

Consider an example. A teacher has given 10 students Fs on a cultural anthropology examination. In attempting to discover what this behavior (assignment of the 10 Fs) reveals about the teacher, you have to determine whether the teacher was responsible for the behavior (the behavior was internally caused) or not (the behavior was externally caused). If you discover that a faculty committee made up the examination and that the committee set the standards for passing or failing, you cannot attribute any particular motives to the teacher. You have to conclude that the behavior was externally caused. In this case, it was caused by the department committee in conjunction with each student's performance on the examination.

On the other hand, assume that this teacher made up the examination and set the standards for passing and failing. Now you will be more apt to attribute the 10 Fs to internal causes. You will be strengthened in your belief that something within this teacher (some personality trait, for example) led to this behavior if you discover that (1) no other teacher gave nearly as many Fs, (2) this particular teacher frequently gives Fs in cultural anthropology, (3) this teacher frequently gives Fs in other courses as well, and (4) this teacher is free to give grades other than F. These four bits of added information may lead you to conclude that something in this teacher motivated the behavior. According to **attribution theory,** each of these new items of information represents one of the principles you use in making causal judgments, or attributions: principles known as consensus, consistency, distinctiveness, and controllability.

Consensus

When you focus on the principle of **consensus,** you ask, "Do other people behave the same way as the person on whom I am focusing?" That is, does this person act in accordance with the general consensus? If the answer is no, you're more likely to attribute the behavior to some internal cause. In the previous example, you were strengthened in your belief that the teacher's behavior had an internal cause when you learned that other teachers did not follow this behavior—there was low consensus.

Consistency

When you focus on *consistency* in making attributions, you ask whether a person repeatedly behaves the same way in similar situations. If the answer is yes, there's high consistency, and you're likely to attribute the behavior to internal motivation. The fact that the teacher frequently gives Fs in cultural anthropology leads you to attribute the cause to the teacher rather than to outside sources.

Distinctiveness

When you focus on the principle of *distinctiveness,* you ask if a person acts in similar ways in different situations. If the answer is yes, you're likely to conclude that the behavior has an internal cause. A finding of "low distinctiveness" indicates that this person acts in similar ways in different situations; it indicates that this situation is not distinctive.

Consider the alternative—high distinctiveness. Assume that this teacher gave all high grades and no failures in all his or her other courses (that is, that the cultural anthropology class situation was distinctive). Then you would probably conclude that the motivation for the failures was unique to this class and was external to the teacher.

Controllability

The term **controllability** refers to the degree to which you think a person was in control of his or her behavior. Let's say, for example, that you invite your friend Desmond to dinner for seven o'clock and he arrives at nine. Consider how you will respond to the reasons he may give you for his lateness:

Reason 1: Oh, I got to watching this old movie and I wanted to see the end.

Reason 2: On my way here I witnessed a robbery and felt I had to report it. At the police station the phones were all tied up.

Reason 3: I got in a car accident and was taken to the hospital.

Assuming you believe all three explanations, you will attribute very different motives to Desmond's behavior. With reasons 1 and 2, you will conclude that Desmond was in control of his behavior; with reason 3, you will conclude that Desmond was not in control of his behavior. Further, you will probably respond negatively to reason 1 (Desmond was selfish and inconsiderate) but positively to reason 2 (Desmond did his duty as a responsible citizen). Because Desmond was not in control of his behavior in reason 3, you will probably not attribute either positive or negative motivation to Desmond's behavior. Instead you will probably feel sorry that he had an accident on the way to your house.

Consider your own tendency to make similar judgments based on controllability in a variety of situations. How would you respond to such situations as the following?

- Doris fails her midterm history exam.
- Sidney's car is repossessed because he failed to make the payments.

- Margie is 150 pounds overweight and is complaining that she feels awful.
- Thomas's wife has just filed for divorce and he is feeling depressed.

Very probably you'd be sympathetic to each of these people if you felt they were not in control of what happened—for example, if the examination was unfair, if Sidney lost his job because of employee discrimination, if Margie has a glandular problem, and if Thomas's wife is leaving him for a wealthy drug dealer. On the other hand, you might blame these people for their problems if you felt that they were in control of the situation—for example, if Doris partied instead of studying, if Sidney gambled his payments away, if Margie ate nothing but junk food and refused to exercise, and if Thomas had been repeatedly unfaithful and his wife finally gave up trying to change him.

Low consensus, high consistency, low distinctiveness, and high controllability lead to an attribution of internal causes. As a result, you praise or blame

---

BUILDING COMMUNICATION SKILLS

How Can You Make Attributions?

Consider how you would explain the following cases in terms of attribution theory. Do you think the individual's behavior in each scenario was due to internal causes (such as personality characteristics or various personal motives) or external causes (such as the particular situation, the demands of others who might be in positions of authority, or the behaviors of others)? The behavior in question appears in italics. As you analyze these situations, consider the information provided concerning (1) consensus, (2) consistency, (3) distinctiveness, and (4) controllability. What combination of these data would lead you to conclude that the behavior was internally motivated? What combination would lead you to conclude that the behavior was externally motivated?

▶ *Mita's performance in the race was disappointing.* For the last few days she had to tend to her sick grandfather and got too little sleep.

▶ *Peter just quit his job.* No one else that you know who has had this same job has ever quit.

▶ *Karla failed her recent chemistry test.* Many other students (in fact, some 40 percent of the class) also failed the test. Karla has never failed a chemistry test before and, in fact, has never failed any other test in her life.

▶ *Russell took the schoolchildren to the zoo.* Russell works for the board of education in a small town, and taking the students on trips is one of his major functions. All people previously on the job have taken the students to the zoo. Russell has never taken any other children to the zoo.

the person for his or her behaviors. High consensus, low consistency, high distinctiveness, and low controllability lead to an attribution of external causes. As a result, you may consider this person lucky or unlucky.

Potential Barriers with Attribution

Of course, the obvious problem with attribution is that we can only make guesses about another person's behaviors. Can we really know if Doris deserved to pass or fail the history exam? Can we really know if Sidney deserved to have his car repossessed? When you realize that such judgments are often based on guesses, you'll be more apt to seek further information before acting as if attributions were facts. In addition, the attribution process is often subject to different kinds of bias and error.

The Self-Serving Bias. The **self-serving bias** is another perceptual barrier and is generally designed to preserve or raise our own self-esteem as we engage in **self-attribution**. When you evaluate your own behaviors by taking credit for the positive and denying responsibility for the negative, you're demonstrating the self-serving bias. You're more likely to attribute your own negative behaviors to uncontrollable factors. For example, you're more likely to attribute getting a D on an exam to the difficulty of the test than to your failure to prepare adequately for it. And you're more likely to attribute your positive behaviors to controllable

UNDERSTANDING THEORY AND RESEARCH

The Just World Hypothesis

Many people believe that the world is just: that good things happen to good people and bad things happen to bad people (Aronson, Wilson, & Akert, 1999; Hunt, 2000). Put differently, you'll get what you deserve! Even when you mindfully dismiss this assumption, you may use it mindlessly when perceiving and evaluating other people. Let's take a particularly vivid example. In certain cultures (for example, in Bangladesh or Iran or Yemen), a woman who is raped is considered by many people (though certainly not all) to have disgraced her family and to deserve severe punishment—in many cases, even death. In this country, too, although most people reading this book would consider this unjust and unfair, it's quite common to blame the victim. Much research, for example, shows that people often blame the victim for being raped (Bell, Kuriloff, & Lottes, 1994). In fact, defense attorneys routinely attack the rape victim in court for "leading him on" or for dressing provocatively. And it's relevant to note that only two states—New York and Florida—currently forbid questions about the victim's clothing. In a similar way, people may blame the poor or the homeless for their plight on the theory that people deserve what they get.

Belief in a just world, although reassuring to those with a comfortable lifestyle, creates perceptual distortions by leading us to deemphasize the influence of situational factors and to overemphasize the influence of internal factors in our attempts to explain the behaviors of other people. Another way in which belief in a just world distorts perception is seen in the egocentric fairness bias; people who have strong beliefs in a just world tend to see their own behaviors as fairer and more moral than those of others (Tanaka, 1999). The reasoning seems to go like this:

▶ *if* I am fairer and more moral than others

▶ *then* I will experience more good than bad

▶ *because* the world is just

Working with Theories and Research. *Can you identify examples of people you know who use the just world hypothesis as a basic assumption in their attitudes and behaviors toward, say, people who are homeless, alcoholic, or unemployed?*

factors—to your own strength or intelligence or personality. For example, after getting an A on an exam, you're more likely to attribute it to your ability or hard work than to luck or the ease of the test (Bernstein, Stephan, & Davis, 1979). To pursue the way you see yourself, take a look at the exercises "How Can You Perceive Yourself?" and "How Can You See Your Many Intelligences?" at www.ablongman.com/devito.

The Fundamental Attribution Error.   Perhaps the major difficulty in making accurate attributions is the **fundamental attribution error:** the tendency to conclude that people do what they do because that's the kind of people they are, not because of the situation they are in. When Pat is late for an appointment, we're more likely to conclude that Pat is inconsiderate or irresponsible than to attribute the lateness to the bus breaking down or

WHAT DO YOU DO WHEN YOU MEET A BLIND PERSON?

Give a Blind Person the Same Respect and Consideration You Would Give Someone Sighted

On the Street
Ask if assistance would be helpful. Sometimes a blind person prefers to proceed unaided. If the person wants your help, offer your elbow. You should walk a half-step ahead so that your body movements will indicate when to change direction, stop and start, and step up or down at curbside.

Giving Directions
Verbal directions should have the blind person as the reference point. Example: "You are facing Lexington Avenue and you will have to cross it as you continue east on 59th Street."

Handling Money
When giving out bills, indicate the denomination of each so that the blind person can identify it and put it away. Coins are identified by touch.

Safety
Half-open doors are a hazard to everyone, particularly to a blind person. Keep doors closed or wide open.

Dining Out
Guide blind people to the table by offering your arm. Then place their hand on the chair back so they can seat themselves. Read the menu aloud and encourage the waiter to speak directly to the blind person rather than to you. Describe placement of food, using an imaginary clock face (e.g., vegetables are at 2 o'clock, salad plate is at 11 o'clock).

Traveling
Just as a sighted person enjoys hearing a tour guide describe unfamiliar scenery, a blind person likes to hear about indoor and outdoor sights.

Guide Dogs
These are working animals, not pets. Do not distract a guide dog by petting it or by seeking its attention.

Remember
Talk with a blind person as you would with a sighted one, in a normal tone. You may use such expressions as "See you later" and "Did you see that?"

   If you enter a room in which a blind person is alone, announce your presence by speaking or introducing yourself. In a group, address blind people by name if they are expected to reply. Excuse yourself when you are leaving.

   Always ask before trying to help. Grabbing an arm or pushing is dangerous and discourteous. When you accompany blind people, offer to describe the surroundings.

Source: From "What Do You Do When You Meet Someone Who Can't See?" Reprinted by permission of Lighthouse International, New York, NY.

to a traffic accident. When we commit the fundamental attribution error, we overvalue the contribution of internal factors and undervalue the influence of external factors.

When we explain our own behavior, we also favor internal explanations, although not to as great an extent as we do when explaining the behaviors of others. In one study, managers who evaluated their own performance and the performance of their subordinates used more internal explanations when evaluating the behavior of their subordinates than when evaluating their own (Martin & Klimoski, 1990). One reason we tend to give greater weight to external factors in explaining our own behavior than in explaining the behavior of others is that we know the situation surrounding our own behavior. We know, for example, what's going on in our love life, and we know our financial condition; so we naturally see the influence of these factors. But we rarely know as much about others, so we're more likely to give less weight to the external factors in their cases.

This fundamental attribution error is at least in part culturally influenced. For example, Americans are likely to explain behavior by saying that people did what they did because of who they are. But when Hindus in India were asked to explain why their friends behaved as they did, they gave greater weight to external factors than did people in the United States (Miller, 1984; Aronson, Wilson, & Akert, 1999). Further, Americans have little hesitation in offering causal explanations of a person's behavior ("Pat did this because . . ."). Hindus, on the other hand, are generally reluctant to explain a person's behavior in causal terms (Matsumoto, 1994).

Overattribution.   Another problem is *overattribution*—attributing everything a person does to one or two obvious characteristics, as when we attribute a person's behavior to alcoholic parents or to being born blind or possessing great wealth. For example, "Sally has difficulty forming meaningful relationships because she grew up in a home of alcoholics," "Alex overeats because he's blind," or "Shandra is irresponsible because she never had to work for her money." Most behaviors and personality characteristics are the product of a wide variety of factors, however; it's almost always a mistake to select one factor and attribute everything to it.

You may find it interesting to review the box on page 70, "What Do You Do When You Meet a Blind Person?" with these seven perceptual processes in mind. Specifically, how are your perceptions of blind and sighted people influenced by these perceptual processes? What types of barriers intrude on communication between blind and sighted persons?

CRITICAL PERCEPTION: MAKING PERCEPTIONS MORE ACCURATE

Successful communication depends largely on the accuracy of your perceptions—perceptions of people, of problems and solutions, of events. We've already identified the potential barriers that can arise with each of the seven perceptual processes; for example, our tendency to see what we expect or want instead of what is and our vulnerability to the self-serving bias. There are, however, additional useful guidelines for improving your **interpersonal perception** skills.

Become Aware of Your Perceptions

Heighten your awareness of the ways you perceive others. Subject your perceptions to logical analysis and critical thinking. Here are a few suggestions:

- Recognize your own role in perception. Your emotional and physiological state will influence the meaning you give to your perceptions. The sight of raw clams may be physically upsetting when you have a stomachache but mouthwatering when you're hungry.

- Avoid early conclusions. On the basis of your observations of behaviors, formulate hypotheses to test against additional information and evidence rather than drawing conclusions you then look to confirm. Delay formulating conclusions until you've had a chance to process a wide variety of cues.

- Avoid the one-cue conclusion. Look for a variety of cues pointing in the same direction. The more cues pointing to the same conclusion, the more likely your conclusion will be correct. Be especially alert to contradictory cues—evidence that seems to refute your initial hypotheses. It's relatively easy to perceive cues that confirm your hypotheses but more difficult to acknowledge contradictory evidence. At the same time, seek validation from others. Do others see things in the same way you do? If not, ask yourself if your perceptions may be in some way distorted.

- Beware of your own biases. Know when your perceptual evaluations are unduly influenced by your own biases; for example, your tendency to perceive only the positive in people you like and only the negative in people you don't like.

- Realize that we all have a tendency to see ourselves as more self-sacrificing, more moral, more altruistic, and fairer than other people (Epley & Dunning, 2000). So, when perceiving yourself in relation to others, ask yourself if this perceptual bias may be operating.

Check Your Perceptions

Perception checking is another way to reduce uncertainty and to make your perceptions more accurate. In its most basic form, **perception checking** consists of two steps:

1. Describe what you see or hear. Recognizing that even descriptions are not really objective but are heavily influenced by who you are, your emotional state, and so on, try to describe what you think is happening as descriptively (not evaluatively) as you can. Sometimes you may wish to offer several possibilities.

   - You've called me from work a lot this week. You seem concerned that everything is all right at home.
   - You haven't talked with me all week.
   - You say that my work is fine, but I haven't been given the same responsibilities that other editorial assistants have.

2. Ask the other person for confirmation. Do be careful, however, that your request for confirmation does not sound as though you already know the answer. Avoid phrasing your questions defensively; for example, "You really don't want to go out, do you? I knew you didn't when you turned on that lousy television." Instead, ask for confirmation in as supportive a way as possible:

   - Would you rather watch TV?
   - Are you worried about me or the kids?
   - Are you pleased with my work? Is there anything I can do to improve my job performance?

MEDIA WATCH

CULTIVATION THEORY

According to cultivation theory, the media, especially television, are the primary means by which you form your perceptions of your society and your culture (Gerbner, Gross, Morgan, & Signorielli, 1980). What you watch and how often you watch it will influence your perception of the world and of people (Signorielli & Lears, 1992; Morgan & Shanahan, 1991; Vergeer, Lubbers, & Scheepers, 2000).

Cultivation theory argues that heavy television viewers form an image of reality that is inconsistent with the facts (Potter, 1986; Potter & Chang, 1990). For example:

- Heavy TV viewers estimate their chances of being a victim of a crime to be 1 in 10. In reality the ratio is 1 in 50.

- Heavy viewers think that 20 percent of the world's population lives in the United States. In reality it's only 6 percent.

- Heavy viewers believe that the percentage of workers in managerial or professional jobs is 25 percent. In reality it's 5 percent.

- Heavy viewers in the United States are more likely to believe that "hard work yields rewards" and that "good wins over evil" than are light viewers.

- Heavy sports program viewers were more likely than others to believe in the values of hard work and good conduct.

- Heavy soap opera viewers are more likely to believe that "luck is important" and that "the strong survive" than are light viewers.

Follow–Up. *What do you think of this theory? Do you think its hypotheses about media influence are valid? How would you go about testing this theory?*

As these examples illustrate, the goal of perception checking is not to prove that your initial perception is correct but to explore further the thoughts and feelings of the other person. With this simple technique, you lessen your chances of misinterpreting another's feelings. At the same time, you give the other person an opportunity to elaborate on his or her thoughts and feelings.

Reduce Uncertainty

We all have a tendency to reduce uncertainty, a process that enables us to achieve greater accuracy in perception. In large part we learned about uncertainty and how to deal with it from our culture.

Culture and Uncertainty

People from different cultures differ greatly in their attitudes toward uncertainty and how to deal with it. These attitudes and ways of dealing with uncertainty have consequences for perceptual accuracy.

People in some cultures do little to avoid uncertainty and have little anxiety about not knowing what will happen next. The people of Singapore, Jamaica, Denmark, Sweden, Hong Kong, and Ireland are examples. Uncertainty to them is a normal part of life and is accepted as it comes. Members of these cultures don't feel threatened by unknown situations. Other cultures do much to avoid uncertainty and have a great deal of anxiety about not knowing what will happen next; uncertainty is seen as threatening and something that must be counteracted. The cultures of Greece, Portugal, Guatamala, Uruguay, Belgium, El Salvador, and Japan are examples.

Because weak-uncertainty-avoidance cultures have great tolerance for ambiguity and uncertainty, they minimize the rules governing communication and relationships (Hofstede, 1997; Lustig & Koester, 1999). People who don't follow the same rules as the cultural majority are readily tolerated. Different approaches and perspectives may even be encouraged in cultures with weak uncertainty avoidance. Strong-uncertainty-avoidance cultures, in contrast, create very clear-cut rules for communication. It's considered unacceptable for people to break these rules.

Students from weak-uncertainty-avoidance cultures appreciate freedom in education and prefer vague assignments without specific timetables. These students will want to be rewarded for creativity and will easily accept the teacher's (sometimes) lack of knowledge. Students from strong-uncertainty-avoidance cultures prefer highly structured experiences and very little ambiguity: specific objectives, detailed instructions, and definite timetables. These students expect to be judged on the basis of the right answers and expect the teacher to have all the answers all the time (Hofstede, 1997).

Strategies for Reducing Uncertainty

Communication involves a gradual process of reducing uncertainty about others (Berger & Bradac, 1982). A variety of **uncertainty reduction strategies** can help reduce uncertainty. Observing a person while he or she is engaged in an active task, preferably interacting informally with others, will often reveal a great deal about the person—because people are less apt to monitor their behaviors and more likely to reveal their true selves in informal social situations.

You can also manipulate the situation so as to observe the person in more specific and more revealing contexts. Employment interviews, theatrical auditions, and student teaching are examples of situations structured to let one person observe how another individual might act and react and hence to reduce uncertainty about that individual.

New members of Internet chat groups usually "lurk" before joining the group discussion. Lurking, or reading the exchanges among other group members without saying anything yourself, will help you learn about the people in the group and about the group itself.

Another way to reduce uncertainty is to collect information about a person by asking others. You might inquire of a colleague if a third person finds you interesting and might like to have dinner with you.

And of course you can interact with the individual. For example, you can ask questions: "Do you enjoy sports?" "What did you think of that computer science course?" "What would you do if you got fired?" You also gain knowledge about another person by disclosing information about yourself. Your self-disclosure can create a relaxed environment that encourages subsequent disclosures from the person about whom you wish to learn more.

You probably use these strategies all the time to learn about people. Unfortunately, many people feel that they know someone well enough after observing the person only from a distance or through rumors. A combination of information—including especially information from your own interactions—is most successful at reducing uncertainty. Consider this idea of reducing uncertainty in terms of your own perceptions of others; see "How Can You Perceive Others?" at **www.ablongman.com/ devito.**

Be Culturally Sensitive

You can increase your accuracy in perception by recognizing and being sensitive to cultural differences, especially those that involve values, attitudes, and beliefs. You can easily see and accept different hairstyles, clothing, and foods. In relation to basic values and beliefs, however, you may assume that down deep we're really all alike. We aren't. When you assume similarities and ignore differences, you may not perceive a situation accurately. Take a simple example. An American invites a Filipino co-worker to dinner. The Filipino politely refuses. The American is hurt, feels that the Filipino does not want to be friendly, and does not try again. As a result the Filipino is hurt and concludes that the invitation was not extended sincerely. Here, it seems, both the American and the Filipino assume that their customs for inviting people to dinner are the same when, in fact, they aren't. In the Philippines people expect to be invited several times before accepting a dinner invitation. When an invitation is given only once it's viewed as insincere.

Within every cultural group there are wide and important differences. As all Americans are not alike, neither are all Indonesians, Greeks, Mexicans, and so on. When we make assumptions that all people of a certain culture are alike, we're thinking in stereotypes.

Recognizing differences between another culture and your own and recognizing differences among members of a particular culture will help you perceive situations more accurately.

REFLECTIONS ON ETHICS IN HUMAN COMMUNICATION

Making Ethical Choices

Imagine that your 16-year-old son has been diagnosed with a rare blood disease and has only a month or two to live. The doctors say that there is no need to tell him about the severity of his illness, as it will only depress him and may even hasten his death. But, they say, it's up to you as his parent.

Keep this example in mind as you read about the ethics of choice, an ethical approach that argues that people have the right to information relevant to the choices they make. In this view, communications are ethical when they facilitate people's freedom of choice by presenting them with accurate information. Communications are unethical when they interfere with people's freedom of choice by preventing them from securing such information—or by giving false or misleading information that will lead people to make choices they would not make if they had more accurate information.

In this ethical system, you have the right to information about yourself that others possess and that will influence the choices you make. Thus, for example, you have the right to face your accusers, to know the witnesses who will be called to testify against you, to see your credit ratings, and to know what Social Security benefits you'll receive. On the other hand, you do not have the right to information that is none of your business, such as information about whether your neighbors are happy or argue a lot or receive food stamps.

At the same time, you also have the obligation to reveal information you possess that bears on the choices of your society. Thus, for example, you have an obligation to speak up when you witness wrongdoing, to identify someone in a police lineup, to report criminal activity, and to testify at a trial if you possess pertinent information. This information is essential for society to accomplish its purposes and to make its legitimate choices.

In this ethic based on choice, we assume that the individual is of an age and mental condition to allow the reasonable execution of free choice. For example, children are not ready to choose their own menu, time for bed, or type of medication to take. In addition, the circumstances under which one is living can restrict free choice. For example, persons serving in the military will at times have to eat hamburger rather than steak, wear uniforms rather than jeans, and march rather than staying in bed. Finally, individuals' free choices must not prevent others

from making their own free choices. A thief cannot be permitted to have the freedom of choice to steal, because the granting of that freedom would prevent the victims from exercising their free choice to own property and to be secure in their possessions.

What would you do? *You are aware that your best friend's husband is currently having an extramarital affair with a 17-year-old girl. Your friend suspects this is going on and asks you if you know anything about it. Would it be ethical for you to lie and say you know nothing, or are you obligated to tell your friend what you know? Are you obligated to tell the police? What would you do in this situation? If you were the parent described in the opening of this ethics box, what would you do?*

 # SUMMARY

In this unit we reviewed the process of perception, the processes influencing perception, and the principles for making perception more accurate.

1. Perception is the process through which you become aware of the many stimuli impinging on your senses.
2. The process of perception consists of three stages: sensory stimulation occurs; sensory stimulation is organized; and sensory stimulation is interpreted–evaluated.
3. The following processes influence perception: (1) implicit personality theory, (2) self-fulfilling prophecy, (3) perceptual accentuation, (4) primacy–recency, (5) consistency, (6) stereotyping, and (7) attribution.
4. The concept of implicit personality theory has to do with the private personality theories that individuals hold and that influence how they perceive other people.
5. The self-fulfilling prophecy occurs when you make a prediction or formulate a belief that comes true because you've made the prediction and acted on it as if it were true.
6. Perceptual accentuation leads you to see what you expect and what you want to see.
7. The phenomenon of primacy–recency involves the relative influence of stimuli in relation to the

order in which you perceive them. If what occurs first exerts the greatest influence, you're influenced by the primacy effect. If what occurs last exerts the greatest influence, you're experiencing a recency effect.
8. The principle of consistency describes your tendency to perceive that which enables you to achieve psychological balance or comfort among various attitude objects and their interconnections.
9. Stereotyping is the tendency to develop and maintain fixed, unchanging perceptions of groups of people and to use these perceptions to evaluate individual members of these groups, ignoring their unique individual characteristics.
10. Attribution is the process through which you try to understand your own and others' behaviors and the motivations for these behaviors. In this process you utilize four types of data: data about consensus, consistency, distinctiveness, and controllability.
11. To increase accuracy in perception, become aware of your perceptions, check your perceptions, reduce uncertainty, and become aware of cultural differences and influences on perception.

KEY TERMS

perception	consistency	controllability
implicit personality theory	stereotyping	self-serving bias
self-fulfilling prophecy	attribution	fundamental attribution error
perceptional accentuation	consensus	overattribution
primacy–recency	distinctiveness	uncertainty avoidance

THINKING CRITICALLY ABOUT

Perception

1. It has been argued that the self-fulfilling prophecy may be used in organizations to stimulate higher performance (Eden, 1992; Field, 1989). For example, managers could be given the belief that workers were able to perform at extremely high levels; managers would then act as if this were true and thus promote this high-level behavior in the workers. How might this approach be used in the college classroom? How might it be used in parenting? Would you consider this tactic ethical?

2. For the next several days, record all examples of people perception on your part—instances in which you draw a conclusion about another person. Try to classify these in terms of the processes identified in this unit; for example, implicit personality theory, stereotyping, attribution, and so on. Record also the specific context in which each instance occurred. After you've identified the various processes, share your findings in groups of five or six or with the entire class. As always, disclose only what you wish to disclose. What processes do you use most frequently? Do these processes lead to any barriers to accurate perception?

3. A study of stereotypes on British television found that gender stereotypes hadn't changed much over 10 years and that these stereotypes were comparable to those found on North American television (Furnham & Bitar, 1993). Other research, however, suggested that gender stereotypes were changing and that television depictions of men and women were helping erase these stereotypes (Vernon, Williams, Phillips, & Wilson, 1990). Do you find gender stereotypes on television? How many can you identify?

4. How would you use perception checking in such situations as these: (a) Your friend says he wants to drop out of college; (b) your cousin hasn't called you in several months, though you have called her at least six times; (c) another student seems totally detached from everything that happens in class?

5. **Researching Perception.** How would you go about finding answers to such questions as these:
   - Are there gender differences in accuracy of perception? Are there age differences?
   - Are men or women more likely to use the self-serving bias in perceiving others?
   - Do people in all cultures demonstrate essentially the same perceptual processes (implicit personality theory, self-fulfilling prophecy, and so on) in the ways they make judgments about others?
   - Does a primacy effect operate in college students' perceptions of instructors? Does a recency effect operate in college instructors' perceptions of students?
   - How do the schemata of college students and, say, people in their 60s and 70s differ for "Japanese people," "gay men and lesbians," or "single mothers"?

UNIT 5
Listening

Unit Contents

There can be little doubt that you listen a great deal. Upon awakening you listen to the radio. On the way to school you listen to friends, people around you, screeching cars, singing birds, or falling rain. In school you listen to the teacher, to other students, and to yourself. You listen to friends at lunch and return to class to listen to more teachers. You arrive home and again listen to family and friends. Perhaps you listen to CDs, radio, or television. All in all, you listen for a good part of your waking day. In this unit you'll learn

▶ how listening works and the types of listening you can engage in

▶ how you can improve your own listening abilities

Before reading about this area of human communication, examine your own listening habits and tendencies by taking the self-test below.

TEST YOURSELF

How Do You Listen?

Respond to each question with the following scale: 1 = always, 2 = frequently, 3 = sometimes, 4 = seldom, and 5 = never.

_____ **1.** I listen actively, communicate acceptance of the speaker, and prompt the speaker to further explore his or her thoughts.

_____ **2.** I listen to what the speaker is saying and feeling; I try to feel what the speaker feels.

_____ **3.** I listen without judging the speaker.

_____ **4.** I listen to the literal meanings that a speaker communicates; I don't look too deeply into hidden meanings.

_____ **5.** I listen without active involvement; I generally remain silent and take in what the other person is saying.

_____ **6.** I listen objectively; I focus on the logic of the ideas rather than on the emotional meaning of the message.

_____ **7.** I listen critically, evaluating the speaker and what the speaker is saying.

_____ **8.** I look for the hidden meanings: the meanings that are revealed by subtle verbal or nonverbal cues.

How did you do? These statements focus on the ways of listening discussed in this unit. All of these ways are appropriate at some times but not at other times. It depends. So the only responses that are really inappropriate are "always" and "never." Effective listening is listening that is tailored to the specific communication situation.

What will you do? Consider how you might use these statements to begin to improve your listening effectiveness. A good way to start is to review these listening behaviors and try to identify situations in which each behavior would be appropriate and situations in which each behavior would be inappropriate. ✔

If you measured the importance of an activity by the time you spent on it, then—according to numerous research studies—listening would be your most important communication activity. Studies conducted from 1929 to 1980 showed that listening is the most often used form of communication, followed by speaking, reading, and writing (Rankin, 1929; Werner, 1975; Barker, Edwards, Gaines, Gladney, & Holley, 1980; Steil, Barker, & Watson, 1983; Wolvin & Coakley, 1982). This was true of high school and college students as well as of adults from a wide variety of fields. With the widespread use of the Internet today, these studies have become dated and their findings of limited value. Your communication patterns are very different from those of someone raised and educated before the widespread use of home computers. However, anecdotal evidence, although not conclusive in any way, still suggests that listening is probably the most used communication activity. Just think of how you spend your day; listening probably occupies a considerable amount of time.

Another way to appreciate the importance of listening is to consider its many benefits. Table 5.1 presents five of these benefits.

TABLE 5.1   The Benefits of Effective Listening

This table identifies some of the benefits you can derive from effective listening. As you read the table, try to visualize the benefits as they might accrue to you in interpersonal, small group, and public communication.

Effective listening will result in increasing your ability to:	For example:
Learn—to acquire knowledge of others, the world, and yourself, so as to avoid problems and make more reasonable decisions	Listening to Peter speak about his travels to Cuba will help you learn more about Peter and about life in another country. Listening to the difficulties of your sales staff may help you offer more pertinent sales training.
Relate, to gain social acceptance and popularity	Others will increase their liking of you once they see your genuine concern for them, communicated through attentive and supportive listening.
Influence the attitudes and behaviors of others	Workers are more likely to follow your advice once they feel you've really listened to their insights and concerns.
Play	Listening to the anecdotes of coworkers will allow you to gain a more comfortable balance between the world of work and the world of play.
Help others	Listening to your child's complaints about her teacher will increase your ability to help your child cope with school and her teacher.

THE PROCESS OF LISTENING

The process of **listening** can be described as a series of five steps: receiving, understanding, remembering, evaluating, and responding. The process is visualized in Figure 5.1 on page 80. Note that the listening process is a circular one. The responses of person A serve as the stimuli for person B, whose responses in turn serve as the stimuli for person A, and so on. As will become clear in the discussion of the five steps that follows, listening is not a process of transferring an idea from the mind of a speaker to the mind of a listener. Rather, it is a process in which speaker and listener work together to achieve a common understanding.

Receiving

Unlike listening, hearing begins and ends with this first stage—receiving. Hearing is something that just happens when you open your ears or when you get within earshot of auditory stimuli.

Listening is quite different. Listening begins, but does not end, with receiving messages the speaker

sends. In listening you receive both the verbal and the nonverbal messages—not only the words but also the gestures, facial expressions, variations in volume and rate, and lots more, as you'll discover when we discuss messages in more detail in Units 7 and 8. For improved reception:

- Focus **attention** on the speaker's verbal and nonverbal messages, on both what is said and what is not said.
- Look for both feedback in response to previous messages as well as feedforward (Unit 1), which can reveal how the speaker would like his or her message viewed.
- Avoid distractions in the environment and focus attention on the speaker rather than on what you'll say next.
- Maintain your role as listener and avoid interrupting the speaker until he or she is finished.

Understanding

Understanding is the stage at which you learn what the speaker means. This understanding must take

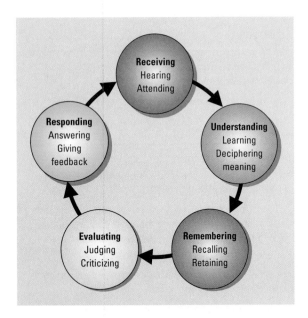

Figure 5.1

A Five-Stage Model of Listening

Of course, at each stage of listening there will be lapses. Thus, for example, at the receiving stage, a listener receives part of the message but because of noise (and perhaps for other reasons) fails to receive other parts. Similarly, at the stage of understanding, a listener understands part of the message but because of the inability to share another's meanings exactly (see Unit 7 for more on this) fails to understand other parts. The same is true for remembering, evaluating, and responding. This model draws on a variety of previous models that listening researchers have developed (e.g., Alessandra, 1986; Barker & Gaut, 2002; Brownell, 1987; Steil, Barker, & Watson, 1983).

into consideration both the thoughts that are expressed and the emotional tone that accompanies these thoughts—the urgency or the joy or sorrow expressed in the message. For improved understanding:

- Relate new information to what you already know.

- See the speaker's messages from the speaker's point of view. Avoid judging the message until you've fully understood it—as the speaker intended it.

- Ask questions to clarify or to secure additional details or examples if necessary.

- Rephrase (paraphrase) the speaker's ideas in your own words.

Remembering

Messages that you receive and understand need to be retained for at least some period of time. In some small group and public speaking situations, you can augment your memory by taking notes or by tape-recording the messages. In most interpersonal communication situations, however, such note taking would be considered inappropriate—although you often do write down a phone number, an appointment, or directions.

You can improve your message memory by:

- identifying the central ideas in a message and the major support advanced for them

The term *false memory syndrome* refers to the tendency to remember a past experience as having occurred but which never did. Most of the studies on false memory syndrome have centered on beliefs of abuse and other traumatic experiences. Often these false memories are implanted by therapists and interviewers whose persistent questioning over a period of time creates such a realistic scenario that the individual comes to believe these things actually occurred (Porter, Brit, Yuille, & Lehman, 2000). In what other, less dramatic ways can false memory syndrome occur?

MEDIA WATCH

TALK RADIO

Talk radio enables listeners to "communicate with the outside world, get quick answers to questions, express opinions, and simply talk to other people. In short, talk radio allows for interpersonal communication" (Armstrong & Rubin, 1989, p. 84). People listen to talk radio for relaxation, entertainment, convenience, voyeurism, escapism, information, passing the time, and companionship—motives not unlike those underlying face-to-face communication (Armstrong & Rubin, 1989; Rubin, Perse, & Barbato, 1988; Hofstetter & Gianos, 1997; Barker, 1998).

In talk radio (and in computer communication), there's significantly less ego involvement and much less potential threat to self-esteem than in face-to-face interaction, largely because both radio and computer communication allow the listener a greater amount of anonymity, and hence psychological security and protection.

Talk radio may also be an extremely persuasive medium. After Timothy McVeigh, an American terrorist, bombed the federal building in Oklahoma City in April 1995, much criticism and defense of talk radio was heard. President Clinton criticized the extremists on talk radio for inciting and nourishing antigovernment sentiment; he connected the bomber's motives to "right-wing hate radio" (*Newsweek*, May 8, 1995, p. 44). Talk radio hosts such as Rush Limbaugh and G. Gordon Liddy rushed to the defense of talk radio

and its right to criticize the government, arguing that the bombing had nothing to do with radio talk shows (*Newsweek*, May 8, 1995, p. 39). Howard Halpern, president of the American Academy of Psychotherapists, writing to the *New York Times* (May 5, 1995, p. A30), argued that extremist talk is dangerous because it cuts the empathic bond of the listener with those who are attacked; it suggests that the members of the attacked group are somehow different and deserving of hate. By doing so, it allows and may even encourage physical attacks and mass violence, argues Halpern.

Talk radio provides outlets for minority points of view in a way similar to cable television. Because the large media—the networks, national magazines, and major newspapers—focus on echoing the majority point of view, these minority voices would not be heard were it not for talk radio and similar niche media. In China, for example, talk radio is clearly offering an outlet for different opinions while encouraging individuals to participate in the political process (Xu, 1998).

Follow-Up. *Do you listen to talk radio? If so, what purposes does it serve for you? How persuasive is talk radio compared to, say, interpersonal interaction with college friends or major network reporting?*

- summarizing the message in a more easily retained form, being careful not to ignore crucial details or qualifications

- repeating names and key concepts to yourself or, if appropriate, aloud

Evaluating

Evaluating consists of judging messages in some way. At times you may try to evaluate the speaker's underlying intent. Often this evaluation process goes on without much conscious thought. For example, Elaine tells you that she is up for a promotion and is really excited about it. You may then try to judge her intention. Does she want you to use your influence with the company president?

Is she preoccupied with her accomplishment and thus telling everyone about it? Is she looking for a pat on the back? Generally, if you know the person well, you'll be able to identify the intention and therefore be able to respond appropriately.

In other situations, evaluation is more in the nature of critical analysis. For example, in listening to proposals advanced in a business meeting, you will at this stage evaluate them. Is there evidence to show that these proposals are practical and will increase productivity? Is there contradictory evidence? Are there alternative proposals that would be more practical and more productive?

In evaluating, try to

- resist evaluation until you fully understand the speaker's point of view

UNDERSTANDING THEORY AND RESEARCH

Reconstructing Memory

When you remember a message, do you remember it as it was spoken, or do you remember what you think you heard? The commonsense theory, of course, claims that you remember what was said. But before accepting this simple explanation, try to memorize the list of 12 words presented below (Glucksberg & Danks, 1975). Don't worry about the order of the words; only the number remembered counts. Take about 20 seconds to memorize as many words as possible. Then close the book and write down as many words as you can remember.

bed	comfort	night
rest	sound	eat
dream	awake	slumber
wake	tired	snore

Don't read any further until you've tried to memorize and reproduce the list of words.

If you're like my students, you not only remembered a good number of the words on the list but also "remembered" at least one word that was not on the list: *sleep*. Most people recall the word *sleep* as being on the list—but, as you can see, it wasn't. What happens is that in remembering you don't simply reproduce the list; you reconstruct it. In this case you gave the list meaning, and part of that meaning included the word *sleep*. Memory for speech, then, is not reproductive—you don't simply reproduce in your memory what the speaker said. Rather, memory is reconstructive: You actually reconstruct the messages you hear into a system that seems to make sense to you. You do this with all types of messages; you reconstruct the messages you hear into meaningful wholes and in the process often remember distorted versions of what was said.

Working with Theories and Research. *Have you ever "remembered" what later proved not to have occurred? What happened?*

- assume that the speaker is a person of goodwill; give the speaker the benefit of any doubt by asking for clarification on issues that you feel you must object to (are there any other reasons for accepting this new proposal?)
- distinguish facts from inferences (see Unit 7), opinions, and personal interpretations by the speaker
- identify any biases, self-interests, or prejudices that may lead the speaker to slant unfairly what is presented

Responding

Responding occurs in two phases: (1) responses you make while the speaker is talking and (2) responses you make after the speaker has stopped talking. These responses are feedback—information that you send back to the speaker and that tells the speaker how you feel and think about his or her messages. Responses made while the speaker is talking should be supportive and should acknowledge that you're listening. These include what researchers on nonverbal communication call **backchanneling cues:** "I see," "yes," "uh-huh," and similar signals that let the speaker know you're attending to the message.

Responses made after the speaker has stopped talking are generally more elaborate and might include expressing empathy ("I know how you must feel"), asking for clarification ("Do you mean that this new health plan is to replace the old one, or will it just be a supplement?"), challenging ("I think your evidence is weak here"), and agreeing ("You're absolutely right on this, and I'll support your proposal when it comes up for a vote"). For effective responding:

- Be supportive of the speaker throughout the speaker's talk by using and varying backchanneling cues; using only one backchanneling

TABLE 5.2   Some Problem-Causing Ways of Responding in Listening

Review this table and try to see if it includes some of your own listening behaviors. An exercise, "How Can You Pass Information from One Person to Another?" will help illustrate some of the major listening problems; visit www.ablongman.com/devito.

Listener Type	Listening (Responding) Behavior	(Mis)interpreting Thoughts
The static listener	Gives no feedback, remains relatively motionless, reveals no expression	Why isn't she reacting? Am I not producing sound?
The monotonous feedback giver	Seems responsive, but the responses never vary; regardless of what you say, the response is the same	Am I making sense? Why is he still smiling? I'm being dead serious.
The overly expressive listener	Reacts to just about everything with extreme responses	Why is she so expressive? I didn't say anything that provocative. She'll have a heart attack when I get to the punchline.
The reader/writer	Reads or writes while "listening" and only occasionally glances up	Am I that boring? Is last week's student newspaper more interesting than me?
The eye avoider	Looks all around the room and at others but never at you	Why isn't he looking at me? Do I have spinach on my teeth?
The preoccupied listener	Listens to other things at the same time, often with headphones turned up so loud that the sound interferes with your own thinking	When is she going to shut that music off and really listen? Am I so boring that my talk needs background music?
The waiting listener	Listens for a cue to take over the speaking turn	Is he listening to me or rehearsing his next interruption?
The thought-completing listener	Listens a little and then finishes your thought	Am I that predictable? Why do I bother saying anything? He already knows what I'm going to say.

cue—for example, saying "uh-huh" throughout—may make it appear that you're not really listening.

- Express support for the speaker in your final responses.
- Be honest; the speaker has a right to expect honest responses, even if these express anger or disagreement.
- State your thoughts and feelings as your own, using I-messages. For example, say "I think the new proposal will entail greater expense than you outlined" rather than "Everyone will object to the plan for costing too much."

Table 5.2 identifies some types of difficult listeners—listeners who don't follow the suggestions for each of the five listening stages—and their problem-causing ways of responding.

LISTENING, CULTURE, AND GENDER

Listening is difficult, in part, because of the inevitable differences in the communication systems between speaker and listener. Because each person has had a unique set of experiences, each person's

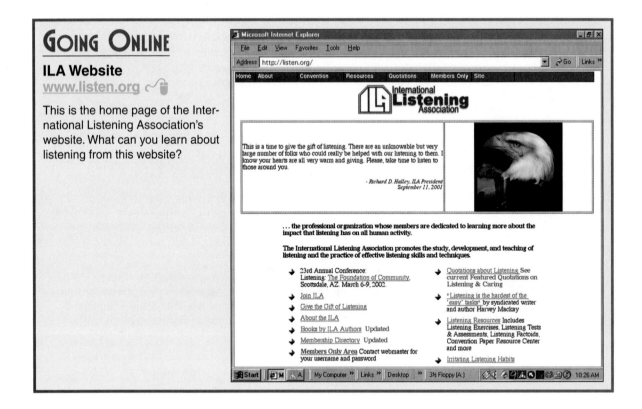

GOING ONLINE

ILA Website
www.listen.org

This is the home page of the International Listening Association's website. What can you learn about listening from this website?

---

communication and meaning system is going to be different from each other person's. When speaker and listener come from different cultures or are of different genders, the differences and their effects are naturally so much greater. Let's look first at culture.

Listening and Culture

The culture in which you were raised will influence your listening in a variety of ways. Here we look at some of these: language and speech, nonverbal behavioral differences, feedback, and credibility.

Language and Speech

Even when speaker and listener speak the same language, they speak it with different meanings and different accents. No two speakers speak exactly the same language. Speakers of the same language will, at the very least, have different meanings for the same terms because they have had different experiences.

Speakers and listeners who have different native languages and who may have learned English as a second language will have even greater differences

in meaning. Translations are never precise and never fully capture the meaning in the other language. If your meaning for "house" was learned in a culture in which everyone lived in their own house with lots of land around it, then talking about houses with someone whose meaning was learned in a neighborhood of high-rise tenements is going to be difficult. Although you'll each hear the same word, the meanings you'll each develop will be drastically different. In adjusting your listening—especially when in an intercultural setting—understand that the speaker's meanings may be very different from yours even though you both know the same language.

Still another aspect of speech is that of accents. In many classrooms throughout the country, there will be a wide range of **accents**. People whose native language is a tonal one such as Chinese (in which differences in pitch signal important meaning differences) may speak English with variations in pitch that may puzzle their hearers. People whose native language is Japanese may have trouble distinguishing *l* from *r,* as Japanese does not include this distinction. The native language acts as a filter and influences the accent given to the second language.

Nonverbal Behavioral Differences

Speakers from different cultures have different display rules—cultural rules that govern which nonverbal behaviors are appropriate and which are inappropriate in a public setting. As you listen to another person, you also "listen" to their nonverbals. If these are drastically different from what you would expect on the basis of the verbal message, they may be seen as a kind of noise or interference or may be seen as contradictory messages. Also, different cultures may give very different meanings to the same nonverbal gesture: The thumb and forefinger forming a circle means "okay" in most of the United States, but it means "money" in Japan, "zero" in some Mediterranean countries, and "I'll kill you" in Tunisia.

Feedback

Members of some cultures give very direct and very honest feedback. Speakers from these cultures—that of the United States is a good example—expect the feedback to be an honest reflection of what their listeners are feeling. In other cultures—those of Japan and Korea are good examples—it's more important to be positive than to be truthful, so people may respond with positive feedback (say, in commenting on a business colleague's proposal) even though they don't feel positive. Listen to

UNDERSTANDING THEORY AND RESEARCH

Cues to Lying

In listening, you normally assume that the speaker is telling the truth and seldom even ask yourself if the speaker is lying. When you do wonder about the speaker's truthfulness, research shows, it may well be because the speaker is exhibiting certain behaviors that often accompany lying. To a great extent, these **deception cues** seem to apply across many different cultures. Here are some verbal and nonverbal behaviors that seem to be associated with lying, a topic we return to in Unit 7 (Knapp & Hall, 1997; Miller & Burgoon, 1990; O'Hair, Cody, Goss, & Krayer, 1988; Leathers, 1997; Bond & Atoum, 2000; Al-Simadi, 2000). As you review these behaviors, ask yourself if you watch for these cues in making assumptions about whether or not people are telling the truth. Be careful that you don't fall into the trap of thinking that because someone emits these cues, he or she is therefore lying. These cues are often used by truth-tellers as well and are far from 100 percent reliable in indicating lying. In fact, in one study participants who held stereotypical views of how liars behave (for example, liars don't look at you, or liars fidget) were *less* effective in detecting lying than were those who did not hold such beliefs (Vrij & Mann, 2001). (Along with this discussion consider the ethical implications of lying by taking the self-test "[When] is lying unethical?" at www.ablongman.com/devito.) Generally, however, research indicates that liars

- smile less
- respond with shorter answers, often simple "yes" or "no" responses
- use fewer specifics and more generalities; for example, "we hung out"
- shift their posture more and use more self-touching movements
- use more and longer pauses
- avoid direct eye contact with listener and blink more often than normal
- appear less friendly and attentive
- make more speech errors

Working with Theories and Research. *Can you recall a situation in which you made the assumption that someone was lying, whereas the person was actually telling the truth? What cues led you to draw the wrong conclusion?*

feedback, as you would to all messages, with a full recognition that various cultures view feedback very differently.

Credibility

What makes a speaker credible, or believable, will vary from one culture to another. In some cultures people would claim that competence is the most important factor in, say, the choice of a teacher for their preschool children. In other cultures the most important factor might be the goodness or morality of the teacher. Similarly, members of different cultures may perceive the credibility of the various media very differently. For example, members of a repressive society in which the government controls television news may come to attribute little credibility to such broadcasts. After all, these listeners might reason, television news is simply what the government wants you to know. This reaction may be hard to understand or even recognize for someone raised in the United States, for example, where the media are largely free of such political control.

Listening and Gender

Deborah Tannen opens her chapter on listening in her best-selling *You Just Don't Understand: Women and Men in Conversation* (1990) with several anecdotes illustrating that when men and women talk, men lecture and women listen. The lecturer is positioned as the superior: as the teacher, the expert. The listener is positioned as the inferior: as the student, the nonexpert.

Women, according to Tannen, seek to build rapport and establish a closer relationship, and so use listening to achieve these ends. For example, women use more listening cues (such as interjecting "yeah," or "uh-uh," nodding in agreement, or smiling) to let the other person know they're paying attention and are interested. Men not only use fewer listening cues but interrupt more, and they will often change the topic to one they know more about or one that is less relational or people oriented or one that is more factual, such as sports statistics, economic developments, or political problems. Men, research shows, tend to play up their expertise, emphasize it, and use it in dominating the conversation. Women often play down their expertise.

Now, you might be tempted to conclude from this that women play fair in conversation and that men don't; for example, that men consistently seek

to put themselves in a position superior to women. But that may be too simple an explanation. Research shows that men communicate this way not only with women but with other men as well. Men are not showing disrespect for their female conversational partners but are simply communicating as they normally do. Women, too, communicate as they do not only with men but also with other women.

Tannen argues that the goal of a man in conversation is to be accorded respect. Therefore, a man seeks to display his knowledge and expertise, even if to do this he has to change the topic to one he knows a great deal about. Women, on the other hand, seek to be liked; so they express agreement, rarely interrupt in order to take their turn as speaker, and give lots of cues (verbally and nonverbally) to indicate that they are listening.

There's no evidence to show that these differences represent any negative motives—for example, motives on the part of men to prove themselves superior or on the part of women to ingratiate themselves. Rather, these differences in listening are largely the result of the ways in which men and women have been socialized. Can men and women change these habitual ways of listening (and speaking)? You can further explore gender differences, and especially the stereotypical male and female listening patterns, with the exercise "How Can You Listen Like a Man? Like a Woman?" at www.ablongman.com/devito.

LISTENING EFFECTIVELY

Because you listen for different reasons, the ways to listen effectively should vary from one situation to another. Here are four dimensions of listening and suggestions for adjusting them depending on the specifics of the communication situation. Along with this discussion visit the exercise "How Can You Reduce Listening Barriers?" at www.ablongman.com/devito.

Empathic and Objective Listening

If you're to understand what a person means and what a person is feeling, you need to listen with some degree of **empathy** (Rogers, 1970; Rogers & Farson, 1981). To empathize with others is to feel with them, to see the world as they see it, to feel what they feel. Only when you achieve this can you understand another person's meaning fully. Empathic listening will also help you enhance your relationships (Barrett & Godfrey, 1988; Snyder, 1992).

Although empathic listening is the preferred mode of responding for most communication situations, there are times when you need to go beyond it to measure the meanings and feelings against some objective reality. It's important to listen as Peter tells you how the entire world hates him and to understand how Peter feels and why he feels this way. But then you need to look a bit more objectively at Peter and perhaps see the paranoia or the self-hatred. Sometimes you have to put your empathic responses aside and listen with **neutrality**—objectivity and detachment.

In adjusting your empathic and objective listening focus, keep the following recommendations in mind:

- Punctuate from the speaker's point of view. If you're to understand the speaker's perspective, you must see the sequence of events as the speaker does and ascertain how this can influence what the speaker says and does.

- Engage in dialogue, not monologue. View the speaker as an equal. To encourage openness and empathy, try to eliminate any physical or psychological barriers to equality (for example, step from behind the large desk separating you from your employees). Avoid interrupting the speaker—a sign that what you have to say is more important.

- Seek to understand both thoughts and feelings. Don't consider your listening task finished until you've understood what the speaker is feeling as well as thinking.

- Avoid "offensive listening," the tendency to listen for bits and pieces of information that will enable you to attack the speaker or find fault with something the speaker has said.

- Strive to be objective especially when listening to friends or foes. Your attitudes may lead you to distort messages—to block out positive messages about a foe and negative messages about a friend. Guard against "expectancy hearing"—failing to hear what the speaker is really saying and instead hearing what you expect.

Nonjudgmental and Critical Listening

Effective listening includes both nonjudgmental and critical responses. You need to listen nonjudgmentally—with an open mind and with a view toward understanding; and you need to listen critically—with a view toward making some kind of evaluation or judgment.

Clearly, you should first listen for understanding and suspend judgment. Only after you've fully understood the relevant messages should you eval-

---

BUILDING COMMUNICATION SKILLS

How Can You Express Empathy?

Think about some typical situations. How would you respond with empathy to each of these comments? Assume that all five people are your peers.

- I just can't seem to get my act together. Everything just falls apart as soon as I get involved.

- I've never felt so alone in my life. Chris left last night and said it was all over. We were together for three years and now—after a ten-minute argument—everything is lost.

- I just got $20,000 from my aunt's estate. She left it to me! Twenty thousand! Now I can get that car and buy some new clothes.

- I just can't bear the thought of going in to work today. I'm really fed up with the company. They treat us all like idiots.

- A Camry! My parents bought me a Camry for graduation. What a bummer. They promised me a Lexus.

uate or judge. If meaningful communication is to take place, however, you need to supplement open-minded listening with critical listening. Listening with an open mind will help you understand the messages better. Listening with a critical mind will help you analyze and evaluate the messages. In adjusting your nonjudgmental and critical listening, focus on the following guidelines:

- Keep an open mind. Avoid prejudging. Delay your judgments until you fully understand the intention and the content the speaker is communicating. Avoid both positive and negative evaluation until you have a reasonably complete understanding.

- Avoid filtering out difficult messages. Avoid over-simplification or **leveling**—the tendency to eliminate details and to simplify complex messages so they're easier to remember. Avoid filtering out undesirable messages. None of us wants to hear that something we believe in is untrue, that peo-

COMMUNICATION @ WORK

Power Listening at Company Meetings

Big people monopolize the listening. Small people monopolize the talking.

—David Schwartz

Much as you communicate power and authority with words and nonverbal expressions, you also communicate power through listening. After all, through your listening you're communicating messages to others that comment in some way on your power. To communicate power through listening:

▶ Respond visibly, but in moderation: An occasional nod of agreement or a facial expression that says "that's interesting" is usually sufficient. Responding with too little or too much reaction is likely to be perceived as demonstrating lack of power; too little response says you aren't listening, and too much response says you aren't listening critically. Backchanneling cues—head nods and brief oral responses that say you're listening—are especially helpful in communicating power.

▶ Avoid "adaptors"—behaviors such as playing with your hair or a pencil or drawing pictures on a Styrofoam cup. Adaptors tend to signal your discomfort and hence your lack of power. The lack of adaptors, on the other hand, makes you appear in control of the situation and comfortable in the role of listener.

▶ Maintain an open posture. When around a table or in an audience, resist covering your face, chest, or stomach with your hands, postures that indicate defensiveness or vulnerability and hence powerlessness.

▶ Take modest notes when appropriate. Taking too many notes may communicate a lack of ability to distinguish between what is and what is not important. Taking too few notes may communicate a lack of interest or unwillingness to deal with the material.

▶ You can also signal power through "visual dominance behavior" (Exline, Ellyson, & Long, 1975). For example, the average speaker maintains a high level of eye contact while listening and a lower level while speaking. When you want to signal dominance, you might reverse this pattern and maintain a high level of eye contact while talking but a lower level while listening.

Thinking about Your Communicating @ Work

Can you identify these listening behaviors in people you've seen at meetings? Did they communicate power (or powerlessness) to you? In what other ways might you enhance your ability to listen with power?

ple we care for are unkind, or that ideals we hold are self-destructive. Yet it's important that educated people reexamine their beliefs by listening to these messages.

- Recognize your own biases. These may interfere with accurate listening and cause you to distort message reception through the process called **assimilation**—the tendency to integrate and interpret what you hear or think you hear to conform to your own biases, prejudices, and expectations. For example, are your ethnic, national, or religious biases preventing you from appreciating a speaker's point of view?

- When you need to make evaluations and judgments, avoid careless listening. Recognize and combat the normal tendency to sharpen—a process in which one or two aspects of the message become highlighted, emphasized, and perhaps embellished. Often the concepts that are sharpened are incidental remarks that somehow stand out from all the other messages.

Surface and Depth Listening

In Shakespeare's *Julius Caesar*, Marc Antony, giving the funeral oration for Caesar, says: "I come to bury Caesar, not to praise him. / The evil that men do lives after them; / The good is oft interred with their bones." And later: "For Brutus is an honourable man; / So are they all, all honourable men." But Antony, as we know, did come to praise Caesar—and to convince the crowd that Brutus was not an honorable man.

In most messages there's an obvious meaning that you can derive from a literal reading of the words and sentences. But there's often another level of meaning. Sometimes, as in *Julius Caesar*, it's the opposite of the literal meaning. At other times it seems totally unrelated. In reality, most messages have more than one level of meaning. Carol asks you how you like her new haircut. On one level, the meaning is clear: Do you like the haircut? But there's also another, perhaps more important level: Carol is asking you to say something positive about her appearance. In the same way, the parent who complains about working hard at the office or in the home may in reality be asking for some expression of appreciation. The child who talks about the unfairness of the other children in the playground may be asking for affection and love, for some

expression of caring. To appreciate these other meanings you need to engage in depth listening.

You need also to respond to the two levels of meaning. If you respond only to the surface-level communication (the literal meaning), you miss the opportunity to make meaningful contact with the other person's feelings and needs. If you say to the parent, "You're always complaining—I bet you really love working so hard," you fail to respond to the call for understanding and appreciation. So important is understanding this deeper level of meaning that Deborah Tannen (2001) makes depth listening the cornerstone of her approach to improving relationship communication.

In regulating your surface and depth listening, consider the following guidelines:

- Focus on both verbal and nonverbal messages. Recognize both consistent and inconsistent "packages" of messages, and use these as guides for drawing inferences about the speaker's meaning. Ask questions when in doubt. Listen also to what is omitted. Remember that speakers communicate by what they leave out as well as by what they include. Listen, therefore, for omissions that may give you a clue to the speaker's meanings.

- Listen for both content and relational messages. The student who constantly challenges the teacher is on one level communicating disagreement over content. However, on another level—the relationship level—the student may be voicing objections to the instructor's authority or authoritarianism. To deal effectively with the student, the instructor must listen and respond to both types of messages.

- Make special note of statements that refer back to the speaker. Remember that people inevitably talk about themselves. Whatever a person says is in part a function of who that person is. Listening for the different levels of meaning means attending to those personal, self-reference messages.

- Don't disregard the literal meaning of interpersonal messages in trying to uncover the more hidden meanings. Balance your listening between surface and depth meanings. Respond to the various levels of meaning in the messages of others as you would like others to respond to yours—sensitively but not obsessively, readily but not overambitiously.

Active and Inactive Listening

Consider the following exchange:

Speaker: I can't believe I have to rewrite this entire budget report. I really worked hard on this, and now I have to do it all over again.

Listener 1:   That's not so bad; most people find they have to redo their first reports. That's the norm here.

Listener 2:   You should be pleased that all you have to do is a rewrite. Peggy and Michael both had to completely redo their entire projects.

Listener 3:   You have to rewrite that report you've worked on for the last three weeks? You sound really angry and frustrated.

All three listeners are probably trying to make the speaker feel better. But they go about it in very different ways and, we can be sure, with very different results. Listener 1 tries to lessen the significance of the rewrite. This well-intended response is extremely common but does little to promote meaningful communication and understanding. Listener 2 tries to give the situation a positive spin. With these responses, however, both these listeners are also suggesting that the speaker should not be feeling the way he or she does. They're also saying the speaker's feelings are not legitimate and should be replaced with more logical feelings.

Listener 3's response is different from the others. Listener 3 uses active listening. **Active listening—** which owes its development to Thomas Gordon (1975), who made it a cornerstone of his P.E.T. (parent effectiveness training) technique—is a process of sending back to the speaker what you as a listener think the speaker meant—both in content and in feelings. Active listening, then, is not merely repeating the speaker's exact words, but rather putting together into some meaningful whole your understanding of the speaker's total message.

Active listening serves several important functions. First, it helps you as a listener check your understanding of what the speaker said and, more important, of what he or she meant. Reflecting back perceived meanings gives the speaker an opportunity to offer clarification. In this way, future messages will have a better chance of being relevant.

Second, through active listening you let the speaker know that you acknowledge and accept his or her feelings. In the sample responses given above, listeners 1 and 2 challenged the speaker's feelings. The active listener (listener 3), who reflected back to the speaker what he or she thought was said, accepted what the speaker was feeling. In addition to accepting the speaker's feelings, listener 3 also explicitly identified them: "You sound really angry and frustrated," allowing the speaker an opportunity to correct the listener.

Third, active listening stimulates the speaker to explore feelings and thoughts. Listener 3's response encourages the speaker to elaborate on his or her feelings. This exploration also helps the speaker to deal with the feelings by giving him or her an opportunity to talk them through.

As an added bonus, active listening contributes heavily to effective group leadership; in fact, research shows that listening techniques are more important in effective leadership than any other factor (Kramer, 1997).

Three simple techniques may help you master the process of active listening: paraphrasing the speaker's meaning, expressing understanding, and asking questions. If you'd like to practice your active listening skill, see "How Can You Practice Active Listening?" at www.ablongman.com/devito.

- *Paraphrase the speaker's meaning.* Stating in your own words what you think the speaker means and feels helps ensure your understanding and also shows interest in the speaker. Paraphrasing gives the speaker a chance to extend what was originally said. Thus, when listener 3 echoes the speaker's thought, the speaker may elaborate on why rewriting the budget report means so much. In your paraphrase be objective; be especially careful not to lead the speaker in the direction you think he or she should go.

  Also, be careful that you don't overdo paraphrasing; only a very small percentage of statements need paraphrasing. Paraphrase when you feel there's a chance for misunderstanding or when you want to express support for the other person and keep the conversation going.

- *Express understanding of the speaker's feelings.* In addition to paraphrasing the content, echo the feelings the speaker expressed or implied ("You must have felt horrible"). This expression of feel-

BUILDING COMMUNICATION SKILLS

How Can You Paraphrase to Ensure Understanding?

For each of the messages presented below, write a paraphrase that you think would be appropriate. After you complete the paraphrases, ask another person if he or she would accept them as objective restatements of the thoughts and feelings expressed in the messages. Rework the paraphrases until the other person agrees that they're accurate. A sample paraphrase is provided for the first one.

▶ I can't deal with my parents' constant fighting. I've seen it for the last 10 years and I really can't stand it anymore.

Paraphrase: You have trouble dealing with their fighting. You seem really upset by this last fight.

▶ I got a C on that paper. That's the worst grade I've ever received. I just can't believe that I got a C. This is my major. What am I going to do?

▶ I can't understand why I didn't get that promotion. I was here longer and did better work than Thompson. Even my two supervisors said I was the next in line for the promotion. And now it looks like another one won't come along for at least a year.

▶ That rotten, inconsiderate pig just up and left. He never even said goodbye. We were together for six months and after one small argument he leaves without a word. And he even took my bathrobe—that expensive one he bought for my last birthday.

▶ I'm just not sure what to do. I really love Karen. She's the sweetest kid I've ever known. I mean she'd do anything for me. But she really wants to get married. I do, too, and yet I don't want to make such a commitment. I mean that's a long-term thing. And, much as I hate to admit it, I don't want the responsibility of a wife, a family, a house. I really don't need that kind of pressure.

ings will help you further check your perception of the speaker's feelings. This will also allow the speaker to see his or her feelings more objectively; this is especially helpful when there are feelings of anger, hurt, or depression.

When you echo the speaker's feelings, you also offer the speaker a chance to elaborate. Most of us hold back our feelings until we're certain they'll be accepted. When we feel acceptance, we feel free to go into more detail. Active listening gives the speaker this important opportunity. In echoing feelings, however, be careful not to over- or understate the speaker's feelings; try to be as accurate as you can.

• *Ask questions.* Asking questions ensures your own understanding of the speaker's thoughts and feel-

ings and secures additional information ("How did you feel when you read your job appraisal report?"). Ask questions to provide just enough stimulation and support for the speaker to feel he or she can elaborate on these thoughts and feelings. These questions should further confirm your interest and concern for the speaker but not pry into unrelated areas or challenge the speaker in any way.

You can practice adjusting your listening by responding to the exercise "How Can You Listen?" at www.ablongman.com/devito.

REFLECTIONS ON ETHICS IN HUMAN COMMUNICATION

Listening Ethically

As a listener you share not only in the success or failure of any communication but also in the moral implications of the communication exchange.

Two major principles govern ethical listening. First, Give the speaker an *honest hearing*. Avoid prejudging the speaker before hearing her or him. Try to put aside prejudices and preconceptions so you can evaluate the speaker's message fairly. At the same time, try to empathize with the speaker. You don't have to agree with the speaker, but try to understand emotionally as well as intellectually what the speaker means. Then accept or reject the speaker's ideas on the basis of the information offered, not on the basis of some bias or prejudice or incomplete understanding.

Second, give the speaker *honest responses* and feedback. In a learning environment such as a communication class, this means giving hon-est and constructive criticism to help speakers improve. It also means reflecting honestly on the questions speakers raise. Much as the listener has a right to expect an active speaker, the speaker has the right to expect a listener who will actively deal with, rather than just passively hear, the message.

What would you do? *You're teaching a class in communication. In the public speaking segment, one of your students, a sincere and devout Iranian Muslim, gives a speech on "why women should be subservient to men." After the first two minutes of the speech, half the class walks out. During the next class you give a lecture on listening. What do you say in your lecture about the events of the preceding class, especially in your discussion of the ethics of lis-tening? What would you say in your listening lecture if the student's speech had been devoted to the virtues of neo-Nazism and, again, half the class walked out?*

SUMMARY

This unit discussed the process of listening, the influ-ence of culture and gender on the way people listen, and the principles for listening more effectively.

1. Effective listening yields a wide variety of benefits, including more effective learning, relating, influenc-ing, playing, and helping.
2. Listening is a five-part process that begins with receiving and continues through understanding, remembering, evaluating, and responding.
3. Receiving consists of hearing the verbal signals and seeing the nonverbal signals.
4. Understanding involves learning what the speaker means, not merely what the words mean.
5. Remembering involves retaining the received mes-sage, a process that involves considerable recon-struction.

6. Evaluating consists in judging the messages you receive.
7. Responding involves giving feedback while the speaker is speaking and taking your turn at speak-ing after the speaker has finished.
8. Listening is influenced by a wide range of cultural factors, such as differences in language and speech, nonverbal behaviors, credibility criteria, and feed-back approaches.
9. Listening is influenced by gender: Men and women seem to view listening as serving different pur-poses.
10. Effective listening involves adjusting our behaviors on the basis of at least four dimensions: empathic and objective listening, nonjudgmental and critical listening, surface and depth listening, and active and inactive listening.

11. Empathic and objective listening involves the degree to which the listener focuses on feeling what the speaker is feeling versus grasping the objective message.
12. Nonjudgmental and critical listening involves the degree to which the listener evaluates what is said.
13. Surface and depth listening has to do with the extent to which the listener focuses on the literal or obvious meanings versus the hidden or less obvious meanings.
14. Active and inactive listening involves the extent to which the listener reflects back and expresses support for the speaker.

KEY TERMS

listening	evaluating	surface and depth listening
receiving	responding	active and inactive listening
understanding	empathic and objective listening	paraphrase
remembering	nonjudgmental and critical listening	

THINKING CRITICALLY ABOUT

Listening

1. Using the four dimensions of listening effectiveness, how would you describe yourself as a listener when listening in class? When listening to your best friend? When listening to a romantic partner? When listening to parents? When listening to superiors at work?

2. What would be an appropriate active listening response for each of these situations?
   - Your friend Phil has just broken up a love affair and is telling you about it. "I can't seem to get Chris out of my mind," he says. "All I do is daydream about what we used to do and all the fun we used to have."
   - A young nephew tells you that he can't talk with his parents. No matter how hard he tries, they just don't listen. "I tried to tell them that I can't play baseball and I don't want to play baseball," he confides. "But they ignore me and tell me that all I need is practice."
   - Your mother has been having a difficult time at work. She was recently passed up for a promotion and received one of the lowest merit raises given in the company. "I'm not sure what I did wrong," she tells you. "I do my work, mind my own business, don't take my sick days like everyone else. How could they give that promotion to

Helen, who's only been with the company for two years? Maybe I should just quit."

3. Would you find it difficult to listen to friends who were complaining that the insurance premium on their Rolls-Royce was going up? Why? Would you find it difficult to listen to friends complain that their rent was going up and that they feared becoming homeless? Why?

4. Researchers have argued that the effective listening skills of salespeople are positively associated with their effectiveness in selling (Castleberrry & Shepherd, 1993). Can you think of examples from your own experience that would support this positive association between effective listening and effective selling?

5. What type(s) of listening would you use in each of the following situations? What types of listening would be obviously inappropriate in each situation?
   - Your steady dating partner for the last five years tells you that spells of depression are becoming more frequent and more long lasting.
   - Your history instructor is giving a lecture on the contributions of the ancient Greeks to modern civilization.
   - Your five-year-old daughter says she wants to become a nurse.

- A salesperson tells you of the benefits of a new computer.
- A gossip columnist details the secret lives of the stars.
- A television advertiser explains the benefits of the new Volvo.

6. **Researching Listening.** How would you go about finding answers to such questions as these?

- Are women and men equally effective as listeners?
- Can empathic listening be taught?
- What kinds of listening make health professional–patient communication more effective? More personally satisfying?
- What attitudes do business executives have toward listening and its importance in the workplace?
- How important is listening in maintaining friendships, romantic relationships, or family connections?

UNIT 6
The Self in Communication

Unit Contents

Self-Concept

Self-Awareness

Self-Esteem

Self-Disclosure

Of all the elements in communication, the most important is the self. Who you are and how you perceive yourself and others greatly influence your communications and your responses to the communications of others. In this unit you'll learn

▶ how self-concept, self-awareness, self-esteem, and self-disclosure work in communication

▶ how you can use this knowledge to communicate more effectively with others and even with yourself

SELF-CONCEPT

Your **self-concept** is your image of who you are. It's how you perceive yourself: your feelings and thoughts about your strengths and weaknesses and your abilities and limitations. Self-concept develops from the image that others have of you and reveal to you; the comparisons you make between yourself and others; your cultural experiences in the realms of race, ethnicity, gender, and gender roles; and your evaluation of your own thoughts and behaviors.

Others' Images of You

If you wished to see how your hair looked, you would probably look in a mirror. But what would you do if you wanted to see how friendly or how assertive you were? According to the concept of the **looking-glass self** (Cooley, 1922), you would look at the image of yourself that others reveal to you through their behaviors and especially through the way they treat you and react to you.

Of course, you would not look to just anyone. Rather, you would look to those who are most important in your life—to your significant others. As a child you would look to your parents and then to your elementary school teachers, for example. As an adult you might look to your friends and romantic partners. If these significant others think highly of you, you'll see a positive image reflected in their behaviors; if they think little of you, you'll see a more negative image.

Comparisons with Others

Another way you develop your self-concept is to compare yourself with others, to engage in what are called **social comparison processes** (Festinger, 1954). Again, you don't choose just anyone. Rather, when you want to gain insight into who you are and how effective or competent you are, you look

to your peers; generally to those who are distinctly similar to you (Miller, Turnbull, & McFarland, 1988) or who have approximately the same level of ability as you do (Foddy & Crundall, 1993). For example, after an examination you probably want to know how you performed relative to the other students in your class. This gives you a clearer idea as to how effectively you performed. If you play on a baseball team, it's important to know your batting average in comparison with the batting averages of others on the team. Your absolute scores on the exam or your batting average alone may be helpful in telling you something about your performance, but you gain a different perspective when you see your score in comparison with those of your peers.

When comparing yourself to others, be careful of what's called the "false consensus effect": our tendency to overestimate the degree to which others share our attitudes and behaviors. For example, college students who smoked marijuana and took amphetamines were more likely to assume other students did likewise than were students who were not users (Wolfson, 2000). Overestimating commonality tends to validate our own attitudes and behaviors: "If others are like me, then I must be pretty normal."

Cultural Teachings

Through your parents, your teachers, and the media, your culture instills in you a variety of beliefs, values, and attitudes—about success (how you define it and how you should achieve it); about the relevance of your religion, race, or nationality; and about the ethical principles you should follow in business and in your personal life. These teachings provide benchmarks against which you can measure yourself. For example, your success in achieving what your culture defines as success will contribute to a positive self-concept. Your failure to achieve what your culture encourages (for example, being married by the time you're 30) will contribute to a negative self-concept.

When you demonstrate the qualities that your culture (or your organization) teaches, you'll see yourself as a cultural success and will be rewarded by other members of the culture (or organization). Seeing yourself as culturally successful and being rewarded by others will contribute positively to your self-concept. When you fail to demonstrate such qualities, you're more likely to see yourself as a cultural failure and to be punished by other members of the culture, an effect that will contribute to a more negative self-concept.

Your Own Interpretations and Evaluations

You also react to your own behavior; you interpret it and evaluate it. These interpretations and evaluations contribute to your self-concept. For example, let's say you believe that lying is wrong. If you lie, you'll probably evaluate this behavior in terms of your internalized beliefs about lying and will react negatively to your own behavior. You might, for example, experience guilt as a result of your behavior's contradicting your beliefs. On the other hand, let's say that you pull someone out of a burning building at great personal risk. You will probably evaluate this behavior positively; you will feel good about this behavior and, as a result, about yourself.

The more you understand why you view yourself as you do, the better you'll understand who you are. You can gain additional insight into yourself by looking more closely at self-awareness, and especially at the Johari model of the self.

SELF-AWARENESS

If you listed some of the qualities you wanted to have, **self-awareness** would surely rank high. Self-awareness is eminently practical: The more you understand yourself, the more you'll be able to control your thoughts and behaviors (Wilson & Hayes, 2000).

The Four Selves

Figure 6.1 explains self-awareness in terms of the Johari window (Luft, 1969, 1984). The window is broken up into four basic areas or quadrants, each of which contains a somewhat different self. Let's assume that this window and the four selves represent you.

The Open Self

The open self represents all the information, behaviors, attitudes, feelings, desires, motivations, ideas, and so on that you know about yourself and that others also know. The information included here

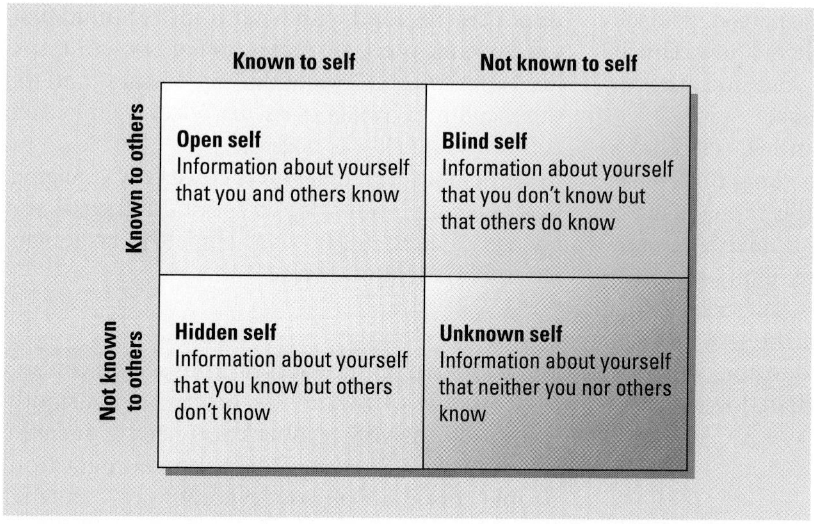

Known to self   **Not known to self**

Known to others

Open self
Information about yourself that you and others know

Blind self
Information about yourself that you don't know but that others do know

Not known to others

Hidden self
Information about yourself that you know but others don't know

Unknown self
Information about yourself that neither you nor others know

Figure 6.1
The Johari Window

Note that a change in any one of the quadrants produces changes in the other quadrants. Visualize the size of the entire window as constant, and the size of each quadrant as variable—sometimes small, sometimes large. As you communicate with others, information is moved from one quadrant to another. So, for example, if you reveal a secret, you shrink the hidden self and enlarge the open self. These several selves, then, are not separate and distinct from one another. Rather, each depends on the others.

Source: From *Group Processes: An Introduction to Group Dynamics*, Third Edition, by Joseph Luft. Copyright © 1984, 1970, 1963 by Joseph Luft. Reprinted by permission of The McGraw-Hill Companies.

might range from your name, skin color, and gender to your age, political and religious affiliations, and job title. Your open self will vary in size depending on the individuals with whom you're dealing. Some people probably make you feel comfortable and support you. To them, you open yourself wide. To others you may prefer to leave most of yourself closed.

The size of the open self also varies from person to person. Some people tend to reveal their innermost desires and feelings. Others prefer to remain silent about both significant and insignificant details. Most of us, however, open ourselves to some people about some things at some times.

The Blind Self

The blind self represents information about yourself that others know but you don't. This may vary from relatively insignificant quirks—using the expression "you know," rubbing your nose when you get angry, or having a peculiar body odor—to something as significant as defense mechanisms, fight strategies, or repressed experiences.

Communication depends in great part on both parties' having the same basic information about themselves and each other. Where blind areas exist, communication will be difficult. Yet blind areas will always exist for each of us. Although we may be able to shrink our blind areas, we can never eliminate them.

The Unknown Self

The unknown self represents those parts of yourself about which neither you nor others know. This is the information that is buried in your unconscious or that has somehow escaped notice.

You gain insight into the unknown self from a number of different sources. Sometimes this area is revealed through temporary changes brought about by drug experiences, special experimental conditions such as hypnosis or sensory deprivation, or various projective tests or dreams. The exploration of the unknown self through open, honest, and empathic interaction with trusted and trusting others—parents, friends, counselors, children, lovers—is an effective way of gaining insight.

The Hidden Self

The hidden self contains all that you know of yourself but keep hidden from others. This area includes all your successfully kept secrets about yourself and

others. At the extremes of this quadrant are overdisclosers and underdisclosers. The overdisclosers tell all, keeping nothing hidden about themselves or others. They will tell you their family history, sexual problems, financial status, goals, failures and successes, and just about everything else. The underdisclosers tell nothing. They will talk about you but not about themselves.

Very likely you fall somewhere between these two extremes; you keep certain things hidden and you disclose other things. Likewise, you disclose to some people and not to others. You are, in effect, a selective discloser.

Growing in Self-Awareness

Embedded in the foregoing discussion are suggestions on how to increase your own self-awareness. Some of these may now be made explicit. You may also want to try the exercise "How Can You Increase Self-Awareness?" at www.ablongman.com/devito.

Dialogue with Yourself

No one knows you better than you do. The problem is that you probably seldom ask yourself about yourself. It can be interesting and revealing. Consider what you know by taking the "Who Am I?" test (Bugental & Zelen, 1950). Head a piece of paper "Who Am I?" and write 10, 15, or 20 times, "I am . . . ." Then complete each of the sentences. Try not to give only positive or socially acceptable responses; respond with what comes to mind first. On another piece of paper, make two columns; head one column "Strengths" or "Virtues" and the other column "Weaknesses" or "Vices." Fill in each column as quickly as possible.

Remember, too, that you're constantly changing. Consequently, your self-perceptions and goals also change, often in drastic ways. Update them at regular and frequent intervals.

Listen

You can learn about yourself from seeing yourself as others do. Conveniently, others are constantly giving you the very feedback you need to increase self-awareness. In every interpersonal interaction, people comment on you in some way—on what you do, what you say, how you look. Sometimes these comments are explicit: "You really look washed-out today." Most often they're only im-

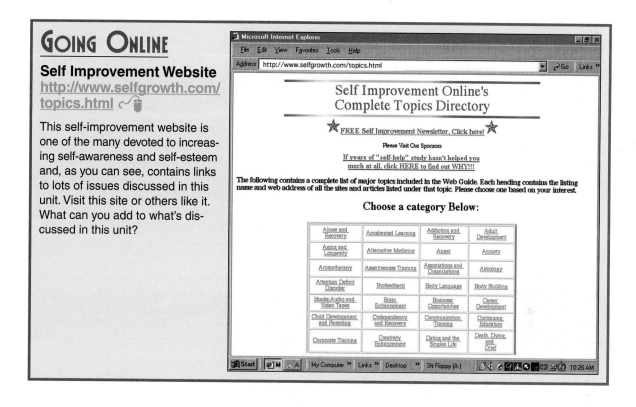

GOING ONLINE

Self Improvement Website
http://www.selfgrowth.com/
topics.html

This self-improvement website is one of the many devoted to increasing self-awareness and self-esteem and, as you can see, contains links to lots of issues discussed in this unit. Visit this site or others like it. What can you add to what's discussed in this unit?

plicit, such as a stare or averted eyes. Often they're "hidden" in the way others look, what they talk about, and the focus of their interest.

Reduce Your Blind Self
Actively seek information to reduce your blind self. People will reveal information they know about you when you encourage them to do so. Use some of the situations that arise every day to gain self-information: "Do you think I came down too hard on the instructor today?" "Do you think I was assertive enough when I asked for the raise?" Don't, of course, seek this information constantly—if you did, your friends would quickly find others with whom to interact. But you can make use of some situations—perhaps those in which you're particularly unsure of what to do or how you appear—to reduce your blind self and increase self-awareness.

See Your Different Selves
To each of your friends and relatives, you're a somewhat different person. Yet you're really all of these. Try to see yourself as do the people with whom you interact. For starters, visualize how you're seen by your mother, your father, your teacher, your best friend, the stranger you sat next to on the bus, your employer, and your neighbor's child. Because you are, in fact, a composite of all of these views, it's important that you see yourself through the eyes of many people.

Increase Your Open Self
Self-awareness generally increases when you increase your open self. When you reveal yourself to others, you learn about yourself at the same time. You bring into clearer focus what you may have buried within. As you discuss yourself, you may see connections that you had previously missed. In receiving feedback from others, you gain still more insight.

Further, by increasing your open self, you increase the likelihood that a meaningful and intimate dialogue will develop. It's through such interactions that you best get to know yourself.

SELF-ESTEEM

Personal **self-esteem** refers to the way you feel about yourself—how much you like yourself, how

UNDERSTANDING THEORY AND RESEARCH

The Value of Self-Esteem

Anecdotal evidence strongly favors the importance of self-esteem. Popular books and magazine articles regularly provide you with ways to raise your self-esteem. When you feel good about yourself—about who you are and what you are capable of doing—you perform more effectively. When you think like a success, you're more likely to act like a success. When you think you're a failure, you're more likely to act like a failure. And success (or failure), in turn, raises (lowers) your self-esteem.

Increasing your self-esteem is thus seen as a way to help you function more effectively in school, in your interpersonal relationships, and in your career. But the scientific evidence on that connection is not conclusive. For example, many people who have extremely low self-esteem have become quite successful in all fields. And a surprisingly large number of criminals and delinquents are found to have extremely high self-esteem (Johnson, 1998).

> **Working with Theories and Research.** *How would you go about studying the relationship between self-esteem and personal effectiveness?*

valuable a person you think you are, how competent you think you are. These feelings reflect the value you place on yourself; they're a measure of your self-esteem.

There's also group self-esteem, or your evaluation of yourself as a member of a particular cultural group (Porter & Washington, 1993). Personal self-esteem is influenced by your group self-esteem. If you view your racial or ethnic group membership negatively, then it's especially difficult to develop high positive self-esteem. Conversely, if you view your membership positively, then you're more likely to develop high positive self-esteem. Pride in one's group (racial, ethnic, religious, or gender, for example) and a supportive community contribute to group self-esteem and consequently to personal self-esteem.

There are also significant cultural differences in the way we're taught to view ourselves (Gudykunst & Ting-Toomey, 1988). For example, in the United States, Australia, and western Europe, people are encouraged to be independent. Members of these cultures are taught to get ahead, to compete, to win, to achieve their goals, to realize their unique potential, to stand out from the crowd. In many Asian and African cultures, on the other hand, people are taught to value an *inter*dependent self. Members of these cultures are taught to get along, to help others, and not to disagree, stand out, or be

conspicuous. Although self-esteem depends largely on achieving your goals, your culture seems to select the specific goals.

Attack Your Self-Destructive Beliefs

Self-destructive beliefs are those beliefs that damage your self-esteem and prevent you from building meaningful and productive relationships. They may be about yourself ("I'm not creative," "I'm boring"), your world ("The world is an unhappy place," "People are out to get me"), and/or your relationships ("All the good people are already in relationships," "If I ever fall in love, I know I'll be hurt"). Identifying these beliefs will help you examine them critically and see that they're both illogical and self-defeating. A useful way to view self-destructive beliefs is given in the Building Communication Skills box entitled "How Do You Attack Self-Defeating Drivers?".

Engage in Self-Affirmation

Remind yourself of your successes from time to time. To enhance self-affirmation focus on your good deeds, strengths, and positive qualities. Also, look carefully at the good relationships you have

BUILDING COMMUNICATION SKILLS

How Can You Attack Self-Defeating Drivers?

Another approach to unrealistic beliefs is to focus on what Pamela Butler (1981) calls "drivers"—beliefs that may motivate you to act in ways that are self-defeating. Because these drivers embody unrealistically high standards, they make it impossible for you to accomplish the very things you feel are essential for gaining approval from others and from yourself. Recognizing that you may have internalized such drivers is the first step to eliminating them. The second step involves recognizing that these drivers are in fact unrealistic and self-defeating. The third step is to substitute realistic and self-affirming beliefs for these self-defeating drivers. How would you restate each of these five drivers as realistic and productive beliefs?

▶ The drive *to be perfect* impels you to try to perform at unrealistically high levels at work, school, and home; anything short of perfection is unacceptable.

▶ The drive *to be strong* tells you that weakness and any of the more vulnerable emotions (like sadness, compassion, or loneliness) are wrong.

▶ The drive *to please* others leads you to seek approval from others; you assume that if you gain the approval of others, then you're a worthy and deserving person—and that if others disapprove of you, then you're worthless and undeserving.

▶ The drive *to hurry up* compels you to do things quickly, to try to do more than can reasonably be expected in any given amount of time.

▶ The drive *to try hard* makes you take on more responsibilities than any one person can be expected to handle.

with friends and relatives. Concentrate on your potential, not your limitations (Brody, 1991):

- I'm a good team worker.
- I keep confidences.
- I respect other people.
- I'm goal directed.
- I'm open to new ideas.
- I nurture others and allow others to nurture me.
- I'm creative.
- I'm willing to share what I have and what I know.
- I like myself.
- I deserve to have good things in my life.

Seek Out Nurturing People

Seek out positive, optimistic people who make you feel good about yourself. Avoid those who find fault with just about everything. Seek to build a network of supportive others (Brody, 1991). At the same time, however, realize that you do not have to be loved by everyone. Many people believe that everyone should love them. This belief traps you into

Television talk show hosts, especially Oprah Winfrey, generally emphasize the importance of self-esteem. Do you feel self-esteem is important to your own personal and professional success?

COMMUNICATION @ **WORK**

Criticism and Praise

People ask you for criticism, but they only want praise.

—Somerset Maugham

In the workplace you'll often be asked to evaluate others: to render some kind of judgment, to criticize and to praise. Both criticism and praise are difficult tasks and will significantly affect the self-esteem of the individuals. Here are a few suggestions for making constructive **criticism.** You may wish to test out these suggestions by responding to the exercise "How Do You Give and Receive Compliments?" at www.ablongman.com/devito.

▶ State criticism positively, if possible. Rather than saying, "You look terrible in black," say, "You look much better in bright colors." If you do express criticism that seems too negative, it may be helpful to offer a direct apology or to disclaim any harmful intentions (Baron, 1990). In giving praise, make sure your facial expressions communicate your positive feelings. Often, when people praise others simply because it's socially expected, they betray their lack of conviction with too little or inappropriate facial affect. Also, avoid "taking it back" or "the left-handed compliment"; for example, saying: "That was a great presentation, though a few more slides would have helped a lot."

▶ Own your thoughts and feelings. Instead of saying, "Your report was unintelligible," say, "I had difficulty following your ideas." Similarly, avoid trying to read the other person's mind. Instead of saying, "Don't you care about the impression you make? This report is terrible," say, "I would use a stronger introduction and a friendlier writing style." Use I-messages when praising as well; instead of saying, "That report was good," say, "I thought that report was good" or "I liked your report."

▶ State your concern for the other person along with your criticism or your praise, if appropriate. Instead of saying, "The introduction to your speech is boring," say, "I really want your speech to be great; how about opening with some humor to get the audience's attention?"

▶ Focus on the event or the behavior rather than on personality. For example, say, "This paper has four errors and needs retyping" rather than "You're a lousy typist; do this over." In your focus on the event, be constructive and specific; explain specifically what could be done to make it better: "I'd like a more detailed abstract on the first page of the report and an itemized summary at the end." Similarly, in praising, focus on the specific accomplishment. Name the behavior you're praising. Instead of saying "That was good," say "I enjoyed your speech" or "I thought your introduction was great."

▶ Avoid ordering or directing the other person to change; try instead to identify possible alternatives. Instead of saying, "Don't be so forward when you're first introduced to someone," say, "I think they might respond better to a less forward approach."

▶ Express criticism face-to-face (rather than by letter, memo, e-mail, or even phone) and in private, whenever possible. Privacy is especially important when dealing with members from cultures where public criticism could result in a serious loss of face. Culture is also important when praising; many Asians, for example, feel uncomfortable when praised because it is often taken as a sign of veiled criticism (Dresser, 1996).

Thinking about Your Communicating @ Work

What type of criticism do you find easiest to accept? That is, what are its major characteristics or qualities? What type of praise do you find most rewarding? What are its major characteristics?

thinking you must always please others so they will like you.

Work on Projects That Will Result in Success

Try to select projects you can complete successfully. Success builds self-esteem. Each success makes achieving the next one a little easier. Remember, too, that the failure of a project is not the failure of you as a person; failure is something that happens, not something inside you. Everyone faces defeat somewhere along the line. Successful people are those who know how to deal with setbacks. Further, one defeat does not mean you'll fail the next time. Put failure in perspective, and don't make it an excuse for not trying again.

Another activity that has been shown to contribute to self-esteem is exercise. In a study of adults between the ages of 60 and 75, those who exercised—and it didn't matter what exercise it was—increased their self-esteem. The exercise seems to have made the individuals feel better physically; this gave them a feeling of increased physical strength and hence control over their environment (McAuley, Blissmer, Katula, Duncan, & Mihalko, 2000).

SELF-DISCLOSURE

Self-disclosure is communication in which you reveal information about yourself. Because self-disclosure is a type of communication, it includes not only overt statements but also, for example, slips of the tongue and unconscious nonverbal signals. It varies from whispering a secret to a best friend to making a public confession on a television talk show (Jourard, 1968, 1971a, b; Petronio, 2000).

As the term implies, self-disclosure concerns you—your thoughts, feelings, and behaviors. It can also, however, refer to your intimates, because information about them usually has some impact on yourself. Thus, self-disclosure can result both from your own actions and from the actions of, say, your parents or your children, as these have a direct relationship to who you are.

Although by definition *self-disclosure* may refer to any information about the self, the term is most often used to refer to information that you nor-

mally keep hidden rather than simply to information that you have not previously revealed.

Before reading further about self-disclosure, its rewards and dangers, and the guidelines to consider before disclosing, explore your own willingness to disclose by taking the self-test below.

TEST YOURSELF

How Willing to Self-Disclose Are You?

Respond to each statement below by indicating the likelihood that you would disclose such items of information to, say, other members of this class. Use the following scale: 1 = would definitely self-disclose; 2 = would probably self-disclose; 3 = don't know; 4 = would probably not self-disclose; and 5 = would definitely not self-disclose.

——— 1. My attitudes toward different nationalities and races.

——— 2. My feelings about my parents.

——— 3. My sexual fantasies.

——— 4. My past sexual experiences.

——— 5. My ideal mate.

——— 6. My drinking and/or drug-taking behavior.

——— 7. My personal goals.

——— 8. My unfulfilled desires.

——— 9. My major weaknesses.

——— 10. My feelings about the people in this group.

How did you do? There are, of course, no right or wrong answers to this self-test. By considering these topics, however, you may be able to pinpoint more precisely the areas about which you're willing to disclose and the areas about which you aren't willing to disclose. How would your answers have differed if the question had asked you to indicate the likelihood of your self-disclosing to your best friend?

What will you do? This test, and ideally its discussion with others who also complete it, should get you started thinking about your own self-disclosing behavior and especially the factors that influence it. Can you identify what factors most influence your willingness to disclose or not to disclose each of these items of information? ✔

MEDIA WATCH

OUTING

Self-disclosure, as already noted, is a process by which you reveal information about yourself to others. Although at times you may be forced to disclose, normally you control what you reveal to others. There is, however, another side to disclosure—the disclosure that occurs when someone else takes information from your hidden self and makes it public. Although this third-party disclosure can concern any aspect of your hidden self, the media have made a special case out of revealing information about affectional orientation, a process called "outing."

Outing as a media process began in a relatively obscure gay magazine (*Outweek*). *Outweek's* article on "The Secret Gay Life of Malcolm Forbes" made public the homosexuality of one of the world's richest men; it "outed" him (Gross, 1991; Johansson & Percy, 1994). On March 3, 1995, the *Wall Street Journal* ran a front-page story on Jann Wenner, the multimillionaire owner and publisher of *Rolling Stone*, *Us*, *Men's Journal*, and *Family Life*. The story was basically financial and focused on the possible effects Wenner's marital breakup would have on his media empire. Somewhat casually noted in the article—without Wenner's permission and against his wishes (Rotello, 1995)—was the fact that the new person in Wenner's life was a man. This article, although not the first to discuss Wenner's gay relationship, has been singled out because of the prestige of the *Wall Street Journal* and because of the many issues this type of forced disclosure raises.

A few weeks later and across the Atlantic, the Church of England's third highest-ranking cleric, the bishop of London, David Hope, was pressured by gay and lesbian groups to announce his homosexuality (*New York Times*, March 19, 1995, p. 10). The bishop called a news conference and condemned the tactics as "seriously intimidatory or worse."

The cases of Wenner and Bishop Hope are especially interesting in terms of self-disclosure and raise the issue of the legitimacy of outing (Gross, 1991; Signorile, 1993). In the first case, if Wenner had been dating a woman, the media would have mentioned it, but few would have raised the privacy issue—because he's a public figure, and divorce is a relevant issue that will likely impact on his financial empire. And if the media reported on only extramarital heterosexual relationships, it would imply that homosexual relationships were illegitimate and not to be spoken of openly.

The David Hope case is different. Here, the bishop wished not to discuss his sexuality; he said that it was "ambiguous" and that he was celibate (*New York Times*, March 19, 1995, p. 10). Gay organizations in England, however, contended that he was a policy maker in the Church of England and that by outing him they were preventing him from taking a negative stand against homosexuality, as the Church of England had done in the past. The outing served the purpose of silencing or weakening any potential antihomosexual stand. It may be noted that at a subsequent meeting, the bishops of the Church of England, who represent 70 million members, issued a condemnation of homophobia and asked that the church reconsider its generally negative position on lesbian and gay relationships (Morales, 1995).

Follow-Up. *How do you feel about outing? What guidelines should the media follow in dealing with issues that individuals wish to keep private? Should the same guidelines apply to all media, or should different guidelines be applied to different media? At what point should the media be allowed to consider a person to be a public figure and hence without the right to privacy?*

Factors Influencing Self-Disclosure

The most important factors influencing self-disclosure are who you are, who your listeners are, and the topic of the impending self-disclosure.

Yourself

Age influences self-disclosure. Researchers have found that people self-disclose more when they talk with those who are approximately the same age (Collins & Gould, 1994). For example, young women disclose more to same-aged partners than to those significantly older than they are. Also, the level of intimacy seems to be more similar in similar-age dyads than in differing-age dyads. Not surprisingly, older people are more likely to engage in painful self-disclosures (talk of illness and loneliness, for example) than are younger people

(Coupland, Coupland, Giles, Henwood, et al., 1988).

Competence and self-esteem also influence self-disclosure: People who are competent and high in self-esteem disclose more than do those who are less competent and lower in self-esteem, perhaps because they're more confident and have more positive things to disclose than do less competent people (McCroskey & Wheeless, 1976).

Naturally enough, highly sociable and extroverted people disclose more than those who are less sociable and more introverted. People who are apprehensive about talking in general also disclose less than do those who are more comfortable in oral communication (Dolgin, Meyer, & Schwartz, 1991).

Culture also influences disclosures. People in the United States, for example, disclose more than do those in Great Britain, Germany, Japan, or Puerto Rico (Gudykunst, 1983). And among the Kabre of Togo, secrecy is a major part of everyday interaction (Piot, 1993). American students also disclose more than do students from nine different Middle East countries (Jourard, 1971a). Similarly, American students self-disclose more on a variety of controversial issues and self-disclose to more different types of people than do Chinese students (Chen, 1992).

Generally, women self-disclose more than men (Naifeh & Smith, 1984; Rosenfeld, 1979). For example, women seem more willing to disclose their feelings with their best friends than men. This gender difference is most pronounced with the negative emotions: Women are more apt to disclose their anxiety, apathy, depression, and fear. Males, on the other hand, rarely disclose such emotions to either same-sex or opposite-sex friends (Kiraly, 2000). There are, however, two situations in which men disclose more than women. First, men disclose more in initial heterosexual encounters (Derlega, Winstead, Wong, & Hunter, 1985). Second, young boys are more likely than girls to disclose family information on the Internet (CNN.com, May 17, 2000).

The gender role that a person plays is probably even more influential than is biological sex (Pearson, 1980; Shaffer, Pegalis, & Cornell, 1992). "Masculine women" disclose less than do women who score low on masculinity, and "feminine men" disclose more than do men who score low on femininity scales (Pearson, 1980). Both men and women resist self-disclosure for fear of projecting an unfa-

An interesting twist on the general finding that women self-disclose more than men is the finding that among married couples in one study, both husbands and wives self-disclosed equally, but wives reported that they made more emotional disclosures than did their husbands (Shimanoff, 1985). Do you think this pattern would also hold for dating couples?

vorable image. Men also avoid disclosing because they fear appearing inconsistent, losing control over the other person, and threatening the relationship. Women, on the other hand, avoid disclosing because they fear revealing information that may be used against them, giving others the impression that they're emotionally disturbed, or hurting their relationships (Rosenfeld, 1979).

Your Listeners

Self-disclosure is more likely to occur between people who like and trust each other than between those who don't. People you like are probably more supportive and positive, qualities that encourage self-disclosure (Derlega, Winstead, Wong, & Greenspan, 1987; Wheeless & Grotz, 1977; Petronio & Bantz, 1991). Interestingly, not only do you disclose to those you like; you probably also come to like those to whom you disclose (Berg & Archer, 1983).

Your relationship with the listener will also influence disclosure. At times self-disclosure is more likely to occur in temporary than in permanent relationships—for example, between strangers on a train or plane, a kind of "in-flight intimacy" (McGill, 1985). In this situation two people often establish an intimate self-disclosing relationship during some brief travel period, knowing that they will never see each other again. In a similar way, you might set up a relationship with one or several people on the Internet and engage in significant disclosure. Perhaps knowing that you'll never see these other people, and that they will never know where you live or work or what you look like, makes it a bit easier.

Self-disclosure occurs more in small groups than in large groups. Dyads (groups of two people) are the most hospitable setting for self-disclosure. With one listener, you can attend carefully to the person's responses. On the basis of this support or lack of support, you can monitor your disclosures, continuing if the situation is supportive and stopping if it's not. Self-disclosure occurs more quickly and at higher levels (for example, includes more intimate details) online than in face-to-face situations (Joinson, 2001; Levine, 2000).

When you self-disclose, you generally expose some weakness or make yourself vulnerable in some way; so it's not surprising to find that intimate self-disclosures are more likely to occur in noncompetitive than in competitive relationships (Busse & Birk, 1993).

You're also more likely to disclose to in-group members than to members of groups of which you're not a member. For example, people from the same race are likely to disclose more to each other than to members of another race, and people with disabilities are more likely to disclose to others with disabilities than to those without disabilities (Stephan, Stephan, Wenzel, & Cornelius, 1991).

Your Topic

If you're like the people studied by researchers, you're more likely to disclose about some topics than about others. For example, you're more likely to self-disclose information about your job, hobbies, interests, attitudes, and opinions on politics and religion than about your sex life, financial situation, personality, or interpersonal relationships (Jourard, 1968, 1971a). These topic differences have been found for people from Great Britain, Germany, the United States, and Puerto Rico (Jourard, 1971a). You're likely also to disclose favorable information more readily than unfavorable information. Generally, the more personal and the more negative the topic, the less likely you are to self-disclose—and this is true for both men and women (Nakanishi, 1986; Naifeh & Smith, 1984). Further, you're more likely to disclose information that reflects positively on the other person than information that reflects negatively (Shimanoff, 1985).

Deciding about Self-Disclosure

Because self-disclosure and its effects can be so significant, think carefully before deciding to disclose or not to disclose; weigh both the potential rewards and the potential dangers.

The Rewards of Self-Disclosure

One reason why self-disclosure is so significant is that its rewards are great. Self-disclosure may increase self-knowledge, coping abilities, communication efficiency, and relationship depth.

Self-Knowledge. When you disclose, you gain a new perspective on yourself and a deeper understanding of your own behavior. In therapy, for example, often the insight comes while the client is self-disclosing. He or she may recognize some previously unknown facet of behavior or relationship. Through self-disclosure, then, you may also come to understand yourself more thoroughly.

Coping Abilities. Self-disclosure may help you deal with your problems, especially guilt. One of the great fears many people have is that they will not be accepted because of some deep, dark secret, because of something they have done, or because of some feeling or attitude they have. By disclosing such feelings and receiving support rather than rejection, you may become better able to deal with any such guilt and perhaps reduce or even eliminate it (Pennebaker, 1991).

Even **self-acceptance** is difficult without self-disclosure. If you accept yourself as you are, you do so in part at least through the eyes of others. So it is essential that you give others the opportunity to know and to respond to the "real" you. Through self-disclosure and subsequent support, you put yourself in a better position to receive positive responses to who you really are, stripped of the facade that the failure to self-disclose erects.

Communication Efficiency. Self-disclosure may help improve communication. You understand the messages of others largely to the extent that you understand the senders of those messages. You can understand what someone says better if you know that individual well. You can tell what certain nuances mean; when the person is serious and when joking; when the person is being sarcastic out of fear and when out of resentment. Self-disclosure is an essential condition for getting to know another individual and for the process of adjustment we considered in Unit 2.

Relational Depth. Self-disclosure is often helpful for establishing a meaningful relationship between two people. Research has found, for example, that marital satisfaction is greater for couples who are mid- to high self-disclosers and significantly less in low-disclosing relationships (Rosenfeld & Bowen, 1991). Without self-disclosure relationships of any meaningful depth seem difficult if not impossible. By self-disclosing in **dyadic communication** (communication between two people), you tell others that you trust them, respect them, and care enough about them and your relationship to reveal yourself to them. This in turn leads the other individual to self-disclose and forms at least the start of a meaningful relationship, one that is honest and open and goes beyond surface trivialities.

The Dangers of Self-Disclosure

In March 1995 television talk show host Jenny Jones did a show on self-disclosing your secret crushes. One panelist, Scott Amedure, disclosed his crush on another man, Jonathan Schmitz. Three days after the taping of the show—a show that was never aired—Scott Amedure was shot in his home. The police arrested Schmitz and charged him with murder (*New York Times,* March 19, 1995, Section 4, p. 16). Although this is an extreme demonstration of the dangers of self-disclosure, there are many everyday risks to self-disclosing (Bochner, 1984). Remember too that self-disclosure, like any communication, is irreversible (see Unit 2). Regardless of how many times you may try to "take it back," once something is said it can't be withdrawn. Nor can you erase the conclusions and inferences listeners have made on the basis of your disclosures. Here, then, are a few potential dangers to keep in mind when you consider disclosing.

UNDERSTANDING THEORY AND RESEARCH

The Dyadic Effect

Generally, self-disclosure is reciprocal. In any interaction, it's more likely to occur if the other person has previously done so. This is the **dyadic effect**—namely, what one person in a dyad does, the other does in response. The dyadic effect in self-disclosure takes a kind of spiral form: Each self-disclosure prompts an additional self-disclosure by the other person, which in turn prompts still more self-disclosure, and so on. It's interesting to note that disclosures made in response to the disclosures of others are generally more intimate than those that are not the result of the dyadic effect (Berg & Archer, 1983).

This dyadic effect is not universal across all cultures, however. For example, Americans are likely to follow the dyadic effect and reciprocate with explicit, verbal self-disclosure, but Koreans aren't (Won-Doornink, 1985).

Working with Theories and Research. *In what types of situations (for example, when first meeting someone, when visiting a childhood friend, when on a date) do you find the dyadic effect most prevalent? In what types of situations does the dyadic effect seem to be weak or not to operate at all?*

Personal and Social Rejection.   Usually you self-disclose to someone you trust to be supportive. Sometimes, however, the person you think will be supportive may turn out to reject you. Parents, normally the most supportive of all in interpersonal relations, have frequently rejected children who self-disclosed their homosexuality, their plans to marry someone of a different race, or their belief in another faith. Your best friends and your closest intimates may reject you for similar self-disclosures.

Material Loss.   Sometimes, self-disclosures result in material losses. Politicians who disclose inappropriate relationships with staff members may later find that their own political party no longer supports them and that voters are unwilling to vote for them. Professors who disclose former or present drug-taking behavior or cohabitation with students may find themselves denied tenure, forced to teach undesirable schedules, and eventually let go because of "budget cuts." In the corporate world, self-disclosures of alcoholism or drug addiction are often met with dismissal, demotion, or transfer.

Intrapersonal Difficulties.   When other people's reactions are not as expected, intrapersonal difficulties may result. When you're rejected instead of supported, when your parents say that you disgust them instead of hugging you, or when your friends ignore you at school rather than seeking you out as before, you're in line for some intrapersonal difficulties.

Guidelines for Self-Disclosing

In making a decision about self-disclosure, consider your motivation, the appropriateness of the disclosure, the disclosures of the other person, and the possible burdens that self-disclosure may create.

The Motivation for Self-Disclosure.   Effective self-disclosure is motivated by a concern for the relationship, for the others involved, and for yourself. Some people self-disclose out of a desire to hurt the listener. For example, a daughter who tells her parents that they hindered rather than helped her emotional development may be disclosing out of a desire to hurt and punish rather than to improve the relationship.

The Appropriateness of Self-Disclosure.   Effective self-disclosure is appropriate to the context and to the relationship between speaker and listener. Before self-disclosing, ask yourself if the context is right or if you could arrange a better time or place. Consider also if the disclosure is appropriate to the relationship. Generally, the more intimate the disclosure, the closer the relationship should be. It's generally recommended that you resist intimate disclosures with nonintimates and casual acquaintances and **premature self-disclosure** in the early stages of any relationship. This suggestion applies especially to negative disclosures; for example, financial or sexual difficulties or a history of drug dependency.

The Disclosures of the Other Person.   Generally, disclosures are reciprocated. If the other person does not also self-disclose, then reassess your own decision to open up. The lack of reciprocity may be a signal that this person—at this time and in this context—does not welcome your disclosures. It is wise to disclose gradually and in small increments so you'll be able to retreat if the responses are not positive enough. An exercise, "How Can You Time Self-Disclosure?" allows you to explore the concept of time appropriateness; see www.ablongman.com/devito.

The Possible Burdens Self-Disclosure Might Entail.   Carefully weigh any problems you could run into as a result of a disclosure. For example, consider whether you can afford to lose your job if you disclose your misstatements on your résumé. Consider whether you're willing to risk losing a relationship if you disclose previous relationship infidelities. Consider also whether you might be making unreasonable demands on your listener. Parents, for example, often place unreasonable burdens on their children by disclosing marital problems, addictions, or self-doubts that children are too young or too emotionally involved to handle.

Guidelines for Responding to Self-Disclosures

As with self-disclosing itself, certain principles govern responding to self-disclosure. A group exercise titled "How Can You Respond to Disclosures?" is at www.ablongman.com/devito. Here are a few suggestions.

Use Effective and Active Listening Skills.   Unit 5 identified the skills of effective listening,

BUILDING COMMUNICATION SKILLS

How Can You Decide about Self-Disclosure?

Here are several instances of impending self-disclosure. For each, indicate whether you think the person should or should not self-disclose and why. In making your decision, consider each of the guidelines identified in this unit.

▶ Cathy has fallen in love with another man and wants to end her relationship with Tom, a coworker. She wants to call Tom on the phone, break the engagement, and disclose her new relationship.

▶ Gregory plagiarized a term paper in anthropology. He's sorry, especially because the plagiarized paper earned a grade of only C+. He wants to disclose to his instructor and redo the paper.

▶ A mother of two teenage children (one boy, one girl) has been feeling guilty for the past year over a romantic affair she had with her brother-in-law while her husband was in prison. The mother has been divorced for the last few months. She wants to disclose this affair and her guilt to her children.

▶ Shandra is 27 years old and has been living in a romantic relationship with another woman for the past several years. Shandra wants to tell her parents, with whom she has been very close throughout her life, but can't seem to get up the courage. She decides to tell them in a long letter.

▶ Roberto, a college sophomore, has just discovered he is HIV positive. He wants to tell his parents and his best friends, but he fears rejection. In his Mexican American culture, information like this is rarely disclosed, especially by men. He wants the support of his friends and family and yet doesn't want them to reject him or treat him differently.

---

and these are especially important when you are listening to self-disclosures. Listen actively, listen for different levels of meaning, listen with empathy, and listen with an open mind. Paraphrase the speaker so that you can be sure you understand both the thoughts and the feelings communicated. Express understanding of the speaker's feelings so as to help the other person see these feelings more objectively and through the eyes of another. Ask questions to ensure your own understanding and to signal your interest and attention.

Support and Reinforce the Discloser.   Express support and make your supportiveness clear through your verbal and nonverbal responses. Maintain eye contact, lean toward the speaker, ask relevant questions, and echo the speaker's thoughts and feelings. Refrain from evaluation during the disclosures; don't say, "You shouldn't have done that" or "Did you really cheat that often?" Instead, concentrate on understanding and empathizing with the person. Allow the speaker to set her or his own pace; don't rush the discloser.

Maintain Confidentiality.   If you tell others information you have learned through another's self-disclosures, be prepared for all sorts of negative effects. Such indiscretion will likely inhibit future disclosures from this individual to anyone in general and to you in particular, and your relationship will probably suffer. Also, those to whom you reveal these disclosures will likely feel that because you've betrayed a confidence once, you'll do so again, perhaps with their own personal details. A general climate of distrust is easily established.

Don't Use Disclosures as Weapons.   Many self-disclosures expose vulnerability or weakness. If you later turn around and use these revelations against the person, you betray that person's confidence and trust. The relationship is sure to suffer and may never fully recover.

REFLECTIONS ON ETHICS IN HUMAN COMMUNICATION

Self-Monitoring

When you self-disclose, or when you interact generally, you may regulate your messages so as to best achieve the effects you want. Examine your own tendency to self-monitor by responding to the following statements. Consider whether each statement is mostly true or mostly false for you:

▶ I can make impromptu speeches even on topics about which I have almost no information.

▶ I guess I put on a show to impress or entertain people.

▶ I would probably make a good actor.

▶ In different situations and with different people, I often act like very different persons.

▶ I'm not always the person I appear to be.

▶ I can look anyone in the eye and tell a lie with a straight face (if for the right end).

▶ I may deceive people by being friendly when I really dislike them.

These statements come from a test of **self-monitoring,** a test that measures the extent to which you try to manipulate the image you present to others in your interpersonal interactions. "Yes" answers to these questions would indicate that you are high in self-monitoring. (A more extensive self-test, "How much do you self-monitor?" may be found at **www.ablongman.com/devito**.) High self-monitors carefully adjust their behaviors on the basis of feedback from others to enable them to produce the most desirable effect. Low self-monitors are not concerned with the image they present to others; they communicate with no attempt to manipulate the impressions they create.

What would you do? *Let's say you want to get a date with a particular person you met in class. You know the kind of person your prospective date likes; and, as a high self-monitor, you have the ability to communicate that you are this kind of person. Would it be ethical for you to do this? What if the situation were at a job interview? Would it be ethical for you to communicate an image of yourself that the interviewer wants but that isn't really you? What would you do in these situations?*

SUMMARY

In this unit we looked at several aspects of the self: self-concept, self-awareness, self-esteem, and self-disclosure.

1. Self-concept is the image you have of yourself. It's developed from the image of you that others have and reveal, the comparisons you make between yourself and others, and the ways you evaluate your own thoughts and behaviors.

2. In the Johari window model of the self, there are four major areas: the open self, the blind self, the hidden self, and the unknown self.

3. To increase self-awareness, ask yourself about yourself, listen to others to see yourself as others do, actively seek information from others about yourself, see yourself from different perspectives, and increase your open self.

4. Self-esteem has to do with the way you feel about yourself, the value you place on yourself, and the positive–negative evaluations you make of yourself. You can boost your self-esteem by attacking your self-destructive beliefs, engaging in self-affirmation, seeking out nurturing people, working on proj-

ects that will result in success, and recognizing that you don't have to be loved by everyone.

5. Self-disclosure is a form of communication in which information about the self (usually information that is normally kept hidden) is communicated to another person.

6. Self-disclosure is more likely to occur when the potential discloser is with one other person, when the discloser likes or loves the listener, when the two people are approximately the same age, when the listener also discloses, when the discloser feels competent, when the discloser is highly sociable and extroverted, and when the topic of disclosure is relatively impersonal and positive.

7. The rewards of self-disclosure include increased self-knowledge, a better ability to cope with difficult

situations and guilt, more efficient communication, and a better chance for a meaningful relationship.

8. The dangers of self-disclosure include personal and social rejection, material loss, and intrapersonal difficulties.

9. Before self-disclosing, consider the motivation and appropriateness of the self-disclosure, the opportunity available for open and honest responses, the disclosures of the other person, and the possible burdens that your self-disclosure might impose on you and your listeners.

10. When listening to disclosures, practice the skills of effective and active listening, support and reinforce the discloser, keep the disclosures confidential, and don't use the disclosures as weapons against the person.

KEY TERMS

self-concept

looking-glass self

social comparison processes

Johari window

self-awareness

unknown self

self-esteem

self-destructive beliefs

self-affirmation

self-disclosure

outing

dyadic effect

THINKING CRITICALLY ABOUT

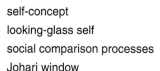

The Self in Communication

1. Do you engage in downward social comparison (comparing yourself to those you know are worse than you are on a particular quality) or upward social comparison (comparing yourself to those who are better than you on a particular quality) (Aspinwall & Taylor, 1993)? What purposes do these comparisons serve? How do they make you feel?

2. Take the self-test "How shy are you?" at <u>www.ablongman.com/devito</u>. In what ways is your shyness related to your self-concept?

3. What effect would you predict Internet communication would have on the self-esteem of adolescents? Would you offer the same predictions for people in their 60s and 70s?

4. Have you self-disclosed more in close relationships, in casual relationships, or in temporary acquaintanceships? What accounts for these differences?

5. As a parent, would you share with your children your financial and personal worries? The answer, it

seems, would depend at least in part on your socioeconomic status and on whether you're a single parent or one of two parents (McLoyd & Wilson, 1992). Research finds that members of middle-class two-parent families are reluctant to share financial problems with their children, preferring to shelter them from some of life's harsher realities. Low-income single mothers, however, feel that sharing their troubles with their children will protect the children, because they will know how hard life is and what they're up against. The researchers argue that this practice of disclosing such information actually creates problems for the child, such as aggressiveness, difficulties in concentrating on learning in school, and anxiety disorders. What would your general advice be to parents about disclosing such matters?

6. What do you think of people's self-disclosing publicly on, say, a television talk show? Would you go

on such a show? What topics would you be willing to discuss? What topics would you be unwilling to discuss?

7. How would you compare the disclosures made in chat groups with disclosures made face-to-face?

8. An interesting way to look at self-disclosure is to examine the right a person has to know information about another person. For example, is it your right to know the past relationship history of your life partner? See the exercise "What Do You Have a Right to Know?" at www.ablongman.com/devito.

9. **Researching the Self in Communication.** How would you go about finding answers to such questions as these?

   - Under what circumstances do people compare themselves with those of less ability, and under what circumstances do people compare themselves with those of greater ability?

   - Is intelligence related to self-awareness? To self-esteem?

   - Do men and women differ in the topics of their self-disclosures when talking with each other? When talking with same-sex others? Do same-sex and opposite-sex couples self-disclose similarly?

   - Does the physical context influence the amount and type of self-disclosure that takes place between two strangers who are meeting for the first time?

   - Are people more likely to disclose in intracultural or in intercultural situations?

UNIT 7
Verbal Messages

Unit Contents

*You can use language to communicate your thoughts and feelings and to create mean-
ingful and lasting relationships. But you can just as easily use language to distort and prevent
meaningful dialogue and destroy relationships. In this unit you'll learn*

▶ how language works

▶ how you can use it to communicate effectively and at the same time avoid the
  pitfalls that create misunderstanding

LANGUAGE AND MEANING

In communicating you use two major signal systems—the verbal and the nonverbal. This unit focuses on the verbal system: language as a system for
communicating meaning. The next unit focuses on
the nonverbal system. In actual practice, of course,
you communicate—in both sending and receiving—with both systems simultaneously. The following principles underlie both verbal and nonverbal
communication systems.

Meanings Are in People

If you wanted to know the meaning of the word
love, you'd probably turn to a dictionary. There
you'd find a definition such as Webster's: "the
attraction, desire, or affection felt for a person who
arouses delight or admiration or elicits tenderness,
sympathetic interest, or benevolence." But where
would you turn if you wanted to know what Pedro
means when he says, "I'm in love?" Of course, you'd
turn to Pedro to discover his meaning. It's in this
sense that meanings are not in words but in people.
Consequently, to uncover meaning, you need to
look into people and not merely into words.

Also recognize that as you change, you also
change the meanings you created out of past messages. Thus, although the message sent may not
have changed, the meanings you created from it yesterday and the meanings you create today may be
quite different. Yesterday, when a special someone
said, "I love you," you created certain meanings. But
today, when you learn that the same "I love you"
was said to three other people, or when you fall in
love with someone else, you drastically change the
meanings you perceive from those three words.

As already noted in Unit 3, this principle is
especially important in intercultural communication where meanings for the same words are often

drastically different between members of different
cultures. This became especially obvious after the
tragedy of the World Trade Center attack, where
terms like *justice, suicide,* and *terrorism* were given
totally different meanings by many in Afghanistan
and in the United States.

The Case of Bypassing

A failure to recognize this important principle is at
the heart of a common pattern of miscommunica-
tion called bypassing. Bypassing is "the miscom-
munication pattern which occurs when the sender
(speaker, writer, and so on) and the receiver (listener, reader, and so forth) miss each other with
their meanings" (Haney, 1973).

Bypassing can take either of two forms. One type
of bypassing occurs when two people use different
words but give them the same meaning; on the surface there's disagreement, but at the level of meaning there's agreement. The two people actually agree
but assume, because they use different words (some
of which may actually never be verbalized), that
they disagree. Here's an example:

Pat: I'm not interested in one-night stands. I
          want a permanent relationship. [Meaning:
          I want an exclusive dating relationship.]

Chris: I'm not ready for that. [Meaning: I'm not
          ready for marriage.]

The second type is more common and occurs
when two people use the same words but give the
words different meanings. On the surface it looks
like the two people agree (simply because they're
using the same words). But if you look more closely,
you see that the apparent agreement masks real disagreement, as in this example:

Pat: I don't really believe in religion. [Meaning:
          I don't really believe in God.]

Chris: Neither do I. [Meaning: I don't really be-
          lieve in organized religions.]

Here Pat and Chris assume they agree, but actually disagree. At some later date the implications of these differences may well become crucial.

Numerous other examples could be cited. Couples who say they're "in love" may mean very different things; one person may be thinking about "a permanent and exclusive commitment" while the other may be referring to "a sexual involvement." "Come home early" may mean one thing to an anxious parent and quite another to a teenager.

Because of bypassing it is a mistake to assume that when two people use the same word, they mean the same thing, or that when they use different words, they mean different things. Words in themselves don't have meaning; meaning is in the people who use those words. Therefore, people can use different words but mean the same thing or use the same words but mean different things.

Meanings Depend on Context

Verbal and nonverbal communications exist in a context, and that context to a large extent determines the meaning of any verbal or nonverbal behavior. The same words or behaviors may have totally different meanings when they occur in different contexts. For example, the greeting "How are you?" means "Hello" to someone you pass regularly on the street but means "Is your health improving?" when said to a friend in the hospital. A wink to an attractive person on a bus means something completely different from a wink that says "I'm kidding."

Similarly, the meaning of a given signal depends on the other behavior it accompanies or is close to in time. Pounding a fist on the table during a speech in support of a politician means something quite different from that same gesture in response to news of a friend's death. Focused eye contact may signify openness and honesty in one culture and defiance in another. In isolation from the context, it's impossible to tell what meaning was intended by merely examining the signals. Of course, even if you know the context in detail, you still may not be able to decipher the meaning of the message.

Messages Are Governed by Rules

Both verbal and nonverbal messages are regulated by a system of rules or norms that state what is and what is not meaningful, appropriate, expected, or permissible in specific social situations. Rules are cultural (and relative) institutions; they're not universal laws and so will vary from one culture to another.

You learned the ways to communicate and the rules of meaningfulness and appropriateness from observing the behaviors of the adult community around you as you grew up. For example, you learned how to express sympathy along with the rules that your culture has established for expressing it. You learned that touch is permissible under certain circumstances but not under others, and you learned which types of touching are permissible and which are not. You learned that women may touch each other in public; for example, they may hold hands, walk arm in arm, engage in prolonged hugging, and even dance together. You also learned (in the United States, at least) that if men did this, many onlookers would criticize them.

Another way of looking at the role of cultural rules in regulating verbal and nonverbal messages is to examine the culture's maxims or general communication principles (Grice, 1975). For example, in much of the United States, you operate with the maxim of quality, which holds that communication must be truthful; that is, you expect that what the other person says will be the truth. And you no doubt follow that maxim by telling the truth yourself. Similarly, you operate with the maxim of relevance; that is, what you talk about will be relevant to the conversation. Thus, if you're talking about A, B, and C, and someone brings up D, you assume that there's a connection between A, B, and C on the one hand and D on the other.

Another maxim that you operate with is that of politeness. Politeness is probably universal across all cultures (Brown & Levinson, 1988). Cultures differ, however, in how they define politeness and in how important politeness is compared with, say, openness or honesty. Cultures also differ in the rules for expressing politeness and in the punishments for violating the accepted rules of politeness (Mao, 1994; Strecker, 1993). Asian cultures, especially Chinese and Japanese, are often singled out because they emphasize politeness more and mete out harsher social punishments for violations than would most people in the United States and western Europe (Fraser, 1990). When this politeness maxim operates, it may actually override other maxims. For example, the maxim of politeness may require that you not tell the truth, a situation that would violate the maxim of quality. There are also gender differences in the expression of politeness (Holmes, 1995). Generally, studies from many different cultures show that women use more polite forms than men (Brown, 1980; Wetzel, 1988; Holmes, 1995). You may want to examine your own politeness by taking the self-test "How polite is your conversation?" at www.ablongman.com/devito.

Politeness on the Net: The Rules of Netiquette

Not surprisingly, politeness has its own rules in Internet culture. The rules of netiquette are the rules for communicating politely over the Internet. Much as the rules of etiquette provide guidance for communicating in social situations, the rules of netiquette provide guidance for communicating over the Net. These rules, as you'll see, are helpful for making Internet communication easier and more pleasant, facilitating greater personal efficiency, and putting less strain on the system and on other users. Here are several guidelines suggested by computer researchers (Shea, 1994; James & Weingarten, 1995; Barron, 1995; *Time* [special issue], Spring 1995). A helpful website to help you pursue this topic, with lots of links to a variety of netiquette-related websites, is www.albion.com/netiquette.

- *Read the FAQs.* Before asking questions about the system, read the Frequently Asked Questions; your question has probably been asked before, and you'll put less strain on the system.
- *Don't shout.* WRITING IN CAPS IS PERCEIVED AS SHOUTING. It's okay to use caps occasionally to achieve emphasis. If you wish to give emphasis without "shouting," underline like _this_ or *like this*
- *Lurk before speaking.* Lurking is reading the posted notices and the conversations without contributing anything; in computer communication, lurking is good, not bad. Lurking will help you learn the rules of the particular group and will help you avoid saying things you'll want to take back.
- Don't contribute to traffic jams. Try connecting during off-hours whenever possible. If you're unable to connect, try again later, but not immediately. Trying immediately only puts added strain on the system, and you're likely still to be unable to connect. To secure information, try local sources before trying more distant sources;

it requires fewer connections and less time. And be economical in using files that may tie up lines for long periods of time, such as photographs.

- Be brief. Follow the maxim of quantity by communicating only the information that is needed; follow the maxim of manner by communicating clearly, briefly, and in an organized way.
- Treat newbies kindly. You were once new to the Internet yourself.

Language Is Both Denotative and Connotative

Denotation refers to the meaning you'd find in a dictionary; it's the meaning that members of the culture assign to a word. **Connotation** refers to the emotional meaning that specific speakers–listeners give to a word. Words have both kinds of meaning. Take as an example the word *death*. To a doctor this word might mean (or denote) the time when brain activity ceases. This is an objective description of a particular event. In contrast, when a mother is informed of her child's death, the word means (or connotes) much more. It recalls her child's youth, ambition, family, illness, and so on. To her it's a highly emotional, subjective, and personal word. These emotional, subjective, or personal reactions are the word's connotative meaning.

Semanticist S. I. Hayakawa (Hayakawa & Hayakawa, 1990) coined the terms "snarl words" and "purr words" to further clarify the distinction between denotative and connotative meaning. Snarl words are highly negative ("She's an idiot," "He's a pig," "They're a bunch of losers"). Sexist, racist, and heterosexist language and hate speech provide lots of other examples. Purr words are highly positive ("She's a real sweetheart," "He's a dream," "They're the greatest"). Although they may sometimes seem to have denotative meaning and refer to the "real world," snarl and purr words are purely connotative in meaning. They don't describe people or events; rather, they reveal the speaker's feelings about these people or events.

Language Varies in Directness

Direct speech communicates your meaning explicitly and leaves little doubt as to the thoughts and feelings you want to convey. Indirect messages, on the other hand, are those that communicate your

COMMUNICATION @ WORK

Upward and Downward Communication

It's sad but true that the further up you get in an organization, the less likely it is that people will tell you what you ought to hear.

—Donald C. Cook

In any hierarchical organization, communication flows both upward and downward. **Upward communication** refers to messages sent from the lower levels of the hierarchy to the upper levels—for example, from line worker to manager or from faculty member to dean. This type of communication is usually concerned with job-related activities and problems; ideas for change and suggestions for improvement; and feelings about the organization, work, other workers, or similar issues.

Upward communication is vital to the growth of the organization. It provides management with feedback on worker morale and possible sources of dissatisfaction and the opportunity to acquire new ideas from workers. And it gives subordinates a sense of belonging to and being a part of the organization. Here are some guidelines for improving upward communication:

- Set up some nonthreatening system for upward communication. And, in this age of the multicultural workplace, make sure these channels are designed with the cultural attitudes and beliefs of the organization's members in mind. For example, asking Asian workers to make suggestions in a public forum would probably prove ineffective, because many Asians prefer not to offer any form of criticism in public.

- Be open to hearing worker comments, and eliminate unnecessary gatekeepers that prevent important messages from traveling up the organizational hierarchy. Like most people, managers think they communicate more often and with greater recognition than their subordinates think they do (Callan, 1993).

- Listen to these upward messages; make sure you receive, understand, remember, evaluate, and respond to worker messages.

Downward communication consists of messages sent from the higher levels of the hierarchy to the lower levels; for example, messages sent by managers to workers or from deans to faculty members. Common forms of downward communication include orders; explanations of procedures, goals, and changes; and appraisals of workers. The following suggestions can help make downward communication more effective:

- Use a vocabulary known to the workers. Keep technical jargon to a minimum. Also, remember that many workers throughout the industrialized world are not native speakers of the managers' language.

- Provide workers with sufficient information for them to function effectively. At the same time, avoid contributing to information overload.

- When making negative communications, be especially careful not to violate deeply held cultural beliefs. For example, members of some cultures (both participants and bystanders) will be offended by even mild criticism given in public. Face-saving is so important that you risk offending an entire workforce with the public criticism of even one worker.

Thinking about Your Communicating @ Work

What other suggestions would you offer for upward and for downward communication in the organization?

meaning in a roundabout way. You don't really say what you mean, but you imply it. Indirect messages have both advantages and disadvantages. You may at this point want to examine your own tendency toward directness by taking the self-test "How direct are you?" at www.ablongman.com/devito.

One of the advantages of **indirect speech** is that it allows you to express a desire without insulting or offending anyone; it allows you to observe the rules of polite interaction. So instead of saying, "I'm bored with this group," you say, "It's getting late and I have to get up early tomorrow," or you look at your watch and pretend to be surprised by the time. In this way you state a preference but express it indirectly so as to avoid offending someone. Sometimes indirect messages allow you to ask for compliments in a socially acceptable manner; for example, a person who says, "I was thinking of getting a nose job" may hope to get a response such as "A nose job? You? Your nose is perfect."

Indirect messages, however, can also create problems. For example, meanings that are expressed too indirectly may be misunderstood; the other person may simply not understand your implied meaning. When this happens, you may come to resent the other person for not seeing beneath the surface—and yourself for not being more up-front. Another disadvantage is that you may be seen as manipulative; that is, as trying to get someone to do something without really saying it. For example, you

might tell a friend, "I really could use a loan until payday but I really don't want to ask anyone."

A popular stereotype in the United States holds that women tend to be indirect in making requests and in giving orders (e.g., Kramarae, 1981). This indirectness is thought to communicate women's powerlessness and discomfort with their own authority. Men, the stereotype continues, generally use **direct speech,** sometimes to the point of being blunt or rude. This directness communicates power and comfort with one's own authority.

Deborah Tannen (1994b) provides an interesting perspective on these stereotypes. She agrees that women are more indirect in giving orders and are more likely to say, for example, "It would be great if these letters could go out today" rather than "Have these letters out by three." But Tannen (1994b, p. 84) argues that "issuing orders indirectly can be the prerogative of those in power" and in no way shows powerlessness. Power, to Tannen, is the ability to chose your own style of communication.

Men, however, are also indirect—but in different situations (Rundquist, 1992). According to Tannen (1994b), men are more likely to use indirectness when they express weakness, reveal a problem, or admit an error. Men are more likely to speak indirectly in expressing emotions other than anger. Men are also more indirect when they refuse expressions of increased romantic intimacy. Men are thus indirect, the theory goes, when they're saying

BUILDING COMMUNICATION SKILLS

How Can You Use Directness Effectively?

Think about how you would respond to someone's saying each of the following sentences.

▶ I'm so bored; I have nothing to do tonight.

▶ Do you feel like hamburgers tonight?

▶ I'd like to go to the movies. Would you like to come?

▶ I'd like hamburgers tonight. How about you?

The first two sentences are relatively indirect; they're attempts to get the listener to say or do

something without committing the speaker. The last two are more direct; they state the speaker's preferences clearly and then ask if the listener agrees. Try identifying at least three situations in which indirect statements would be more appropriate than direct ones and three situations in which direct statements would be more appropriate than indirect ones.

something that goes against the masculine stereotype. If you wish to pursue some of these and other gender differences in language, take a look at the exercise "How Can Men and Women Talk?" at www.ablongman.com/devito.

Many Asian and Latin American cultures stress the values of indirectness largely because it enables a person to avoid appearing criticized or contradicted and thereby losing face. A somewhat different kind of indirectness is seen in the greater use of intermediaries to resolve conflict among the Chinese than among North Americans, for example (Ma, 1992). In most of the United States, you're taught that directness is the preferred style. "Be upfront" and "Tell it like it is" are commonly heard communication guidelines.

Another way in which language varies is in abstraction—from the very general and abstract ("emotion," "animal") to the very specific and concrete ("happiness," "Fifi"). For a discussion of this language characteristic see "Language Varies in Abstraction" at www.ablongman.com/devito.

DISCONFIRMATION AND CONFIRMATION

Before reading about disconfirmation and confirmation, take the following self-test to examine your own behavior.

TEST YOURSELF

How Confirming Are You?

In your typical communications, how likely are you to display the following behaviors? Use this scale in responding to each statement: 5 = always; 4 = often; 3 = sometimes; 2 = rarely; and 1 = never.

_____ 1. I acknowledge the presence of another person both verbally and nonverbally.

_____ 2. I acknowledge the contributions of the other person by, for example, supporting or taking issue with what the person says.

_____ 3. During the conversation, I make nonverbal contact by maintaining direct eye contact, touching, hugging, kissing, and otherwise

demonstrating acknowledgment of the other person.

_____ 4. I communicate as both speaker and listener, with involvement, and with a concern and respect for the other person.

_____ 5. I signal my understanding of the other person both verbally and nonverbally.

_____ 6. I reflect back the other person's feelings as a way of showing that I understand these feelings.

_____ 7. I ask questions as appropriate concerning the other person's thoughts and feelings.

_____ 8. I respond to the other person's requests by, for example, returning phone calls and answering letters within a reasonable time.

_____ 9. I encourage the other person to express his or her thoughts and feelings.

_____ 10. I respond directly and exclusively to what the other person says.

How did you do? All 10 statements express confirming behaviors. Therefore, high scores (above 35) reflect a strong tendency to engage in confirmation. Low scores (below 25) reflect a strong tendency to engage in disconfirmation.

What will you do? Provide at least one specific message to illustrate how you might express confirmation in each of the 10 statements in the self-test. For example, for the first statement you might say: "Hi, Pat, come over and join us" or simply smile and wave Pat to join your group. If you feel you are not as confirming as you'd like to be, what steps might you take to increase your tendency to be confirming? Don't assume, however, that all situations call for confirmation and that only insensitive people are disconfirming. You may wish to consider situations in which disconfirmation would be, if not an effective response, at least a legitimate one. To gain some practice in identifying and framing confirmation, try the exercise "How Do You Confirm, Reject, and Disconfirm?" at www.ablongman.com/devito. ✔

Disconfirmation is a communication pattern in which you ignore someone's presence as well as that person's communications. You say, in effect, that this person and what this person has to say are not worth serious attention or effort, that this person and this person's contributions are so unimportant or insignificant that there's no reason to concern yourself with them. In doing so, you insult the other person. In fact, you can look at disconfirmation as any communication that insults another person by, say, excluding them, talking about them in stereotypes, or ignoring them (Gabriel, 1998). A perfect example of disconfirmation comes from research that finds homosexual couples are often ignored (disconfirmed) by salespeople; for example, homosexual couples have to wait significantly longer for sales assistance than do heterosexual couples (Walters & Curran, 1996). Gay men and lesbians tend also to be ignored and devalued at weddings (Oswald, 2000).

Note that disconfirmation is not the same as rejection. In rejection you disagree with the person; you indicate your unwillingness to accept something the other person says or does. In disconfirming someone, however, you deny that person's significance; you claim that what this person says or does simply does not count.

Confirmation is the opposite communication pattern. In confirmation you not only acknowledge the presence of the other person but also indicate your acceptance of the person, of the person's definition of self, and of your relationship as defined or viewed by the person. An excellent opportunity to examine your confirmation skills occurs when you talk with those who are experiencing grief. For a discussion of "Talking with the Grief-Stricken," visit **www.ablongman.com/devito**.

You can gain insight into a wide variety of offensive language practices by viewing them as types of disconfirmation—as language that alienates and separates. Three obvious practices are sexism, heterosexism, and racism.

Sexism

The National Council of Teachers of English (NCTE) has proposed guidelines for nonsexist (gender-free, gender-neutral, or sex-fair) language. These concern **sexist language** practices such as the use of generic "man," the use of generic "he" and "his," and sex-role stereotyping (Penfield, 1987).

Generic *Man*
The word *man* refers most clearly to an adult male. To use the term to refer to both men and women emphasizes maleness at the expense of femaleness. Similarly, the terms *mankind* or *the common man* or even *cavemen* imply a primary focus on adult males.

Gender-neutral terms can easily be substituted. Instead of talking about mankind, you can refer to humanity, people, or human beings. Instead of citing the common man, you can discuss the average person or ordinary people. Instead of portraying cavemen, you can describe prehistoric people or cave dwellers.

Similarly, terms such as *policeman* and *fireman*, and other terms that presume maleness as the norm and femaleness as a deviation from this norm, are clear and common examples of sexist language. Consider using nonsexist alternatives for these and similar terms; make these alternatives (for example, police officer and firefighter) a part of your active vocabulary. What alternatives can you offer for each of these words: *man, countryman, manmade, manpower, repairman, doorman, fireman, stewardess, waitress, salesman, mailman,* and *actress*?

Generic *He* and *His*
The use of the masculine pronoun to refer to any individual regardless of gender is certainly declining. But it was only as far back as 1975 that all college textbooks, for example, used the masculine pronoun as generic. There seems to be no legitimate reason why authors cannot alternate the feminine pronoun with the masculine pronoun in referring to hypothetical individuals, or why such terms as *he and she* or *her and him* cannot be used instead of just *he* or *him*. Alternatively, you can restructure your sentences to eliminate any reference to gender. For example, the NCTE guidelines (Penfield, 1987) suggest that instead of saying, "The average student worries about his grades," say, "The average student worries about grades." Instead of saying, "Ask the student to hand in his work as soon as he is finished," say, "Ask students to hand in their work as soon as they're finished."

Sex-Role Stereotyping
The words you use often reflect a sex-role bias—the assumption that certain roles or professions belong to men and others to women. To eliminate sex-role stereotyping avoid, for example, making the hypothetical elementary school teacher female and the college professor male. Avoid referring to doctors as male and nurses as female. Avoid noting the sex of a professional with phrases such as "female doctor" or "male nurse." When you're referring to a specific doctor or nurse, the person's sex will become clear when you use the appropriate pronoun: "Dr. Smith

In recent research only 45 percent of women actually confronted a man who made a sexist comment. And of these only 15 percent responded directly. Among the reasons for such lack of confrontation are the social norms that teach us that it's best not to say anything, the pressure to be polite, and concerns about a prolonged confrontation (Swim & Hyers, 1999). Do you generally confront sexist remarks? Are you equally likely to confront racist and heterosexist remarks?

wrote the prescription for her new patient" or "The nurse recorded the patient's temperature himself."

Heterosexism

A close relative of sexism is heterosexism. The term is a relatively new addition to the list of linguistic prejudices. As the term implies, **heterosexist language** is language used to disparage gay men and lesbians. As with racist language, you see heterosexism in the derogatory terms used for lesbians and gay men as well as in more subtle forms of language usage. For example, when you qualify a member of a profession—as in "gay athlete" or "lesbian doctor"—you're in effect stating that athletes and doctors are not normally gay or lesbian. Further, you're highlighting the affectional orientation of the athlete and the doctor in a context where it may have no relevance. This practice, of course, is the same as qualifying by race or gender.

Still another form of heterosexism—and perhaps the most difficult to deal with—is the presumption of heterosexuality. Usually people assume the person they're talking to or about is heterosexual. Usually they're correct, because the great majority of the population is heterosexual. At the same time, however, note that this assumption denies the lesbian and gay identity a certain legitimacy. The practice is very similar to the presumption of whiteness and maleness that we have made significant inroads in eliminating. Here are a few additional suggestions for avoiding heterosexist, or what some call "homophobic," language.

- Avoid "complimenting" gay men and lesbians by saying "they don't look it." To gay men and lesbians, this comment is not a compliment. Similarly, expressing disappointment that a person is gay—often thought to be flattering, as in such remarks as "What a waste!"—is not really a compliment.

- Avoid the assumption that every gay man or lesbian knows what every other gay man or lesbian is thinking. Making this assumption is very similar to asking a Japanese person why Sony is investing heavily in the United States or, as one comic put it, asking an African American, "What do you think Jesse Jackson meant by that last speech?"

- Avoid denying individual differences. Sweeping statements such as "Lesbians are so loyal" or "Gay men are so open with their feelings," which ignore the reality of wide differences within any group, are potentially insulting to all groups.

- Avoid overattribution, the tendency to attribute just about everything a person does, says, and believes to the fact that the person is gay or lesbian. This tendency helps to recall and perpetuate stereotypes (see Unit 4).

- Understand that relationship milestones are important to homosexual as well as heterosexual couples. Remembering anniversaries or, say, the birthday of a relative's partner will convey thoughtfulness and respect.

Racism

According to Andrea Rich (1974), "any language that, through a conscious or unconscious attempt by the user, places a particular racial or ethnic group in an inferior position is racist." **Racist language** expresses racist attitudes. It also contributes to the development of racist attitudes in those who use or hear the language.

Racist terms are used by members of one culture to disparage members of other cultures, their cus-

MEDIA WATCH

HATE SPEECH

Hate speech is speech that is hostile, offensive, degrading, or intimidating to a particular group of people. Women, African Americans, Jews, Asians, Hispanics, and gay men and lesbians are among the major targets of hate speech in the United States.

Hate speech occurs in all forms of human communication. For example, it occurs when

- people utter insults to someone passing by
- posters and fliers degrade specific groups
- radio talk shows denigrate members of certain groups
- computer games are reconfigured to target members of minority groups
- websites insult and demean certain groups and at the same time encourage hostility toward members of these groups

Because the media reach so many people and are so powerful in influencing opinions, the issue of hate speech in the media takes on special importance (Ruscher, 2001).

One of the difficulties in attacking and eliminating hate speech is that it's often difficult to draw a clear line between speech that is protected by the First Amendment right to freedom of expression but is simply at odds with the majority viewpoint and speech that is designed to denigrate and encourage hostility against members of certain cultural groups.

Some colleges are instituting hate speech codes—written statements of what constitutes hate speech as well as the penalties for hate speech. (For example, see the hate speech code adopted by St. Edwards University in Austin, Texas, at **www.stedwards.edu/hum/Drummond/hc3. html**.) Proponents of such codes argue that they teach students that hate speech is unacceptable, is harmful to all people (but especially to minority members who are the targets of such attacks), and may be curtailed in the same way as other undesirable acts (such as child pornography or rape). Opponents argue that such codes do not address the underlying prejudices and biases that give rise to hate speech, that they stifle free expression, and that they may be used unfairly by the majority to silence minority opinion and dissent.

Follow-Up. *Using a good search engine such as Google (*www.google.com*), Dogpile (*www. dogpile.com*), or AskJeeves (*www.aj.com*), look up "hate speech," especially campus codes on hate speech. After reading about hate speech and the codes that have been developed, formulate your own position on campus codes for hate speech. Are you in favor of such codes? Against such codes? What reasons can you develop in support of your position? If you're in favor of codes on hate speech, how would you write such a code of conduct?*

---

toms, or their accomplishments. Racist language emphasizes differences rather than similarities and separates rather than unites members of different cultures. Generally, racist language is used by a dominant group to establish and maintain power over other groups. The social consequences of racist language in terms of employment, education, housing opportunities, and general community acceptance are well known.

Many people feel that it's permissible for members of a culture to use racist language when referring to themselves. That is, Asians may use negative terms referring to Asians, Italians may use negative terms referring to Italians, and so on. This pattern is seen clearly in rap music (*New York Times,* January 24, 1993, Sec. 1, p. 31). The reasoning seems to be that groups should be able to laugh at themselves.

One possible problem, though, is that such language may not lose its negative connotations and may simply reinforce the negative stereotypes that society has already assigned to certain groups. By using racist terms, group members may come to accept the labels with their negative connotations and thus contribute to their own stereotyping.

It has often been pointed out (Davis, 1973; Bosmajian, 1974) that there are aspects of language that may be inherently racist. For example, one analysis of the English language found 134 synonyms for *white.* Of these, 44 have positive connotations (for example, clean, chaste, and unblemished), and only 10 have negative connotations (for example, whitewash and pale). The remaining are relatively neutral. Of the 120 synonyms for *black*, 60 have unfavorable connotations (unclean, foreboding, and deadly), and none have positive connotations.

Racist, Sexist, and Heterosexist Listening

Just as racist, sexist, and heterosexist attitudes can influence your language, they also influence your listening. Under the influence of these attitudes, you hear what the speaker is saying only through your stereotypes. You assume that what the speaker is saying is unfairly influenced by the speaker's gender, race, or affectional orientation.

Sexist, racist, and heterosexist listening occurs in a wide variety of situations. For example, when you dismiss a valid argument or accept an invalid argument, when you refuse to give someone a fair hearing, or when you give less credibility (or more credibility) to a speaker because the speaker is of a particular sex, race, or affectional orientation, you're practicing sexist, racist, or heterosexist listening. Put differently, sexist, racist, or heterosexist listening occurs when you listen differently to a person because of his or her sex, race, or affectional orientation despite the fact that these characteristics are irrelevant to the communication.

There are many instances, to be sure, in which these characteristics are relevant and pertinent to your evaluation of the message. For example, the gender of a person talking about pregnancy, fathering a child, birth control, or surrogate fatherhood is, most would agree, probably relevant to the message. So in these examples it would not be sexist to listen with awareness of the sex of the speaker. But it is sexist listening to assume that only one gender has anything to say that's worth hearing or that what one gender says can be discounted without a fair hearing. The same is true in relation to a person's race or affectional orientation.

Cultural Identifiers

Perhaps the best way to avoid sexism, heterosexism, and racism is to be conscious of the preferred cultural identifiers to use (and not to use) in talking about members of different cultures. As always, when in doubt, find out. The preferences and many of the specific examples identified here are drawn largely from the findings of the Task Force on Bias-Free Language of the Association of American University Presses (Schwartz, 1995). Do realize that not everyone would agree with these recommendations;

UNDERSTANDING THEORY AND RESEARCH

Theories of Gender Differences

Throughout this text, gender differences are discussed in a wide variety of contexts. Holmes (1995) distinguishes three perspectives on gender differences in communication:

▶ Gender differences are due to innate biological differences. Thus, gender differences in communication—such as in politeness or in listening behavior—are the result of innate biological differences.

▶ Gender differences are due to different patterns of socialization, which lead to different forms of communication. Thus, the gender differences that you observe are due to the ways in which boys and girls are raised and taught.

▶ Gender differences are due to inequalities in social power. For example, because of women's lesser social power, they're more apt to communicate with greater deference and politeness than are men.

Working with Theories and Research. *What do you think of these three positions? Can you find arguments to support or contradict any of these positions?*

they're presented here, in the words of the Task Force, "to encourage sensitivity to usages that may be imprecise, misleading, and needlessly offensive" (Schwartz, 1995, p. ix).

Generally: The term *girl* should be used only to refer to very young females and is equivalent to *boy*. Neither term should be used for people older than, say, 13 or 14. *Girl* is never used to refer to a grown woman, nor is *boy* used to refer to persons in blue-collar positions. *Lady* is negatively evaluated by many because it evokes the stereotype of the prim and proper woman. *Woman* or *young woman* is preferred. *Older person* is preferred to *elder, elderly, senior,* or *senior citizen* (which technically refers to someone older than 65).

Generally: *Gay* is the preferred term for a man who has an affectional preference for men, and *lesbian* is the preferred term for a woman who has an affectional preference for women. (Lesbian means "homosexual woman," so the phrase "lesbian woman" is redundant.) This preference for the term *lesbian* is not universal among homosexual women, however; in one survey, for example, 58 percent preferred *lesbian*, but 34 percent preferred *gay* (Lever, 1995). *Homosexual* refers to both gay men and lesbians, but more often to a sexual orientation to members of one's own sex. *Gay* and *lesbian* refer to a lifestyle, not simply to sexual orientation. *Gay* as a noun, although widely used, may prove offensive in some contexts, as in "We have two gays on the team." Although used within the gay community in an effort to remove the negative stigma through frequent usage, the term *queer*—as in "queer power"—is often resented when used by outsiders. Because most scientific thinking holds that one's sexuality is genetically determined rather than being a matter of choice, the term *sexual orientation* rather than sexual preference or sexual status (which is also vague) is preferred.

Generally: Most African Americans prefer *African American* to *black* (Hecht, Collier, & Ribeau, 1993), though *black* is often used with *white* and in a variety of other contexts (for example, Department of Black and Puerto Rican Studies, the *Journal of Black History,* and Black History Month). The American Psychological Association recommends that both *black* and *white* be capitalized, but *The Chicago Manual of Style* (a manual used by many newspapers and publishing houses) recommends using lowercase. The terms *negro* and *colored,* although used in the names of some organizations (for example, the United Negro College Fund and the National Association for the Advancement of Colored People) are not used outside of these contexts. *White* is generally used to refer to those whose roots are in European cultures and usually does not include Hispanics. Analogous to *African American* is the phrase *European American.* Few European Americans, however, would want to be called that; most would prefer their national origins emphasized, as in *German American* or *Greek American.* This preference may well change if Europe evolves into a more cohesive and united entity. *People of color*—a somewhat literary-sounding term, appropriate perhaps to public speaking but awkward in most conversations—is preferred to *nonwhite,* which implies that whiteness is the norm and nonwhiteness a deviation from that norm. The same is true of the term non-Christian.

Generally: *Hispanic* is used to refer to anyone who identifies himself or herself as belonging to a Spanish-speaking culture. *Latina* (female) and *Latino* (male) refer to people whose roots are in one of the Latin American countries; for example, in the Dominican Republic, Nicaragua, or Guatemala. *Hispanic American* refers to U.S. residents whose ancestry is a Spanish culture and includes Mexican, Caribbean, and Central and South Americans. Because it emphasizes a Spanish heritage, however, the term is really inadequate as a designation for the many people in the Caribbean and in South America whose origins are French or Portuguese. *Chicana* (female) and *Chicano* (male) refer to people with roots in Mexico, though they often connote a nationalist attitude (Jandt, 2000) and are considered offensive by many Mexican Americans. Mexican American is preferred.

Inuk (plural: *Inuit*) was officially adopted at the Inuit Circumpolar Conference to refer to the indigenous peoples of Alaska, northern Canada, Greenland, and eastern Siberia. This term is preferred to *Eskimo* (the term the U.S. Census Bureau uses), which was applied to the indigenous peoples of Alaska by Europeans and derives from a term that means "raw meat eaters" (Maggio, 1997).

Indian refers only to someone from India and is incorrectly used when applied to members of other Asian countries or to the indigenous peoples of North America. *American Indian* or *Native American* is preferred, even though many Native Americans refer to themselves as Indians and Indian people. The term *native American* (with a lowercase *n*) is most often used to refer to persons born in the United States. Although the term technically could refer to anyone born in North or South America, people outside the United States generally prefer more specific designations such as Argentinean, Cuban, or Canadian. The term *native* means an indigenous inhabitant; it's not used to mean "someone having a less developed culture."

Muslim is the form preferred (rather than the older Moslem) to refer to a person who adheres to the religious teachings of Islam. *Quran* (rather than Koran) is the preferred term for the scriptures of Islam. The terms *Mohammedan* or *Mohammedanism* are not considered appropriate, because they imply worship of the prophet Muhammad; such worship would be "considered by Muslims to be a blasphemy against the absolute oneness of God" (Maggio, 1997, p. 277).

Although there's no universal agreement, generally *Jewish people* is preferred to *Jews;* and *Jewess* (to refer to a Jewish female) is considered derogatory. *Jew* should be used only as a noun and is never correctly used as a verb or an adjective; the appropriate adjective form is *Jewish* (Maggio, 1997).

When history was being written from a European perspective, Europe was taken as the focal point, and other parts of the world were defined in terms of their locations relative to Europe. Thus, Asia became *the east* or *the orient,* and Asians became *Orientals*—a term that is today considered inappropriate or "Eurocentric." Thus, people from Asia are referred to as *Asians,* just as people from Africa are Africans and people from Europe are Europeans.

USING VERBAL MESSAGES EFFECTIVELY

A chief concern in using verbal messages is to recognize what critical thinking theorists call "conceptual distortions"; that is, mental mistakes, misinterpretations, or reasoning fallacies. Avoiding these distortions and substituting a more critical, more realistic analysis is probably the best way to improve your own use of verbal messages (DeVito, 1974).

Language Symbolizes Reality (Partially)

Language symbolizes reality; it's not the reality itself. Of course, this is obvious. But consider: Have

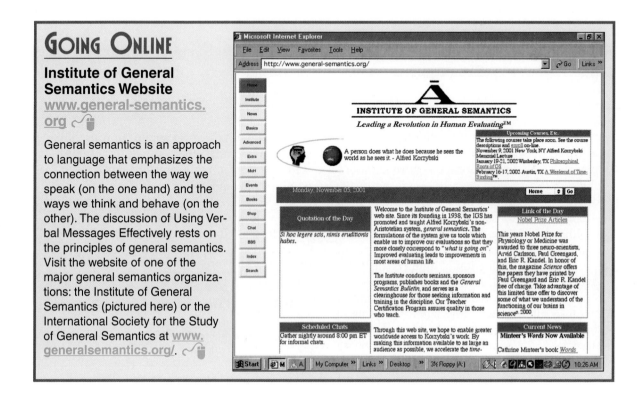

GOING ONLINE

Institute of General Semantics Website

www.general-semantics. org

General semantics is an approach to language that emphasizes the connection between the way we speak (on the one hand) and the ways we think and behave (on the other). The discussion of Using Verbal Messages Effectively rests on the principles of general semantics. Visit the website of one of the major general semantics organizations: the Institute of General Semantics (pictured here) or the International Society for the Study of General Semantics at www. generalsemantics.org/.

you ever reacted to the way something was labeled or described rather than to the actual item? Have you ever bought something because of its name rather than because of the actual object? If so, you were probably responding as if language were the reality, a distortion called intensional orientation.

Intensional Orientation

Intensional orientation (the *s* in intensional is intentional) is the tendency to view people, objects, and events according to way they're talked about—the way they're labeled. For example, if Sally were labeled "uninteresting," you would, responding intensionally, evaluate her as uninteresting even before listening to what she had to say. You'd see Sally through a filter imposed by the label "uninteresting." **Extensional orientation**, on the other hand, is the tendency to look first at the actual people, objects, and events and only afterwards at their labels. In this case, it would mean looking at Sally without any preconceived labels, guided by what she says and does, not by the words used to label her.

To avoid intensional orientation, extensionalize. Labels should never be given greater attention than the actual thing. Give your main attention to the people, things, and events in the world as you see them and not as they're presented in words. For example, when you meet Jack and Jill, observe and interact with them. Then form your impressions. Don't respond to them as "greedy, money-grubbing landlords" because Harry labeled them this way. Don't respond to George as "lazy" just because Elaine told you he was.

Allness

A related distortion is to forget that language symbolizes only a portion of reality, never the whole. When you assume that you can know all or say all about anything, you're into a pattern of behavior called **allness.** In reality, you can never see all of anything. You can never experience anything fully. You see a part, then conclude what the whole is like. You have to draw conclusions on the basis of insufficient evidence (because you always have insufficient evidence). A useful **extensional device** to help combat the tendency to think that all can or has been said about anything is to end each statement mentally with **et cetera**—a reminder that there's more to learn, more to know, and more to say and that every statement is inevitably incomplete. Some people overuse the "et cetera." They use it not as a mental reminder but as a substitute for being specific. This obviously is to be avoided and merely adds to the conversational confusion.

UNDERSTANDING THEORY AND RESEARCH

The Verb "To Be"

The theory of "E-prime" argues that if you wrote and spoke without the verb *to be* (*E-prime*, or *E'*, is simply normal English without the verb *to be*), you'd describe events more accurately (Bourland, 1965–66; Wilson, 1989; Klein, 1992). For example, when you say, "Johnny is a failure," the verb *is* implies that "failure" is *in* Johnny rather than in your observation or evaluation of Johnny. The verb *to be* (in forms such as *is, are,* and *am*) also implies permanence; the implication is that because failure is *in* Johnny, it will always be there; Johnny will always be a failure. A more accurate and descriptive statement might be "Johnny failed his last two math exams."

Consider this theory as applied to your thinking about yourself. When you say, for example, "I'm not good at public speaking" or "I'm unpopular" or "I'm lazy," you imply that these qualities are *in* you. But these are simply evaluations that may be incorrect or, if at least partly accurate, may change (Joyner, 1993).

Working with Theories and Research. *Do you find this approach to language a useful one? Does it seem applicable to your own evaluations—of yourself and of others?*

To avoid allness, recognize that language symbolizes only a part of reality, never the whole. Whatever someone says—regardless of what it is or how extensive it is—represents only part of the story.

Language Expresses Both Facts and Inferences

Language enables you to form statements of both facts and inferences without making any linguistic distinction between the two. Similarly, in speaking and listening you often don't make a clear distinction between statements of fact and statements of inference. Yet there are great differences between the two. Barriers to clear thinking can be created when inferences are treated as facts, a tendency called **fact–inference confusion.**

For example, you can say, "She's wearing a blue jacket," and you can say, "He's harboring an illogical hatred." Although the sentences have similar structures, they're different. You can observe the jacket and its color, but how do you observe "illogical hatred"? Obviously, this is not a **factual statement** but an **inferential statement.** It's a statement you make on the basis not only of what you observe, but of what you infer. For a statement to be considered factual, it must be made by the observer after observation and must be limited to what is observed (Weinberg, 1958).

There's nothing wrong with making inferential statements. You must make them in order to talk about much that is meaningful to you. The problem arises when you act as if those inferential statements were factual. You may test your ability to distinguish facts from inferences by taking the fact–inference self-test below (based on the tests constructed in Haney, 1973).

TEST YOURSELF

Can You Distinguish Facts from Inferences?

Carefully read the following report and the observations based on it. Indicate whether you think the observations are true, false, or doubtful on the basis of the information presented in the report. Write T if the observation is definitely true, F if the observation is definitely false, and ? if the observation may be either true or false. Judge each observation in order. Don't reread the observations after you've indicated your judgment, and don't change any of your answers.

A well-liked college teacher had just completed making up the final examinations and had turned off the lights in the office. Just then a tall, broad figure with dark glasses appeared and demanded the examination. The professor opened the drawer. Everything in the drawer was picked up and the individual ran down the corridor. The dean was notified immediately.

_____ 1. The thief was tall and broad and wore dark glasses.

_____ 2. The professor turned off the lights.

_____ 3. A tall figure demanded the examination.

_____ 4. The examination was picked up by someone.

_____ 5. The examination was picked up by the professor.

_____ 6. A tall, broad figure appeared after the professor turned off the lights in the office.

_____ 7. The man who opened the drawer was the professor.

_____ 8. The professor ran down the corridor.

_____ 9. The drawer was never actually opened.

_____ 10. Three persons are referred to in this report.

How did you do? Number 3 is true, number 9 is false, and all the rest are "?" Review your answers by referring back to the story. To get you started, consider: Is there necessarily a thief? Might the dean have demanded to see the instructor's examination (statement 1)? Did the examination have to be in the drawer (statements 4 and 5)? How do you know it was the professor who turned off the lights (statement 6)? Need the professor have been a man (statement 7)? Do the instructor and the professor have to be the same person (statement 10)?

What will you do? Again, recognize that there's nothing wrong with making inferences. When you hear inferential statements, however, treat them as inferences and not as facts. Be mindful of the possibility that such statements may prove to be wrong. As you read this chapter, try to formulate specific guidelines that will help you distinguish facts from inferences. ✔

To avoid fact–inference confusion, phrase inferential statements in such a way as to show that they are tentative. Inferential statements should leave open the possibility of alternatives. If, for example, you treat the statement "Our biology teacher was fired for poor teaching" as factual, you eliminate any alternatives. But if you preface your statement with, say, "Pat told me . . ." or "I'm wondering if . . .," the inferential nature of your statement will be clear. Be especially sensitive to this distinction when you're listening. Most talk is inferential. Beware of the speaker who presents everything as fact. Analyze closely and you'll uncover a world of inferences.

Language Is Relatively Static

Language changes only very slowly, especially when compared to the rapid change in people and things. **Static evaluation** is the tendency to retain evaluations without change while the reality to which they refer is changing. Often a verbal statement you make about an event or person remains static ("That's the way he is; he's always been that way") while the event or person may change enormously. Alfred Korzybski (1933) used an interesting illustration. In a tank you have a large fish and many small fish, the natural food for the large fish. Given freedom in the tank, the large fish will eat the small fish. If you partition the tank, separating the large fish from the small fish by a clear piece of glass, the large fish will continue to attempt to eat the small fish but will fail, knocking instead into the glass partition.

Eventually, the large fish will learn the futility of attempting to eat the small fish. If you now remove the partition, the small fish will swim all around the big fish, but the big fish will not eat them. In fact, the large fish will die of starvation while its natural food swims all around. The large fish has learned a pattern or "map" of behavior, and even though the actual territory has changed, the map remains static.

The mental **date** is a device that helps you keep your language (and your thinking) up to date and helps you guard against static evaluation. The procedure is simple: date your statements and especially your evaluations. Remember that Pat Smith$_{1989}$ is not Pat Smith$_{2002}$; academic abilities$_{1995}$ are not academic abilities$_{2002}$. T. S. Eliot, in *The Cocktail Party*, said, "What we know of other people is only our memory of the moments during which we knew them. And they have changed since then . . . at every meeting we are meeting a stranger." In listening, look carefully at messages that claim that what was true still is. It may or may not be. Look for change.

Language Can Obscure Distinctions

Language can obscure distinctions among people or events that are covered by the same label but are really quite different (indiscrimination); it can also make it easy to focus on extremes rather than on the vast middle ground between opposites (polarization).

Indiscrimination
Indiscrimination is the failure to distinguish between similar but different people, objects, or

Using this photo as a basis, develop hypothetical scenarios to illustrate some of the major barriers to effective verbal interaction—such as intensional orientation, allness, fact–inference confusion, static evaluation, indiscrimination, or polarization.

events. It occurs when you focus on classes and fail to see that each phenomenon is unique and needs to be looked at individually.

Everything is unlike everything else. Our language, however, provides you with common nouns, such as *teacher, student, friend, enemy, war, politician,* and *liberal.* These lead you to focus on similarities—to group together all teachers, all students, and all politicians. At the same time, the terms divert attention away from the uniqueness of each person, each object, and each event.

This misevaluation is at the heart of stereotyping on the basis of nationality, race, religion, sex, and affectional orientation. A stereotype, you'll remember from Unit 4, is a fixed mental picture of a group that is applied to each individual in the group without regard to his or her unique qualities. Whether stereotypes are positive or negative, they create the same problem: They provide you with shortcuts that are often inappropriate.

A useful antidote to indiscrimination (and stereotyping) is another extensional device called the **index.** This mental subscript identifies each individual as an individual even though both may be covered by the same label. Thus, politician$_1$ is not politician$_2$, teacher$_1$ is not teacher$_2$. The index helps you to discriminate among without discriminating against. Although the label ("politician," for example) covers all politicians, the index makes sure that each is thought about as an individual.

Polarization

Another way in which language can obscure differences is in its preponderance of extreme terms and its relative lack of middle terms, a characteristic that often leads to polarization. **Polarization** is the tendency to look at the world in terms of opposites and to describe it in extremes—good or bad, positive or negative, healthy or sick, intelligent or stupid. Polarization is often referred to as the fallacy of "either/or" or "black or white." Most people exist somewhere between the extremes. Yet there's a strong tendency to view only the extremes and to categorize people, objects, and events in terms of polar opposites.

Problems are created when opposites are used in inappropriate situations. For example, "So-and-so is either for us or against us." These options don't include all possibilities. The person may be for us in some things and against us in other things, or may be neutral.

BUILDING COMMUNICATION SKILLS

How Can You Talk about the Middle?

Think about your own tendency to polarize. Try filling in the word that would logically go where the question mark appears, a word that is the opposite of the term on the left.

hot	_____	?
high	_____	?
good	_____	?
popular	_____	?
sad	_____	?

Filling in these opposites was probably easy for you. Also, the words you supplied were probably short. Further, if several different people supplied opposites, you would find a high degree of agreement among them.

Now try to fill in the middle positions with words meaning, for example, "midway between hot and cold," "midway between high and low." You probably had greater difficulty here. You probably took more time to think of these middle terms; you also probably used multi-word phrases. Further, you would probably find less agreement among different people completing this same task. Although most things and people fall between extremes, the common tendency is to concentrate on the extremes and ignore the middle. What implications can you draw about polarization from this brief experience?

To correct this polarizing tendency, beware of implying (and believing) that two extreme classes include all possible classes—that an individual must be one or the other, with no alternatives ("Are you pro-choice or pro-life?"). Most people, most events, most qualities exist between polar extremes. When others imply that there are only two sides or alternatives, look for the middle ground.

REFLECTIONS ON ETHICS IN HUMAN COMMUNICATION

Lying

Lying occurs when you intend to mislead someone, when you do it deliberately and without warning, and when you have not been asked to do so by the person you intend to mislead (Ekman, 1985, p. 28). You can lie by commission (making explicitly false statements) or by omission (omitting relevant information and thus allowing others to draw incorrect inferences). Similarly, you can lie verbally (in speech or writing) or nonverbally (with the innocent facial expression despite the commission of some wrong or the knowing nod instead of the honest expression of ignorance) (O'Hair, Cody, & McLaughlin, 1981). Lies may range from "white lies" and truth stretching to lies that constitute infidelity in a relationship, libel, or perjury.

And, not surprisingly, lies have ethical implications. Some lies are considered innocent, acceptable, and ethical; for example, lying to a child to protect a fantasy belief in Santa Claus or the Tooth Fairy, or publicly agreeing with someone to enable the person to save face. Other lies are considered unacceptable and unethical; for example, lying to defraud investors or to falsely accuse someone of a crime. Still other lies, however, are not so easy to classify as ethical or unethical.

What would you do? *You've been asked to serve as a witness in a trial involving the robbery of a local grocery store. You really don't want to get involved; in fact, you're afraid to get involved. Yet you wonder if you can ethically refuse and say you didn't see anything (although you did). There are other witnesses, and your testimony is not likely to make a significant difference. What would you do? More generally, in what situations would lying be unethical? In what situations would lying be ethical?*

SUMMARY

This unit focused on verbal messages, and specifically on the nature of language and the ways language works; the concept of disconfirmation and how it relates to sexism, heterosexism, and racist language; and the ways in which language can be used more effectively.

1. Meanings are in people, not in things.
2. Meanings are context based; the same message in a different context will likely mean something different.
3. Language is both denotative (objective and generally easily agreed upon) and connotative (subjective and generally highly individual in meaning).
4. Language varies in directness; language can state exactly what you mean or it can hedge and state your meaning very indirectly.
5. Language is a cultural institution; each culture has its own rules identifying the ways in which language should be used.

6. Language varies in abstraction; language can vary from extremely general to extremely specific.
7. Disconfirmation is the process of ignoring the presence and the communications of others. Confirmation is accepting, supporting, and acknowledging the importance of the other person.
8. Sexist, heterosexist, and racist language puts down and negatively evaluates various cultural groups.
9. Using language effectively involves eliminating conceptual distortions and substituting more accurate assumptions about language, the most important of which are:

- Language symbolizes reality; it's not the reality itself.
- Language can express both facts and inferences, and distinctions need to be made between them.
- Language is relatively static; because reality changes so rapidly, you need to constantly revise the way you talk about people and things.
- Language can obscure distinctions in its use of general terms and in its emphasis on extreme rather than middle terms.

KEY TERMS

language	disconfirmation	allness
bypassing	sexist language	fact–inference confusion
netiquette	heterosexist language	static evaluation
connotation	racist language	indiscrimination
denotation	intensional orientation	polarization
confirmation	extensional orientation	lying

THINKING CRITICALLY ABOUT

Verbal Messages

1. When asked what they would like to change about the communication habits of the opposite sex, men said they wanted women to be more direct and women said they wanted men to stop interrupting and offering advice (Noble, 1994). What one change would you like to see in the communication style of the opposite sex? Of your own sex?

2. Visit http://www.ccil.org/jargon/ or any electronic dictionary and browse through the terms and definitions. How is an online dictionary different from a print dictionary? What would a connotative dictionary look like?

3. One theory of politeness claims that you are most polite with friends and considerably less polite with both strangers and intimates (Wolfson, 1988; Holmes, 1995). Do you find this theory a generally accurate representation of your own level of politeness in different types of relationships?

4. What cultural identifiers that describe you do you prefer? Have these preferences changed over time? How can you let other people know the des-

ignations that you prefer and those that you don't prefer? An interesting exercise—especially in a large and multicultural class—is for each student to write his or her preferred cultural identification anonymously on an index card and have them all read aloud.

5. Do you find the ideas expressed in this unit's discussions of sexist, racist, and heterosexist listening reasonable? If not, how would you define sexist, racist, and heterosexist listening? Do you find this a useful concept in understanding effective communication? Do you notice these types of listening in your classes? In your family? In your community? If you wanted to reduce these types of listening, how would you do it?

6. A widely held assumption in anthropology, linguistics, and communication is that the importance of a concept to a culture can be measured by the number of words the language has for talking about the concept. So, for example, in English there are lots of words for money or for transportation or communi-

cation. With this principle in mind, consider the findings of Julia Stanley, for example, who researched terms in English indicating sexual promiscuity (Thorne, Kramarae, & Henley, 1983). Stanley found 220 terms referring to a sexually promiscuous woman but only 22 terms for a sexually promiscuous man. What does this finding suggest about the culture's attitudes and beliefs concerning promiscuity in men and women?

7. Consider this situation: An instructor at your college or university persists in calling the female students girls, refers to gay men and lesbians as queers, and refers to various racial groups with terms that most people would consider inappropriate. When told that these terms are offensive, the instructor claims the right to free speech and argues that to prevent instructors from using such terms would be to restrict free speech, which would be a far greater wrong than being culturally or politically incorrect. How would you comment on this argument?

8. **Researching Verbal Messages.** How would you go about finding answers to questions such as these?

   - Does the use of derogatory language about your own groups influence your self-concept?
   - What are the effects of your using racist, sexist, and heterosexist language on your campus? At home? With your close friends?
   - Do definitions of what constitutes confirmation, rejection, and disconfirmation vary from one culture to another?
   - What effects do campus hate speech codes have?
   - Are people who use sexist, heterosexist, or racist language more likely to be sexist, heterosexist, or racist than those who don't use such language?

UNIT 8
Nonverbal Messages

Unit Contents

Nonverbal Communication

The Channels of Nonverbal Communication

Culture and Nonverbal Communication

When you smile, nod your head in agreement, or wave your hand to someone, you're communicating nonverbally. In fact, some researchers argue that you actually communicate more information nonverbally than you do with words. In this unit we explore this nonverbal communication system; here you'll learn

▶ how nonverbal communication works and the various forms it takes

▶ how you can use these nonverbal channels to communicate your thoughts and feelings more effectively

NONVERBAL COMMUNICATION

Nonverbal communication is communication without words. You communicate nonverbally when you gesture, smile or frown, widen your eyes, move your chair closer to someone, wear jewelry, touch someone, or raise your vocal volume—*and* when someone receives these signals. Even if you remained silent and someone attributed meaning to your silence, communication would have taken place. If, on the other hand, you gestured or smiled and no one perceived these movements, then communication would not have taken place. This doesn't mean that both sender and receiver have to give the same meanings to the signals (the gestures, the smile). It merely means that for communication to be said to have occurred, someone must send and someone must receive the message signals.

Nonverbal messages may communicate specific meanings, just as verbal messages do; they may also metacommunicate, or communicate about other messages. Let's look at each of these functions.

To Communicate Meaning

Nonverbal messages may communicate the exact same meanings as verbal messages. The same purposes that were identified for communication in general (Unit 1) are served by nonverbal signals as well. First, nonverbal messages help us *to discover—* to learn, to acquire information about the world and about other people.

Nonverbal messages—the smile, the focused eye contact, the leaning forward, and of course the kiss—also help us *to establish and maintain relationships.* We signal that we like another person first though nonverbal signals; then, usually at least, we follow up with verbal messages. At the same time, of course, our nonverbal messages can help destroy and dissolve interpersonal relationships. When you avoid eye contact and touching, when you frown more than smile, and when your voice is without warmth, you're using nonverbal signals to distance yourself from the other person.

You can also use nonverbal messages *to help.* Gently touching an ill person's face, hugging someone who's in pain, or helping an old person walk are common examples.

You use nonverbal messages *to persuade;* for example, when your posture and clothing communicate your self-confidence, when your steady gaze communicates conviction that you're right, or when your facial expression communicates that the advertised product tastes great.

Nonverbal messages may also be used *to play.* Tickling or playing patty-cake with a young child, making funny faces, and drawing cartoons are simple examples.

To Metacommunicate

Much of nonverbal communication, however, occurs in combination with verbal messages and serves a metacommunication function (see Unit 1). That is, nonverbal messages often comment on or communicate something about other messages (often verbal messages). Six general ways in which nonverbal communication blends with verbal communication have been identified and will illustrate the wide variety of metacommunication functions that nonverbal messages may serve (Knapp & Hall, 1997).

Nonverbal messages are often used to *accent* or emphasize some part of the verbal message. You might, for example, raise your voice to underscore a particular word or phrase, bang your fist on the desk to stress your commitment, or look longingly into someone's eyes when saying "I love you."

You use nonverbal communication to *complement*, to add nuances of meaning not communicated by your verbal message. Thus, you might smile when telling a story (to suggest that you find it humorous) or frown and shake your head when recounting someone's deceit (to suggest your disapproval).

You may deliberately *contradict* your verbal messages with nonverbal movements—for example, by crossing your fingers or winking to indicate that you're lying.

Movements may be used to *regulate* or control the flow of verbal messages, as when you purse your lips, lean forward, or make hand gestures to indicate that you want to speak. You might also put up your hand or vocalize your **pauses** (for example, with "um" or "ah") to indicate that you've not finished and aren't ready to relinquish the floor to the next speaker.

You can *repeat* or restate the verbal message nonverbally. You can, for example, follow your verbal "Is that all right?" with raised eyebrows and a questioning look, or motion with your head or hand to repeat your verbal "Let's go."

You may also use nonverbal communication to *substitute for* or take the place of verbal messages. For instance, you can signal "OK" with a hand gesture. You can nod your head to indicate yes or shake your head to indicate no.

An exercise that asks you to look at the functions of verbal and nonverbal messages, "How Can You Recognize Verbal and Nonverbal Message Functions?" is available at **www.ablongman.com/ devito**.

COMMUNICATION @ WORK

Communicating Power Nonverbally

The body says what words cannot.

—Martha Graham

If you want to signal power nonverbally, try these suggestions (Lewis, 1989; Burgoon, Buller, & Woodall, 1996).

▶ Walk slowly and deliberately. To appear hurried is to appear powerless, as if you were rushing to meet the expectations of those who have power over you.

▶ Use facial expressions and gestures as appropriate; these help you express your concern for the other person and the interaction and help you communicate your comfort and control of the situation.

▶ Consider standing relatively close to your listeners (even in public speaking); it will create greater immediacy and is likely to be more persuasive.

▶ Other things being equal, dress relatively conservatively if you want to influence others; conservative clothing is associated with power and status.

▶ Select chairs you can get in and out of easily; avoid deep plush chairs that you will sink into and have trouble getting out of.

▶ To communicate dominance with your handshake, exert more pressure than usual and hold the grip a bit longer than normal.

▶ Use consistent packaging; be careful that your verbal and nonverbal messages do not contradict each other, a signal of uncertainty and a lack of conviction.

▶ Be sure to respond in kind to another's eyebrow flash (raising the eyebrow as a way of acknowledging another person).

▶ When you break eye contact, direct your gaze downward; otherwise you will communicate a lack of interest in the other person.

Thinking about Your Communicating @ Work

Do you recognize these nonverbal cues in the communication behavior of those in power? Do you recognize these nonverbal cues in your own behaviors?

THE CHANNELS OF NONVERBAL COMMUNICATION

Nonverbal communication is probably most easily explained in terms of the various channels through which messages pass. Here we'll survey 10 channels: body, face, eye, space, artifactual, touch, paralanguage, silence, time, and smell.

The Body

Two areas of the body are especially important in communicating messages. First, the movements you make with your body communicate; second, the general appearance of your body communicates.

Body Movements

Researchers in **kinesics**, or the study of nonverbal communication through face and body movements, identify five major types of movements: emblems, illustrators, affect displays, regulators, and adaptors (Ekman & Friesen, 1969; Knapp & Hall, 1997).

Emblems are body gestures that directly translate into words or phrases; for example, the OK sign, the thumbs-up for "good job," and the V for victory. You use these consciously and purposely to communicate the same meaning as the words. But emblems are culture specific, so be careful when using your culture's emblems in other cultures. For example, when President Nixon visited Latin America and gestured with the OK sign, intending to communicate something positive, he was quickly informed that this gesture was not universal. In Latin America the gesture has a far more negative meaning. Here are a few cultural differences in the emblems you may commonly use (Axtell, 1993):

- In the United States, to say "hello" you wave with your whole hand moving from side to side, but in a large part of Europe that same signal means "no." In Greece such a gesture would be considered insulting.

- The V for victory is common throughout much of the world; but if you make this gesture in England with the palm facing your face, it's as insulting as the raised middle finger is in the United States.

- In Texas the raised fist with little finger and index finger held upright is a positive expression of support, because it represents the Texas longhorn

steer. But in Italy it's an insult that means "Your spouse is having an affair with someone else." In parts of South America it's a gesture to ward off evil, and in parts of Africa it's a curse: "May you experience bad times."

- In the United States and in much of Asia, hugs are rarely exchanged among acquaintances; but among Latins and southern Europeans, hugging is a common greeting gesture, and failing to hug someone may communicate unfriendliness.

Illustrators enhance (literally "illustrate") the verbal messages they accompany. For example, when referring to something to the left, you might gesture toward the left. Most often you illustrate with your hands, but you can also illustrate with head and general body movements. You might, for example, turn your head or your entire body toward the left. You might also use illustrators to communicate the shape or size of objects you're talking about.

Affect displays are movements of the face (smiling or frowning, for example) but also of the hands and general body (body tension or relaxation, for example) that communicate emotional meaning. Affect displays are often unconscious; you smile or frown, for example, without awareness. At other times, however, you may smile consciously, trying to convey your pleasure or satisfaction.

Regulators are behaviors that monitor, control, coordinate, or maintain the speaking of another individual. When you nod your head, for example, you tell the speaker to keep on speaking; when you lean forward and open your mouth, you tell the speaker that you would like to say something.

Adaptors are gestures that satisfy some personal need, such as scratching to relieve an itch or moving your hair out of your eyes. **Self-adaptors** are self-touching movements (for example, rubbing your nose). **Alter-adaptors** are movements directed at the person with whom you're speaking, such as removing lint from someone's jacket or straightening a person's tie or folding your arms in front of you to keep others a comfortable distance from you. **Object-adaptors** are gestures focused on objects, such as doodling on or shredding a Styrofoam coffee cup.

Body Appearance

Your general body appearance also communicates. Height, for example, has been shown to be significant in a wide variety of situations. Tall presidential

MEDIA WATCH

LEGIBLE CLOTHING

Legible clothing is anything that you wear that contains some verbal message; it's clothing that literally can be read. In some instances the message proclaims status; it tells others that you are, for example, rich or stylish or youthful. The Gucci or Louis Vuitton logos on your luggage communicate your financial status. Your Bulls or Pirates sweatshirt communicates your interest in sports and your favorite team.

Items of legible clothing are being bought and worn in record numbers. Many designers and manufacturers have their names integrated into the design of the clothing: DKNY, Calvin Klein, Armani, L. L. Bean, the Gap, and Old Navy are just a few examples. At the same time that you're paying extra to buy the brand name, you're also providing free advertising.

T-shirts and sweatshirts are especially popular as message senders. One study surveyed 600 male and female students as to the types of T-shirt messages they preferred (Sayre, 1992). Four kinds of messages were cited most often:

▶ Affiliation messages, such as a club or school name, communicate that you're a part of a larger group.

▶ Trophy names, such as those of a high-status concert or perhaps a ski lodge, say that you were in the right place at the right time.

▶ Metaphorical expressions, such as pictures of rock groups or famous athletes, reveal that you're a part of the current trend.

▶ Personal messages, such as statements of beliefs or philosophies, tell others that you're willing to express your beliefs publicly.

Follow-Up. *Affiliation messages may create problems when they identify the wearer as a member of a gang, because wearing gang colors can contribute to violence, especially in schools (Burke, 1993). And personal messages may create conflict when they insult one gender, group, or popular and cherished belief. For example, the* Wall Street Journal *reports that boy-bashing slogans ("Boys are great. Every girl should own one" or "I make boys cry" or "Boys make good pets") are becoming increasingly popular with teenage girls, although they don't have the same sexual harassment connotations that girl-bashing slogans seem to have (Zimmerman, 2000). How do you feel about these types of clothing messages? Do you feel that some clothing messages should be prohibited? If so, which ones? Or do you feel that such messages should be protected by the First Amendment guarantee of freedom of speech?*

candidates have a much better record of winning the election than do their shorter opponents. Tall people seem to be paid more and are favored by interviewers over shorter applicants (Keyes, 1980; Guerrero, DeVito, & Hecht, 1999; Knapp & Hall, 1997).

Your body also reveals your race (through skin color and tone) and may also give clues as to your more specific nationality. Your weight in proportion to your height will also communicate messages to others, as will the length, color, and style of your hair.

Your general **attractiveness** is also a part of body communication. Attractive people have the advantage in just about every activity you can name. They get better grades in school, are more valued as friends and lovers, and are preferred as coworkers (Burgoon, Buller, & Woodall, 1996). Although we

normally think that attractiveness is culturally determined—and to some degree it is—research seems to indicate that definitions of attractiveness are becoming universal (Brody, 1994). A person rated as attractive in one culture is likely to be rated as attractive in other cultures—even in cultures whose people are widely different in appearance.

Facial Communication

Throughout your interactions, your face communicates various messages, especially your emotions. Facial movements alone seem to communicate the degree of pleasantness, agreement, and sympathy felt; the rest of the body doesn't provide any additional information. But for other emotional messages—for example, the intensity with which an

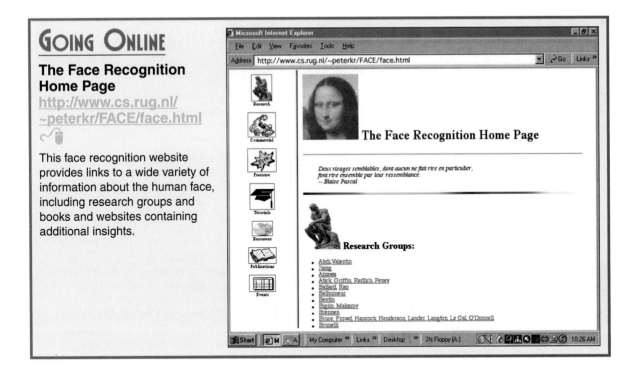

GOING ONLINE

The Face Recognition Home Page

http://www.cs.rug.nl/
~peterkr/FACE/face.html

This face recognition website provides links to a wide variety of information about the human face, including research groups and books and websites containing additional insights.

emotion is felt—both facial and bodily cues are used (Graham, Bitti, & Argyle, 1975; Graham & Argyle, 1975).

So important are these cues in communicating your full meaning that graphic representations are now commonly used in Internet communication. In graphic user interface chat groups, buttons are available to help you encode your emotions graphically. Table 8.1 identifies some of the more common "emoticons," icons that communicate emotions.

Some researchers in nonverbal communication claim that facial movements may express at least

TABLE 8.1   Some Popular Emoticons

Here are a few of the many popular emoticons used in computer communication. The first six are popular in the United States; the last three are popular in Japan and illustrate how culture influences such symbols. That is, because Japanese culture considers it impolite for women to show their teeth when smiling, the emoticon for a woman's smile shows a dot signifying a closed mouth. Two excellent websites that contain extensive examples of smileys, emoticons, acronyms, and shorthand abbreviations are wysiwyg://5http://www.netlingo.com/smiley.cfm and wysiwyg://3http://www.netlingo.com/emailsh.cfm.

Emoticon	Meaning	Emoticon	Meaning
:-)	Smile; I'm kidding	*This is important*	Substitutes for underlining or italics
:-(	Frown; I'm feeling down	<G>	Grin; I'm kidding
*	Kiss	<grin>	Grin; I'm kidding
{}	Hug	^.^	Woman's smile
{*****}	Hugs and kisses	^_^	Man's smile
This is important	Gives emphasis, calls special attention to	^ o ^	Happy

the following eight emotions: happiness, surprise, fear, anger, sadness, disgust, contempt, and interest (Ekman, Friesen, & Ellsworth, 1972). Facial expressions of these emotions are generally called primary affect displays: They indicate relatively pure, single emotions. Other emotional states and other facial displays are combinations of these various primary emotions and are called affect blends. You communicate these blended feelings with different parts of your face. Thus, for example, you may experience both fear and disgust at the same time. Your eyes and eyelids may signal fear, and movements of your nose, cheek, and mouth area may signal disgust. You may wish to explore facial expressions with the exercise "How Can You Make a Face?" at www.ablongman.com/devito.

Facial Management Techniques

As you grew up, you learned your culture's nonverbal system of communication. You also learned certain **facial management techniques;** for exam-

ple, to hide certain emotions and to emphasize others. Here are four facial management techniques that you will quickly recognize (Malandro, Barker, & Barker, 1989):

- *Intensifying* helps you to exaggerate a feeling; for example, to exaggerate your surprise when friends throw you a party, so as to make your friends feel better.
- *Deintensifying* helps you to underplay a feeling; for example, to cover up your own joy in the presence of a friend who didn't receive such good news.
- *Neutralizing* helps you to hide feelings; for example, to cover up your sadness so as not to depress others.
- *Masking* helps you to replace or substitute the expression of one emotion for the emotion you're really feeling; for example, to express happiness in order to cover up your disappointment about not receiving the gift you had expected.

UNDERSTANDING THEORY AND RESEARCH

Expressions and Attitudes

The **facial feedback hypothesis** holds that your facial expressions influence physiological arousal (Lanzetta, Cartwright-Smith, & Kleck, 1976; Zuckerman, Klorman, Larrance, & Spiegel, 1981). In one study, for example, participants held a pen in their teeth to simulate a sad expression and then rated a series of photographs. Results showed that mimicking sad expressions actually increased the degree of sadness the subjects reported feeling when viewing the photographs (Larsen, Kasimatis, & Frey, 1992). Further support for this hypothesis comes from a study that compared (1) participants who felt emotions such as happiness and anger with (2) participants who both felt and expressed these emotions. In support of the facial feedback hypothesis, subjects who felt and expressed the emotions became emotionally aroused faster than did those who only felt the emotions (Hess, Kappas, McHugo, & Lanzetta, 1992).

Generally, research finds that facial expressions can produce or heighten feelings of sadness, fear, disgust, and anger. But this effect does not occur with all emotions; smiling, for example, doesn't seem to make us feel happier (Burgoon, Buller, & Woodall, 1996). Further, it has not been demonstrated that facial expressions can eliminate one feeling and replace it with another: If you're feeling sad, smiling will not eliminate the sadness and replace it with gladness. A reasonable conclusion seems to be that your facial expressions can influence some feelings but not all (Burgoon, Buller, & Woodall, 1996; Cappella, 1993).

Working with Theories and Research. *Test out this theory yourself or with a few friends. Do your findings support the theory?*

These facial management techniques are learned along with display rules, which tell you what emotions to express when; they're the rules of appropriateness. For example, when someone gets bad news in which you may secretly take pleasure, the display rule dictates that you frown and otherwise nonverbally signal your displeasure. If you violate this kind of display rule, you'll be judged insensitive.

Encoding–Decoding Accuracy

One popular question concerns the accuracy with which people can encode and decode emotions through facial expressions. One problem confronting us as we try to answer this question is that it's difficult to separate the ability of the encoder from the ability of the decoder. Thus, a person may be quite adept at communicating emotions nonverbally, but the receiver may prove insensitive. On the other hand, the receiver may be good at deciphering emotions, but the sender may be inept. For example, introverts are not as accurate at decoding nonverbal cues as are extroverts (Akert & Panter, 1986).

Research in 11 different countries shows that women are better than men at both encoding and decoding nonverbal cues (Rosenthal & DePaulo, 1979). It may be argued that because men and women play different roles in society, they've learned different adaptive techniques and skills to help them perform these roles. Thus, in most societies women are expected to be more friendly, nurturing, and supportive and so learn these skills (Eagly & Crowley, 1986).

Accuracy also varies with the emotions themselves. Some emotions are easier to encode and decode than others. In one study, for example, people judged facial expressions of happiness with an accuracy ranging from 55 to 100 percent, surprise from 38 to 86 percent, and sadness from 19 to 88 percent (Ekman, Friesen, & Ellsworth, 1972).

Eye Communication

Research on the messages communicated by the eyes (a study known technically as oculesis) shows that these messages vary depending on the duration, direction, and quality of the eye behavior. For example, in every culture there are strict, though unstated, rules for the proper duration for eye contact. In U.S. culture the average length of gaze is 2.95 seconds. The average length of mutual gaze (two persons gazing at each other) is 1.18 seconds

(Argyle & Ingham, 1972; Argyle, 1988). When eye contact falls short of this amount, you may think the person is uninterested, shy, or preoccupied. When the appropriate amount of time is exceeded, you may perceive the person as showing unusually high interest. An exercise, "How Can You Make Eye Contact?" will allow you to explore further the nature of eye contact and may be found at www.ablongman.com/devito.

The direction of the eye also communicates. In much of the United States, you're expected to glance alternately at the other person's face, then away, then again at the face, and so on. The rule for the public speaker is to scan the entire audience, not focusing for too long on or ignoring any one area of the audience. When you break these directional rules, you communicate different meanings—abnormally high or low interest, self-consciousness, nervousness over the interaction, and so on. The quality of eye behavior—how wide or how narrow your eyes get during interaction—also communicates meaning, especially interest level and such emotions as surprise, fear, and disgust.

The Functions of Eye Contact and Eye Avoidance

Eye contact can serve a variety of functions. One such function is to seek feedback. In talking with someone, we look at her or him intently, as if to say, "Well, what do you think?" As you might predict, listeners gaze at speakers more than speakers gaze at listeners. In public speaking, you may scan hundreds of people to secure this feedback.

A second function is to inform the other person that the channel of communication is open and that he or she should now speak. You see this regularly in conversation, when one person asks a question or finishes a thought and then looks to you for a response. And one study found that eye contact was the most frequently noted nonverbal behavior used to tell library users that the librarian was approachable (Radford, 1998).

Eye movements may also signal the nature of a relationship, whether positive (an attentive glance) or negative (eye avoidance). You can also signal your power through **visual dominance** behavior (Exline, Ellyson, & Long, 1975). The average speaker, for example, maintains a high level of eye contact while listening and a lower level while speaking. When people want to signal dominance, they may reverse this pattern—maintaining a high level of eye contact while talking but a much lower level while listening.

By making eye contact you psychologically lessen the physical distance between yourself and another person. When you catch someone's eye at a party, for example, you become psychologically close though physically far apart.

Eye avoidance can also serve several different functions. When you avoid eye contact or avert your glance, you may help others maintain their privacy. For example, you may do this when you see a couple arguing in public. You turn your eyes away (though your eyes may be wide open) as if to say, "I don't mean to intrude; I respect your privacy," a behavior referred to as **civil inattention** (Goffman, 1971).

Eye avoidance can also signal lack of interest—in a person, a conversation, or some visual stimulus. At times, too, you may hide your eyes to block out unpleasant stimuli (a particularly gory or violent scene in a movie, for example) or close your eyes to block out visual stimuli and thus heighten other senses. For example, you may listen to music with your eyes closed. Lovers often close their eyes while kissing, and many prefer to make love in a dark or dimly lit room.

Pupil Dilation

In the fifteenth and sixteenth centuries, Italian women put drops of belladonna (which literally means "beautiful woman") into their eyes to enlarge the pupils so that they would look more attractive. Contemporary **pupillometrics** research supports the intuitive logic of these women; dilated pupils are judged more attractive than constricted ones (Hess, 1975; Marshall, 1983). In one study, researchers retouched photographs of women; in half they enlarged the pupils, and in the other half they made them smaller (Hess, 1975). Men were then asked to judge the women's personalities from the photographs. The photos of women with small pupils drew responses such as "cold," "hard," and "selfish"; those with dilated pupils drew responses such as "feminine" and "soft." Interestingly, the male observers could not verbalize the reasons for their different perceptions. Pupil dilation and our reactions to changes in the pupil size of others may function below the level of conscious awareness.

Pupil size also reveals your interest and level of emotional arousal. Your pupils enlarge when you're interested in something or when you are emotion-ally aroused. When homosexuals and heterosexuals were shown pictures of nude bodies, the homosexuals' pupils dilated more when they viewed same-sex bodies, whereas the heterosexuals' pupils dilated more when they viewed opposite-sex bodies (Hess, Seltzer, & Schlien, 1965). These pupillary responses are also observed in persons with profound mental retardation (Chaney, Givens, Aoki, & Gombiner, 1989). Perhaps we judge dilated pupils as more attractive because we respond to them as indicative of a person's interest in us. And that may be the reason why both models and fuzzy beanbag toys have exceptionally large pupils.

Space Communication

Your use of space to communicate—an area of study known technically as **proxemics**—speaks as surely and as loudly as words and sentences. Speakers who stand close to their listener, with their hands on the listener's shoulders and their eyes focused directly on those of the listener, communicate something very different from speakers who stand in a corner with arms folded and eyes downcast.

Spatial Distances

Edward Hall (1959, 1963, 1976) distinguishes four **proxemic distances**: types of **spatial distances** that define the types of relationships between people and the types of communication in which they're likely to engage (see Table 8.2). In **intimate distance**, ranging from actual touching to 18 inches, the presence of the other individual is unmistakable. Each person experiences the sound, smell, and feel of the other's breath. You use intimate distance for lovemaking, comforting, and protecting. This distance is so short that most people don't consider it proper in public.

Personal distance refers to the protective "bubble" that defines your personal space, ranging from 18 inches to 4 feet. This imaginary bubble keeps you protected and untouched by others. You can still hold or grasp another person at this distance, but only by extending your arms; this allows you to take certain individuals such as loved ones into your protective bubble. At the outer limit of personal distance, you can touch another person only if both of you extend your arms. This is the distance at which you conduct most of your interpersonal interactions; for example, talking with friends and family.

TABLE 8.2 Relationships and Proxemic Distances

Note that these four distances can be further divided into close and far phases and that the far phase of one level (say, personal) blends into the close phase of the next level (social). Do your relationships also blend into one another? Or are, say, your personal relationships totally separate from your social relationships?

Relationship		Distance	
Intimate relationship		Intimate distance	
		0 ——————— 18 inches	
		close phase	far phase
Personal relationship		Personal distance	
		1½ ——————— 4 feet	
		close phase	far phase
Social relationship		Social distance	
		4 ——————— 12 feet	
		close phase	far phase
Public relationship		Public distance	
		12 ——————— 25+ feet	
		close phase	far phase

At **social distance,** ranging from 4 to 12 feet, you lose the visual detail you have at personal distance. You conduct impersonal business and interact at a social gathering at this social distance. The more distance you maintain in your interactions, the more formal they appear. In offices of high officials, the desks are positioned so the official is assured of at least this distance from clients.

Public distance, from 12 to more than 25 feet, protects you. At this distance you could take defensive action if threatened. On a public bus or train, for example, you might keep at least this distance from a drunken passenger. Although at this distance you lose fine details of the face and eyes, you're still close enough to see what is happening.

Influences on Space Communication

Several factors influence the way you relate to and use space in communicating. Here are a few examples of how status, culture, subject matter, gender, and age influence space communication (Burgoon, Buller, & Woodall, 1996).

People of equal *status* maintain shorter distances between themselves than do people of unequal status. When status is unequal, the higher-status person may approach the lower-status person more closely than the lower-status person would approach the higher-status person.

Members of different *cultures* treat space differently. For example, people from northern European cultures and many Americans stand fairly far apart when conversing; those from southern European and Middle Eastern cultures stand much closer. It's easy to see how people who normally stand far apart may interpret the close distances of others as pushy and overly intimate. It's equally easy to appreciate how those who normally stand close may interpret the far distances of others as cold and unfriendly.

When discussing personal *subjects* you maintain shorter distances than with impersonal subjects.

BUILDING COMMUNICATION SKILLS

How Can You Choose a Seat?

With your recently acquired sensitivity to nonverbal cues, where would you sit in each of the following situations to best achieve the purposes identified? What would be your first choice? Your second choice?

▶ You want to polish the apple and ingratiate yourself with your boss.

▶ You aren't prepared and want to be ignored.

▶ You want to challenge your boss on a certain policy that will come up for a vote.

▶ You want to be accepted as a new (but important) member of the company.

▶ You want to get to know the person already seated at position number 5.

After making your choices, consider why you made them. Do you normally make choices based on such factors as these? What interpersonal factors—for example, the desire to talk to or get a closer look at someone—influence your day-to-day seating behavior?

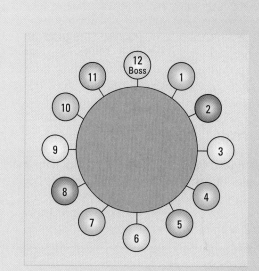

Also, you stand closer to someone who is praising you than to someone criticizing you.

Your *gender* also influences your spatial relationships. Women generally stand closer to each other than men do. Similarly, when someone approaches another person, he or she will come closer to a woman than to a man. With increasing *age* there's a tendency for the spaces to become larger. Children stand much closer to each other than do adults. These research findings provide some evidence that maintaining distance is a learned behavior.

The evaluation you make of a person (whether positive or negative) will also influence your space. For example, you stand farther from enemies, authority figures, and higher-status individuals than from friends and peers. You maintain a greater distance from people you see as different from yourself; for example, different in race or in physical condition. Typically, you maintain more distance between yourself and people you may unconsciously evaluate negatively.

Territoriality

One of the most interesting concepts in ethology (the study of animals in their natural surroundings) is **territoriality,** a possessive or ownership reaction to an area of space or to particular objects. Two interesting dimensions of territoriality are territorial types and territorial markers.

Territory Types

Three types of territory are often distinguished: primary, secondary, and public (Altman, 1975). **Primary territories** are your exclusive preserve: your desk, room, house, or backyard, for example. In these areas you're in control. The effect is similar to

UNDERSTANDING THEORY AND RESEARCH

Space Violations

Expectancy violations theory explains what happens when you increase or decrease the distance between yourself and another person in an interpersonal interaction (Burgoon, 1978; Burgoon, Buller, & Woodall, 1996). Each culture has certain expectancies about the distance that people should normally maintain in their conversations. And, of course, each person has certain idiosyncrasies. Together these determine "expected distance." If you violate the expected distance to a great extent (small violations most often go unnoticed), then the relationship itself comes into focus. Then the other person begins to turn attention away from the topic of conversation and toward you and your relationship with him or her.

If this other person perceives you positively—for example, if you're a high-status person or you're particularly attractive—then you'll be perceived even more positively if you violate the expected distance. If, on the other hand, you're perceived negatively and you violate the norm, you'll be perceived even more negatively.

Working with Theories and Research. *Do your own experiences support this theory of space violations? What do you see happen when space expectations are violated?*

the **home field advantage** that a sports team has when playing in its own ballpark. When you're in these **home territories,** you generally have greater influence over others than you would in someone else's territory. For example, in their own home or office people generally take on a kind of leadership role; they initiate conversations, fill in silences, assume relaxed and comfortable postures, and maintain their positions with greater conviction. Because the territorial owner is dominant, you stand a better chance of getting your raise approved, your point accepted, or a contract resolved in your favor if you're in your own primary territory (home, office) rather than in someone else's (Marsh, 1988).

Secondary territories, although they don't belong to you, are associated with you—perhaps because you've occupied them for a long time or they were assigned to you. For example, your desk in a classroom may become a secondary territory if it is assigned to you or if you regularly occupy it and others treat it as yours. Your neighborhood turf, a cafeteria table where you usually sit, or a favorite corner of a local coffee shop may be secondary territories. You feel a certain "ownership-like" attachment to the place, even though it's really not yours in any legal sense.

Public territories are areas that are open to all people, such as a park, movie house, restaurant, or beach. European cafés, food courts in suburban malls, and the open areas in large city office buildings are public spaces that bring people together and stimulate communication.

The electronic revolution, however, may well change the role of public space in stimulating communication (Drucker & Gumpert, 1991; Gumpert & Drucker, 1995). For example, home shopping clubs make it less necessary for people to go downtown or to the mall, and shoppers consequently have less opportunity to run into other people and to talk and exchange news. Similarly, electronic mail permits us to communicate without talking and without even leaving the house to mail a letter. Perhaps the greatest change is telecommuting (Giordano, 1989), in which workers can go to work without even leaving their homes. The face-to-face communication that normally takes place in an office is replaced by communication via computer.

Territoriality is closely linked to **status.** Generally, the size and location of your territories signal your status within your social group. For example, male animals will stake out a particular territory and consider it their own. They will allow prospective mates to enter but will defend the territory against entrance by others, especially by other males of the same species. The larger the animal's territory, the higher the animal is in status within the herd. The size and location of human territories also say something about status (Mehrabian, 1976; Sommer, 1969). An apartment or office in midtown Manhattan or downtown Tokyo, for example, is extremely high-status territory. The cost of the territory restricts it to those who have lots of money.

Territorial Markers

Much as animals mark their territory, humans mark theirs with three types of **markers:** central markers, boundary markers, and earmarkers (Hickson & Stacks, 1993). **Central markers** are items you place in a territory to reserve it. For example, you place a drink at the bar, books on your desk, or a sweater over the chair to let others know that these territories belong to you.

Boundary markers set boundaries that divide your territory from "theirs." In the supermarket checkout line, the bar placed between your groceries and those of the person behind you is a boundary marker. Similarly, the armrests separating your seat from those of the people on either side at a movie theater and the molded plastic seats on a bus or train are boundary markers.

Earmarkers—a term taken from the practice of branding animals on their ears—are those identifying marks that indicate your possession of a territory or object. Trademarks, nameplates, and initials on a shirt or attaché case are all examples of earmarkers.

Artifactual Communication

Artifactual communication is communication via objects made by human hands. Thus, color, clothing, jewelry, and the decoration of space would be considered artifactual. Let's look at each of these briefly. Another aspect of artifactual communication—gift giving and the meanings that different gifts can communicate in different cultures—is explored in the exercise "How Can You Give Gifts in Different Cultures?" available at www.ablongman.com/devito.

Color Communication

There is some evidence that colors affect us physiologically. For example, respiratory movements increase with red light and decrease with blue light. Similarly, eye blinks increase in frequency when eyes are exposed to red light and decrease when exposed to blue. These responses seem consistent with our intuitive feelings about blue being more soothing and red more arousing. When a school changed the color of its walls from orange and white to blue, the blood pressure of the students decreased and their academic performance increased (Ketcham, 1958; Malandro, Barker, & Barker, 1989).

Color communication also influences perceptions and behaviors (Kanner, 1989). People's acceptance of a product, for example, is largely determined by its packaging, especially its color. In one study the very same coffee taken from a yellow can was described as weak, from a dark brown can as too strong, from a red can as rich, and from a blue can as mild. Even your acceptance of a person may depend on the colors he or she wears. Consider, for example, the comments of one color expert (Kanner, 1989): "If you have to pick the wardrobe for your defense lawyer heading into court and choose anything but blue, you deserve to lose the case." Black is so powerful it could work against the lawyer with the jury. Brown lacks sufficient authority. Green would probably elicit a negative response. If you wish to pursue this role of color in communication, take a look at "How Can You Express Meanings with Color?" at www.ablongman.com/devito.

Clothing and Body Adornment

People make inferences about who you are, at least in part, from the way you dress. Whether these inferences are accurate or not, they will influence what people think of you and how they react to you. Your socioeconomic class, your seriousness, your attitudes (for example, whether you're conservative or liberal), your concern for convention, your sense of style, and perhaps even your creativity will all be judged in part by the way you dress (Molloy, 1975, 1977, 1981; Burgoon, Buller, & Woodall, 1996; Knapp & Hall, 1997). Similarly, college students will perceive an instructor dressed informally as friendly, fair, enthusiastic, and flexible; they will see the same instructor dressed formally as prepared, knowledgeable, and organized (Malandro, Barker, & Barker, 1989).

The way you wear your hair says something about your attitudes—from a concern about being up to date to a desire to shock to perhaps a lack of interest in appearances. Men with long hair will generally be judged as less conservative than those with shorter hair. Your jewelry also communicates about you. Wedding and engagement rings are obvious examples that communicate specific messages. College rings and political buttons likewise communicate specific messages. If you wear a Rolex watch or large precious stones, others are likely to infer that you're rich. Men who wear earrings will be judged differently from men who don't. What judgments are made will depend on who the receiver is, the communication context, and all the factors identified throughout this text.

Space Decoration

The way you decorate your private spaces also communicates about you. The office with a mahogany desk and bookcases and oriental rugs communicates your importance and status within an organization, just as a metal desk and bare floor indicate a worker much farther down in the hierarchy.

Similarly, people will make inferences about you based on the way you decorate your home. The expensiveness of the furnishings may communicate your status and wealth; their coordination may convey your sense of style. The magazines may reflect your interests, and the arrangement of chairs around a television set may reveal how important watching television is to you. The contents of bookcases lining the walls reveal the importance of reading in your life. In fact, there's probably little in your home that would not send messages from which others would draw inferences about you. Computers, wide-screen televisions, well-equipped kitchens, and oil paintings of great grandparents, for example, all say something about the people who live in the home.

Similarly, the absence of certain items will communicate something about you. Consider what messages you'd get from a home where no television, phone, or books could be seen.

Touch Communication

The study of **touch communication,** technically referred to as **haptics,** suggests that touch is perhaps the most primitive form of communication (Montagu, 1971). Developmentally, touch is probably the first sense to be used. Even in the womb the child is stimulated by touch. Soon after birth the child is fondled, caressed, patted, and stroked. In turn, the child explores its world through touch. In

a short time the child learns to communicate a wide variety of meanings through touch.

The Meanings of Touch

Touch communicates a wide variety of messages (Jones & Yarbrough, 1985). Here are five major ones that will illustrate this great variety.

● Touch communicates positive feelings; for example, support, appreciation, inclusion, sexual interest or intent, composure, immediacy, affection, trust, similarity and quality, and informality (Jones & Yarbrough, 1985; Burgoon, 1991). Touch also stimulates self-disclosure (Rabinowitz, 1991).

● Touch often communicates your intention to play, either affectionately or aggressively.

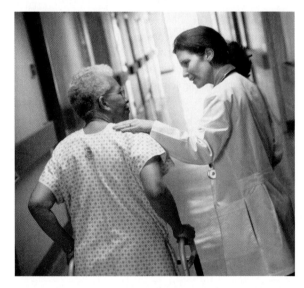

Consider, as Nancy Henley suggests in her *Body Politics* (1977), who would touch whom (say, by putting an arm on the other person's shoulder or by putting a hand on the other person's back) in the following dyads: teacher and student, doctor and patient, manager and worker, minister and parishioner, business executive and secretary. Do your answers reveal that the higher-status person initiates touch with the lower-status person? Henley further argues that in addition to indicating relative status, touching demonstrates the assertion of superior male status, power, and dominance over women. When women touch men, Henley says, the interpretation that it designates a female-dominant relationship is not acceptable (to men) and so the touching is interpreted as a sexual invitation. What do you think of this argument?

- Touch may control the behaviors, attitudes, or feelings of the other person. To obtain compliance, for example, you touch the other person to communicate "move over," "hurry," "stay here," or "do it." You might also touch a person to gain his or her attention, as if to say "look at me" or "look over here." In some situations touching can even amount to a kind of **nonverbal dominance behavior**.

- Ritualistic touching centers on greetings and departures; examples are shaking hands to say "hello" or "good-bye," hugging, kissing, or putting your arm around another's shoulder when greeting or saying farewell.

- Task-related touching is associated with the performance of some function, as when you remove a speck of dust from another person's coat, help someone out of a car, or check someone's forehead for fever.

Touch Avoidance

Much as you have a need and desire to touch and be touched, you also have a tendency to avoid touch from certain people or in certain circumstances (Andersen & Leibowitz, 1978). You may wish to examine your own **touch avoidance** tendency by taking the self-test below.

TEST YOURSELF

Do You Avoid Touch?

This test is composed of 18 statements concerning how you feel about touching other people and being touched. Please indicate the degree to which each statement applies to you according to the following scale: 1 = strongly agree; 2 = agree; 3 = undecided; 4 = disagree; and 5 = strongly disagree.

_____ 1. A hug from a same-sex friend is a true sign of friendship.

_____ 2. Opposite-sex friends enjoy it when I touch them.

_____ 3. I often put my arm around friends of the same sex.

_____ 4. When I see two friends of the same sex hugging, it revolts me.

_____ 5. I like it when members of the opposite sex touch me.

_____ 6. People shouldn't be so uptight about touching persons of the same sex.

_____ 7. I think it is vulgar when members of the opposite sex touch me.

_____ 8. When a member of the opposite sex touches me, I find it unpleasant.

_____ 9. I wish I were free to show emotions by touching members of same sex.

_____ 10. I'd enjoy giving a massage to an opposite-sex friend.

_____ 11. I enjoy kissing a person of the same sex.

_____ 12. I like to touch friends that are the same sex as I am.

_____ 13. Touching a friend of the same sex does not make me uncomfortable.

_____ 14. I find it enjoyable when my date and I embrace.

_____ 15. I enjoy getting a back rub from a member of the opposite sex.

_____ 16. I dislike kissing relatives of the same sex.

_____ 17. Intimate touching with members of the opposite sex is pleasurable.

_____ 18. I find it difficult to be touched by a member of my own sex.

How did you do? To score your touch avoidance questionnaire:

1. Reverse your scores for items 4, 7, 8, 16, and 18. Use these reversed scores in all future calculations.

2. To obtain your same-sex touch avoidance score (the extent to which you avoid touching members of your sex), total the scores for items 1, 3, 4, 6, 9, 11, 12, 13, 16, and 18.

3. To obtain your opposite-sex touch avoidance score (the extent to which you avoid touching members of the opposite sex), total the scores for items 2, 5, 7, 8, 10, 14, 15, and 17.

4. To obtain your total touch avoidance score, add the subtotals from steps 2 and 3.

The higher the score, the higher the touch avoidance—that is, the greater your tendency to avoid touch. In studies by Andersen and Leibowitz (1978), who constructed this test, average opposite-sex touch avoidance scores were 12.9 for males and 14.85 for females. Average same-sex touch avoidance scores were 26.43 for males and 21.70 for females. How do your scores compare with those of the college students in Andersen and Leibowitz's study? Is your touch avoidance likely to be higher when you are interacting with persons who are culturally different from you? Can you identify types of people and types of situations in which your touch avoidance would be especially high? Especially low?

What will you do? Are you satisfied with your score? Would you like to change your touch avoidance tendencies? What might you do about them?

Source: From "Development and Nature of the Construct Touch Avoidance" by Peter Andersen and Ken Leibowitz in *Environmental Psychology and Nonverbal Behavior*, Vol. 3, 1978, pp. 89–106. Copyright © 1978 Plenum Publishing Corporation. Reprinted by Plenum Publishing Corporation as publisher. ✔

Based on the self-test presented here, several interesting connections between touch avoidance and other factors have been found (Andersen & Liebowitz, 1978). For example, touch avoidance is positively related to communication apprehension. If you have a strong fear of oral communication, then you probably also have strong touch avoidance tendencies. Touch avoidance is also high in those who self-disclose less.

Both touch and self-disclosure are intimate forms of communication. People who are reluctant to get close to another person by self-disclosing also seem reluctant to get close by touching.

Older people avoid touch with opposite-sex persons more than do younger people. As people get older they're touched less by members of the opposite sex; this decreased frequency of touching may lead them to avoid touching.

Paralanguage: The Vocal Channel

Paralanguage is the vocal but nonverbal dimension of speech. It has to do not with what you say but with how you say it. A traditional exercise students use to increase their ability to express different emotions, feelings, and attitudes is to repeat a sentence while accenting or stressing different words. One popular sentence is, "Is this the face that launched a thousand ships?" Significant differences in meaning are easily communicated depending on where the speaker places the stress. Consider the following variations:

- Is *this* the face that launched a thousand ships?
- Is this the *face* that launched a thousand ships?
- Is this the face that *launched* a thousand ships?
- Is this the face that launched *a thousand ships*?

Each sentence communicates something different; in fact, each asks a different question, even though the words are exactly the same. All that distinguishes the sentences is stress, one aspect of paralanguage. In addition to stress and **pitch** (highness or lowness), paralanguage includes such **voice qualities** as **rate** (speed), **volume** (loudness), and rhythm as well as the vocalizations you make in crying, whispering, moaning, belching, yawning, and yelling (Trager, 1958, 1961; Argyle, 1988). A variation in any of these features communicates. When you speak quickly, for example, you communicate something different from when you speak slowly. Even though the words may be the same, if the speed (or volume, rhythm, or pitch) differs, the meanings people receive will also differ.

Judgments about People

Paralanguage cues are often used as a basis for judgments about people; for example, evaluations of their emotional state or even their personality. A listener can accurately judge the emotional state of a speaker from vocal expression alone, if both speaker and listener speak the same language. Paralanguage cues are not so accurate when used to communicate emotions to those who speak a different language (Albas, McCluskey, & Albas, 1976). Also, some emotions are easier to identify than others; it's easy to distinguish between hate and sympathy but more difficult to distinguish between fear and anxiety. And, of course, listeners vary in their ability to decode, and speakers in their ability to encode emotions (Scherer, 1986).

Judgments about Communication Effectiveness

In one-way communication (when one person is doing all or most of the speaking and the other person is doing all or most of the listening), those who talk fast (about 50 percent faster than normal) are more persuasive (MacLachlan, 1979). People agree more with a fast speaker than with a slow speaker and find the fast speaker more intelligent and objective.

When we look at comprehension, rapid speech shows an interesting effect. When the speaking rate is increased by 50 percent, the comprehension level

BUILDING COMMUNICATION SKILLS

How Can You Praise and Criticize?

Consider how paralanguage variations can communicate praise and criticism by reading each of the following 10 statements aloud—first to communicate praise in each case and second, criticism. Then consider what paralanguage cues you used to convey the praise and criticism. Did you read the statements with different facial expressions, eye movements, and body postures depending on your desire to communicate praise or criticism?

▶ Now that looks good on you.

▶ You lost weight.

▶ You look younger than that.

▶ You're gonna make it.

▶ That was some meal.

▶ You really know yourself.

▶ You're an expert.

▶ You're so sensitive. I'm amazed.

▶ Your parents are really something.

▶ Are you ready? Already?

---

drops by only 5 percent. When the rate is doubled, the comprehension level drops only 10 percent. These 5 and 10 percent losses are more than offset by the increased speed; thus the faster rates are much more efficient in communicating information. If speeds are more than twice the rate of normal speech, however, comprehension begins to fall dramatically.

Do exercise caution in applying this research to all forms of communication (MacLachlan, 1979). For example, if you increase your rate to increase efficiency, you may create an impression so unnatural that others will focus on your speed instead of your meaning.

Silence

Like words and gestures, **silence,** too, communicates important meanings and serves important functions (Johannesen, 1974; Jaworski, 1993). Silence allows the speaker *time to think*, time to formulate and organize his or her verbal communications. Before messages of intense conflict, as well as before those confessing undying love, there's often silence. Again, silence seems to prepare the receiver for the importance of these future messages.

Some people use silence as a *weapon* to hurt others. We often speak of giving someone "the silent treatment." After a conflict, for example, one or

both individuals may remain silent as a kind of punishment. Silence used to hurt others may also take the form of refusing to acknowledge the presence of another person, as in disconfirmation (see Unit 7); here silence is a dramatic demonstration of the total indifference one person feels toward the other.

Sometimes silence is used as a *response to personal anxiety*, shyness, or threats. You may feel anxious or shy among new people and prefer to remain silent. By remaining silent you preclude the chance of rejection. Only when you break your silence and make an attempt to communicate with another person do you risk rejection.

Silence may be used *to prevent communication* of certain messages. In conflict situations silence is sometimes used to prevent certain topics from surfacing and to prevent one or both parties from saying things they may later regret. In such situations silence often allows us time to cool off before expressing hatred, severe criticism, or personal attacks—which, as we know, are irreversible.

Like the eyes, face, and hands, silence can also be used to *communicate emotional responses* (Ehrenhaus, 1988). Sometimes silence communicates a determination to be uncooperative or defiant; by refusing to engage in verbal communication, you defy the authority or the legitimacy of the other person's position. Silence is often used to communicate annoyance, particularly when accompanied by a pouting expression, arms crossed in front of the chest, and nostrils flared. Silence may express affection or love, especially when coupled with long and longing stares into each other's eyes.

Of course, you may also use silence when you simply have *nothing to say*, when nothing occurs to you, or when you don't want to say anything. James Russell Lowell expressed this best: "Blessed are they who have nothing to say, and who cannot be persuaded to say it." Silence may also be used to avoid responsibility for any wrongdoing (Beach, 1990–91).

Time Communication

The study of **temporal communication,** known technically as **chronemics,** concerns the use of time—how you organize it, react to it, and communicate messages through it (Bruneau, 1985, 1990). Consider, for example, your **psychological time** orientation; the emphasis you place on the past, present, and future. In a past orientation, you have special reverence for the past. You relive old times and regard old methods as the best. You see events as circular and recurring, so the wisdom of yesterday is applicable also to today and tomorrow. In a present orientation, however, you live in the present: for now, not tomorrow. In a future orientation, you look toward and live for the future. You save today, work hard in college, and deny yourself luxuries because you're preparing for the future. Before reading more about time, take the self-test below.

TEST YOURSELF

What Time Do You Have?

For each statement, indicate whether the statement is true (T) or false (F) in relation to your general attitude and behavior. (A few statements are purposely repeated to facilitate scoring and analysis of your responses.)

_____ **1.** Meeting tomorrow's deadlines and doing other necessary work comes before tonight's partying.

_____ **2.** I meet my obligations to friends and authorities on time.

_____ **3.** I complete projects on time by making steady progress.

_____ **4.** I am able to resist temptations when I know there is work to be done.

_____ **5.** I keep working at a difficult, uninteresting task if it will help me get ahead.

_____ **6.** If things don't get done on time, I don't worry about it.

_____ **7.** I think that it's useless to plan too far ahead, because things hardly ever come out the way you planned anyway.

_____ **8.** I try to live one day at a time.

_____ **9.** I live to make better what is rather than to be concerned about what will be.

_____ **10.** It seems to me that it doesn't make sense to worry about the future, since fate determines that whatever will be, will be.

_____ **11.** I believe that getting together with friends to party is one of life's important pleasures.

_____ **12.** I do things impulsively, making decisions on the spur of the moment.

_____ **13.** I take risks to put excitement in my life.

_____ **14.** I get drunk at parties.

_____ **15.** It's fun to gamble.

_____ **16.** Thinking about the future is pleasant to me.

_____ **17.** When I want to achieve something, I set subgoals and consider specific means for reaching those goals.

_____ **18.** It seems to me that my career path is pretty well laid out.

_____ **19.** It upsets me to be late for appointments.

_____ **20.** I meet my obligations to friends and authorities on time.

_____ **21.** I get irritated at people who keep me waiting when we've agreed to meet at a given time.

_____ **22.** It makes sense to invest a substantial part of my income in insurance premiums.

_____ **23.** I believe that "A stitch in time saves nine."

_____ **24.** I believe that "A bird in the hand is worth two in the bush."

_____ **25.** I believe it is important to save for a rainy day.

_____ **26.** I believe a person's day should be planned each morning.

_____ **27.** I make lists of things I must do.

_____ **28.** When I want to achieve something, I set sub-goals and consider specific means for reaching those goals.

_____ **29.** I believe that "A stitch in time saves nine."

How did you do? This time test measures seven different factors. If you selected true (T) for all or most of the statements within any given factor, you are probably high on that factor. If you selected false (F) for all or most of the statements within any given factor, you are probably low on that factor.

The first factor, measured by items 1–5, is a future, work motivation, perseverance orientation. These people have a strong work ethic and are committed to completing a task despite difficulties and temptations. The second factor (items 6–10) is a present, fatalistic, worry-free orientation. High scorers on this factor live one day at a time, not necessarily to enjoy the day but to avoid planning for the next day or anxiety about the future.

The third factor (items 11–15) is a present, pleasure-seeking, partying orientation. These people enjoy the present, take risks, and engage in a variety of impulsive actions. The fourth factor (items 16–18) is a future, goal-seeking, planning orientation. These people derive special pleasure from planning and achieving a variety of goals.

The fifth factor (items 19–21) is a time-sensitivity orientation. People who score high are especially sensitive to time and its role in social obligations. The sixth factor (items 22–25) is a future, practical action orientation. These people do what they have to do—take practical actions—to achieve the future they want.

The seventh factor (items 26–29) is a future, somewhat obsessive daily planning orientation. High scorers on this factor make daily "to do" lists and devote great attention to specific details.

What will you do? Now that you have some idea of how you treat time, consider how these attitudes and behaviors work for you. For example, will your time orientations help you achieve your social and professional goals? If not, what might you do about changing these attitudes and behaviors?

Source: From "Time in Perspective" by Alexander Gonzalez and Philip G. Zimbardo in *Psychology Today*, V. 19, pp. 20–26. Reprinted with permission from *Psychology Today* magazine. Copyright © 1985 Sussex Publishers, Inc. ✔

The time orientation you develop depends to a great extent on your socioeconomic class and your personal experiences. Gonzalez and Zimbardo (1985), who developed the time quiz and on whose research the scoring is based, observe: "A child with parents in unskilled and semiskilled occupations is usually socialized in a way that promotes a present-oriented fatalism and hedonism.

UNDERSTANDING THEORY AND RESEARCH

The Social Clock

Your culture or, more specifically, your society maintains a schedule of the right times for doing a variety of important things; for example, the right times to start dating, to finish college, to buy your own home, or to have a child. This unwritten schedule provides you with a "social clock"—a clock that will tell you if you're keeping pace with your peers, are ahead of them, or are falling behind (Neugarten, 1979). And although the social clock is becoming more flexible and more tolerant of deviations from the standard timetable, it still exerts pressure on you to keep pace with your peers (Peterson, 1996). On the basis of this social clock, which you learned as you grew up, you evaluate your own social and professional development. If you're in step with the rest of your peers—for example, you started dating at the "appropriate" age or you're finishing college at the "appropriate" age—then you'll feel well adjusted, competent, and a part of the group. If you're late, you'll probably experience feelings of dissatisfaction.

Working with Theories and Research. *How important is the social clock to you? Have you ever felt out of step with your peers in some area? Did your feeling influence your behavior in any way?*

A child of parents who are managers, teachers, or other professionals learns future-oriented values and strategies designed to promote achievement." Not surprisingly, in the United States income is positively related to future orientation; the more future oriented you are, the greater your income is likely to be.

Different **cultural time** perspectives also account for much intercultural misunderstanding, as different cultures often teach their members drastically different time orientations. For example, members of some Latin cultures would rather be late for an appointment than end a conversation abruptly or before it has come to a natural end. So the Latin may see lateness as a result of politeness. But others may see this as impolite to the person with whom he or she had the appointment (Hall & Hall, 1987).

Smell Communication

Smell communication, or **olfactory communication,** is extremely important in a wide variety of situations and is now big business (Kleinfeld, 1992). For example, there's some evidence (though clearly not very conclusive evidence) that the smell of lemon contributes to a perception of heath, the smells of lavender and eucalyptus increase alertness, and the smell of rose oil reduces blood pressure. Findings such as these have contributed to the growth of aromatherapy and to a new profession of aromatherapists (Furlow, 1996). Because humans possess "denser skin concentrations of scent glands than almost any other mammal," it has been argued that it only remains for us to discover how we use scent to communicate a wide variety of messages (Furlow, 1996, p. 41). Here are some of the most important messages scent seems to communicate.

- *Attraction messages.* Humans use perfumes, colognes, after-shave lotions, powders, and the like to enhance their attractiveness to others and to themselves. After all, you also smell yourself. When the smells are pleasant, you feel better about yourself.

- *Taste messages.* Without smell, taste would be severely impaired. For example, without smell it would be extremely difficult to taste the difference between a raw potato and an apple. Street vendors selling hot dogs, sausages, and similar foods are aided greatly by the smells, which stimulate the appetites of passersby.

- *Memory messages.* Smell is a powerful memory aid; you often recall situations from months and even years ago when you encounter a similar smell.

- *Identification messages.* Smell is often used to create an image or an identity for a product. Advertisers and manufacturers spend millions of dollars each year creating scents for cleaning products and toothpastes, for example, which have nothing to do with their cleaning power. There's also evidence that we can identify specific significant others by smell. For example, young children were able to identify the T-shirts of their brothers and sisters solely on the basis of smell (Porter & Moore, 1981).

CULTURE AND NONVERBAL COMMUNICATION

Not surprisingly, nonverbal communication is heavily influenced by culture. Consider a variety of differences. At the sight of unpleasant pictures, members of some cultures (American and European, for example) will facially express disgust. Members of other cultures (Japanese, for example) will avoid facially expressing disgust (Ekman, 1985; Matsumoto, 1991).

Although Americans consider direct eye contact an expression of honesty and forthrightness, the Japanese often view this as showing a lack of respect. The Japanese will glance at the other person's face rarely and then only for very short periods (Axtell, 1993). Among some Latin Americans and Native Americans, direct eye contact between, say, a student and a teacher is considered inappropriate, perhaps aggressive; appropriate student behavior is to avoid eye contact with the teacher. Folding your arms over your chest is considered disrespectful in Fiji; pointing with the index finger is considered impolite in many Middle Eastern countries; and waving your hand can be considered insulting in Greece and Nigeria (Axtell, 1993).

In the United States living next door to someone means that you're expected to be friendly and to interact with that person. This cultural expectation seems so natural that Americans and members of many other cultures probably don't even consider that it is not shared by all cultures. In Japan, the fact that your house is next to another's does not imply that you should become close or visit each other. Consider, therefore, the situation in which a Japanese person buys a house next to an American. The Japanese may see the American as overly familiar and as taking friendship for granted. The American may see the Japanese as distant, unfriendly, and unneighborly. Yet each person is merely fulfilling the expectations of his or her own culture (Hall & Hall, 1987).

Different cultures also assign different meanings to colors. Some of these cultural differences are illustrated in Table 8.3—but before looking at the table, think about the meanings your own culture gives to such colors as red, green, black, white, blue, yellow, and purple.

Touching varies greatly from one culture to another. For example, African Americans touch one another more than do whites. Similarly, touching declines from kindergarten to the sixth grade for white but not for African American children (Burgoon, Buller, & Woodall, 1996). Japanese people touch one another much less than do Anglo-Saxons, who in turn touch one another much less than do southern Europeans (Morris, 1977; Burgoon, Buller, & Woodall, 1996). In one study students in the United States reported being touched twice as much as did students from Japan (Barnlund, 1989). In Japan there's a strong taboo against touching between strangers. The Japanese are therefore especially careful to maintain sufficient distance.

Another obvious cross-cultural contrast is presented by the Middle East, where same-sex touching

---

TABLE 8.3   Some Cultural Meanings of Color

This table, constructed from the research reported by Henry Dreyfuss (1971), Nancy Hoft (1995), and Norine Dresser (1996), illustrates only some of the different meanings that colors may communicate, especially in different cultures. Before looking at the table, jot down on a separate piece of paper the meanings given by your own culture(s) to colors such as red, green, black, white, blue, yellow, and purple.

Color	Cultural Meanings and Comments
Red	In China, red signifies prosperity and rebirth and is used for festive and joyous occasions; in France and the United Kingdon, masculinity; in many African countries, blasphemy or death; in Japan, anger and danger. Red ink, especially among Korean Buddhists, is used only to write a person's name at the time of death or on the anniversary of the person's death, and creates lots of problems when American teachers use red ink to mark homework.
Green	In the United States, green signifies capitalism, go-ahead, and envy; in Ireland, patriotism; among some Native Americans, femininity; to the Egyptians, fertility and strength; and to the Japanese, youth and energy.
Black	In Thailand, black signifies old age; in parts of Malaysia, courage; and in much of Europe, death.
White	In Thailand, white signifies purity; in many Muslim and Hindu cultures, purity and peace; and in Japan and other Asian countries, death and mourning.
Blue	In Iran, blue signifies something negative; in Egypt, virtue and truth; in Ghana, joy; and among the Cherokee, defeat.
Yellow	In China, yellow signifies wealth and authority; in the United States, caution and cowardice; in Egypt, happiness and prosperity; and in many countries throughout the world, femininity.
Purple	In Latin America, purple signifies death; in Europe, royalty; in Egypt, virtue and faith; in Japan, grace and nobility; and in China, barbarism.

in public is extremely common. Middle Easterners, Latin Americans, and southern Europeans touch one another while talking a great deal more than do people from "noncontact cultures" such as those of Asia and northern Europe. Even such seemingly minor nonverbal differences as these can create difficulties when members of different cultures interact. Southern Europeans may perceive northern Europeans or Japanese, for example, as cold, distant, and uninvolved. Southern Europeans in turn may be perceived as pushy, aggressive, and inappropriately intimate.

In the study of touch avoidance discussed earlier, women said that they avoid touching members of the opposite sex more than do men. This male–female difference, however, seems to conflict with a study by Jones (1986), who reported that women initiated more opposite-sex touching than did men (especially more opposite-sex touching designed to control). Yet women also report feeling less positive about opposite-sex touching than do men (Guerrero & Andersen, 1994).

Opposite-sex friends touch more than do same-sex friends. Both male and female college students report that they touch and are touched more by their opposite-sex friends than by their same-sex friends. The strong societal bias against same-sex touching may have influenced these self-reports; people may have reported as they did in order to conform to what they saw as culturally accepted and expected.

Not surprisingly, the role of silence is seen differently in different cultures (Basso, 1972). Among the Apache, for example, mutual friends don't feel the need to introduce strangers who may be working in the same area or on the same project. The strangers may remain silent for several days. During this time they're looking each other over, trying to determine if the other person is all right. Only after this period do the individuals talk. When courting, especially during the initial stages, the Apache remain silent for hours; if they do talk, they generally talk very little. Only after a couple has been dating for several

months will they have lengthy conversations. These periods of silence are generally attributed to shyness or self-consciousness; but the use of silence is explicitly taught to Apache women, who are especially discouraged from engaging in long discussions with their dates. To many Apache, silence during courtship is a sign of modesty.

In Iranian culture there's an expression, *qahr*, which means not being on speaking terms with someone, giving someone the silent treatment. For example, when children disobey their parents, are disrespectful, or fail to do their chores as they should, they're given this silent treatment. With adults *qahr* may be instituted when one person insults or injures another. After a cooling-off period, *ashti* (making up after *qahr*) may be initiated. *Qahr* lasts for a relatively short time between parents and children, but longer when between adults. *Qahr* is more frequently initiated between two women than between two men, but when men experience *qahr* it lasts much longer and often requires the intercession of a mediator to establish *ashti* (Behzadi, 1994).

An interesting cultural difference in time orientation is that between **monochronic** and **polychronic time orientations** (Hall, 1959, 1976; Hall & Hall, 1987). Monochronic people or cultures (the United States, Germany, Scandinavia, and Switzerland are good examples) schedule one thing at a time. Time is compartmentalized; there's a time for everything, and everything has its own time. Polychronic people or cultures (Latin Americans, Mediterranean people, and Arabs are good examples), on the other hand, schedule a number of things at the same time. Eating, conducting business with several different people, and taking care of family matters may all be conducted at the same time. No culture is entirely monochronic or polychronic; rather, these are general tendencies that are found across a large part of the culture. Some cultures combine both time orientations; for example, in Japan and in some areas of American culture, both orientations are found.

REFLECTIONS ON ETHICS IN HUMAN COMMUNICATION

Interpersonal Silence

Often, though not always, you have the right to remain silent in order to maintain your privacy—to withhold information that has no bearing on the matter at hand. Thus, for example, your previous relationship history, affectional orientation, or religion is usually irrelevant to your ability to function in a job, and thus may be kept private in most job-related situations. On the other hand, these issues may be relevant when, for example, you're about to enter a new relationship—and then there *may* be an obligation to reveal your relationship history, affectional orientation, or religion.

In court, of course, you have the right to refuse to incriminate yourself or to reveal information about yourself that could be used against you. But you don't generally have the right to refuse to reveal information about the criminal activities of others (although psychiatrists, clergy, and lawyers are often exempt from this rule).

What would you do? *You're the assistant manager of a store that sells high-tech equipment. You discover that over the last several weeks your brother-in-law, who also works in the store, has stolen equipment worth well over $20,000. You wonder if you should say something or remain silent. Would your answer be different depending on whether the store owner or the insurance company had to cover the loss? What would you do in this situation? More generally, what obligation do you have to reveal wrongdoing that you've witnessed?*

SUMMARY

In this unit we explored nonverbal communication—communication without words—and considered such areas as body movements, facial and eye movements, spatial and territorial communication, artifactual communication, touch communication, paralanguage, silence, and time communication.

1. Nonverbal messages may communicate meaning by themselves and may be used to serve a variety of functions: to discover, establish and maintain relationships, help, persuade, and play.

2. Nonverbal messages may occur with other messages and metacommunicate (comment on other messages); such messages may accent, complement, contradict, regulate, repeat, or substitute for other messages.

3. The five categories of body movements are emblems (nonverbal behaviors that directly translate words or phrases), illustrators (nonverbal behaviors that accompany and literally "illustrate" verbal messages), affect displays (nonverbal movements that communicate emotional meaning), regulators (nonverbal movements that coordinate, monitor, maintain, or control the speaking of another individual), and adaptors (nonverbal behaviors that are emitted without conscious awareness and that usually serve some kind of need, as in scratching an itch).

4. Facial movements may communicate a variety of emotions. The most frequently studied are happiness, surprise, fear, anger, sadness, disgust, and contempt. Facial management techniques enable you to control the extent to which you reveal the emotions you feel.

5. The facial feedback hypothesis claims that facial display of an emotion can lead to physiological and psychological changes.

6. Eye contact may seek feedback, signal others to speak, indicate the nature of a relationship, or compensate for increased physical distance. Eye avoidance may help you avoid prying or may signal a lack of interest.

7. Pupil size shows one's interest and level of emotional arousal. Pupils enlarge when one is interested in something or is emotionally aroused in a positive way.

8. Proxemics is the study of the communicative functions of space and spatial relationships. Four major proxemic distances are (1) intimate distance, ranging from actual touching to 18 inches; (2) personal distance, ranging from 18 inches to 4 feet; (3) social distance, ranging from 4 to 12 feet; and (4) public distance, ranging from 12 to more than 25 feet.

9. Your treatment of space is influenced by such factors as status, culture, context, subject matter, gender, age, and positive or negative evaluation of the other person.

10. Territoriality has to do with your possessive reaction to an area of space or to particular objects.

11. Artifactual communication consists of messages that are human-made; for example, communication through color, clothing and body adornment, and space decoration.

12. The study of haptics indicates that touch communication may convey a variety of meanings, the most important being positive affect, playfulness, control, ritual, and task-relatedness. Touch avoidance is the desire to avoid touching and being touched by others.

13. Paralanguage involves the vocal but nonverbal dimensions of speech. It includes rate, pitch, volume, rhythm, and vocal quality as well as pauses and hesitations. Paralanguage helps us make judgments about people, their emotions, and their believability.

14. We us silence to communicate a variety of meanings, from messages aimed at hurting another (the silent treatment) to deep emotional responses.

15. The study of time communication (chronemics) explores the messages communicated by our treatment of time.

16. Smell can communicate messages of attraction, taste, memory, and identification.

17. Cultural variations in nonverbal communication are great. Different cultures, for example, assign different meanings to facial expressions and colors, have different spatial rules, and treat time very differently.

KEY TERMS

emblems	facial management techniques	artifactual communication
illustrators	civil inattention	haptics
affect displays	pupil dilation	paralanguage
regulators	proxemics	chronemics
adaptors	territoriality	social clock

THINKING CRITICALLY ABOUT

Nonverbal Messages

1. Status is signaled not only by the nature of a person's territory but by the unwritten law granting the right of invasion. Higher-status individuals have more of a right to invade the territory of others than vice versa. The boss of a large company, for example, can invade the territory of a junior executive by barging into her or his office, but the reverse would be unthinkable. Do you observe this "right" of territorial invasion?

2. A popular defense tactic in sex crimes against women, gay men, and lesbians is to blame the victim by referring to the way the victim was dressed and to imply that the victim, by wearing a certain type of clothing, provoked the attack. Currently, New York and Florida are the only states that prohibit defense attorneys from referring to the way a sex-crime victim was dressed at the time of the attack (*New York Times,* July 30, 1994, p. 22). What do you

think of this? If you don't live in New York or Florida, have there been proposals in your state to similarly limit this popular defense tactic?

3. Here are a few findings from research on nonverbal gender differences (Burgoon, Buller, & Woodall, 1996; Eakins & Eakins, 1978; Pearson, West, & Turner, 1995; Arliss, 1991; Shannon, 1987): (1) Women smile more than men. (2) Women stand closer to each other than men do and are generally approached more closely than men. (3) Both men and women, when speaking, look at men more than at women. (4) Women both touch and are touched more than men. (5) Men extend their bodies, taking up greater areas of space, more than women. What problems might these differences create when men and women communicate with each other?

4. Visit the website of a large multinational corporation. Most corporations have Web addresses like this: www.CompanyName.com. What can you learn about nonverbal communication from such elements as the website's general design, colors, movement, fonts, or spacing? Can you point out any ways the website could be visually improved?

5. Test your ability to identify emotions on the basis of verbal descriptions. Try to "hear" the following voices and to identify the emotions being communicated. Do you hear affection, anger, boredom, or joy (Davitz, 1964)?
   • This voice is soft, with a low pitch, a resonant quality, a slow rate, and a steady and slightly upward inflection. The rhythm is regular, and the enunciation is slurred.
   • This voice is loud, with a high pitch, a moderately blaring quality, a fast rate, an upward inflection, and a regular rhythm.
   • This voice is loud, with a high pitch, a blaring quality, a fast rate, and an irregular up-and-down inflection. The rhythm is irregular, and the enunciation is clipped.
   • This voice is moderate to low in volume, with a moderate-to-low pitch, a moderately resonant quality, a moderately slow rate, and a monotonous or gradually falling inflection. The enunciation is somewhat slurred.

6. What nonverbal cues should you look for in judging whether someone likes you? List them in the order of their importance, using 1 for the cue that is of most value in helping you make your judgment, 2 for the cue that is next most valuable, and so on down to perhaps 10 or 12. Do you really need two lists? One for judging a woman's liking and one for a man's?

7. **Researching Nonverbal Messages.** How would you go about seeking answers to questions such as these?
   • Do higher-status people touch each other with the same frequency as do lower-status people?
   • Do children who were born blind express emotions with the same facial expressions that sighted children use?
   • Do men and women differ in the way they view time?
   • What is the ideal outfit for a college instructor to wear on the first day of class?
   • Do family photos on an executive's desk contribute to the executive's credibility? Is the relationship between photos and credibility the same for male and female executives?

UNIT 9
Interpersonal Communication: Conversation

CBS Photo Archive

Unit Contents

Talking with another person seems so simple and so natural that most people are surprised to learn that the process actually follows a complex set of rules and customs. In this unit we dissect this process and explain how it operates and the kinds of problems that can be created when these rules and customs are broken. In this excursion into conversation, you'll learn

▶ how the process of conversation works

▶ how you can become a more satisfying and more effective conversationalist

CONVERSATION

Conversation is the essence of interpersonal communication; in many scholarly views they're equivalent, and among nonscholars the words *conversation* and *interpersonal communication* often mean the same thing (though consider the qualifications noted in Understanding Theory and Research: The Development of Interpersonal Communication on page 166). **Conversation** occurs when two or three people exchange messages—whether face-to-face, over the telephone, through apartment walls, or on the Internet.

E-mail, originally a business convenience, has now become a major channel of conversation. In fact, according to a recent Gallop poll (http://www.gallup.com/poll/releases/pr010723.asp, July 23, 2001), e-mail is the most common Internet activity. Of those surveyed, 90 percent say they use e-mail at home and 80 percent say they use it at work. Of these, 61 percent of the women and only 44 percent of the men said that e-mail was their main online activity. As a means of communication, e-mail is extremely well liked; 97 percent of those surveyed said that e-mail has made their lives better. Instant messaging, which enables you to communicate with others who are also at their computers in near real time, is used by only 2 percent of computer users.

Along with chat groups and mailing lists (which share many characteristics of small groups, and so are discussed in Unit 13) and newsgroups (which are covered in our discussion of public speaking in Unit 15), e-mail is an ever increasingly popular means of conversing. Among college students in the United States e-mail is near universal, and it is becoming standard throughout the world.

Another type of e-mail that is becoming increasingly popular is text messaging, in which you type and send very short messages to another person using your pager or cell phone. The New York City Police Department, for example, uses text messaging to check on license plates and some airlines are using it to notify passengers if their flights will be delayed. Although text messaging lacks the advantages of face-to-face interaction, it has advantages of its own; for example, you can reach lots of people at once at a relatively low cost and the necessary equipment (the pager or the cell phone) is always with you. Although instant messaging has the advantage of near real time interaction, it also has the disadvantage that you can only communicate with those who are at their computers at the same time you are.

In face-to-face interaction the messages exchanged are both verbal and nonverbal. In e-mail today most messages are basically verbal. But with the addition of emoticons and the popularity of digital video cameras and voice software, e-mail messages are increasingly blending the verbal with the nonverbal in much the same way as face-to-face conversation.

The Conversation Process in Five Stages

Figure 9.1 on page 160 provides a model of the process of conversation and divides the process into five main stages: opening, feedforward, business, feedback, and closing. Examining each stage will give you an overview of what goes on when two people talk.

The Opening

The first step is to open the conversation, usually with some kind of greeting. Greetings can be verbal or nonverbal and are usually both (Krivonos & Knapp, 1975; Knapp & Vangelisti, 2000). Verbal greetings include, for example, verbal salutes ("Hi," "Hello"), initiation of the topic ("The reason I called . . ."), making reference to the other ("Hey, Joe, what's up?"), and personal inquiries ("What's

Figure 9.1
The Process of Conversation

This model of the stages of conversation is best seen as a way of looking at conversation and not as defining unvarying stages that all conversations follow. As you read about conversation, consider how accurately you think this model reflects the progression of your last conversation.

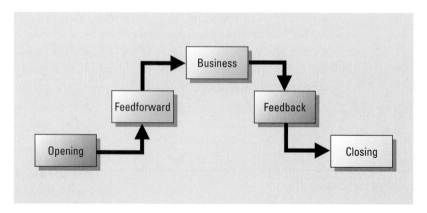

Greetings serve different functions (Knapp & Vangelisti, 2000; Krivonos & Knapp, 1975). For example, greetings may signal a stage of access, opening up the channels of communication for more meaningful interaction. Greetings may also reveal important information about the relationship; for example, a big smile and a warm "Hi, it's been a long time" signal a friendly relationship. Greetings may also help maintain the relationship. When two workers in an office greet each other as they pass through the office, it assures them that even though they don't stop and talk for an extended period, they still have access to each other. What functions did your last three greetings serve?

new?" "How are you doing?"). Nonverbal greetings include waving, smiling, shaking hands, and winking. Usually you greet another person both verbally and nonverbally: You smile when you say "Hello."

In normal conversation, your greeting is reciprocated with a greeting from the other person that is similar in degree of formality or informality and in intensity. When it isn't—when the other person turns away or responds coldly to your friendly "good morning"—you know that something is wrong. Openings are also generally consistent in tone with the main part of the conversation; a cheery "How ya doing today, big guy?" is not normally followed by news of a family death. This, however, is distinctly cultural; in Finland, for example, the "How are you?" opening is interpreted as a genuine request for information and not simply as a "hello" (Halmari, 1995). In e-mail the opening is the header and the announcement from your ISP of "You got mail" or "Mail truck."

In opening a conversation, consider two general guidelines. First, be positive. Lead off with something positive rather than something negative. Say, for example, "I really enjoy coming here" instead of "Don't you just hate this place?" Second, don't be too revealing; don't self-disclose too early in an interaction. If you do, you risk making the other person feel uncomfortable.

Feedforward

At the second step there's usually some kind of feedforward. Here you give the other person a general idea of what the conversation will focus on: "I've got to tell you about Jack," "Did you hear what happened in class yesterday?" or "We need to talk about our vacation plans." Feedforward may also identify the tone of the conversation ("I'm really depressed

BUILDING COMMUNICATION SKILLS

How Can You Open a Conversation?

Think about how you might open a conversation with the persons described in each of these situations. What general approaches would meet with a favorable response? What general approaches seem frowned on?

▶ On the first day of class, you and another student are the first to come into the classroom and are seated in the room alone.

▶ You're a guest at a friend's party. You're one of the first guests to arrive and are now there with several other people to whom you've

only just been introduced. Your friend, the host, is busy with other matters.

▶ You've just started a new job in a large office where you're one of several computer operators. It seems as if most of the other people know one another.

▶ You're in the college cafeteria eating alone. You see another student who is also eating alone and whom you've seen in your English literature class. You're not sure if this person has noticed you in class.

and need to talk with you") or the time required ("This will just take a minute") (Frentz, 1976; Reardon, 1987); or you may use it to preface the conversation to ensure that your message will be understood and will not reflect negatively on you (see Unit 1).

UNDERSTANDING THEORY AND RESEARCH

Opening Lines

How do you strike up a conversation? How have people tried to open a conversation with you? Researchers investigating this question have found three basic types of opening lines (Kleinke, 1986):

Cute–flippant openers are humorous, indirect, and ambiguous as to whether or not the person opening the conversation really wants an extended encounter. Examples: "Is that really your hair?" "Bet I can outdrink you." "I bet the cherries jubilee isn't as sweet as you are."

Innocuous openers are highly ambiguous as to whether they are simple comments that might be made to just anyone or are in fact openers designed to initiate an extended encounter. Examples: "What do you think of the band?" "I haven't been here before. What's good on the menu?" "Could you show me how to work this machine?"

Direct openers clearly demonstrate the speaker's interest in meeting the other person. Examples: "I feel a little embarrassed about this, but I'd like to meet you." "Would you like to have a drink after dinner?" "Since we're both eating alone, would you like to join me?"

The opening lines most preferred by both men and women are generally those that are direct or innocuous (Kleinke & Dean, 1990). The lines least preferred by both men and women are those that are cute–flippant—and women dislike these openers even more than men (Kleinke & Dean, 1990).

> **Working with Theories and Research.** *Do you find support for these research conclusions from your own experience? What openers do you find most effective?*

In e-mail the title serves as feedforward; it gives the reader some idea of what to expect in the e-mail. Conveniently, this allows for quick deletion of spam and a concentrated focus on e-mail titled "sad news" or "family problem."

Business

The third step is the "business," the substance or focus of the conversation. This is obviously the longest part of the conversation and the reason for both the opening and the feedforward. *Business* is a good term to use for this stage, because it emphasizes that most conversations—whether face-to-face, on the phone, or via e-mail—are goal directed. You converse to fulfill one or several of the general purposes of interpersonal communication: to learn, relate, influence, play, or help (Unit 1). The term is also sufficiently general to incorporate all kinds of interactions. In e-mail you can easily supplement your message by attaching hotlinks to websites and to word, sound, and video files, as well as to other e-mails. Although you can also distribute supplementary materials in conversation, it's not as common as it is in e-mail communication.

The business is conducted through an exchange of speaker and listener roles. Usually, brief (rather than long) speaking turns characterize the most satisfying conversations. Here you talk about Jack, what happened in class, or your vacation plans. Here is where the similarity between e-mail and face-to-face conversation breaks down a bit. E-mail doesn't have the spontaneity and the frequent interchange of sender-receiver roles—although with voice and video advancements, this distinction between face-to-face and electronic communication will probably blur in coming years.

Another important difference is that in normal face-to-face communication there is no permanent record of the conversation; the record exists only in the memories of those who are present. In e-mail there is a permanent record of the interaction, a record that can easily be sent to third parties. In large organizations employees' e-mails are stored on hard disk or on backup tapes and may be retrieved from archives long thought destroyed. Recently, for example, Dow Chemical fired 24 employees for sending offensive e-mail messages.

Feedback

The fourth step is the reverse of the second. In feedback (see Unit 1) you reflect back on the conversation to signal that as far as you're concerned, the business is completed: "So, you may want to send Jack a get-well card," "Wasn't that the craziest class you ever heard of?" or "I'll call for reservations while you shop for what we need."

Of course, the other person may not agree that the business is completed and may therefore counter with, for example, "But what hospital is he in?" When this happens, you normally go back a step and continue the business.

Closing

The fifth and last step, the opposite of the first step, is the closing, the good-bye (Knapp, Hart, Friedrich, & Shulman, 1973; Knapp & Vangelisti, 2000). Like the opening, the closing may be verbal or nonverbal but is usually a combination of both. Most obviously, the closing signals the end of accessibility. Just as the opening signaled access, the closing signals the end of access. The closing usually also signals some degree of supportiveness; for example, you express your pleasure in interacting, as in "Well, it was good talking with you." The closing may also summarize the interaction.

In e-mail the closing is similar to that in face-to-face conversation but has the added capability of including a "signature," perhaps along with a favorite quotation or saying or a phone number through which you can be reached.

Closing a conversation is almost as difficult as opening a conversation. It's frequently an awkward and uncomfortable part of interpersonal interaction. Here are a few leave-taking cues you might consider for closing a conversation.

- Reflect back on the conversation and briefly summarize it so as to bring it to a close. For example, "I'm glad I ran into you and found out what happened at that union meeting. I'll probably be seeing you at the meetings."

- State the desire to end the conversation directly and to get on with other things. For example, "I'd like to continue talking but I really have to run. I'll see you around."

- Refer to future interaction. For example, "E-mail me when after you've had a chance to read the report," or "Why don't we get together next week sometime and continue this discussion?"

- Ask for closure. For example, "Have I explained what you wanted to know?"

BUILDING COMMUNICATION SKILLS

How Can You Close a Conversation?

How might you bring each of the following conversations to an end? What types of closings seem most effective? Which seem least effective?

▶ You and a friend have been talking on the phone for the last hour, but not much new is being said. You have a great deal of work to get to and would like to close the conversation. Your friend just doesn't seem to hear your subtle cues.

▶ You're at a party and are anxious to meet a person with whom you've exchanged eye contact for the last 10 minutes. The problem is that a friendly and talkative older relative of yours is demanding all your attention. You don't want to insult your relative, but at

the same time you want to make contact with this other person.

▶ You've had a conference with a teacher and learned what you needed to know. This teacher, however, doesn't seem to know how to end the conversation and just continues to go over what has already been said. You have to get to your next class and must close the conversation.

▶ You're at a party and notice someone you would like to get to know. You initiate a conversation but after a few minutes realize that this individual is not the kind of person with whom you would care to spend any more time. You want to close the conversation as soon as possible.

• State that you enjoyed the interaction. For example, "I really enjoyed talking with you."

With any of these closings, it should be clear to the other person that you're attempting to end the conversation. Obviously, you'll have to use more direct methods with those who don't take these subtle hints—those who don't realize that both persons are responsible for bringing the conversation to a satisfying close.

MAINTAINING CONVERSATIONS

The defining feature of conversation is that the roles of speaker and listener are exchanged throughout the interaction. You accomplish this exchange, or **conversational management,** by using a wide variety of verbal and nonverbal cues to signal **conversational turns**—the changing (or maintaining) of the speaker or listener role during the conversation. The majority of today's e-mail lacks this frequent exchange of roles between sender and receiver; the exchanges take place with hours, days, or even weeks intervening between the sending and the responding. Such feedback lacks the immediacy that's com-

mon in face-to-face conversation—though, again, with video and voice capabilities, this distinction may fade.

Conversational Turns

Combining the insights of a variety of communication researchers (Burgoon, Buller, & Woodall, 1996; Duncan, 1972; Pearson & Spitzberg, 1990), we can look at conversational turns in terms of speaker cues and listener cues.

Speaker Cues

Speakers regulate the conversation through two major types of cues: turn-maintaining cues and turn-yielding cues. Using these cues effectively not only ensures communication efficiency but also increases likeability (Place & Becker, 1991; Heap, 1992). The ways of using the conversational turns identified here have been derived largely from studies conducted in the United States. Each culture appears to define the types and appropriateness of turns differently (e.g., Iizuka, 1993). In polychronic cultures, for example, people will often disregard the turn-taking rules used in monochronic cultures.

The effect is that to monochronic people—who carefully follow these rules—polychronic people may appear rude as they interrupt and overlap conversations (Lee, 1984; Grossin, 1987). In some cultures (largely individualistic ones) the conversational turn is more often passed to one person; in other cultures (largely collectivist ones) the turn is more often passed to several individuals (Ng, Loong, He, Liu, & Weatherall, 2000).

Turn-Maintaining Cues. Turn-maintaining cues are designed to enable a person to maintain the role of speaker and may be communicated in a variety of ways (Burgoon, Buller, & Woodall, 1996; Duncan, 1972):

- audibly inhaling breath to show that the speaker has more to say
- continuing a gesture or series of gestures to show that the thought is not yet complete
- avoiding eye contact with the listener so as not to indicate that the speaking turn is being passed along
- sustaining the intonation pattern to indicate that more will be said
- vocalizing pauses ("er," "umm") to prevent the listener from speaking and to show that the speaker is still talking

In most cases you expect the speaker to maintain relatively brief speaking turns and to turn over the speaking role to the listener willingly (when so signaled by the listener). People who don't follow those unwritten rules are likely to be evaluated negatively.

Turn-Yielding Cues. Turn-yielding cues tell the listener that the speaker is finished and wishes to exchange the role of speaker for the role of listener. They tell the listener (and sometimes they're addressed to a specific listener rather than to just any listener) to take over the role of speaker. For example, you may at the end of a statement add some cue such as "okay?" or "right?" which asks one of the listeners to assume the role of speaker. You can also indicate that you've finished speaking by dropping your intonation, by a prolonged silence, by making direct eye contact with a listener, by asking some question, or by nodding in the direction of a particular listener.

In much the same way that you expect a speaker to yield the role of speaker, you also expect the listener to assume the speaking role willingly. Those who don't may be regarded as reticent or unwilling to involve themselves and take equal responsibility for the conversation. For example, in an analysis of turn-taking violations in the conversations of married couples, the most common violation found was that of no response (DeFrancisco, 1991). Forty-five percent of the 540 violations identified involved a lack of response to an invitation to take on the role of speaker. Of these "no response" violations, 68 percent were committed by men and 32 percent by women. Other turn-taking violations include delayed responses and inappropriately brief responses. DeFrancisco (1991) argues that with these violations, all of which are committed more frequently by men, men silence women in marital interactions. Perhaps the most important violation is interruption. Much research has addressed this issue, especially the question of whether men or women interrupt more. The research that has found a difference indicates that men interrupt more often than women, though much research finds no differences (Stratford, 1998; Crown & Cummins, 1998; Smith-Lovin & Brody, 1989; Donaldson, 1992).

Listener Cues

As a listener you can regulate the conversation by using three types of cues: turn-requesting cues, turn-denying cues, and backchanneling cues.

Turn-Requesting Cues. Turn-requesting cues let the speaker know that you would like to say something and take a turn as speaker. Sometimes you can do this simply by saying, "I'd like to say something," but often it's done more subtly through some vocalized *er* or *um* that tells the speaker that you would now like to speak. The request to speak is also often made with facial and mouth gestures. Frequently a listener will indicate a desire to speak by opening his or her eyes and mouth wide as if to say something, by beginning to gesture with a hand, or by leaning forward.

Turn-Denying Cues. You can use turn-denying cues to indicate your reluctance to assume the role of speaker; for example, by intoning a slurred "I don't know" or by giving some brief grunt that signals you have nothing to say. Often people accomplish turn denying by avoiding eye contact with the speaker (who wishes them now to take on the role of speaker) or by engaging in some behavior that is incompatible with speaking—for example, coughing or blowing their nose.

Backchanneling Cues. People use backchanneling cues to communicate various types of information back to the speaker without assuming the role of the speaker. You can send a variety of messages with backchanneling cues (Burgoon, Buller, & Woodall, 1996; Pearson & Spitzberg, 1990). You can indicate your agreement or disagreement with the speaker through smiles or frowns, gestures of approval or disapproval, brief comments such as "right" or "never," or a vocalization such as *uh-huh*.

You can also indicate your degree of involvement or boredom with the speaker. Attentive posture, forward leaning, and focused eye contact will tell the speaker that you're involved in the conversation—and an inattentive posture, backward leaning, and avoidance of eye contact will communicate your lack of involvement.

Giving the speaker pacing cues helps regulate the speed of speech. You can, for example, ask the speaker to slow down by raising your hand near your ear and leaning forward and to speed up by continuously nodding your head. You can also do this verbally by simply asking the speaker to slow down ("Slow down, I want to make sure I'm getting all this"). Similarly, you can tell the speaker to speed up by saying something like "and—?" or "go on, go on."

A request for clarification is still another function of backchanneling cues. A puzzled facial expression, perhaps coupled with a forward lean, will probably tell most speakers that you want some clarification. Similarly, you can ask for clarification by interjecting some interrogative: "Who?" "When?" "Where?"

Some of these backchanneling cues are actually interruptions. These interruptions, however, are generally confirming rather than disconfirming. They tell the speaker that you are listening and are involved (Kennedy & Camden, 1988).

Figure 9.2 provides an illustration of the various turn-taking cues and how they correspond to the conversational wants of speaker and listener.

	Conversational Wants	
	To speak	**To listen**
Speaker	1 Turn-maintaining cues	2 Turn-yielding cues
Listener	3 Turn-requesting cues	4 Turn-denying cues

Figure 9.2

Turn-Taking and Conversational Wants

Quadrant 1 represents the speaker who wants to speak (continue to speak) and uses turn-maintaining cues; quadrant 2, the speaker who wants to listen and uses turn-yielding cues; quadrant 3, the listener who wants to speak and uses turn-requesting cues; and quadrant 4, the listener who wants to listen (continue listening) and uses turn-denying cues. Backchanneling cues would appear in quadrant 4, because they are cues that listeners use while they continue to listen.

Reflections on the Model

Not all conversations will be easily divided into the five steps described earlier. Often the opening and the feedforward are combined, as when you see someone on campus and say, "Hey, listen to this," or when in a work situation someone says, "Well, folks, let's get the meeting going." In a similar way, the feedback and the closing might be combined: "Look, I've got to think more about this commitment, okay?"

As already noted, the business is the longest part of the conversation. The opening and the closing are usually about the same length, and the feedforward and feedback are usually about equal in length. When these relative lengths are severely distorted, you may feel that something is wrong. For example, if someone used a long feedforward or a too-short opening, you might suspect that what was to follow was extremely serious.

It's also important to note that effectiveness or competence in conversation and skill in following the appropriate conversational rules will contribute to your own interpersonal attractiveness. For example, researchers studied four conversational skills in 10-year-old girls: making an appropriate request,

UNDERSTANDING THEORY AND RESEARCH

The Development of Interpersonal Communication

You can view interpersonal communication as the end portion of a continuum with impersonal communication at one extreme and highly personal or intimate communication at the other extreme. Interpersonal communication (or interpersonal conversation) occupies a part of the continuum toward the more personal and intimate extreme and is distinguished from impersonal communication by three factors: psychologically based predictions, explanatory knowledge, and personally established rules (Miller, 1978).

In impersonal encounters, you respond to another person on the basis of sociological data—the classes or groups to which the person belongs. For example, a student responds to a particular college professor the way students respond to college professors generally. Similarly, the college professor responds to a particular student in the way professors respond to students generally. As the relationship becomes more personal, however, both professor and student begin to respond to each other not just as members of their groups but as individuals. They respond (to some degree) on the basis of *psychological data;* that is, on the ways each individual differs from the members of his or her group.

In interpersonal interactions you also base your communications on *explanatory knowledge* of each other. When you know a particular person, you can predict how that person will act in a variety of situations. But as you get to know that person better, you can predict not only how the person will act, but also why the person behaves as he or she does. In an impersonal relationship the professor may be able to predict Pat's behavior and know that Pat will be late to class each Friday. But in an interpersonal situation the professor can also offer explanations for the behavior because he or she understands the reasons for Pat's lateness.

Society sets up rules for interaction in impersonal situations. As noted in the example of the student and professor, however, the social rules of interaction set up by the culture lose importance as the relationship becomes more personal. In the place of these social rules, the individuals set up *personal rules.* When individuals establish their own rules for interacting with each other rather than using the rules set down by the society, the situation becomes increasingly interpersonal.

Working with Theories and Research. *Are these three factors helpful as you think about defining or classifying your own interactions? Try applying them to an interpersonal relationship you have developed with someone. Can you categorize your interactions along these three dimensions? Did you experience the kind of progression identified here?*

turn taking, responding without excessive delay when spoken to, and following the logic of the conversation. The girls who demonstrated these skills were liked more and were described in more positive terms than those who lacked these conversational skills (Place & Becker, 1991). Conversational competence is also likely to contribute to the satisfaction or enjoyment you experience when interacting with others. Examine your own conversational satisfaction by taking the self-test "How satisfying is your conversation?" at www.ablongman.com/devito.

Of course, each culture will alter these basic steps in different ways. In some cultures the openings are especially short; in others the openings are elaborate, lengthy, and, in some cases, highly ritualized. It's easy in intercultural communication situations to violate another culture's conversational rules.

Being overly friendly, too formal, or too forward may easily hinder the remainder of the conversation (Murata, 1994).

The reasons such violations may have significant consequences is that you may not be aware of these rules and hence may see violations not as cultural differences but rather as aggressiveness, stuffiness, or pushiness—and thus may almost immediately dislike the person and put a negative cast on the future conversation. Some of the more common conversational problems include:

- Openings that are insensitive; for example, "Wow, you've gained a few pounds!"
- Overly long feedforwards that make you wonder if the other person will ever get to the business.

COMMUNICATION @ WORK

Grapevine Communication

Electronic engineers have yet to devise a better interoffice communication system than the water cooler.

—Leo Ellis

Grapevine messages don't follow any of the formal lines of communication established in an organization; rather, they seem to have a life of their own and are concerned primarily with personal and social matters rather than with the organization itself. Grapevine communications grow along with the formal communications; the more active the formal communication system, the more active the informal system. Not surprisingly, the grapevine also grows as the size of the organization increases.

The organizational grapevine is most likely to be used when there is great upheaval or change within the organization (Davis, 1977, 1980). In fact, one research study notes that during a crisis workers spend between 65 and 70 percent of their time on the grapevine. And even in noncrisis times they spend between 10 and 15 percent on the grapevine (Smith, 1996). The grapevine is also surprisingly accurate, with estimates of accuracy ranging from 75 to 95 percent (Davis, 1980; Hellweg, 1992; Smith, 1996).

Here are a few useful suggestions for dealing with the inevitable grapevine:

▶ Understand the variety of purposes the grapevine serves. Its speed and general accuracy make it an ideal medium to carry a great proportion of the social communications that so effectively bind workers together.

▶ Although grapevine information is generally accurate, it's usually incomplete and may contain crucial distortions. So treat grapevine information you receive as tentative, as possibly not necessarily true.

▶ Tap into the grapevine. Whether you are a worker or a member of management, it's important to hear grapevine information. It may clue you in to events that will figure in your future with the organization. And, of course, it will help you bond and network with others in the organization.

▶ Always assume that what you say in grapevine communication will be repeated to others (Smith, 1996; Hilton, 2000). Be especially careful of that potentially offensive joke that you e-mail a colleague; it can easily be forwarded to the very people who may take offense.

Thinking about Your Communicating @ Work

How does the grapevine work at your place of employment? How does it work on campus? What roles do you play in grapevine communication?

- Omission of feedforward before a truly shocking message (for example, the death or illness of a friend or relative), which can lead you to see the other person as insensitive or uncaring.

- Introduction of business without the normally expected greeting, as when you go to a doctor who begins the conversation by saying, "Well, what's wrong?"

- Omission of feedback, which leads you to wonder if the other person heard what you said or cared about it.

- Omission of an appropriate closing, which makes you wonder if the other person is disturbed or angry.

MANAGING CONVERSATION

To develop conversational competence or effectiveness, we need to look at interpersonal skills on two levels. On one level are the skills of effectiveness, such as openness and supportiveness. On another level, however, are skills that guide us in regulating our openness and our supportiveness. They're skills about skills, or **metaskills**. These qualities will provide a good foundation for communicating interpersonally, in small groups, in public speaking, and especially in intercultural communication. Additional skills and guidelines for effective conversation are provided in the full-length unit "Emotional Communication" at **www.ablongman.com/devito**. ⌐🖱

Metaskills

Because each conversation is unique, the qualities of interpersonal competence can't be applied indiscriminately. You need to have metaskills—to know how the skills themselves should be applied. You should be mindful, flexible, and culturally sensitive.

Mindfulness

After you've learned a skill or a rule, you often apply it without thinking; you apply it mindlessly, without considering the unique aspects of each situation. Instead, conversational skills need to be applied in accordance with the concept of **mind-fulness and mindlessness,** as introduced briefly in Unit 3 (Langer, 1989; Burgoon, Berger, & Waldron, 2000). For example, after learning the skills of active listening, many will respond to all situations with active listening responses. Some of these responses will be appropriate, but others will prove inappropriate and ineffective. Before responding, think about the unique communication situation you face and consider your alternatives. Be alert and responsive to small changes in the situation that may cue which behaviors will be effective and which ineffective. Be especially mindful of the cultural differences among people, as outlined in the section "Cultural Sensitivity" below.

Langer (1989) offers several ideas for increasing mindfulness that will prove useful in most conversations and, in fact, in most communications generally. As you read through these suggestions, try to provide a specific example or application for each recommendation.

- Create and recreate categories. See an object, event, or person as belonging to a wide variety of categories. Avoid storing in memory an image of a person, for example, with only one specific label; it will be difficult to recategorize that image later.

- Be open to new information even if it contradicts your most firmly held stereotypes.

- Be open to different points of view. This will help you avoid the tendency to blame outside forces for your negative outcomes ("That test was unfair") and internal forces for the negative outcomes of others ("Pat didn't study," "Pat isn't very bright"). Be willing to see your own and others' behaviors from a variety of perspectives.

- Beware of relying too heavily on first impressions, what psychologists call "premature cognitive commitment" (Chanowitz & Langer, 1981; Langer, 1989). Treat your first impressions as tentative, as hypotheses.

Flexibility

You can best understand the concept of **flexibility** by examining specific communication situations and thinking about the way you would act in each. The following self-test, "How flexible are you in communication?" will help you with this introspection.

TEST YOURSELF

How Flexible Are You in Communication?

Here are some situations that illustrate how people sometimes act when communicating with others. The first part of each situation asks you to imagine that you are in the situation; then a course of action is identified, and you are asked to determine how much your own behavior would be like the action described in the scenario. If it is exactly like you, mark a 5; if it is a lot like you, mark a 4; if it is somewhat like you, mark a 3; if it is not much like you, mark a 2; and if it is not at all like you, mark a 1.

Imagine

_____ 1. Last week, as you were discussing your strained finances with your family, family members came up with several possible solutions. Even though you already decided on one solution, you decided to spend more time considering all the possibilities before making a final decision.

_____ 2. You were invited to a Halloween party, and assuming it was a costume party, you dressed as a pumpkin. When you arrived at the party and found everyone else dressed in formal attire, you laughed and joked about the misunderstanding, and decided to stay and enjoy the party.

_____ 3. You have always enjoyed being with your friend Chris, but do not enjoy Chris's habit of always interrupting you. The last time you met, every time Chris interrupted you, you then interrupted Chris to teach Chris a lesson.

_____ 4. Your daily schedule is very structured and your calendar is full of appointments and commitments. When asked to make a change in your schedule, you replied that changes are impossible before even considering the change.

_____ 5. You went to a party where over 50 people attended. You had a good time, but spent most of the evening talking to one close friend rather than meeting new people.

_____ 6. When discussing a personal problem with a group of friends, you noticed that many different solutions were offered. Although several of the solutions seemed feasible, you already had your opinion and did not listen to any of the alternative solutions.

_____ 7. You and a friend planned a fun evening and you were dressed and ready ahead of time. You found that you are unable to do anything else until your friend arrived.

_____ 8. When you found your seat at the ball game, you realized you did not know anyone sitting nearby. However, you introduced yourself to the people sitting next to you and attempted to strike up a conversation.

_____ 9. You had lunch with your friend Chris, and Chris told you about a too-personal family problem. You quickly finished your lunch and stated that you had to leave because you had a lot to do that afternoon.

_____ 10. You were involved in a discussion about international politics with a group of acquaintances and you assumed that the members of the group were as knowledgeable as you on the topic; but, as the discussion progressed, you learned that most of the group knew little about the subject. Instead of explaining your point of view, you decided to withdraw from the discussion.

_____ 11. You and a group of friends got into a discussion about gun control and, after a while, it became obvious that your opinions differed greatly from the rest of the group. You explained your position once again, but you agreed to respect the group's opinion also.

_____ 12. You were asked to speak to a group you belong to, so you worked hard preparing a 30-minute presentation; but at the meeting, the organizer asked you to lead a question-and-answer session instead of giving your presentation. You agreed, and answered the group's questions as candidly and fully as possible.

_____ 13. You were offered a managerial position where every day you would face new tasks and challenges and a changing day-to-day routine. You decided to accept this position instead of one that has a stable daily routine.

_____ 14. You were asked to give a speech at a Chamber of Commerce breakfast. Because you did not know anyone at the breakfast and would feel uncomfortable not knowing anyone in the audience, you declined the invitation.

How did you do? To compute your score:

1. Reverse the scoring for items 4, 5, 6, 7, 9, 10, and 14. That is, for each of these questions, substitute as follows:
   a. If you answered 5, reverse it to 1.
   b. If you answered 4, reverse it to 2.
   c. If you answered 3, keep it as 3.
   d. If you answered 2, reverse it to 4.
   e. If you answered 1, reverse it to 5.

2. Add the scores for all 14 items. Be sure that you use the reversed scores for items 4, 5, 6, 7, 9, 10, and 14. Use your original scores for items 1, 2, 3, 8, 11, 12, and 13.

    In general, you can interpret your score as follows:
    - 65–70 = much more flexible than average
    - 57–64 = more flexible than average
    - 44–56 = about average
    - 37–43 = less flexible than average
    - 14–36 = much less flexible than average

What will you do? Are you satisfied with your level of flexibility? What might you do to cultivate flexibility in general and communication flexibility in particular?

Source: From "Development of a Communication Flexibility Measure" by Matthew M. Martin and Rebecca B. Rubin in *The Southern Communication Journal*, V. 59, Winter 1994, pp. 171–178. Reprinted by permission of the Southern States Communication Association.   ✔

Keep in mind this concept of flexibility as you examine the general principles for conversational effectiveness presented under "Skills in Conversational Competence" below. For example, you may need to be frank and spontaneous when talking with a close friend about your feelings, but you may not want to be so open when talking with your grandmother about a dinner she prepared that you disliked.

Cultural Sensitivity

In applying the skills for interpersonal effectiveness, be sensitive to the cultural differences among people, as discussed in Unit 3 (Guo-Ming & Starosta, 1995). What may prove effective for upper-income people working in the IBM subculture in Boston or New York may prove ineffective for lower-income people working as fruit pickers in Florida or California. What works in Germany may not work in Mexico. Direct eye contact signals immediacy (see "Skills in Conversational Competence," below) among most groups in the United States, but may be considered rude or too intrusive in other cul-tures. The specific skills discussed in the next section are considered to be generally effective among most people living in the United States; but do be aware that these skills and the ways you communicate them may not apply to other cultures (Kim, 1991).

Effectiveness in intercultural settings, according to Kim, requires that you be

- open to new ideas and to differences among people
- flexible in ways of communicating and in adapting to the communications of people who are culturally different
- tolerant of other attitudes, values, and ways of doing things
- creative in seeking varied ways to communicate

From another perspective, research suggests that the successful sojourner—someone who enters another culture for a relatively short period of time, such as a traveler or a person who spends a year or so working in this other culture—is self-confident, interested in others, open, flexible, and competent professionally (Kealey & Ruben, 1983; Berry, Poortinga, Segall, & Dasen, 1992).

In another study, persons were more likely to be competent in intercultural communication when they had a high positive self-concept and when they were appropriate self-disclosers, high self-monitors, behaviorally flexible, highly involving (attentive and responsive, for example), adaptable, and culturally aware (Chen, 1990).

These qualities—along with some knowledge of the other culture and the general skills of effectiveness discussed next—"should enable a person to approach each intercultural encounter with the psychological posture of an interested learner . . . and to strive for the communication outcomes that are as effective as possible under a given set of relational and situational constraints" (Kim, 1991).

Skills in Conversational Competence

The skills of conversational competence discussed here are (1) openness, (2) empathy, (3) positiveness, (4) immediacy, (5) interaction management, (6) expressiveness, and (7) other-orientation (Bochner & Kelly, 1974; Bochner & Yerby, 1977; Spitzberg & Hecht, 1984; Spitzberg & Cupach, 1984). As you read the discussions of these concepts, keep in mind

MEDIA WATCH

THE SPIRAL OF SILENCE

Are you as likely to voice opinions that disagree with those of others as to express opinions that agree? The "spiral of silence" theory argues that you're more likely to voice agreement than disagreement (Noelle-Neumann, 1973, 1980, 1991; Windahl, Signitzer, & Olson, 1992). The theory claims that when a controversial issue arises, you try to estimate public opinion on the issue and figure out which views are popular and which are not, largely by attending to the media (Gonzenbach, King, & Jablonski, 1999). At the same time, you also judge the likelihood of being punished for expressing minority opinions and the severity of that potential punishment. You then use these estimates to regulate your expression of opinions.

When you're in agreement with the majority views articulated in the media, you're more likely to voice your opinions than if you're in disagreement. You may do so to avoid being isolated from the majority or confronting the unpleasant possibility of being proven wrong. Alternatively, you may assume that people in the majority, because they're a majority, are right.

Not all people seem affected equally by this spiral (Noelle-Neumann, 1991). For example, younger peo-ple and men are more likely to express minority opinions than are older people and women. Educated people are more likely to express minority opinions than are those who are less educated. Similarly, the tendency to voice minority opinions will vary from one culture to another (Scheufele & Moy, 2000).

As people with minority views remain silent, the media position gets stronger—because those who agree with it are the only ones speaking. Thus, when you hear opinions from the media, you're likely to assume that nearly everyone is in agreement—after all, those who do disagree are remaining silent. As the media's position grows stronger, the silence of the opposition also grows, and the situation becomes an ever widening spiral.

Follow-Up. *Do you contribute to this spiral of silence? Do your peers and your family? Does your college provide opportunities for the presentation of minority values, opinions, and beliefs? Can you apply this theory to the way that small groups within organizations operate? To contemporary political speaking?*

---

that the most effective communicator is the person who is flexible and who adapts to the individual situation. To be always open or empathic, for example, will probably prove ineffective. Although these qualities are generally appropriate to most interpersonal interactions, do remember that the ability to control these qualities—rather than exhibiting them reflexively—should be your aim.

Also, these qualities would not be effective in all cultures; nor would the specific verbal and nonverbal behaviors carry the same meanings in all cultures. For example, assertiveness is evaluated differently by African Americans and Hispanics (Rodriguez, 1988). Similarly, whites, African Americans, and Hispanics define "satisfying communication" in different ways. The following general suggestions should prove useful most of the time—but always go to the specific culture for specific recommendations.

Openness

Openness embraces three aspects of interpersonal communication. First, you should be willing to self-disclose—to reveal information about yourself. Of course, these disclosures need to be appropriate to the entire communication act (see Unit 6). There must also be openness in regard to listening to the other person; you should be open to the thoughts and feelings of the person with whom you're communicating.

A second aspect of openness refers to your willingness to listen and react honestly to the messages and situations that confront you. You demonstrate openness by responding spontaneously and honestly to the communications and the feedback of others.

Third, openness calls for **owning feelings**. To be open in this sense is to acknowledge that the feelings and thoughts you express are yours and that you bear the responsibility for them; you don't try to shift the responsibility for your feelings to others. For example, consider these comments:

1. Your behavior was grossly inconsiderate.
2. Everyone thought your behavior was grossly inconsiderate.
3. I was really disturbed when you told my father he was an old man.

Comments 1 and 2 don't evidence ownership of feelings. In 1, the speaker accuses the listener of being inconsiderate without assuming any of the responsibility for the judgment. In 2, the speaker assigns responsibility to the convenient but elusive "everyone" and again assumes none of the responsibility. In comment 3, however, a drastic difference appears. Note that here the speaker is taking responsibility for his or her own feelings ("I was really disturbed").

When you own your own messages you use **I-messages** instead of **you-messages.** Instead of saying, "You make me feel so stupid when you ask what everyone else thinks but don't ask my opinion," the person who owns his or her feelings says, "I feel stupid when you ask everyone else what they think but don't ask me." When you own your feelings and thoughts, when you use I-messages, you say in effect, "This is how I feel," "This is how I see the situation," "This is what I think," with the "I" always paramount. Instead of saying, "This discussion is useless," say, "I'm bored by this discussion," or "I want to talk more about myself," or any other such statement that includes a reference to the fact that "I" am making an evaluation and not describing objective reality. By doing so, you make it explicit that your feelings are the result of the interaction between what is going on in the world outside your skin (what others say, for example) and what is going on inside your skin (your preconceptions, attitudes, and prejudices, for example).

Empathy

When you empathize with someone, you're able to experience what the other is experiencing from that person's point of view. Empathy does not necessarily mean that you agree with what the other person says or does. You never lose your own identity or your own attitudes and beliefs. To empathize is to feel the same feelings in the same way as the other person does. (To sympathize, on the other hand, is to feel for the individual—to feel sorry for the person.) *Empathy,* then, enables you to understand, emotionally and intellectually, what another person is experiencing.

Most people find it easier to communicate empathy in response to another person's positive statements (Heiskell & Rychiak, 1986). Similarly, empathy is more difficult to achieve with persons who are culturally different from you than with persons who are culturally similar. So perhaps you'll have to exert special effort to communicate empathy for negative statements and in intercultural situations.

Of course, empathy will mean little if you're not able to communicate this empathic understanding back to the other person. Here are a few suggestions for communicating empathy both verbally and nonverbally:

- Confront mixed messages. To show you're trying to understand the other person's feelings, confront messages that seem to be communicating conflicting feelings. For example, "You say that it doesn't bother you, but I seem to hear a lot of anger coming through."

- Avoid judgmental and evaluative (nonempathic) responses. Avoid *should* and *ought* statements that try to tell the other person how he or she should feel. For example, avoid expressions such as "Don't feel so bad," "Cheer up," "In time you'll forget all about this," and "You should start looking for another job; by next month you won't even remember this place."

- Use reinforcing comments. Let the speaker know that you understand what the speaker is saying, and encourage the speaker to continue talking about this issue. For example, use comments such as "I see," "I get it," "I understand," "Yes," and "Right."

- Demonstrate interest by maintaining eye contact (avoid scanning the room or focusing on objects or persons other than the person with whom you're interacting); maintaining physical closeness; leaning toward (not away from) the other person; and showing your interest and agreement through your facial expressions, nods, and eye movements.

Although empathy is almost universally considered positive, there's some evidence to show that even empathy has a negative side. For example, people are most empathic with those who are similar racially and ethnically, as well as in appearance and social status. The more empathy we feel toward our own group, the less empathy—possibly even the more hostility—we feel toward other groups. That is, the same empathy that increases our understanding of our own group can decrease our understanding of other groups. So although empathy may encourage group cohesiveness and identification, it can also create dividing lines between our own group and "them" (Angier, 1995).

Positiveness

You can communicate **positiveness** in interpersonal communication in at least two ways. First, you can state positive attitudes. Second, you can "stroke" the person with whom you interact.

People who feel negative about themselves invariably communicate these feelings to others, who in turn probably develop similar negative feelings. On the other hand, people who feel positive about themselves convey this feeling to others, who then return the positive regard. Positiveness in attitudes also involves a positive feeling for the general communication situation. A negative response to a communication makes you feel almost as if you're intruding, and communication is sure to break down.

Positiveness is most clearly evident in the way you phrase statements. Consider these two sentences:

1. You look horrible in stripes.
2. You look your best, I think, in solid colors.

The first sentence is critical and will almost surely encourage an argument. The second sentence, on the other hand, expresses the speaker's thought clearly and positively and should encourage responses that are cooperative.

You also communicate positiveness through positive "stroking." Stroking behavior acknowledges the importance of the other person. It's the opposite of indifference. When you stroke someone, whether positively or negatively, you acknowledge him or her as a person, as a significant human being.

Stroking may be verbal, as in "I like you," "I enjoy being with you," or "You're a pig." Stroking may also be nonverbal. A smile, a hug, or a slap in the face are also examples of stroking. Positive stroking generally takes the form of compliments or rewards. Positive strokes bolster listeners' self-image and make people feel a little bit better than they did before they received them. Negative strokes, on the other hand, are punishing. Sometimes, like cruel remarks, they hurt people emotionally. Sometimes, like a punch in the mouth, they hurt them physically.

Immediacy

The term **immediacy** refers to the joining of the speaker and listener, the creation of a sense of togetherness. The communicator who demonstrates immediacy conveys a sense of interest and attention, a liking for and an attraction to the other person. Here are a few ways immediacy may be communicated nonverbally and verbally:

- Maintain appropriate eye contact and limit looking around at others.

- Maintain a physical closeness, which suggests a psychological closeness.

- Use a direct and open body posture; for example, by arranging your body to keep others out.

- Smile and otherwise express your interest and concern for the other person.

- Use the other person's name; for example, say "Joe, what do you think?" instead of "What do you think?" Say, "I like that, Mary" instead of "I like that."

- Focus on the other person's remarks. Make the speaker know that you heard and understood what was said and will base your feedback on it. For example, use questions that ask for clarification or elaboration, such as "Do you think the same thing is true of baseball?" or "How would your argument apply to the Midwest?" Also, refer to the speaker's previous remarks, as in "I never thought of that being true of all religions" or "Colorado does sound like a great vacation spot."

- Reinforce, reward, or compliment the other person. Make use of such expressions as "I like your new outfit" or "Your comments were really to the point."

- Incorporate self-references into evaluative statements rather than depersonalizing them. Say, for example, "I think your report is great" rather than "Your report is great" or "Everyone likes your report."

Be aware that these immediacy behaviors will be evaluated differently in different cultures. For example, in the United States these immediacy behaviors are generally seen as friendly and appropriate. In other cultures, however, the same immediacy behaviors may be viewed as overly familiar—as presuming that a close relationship exists when it's only one of acquaintanceship. In the United States, to take one specific example, we move rather quickly from Mr. LastName and Ms. LastName to Fred and Ginger. In more formal countries (Japan and Germany are two examples) a much longer period of acquaintanceship would be necessary before first names would be considered appropriate (Axtell, 1993).

Interaction Management

The effective communicator controls the interaction to the satisfaction of both parties. In effective **interaction management,** neither person feels ignored or on stage. Each contributes to the total communication interchange. Maintaining your role as speaker or listener and passing back and forth the opportunity to speak are interaction management skills. If one person speaks all the time and the other listens all the time, effective conversation becomes difficult if not impossible. Depending on the situation, one person may speak more than the other person. This imbalance, however, should occur because of the situation and not because one person is a "talker" and another a "listener."

Generally, effective interaction managers also avoid interrupting the other person. Interruptions often signal that what you have to say is more important than what the other person is saying and put the other person in an inferior position. The result is dissatisfaction with the conversation. In the United States some interruptions may be seen as signs of involvement and interest in the conversation. In other cultures, however, these same interruptions may be seen as rude and insulting. Similarly, effective interaction management includes keeping the conversation flowing and fluent without long and awkward pauses that make everyone uncomfortable.

Another aspect of interaction management is the effective management and control of any signs of nervousness or apprehension. You may want to examine your own apprehension in conversations by taking the self-test "How apprehensive are you in conversations?" at **www.ablongman.com/ devito**. 🖰

Expressiveness

Expressiveness communicates genuine involvement in the interpersonal interaction. The expressive speaker plays the game instead of just watching it as a spectator. Expressiveness is similar to openness in its emphasis on involvement (Cegala, Savage, Brunner, & Conrad, 1982). It includes taking responsibility for your thoughts and feelings, encouraging expressiveness or openness in others, and providing appropriate feedback. Do recognize, however, that here too wide cultural differences exist. For example, in the United States women are expected to participate fully in business discussions and to smile, laugh, and initiate interactions. These behaviors are so expected and seemingly so natural that it seems strange even mentioning them. But in many other countries (Arab countries and many Asian countries) this expressiveness would be considered inappropriate (Lustig & Koester, 1999; Axtell, 1993; Hall & Hall, 1987).

Expressiveness also includes taking responsibility for both talking and listening and in this way is similar to equality. In conflict situations, expressiveness involves fighting actively and stating disagreement directly. It means using I-messages in which you accept responsibility for your thoughts and feelings ("I'm bored when I don't get to talk" or "I want to talk more") rather than you-messages ("You ignore me," "You don't ask my opinion"). It's the opposite of fighting passively, withdrawing from the encounter, or attributing responsibility to others.

You can communicate expressiveness in a variety of ways:

- Practice active listening by paraphrasing, expressing understanding of the thoughts and feelings of the other person, and asking relevant questions (as explained in Unit 5).

- Avoid **clichés**—trite expressions that signal a lack of personal involvement and originality.

- Address mixed messages—messages (verbal or nonverbal) that are communicated simultaneously but that contradict each other.

- Address messages that somehow seem unrealistic to you—for example, statements claiming that the breakup of a long-term relationship is completely forgotten or that failing a course doesn't mean anything.

- Use I-messages to signal personal involvement and a willingness to share your feelings. Instead of saying, "You never give me a chance to make any decisions," say, "I'd like to contribute to the decisions that affect both of us."

- Communicate expressiveness nonverbally by using appropriate variations in vocal rate, pitch, volume, and rhythm to convey involvement and interest, and by allowing your facial muscles to reflect and echo this inner involvement.

- Similarly, use gestures appropriately to communicate involvement. Too few gestures signal disinterest; too many may communicate discomfort, uneasiness, and awkwardness.

Other-Orientation

Some people are primarily self-oriented and talk mainly about themselves, their experiences, their interests, and their desires. They do most of the talking, and they tend to pay little attention to verbal and nonverbal feedback from the other person. **Other-orientation** is the opposite of self-orientation. It involves the ability to communicate attentiveness and interest in the other person and in what is being said. Without other-orientation each person pursues his or her own goal instead of cooperating and working with others to achieve a common goal.

Other-orientation is especially important (and especially difficult) when you're interacting with people who are very different from you; for example, when you are talking with people from other cultures. Here are some methods to improve your other-orientation:

- Use focused eye contact, smiles, and head nods.
- Lean toward the other person.
- Display feelings and emotions through appropriate facial expression.
- Avoid focusing on yourself (as in preening, for example)—or, through frequent or prolonged eye contact or body orientation, on anyone other than the person to whom you're speaking.
- Ask the other person for suggestions, opinions, and clarification as appropriate. Questions such as "How do you feel about it?" or "What do you think?" will go a long way toward focusing the communication on the other person.
- Express agreement when appropriate. Comments such as "You're right" or "That's interesting" help

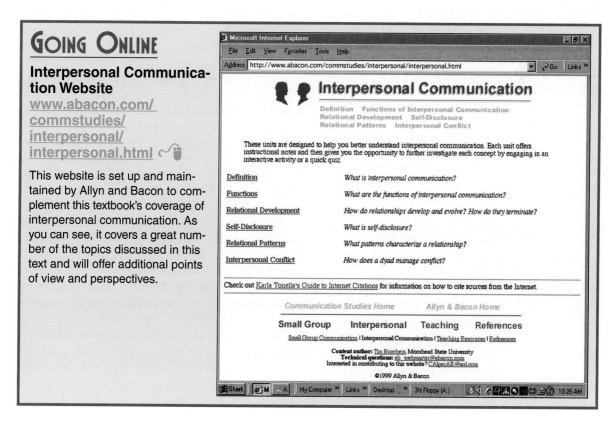

Going Online

Interpersonal Communication Website

www.abacon.com/
commstudies/
interpersonal/
interpersonal.html

This website is set up and maintained by Allyn and Bacon to complement this textbook's coverage of interpersonal communication. As you can see, it covers a great number of the topics discussed in this text and will offer additional points of view and perspectives.

to focus the interaction on the other person, which encourages greater openness.

- Use minimal responses to encourage the other person to express himself or herself. Minimal responses are those brief expressions that encourage another to continue talking without intruding on their thoughts and feelings or directing them to go in any particular direction. For example, "yes," "I see," or even "aha" or "hmm" are minimal responses that tell the other person that you're interested in his or her continued comments.

- Use positive affect statements to refer to the other person and to his or her contributions to the interaction. Comments such as "I really enjoyed your presentation at the department meeting today" or "That was a clever way of looking at things" are positive affect statements that are often felt but rarely expressed.

Other-orientation includes demonstrating consideration and respect—for example, asking if it's all right to dump your troubles on someone before doing so or asking if your phone call comes at an inopportune time before launching into your conversation. Other-orientation also involves acknowledging others' feelings as legitimate: "I can understand why you're so angry; I would be, too."

Now that you've read about conversation, try working actively with some of the concepts and principles through exercises at **www.ablongman. com/devito**. "How Do You Analyze a Conversation?" provides a dialogue for analyzing some of the problems that occur in conversation, and "How Do You Give and Take Directions?" will demonstrate that even "simple" directions often prove difficult.

CONVERSATION PROBLEMS: PREVENTION AND REPAIR

In conversation, you may anticipate a problem and seek to prevent it. Or you may discover that you said or did something that will lead to disapproval, and you may seek to excuse yourself. Here we'll look at one example of a device to prevent potential conversational problems (the disclaimer) and one example of a device to repair conversational problems (the excuse). The purpose of these exam-

ples is simply to illustrate the complexity of these processes and not to present an exhaustive listing of the ways in which conversational problems may be prevented or repaired.

Preventing Conversational Problems: The Disclaimer

Suppose, for example, you fear that your listeners will think your comment is inappropriate in the present context, or that they may rush to judge you without hearing your full account, or that they may wonder if you're not in full possession of your faculties. In these cases, you may use some form of disclaimer. A **disclaimer** is a statement that aims to ensure that your message will be understood and will not reflect negatively on you.

Think about your own use of disclaimers as you read about these five types (Hewitt & Stokes, 1975; McLaughlin, 1984). *Hedging* helps you to separate yourself from the message so that if your listeners reject your message, they won't reject you (for example, "I may be wrong here, but . . ." or "I didn't read the entire book, but it seems that . . ."). *Credentialing* argues that you should not be disqualified for saying what you're about to say (for example, "Don't get me wrong, I'm not homophobic . . ."). *Sin licenses* ask listeners for permission to deviate in some way from some normally accepted convention (for example, "I know this may not be the place to discuss business, but . . ."). *Cognitive disclaimers* help you make the case that you're in full possession of your faculties (for example, "I know you'll think I'm crazy, but let me explain the logic of the case"). *Appeals for the suspension of judgment* ask listeners to hear you out before making a judgment (for example, "Don't hang up on me until you hear my side of the story").

Disclaimers do work in some situations. For example, disclaimers are generally effective when you think you might offend listeners by telling a joke ("I don't usually like these types of jokes, but . . ."). In one study, 11-year-old children were read a story about someone whose actions created negative effects. Some children heard the story with a disclaimer, and others heard the same story without the disclaimer. When the children were asked to indicate how the person should be punished, those who heard the story with the disclaimer recommended significantly lower punishments (Bennett, 1990).

Disclaimers also can get you into trouble, however. For example, to inappropriately preface remarks with "I'm no liar" may well lead listeners to think that perhaps you are a liar. And if you use too many disclaimers, you may be perceived as someone who doesn't have any strong convictions or who wants to avoid responsibility for just about everything. This seems especially true of hedges.

In responding to statements containing disclaimers, it's often necessary to respond both to the disclaimer and to the statement. By doing so, you let the speaker know that you heard the disclaimer and that you aren't going to view this communication negatively. Appropriate responses might be: "I know you're no sexist, but I don't agree that . . ." or "Well, perhaps we should discuss the money now even if it doesn't seem right."

Repairing Conversational Problems: The Excuse

Earlier we examined the concept of irreversibility—the fact that once something is communicated, it cannot be uncommunicated (Unit 2). In part because of this fact, we need at times to defend or justify messages that may be perceived negatively. Perhaps the most common method for doing so is the excuse (Fraser, 2000). Excuses pervade all forms of communication and behavior. Although this discussion emphasizes their role in conversation, recognize that excuses occur in all forms of communication—interpersonal, group, public, and mass. You may at this point want to try your hand at phrasing excuses; see "How Can You Make Excuses?" at www.ablongman.com/devito.

You learn early in life that when you do something that will be perceived negatively, an excuse is needed to justify your poor performance. The excuse usually follows from three conditions (Snyder, 1984):

- You say something.
- Your statement is viewed negatively; you desire to disassociate yourself from it.
- Someone hears the message or the results of the message. The "witness" may be an outsider (for example, a boss, a friend, or a colleague) but also could be yourself—you're a witness to your own messages.

For 6,000 yen a month (about $70), a Japanese cable radio network provides listeners with several "excuse" stations. These stations broadcast background noise; for example, the sound of a train station, coffee shop, or telephone booth. Thus, when you want to have someone believe you're at a train station, you can play the radio while you're on the phone to say that you can't be home on time (*New York Times Magazine*, July 16, 1995, p. 8). What do you think of this service? Would you subscribe to it? Would you invest money in it? Would it be more popular with one gender than the other? Would it be more popular in some cultures than in others?

More formally, Snyder (1984; Snyder, Higgins, & Stucky, 1983) defines **excuses** as "explanations or actions that lessen the negative implications of an actor's performance, thereby maintaining a positive image for oneself and others."

Excuses seem especially in order when we say or are accused of saying something that runs counter to what is expected, sanctioned, or considered "right" by the people involved or by society in general. The excuse, ideally, lessens the negative impact of the message.

Three kinds of excuses can be identified (Snyder, 1984; Snyder, Higgins, & Stucky, 1983). In the *I didn't do it* type, you claim not to have done the behavior of which you're accused: "I didn't say that." "I wasn't even near the place when it happened." In the *It wasn't so bad* type, you claim that the behavior was not really so bad, certainly not as bad as others may at first think: "I only copied one answer." In the *Yes, but* type, you claim that extenuating circumstances accounted for the behavior: "It was the liquor talking." "I really tried to help him; I didn't mean to hurt his feelings."

Some Motives for Excuse Making

The major motive for excuse making seems to be to maintain our self-esteem, to project a positive image to ourselves and to others. Excuses are also offered to reduce the stress that may be created by a bad performance. We feel that if we can offer an excuse—especially a good one that is accepted by those around us—it will lessen the negative reaction and the subsequent stress that accompanies a poor performance.

Anticipatory excuses enable you to take risks and engage in behavior that may be unsuccessful: "My throat's a bit sore, but I'll give the speech a try." The excuse is designed to lessen the criticism should you fail to deliver an acceptable speech.

Excuses also enable us to maintain effective interpersonal relationships even after some negative interaction. For example, after criticizing a friend's behavior and observing the negative reaction to our criticism, we might offer an excuse such as "Please forgive me; I'm really exhausted. I'm just not thinking straight." Excuses enable us to place our messages—even our possible failures—in a more favorable light.

Good and Bad Excuses

To most people the most important question is what makes a good excuse and what makes a bad excuse (Snyder, 1984; Slade, 1995; Schlenker, Pontari, & Christopher, 2001). How can you make good excuses and thus get out of problems, and how can you avoid bad excuses that only make matters worse? Good excuse-makers use excuses in moderation; bad excuse-makers rely on excuses too often. Similarly, unnecessary excuses (which are often disguised attempts to ingratiate yourself) rarely create a positive impression (Levesque, 1995). Good excuse-makers avoid using excuses in the presence of those who know what really happened; bad excusemakers make excuses even in these inopportune situations. Good excuse-makers avoid blaming others, especially those they work with; bad excuse-makers blame even their work colleagues. In a similar way, good excuse-makers don't attribute their failure to others or to the organization; bad excuse-makers do. Good excuse-makers acknowledge their own responsibility for the failure by noting that they did something wrong; bad excuse-makers refuse to accept any responsibility for their failure.

The best excuses are **apologies** because they contain three essential elements for a good excuse (Slade, 1995); they

- acknowledge some of the responsibility
- ask forgiveness
- suggest that things will be done better in the future

The worst excuses are the "I didn't do it" type, because they fail to acknowledge responsibility and offer no assurance that this failure will not happen again.

REFLECTIONS ON ETHICS IN HUMAN COMMUNICATION

Gossip

There can be no doubt that we spend a great deal of time gossiping. In fact, gossiping seems universal among all cultures (Laing, 1993), and among some it's a commonly accepted ritual (Hall, 1993). **Gossip** involves making social evaluations about a person who is not present during the conversation (Eder & Enke, 1991). Gossip generally occurs when two people talk about a third party and profit in some way—for example, get to hear more gossip, gain social status or control, have fun, cement social bonds (Rosnow, 1977; Miller & Wilcox, 1986), or make social comparisons (Leaper & Holliday, 1995).

What would you do? *Laura and Linda have been friends ever since high school and are now competing for the position of sales manager. Laura, Linda knows, has lied on her résumé, claiming much more experience than she really has, and this purported experience is likely to land Laura the position over Linda. Laura's lying on the résumé has not bothered Linda until now—but now it's likely to work against her own promotion. Linda wonders if it would be ethical to let it be known, through informal gossip channels, that Laura doesn't really have all the experience she claims to have. After all, Linda reasons, each person should be judged on the basis of actual accomplishments and experience and not on fabrications. If you were Linda, what would you do? More generally, what ethical obligations do you have in gossiping, as sender and as receiver?*

SUMMARY

In this unit we examined the conversation process from opening to closing; the principles of conversational effectiveness; and conversational problems and their prevention and repair.

1. Conversation consists of five general stages: opening, feedforward, business, feedback, and closing.
2. Conversations can be initiated in various ways; for example, with self, other, relational, and context references.
3. The business of conversation is maintained by the passing of speaking and listening turns; turn-maintaining and turn-yielding cues are used by the speaker, and turn-requesting, turn-denying, and backchanneling cues are used by the listener.
4. The closing of a conversation may be achieved through a variety of methods. For example, you may reflect back on the conversation, as in summarizing; directly state your desire to end the conversation; refer to future interaction; ask for closure; and/or state your pleasure in the interaction.
5. The metaskills of conversational effectiveness include mindfulness, flexibility, and cultural sensitivity (as appropriate).
6. Among the skills of conversational effectiveness are openness, empathy, positiveness, immediacy, interaction management, expressiveness, and other-orientation.
7. One way to avert potential conversational problems is through the disclaimer, a statement that helps ensure that your message will be understood and will not reflect negatively on you.
8. One way to repair a conversational problem is with the excuse, a statement designed to lessen the negative impact of a speaker's messages.

KEY TERMS

conversation	metaskills	interaction management
conversational turns	mindfulness	expressiveness
turn-maintaining cues	flexibility	other-orientation
turn-yielding cues	openness	disclaimer
turn-requesting cues	empathy	excuse
turn-denying cues	positiveness	gossip
backchanneling cues	immediacy	

THINKING CRITICALLY ABOUT

Conversation

1. After reviewing the research on the empathic and listening abilities of men and women, Pearson, West, and Turner (1995) conclude: "Men and women do not differ as much as conventional wisdom would have us believe. In many instances, she thinks like a man, and he thinks like a woman because they both think alike." Does your experience support or contradict this observation?

2. Animal researchers have argued that some animals show empathy. For example, consider the male gorilla who watched a female try in vain to get water that had collected in an automobile tire and who then secured the tire and brought it to the female. This gorilla, it has been argued, demonstrated empathy; he felt the other gorilla's thirst (Angier, 1995). Similarly, the animal who cringes when another of its species gets hurt seems also to be showing empathy. What evidence would you demand before believing that animals possess empathic abilities? What evidence would you want before believing that a relationship partner or a friend feels empathy for you?

3. Try collecting examples of disclaimers from your interpersonal interactions as well as from the media. Consider, for example: What type of disclaimer is being used? Why is it being used? Is the disclaimer appropriate? What other kinds of disclaimers could have been used more effectively?

4. Access ERIC, Medline, PsycINFO, or Sociological Abstracts (databases of citations and abstracts of thousands of articles on communication and education, medicine, psychology, and sociology) and locate an article dealing with some aspect of conversation. What can you learn about conversation and interpersonal communication from this article?

5. Visit one of the many online chat groups and lurk for 5 to 10 minutes. What characterizes the conversation on the channel you observed? What is the topic of conversation? What is the most obvious purpose of the group? If possible, try comparing your reactions with those of others who visited other channels.

6. Another way of looking at conversational rule violations is as breaches of etiquette. A variety of websites focus on etiquette in different communication situations. For general etiquette guidelines see www.westernsilver.com/etiquette.html; for the etiquette of online conversation see www.geocities.com/SouthBeach/Breakders/5257/chatet.htm; for web etiquette see http://www.w3.org/Provider/Style/Etiquette.html; and for dating etiquette see http://www.adolescentadulthood.com/tanya/showarticle.php?id=6. Visit one or more of these websites and record any rules that you find particularly applicable to interpersonal communication and conversation.

7. Research shows that hedging reflects negatively on both men and women when it indicates a lack of certainty or conviction resulting from some inadequacy of the speaker's. Hedging will be more positively received, however, if listeners feel it reflects the speaker's belief that tentative statements are the only kinds that can reasonably be made (Wright & Hosman, 1983; Hosman, 1989; Pearson, West, & Turner, 1995). Do you find this true from your experience in using and listening to hedges?

8. After the World Trade Center and Pentagon attacks comedian Bill Maher criticized the use of "cowardly" to define those who committed these acts. "We have been the cowards lobbing cruise missiles from 2,000 miles away. . . . Staying in the airplane when it hits the building, say what you want about it, that's not cowardly." As a result Sears and FedEx cancelled their ads and various ABC affiliates suspended the program. Actually, as *Business Week Online* (September 26, 2001) notes, Maher was not making a case for the terrorists. On Jay Leno's "Tonight Show," Maher excused his comments, saying that he was not implying that the United States military was cowardly but was simply angry at policymakers for not letting our military personnel do their jobs. What do you think of this excuse? If you were Maher and on the "Tonight Show," what would you have said?

9. **Researching Conversation.** How would you go about answering such questions as these?
   - Do happy and unhappy couples use disclaimers in the same way? Do effective and ineffective managers use disclaimers in the same way?
   - Are people who demonstrate the qualities of effective conversational management better liked than those who don't?
   - Which quality of effectiveness is the most important in communication between health care provider and patient?
   - What role does other-orientation play in first dates?
   - Do men and women use the same kind of excuses?

UNIT 10
Interpersonal Relationships

Unit Contents

Relationship Processes

Relationship Types

Relationship Theories

Much of your life is spent in relationships; friendships, romantic relationships, and family relationships occupy an enormous part of your day-to-day thoughts and experiences. In this unit you'll learn

▶ how relationships can develop, be maintained, deteriorate, and be repaired

▶ how you can make your relationships more satisfying and more productive

You establish your interpersonal relationships in stages. You don't become intimate friends with someone immediately upon meeting. Rather, you grow into an intimate relationship gradually, through a series of steps—from the initial contact, through intimacy, and perhaps on to dissolution. And the same is probably true with most other relationships as well.

In all, six major stages are identifiable (see Figure 10.1): contact, involvement, intimacy, deterioration, repair, and dissolution. Each stage can be divided into an early and a late phase, as noted in the diagram. For each specific relationship, you might wish to modify and revise the basic model in various ways. As a general description of relationship development, however, the stages seem fairly standard. These stages occur in all interpersonal relationships—whether developed and maintained through face-to-face interaction or through Internet hookups.

In fact, so many relationships are begun on the Internet that they need to be integrated into our

Figure 10.1

A Six-Stage Relationship Model

This model of relationships is best viewed as a tool for talking about relationships rather than as a specific map that indicates how you move from one relationship position to another.

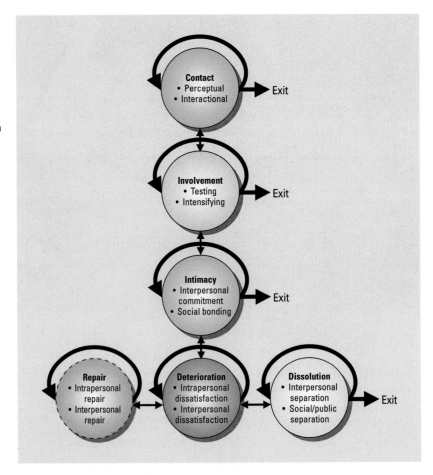

traditional thinking about relationships. The number of Internet users is rapidly increasing, and commercial websites devoted to meeting other people are proliferating, making it especially easy to develop online relationships. Some people now use the Internet as their only means of interaction; others use it as a way of beginning a friendship or romance and intend later to supplement computer talk with photographs, phone calls, and face-to-face meetings. In a 1998 study 36 percent of people responding to a survey established friendships on the Internet, and 22 percent of these defined their online interaction as a "close romantic relationship" (Nice & Katzev, 1998). This study found that among university students the frequency of romantic online relationships was almost 8 percent: approximately 8 students out of 100. Even more interesting is that online relationships were rated superior to those established offline in satisfaction and in ease of communication.

Other researchers found that almost two-thirds of newsgroup users had formed new acquaintances, friendships, or other personal relationships with someone they met on the Internet. Almost one-third said that they communicated with their partner at least three or four times a week; more than half communicated on a weekly basis (Parks & Floyd, 1996). Women, it seems, are more likely to form relationships on the Internet than men. About 72 percent of women and 55 percent of men had formed personal relationships online (Parks & Floyd, 1996). Not surprisingly, those who communicated more frequently formed more relationships.

As relationships develop on the Internet, network convergence occurs; that is, as a relationship develops between two people, they begin to share their network of other communicators with each other (Parks, 1995; Parks & Floyd, 1996). This, of course, is similar to what happens in relationships formed through face-to-face contact.

There are lots of advantages to establishing relationships online. For example, it's safe in terms of avoiding any risk of physical violence or sexually transmitted diseases. Unlike relationships established in face-to-face encounters, in which (initially) physical appearance tends to outweigh personality, Internet relationships let you communicate your inner qualities first. Friendships and romantic interactions on the Internet are a natural boon to shut-ins and the extremely shy, for whom traditional ways of meeting someone are often difficult. Computer talk is more empowering for those with "physical disabilities or disfigurements," for whom face-to-face interactions are often superficial and often end with withdrawal (Lea & Spears, 1995; Bull & Rumsey, 1988). By eliminating the physical cues, computer talk equalizes the interaction and doesn't put the disfigured person, for example, at an immediate disadvantage in a society that values physical attractiveness so highly. Online you're free to reveal as much or as little about your physical self as you wish, when you wish. Another obvious advantage is that the number of people you can reach is so vast that it's relatively easy to find someone who matches what you're looking for. The situation is like finding a book that covers just what you need from a library of millions of volumes rather than from one of only several thousand. Still another advantage for many is that the socio-economic and educational status of people on the Net is significantly higher than you're likely to find in a bar or singles group.

But of course there are also disadvantages. For one thing, you can't see the person; unless you exchange photos or meet face-to-face, you won't know what the person looks like. And even if photos are exchanged, how certain can you be that the photos are of the person or that they were taken recently? In addition, you can't hear the other person's voice, and this too hinders you in formulating a total picture. Of course, you can always add an occasional phone call to give you this added information.

Online, people can present a false self with little chance of detection. For example, minors may present themselves as adults—and adults may present themselves as children for illicit and illegal sexual communications and, perhaps, meetings. Similarly, people can present themselves as poor when they're rich, as mature when they're immature, as serious and committed when they're just enjoying the experience. Recently it was discovered that one of the most sought-after legal "experts" on the AskMe.com website was a self-taught 15-year-old (Lewis, 2001).

Another potential disadvantage—though some might argue it is actually an advantage—is the fact that computer interactions may become all consuming and may substitute for face-to-face interpersonal relationships. But recent studies seem to show that this may not be true. For example, regu-

MEDIA WATCH

PARASOCIAL RELATIONSHIPS

Parasocial relationships are relationships that TV or film viewers perceive themselves to have with a media personality (Rubin & McHugh, 1987). Some viewers develop these imaginary relationships with real media personalities—Rosie O'Donnell, Regis Philbin, Oprah Winfrey, or Matt Lauer, for example. As a result they may watch these people faithfully and communicate with them in their own imaginations. Other viewers form parasocial relationships with fictional characters—a doctor on *ER,* a lawyer on *Ally McBeal,* or a police officer on *Third Watch.* In fact, actors who portray doctors frequently get mail asking for medical advice. And soap opera stars who are about to be "killed" frequently get warning letters from their parasocial relationship fans. (Obviously, most people don't go quite this far.)

The chat sessions that celebrities hold on the Internet (usually on one of the commercial carriers, such as AOL or MSN) help further create the illusion of a real interpersonal relationship. And the screen savers of television performers make it difficult not to think of these people in relationship terms when they face you every time you leave your computer idle for a few minutes.

Parasocial relationships begin with an initial attraction to the media figure's social and task roles, then develop into a perceived relationship and finally into a sense that this relationship is an important one (Rubin & McHugh, 1987). The more you can predict the behavior of a character, the more likely you are to develop a parasocial relationship with that character (Perse & Rubin, 1989). As can be expected, these parasocial relationships are most important to individuals who spend a great deal of time with the media, have few real-life interpersonal relationships, and are generally anxious (Rubin, Perse, & Powell, 1985; Cole & Leets, 1999).

Follow-Up. *Some research indicates that parasocial relationships actually facilitate interpersonal interaction (May, 1999). How might parasocial relationships facilitate interpersonal interaction? Can you think of how parasocial relationships might hinder interpersonal interaction?*

---

lar Internet users were found to have more offline social interactions than nonusers and reported that they had a significantly larger number of friends and relatives to go to in time of need. Further, only 8 percent of Internet users reported that they felt socially isolated, whereas 18 percent of nonusers reported feelings of social isolation (Raney, 2000).

Another disadvantage of developing online relationships is that you may become unforgiving of what you see as deficiencies in the other person because there are so many others out there (Cohen, 2001). As a result you may spend all your time looking for an ideal that may not exist. In offline relationships you have many fewer choices, so you may be more likely to deal with the deficiencies (or any problems in the relationship) rather than giving up and moving on to someone else.

All relationships (including parasocial relationships, discussed in the Media Watch box) will bring both advantages and disadvantages; in an imperfect world, that's to be expected. The insights and skills of interpersonal communication and relationships, however, should stack the odds in favor of greater and longer-lived advantages and fewer and shorter-lived disadvantages.

RELATIONSHIP PROCESSES

Relationship processes include those of development (the contact, involvement, and intimacy stages noted in the six-stage model presented in Figure 10.1); deterioration and dissolution; **maintenance** (in which you maintain a certain level of involvement—neither moving toward more intimacy nor moving toward deterioration); and repair (both of the relationship and of yourself). During your reading of this section take a look at the self-test "What do you believe about relationships?" at www.ablongman.com/devito.

The models and explanations of interpersonal relationships presented in this unit come mainly from research conducted in the United States and reflect the way relationships are generally viewed in the United States. So it's important to pause and consider some of the ways in which this reporting is culturally biased. For example, we assume—in the model and in the discussion of relationship development—that we voluntarily choose our relationship partners. In some cultures, however, your parents choose your romantic partner, perhaps to solidify two families or to bring some financial advantage to your family or village.

Similarly, in the United States researchers study, and textbook authors write about, dissolving relationships and how to manage after a relationship breaks up. We assume that the individual has the right to exit an undesirable relationship. But that's not always true. In some cultures you simply can't dissolve a relationship once it's formed or once there are children. In other cultures only the man may dissolve a relationship.

In most of the United States, interpersonal friendships are drawn from a relatively large pool. Out of all the people you come into regular contact with, you choose relatively few as friends. And now with computer chat groups, the number of friends you can have has increased enormously, as has the range of people from which you can choose these friends. In rural areas and in small villages throughout much of the world, however, you would have very few choices. The two or three other children your age would become your friends; there would be no real choice, because these would be the only possible friends you could make.

A cultural bias is also seen in the research on relationship maintenance: It's assumed that relationships should be permanent or at least long lasting. It's also assumed that people want to keep relationships together. There's little research that studies how people move from one intimate relationship to another or that advises you how to do this effectively and efficiently. Further discussion of the impact of culture and gender on relationships may be found at www.ablongman.com/devito : See "Culture, Gender, and Friendship" and "Culture, Gender, and Love."

Relationship Development

There's probably nothing as important to most people than contact with others. So important is this contact that when it's absent for prolonged periods, depression sets in, self-doubt surfaces, and people find it difficult to conduct even the basics of daily living. **Relationship development** includes the initial **contact** stage as well as increasing **involvement** and **intimacy**.

Reasons for Relationship Development

Each person pursues a relationship for unique reasons, of course. Yet there are also some general reasons for developing relationships: to lessen loneliness, to secure stimulation, to acquire self-knowledge, and to maximize pleasures and minimize pain.

Think about the development of your own relationships as you read on. Are the reasons described here adequate to explain why you've developed the relationships you did? Are there other reasons that motivated your relationships that are not noted here?

One reason we enter relationships is that contact with another human being helps lessen loneliness. It doesn't always, of course. At times, for example, you may experience loneliness even though you're with other people. And at other times you don't feel lonely even when physically alone (Perlman & Peplau, 1981). Yet generally, contact with other people helps lessen the uncomfortable feelings of loneliness (Peplau & Perlman, 1982; Rubenstein & Shaver, 1982).

Human beings need stimulation, and interpersonal relationships provide one of the best ways to get this stimulation. Because you are in part an intellectual creature and need intellectual stimulation, you talk about ideas, attend classes, and argue about different interpretations of a film or novel. Because you're also a physical creature and need physical stimulation, you touch and are touched, hold and are held. Because you're an emotional creature and need emotional stimulation, you laugh and cry, feel hope and surprise, and experience warmth and affection. Such stimulation comes most easily within an interpersonal relationship—a friendship, love, or family relationship.

It's largely through contact with other human beings that you gain self-knowledge. As noted in the discussion of self-awareness (Unit 6), you see yourself in part through the eyes of others. And those with the best eyesight are usually your friends, lovers, or family members.

The most general reason to establish relationships, and one that could include all the others, is that we seek human contact to maximize our pleasures and minimize our pains. Most people want to share with others both their good fortune and their emotional or physical pain. Our first impulse, when something extreme happens (positive or negative), is often to talk about it to a relationship partner.

Initiating Relationships: The First Encounter

Perhaps the hardest and yet the most important aspect of relationship development is the beginning. Meeting the person, presenting yourself, and somehow moving to another stage is a difficult process. Three major phases can be identified in the first encounter: examining the qualifiers, determining clearance, and communicating your desire for contact.

Your first step is to examine the *qualifiers,* those qualities that make the individual you wish to meet an appropriate choice (Davis, 1973). Some qualifiers are obvious, such as beauty, style of clothes, jewelry, and the like. Others are hidden, such as personality, health, wealth, talent, and intelligence. These qualifiers tell you something about who the person is and help you to decide if you wish to pursue this initial encounter.

Your second step is to determine *clearance*—to see if the person is available for the type of meeting you're interested in (Davis, 1973). If you're hoping for a date, then you might look to see if the person is wearing a wedding ring. Does the person seem to be waiting for someone else?

The next stage is to make *contact.* You need to open the encounter nonverbally and verbally. Nonverbally you might signal this desire for contact in a variety of ways. Here are just a few things you might do:

- Establish eye contact. The eyes communicate awareness of and interest in the other person.

- While maintaining eye contact, smile and further signal your interest in and positive response to the other person.

- Concentrate your focus. Nonverbally shut off from your awareness the rest of the room. Be careful, however, that you don't focus so directly that you make the person uncomfortable.

- Establish physical closeness, or at least lessen the physical distance between the two of you. Approach the other person, though not to the point of discomfort, so your interest in making contact is obvious.

- Maintain an open posture. Throughout the encounter, maintain a posture that communicates a willingness to enter into interaction with the other person. Hands crossed over the chest or clutched around your stomach communicate a closedness, an unwillingness to let others enter your space.

- Reinforce the positive behaviors of the other person so as to signal continued interest and a further willingness to make contact. Again, nod, smile, or somehow communicate your favorable reaction.

Although nonverbal contact is signaled first, much of the subsequent nonverbal contact takes place at the same time that you're communicating verbally. Here are some methods for making verbal contact:

- Introduce yourself. Try to avoid trite opening lines, such as "Haven't I seen you here before?" It's best simply to say, "Hi, my name is Pat."

- Focus the conversation on the other person. Get the other person talking about himself or herself. No one enjoys talking about any topic more than this one. Also, you'll gain an opportunity to learn something about the person you want to get to know. For example, hidden qualifiers, or disqualifiers, such as intelligence or the lack of it, will begin to emerge.

- Exchange favors and rewards. Compliment the other person. If you can't find anything to compliment, then you might want to reassess your interest in this person.

- Stress the positives. Positiveness contributes to a good first impression simply because people are more attracted to positive than to negative people.

- Avoid self-disclosures that are negative or too intimate. Enter a relationship gradually and gracefully. Disclosures should come slowly and should be reciprocal (see Unit 6). Anything too intimate or too negative, when revealed too early in the relationship, will create a negative image. If you can't resist self-disclosing, try to stick to the positives and to issues that are not overly intimate.

- Establish commonalities. Seek to discover in your interaction those things you have in common with the other person—attitudes, interests,

BUILDING COMMUNICATION SKILLS

How Can You Get Someone to Like You?

One way to make yourself more attractive to another person is to use a broad class of behaviors known as **affinity-seeking strategies** (Bell & Daly, 1984; Frymier & Thompson, 1992). For example, it's been found that when teachers use these affinity-seeking strategies, students evaluate them as being more competent than teachers who don't use the strategies (Prisbell, 1994). Students also come to like the instructors who use affinity-seeking strategies (an indication that these strategies work) and feel they're learning more (Roach, 1991). As you read down the list of these strategies, try to develop one way in which you could use each strategy.

▶ Altruism: Be of help to Other.

▶ Control: Appear to be "in control"—to be a leader, a person who takes charge.

▶ Equality: Present yourself as socially equal to Other.

▶ Comfortable self: Present yourself as comfortable and relaxed when with Other.

▶ Dynamism: Appear active, enthusiastic, and dynamic.

▶ Disclosures: Stimulate and encourage Other to talk about himself or herself; reinforce the disclosures and contributions of Other.

▶ Inclusion of Other: Include Other in your social activities and groupings.

▶ Listening: Listen to Other attentively and actively.

▶ Openness: Engage in self-disclosure with Other.

▶ Optimism: Appear optimistic and positive rather than pessimistic and negative.

▶ Self-concept confirmation: Show respect for Other and help Other to feel positively about himself or herself.

▶ Self-inclusion: Arrange circumstances so that you and Other come into frequent contact.

▶ Sensitivity: Communicate warmth and empathy to Other.

▶ Similarity: Demonstrate that you share significant attitudes and values with Other.

▶ Trustworthiness: Appear to Other as honest and reliable.

---

personal qualities, third parties, places—anything that will stress a connection.

Relationship Deterioration

The opposite end of relationship development is **deterioration** and possible dissolution. Relational deterioration, the weakening of the bonds that hold people together, may be gradual or sudden, slight or extreme. Murray Davis (1973), in his book *Intimate Relations,* uses the terms "passing away" to designate gradual deterioration and "sudden death" to designate abrupt deterioration. An example of passing away occurs when one of the parties develops close ties with a new intimate and this new relationship gradually pushes out the old. An example of sudden death occurs when one or both of the parties

break a rule that was essential to the relationship (for example, the rule of fidelity). As a result, both realize that the relationship must be terminated immediately.

Although you may be accustomed to thinking of relationship breakup as negative, this is not necessarily so. If a relationship is unproductive for one or both parties, a breakup may be the best thing that could happen. The end of a relationship may provide an opportunity for the individuals to regain their independence and self-reliance. Some relationships are so absorbing that there's little time for the partners to reflect about themselves, others, and the relationship itself. In these cases, distance often helps. For the most part, it's up to you to draw from any decaying relationship some positive characteristics and some learning that can be used later on.

Causes of Relationship Deterioration

The causes of **relationship deterioration** are as numerous as the individuals involved. All these causes may also be seen as effects of relational deterioration. For example, when things start to go sour, the individuals may remove themselves physically from each other in response to the deterioration. This physical separation may in turn cause further deterioration by driving the individuals farther apart emotionally and psychologically. Or it may encourage them to seek other partners. Gossip and news items frequently note what might be called "relationship addiction": a tendency among some people to move rapidly from one relationship to another to another. Exactly how widespread this is hasn't been documented. But some researchers have argued that anonymity, convenience, and ease of escape (ACE) make these fleeting relationships especially easy to enter, and that such encounters can take up a significant part of a person's relationship life (Young, et al., 2000).

When the reasons you developed the relationship change drastically, your relationship may deteriorate. For example, when loneliness is no longer lessened, the relationship may be on the road to decay. When the stimulation is weak, one or both may begin to look elsewhere. If self-knowledge and self-growth prove insufficient, you may become dissatisfied with yourself, your partner, and your relationship. When the pains (costs) begin to exceed the pleasures (rewards), you begin to look for ways to exit the relationship or in some cases ways to improve or repair it.

Relational changes in one or both parties may encourage relational deterioration. Psychological changes such as the development of different intellectual interests or incompatible attitudes may create relational problems. Behavioral changes such as preoccupation with business or schooling may strain the relationship and create problems. Status changes may also create difficulties for a couple.

Sometimes one or both parties have unrealistic expectations. This often occurs early in a relationship—when, for example, individuals often think that they will want to spend all their time together. When they discover that both of them need more "space," each may resent this "lessening" of feeling in the other. The resolution of such conflicts lies not so much in meeting these unrealistic expectations as in discovering why they were unrealistic and substituting more attainable expectations.

Few sexual relationships are free of sexual difficulties. In fact, sexual problems rank among the top three problems in almost all studies of newlyweds (Blumstein & Schwartz, 1983). Although sexual frequency is not related to relational breakdown, sexual satisfaction is. It's the quality and not the quantity of a sexual relationship that is crucial. When the quality is poor, the partners may seek sexual satisfaction outside the primary relationship. Extrarelational affairs contribute significantly to breakups for all couples, whether married or cohabiting, whether heterosexual or homosexual. Even "open relationships"—ones that are based on sexual freedom outside the primary relationship—experience these problems and are more likely to break up than the traditional "closed" relationship.

Unhappiness with work often leads to difficulties in relationships. Most people can't separate problems with work from their relationships (Blumstein & Schwartz, 1983). This is true for all types of couples. With heterosexual couples (both married and cohabiting), if the man is disturbed over the woman's job—for example, if she earns a great deal more than he does or devotes a great deal of time to the job—the relationship is in for considerable trouble. And this is true whether the relationship is in its early stages or is well established. One research study, for example, found that husbands whose wives worked were less satisfied with their own jobs and their own lives than were men whose wives did not work (Staines, Pottick, & Fudge, 1986). Often the man expects the woman to work but does not reduce his expectations concerning her household responsibilities. The man may become resentful if the woman does not fulfill these expectations, and the woman may become resentful if she takes on both outside work and full household duties.

In surveys of problems among couples, financial difficulties loom large. Money is seldom discussed by couples beginning a relationship—yet it proves to be one of the major problems faced by all couples as they settle into their relationship. Dissatisfaction with money usually leads to dissatisfaction with the relationship. This is true for married and cohabiting heterosexual couples and gay male couples. It's not true for lesbian couples, who seem to care a great deal less about financial matters. This

Romance in the Workplace

Love is a gross exaggeration of the difference between one person and everyone else.

—George Bernard Shaw

O pinions vary widely concerning workplace romances. On the positive side, the work environment seems a perfect place to meet a potential romantic partner. After all, by virtue of the fact that you're working in the same office, you're probably both interested in the same field, have similar training and ambitions, and spend considerable time together—all factors that foster the development of a successful interpersonal relationship.

If you're romantically attracted to another worker, it can make going to work, working together, and even working added hours more enjoyable and more satisfying. If the relationship is mutually satisfying, you're likely to develop empathy for each other and act in ways that are supportive, cooperative, friendly, and thus beneficial to the organization.

On the negative side, even when the relationship is good for the lovers, it may not necessarily be good for other workers. Others may see the couple as a team that has to be confronted as a pair; they may feel that to criticize one partner would be to incur the wrath of the other. Such relationships may also cause problems for management—for example, when a promotion is to be made or when relocation decisions are necessary. Can you legitimately ask one lover to move to Boston and the other to move to San Francisco? Will it prove difficult for management to promote one lover to a supervisory position over the other?

The workplace also puts pressure on the individuals. Most organizations, at least in the United States, are highly competitive; one person's success often means another's failure. In this environment, a romantic couple may find that the normal self-disclosures of intimacy (which often reveal weaknesses, doubts, and misgivings) may actually prove a liability.

Of course, when the romance goes bad or when it's one-sided, it can be stressful for the individuals to see each other regularly and perhaps even to work together. And other workers may feel they have to take sides, being supportive of one partner and critical of the other. This can easily cause friction throughout the organization.

Thinking about Your Communicating @ Work

What other advantages and disadvantages can you identify for workplace romances? Do these same advantages and disadvantages hold for workplace friendships? Would you be likely to enter into a workplace romance? What reasons might you give to justify your decision?

difference has led some researchers to speculate that tendencies to equate money with power and relational satisfaction represent largely male attitudes (Blumstein & Schwartz, 1983).

Money also creates problems in heterosexual relationships because men and women view it differently. To many men, money is power. To women, it more often means security and independence.

Such different perceptions can easily precipitate conflicts over how a couple's money is to be spent or invested (Blumstein & Schwartz, 1983).

Communication in Relationship Deterioration

Like relational development, relational deterioration involves unique and specialized communication. These communication patterns are in part a response to the deterioration itself. However, these patterns are also causative; that is, the way you communicate influences the course of a relationship.

Nonverbally, **withdrawal** is seen in the greater space each person seems to require and the ease with which tempers are aroused when that space is encroached on. When people are close emotionally, they can comfortably occupy close physical quarters; when they're growing apart, they need wider spaces. Withdrawal of another kind may be seen in a decrease in similarities in clothing and in a decline in the display of "intimate trophies" such as bracelets, photographs, and rings (Knapp & Vangelisti, 2000). Other nonverbal signs include failure to engage in eye contact, to look at each other generally, or to touch each other (Miller & Parks, 1982).

Verbally, withdrawal is seen in many different forms. Where once there was a great desire to talk and listen, there's now less desire—perhaps none. At times small talk is engaged in as an end in itself. Whereas small talk is usually a preliminary to serious conversation, here it's used as an alternative to or a means of forestalling serious talk. Thus people in the throes of dissolution may talk a great deal about insignificant events—the weather, a movie on television, a neighbor down the hall. By focusing on these topics, they avoid confronting serious issues.

Self-disclosure declines significantly when a relationship deteriorates. Self-disclosure may not be thought worth the effort if the relationship is dying. Or people may also limit self-disclosures because they feel that their partner will not be supportive or may use the disclosures against them. Probably the most general reason is that people no longer have a desire to share intimate thoughts and feelings with someone for whom their positive feelings are decreasing.

Deception generally increases as relationships break down. Lies may be seen as a way to avoid arguments—such as quarrels over staying out all night, not calling, or being seen in the wrong place with the wrong person. At other times lies are used because of some feeling of shame. Perhaps you want to save the relationship and don't want to add another obstacle or to appear to be the cause of any further problems, so you lie. Sometimes deception takes the form of avoidance—the lie of omission. You talk about everything except the crux of the dif-ficulty. Whether by omission or commission, deception has a way of escalating and creating a climate of distrust and disbelief.

Relational deterioration often brings an increase in negative evaluations and a decrease in positive evaluations. Where once you praised the other's behaviors, talents, or ideas, you now criticize them. Often the behaviors have not changed significantly. What has changed is your way of looking at them. Negative evaluation frequently leads to outright fighting and conflict. And although conflict is not necessarily bad (see Unit 11), in relationships that are deteriorating, unresolved conflict (often coupled with withdrawal) frequently adds to the partners' problems.

Finally, during relational deterioration there's little favor exchange. Compliments, once given frequently and sincerely, are now rare. Positive stroking is minimal. Positive nonverbal behaviors such as eye contact, smiling, touching, caressing, and holding each other occur less frequently.

Relationship Maintenance

Relationship maintenance consists of the relationship processes in which you act to keep the relationship

- *intact*—to retain the semblance of a relationship, to prevent completely dissolving the relationship
- *at its present stage*—to prevent it from moving too far toward either less or more intimacy
- *satisfying*—to maintain a favorable balance between rewards and penalties

Some people, after entering a relationship, assume that the relationship will continue unless something catastrophic happens. And so, although they may seek to prevent any major mishaps, they're unlikely to engage in much maintenance behavior. Others will be ever on the lookout for something wrong and will seek to patch up any difficulties as quickly and as effectively as possible. In between lie most people, who will engage in maintenance behaviors when things are going wrong and when there's the possibility that the relationship can be improved. Behaviors directed at improving badly damaged or even broken relationships are considered under the topic of "repair," later in this unit.

Reasons for Maintaining a Relationship

The most obvious reason for maintaining a relationship is that the individuals have an emotional attachment; they like or love each other and want to preserve their relationship. They don't find potential alternative partnerships as inviting or as potentially enjoyable—the individuals' needs are being satisfied, so the relationship is maintained.

Often a relationship involves neither great love nor great need satisfaction but is maintained for reasons of convenience. Perhaps the partners may jointly own a business or may have mutual friends who are important to them. In these cases it may be more convenient to stay together than to break up and go through the difficulties involved in finding another person to live with or another business partner or another social escort. Another factor is children; relationships are often maintained, rightly or wrongly, because children are involved.

Fear motivates many couples to stay together. The individuals may fear the outside world; they may fear being alone and facing others as "singles." As a result they may elect to preserve their current relationship as the better alternative. Sometimes the fear concerns the consequences of violating some religious or parental tenet that tells you to stay together, no matter what happens.

Financial advantages motivate many couples to stick it out. Divorces and separations are expensive both emotionally and financially. Some people fear a breakup that may cost them half their wealth or even more. And, depending on where the individuals live and their preferred lifestyle, being single can be expensive.

A major reason for the preservation of many relationships is inertia—in physics, the tendency for a body at rest to remain at rest and for a body in motion to remain in motion. In terms of relationships, many people simply go along with the program, and it hardly occurs to them to consider changing their status; change seems too much trouble. Inertia is greatly aided by the media and the Internet. That is, it's easier for many individuals to remain in their present relationship and to seek vicarious satisfactions from television dramas or chat room interactions than to act to change their circumstances.

UNDERSTANDING THEORY AND RESEARCH

Relationship Commitment

An important factor influencing the course of relationship deterioration (as well as relationship maintenance) is the degree of commitment the individuals have toward each other and toward the relationship. Our level of commitment depends on our answers to such questions as these: Do I want to stay in this relationship? Do I have a moral obligation to stay in this relationship? Do I have to stay in this relationship—are there no acceptable alternatives? (Johnson, 1973, 1982, 1991; Knapp & Taylor, 1995; Kurdek, 1995). All relationships are held together, in part, by one or some combination of these elements of desire, obligation, and/or necessity. And the strength of the relationship, including its resistance to possible deterioration, is also related to this degree of commit-

ment. When a relationship shows signs of deterioration and yet there's a strong commitment to preserving it, the individuals may well surmount the obstacles and reverse the process. When commitment is weak and the individuals doubt that there are good reasons for staying together, the relationship deteriorates faster and more intensely. For an interesting self-test, "How Committed Are You?" visit www.ablongman.com/devito.

Working with Theories and Research. *How does commitment figure into your own friendships and romantic relationships? Has commitment or the lack of it (from either or both of you) ever influenced the progression of one of your relationships? What happened?*

Maintenance Strategies

Among the most significant **maintenance strategies** used in relationships are those of **relational communication.** The kind of relational communication that effectively helps maintain a relationship is the same as that described for effective conversation: It is open, empathic, positive, immediate, managed effectively, expressive, and other-oriented, and it is performed mindfully, flexibly, and with

cultural sensitivity (Unit 9). Add to these qualities the skills of appropriate self-disclosure, active listening, and confirmation—and in fact all the skills considered throughout this text—and you have a pretty comprehensive list of potentially useful communication tools for maintaining a relationship.

Other maintenance strategies include the following (Ayres, 1983; Canary & Stafford, 1994a, 1994b; Dindia & Baxter, 1987; Canary, Stafford, Hause, &

UNDERSTANDING THEORY AND RESEARCH

Relationship Dialectics

An interesting theory of relationships, **relationship dialectics theory,** argues that people in a relationship experience dynamic tensions between opposite motives or desires. Research generally finds three key pairs of opposites (Baxter, 1988, 1990; Baxter & Simon, 1993; Rawlins, 1989, 1992). The tension between *closedness and openness* has to do with your desire to be in a closed, exclusive relationship or, at the other extreme, in a relationship that is open to different people. This closedness–openness tension is especially in evidence during the early stages of relationship development. The tension between *autonomy and connection* involves your desire to remain an autonomous, independent individual but also to connect intimately to another person and to a relationship. This theme, by the way, has been found to be popular in women's magazines, which teach readers to want both autonomy and connection (Prusank, Duran, & DeLillo, 1993). The tension between *novelty and predictability* centers on your desire for newness, different experiences, and adventure on the one hand and sameness, stability, and predictability on the other. Both the autonomy–connection and the novelty–predictability tensions are more in evidence as the relationship progresses.

Each individual in the relationship will experience a somewhat different set of desires. One person may want exclusivity and another want openness. In some cases a happy combination can be negotiated; in other instances these dif-

ferences are irreconcilable, with the result that the couple become dissatisfied with their relationship or dissolve it.

Desires change as the relationship progresses. For example, at the beginning of a romantic relationship, partners often want to spend all their time together, always connected. As the relationship newness wears off, however, the need for greater autonomy may surface.

Perhaps the major implication of relationship dialectics theory is that these tensions will influence a wide variety of behaviors. For example, the person who finds the primary relationship overwhelmingly predictable may seek novelty elsewhere, perhaps with a different partner, perhaps with a vacation to exotic places. The person who finds the primary relationship too connected may need physical and psychological space to meet his or her autonomy needs. Meeting your partner's needs—insofar as possible, given your own needs—is one of the major challenges in maintaining a relationship.

Working with Theories and Research. *How do your needs for closedness–openness, autonomy–connection, and novelty–predictability influence your own relationship behavior? For example, how do these needs influence the type of partner you look for? How do they influence your responsiveness to the needs of your friends or your romantic partner?*

Wallace, 1993; Dainton & Stafford, 1993; Guerrero, Eloy, & Wabnik, 1993):

- *Prosocial behaviors:* Being polite, cheerful, and friendly; avoiding criticism; and compromising even when it involves self-sacrifice. Prosocial behaviors also include talking about a shared future; for example, talking about planning a future vacation or buying a house together.

- *Ceremonial behaviors:* Celebrating birthdays and anniversaries, discussing past pleasurable times, and eating at a favorite restaurant.

- *Communication behaviors:* Calling just to say, "How are you?," talking about the honesty and openness in the relationship, and talking about shared feelings. Responding constructively in a conflict (even when your partner may act in ways harmful to the relationship) is another type of communicative maintenance strategy (Rusbult & Buunk, 1993).

- *Togetherness behaviors:* Spending time together visiting mutual friends, doing specific things as a couple, and sometimes just being together with no concern for what is done. Controlling extra-relational activities constitutes another type of togetherness behavior (Rusbult & Buunk, 1993).

- *Assurance behaviors:* Assuring the other of the significance of the relationship; for example, comforting each other, putting the partner first, and expressing love for the person.

- *Sharing joint activities:* Spending time with the other; for example, playing ball together, going to events together, simply talking, or even cleaning the house together.

- *Using social networks:* Relying on friends and relatives for support and help with various problems.

Researchers have also identified such strategies as openness (engaging in direct discussion); humor (making jokes or teasing the other); talk (engaging in small talk and establishing specific times for talking); affection, including sexual intimacy (acting affectionately and romantically); and focus on self (making oneself look good) (Canary, Stafford, Hause, & Wallace, 1993; Dainton & Stafford, 1993).

Relationship Repair

When a relationship begins to deteriorate, you may wish to try to save it by repairing the problems and differences. Sometimes, too, you'll suffer emotional damage from relationships and may need to repair yourself. Each of these types of **relationship repair** is considered here.

Interpersonal Repair

If you wish to salvage a relationship, you may try to do so by changing your communication patterns and, in effect, putting into practice the insights and skills learned in this course. You can look at the strategies for interpersonal repair in terms of the following six suggestions, which conveniently spell out the word REPAIR:

<u>R</u>ecognize the problem

<u>E</u>ngage in productive conflict resolution

<u>P</u>ropose possible solutions

<u>A</u>ffirm each other

<u>I</u>ntegrate solutions into normal behavior

<u>R</u>isk

Your first step is to *recognize the problem* and to recognize it both intellectually and emotionally. Specify what is wrong with your present relationship (in concrete, specific terms) and what changes would be needed to make it better (again, in specific terms). Without this first step there's little hope for improving any interpersonal relationship. It sometimes helps to create a picture of your relationship as you would want it to be and to compare that picture to the way the relationship looks now. You can then specify the changes that would have to take place to transform the present picture into the idealized picture.

Engage in productive conflict resolution. Interpersonal conflict is an inevitable part of relationship life. It's not so much the conflict that causes relationship difficulties but rather the way in which the conflict is pursued. If the partners confront a conflict by means of productive strategies, the conflict may be resolved and the relationship may actually emerge stronger and healthier. If, on the other hand, the partners use unproductive and destructive strategies, the relationship may well deteriorate further. Because this topic is so crucial, Unit 11 is devoted exclusively to the process of conflict and especially to the ways people can engage in productive interpersonal conflict.

After the problem is identified, *propose possible solutions* to identify ways to lessen or eliminate the

BUILDING COMMUNICATION SKILLS

How Can You Talk Cherishing?

Cherishing behaviors are an especially insightful way to affirm another person and to increase favor exchange, a concept that comes from the work of William Lederer (1984). **Cherishing behaviors** are those small gestures you enjoy receiving from your partner (a smile, a wink, a squeeze, a kiss). If you think this idea has merit, consider exchanging cherishing behaviors with a partner—a lover, best friend, or sibling, for example. You would each make a list of, say, 10 behaviors that you'd like to receive from your partner—on occasion and as appropriate. Identify cherishing behaviors that are (1) specific and positive—nothing

overly general or negative; (2) focused on the present and future rather than related to issues about which you may have argued in the past; (3) capable of being performed daily; and (4) easily executed—nothing you really have to go out of your way to accomplish. Once you had each prepared your list, you would exchange them and, ideally, perform the cherishing behaviors your partner would like. At first these behaviors might seem self-conscious and awkward. In time, however, they'd become a normal part of your interaction, which is exactly what you would hope to achieve.

difficulty. Look for solutions that will enable both of you to win. Try to avoid "solutions" whereby one person wins and the other person loses; in such circumstances resentment and hostility are likely to fester. The suggestions offered in Unit 13's discussion of problem-solving groups are especially applicable to this phase of relationship repair.

It should come as no surprise that happily married couples *affirm each other*. That is, they engage in greater positive behavior exchange—they communicate more agreement, approval, and positive affect—than do unhappily married couples (Dindia & Fitzpatrick, 1985). Clearly, these behaviors result from the positive feelings these spouses have for each other. But it can also be argued that these expressions help to increase the positive regard that each person has for his or her partner. Other affirming messages include the exchange of favors, compliments, positive stroking, and all the nonverbals that say "I care."

Often solutions that are reached after an argument are followed for only a very short time; then the couple goes back to its previous unproductive behavior patterns. Instead, *integrate solutions into your normal behavior* so that the solutions become integral to your everyday relationship interactions. Favors, compliments, and cherishing behaviors need to become a part of everyday communication.

Risk. Take risks in trying to improve your relationship. Risk giving favors without any certainty of reciprocity. Risk rejection; make the first move to make up or say you're sorry. Be willing to change, to adapt, and to take on new tasks and responsibilities. And, of course, be willing to try new and different communication strategies.

An exercise, "How Can You Repair Relationships?" will enable you to apply some of these insights to specific situations and is available at www.ablongman.com/devito.

Self-Repair

Of course, some relationships end. Sometimes there's simply not enough to hold the couple together or there are problems that can't be resolved. Sometimes the costs are too high and the rewards too few, or the relationship is recognized as destructive and escape seems the only alternative. Given the inevitability that some relationships will end in **dissolution**, here are some suggestions for self-repair to ease the difficulty that is sure to follow. These suggestions can apply to the termination of any type of relationship, whether between friends or lovers or through death, separation, or marital breakup. I shall use the language of romantic breakups, however, because these are the ones we deal with most frequently.

Break the loneliness–depression cycle. Loneliness and depression, the two feelings experienced most after the end of a relationship, are serious. Depression, for example, may lead to physical illness. Ulcers, high blood pressure, insomnia, stomach pains, and sexual difficulties frequently accompany or are seriously aggravated by depression. In most cases loneliness and depression are temporary. Your task then is to eliminate or lessen these uncomfortable and potentially dangerous feelings by changing the situation. When depression does last or proves particularly upsetting, it's time to seek professional help.

Take time out. Take time out for yourself. Renew your relationship with yourself. If you were in a long-term relationship, you probably saw yourself as part of a team, as part of a couple. Now get to know yourself as a unique individual, standing alone now but fully capable of entering a meaningful relationship in the near future.

Bolster your self-esteem. When relationships fail, self-esteem often falls. You may feel guilty for having been the cause of the breakup or inadequate for not holding on to a permanent relationship. You may feel unwanted and unloved. All of these feelings contribute to a lowering of self-esteem. Your task here is to regain the positive self-image you need to function effectively as an individual and as a member of another relationship. Take positive action to raise your self-esteem (see Unit 6).

Avoid repeating negative patterns. Many people enter second and third relationships with the same blinders, faulty preconceptions, and unrealistic expectations with which they entered their earlier relationship. It's possible, however, to learn from failed relationships and not repeat the same patterns. Ask yourself at the start of a new involvement if you're entering a relationship modeled on the previous one. If the answer is yes, be especially careful not to fall into old behavior patterns. At the same time, don't become a prophet of doom. Don't see in every new relationship vestiges of the old. Treat the new relationship as the unique relationship it is and don't evaluate it through past experiences. Past relationships and experiences should be guides, not filters.

For additional guidelines for improving relationship communication see "A POSITIVE Communication Approach to Relationship Effectiveness" at www.ablongman.com/devito. 🖱

RELATIONSHIP TYPES

Each relationship, whether friendship, love, or a primary relationship, is unique. Yet there are general types that research has identified—and these categories offer unusual insight into interpersonal relationships.

The types of relationships discussed here are not the only ones that might be considered. Rather, they're examples of the best available typologies, the ones that provide the most insight into both relationships and communication. For other classifications see "The Needs Friendships Serve," "Stages and Communication in Friendship Development," "Other Views of Love," "Family Rules," and "Family Communication Patterns" at www.ablongman.com/devito. 🖱

Types of Friendships

One theory of **friendship** identifies three major types: reciprocity, receptivity, and association (Reisman, 1979, 1981). The *friendship of reciprocity,* the ideal type, is characterized by loyalty, self-sacrifice, mutual affection, and generosity. A friendship of reciprocity is based on equality: Each individual shares equally in giving and receiving the benefits and rewards of the relationship.

In the *friendship of receptivity,* in contrast, there is an imbalance in giving and receiving; one person is the primary giver and the other the primary receiver. This is a positive imbalance, however, because each person gains something from the relationship. The different needs of both the person who receives affection and the person who gives it are satisfied. This is the friendship that may develop between a teacher and a student or between a doctor and a patient. In fact, a difference in status is essential for the friendship of receptivity to develop.

The *friendship of association* is transitory; it might be described as a friendly relationship rather than a true friendship. Associative friendships are the kind we often have with classmates, neighbors, or co-workers. There is no great loyalty, no great trust, no great giving or receiving. The association is cordial but not intense.

Types of Lovers

Like friends, lovers come in different styles as well. Before reading about these styles, take the following self-test to identify your own love style.

TEST YOURSELF

What Kind of Lover Are You?

Respond to each of the following statements with T for "true" (if you believe the statement to be a generally accurate representation of your attitudes about love) or F for "false" (if you believe the statement does not adequately represent your attitudes about love).

_____ 1. My lover and I have the right physical "chemistry" between us.

_____ 2. I feel that my lover and I were meant for each other.

_____ 3. My lover and I really understand each other.

_____ 4. I believe that what my lover doesn't know about me won't hurt him/her.

_____ 5. My lover would get upset if he/she knew of some of the things I've done with other people.

_____ 6. When my lover gets too dependent on me, I want to back off a little.

_____ 7. I expect to always be friends with my lover.

_____ 8. Our love is really a deep friendship, not a mysterious, mystical emotion.

_____ 9. Our love relationship is the most satisfying because it developed from a good friendship.

_____ 10. In choosing my lover, I believed it was best to love someone with a similar background.

_____ 11. An important factor in choosing a partner is whether or not he/she would be a good parent.

_____ 12. One consideration in choosing my lover was how he/she would reflect on my career.

_____ 13. Sometimes I get so excited about being in love with my lover that I can't sleep.

_____ 14. When my lover doesn't pay attention to me, I feel sick all over.

_____ 15. I cannot relax if I suspect that my lover is with someone else.

_____ 16. I would rather suffer myself than let my lover suffer.

_____ 17. When my lover gets angry with me, I still love him/her fully and unconditionally.

_____ 18. I would endure all things for the sake of my lover.

How did you do? This scale, from Hendrick and Hendrick (1990), is based on the work of Lee (1976), as is the discussion of the six types of love that follows. This scale is designed to enable you to identify your own beliefs about love. The statements refer to the six types of love that we discuss below: eros, ludus, storge, pragma, mania, and agape. Statements 1–3 are characteristic of the eros lover. If you answered "true" to these statements, you have a strong eros component to your love style. If you answered "false," you have a weak eros component. Statements 4–6 refer to ludus love, 7–9 to storge love, 10–12 to pragma love, 13–15 to manic love, and 16–18 to agapic love.

What will you do? Are there things you can do to become more aware of the different love styles and to become a more well-rounded lover? Incorporating the qualities of effective interpersonal communication—for example, being more flexible, more polite, and more other-oriented—will go a long way toward making you a more responsive love partner.

Source: From "A Relationship-Specific Version of the Love Attitudes Scale" by C. Hendrick and S. Hendrick. Copyright © 1990 Select Press, *Journal of Social Behavior and Personality 5*, 1990. Reprinted by permission. ✔

Eros love seeks beauty and sensuality and focuses on physical attractiveness, sometimes to the exclusion of qualities we might consider more important and more lasting. The erotic lover has an idealized image of beauty that is unattainable in reality. Consequently, the erotic lover often feels unfulfilled.

Ludic love seeks entertainment and excitement and sees love as fun, a game. To the ludic lover, love is not to be taken too seriously; emotions are to be held in check lest they get out of hand and make trouble. The ludic lover retains a partner only so long as the partner is interesting and amusing. When the partner is no longer interesting enough, it's time to change.

Storge love is a peaceful and tranquil love. Like ludus, storge lacks passion and intensity. Storgic lovers set out not to find a lover but to establish a companionlike relationship with someone they know and with whom they can share interests and activities. Storgic love is a gradual process of unfolding thoughts and feelings and is sometimes difficult to separate from friendship.

Pragma love is practical and traditional and seeks compatibility and a relationship in which important needs and desires will be satisfied. The pragma lover is concerned with the social qualifications of a potential mate even more than with personal qualities; family and background are extremely important to the pragma lover, who relies not so much on feelings as on logic.

Manic love is an obsessive love that needs to give and receive constant attention and affection. When this is not given or received, or when an expression of increased commitment is not returned, reactions such as depression, jealousy, and self-doubt are often experienced and can lead to the extreme lows characteristic of the manic lover.

Agapic love is compassionate and selfless. The agapic lover loves both the stranger on the road and the annoying neighbor. Jesus, Buddha, and Gandhi practiced and preached this unqualified spiritual love—a love that is offered without concern for personal reward or gain and without any expectation that the love will be returned or reciprocated.

Types of Primary Relationships

A **primary relationship** is a relationship between two people that the partners see as their most important interpersonal relationship. An interesting typology of primary relationships (based on more than 1,000 couples' responses to questions concerning their degree of sharing, their space needs, their conflicts, and the time they spend together) identifies three basic types: traditionals, independents, and separates (Fitzpatrick, 1983, 1988, 1991; Noller & Fitzpatrick, 1993). At this point you may wish to examine your own relational attitudes and style by taking the "What type of relationship do you prefer?" self-test at www.ablongman.com/devito. 🖱 If you have a relational partner, you might wish to have him or her also complete the test and then compare your results.

Traditional couples share a basic belief system and philosophy of life. They see themselves as a blending of two persons into a single couple rather than as two separate individuals. They're interdependent and believe that each individual's independence must be sacrificed for the good of the relationship. Traditionals believe in mutual sharing and do little separately. This couple holds to the traditional sex roles, and there are seldom any role conflicts. There are few power struggles and few conflicts, because each person knows and adheres to a specified role within the relationship. In their communications traditionals are highly responsive to each other. Traditionals lean toward each other, smile, talk a lot, interrupt each other, and finish each other's sentences.

Independents stress their individuality. The relationship is important but never more important than each person's individual identity. Although independents spend a great deal of time together, they don't ritualize it, for example, with schedules. Each individual spends time with outside friends. Independents see themselves as relatively androgynous—as individuals who combine traditionally feminine and traditionally masculine roles and qualities. The communication between independents is responsive. They engage in conflict openly and without fear. Their disclosures are quite extensive and include high-risk and negative disclosures that are typically absent among traditionals.

Separates live together but view their relationship more as a matter of convenience than a result of their mutual love or closeness. They seem to have little desire to be together and, in fact, usually are together only at ritual occasions such as mealtime or holiday get-togethers. It's important to these separates that each has his or her own physical as well as psychological space. Separates share little; each seems to prefer to go his or her own way. Separates hold relatively traditional values and beliefs about sex roles, and each person tries to follow the behaviors normally assigned to each role. What best characterizes this type, however, is that each person sees himself or herself as a separate individual and not as a part of a "we."

In addition to these three pure types, there are also combinations. For example, in the separate–traditional couple one individual is a separate and one a traditional. Another common pattern is the traditional–independent, in which one individual believes in the traditional view of relationships and one in autonomy and independence.

RELATIONSHIP THEORIES

Several theories offer insight into why and how we develop and dissolve our relationships. Here we'll examine five such theories: attraction, relationship rules, social penetration, social exchange, and equity. A chart, "Relationship Theories and Relationship Movement," summaries these five theories and their predictions and may be found at **www.ablongman.com/devito.** After reading this section, you may want to try your hand applying these theories; see "How Can You Make Relationship Predictions?" at **www.ablongman.com/ devito.**

Attraction Theory

Attraction theory holds that people form relationships on the basis of **attraction.** You are no doubt drawn, or attracted, to some people and not attracted to others. In a similar way, some people are attracted to you and some are not. If you're like most people, then you're attracted to others on the basis of four major factors:

- *Similarity.* If you could construct your mate, according to the **similarity** principle, it's likely that your mate would look, act, and think very much like you (Burleson, Samter, & Luccetti, 1992; Burleson, Kunkel, & Birch, 1994). Generally, people like those who are similar to them in nationality, race, abilities, physical characteristics, intelligence, and attitudes. Sometimes people are attracted to their opposites in a pattern called **complementarity;** for example, a dominant person might be attracted to someone who is more submissive. Generally, however, people prefer those who are similar.

- *Proximity.* If you look around at people you find attractive, you will probably find that they are the people who live or work close to you. People who become friends are the people who have the greatest opportunity to interact with each other. **Proximity,** or physical closeness, is most important in the early stages of interaction—for example, during the first days of school (in class or in dormitories). It decreases, though always remaining significant, as the opportunity to interact with more distant others increases.

It has been argued that you don't actually develop an attraction to those who are similar to you but rather develop a repulsion for those who are dissimilar (Rosenbaum, 1986). For example, you may be repulsed by those who disagree with you and therefore exclude them from those with whom you might develop a relationship. You're therefore left with a pool of possible partners who are similar to you. What do you think of this repulsion hypothesis? How would you go about testing it?

- *Reinforcement.* Not surprisingly, **reinforcement theory** points out that you're attracted to people who give rewards or reinforcements, which can range from a simple compliment to an expensive cruise. You're also attracted to people you reward (Jecker & Landy, 1969; Aronson, Wilson, & Akert, 1999). That is, you come to like people for whom you do favors; for example, you've probably increased your liking for persons after buying them an expensive present or going out of your way to do them a special favor. In these situations you justify your behavior by believing that the person was worth your efforts; otherwise, you'd have to admit to spending effort on people who don't deserve it.

- *Physical attractiveness and personality.* For the most part you probably like physically attractive people rather than physically unattractive people. And you probably tend to like people who have a pleasant rather than an unpleasant personality.

Relationship Rules Approach

You can gain an interesting perspective on interpersonal relationships by looking at them in terms of the rules that govern them (Shimanoff, 1980). The general assumption of **rules theory** is that relationships—friendship and love in particular—are held together by adherence to certain rules. When those rules are broken, the relationship may deteriorate and even dissolve.

Relationship rules theory helps us clarify several aspects of relationships. First, these rules help identify successful versus destructive relationship behavior. In addition, these rules help pinpoint more specifically why relationships break up and how they may be repaired. Further, if we know what the rules are, we will be better able to master the social skills involved in relationship development and maintenance. And because these rules vary from one culture to another, it is important to identify those unique to each culture so that intercultural relationships may be more effectively developed and maintained.

Friendship Rules

One approach to friendship argues that friendships are maintained by rules (Argyle & Henderson, 1984; Argyle, 1986). When these rules are followed, the friendship is strong and mutually satisfying. When these rules are broken, the friendship suffers and may die. For example, the rules for keeping a friendship include such behaviors as these: standing up for your friend in his or her absence, sharing information and feelings about successes, demonstrating emotional support for your friend, trusting and offering to help your friends when in need, and trying to make your friend happy when you're together. On the other hand, a friendship is likely to be in trouble when one or both friends are intolerant of the other's friends, discuss confidences with third parties, fail to demonstrate positive support, nag, and/or fail to trust or confide in the other. The strategy for maintaining a friendship then depends on your knowing the rules and having the ability to apply the appropriate interpersonal skills (Trower, 1981; Blieszner & Adams, 1992).

Romantic Rules

Other research has identified the rules that romantic relationships establish and follow. These rules, of course, will vary considerably from one culture to another. For example, different attitudes toward permissiveness and sexual relations with which Chinese and American college students view dating influence the romantic rules each group will establish and live by (Tang & Zuo, 2000). Leslie Baxter (1986) has identified eight major romantic rules. Baxter argues that these rules keep the relationship together—or, when broken, lead to deterioration and eventually dissolution. The general form for each rule, as Baxter phrases it, is, "If parties are in a close relationship, they should . . .":

1. acknowledge each other's individual identities and lives beyond the relationship
2. express similar attitudes, beliefs, values, and interests
3. enhance each other's self-worth and self-esteem
4. be open, genuine, and authentic with each other
5. remain loyal and faithful to each other
6. have substantial shared time together
7. reap rewards commensurate with their investments relative to the other party
8. experience a mysterious and inexplicable "magic" in each other's presence

If you wish to explore your own level of romanticism, see the self-test "How romantic are you?" at www.ablongman.com/devito.

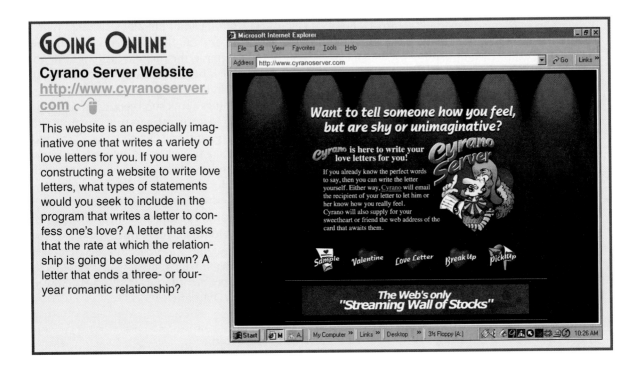

Social Penetration Theory

Social penetration theory is a theory not of why relationships develop but of what happens when they do develop; it describes relationships in terms of the number of topics that people talk about and their degree of "personalness" (Altman & Taylor, 1973). The **breadth** of a relationship has to do with the number of topics you and your partner talk about. The **depth** of a relationship involves the degree to which you penetrate the inner personality—the core—of the other individual. We can represent an individual as a circle and divide that circle into various parts. These parts represent the topics or areas of interpersonal communication, or breadth. Further, visualize the circle and its parts as consisting of concentric inner circles, rather like an onion. These represent the different levels of communication, or the depth.

When a relationship begins to deteriorate, the breadth and depth will, in many ways, reverse themselves, in a process called **depenetration.** For example, while ending a relationship, you might cut out certain topics from your interpersonal communications. At the same time you might discuss the remaining topics in less depth. In some instances of relational deterioration, however, both the breadth

and the depth of interaction increase. For example, when a couple breaks up and each is finally free from an oppressive relationship, they may—after some time—begin to discuss problems and feelings they would never have discussed when they were together. In fact, they may become extremely close friends and come to like each other more than when they were together. In these cases the breadth and depth of their relationship may increase rather than decrease (Baxter, 1983).

Social Exchange Theory

Social exchange theory claims that you develop relationships that will enable you to maximize your profits (Chadwick-Jones, 1976; Gergen, Greenberg, & Willis, 1980; Thibaut & Kelley, 1986)—a theory based on an economic model of profits and losses. The theory begins with the following equation: Profits = Rewards − Costs. Rewards are anything that you would incur costs to obtain. Research has identified six types of rewards in a love relationship: money, status, love, information, goods, and services (Baron & Byrne, 1984). For example, to get the reward of money, you might have to work rather than play. To earn the status of an A in an interpersonal communication course, you might have to write a term paper or study more than you want to.

Costs are things that you normally try to avoid, that you consider unpleasant or difficult. Examples might include working overtime; washing dishes and ironing clothes; watching your partner's favorite television show, which you find boring; or doing favors for those you dislike.

Using this basic economic model, social exchange theory claims that you seek to develop the friendships and romantic relationships that will give you the greatest profits; that is, relationships in which the rewards are greater than the costs. The most preferred relationships, according to this theory, are those that give you the greatest rewards with the least costs.

When you enter a relationship you have in mind a comparison level—a general idea of the kinds of rewards and profits that you feel you ought to get out of such a relationship. This comparison level consists of your realistic expectations concerning what you feel you deserve from this relationship. For example, in a study of married couples it was found that most people expect high levels of trust, mutual respect, love, and commitment. Couples' expectations are significantly lower for time spent together, privacy, sexual activity, and communication (Sabatelli & Pearce, 1986). When the rewards that you get equal or surpass your comparison level, you feel satisfied with your relationship.

However, you also have a comparison level for alternatives. That is, you compare the profits that you get from your current relationship with the profits you think you can get from alternative relationships. Thus, if you see that the profits from your present relationship are below the profits that you could get from an alternative relationship, you may decide to leave your current relationship and enter a new, more profitable relationship.

Equity Theory

Equity theory uses the ideas of social exchange but goes a step farther and claims that you develop and maintain relationships in which the ratio of your rewards relative to your costs is approximately equal to your partner's (Walster, Walster, & Berscheid, 1978; Messick & Cook, 1983). For example, if you and a friend start a business and you put up two-thirds of the money and your friend puts up one-third, equity would demand that you get two-thirds of the profits and your friend get one-third. An equitable relationship, then, is simply one in which each party derives rewards that are proportional to their costs. If you contribute more toward the relationship than your partner, then equity requires that you should get greater rewards. If you both work equally hard, then equity demands that you should both get approximately equal rewards. Conversely, inequity will exist in a relationship if you pay more of the costs (for example, if you do more of the unpleasant tasks) but your partner enjoys more of the rewards. Inequity will also exist if you and your partner work equally hard but one of you gets more of the rewards.

Much research supports this idea that people want equity in their interpersonal relationships (Ueleke et al., 1983). The general idea behind the theory is that if you are underbenefited (you get less than you put in), you'll be angry and dissatisfied. If, on the other hand, you are overbenefited (you get more than you put in), you'll feel guilty. Some research, however, has questioned this rather neat but intuitively unsatisfying assumption and finds that the overbenefited person is often quite happy and contented; guilt from getting more than you deserve seems easily forgotten (Noller & Fitzpatrick, 1993).

Equity theory puts into clear focus the sources of relational dissatisfaction seen every day. For example, in a relationship both partners may have full-time jobs, but one partner may also be expected to do the major share of the household chores. Thus, although both may be deriving equal rewards— they have equally good cars, they live in the same three-bedroom house, and so on—one partner is paying more of the costs. According to equity theory, this partner will be dissatisfied because of this lack of equity.

Equity theory claims that you will develop, maintain, and be satisfied with relationships that are equitable. You will not develop, will terminate, and will be dissatisfied with relationships that are inequitable. The greater the inequity, the greater the dissatisfaction and the greater the likelihood that the relationship will end.

REFLECTIONS ON ETHICS IN HUMAN COMMUNICATION

Ethics on the Job

The ethical issues and guidelines that operate within a workplace environment can be summarized with the acronym ETHICS: empathy (Cheney & Tompkins, 1987), talk rather than force, honesty (Krebs, 1990), interaction management, confidentiality, and supportiveness (Johannesen, 1995).

Empathy. Workers in an organization have an ethical obligation to try to understand what others are feeling as well as thinking from the others' point of view. This is especially important when members from vastly different rungs of the organizational ladder communicate.

Talk. Decisions in an organization should be arrived at by talk, rather than by force—by persuasion, rather than by coercion.

Honesty. Organizational communication—whether from the highest levels of management or from the trainees in the mailroom—should be honest and truthful.

Interaction management. Organizational communication and relationships should be satisfying and comfortable.

Confidentiality. Members have a right to expect that what they say in confidence will not be made public or even whispered about at the water cooler.

Supportiveness. A supportive and cooperative climate should characterize interpersonal interactions throughout the organization.

What would you do? *You're managing a work team of three colleagues charged with redesigning the company website. The problem is that Jack doesn't do any work and misses most of the meetings. You spoke with Jack about it and he confided that he's going through a divorce and child custody battle and really can't concentrate on the project. You feel sorry for Jack and have been carrying him for the last few months, but you realize now that you'll never be able to bring the project in on time if you don't replace Jack. In addition, you really don't want to get a negative appraisal because of Jack; in fact, you were counting on the raise that this project was going to get you. What would you do in this situation?*

 SUMMARY

In this unit we looked at interpersonal relationships; at their nature, stages, and types; and at the theories that try to explain what happens in an interpersonal relationship.

1. People enter into relationships for a variety of reasons; some of the most important are to lessen loneliness, secure stimulation, gain self-knowledge, and maximize pleasures and minimize pain.

2. Relationships tend to develop in stages. Recognize at least these: contact, involvement, intimacy, deterioration, repair, and dissolution.

3. Three main phases in initiating relationships are examining qualifiers, determining clearance, and communicating a desire for contact.

4. In initiating relationships, the following nonverbal behaviors are useful: establish eye contact, signal positive response, concentrate your focus, establish proximity, maintain an open posture, respond visibly, use positive behaviors, and avoid overexposure. The following verbal behaviors are helpful: introduce yourself, focus the conversation on the other person, exchange favors and rewards, be energetic,

stress the positives, avoid negative or too intimate self-disclosures, and establish commonalities.

5. Relationship deterioration—the weakening of the bonds holding people together—may be gradual or sudden and may have positive as well as negative effects.

6. Among the causes for relationship deterioration are diminution of the reasons for establishing the relationship, relational changes, unrealistic expectations, sex conflicts, work problems, financial difficulties, and the inequitable distribution of rewards and costs.

7. Among the communication changes that take place during relationship deterioration are general withdrawal, a decrease in self-disclosure, an increase in deception, a decrease in positive and an increase in negative evaluative responses, and a decrease in the exchange of favors.

8. Relationship maintenance focuses on behaviors designed to continue the relationship, to keep it intact, to keep it at its present stage, or to keep it from deteriorating.

9. Relationships may stay together because of emotional attachments, convenience, children, fear, financial considerations, and/or inertia. Mutual commitment and effective communication patterns also tend to sustain ongoing relationships.

10. A useful approach to relationship repair is to recognize the problem, engage in productive conflict resolution, pose possible solutions, affirm each other, integrate solutions into relationship behaviors, and take risks.

11. If the relationship does end, engage in self-repair. Break the loneliness–depression cycle, take time out, bolster self-esteem, seek emotional support, and avoid repeating negative patterns.

12. Friendships may be classified as those of reciprocity, receptivity, and association.

13. Six primary love styles have been identified: eros, ludus, storge, mania, pragma, and agape.

14. Couples in primary relationships may be classified into traditionals, independents, and separates.

15. Attraction, relationship rules, social penetration, social exchange, and equity theories are five explanations of what happens when you develop, maintain, and dissolve interpersonal relationships.

16. Attraction depends on four factors: attractiveness (physical and personality), similarity (especially attitudinal), proximity (physical closeness), and reinforcement.

17. The relationship rules approach views relationships as held together by agreement and adherence to an agreed-upon set of rules.

18. Social penetration theory describes relationships in terms of breadth and depth: respectively, the number of topics we talk about, and the degree of personalness with which we pursue topics.

19. Social exchange theory holds that we develop relationships that yield the greatest profits. We seek relationships in which the rewards exceed the costs and are more likely to dissolve relationships when the costs exceed the rewards.

20. Equity theory claims that we develop and maintain relationships in which rewards are distributed in proportion to costs. When our share of the rewards is less than would be demanded by equity, we are likely to experience dissatisfaction and exit the relationship.

KEY TERMS

interpersonal relationship

relationship development

relationship deterioration

relationship maintenance

commitment

interpersonal repair

self-repair

friendships of reciprocity, receptivity, and association

eros, ludus, storge, pragma, mania, and agape love styles

traditional, independent, and separate styles in primary relationships

attraction theory

similarity

proximity

reinforcement

relationship rules theory

social penetration theory

breadth

depth

depenetration

social exchange theory

comparison level

comparison level for alternatives

equity theory

THINKING CRITICALLY ABOUT

Interpersonal Relationships

1. It was not until 1967—after nine years of trials and appeals—that the U.S. Supreme Court forbade any state laws against interracial marriage (Crohn, 1995). How would you describe the state of interracial romantic relationships today? What obstacles do such relationships face? What advantages do they offer?

2. One way to improve communication during difficult times is to ask your partner for positive behaviors rather than complaining about negative behaviors. How might you use this suggestion to replace such statements as the following? (1) I hate it when you ignore me at business functions. (2) I can't stand going to these cheap restaurants; when are you going to start spending a few bucks? (3) Stop being so negative; you criticize everything and everyone.

3. The **matching hypothesis** claims that people date and mate people who are similar to themselves in degree of physical attractiveness (Walster & Walster, 1978). When this does not happen—for example, when a very attractive person dates someone of average attractiveness—there may be "compensating factors," qualities the less attractive person possesses that compensate or make up for his or her being less physically attractive. What evidence can you find to support or contract this theory? How would you go about testing this theory?

4. Test out the predictions of the five theories on your own relationships. For example:
   • Are you attracted to people who are physically attractive, have a pleasing personality, live and/or work near you, are similar to you, and reinforce you?
   • Do you maintain relationships when rules are followed and break up when rules are broken?

   • Do you talk about more topics and in greater depth in close relationships than in mere acquaintanceships?
   • Do you pursue and maintain relationships that give you profits (that is, in which rewards are greater than costs)? Were the relationships that you did not pursue or that you ended unprofitable (that is, involving costs greater than their rewards)?
   • Are you more satisfied with equitable relationships than with inequitable ones?

5. Research finds that relationship dissolution has a significant influence on suicide rates among men but not among women (Kposowa, 2000). Can you identify any reasons for this finding?

6. Research generally indicates that the romantic relationships of heterosexuals, gay men, and lesbians are substantially similar (Spiers, 1998). Do you find the media generally reflect this research in their depiction of these relationships?

7. **Researching Interpersonal Relationships.** How would you go about finding answers to such questions as these?
   • Are the reasons for developing relationships similar for female–male, female–female, or male–male relationships?
   • Do the reasons for developing relationships change with age? How do the reasons differ between, say, those of 20-year-olds, on the one hand, and 50- to 60-year-olds, on the other?
   • Do men and women use the same relationship maintenance strategies?
   • How do the maintenance strategies differ for friends and for romantic relationships?

UNIT 11
Interpersonal Conflict

Unit Contents

No matter how effective a communicator you are, you'll still experience interpersonal conflict and disagreements. At some point in your personal, social, and work relationships you'll find yourself in conflict with another person. Conflict is an inevitable part of your interpersonal life, so it's essential to learn how it works, how it can go wrong, and what you can do to revolve conflicts effectively. In this unit you'll learn

▶ what conflict is and how it operates

▶ how you can engage in conflict so that differences can be resolved and your relationships can emerge from the conflict stronger rather than weaker

INTERPERSONAL CONFLICT

Pat wants to go to the movies with Chris; Chris wants to stay home. Pat's insisting on going to the movies interferes with Chris's staying home, and Chris's determination to stay home interferes with Pat's going to the movies. Carl and Bernard own a small business. Carl wants to expand the business and open a branch in California. Bernard wants to sell the business and retire. Each person in these scenarios has goals that interfere with the other person's attaining opposing goals.

Interpersonal conflicts can be of various types. They may concern goals to be pursued ("We want you to go to college and become a teacher or a doctor, not an actor"), the allocation of resources such as money or time ("I want to spend the tax refund on a car, not on new furniture"), decisions to be made ("I refuse to have the Jeffersons over for dinner"), or behaviors that are considered appropriate or desirable by one person but inappropriate or undesirable by the other ("I hate it when you get drunk/pinch me/ridicule me in front of others/flirt with others/dress provocatively").

As these examples illustrate, **interpersonal conflict** occurs when people

- are interdependent; what one person does has an effect on the other person
- perceive their goals to be incompatible; if one person's goal is achieved the other's cannot be (for example, if one person wants to buy a new car and the other person wants to save the money for a house)
- see the other person as interfering with their own chances of achieving their goal (Hocker & Wilmot, 1985; Folger, Poole, & Stutman, 1997)

Myths about Conflict

One of the problems we often encounter in studying and in dealing with interpersonal conflict is the predominance of false assumptions about what conflict is and what it means. Think about your own assumptions about conflict, which are probably derived from communications you have witnessed in your family and in your social interactions. For example, do you think the following are true or false?

- If two people are in a relationship fight, it means their relationship is a bad one.
- Fighting damages an interpersonal relationship.
- Fighting is bad because it reveals our negative selves—our pettiness, our need to be in control, our unreasonable expectations.

Simple answers are usually wrong. Each of the three assumptions above may be true or may be false. It depends. In and of itself, conflict is neither good nor bad. **Conflict** is a part of every interpersonal relationship—of relationships between parents and children, brothers and sisters, friends, lovers, and coworkers. If it isn't, then the relationship is probably dull, irrelevant, or insignificant. Conflict is inevitable in any meaningful relationship.

It's not so much the conflict that creates the problem as the way in which you approach and deal with the conflict. Some ways of approaching conflict can resolve difficulties and actually improve the relationship. Other ways can hurt the relationship; they can destroy self-esteem, create bitterness, and foster suspicion. Your task, therefore, is not to try to create relationships that will be free of conflict but rather to learn appropriate and productive ways of managing conflict.

MEDIA WATCH

VIOLENCE AND THE MEDIA

Does violence in the media lead to violent acts by viewers? And if it does, should violence on television, in movies, in video games, and in music be censored? Most of the research on media violence has focused on television and, to a lesser extent, on films, as these are media used extensively by children. But video games and music are increasingly under scrutiny for their violent content and potential influence on children. For example, a study of Nintendo and Sega Genesis video games showed that approximately 80 percent of the games included aggression or violence as an essential part of the strategy (Dietz, 1998).

Generally, research finds that violence in the media can contribute to a variety of effects (Rodman, 2001; Bok, 1998):

▶ The viewing of violence can teach young people how to be violent; it can teach them the techniques of violence.

▶ Media violence often gives people (and children especially) role models to emulate. Many films made in India, for example, eroticize violence against women; males are encouraged to identify with heroes who use violence to win women. In interviews Indian males revealed that they felt that the depiction of male–female relationships in the films paralleled what they felt was the ideal male–female relationship (Derne, 1999).

▶ Media violence, because it is so prevalent, can desensitize people to the violence around them—which often is not as extreme as that regularly shown on television and in the movies.

▶ Media violence can make viewers afraid of becoming victims of violence.

▶ Media violence creates a desire for depiction of still greater violence. For example, films have become increasingly violent over the years, largely because viewers want to see more violence than they've seen in the last movie.

The extent to which media violence contributes to actual violence, however, has not been determined. The National Institute of Mental Health (1982) has reported that heavy viewing of violence is related to aggressive behavior, and that the more a person is exposed to media violence, the more likely the person is to be aggressive. But there are probably other factors that lead some people to watch violent films, and these factors may help cause the aggressive behavior. Many factors contribute to a viewer's becoming violent, and media portrayals are only part of the total picture. Family and social factors, developmental and affective disorders, and substance abuse, for example, interact with exposure to media violence to produce violent behavior (Withecomb, 1997).

Follow-Up. *How do you feel about violence in the media? If you're unhappy with the current state of media violence, what would you like to see changed? How might you go about effecting these changes? Do you think viewing real-life violence, as on September 11, 2001, influences how you perceive fake, staged violence?*

Similarly, it's not the conflict itself that will reveal your negative side but the fight strategies you use. Thus, if you personally attack the other person, use force, or use personal rejection or manipulation, you'll reveal your negative side. But in fighting you can also reveal your positive self—your openness to hearing opposing points of view, your readiness to change unpleasant behaviors, and your willingness to accept imperfection in others.

Content and Relationship Conflict

Using concepts developed in Unit 2, we may distinguish between content conflict and relationship conflict. *Content conflicts* center on objects, events, and persons in the world that are usually, though not always, external to the parties involved in the conflict. These include the millions of issues that you argue and fight about every day—the value of a particular movie, what to watch on television, the fairness of the last examination or job promotion, and the way to spend your savings.

Relationship conflicts are equally numerous and include such conflict situations as a younger brother who does not obey his older brother, two partners who each want an equal say in making vacation plans, and the mother and daughter who each want to have the final word concerning the daughter's

UNDERSTANDING THEORY AND RESEARCH

Conflict Issues

Think about your own interpersonal conflicts and particularly about the issues you fight over. Here are the results of two studies that investigated what couples fight about. In one study, focusing on heterosexual couples, four conditions led up to a couple's "first big fight" (Siegert & Stamp, 1994):

- uncertainty over commitment
- jealousy
- violation of expectations
- personality differences

Another study examined the issues heterosexual, gay, and lesbian couples argued about most. All three types of couples were amazingly similar in the six main issues they argued about (Kurdek, 1994):

- intimacy issues such as affection and sex

- power issues such as excessive demands or possessiveness, lack of equality in the relationship, friends, and leisure time
- personal flaws issues such as drinking or smoking, personal grooming, and driving style
- personal distance issues such as frequent absences and heavy school or job commitments
- social issues such as political and social questions, parents, and personal values
- distrust issues such as previous lovers and lying

Working with Theories and Research. *What do you fight about? What three issues cause the most conflict in your own interpersonal relationships?*

lifestyle. Here the conflicts are concerned not so much with some external object as with the relationships between the individuals—with such issues as who is in charge, how equal the partners in a primary relationship really are, or who has the right to set down rules of behavior.

Content conflicts are usually manifest; they're clearly observable and identifiable. Relationship conflicts are often latent; they tend to be hidden and much more difficult to identify. Thus, a conflict over where you should vacation may on the surface, or manifest, level center on the advantages and disadvantages of Mexico versus Hawaii. On a relationship and often latent level, however, the conflict may be about who has the greater right to select the place to vacation, who should win the argument, who is the decision maker in the relationship, and so on.

The Context of Conflict

Conflict, like any form of communication, takes place in a context that is physical, sociopsychological, temporal, and cultural.

The physical context—for example, whether you engage in conflict privately or publicly, alone or in front of children or relatives—will influence the way the conflict is conducted as well as the effects the conflict will have.

The sociopsychological context will also influence the conflict. For example, if the atmosphere is one of equality, the conflict is likely to progress very differently than if in an atmosphere of inequality. A friendly or a hostile context will exert different influences on the conflict.

The temporal context will likewise prove important to understand. A conflict after a series of similar conflicts will be seen differently than the same conflict following a series of enjoyable experiences and an absence of conflict. A conflict immediately after a hard day of work will engender different feelings than will a conflict after an enjoyable dinner.

The cultural context will exert considerable influence both on the issues people fight about and on how they engage in conflict. A particularly clear example occurs frequently in many large cities throughout the country; it's seen in the conflict between African American customers, who prefer a personal involvement with the people with whom they do business, and Korean storekeepers, who prefer to maintain considerable distance between themselves and their customers. To the African American customer, the Korean merchant seems to be disconfirming and unwilling to provide courteous service. To the Korean, the African American's personal approach is seen as disrespectful (Bailey, 1997).

Another frequent example concerns the issue of cohabitation. Eighteen-year-olds are more likely to experience conflict with their parents about their living style if they live in the United States than if they live in Sweden, where cohabitation is much more accepted. Similarly, male infidelity is more likely to cause conflict among American couples than among southern European couples. Students from the United States are more likely to engage in conflict with another U.S. student than with someone from another culture; Chinese students, on the other hand, are more likely to engage in a conflict with a non-Chinese student than with another Chinese (Leung, 1988). In a comparison of German and Indonesian adolescents, German students preferred a more confrontational style; Indonesian students preferred a more submissive response style (Haar & Krahe, 1999). Vietnamese people are more likely to avoid conflict than are people from the United States (Dsilva & Whyte, 1998).

When American and Chinese students were asked to analyze a conflict episode, say between a mother and her daughter, they saw it quite differently (Goode, 2000). American students, for example, were more likely to decide in favor of the mother or the daughter—to see one side as right and one side as wrong. The Chinese students, however, were more likely to see the validity of both sides—to conclude that both mother and daughter were right but both were also wrong. This finding is consistent with the Chinese preference for proverbs that contain a contradiction (for example, "Too modest is half boastful") and Americans' reaction to these as "irritating."

The ways in which members of different cultures express conflict also differ. In Japan, for example, it's especially important that you not embarrass the person with whom you are in conflict, especially if the disagreement occurs in public. This face-saving principle prohibits the use of such strategies as personal rejection or verbal aggressiveness. In the United States men and women, ideally at least, are both expected to express their desires and complaints openly and directly. Many Middle Eastern

and Pacific rim cultures, however, would discourage women from such expressions; rather, a more agreeable and submissive posture would be expected.

Even within a given general culture, more specific cultures differ from one another in their methods of conflict management. African American men and women and European American men and women, for example, engage in conflict in very different ways (Kochman, 1981). The issues that cause conflict and aggravate conflict, the conflict strategies that are expected and accepted, and the entire attitude toward conflict vary from one group to the other. For example, African American men prefer to manage conflict with clear arguments and a focus on problem solving. African American women, however, deal with conflict by expressing assertiveness and respect (Collier, 1991). Another study found that African American females used more direct controlling strategies (for example, assuming control over the conflict and arguing persistently for their point of view) than did European American females. European American females, on the other hand, used more problem solution–oriented conflict management styles than did African American women. Interestingly, African American and European American men were very similar in their conflict management strategies: Both tended to avoid or withdraw from relationship conflict. They preferred to keep quiet about their differences or downplay their significance (Ting-Toomey, 1986).

Among Mexican Americans, studies found that men preferred to achieve mutual understanding by discussing the reasons for the conflict, whereas women focused on being supportive of the relationship. Among Anglo Americans, men preferred direct and rational argument; women preferred flexibility. Similarly, Mexicans (whose culture is collectivist) preferred conflict styles that emphasized concern for the others involved more than did people from the United States (an individualistic culture) (Gabrielides, Stephan, Ybarra, Pearson, & Villareal, 1997). An extended example, "The Influence of Culture on Conflict," is available at www.ablongman.com/devito.

The Negatives and Positives of Conflict

The kind of conflict focused on here is conflict among or between "connected" individuals. Inter-

UNDERSTANDING THEORY AND RESEARCH

Conflict and Gender

D o men and women engage in conflict differently? Research shows that men are more apt to withdraw from a conflict situation than women. It has been argued that this may be due to the fact that men become more psychologically and physiologically aroused during conflict (and retain this heightened level of arousal much longer) than women do and so may try to distance themselves and withdraw from the conflict to prevent further arousal (Gottman & Carrere, 1994; Canary, Cupach, & Messman, 1995; Goleman, 1995). Women, in contrast, want to get closer to the conflict; they want to talk about it and resolve it. Even adolescents reveal these differences; in a study of boys and girls aged 11 to 17, boys withdrew more than girls but were more aggressive when they didn't withdraw (Lindeman, Harakka, & Keltikangas-Jarvinen, 1997; Heasley, Babbitt, & Burbach, 1995).

Other research has found that women are more emotional and men are more logical when they argue (Schaap, Buunk, & Kerkstra, 1988; Canary, Cupach, & Messman, 1995). Women have been characterized as conflict "feelers" and men as conflict "thinkers" (Sorenson, Hawkins, & Sorenson, 1995). Another difference found is that women are more apt to reveal their negative feelings than men are (Schaap, Buunk, & Kerkstra, 1988; Canary, Cupach, & Messman, 1995).

It should be noted that many research findings fail to support the supposed gender differences in conflict style that cartoons, situation comedies, novels, and films portray so readily and so clearly. For example, in numerous studies of both college students and men and women in business, no significant differences were found in the way men and women engage in conflict (Wilkins & Andersen, 1991; Canary & Hause, 1993; Canary, Cupach, & Messman, 1995; Gottman & Levenson, 1999).

Working with Theories and Research. *Do you observe gender differences in conflict? What does it mean to "fight like a woman"? What does it mean to "fight like a man"?*

---

personal conflict occurs frequently between lovers, best friends, siblings, and parents and their offspring. Interpersonal conflict is all the more difficult because, unlike many other conflict situations, it involves disagreement with individuals you often care for, like, even love. There are both negative and positive aspects or dimensions to interpersonal conflict, and each of these should be noted.

Some Negatives

Conflict often leads to increased negative regard for the opponent—and when this opponent is someone you love or care for very deeply, this effect can create serious problems for the relationship. One reason is that many conflicts involve unfair fighting methods that aim largely to hurt the other person.

When one person hurts the other, increased negative feelings are inevitable; even the strongest relationship has limits.

Conflict frequently leads to a depletion of energy better spent on other areas. This is especially true when unproductive conflict strategies are used, as we'll examine later in this unit.

At times conflict leads you to close yourself off from the other individual. Though it would not be to your advantage to reveal your weaknesses to your "enemy," when you hide your true self from an intimate, you may prevent meaningful communication from taking place. One possible consequence is that one or both parties may seek intimacy elsewhere. This often leads to further conflict, mutual hurt, and resentment—all of which add heavily to the costs carried by the relationship. As these costs increase, exchanging rewards may become difficult, perhaps impossible. The result is a situation in which the costs increase and the rewards decrease—a situation that often results in relationship deterioration and eventual dissolution.

Some Positives

The major value of interpersonal conflict is that it forces you to examine a problem and work toward a potential solution. And if you use productive conflict strategies, the relationship may well emerge from the encounter stronger, healthier, and more satisfying than before.

Conflict enables each of you to state what you want and—if the conflict is resolved effectively—perhaps to get it. In fact, a better understanding of each other's feelings has been found to be one of the main results of the "first big fight" (Siegert & Stamp, 1994).

Conflict also prevents hostilities and resentments from festering. Suppose you're annoyed at your partner's e-mailing colleagues for two hours after work instead of devoting that time to you. If you say nothing, your annoyance and resentment are likely to grow. Further, by saying nothing you implicitly approve of such behavior and make it more likely that the hours of e-mail will be repeated. In contrast, through conflict and its resolution, you can stop resentment from increasing. In the process you each can let your own needs be known—for example, that you need lots of attention when you come home from work and that your partner needs to review and get closure on his or her day's work. If you both can appreciate the legitimacy of each other's needs, then solutions may be easily identified. Perhaps the e-mailing can be done after your attention needs are met, or perhaps you can delay your need for attention until your partner gets closure about work. Or perhaps you can learn to provide for your partner's closure needs—and in doing so also get the attention you need.

Consider, too, that when you try to resolve conflict within an interpersonal relationship, you're saying in effect that the relationship is worth the effort; otherwise you would walk away from such a conflict. Although there may be exceptions—as when you engage in conflict to save face or to gratify some ego need—usually confronting a conflict

indicates concern, commitment, and a desire to preserve the relationship.

Online Conflicts

Just as you experience conflict in face-to-face communication, you can experience the same conflicts online. A few conflict situations that are unique to online communication may be noted here.

Sending commercial messages to those who didn't request them often creates conflict. Junk mail is junk mail; but on the Internet the receiver has to pay for the time it takes to read and delete these unwanted messages.

Spamming often causes conflict. Spamming is sending someone unsolicited mail, repeatedly sending the same mail, or posting the same message on lots of bulletin boards even when the message is irrelevant to the focus of the group. One of the very practical reasons spamming is frowned on is that it generally costs people money; and even if the e-mail is free, it makes you spend valuable time and energy to read something you didn't want in the first place. Another reason, of course, is that it clogs the system, slowing it down for everyone.

Flaming, especially common in newsgroups, is sending messages that personally attack another user. Flaming frequently leads to flame wars in which everyone in the group gets into the act and attacks other users. Generally, flaming and flame wars prevent us from achieving our goals and so are counterproductive.

In what other ways is face-to-face conflict different from online conflict?

CONFLICT MANAGEMENT

In managing conflict you can choose from a variety of strategies, which this section will describe. Realize, however, that the strategies you choose will be influenced by several different factors. Understanding these factors may help you select more appropriate and more effective strategies.

For example, the goals (short-term and long-term) you wish to achieve will influence what strategies seem appropriate to you. If all you want is to salvage today's date, you may want to simply give in and ignore the difficulty. If you want to build a long-term relationship, on the other hand, you may want to fully analyze the cause of the problem and look for strategies that will enable both parties to win.

Your emotional state will influence your strategies. You're unlikely to select the same strategies when you're sad as when you're angry. You'll turn to different strategies if you're seeking to apologize than you would use if you were looking for revenge.

Your cognitive assessment of the situation will have an important impact. For example, your attitudes and beliefs about what is fair and equitable will influence your readiness to acknowledge the fairness in the other person's position. Your own assessment of who (if anyone) is the cause of the problem will also have a bearing on your conflict style. You may also assess the likely effects of your various strategies. For example, what do you risk if you use blame or personal rejection in a confrontation with your boss? Do you risk alienating your teenager if you use force?

Your personality and level of communication competence, too, will affect the way you engage in conflict. For example, if you're shy and unassertive, you may be more likely to try to avoid a conflict than to fight actively. If you're extroverted and have a strong desire to state your position, then you may be more likely to fight actively and to argue forcefully.

Your culture and gender will influence your strategies. As noted earlier, many Asian cultures emphasize the importance of saving face; consequently, Asians are less likely to use conflict strategies such as blame and personal rejection, because these are likely to cause a loss of face. People from cultures that look favorably on open conflict may be more apt to use argumentativeness and to fight actively. Students from collectivist cultures prefer mediation and bargaining as conflict resolution strategies, whereas students from individualistic cultures prefer a more adversarial and confrontational conflict style (Leung, 1987; Berry, Poortinga, Segal, & Dasen, 1992). Asian women are expected to be exceptionally polite, especially when in public conflict with men (Tannen, 1994a, 1994b). Even in the United States, although conflict equality may be verbalized, many people expect women to be more polite and to pursue conflict is a nonargumentative way, whereas men are expected to argue forcefully and logically.

Win–Lose and Win–Win Strategies

In any interpersonal conflict, you have a choice. You can look for solutions in which one person wins (usually you) and the other person loses (usually the other person): *win–lose solutions.* Or you can look for solutions in which you and the other person both win: *win–win solutions.* Obviously, win–win strategies are the more desirable, at least when the conflict is interpersonal. Too often, however, we fail even to consider the possibility of win–win solutions and what they might be.

For example, let's say that I want to spend our money on a new car (my old one is unreliable) and you want to spend it on a vacation (you're exhausted and feel the need for a rest). If we can engage in productive conflict and come to a resolution, we can learn what each really wants. We may then be able to figure out a way for each of us to get what we want. Perhaps I might accept a good used car and you might accept a less expensive vacation. Or we might buy a used car and take an inexpensive road trip. Each of these win–win solutions will satisfy both of us; each of us wins, in the sense that each of us gets what we wanted. Additional examples of win–win strategies as they might be used in actual problem situations are provided in the Building Communication Skills box, "How Can You Find Win–Win Solutions?" on page 214.

Avoidance and Active Fighting

One nonproductive conflict strategy is **avoidance.** Avoidance may involve actual physical flight: You may leave the scene of the conflict (walk out of the apartment or go to another part of the office), fall asleep, or blast the stereo to drown out all conversation. It may also take the form of emotional or

Sexual Harassment

All human beings are born free and equal in dignity and rights.

—United Nations Declaration of Human Rights, Article 1

Hearing and recognizing messages that may be perceived as sexual harassment is a first step to avoiding them and responding appropriately to them. Petrocelli and Repa (1992) note that under the law, workplace **sexual harassment** is "any unwelcome sexual advance or conduct on the job that creates an intimidating, hostile or offensive working environment." According to these attorneys, behavior constitutes sexual harassment when it is

▶ sexual in nature—for example, making sexual advances, showing pornographic pictures, telling jokes that revolve around sex, commenting on anatomy

▶ unreasonable—for example, behavior that a reasonable person would object to

▶ severe or pervasive—for example, physical molestation or creating an intimidating environment

▶ unwelcome and offensive—for example, behavior that you have let others know offends you and that you want stopped

You can avoid conveying messages that might be considered sexual harassment (Bravo & Cassedy, 1992) by following these guidelines:

▶ Begin with the assumption that others at work are not interested in your sexual advances, sexual stories and jokes, or sexual gestures.

▶ Listen and watch for negative reactions to any sex-related discussion. Use the suggestions and techniques discussed in this book (such as perception checking and critical listening) to become aware of such reactions. When in doubt, find out; ask questions, for example.

▶ Avoid saying or doing anything you think your parent, partner, or child would find offensive in the behavior of someone with whom she or he worked.

If you think you're being sexually harassed, consider these suggestions (Petrocelli & Repa, 1992; Bravo & Cassedy, 1992; Rubenstein, 1993):

▶ Talk to the harasser. Tell this person, assertively, that you do not welcome the behavior and that you find it offensive. If this doesn't solve the problem, then consider the following additional suggestions.

▶ Collect evidence—perhaps get corroboration from others who have experienced similar harassment, and/or perhaps keep a log of the offensive behaviors.

▶ Use the channels within the organization to deal with your grievances. If this doesn't stop the harassment, consider going farther.

▶ File a complaint with an organization or governmental agency or perhaps take legal action.

▶ Don't blame yourself. Like many who are abused, you may tend to blame yourself, feeling that you are responsible for being harassed. You aren't; however, you may need to secure emotional support from friends or perhaps from trained professionals.

Thinking about Your Communicating @ Work

Have you ever witnessed sexual harassment? What was its nature? How was it dealt with?

BUILDING COMMUNICATION SKILLS

How Can You Find Win-Win Solutions?

As this section explains, in interpersonal conflicts win–win strategies are preferable to win–lose approaches. To get into the habit of looking for win–win solutions, consider the following conflict situations, either alone or in groups of five or six. For each of the situations, try generating as many win–win solutions as possible—solutions that you feel the individuals involved in the conflict could reasonably accept. Give yourself two minutes for each case. Write down all win–win solutions that you (or the group) think of; don't censor yourself or any member of the group.

1. Pat and Chris plan to take a two-week vacation in August. Pat wants to go to the shore and relax by the water. Chris wants to go the mountains and go hiking and camping.
2. Pat recently got a totally unexpected $3,000 bonus. Pat wants to buy a new computer and printer to augment the home office; Chris wants to take a much needed vacation.
3. Pat hangs around the house in underwear. Chris really hates this, and they argue about it almost daily.

4. Philip has recently come out as gay to his parents. He wants them to accept him and his lifestyle (which includes a committed relationship with another man). His parents refuse to accept him; they want him to seek religious counseling for help in changing his orientation.
5. Workers at the local bottling plant want a 20 percent raise to bring their pay into line with the salaries of similar workers at other plants. Management has repeatedly turned down their requests.

If possible, share your win–win solutions with other individuals or groups. From this experience it should be clear that win–win solutions exist for most conflict situations—but not necessarily for all. And, of course, some situations will allow for the easy generation of a lot more win–win solutions than others. Not all conflicts are equal. How might you incorporate win–win strategies into your own conflict management behavior?

---

intellectual avoidance, in which you may leave the conflict psychologically by not dealing with any of the arguments or problems raised. In the United States men are more likely to use avoidance than women (Markman, Silvern, Clements, & Kraft-Hanak, 1993; Oggins, Veroff, & Leber, 1993), often additionally denying that anything is wrong (Haferkamp, 1991–92).

Nonnegotiation is a special type of avoidance—refusal to discuss the conflict or to listen to the other person's argument. At times nonnegotiation takes the form of hammering away at one's own point of view until the other person gives in, a method referred to as steamrolling.

Instead of avoiding the issues, take an active role in your interpersonal conflicts. Don't close your ears (or mind), blast the stereo, or walk out of the house during an argument. This is not to say that a

cooling-off period is not at times desirable. But if you wish to resolve conflicts, you need to confront them actively.

Involve yourself on both sides of the communication exchange. Participate actively as a speaker–listener; voice your own feelings and listen carefully to your opponent's voicing of his or her feelings. Although periodic moratoriums are sometimes helpful, be willing to communicate as both sender and receiver—to say what is on your mind and to listen to what the other person is saying.

Another part of active fighting involves taking responsibility for your thoughts and feelings. For example, when you disagree with your partner or find fault with her or his behavior, take responsibility for these feelings. Say, for example, "I disagree with . . ." or "I don't like it when you . . . ." Avoid statements that deny your responsibility, as in

"Everybody thinks you're wrong about . . ." or "Even Chris thinks you shouldn't . . . ."

Force and Talk

When confronted with conflict, many people prefer not to deal with the issues but rather to force their position on the other person. **Force** may be emotional or physical. In either case, the issues are avoided and the person who "wins" is the one who exerts the most force. This nonproductive strategy is the technique of warring nations, children, and even some normally sensible and mature adults. The use of force is surely one of the most serious problems confronting relationships today, although many approach it as if it were a minor—or even humorous—issue. Another aspect of force is the use of **power plays;** see "How Can You Manage Power Plays?" at www.ablongman.com/devito.

Researchers found that more than 50 percent of both married and unmarried couples had experienced physical violence in their relationship. If we add symbolic violence (for example, threatening to hit the other person or throwing something), the rates are above 60 percent for singles and above 70 percent for marrieds (Marshall & Rose, 1987). In a study of divorced couples, 70 percent reported at least one episode of violence in their premarital, marital, or postmarital relationship. Violence during marriage was higher than in pre- or postmarital relationships (Olday & Wesley, 1990). In another study, 47 percent of a sample of 410 college students reported some experience with violence in a dating relationship (Deal & Wampler, 1986). In most cases the violence was reciprocal—each person in the relationship used violence. In cases in which only one person was violent, the research results are conflicting. For example, in cases in which only one partner was violent, the aggressor was significantly more often the female partner (Deal & Wampler, 1986). Earlier research found similar gender differences (e.g., Cate et al., 1982). Other research, however, has tended to confirm the widespread view that men are more likely to use force than women (DeTurck, 1987): Men are more apt than women to use violent methods to achieve compliance.

Findings such as these point to problems well beyond the prevalence of unproductive conflict

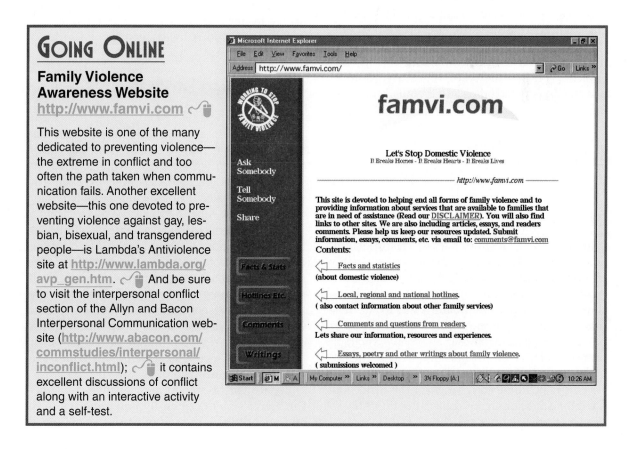

GOING ONLINE

Family Violence Awareness Website
http://www.famvi.com

This website is one of the many dedicated to preventing violence—the extreme in conflict and too often the path taken when communication fails. Another excellent website—this one devoted to preventing violence against gay, lesbian, bisexual, and transgendered people—is Lambda's Antiviolence site at http://www.lambda.org/avp_gen.htm. And be sure to visit the interpersonal conflict section of the Allyn and Bacon Interpersonal Communication website (http://www.abacon.com/commstudies/interpersonal/inconflict.html); it contains excellent discussions of conflict along with an interactive activity and a self-test.

One of the most puzzling findings on violence is that many victims interpret it as a sign of love. For some reason, they see being beaten or verbally abused as a sign that their partner is fully in love with them. Also, many victims blame themselves for the violence instead of blaming their partners (Gelles & Cornell, 1985). Why do you think this is so? What part does force or violence play in your own interpersonal conflicts?

strategies that we want to identify and avoid. They demonstrate the existence of underlying pathologies that we are discovering are a lot more common than were thought previously, when issues like these were never mentioned in college textbooks or lectures. Awareness, of course, is only a first step in understanding and eventually combating such problems.

The only real alternative to force is talk. Instead of using force, you need to talk and listen. The qualities of empathy, openness, and positiveness (see Unit 9), for example, are suitable starting points.

Blame and Empathy

Conflict is rarely caused by a single, clearly identifiable problem or by only one of the parties. Usually conflict is caused by a wide variety of factors, in which both individuals play a role. Any attempt to single out one person for **blame** is sure to fail. Yet a frequently used fight strategy is to blame the other person. Consider, for example, the couple who fight over their child's getting into trouble with the police. Instead of dealing with the problem itself, the parents may blame each other for the child's behavior. Such blaming, of course, does nothing to change the behavior or to help the child.

Often when you blame someone you attribute motives to the person, a process often referred to as "mind reading." Thus, if the person forgot your birthday and this disturbs you, tackle the actual behavior—the forgetting of the birthday. Try not to presuppose motives: "Well, it's obvious you just don't care about me. If you really cared, you could never have forgotten my birthday!"

Empathy is an excellent alternative to blame. Try to feel what the other person is feeling and to see the situation as the other person does. Try to see the situation as punctuated by the other person and think about how this view differs from your own punctuation.

Demonstrate empathic understanding (Unit 9). Once you've empathically understood your opponent's feelings, validate those feelings as appropriate. If your partner is hurt or angry and you feel that such feelings are legitimate and justified (from the other person's point of view), say so; say, "You have a right to be angry; I shouldn't have called your mother a slob. I'm sorry. But I still don't want to go on vacation with her." In expressing validation you're not necessarily expressing agreement on the point at issue; you're merely stating that your partner has feelings that are legitimate and that you recognize them as such.

Silencers and Facilitating Open Expression

The term *silencers* covers a wide variety of fighting techniques that literally silence the other individual. One frequently used silencer is crying. When a person is unable to deal with a conflict or when winning seems unlikely, he or she may begin to cry and thus silence the other person.

Another silencer is to feign extreme emotionalism—to yell and scream and pretend to be losing control. Still another is to develop some "physical" reaction—headaches and shortness of breath are probably the most popular. One of the major problems with silencers is that we can never be certain whether they are mere tactics to win the argument or real physical reactions that we should pay attention to. Regardless of what we do, the conflict remains unexamined and unresolved.

To facilitate open expression, grant the other person permission to express himself or herself freely and openly, to be himself or herself. Avoid power tactics that suppress or inhibit freedom of expression. Such tactics are designed to put the other person down and to subvert real interpersonal equality.

Gunnysacking and Present Focus

A gunnysack is a large bag, usually made of burlap. As a conflict strategy, **gunnysacking** is the unproductive practice of storing up grievances so as to unload them at another time (Bach & Wyden, 1968). The immediate occasion for unloading may be relatively simple (or so it may seem at first); for example, you come home late without calling. Instead of arguing about this, the gunnysacker pours out all past grievances: the birthday you forgot, the time you arrived late for dinner, the hotel reservations you forgot to make. As you probably know from experience, gunnysacking begets gunnysacking. When one person gunnysacks, the other person gunnysacks. The result is two people dumping their stored-up grievances on each other. Frequently the trigger problem never gets addressed. Instead, resentment and hostility escalate.

Focus your conflict on the here and now rather than on issues that occurred two months ago. Similarly, focus your conflict on the person with whom you're fighting, not on the person's mother, child, or friends.

Manipulation and Spontaneity

Manipulation involves an avoidance of open conflict. The manipulative individual attempts to divert conflict by being especially charming (disarming, actually). The manipulator gets the other person into a receptive and noncombative frame of mind, then presents his or her demands to a weakened opponent. The manipulator relies on our tendency to give in to people who are especially nice to us.

Instead of manipulating, try expressing your feelings with **spontaneity** and honesty. Remember that in interpersonal conflict situations, there's no need to plan a strategy to win a war. The objective is not to "win" but to increase mutual understanding and to reach a solution that both parties can accept.

Personal Rejection and Acceptance

A person practicing **personal rejection** withholds love and affection from his or her opponent in conflict, seeking to win the argument by getting the other person to break down in the face of this withdrawal. The individual acts cold and uncaring in an effort to demoralize the other person. In withdrawing affection, the individual hopes to make the other person question his or her own self-worth. Once the other is demoralized and feels less than worthy, it's relatively easy for "rejectors" to get their way. And they can hold out the renewal of love and affection as a reward for a resolution favorable to themselves.

Instead of **rejection**, express positive feelings for the other person and for the relationship between the two of you. Throughout any conflict, harsh words will probably be exchanged, later to be regretted. The words cannot be unsaid or uncommunicated, but they can be partially offset by the expression of positive statements. If you're engaged in combat with someone you love, remember that you're fighting with a loved one and express that feeling. "I love you very much, but I still don't want your mother on vacation with us. I want to be alone with you."

Fighting below and above the Belt

Like fighters in a ring, each of us has a "belt line." When you hit someone below the emotional belt line, a tactic called **beltlining,** you can inflict serious injury. When you hit above the belt, however, the person is able to absorb the blow. With most interpersonal relationships, especially those of long standing, we know where the belt line is. You know, for example, that to hit Pat with the inability to have children is to hit below the belt. You know that to hit Chris with the failure to get a permanent job is to hit below the belt. Hitting below the belt line causes everyone involved added problems. Keep blows to areas your opponent can absorb and handle.

Remember that the aim of a relationship conflict is not to win and have your opponent lose. Rather, it's to resolve a problem and strengthen the relationship. Keep this ultimate goal always in clear focus, especially when you're angry or hurt.

Face-Detracting and Face-Enhancing Strategies

Another dimension of conflict strategies is that of *face orientation*. A face-detracting or face-attacking conflict orientation involves treating the other person as incompetent or untrustworthy, as unable or bad (Donohue & Kolt, 1992). Such attacks can vary from mildly embarrassing to severely damaging to the other person's ego or reputation (Imahori & Cupach, 1994). When such attacks become extreme, they may be similar to verbal aggressiveness—a tactic explained in the next section.

Face-enhancing techniques, in contrast, involve helping the other person to maintain a positive image—an image as competent and trustworthy, able and good. There's some evidence to show that even when, say, you get what you want in a bargaining situation, it is wise to help the other person retain positive face. This makes it less likely that future conflicts will arise (Donohue & Kolt, 1992). Not surprisingly, people are more likely to make a greater effort to support the listener's "face" if they like the listener than if they don't (Meyer, 1994).

Confirming the other person's definition of self (Unit 7), avoiding attack and blame, and using excuses and apologies as appropriate are some generally useful face-positive strategies.

Aggressiveness and Argumentativeness

An especially interesting perspective on conflict is emerging from researchers' work on verbal aggressiveness and argumentativeness (Infante, 1988; Rancer, 1998; Wigley, 1998). Understanding these two concepts will help you understand some of the reasons why conflicts go wrong and some of the ways in which you can use conflict to actually improve your relationships.

Verbal Aggressiveness

Verbal aggressiveness is a method of winning an argument by inflicting psychological pain, by attacking the other person's self-concept. The technique relies on many of the unproductive conflict strategies just considered. It amounts to a type of disconfirmation, in that it seeks to discredit the individual's view of self (see Unit 7). To explore this tendency further, take the following self-test of verbal aggressiveness.

TEST YOURSELF

How Verbally Aggressive Are You?

This scale is designed to measure how people try to win arguments through verbal aggression. For each state-

ment, indicate the extent to which you feel it's true for you. Use the following scale: 1 = almost never true; 2 = rarely true; 3 = occasionally true; 4 = often true; and 5 = almost always true.

_____ 1. I am extremely careful to avoid attacking individuals' intelligence when I attack their ideas.

_____ 2. When individuals are very stubborn, I use insults to soften the stubbornness.

_____ 3. I try very hard to avoid having other people feel bad about themselves when I try to influence them.

_____ 4. When people refuse to do a task I know is important, without good reason, I tell them they are unreasonable.

_____ 5. When others do things I regard as stupid, I try to be extremely gentle with them.

_____ 6. If individuals I am trying to influence really deserve it, I attack their character.

_____ 7. When people behave in ways that are really in very poor taste, I insult them in order to shock them into proper behavior.

_____ 8. I try to make people feel good about themselves even when their ideas are stupid.

_____ 9. When people simply will not budge on a matter of importance, I lose my temper and say rather strong things to them.

_____ 10. When people criticize my shortcomings, I take it in good humor and do not try to get back at them.

_____ 11. When individuals insult me, I get a lot of pleasure out of really telling them off.

_____ 12. When I dislike individuals greatly, I try not to show it in what I say or how I say it.

_____ 13. I like poking fun at people who do things which are very stupid in order to stimulate their intelligence.

_____ 14. When I attack a person's ideas, I try not to damage their self-concepts.

_____ 15. When I try to influence people, I make a great effort not to offend them.

_____ 16. When people do things which are mean or cruel, I attack their character in order to help correct their behavior.

_____ 17. I refuse to participate in arguments when they involve personal attacks.

_____ **18.** When nothing seems to work in trying to influence others, I yell and scream in order to get some movement from them.

_____ **19.** When I am not able to refute others' positions, I try to make them feel defensive in order to weaken their positions.

_____ **20.** When an argument shifts to personal attacks, I try very hard to change the subject.

How did you do? In order to compute your verbal aggressiveness score, follow these steps:

1. Add your scores on items 2, 4, 6, 7, 9, 11, 13, 16, 18, and 19.
2. Add your scores on items 1, 3, 5, 8, 10, 12, 14, 15, 17, and 20.
3. Subtract the sum obtained in step 2 from 60.
4. To compute your verbal aggressiveness score, add the total obtained in step 1 to the result obtained in step 3.

If you scored between 59 and 100, you're high in verbal aggressiveness; if you scored between 39 and 58, you're moderate in verbal aggressiveness; and if you scored between 20 and 38, you're low in verbal aggressiveness. In looking over your responses, make special note of the characteristics identified in the 20 statements that refer to the tendency to act verbally aggressive. Note those inappropriate behaviors that you're especially prone to commit. High agreement (4s or 5s) with statements 2, 4, 6, 7, 9, 11, 13, 16, 18, and 19 and low agreement (1s and 2s) with statements 1, 3, 5, 8, 10, 12, 14, 15, 17, and 20 will help you highlight any significant verbal aggressiveness you might have.

What will you do? Because verbal aggressiveness is likely to seriously reduce interpersonal effectiveness, you probably want to reduce your tendencies to respond aggressively. Review the times when you acted verbally aggressive. What effect did such actions have on your subsequent interaction? What effect did they have on your relationship with the other person? What alternative ways might you have used to get your point across? Might these have proved more effective? Perhaps the most general suggestion for reducing verbal aggressiveness is to increase your argumentativeness.

Source: From "Verbal Aggressiveness" by Dominic Infante and C. J. Wigley in _Communication Monographs,_ V. 53, 1986, pp. 61–69. Used by permission of the National Communication Association and authors. ✔

Argumentativeness

Contrary to popular usage, **argumentativeness** is a quality to be cultivated rather than avoided. Your argumentativeness is your willingness to argue for a point of view, your tendency to speak your mind on significant issues. It's the mode of dealing with disagreements that is the preferred alternative to verbal aggressiveness (Infante & Rancer, 1995). Before reading about ways to cultivate productive argumentativeness, take the following self-test.

TEST YOURSELF

How Argumentative Are You?

This questionnaire, which is based on extensive research, contains statements about controversial issues. Indicate how often each statement is true for you personally according to the following scale: 1 = almost never true; 2 = rarely true; 3 = occasionally true; 4 = often true; and 5 = almost always true.

_____ **1.** While in an argument, I worry that the person I am arguing with will form a negative impression of me.

_____ **2.** Arguing over controversial issues improves my intelligence.

_____ **3.** I enjoy avoiding arguments.

_____ **4.** I am energetic and enthusiastic when I argue.

_____ **5.** Once I finish an argument, I promise myself that I will not get into another.

_____ **6.** Arguing with a person creates more problems for me than it solves.

_____ **7.** I have a pleasant, good feeling when I win a point in an argument.

_____ **8.** When I finish arguing with anyone, I feel nervous and upset.

_____ **9.** I enjoy a good argument over a controversial issue.

_____ **10.** I get an unpleasant feeling when I realize I am about to get into an argument.

_____ **11.** I enjoy defending my point of view on an issue.

_____ **12.** I am happy when I keep an argument from happening.

_____ **13.** I do not like to miss the opportunity to argue a controversial issue.

_____ **14.** I prefer being with people who rarely disagree with me.

_____ **15.** I consider an argument an exciting intellectual challenge.

_____ **16.** I find myself unable to think of effective points during an argument.

_____ **17.** I feel refreshed and satisfied after an argument on a controversial issue.

_____ **18.** I have the ability to do well in an argument.

_____ **19.** I try to avoid getting into arguments.

_____ **20.** I feel excitement when I expect that a conversation I am in is leading to an argument.

How did you do? To compute your argumentativeness score follow these steps:

1. Add your scores on items 2, 4, 7, 9, 11, 13, 15, 17, 18, and 20.

2. Add 60 to the sum obtained in step 1.

3. Add your scores on items 1, 3, 5, 6, 8, 10, 12, 14, 16, and 19.

4. To compute your argumentativeness score, subtract the total obtained in step 3 from the total obtained in step 2.

If you scored between 73 and 100, you are high in argumentativeness; if you scored between 56 and 72, you are moderate in argumentativeness; and if you scored between 20 and 55, you are low in argumentativeness.

What will you do? The researchers who developed this test note that both high and low argumentatives may experience communication difficulties. The high argumentative, for example, may argue needlessly, too often, and too forcefully. The low argumentative, on the other hand, may avoid taking a stand even when it seems necessary. Persons scoring somewhere in the middle are probably the more interpersonally skilled and adaptable, arguing when it is necessary but avoiding arguments that are needless and repetitive. Does your experience support these observations? What specific actions might you take to improve your argumentativeness? A closely related and relevant concept is that of **assertiveness.** Read more about this topic and get an idea of your own assertiveness by taking the self-test, "How Assertive Are Your Messages?" at www.ablongman,com/devito. ᗑ🖱

Source: Scale from "A Conceptualization and Measure of Argumentativeness," by Dominic Infante and Andrew Rancer from *Journal of Personality Assessment,* V. 46, 1982, pp. 72–80. Reprinted by permission of Lawrence Erlbaum Associates.   ✔

Generally, those who score high in argumentativeness have a strong tendency to state their position on controversial issues and to argue against the positions of others. A high scorer sees arguing as exciting and intellectually challenging, and an argument as an opportunity to win a kind of contest. The person who scores low in argumentativeness tries to prevent arguments. This person experiences satisfaction not from arguing but from avoiding arguments. The low argumentative sees arguing as unpleasant and unsatisfying. Not surprisingly, this person has little confidence in his or her ability to argue effectively. The moderately argumentative person possesses some of the qualities of the high argumentative and some of the qualities of the low argumentative.

Men generally score higher in argumentativeness (and in verbal aggressiveness) than women. Men are also apt to be perceived by both men and women as more argumentative (and more verbally aggressive) than women (Nicotera & Rancer, 1994). High and low argumentatives also differ in the way in which they view argument (Rancer, Kosberg, & Baukus, 1992). High argumentatives see arguing as enjoyable and its outcomes as pragmatic. They see arguing as having a positive impact on their self-concept, having functional outcomes, and being highly ego involving. Low argumentatives, on the other hand, believe that arguing has a negative impact on their self-concept, that it has dysfunctional outcomes, and that it's not very ego involving. They see arguing as offering little in the way of enjoyment or pragmatic outcomes.

Given that persons scoring somewhere in the middle on the argumentativeness scale are likely to be the most interpersonally skilled and adaptable, here are some suggestions for cultivating appropriate argumentativeness and for preventing argumentativeness from degenerating into aggressiveness (Infante, 1988).

- Treat disagreements as objectively as possible; avoid assuming that because someone takes issue with your position or your interpretation, they're attacking you as a person.

- Avoid attacking the other person (rather than the person's arguments), even if this would give you a tactical advantage; it will probably backfire at some later time and make your relationship more difficult. Center your arguments on issues rather than personalities.

- Reaffirm the other person's sense of competence; compliment the other person as appropriate.

BUILDING COMMUNICATION SKILLS

How Can You Engage in Conflict?

Think about the major productive and unproductive conflict strategies discussed in this section as they might apply to the specific situations described below. Assume that each of the following statements is made by someone close to you. Try developing an unproductive approach and an alternative productive strategy to deal with each situation.

1. You're late again. You're always late. Your lateness is so inconsiderate of my time and my interests. What is wrong with you?
2. I just can't bear another weekend of sitting home watching television. You never want to do anything. I'm just not going to do that again and that's final.
3. Guess who forgot to phone for reservations again? Don't you remember anything?
4. You can't possibly go out with Pat. We're your parents and we simply won't allow it. And we don't want to hear any more about it. It's over.
5. Why don't you stay out of the neighbors' business? You're always butting in and telling people what to do. Why don't you mind your own business and take care of your own family instead of trying to run everybody else's?

- Avoid interrupting; allow the other person to state her or his position fully before you respond.
- Stress equality and emphasize the similarities that you have with the other person; verbalize your areas of agreement before attacking the disagreements.
- Express interest in the other person's position, attitude, and point of view.
- Avoid presenting your arguments too emotionally; using a loud voice or interjecting vulgar expressions will prove offensive and eventually ineffective.
- Allow the other person to save face; never humiliate the other person.

BEFORE AND AFTER THE CONFLICT

To make conflict truly productive, consider a few suggestions for preparing for conflict and for using conflict as a method for relational growth.

Before the Conflict

Try to fight in private. When you air your conflicts in front of others, you create a wide variety of other problems. You may not be willing to be totally honest when third parties are present; you may feel you have to save face and therefore must win the fight at all costs. This may lead you to use strategies to win the argument rather than strategies to resolve the conflict. Also, of course, you run the risk of embarrassing your partner in front of others, and that may build resentment and hostility.

Be sure you're both ready to fight. Although conflicts arise at the most inopportune times, you can choose the time when you will try to resolve them. Confronting your partner when she or he comes home after a hard day of work may not be the right tactic for resolving a conflict. Make sure you're both relatively free of other problems and ready to deal with the conflict at hand.

Know what you're fighting about. Sometimes people in a relationship become so hurt and angry that they lash out at the other person just to vent their own frustration. The "content" of the conflict may merely be an excuse to express anger. Any attempt at resolving such a "problem" will of course be doomed to failure, because the problem addressed is not the true source of the conflict. Instead, it may be underlying hostility, anger, and frustration that need to be dealt with.

At other times, people argue about general and abstract issues that are poorly specified; for example, a partner's lack of consideration or failure to accept responsibility. Only when you define issues in specific, concrete terms can you begin to understand them and thus resolve them.

Fight about problems that can be solved. Fighting about past behaviors or about family members or situations over which you have no control solves nothing; instead, it creates additional difficulties. Any attempt at resolution is doomed, because by definition you can't solve such problems. Often such conflicts are actually concealed attempts at expressing frustration or dissatisfaction.

Consider what beliefs you hold that may need to be reexamined. Unrealistic beliefs are often at the heart of interpersonal conflict. Such beliefs include "If my partner really cared, he or she would do what I ask," "If people really love each other, they should not have to work on their relationship," and "My partner doesn't listen to what I have to say."

After the Conflict

After the conflict is resolved, there's still work to be done. Often after one conflict is supposedly settled, another conflict will emerge—because, for example, one person may feel harmed and may feel the need to retaliate and take revenge in order to restore self-worth (Kim & Smith, 1993). So it's especially important that the conflict be resolved in such a way that it does not generate other, perhaps more significant, conflicts.

Learn from the conflict and from the process you went through in trying to resolve it. For example, can you identify the fight strategies that aggravated the situation? Does the other person need a cooling-off period? Do you need extra space when upset? Can you identify when minor issues are going to escalate into major arguments? Does avoidance make matters worse? What issues are particularly disturbing and likely to cause difficulties? Can these be avoided?

Keep the conflict in perspective. Be careful not to blow it out of proportion—to define your relationship in terms of the conflict. Conflicts in most relationships actually occupy a very small percentage of real time, yet in recollection they often loom extremely large. Also, avoid the tendency to see disagreements as inevitably leading to major blowups. And don't allow conflict to undermine your own or your partner's self-esteem. Don't view yourself, your partner, or your relationship as a failure just because you have had an argument—or even lots of arguments.

Negative feelings frequently arise after an interpersonal conflict, most often because unfair fight strategies were used to undermine the other person—strategies such as personal rejection, manipulation, or force. Resolve surely to avoid such unfair tactics in the future, but at the same time let go of guilt and blame for yourself and your partner. If you think it would help, discuss these feelings with your partner or even with a therapist.

Increase the exchange of rewards and cherishing behaviors to demonstrate your positive feelings and to show that you're over the conflict. It's a good way of saying you want the relationship to endure and to flourish.

REFLECTIONS ON ETHICS IN HUMAN COMMUNICATION

Libel, Slander, and More

The First Amendment to the U.S. Constitution states that

> Congress shall make no law . . . abridging the freedom of speech, or of the press; or the right of the people peaceably to assemble and to petition the Government for a redress of grievances.

But speech is not always free; in fact, speech can be unlawful and unethical in a variety of situations. For example, it's considered unethical (and illegal as well) to defame another person—to falsely attack his or her reputation, causing damage to it. When this attack is done in print or in pictures, it's called *libel*. When done through speech, it's called *slander*.

People are becoming increasingly sensitive to and accepting of cultural differences. Whereas just decades ago it was widely considered normal to use racial, sexist, or homophobic terms in conversation or to tell jokes at the expense of various cultural groups, today it's considered inappropriate. Today it is generally considered unethical to demean another person because of that person's gender, age, race, nationality, affectional orientation, or religion or to speak in cultural stereotypes—fixed images of groups that promote generally negative pictures.

Sexual harassment is unethical and a form of speech that is not protected by the First Amendment. The courts have ruled that sexual harassment can take place by either sex against either sex.

Verbal abuse of people because of their position on a particular issue or their cultural identifi-

cation, or because of something they've done that a person disapproves of, is considered unethical.

What would you do? *At the water cooler in the office, you join two of your colleagues only to discover that they're exchanging racist jokes. You don't want to criticize them, for fear that you'll become unpopular; these colleagues could make it harder for you to get ahead in the organization. At the same time, however, you don't want to remain silent, for fear it would imply that you're accepting of this type of talk. What would you do in this situation? In this connection you may want to visit the Freedom Forum for all sorts of information on freedom of speech (*www.freedomforum.org*).*

SUMMARY

In this unit we explored interpersonal conflict, the types of conflicts that occur, the don'ts and dos of conflict management, and what to do before and after the conflict.

1. Relationship conflict is a situation in which two persons have opposing goals and interfere with each other's attaining these goals. Conflicts may occur face-to-face or on the Internet; for example, through e-mail or newsgroups.

2. Content conflict centers on objects, events, and persons in the world that are usually, but not always, external to the parties involved in the conflict.

3. Relationship conflicts are concerned not so much with external objects as with relationships between individuals: with such issues as who is in charge, how equal the partners are in a primary relationship, or who has the right to set down rules of behavior.

4. Unproductive and productive conflict strategies include win–lose and win–win approaches, avoidance and fighting actively, force and talk, blame and

empathy, silencers and open expression, gunnysacking and present focus, manipulation and spontaneity, personal rejection and acceptance, fighting below and above the belt, and fighting aggressively and argumentatively.

5. To cultivate argumentativeness, treat disagreements objectively and avoid attacking the other person; reaffirm the other's sense of competence; avoid interrupting; stress equality and similarities; express interest in the other's position; avoid presenting your arguments too emotionally; and allow the other to save face.

6. Prepare for the conflict, and try to fight in private and when you're both ready to fight. Have a clear idea of what you want to fight about, be specific, and fight about things that can be solved.

7. After the conflict, assess what you've learned, keep the conflict in perspective, let go of negative feelings, and increase the positiveness in the relationship.

KEY TERMS

interpersonal conflict

content conflict

relationship conflict

win–lose solutions

win–win solutions

avoidance

nonnegotiation

blame

empathy

silencers

gunnysacking

manipulation

beltlining

verbal aggressiveness

argumentativeness

 THINKING CRITICALLY ABOUT

Interpersonal Conflict

1. Why are men more likely to withdraw from a conflict than women? What arguments can you present for or against any of these reasons (Noller, 1993): Because men have difficulty dealing with conflict? Because the culture has taught men to avoid it? Because withdrawal is an expression of power?

2. Access ERIC, Medline, PsycLit, or Sociofile and locate an article dealing with interpersonal conflict. What can you learn about conflict and interpersonal communication from this article?

3. Visit some game websites (for example, http://www.gamesdomain.co.uk or http://www.gamepen.com/yellowpages/) and examine the rules of the games. What kinds of conflict strategies do these game rules embody? Do you think these games influence people's interpersonal conflict strategies?

4. What does your own culture teach about conflict and its management? For example, what strategies does your culture prohibit? Are some strategies prohibited in conflicts with certain people (say, your parents) but not in disagreements with others (say, your friends)? Does your culture prescribe certain ways of dealing with conflict? Does it have different expectations for men and for women? To what degree have you internalized these cultural teachings? What effect do these teachings have on your actual conflict behaviors?

5. **Researching Interpersonal Conflict.** How would you go about finding answers to such questions as these?
   - What topics cause the most conflict among college friends?
   - Are more-educated people less likely to use verbal aggressiveness and more likely to use argumentativeness than less-educated people?
   - Do men and women differ in the satisfaction or dissatisfaction they derive from a conflict experience?
   - What types of strategies are more likely to be used by happy couples than by unhappy couples?
   - How do man–man, woman–woman, and woman–man interpersonal conflicts differ from one another?

UNIT 12
Interviewing

Unit Contents

The Interview Process

The Information Interview

The Employment Interview

The Lawfulness of Questions

You'll no doubt find yourself in a wide variety of interview situations throughout your social and professional life. And, as you'll see throughout this unit, your effectiveness in this form of communication will prove crucial in helping you achieve many of your life goals. In this unit you'll learn

▶ how interviewing works and the many forms it takes

▶ how you can be a more effective interviewer or interviewee, especially in employment and information interviews

THE INTERVIEW PROCESS

Interviewing is a particular form of communication in which you interact largely through a question-and-answer format to achieve a variety of specific goals. Here are just a few examples:

- A salesperson tries to sell a client a new car.
- A teacher talks with a student about the reasons the student failed the course.
- A counselor talks with a family about their communication problems.
- A recent graduate applies to IBM for a job in the product development division.
- A building owner talks with a potential apartment renter.
- A minister talks with a church member about relationship problems.
- A lawyer examines a witness during a trial.
- A theatrical agent talks with a producer.
- A client discusses the qualities desired in a potential mate with a dating service employee.
- An employer talks with an employee about the reasons for terminating his or her employment.

The specific goals of an interview will guide and structure both its content and its format. In an employment interview, for example, the goal for the interviewer is to find an applicant who can fulfill the tasks of the position. The interviewee's goal is to get the job, if it seems desirable. These goals, which guide the behaviors of both parties, are relatively specific and are usually clear to both parties.

The **interview** is distinctly different from other forms of communication because it proceeds through questions and answers. Both parties in the interview can ask and answer questions, but generally the interviewer asks most of the questions and the interviewee answers them.

Usually we think of interviewing as a face-to-face experience, and often it is. But interviewing is increasingly being conducted through e-mail, chat groups, and video conferences and, of course, by telephone. Especially when a company, say, interviews candidates in a series of three or four interviews, the first one or two interviews may well be held through chat groups or by telephone and the later ones in a face-to-face setting.

Two-Person and Team Interviews

Most interviews follow a two-person structure, but team interviews are becoming more popular. On *Nightline,* for example, several journalists may interview a political candidate, or one journalist may interview several candidates. On the ubiquitous television talk show (see the Media Watch box in this unit), a moderator interviews several people at the same time.

In employment situations team interviews are extremely important, especially as you go up the organizational hierarchy. It's not uncommon, for example, for an entire academic department to interview a candidate for a teaching position; and a similar team interview with the administration often follows. In business organizations three or four vice presidents may interview a candidate for a middle management position.

The main advantage of the team interview is that it gives the audience or the organization different viewpoints and perspectives on the person being interviewed. It also helps ensure that the interview does not lag but follows a relatively rapid pace.

Team interviews, however, are expensive (in an organization, time is money); they occasionally degenerate into what may appear to be an interrogation (which may be desirable on television but is inappropriate in an employment setting); and they may allocate too much time to those conducting the interview and not enough to the person being interviewed (see Kanter, 1995).

General Interview Structures

Interviews vary from relatively informal talks that resemble everyday conversations to rigidly prescribed questions that are posed in a set order (Hambrick, 1991). Depending on your specific purpose, you can select the interview structure—or combine various types to create a unique interview structure—to meet your particular needs.

In the *informal interview* two friends might discuss what happened on their respective dates or in their employment interviews. This type of interview resembles conversation; a general theme for the interview is chosen in advance, but the specific questions are formed during the interaction. You use this type of interview to obtain information informally.

In the *guided interview* a guest on, say, *The Tonight Show* might be interviewed about a new television series or CD. Here the topics are chosen in advance, but specific questions and wordings are guided by the ongoing interaction. The guided interview is useful because it ensures maximum flexibility and responsiveness to the dynamics of the situation.

The *standard open interview* might be used for interviewing several candidates for a job. Open-ended questions and their order are selected in advance. This type of interview is useful when standardization is needed: when you want to be sure to ask each person the same question in exactly the same way.

In the *quantitative interview* a researcher might survey, for example, students' political opinions. In this type, questions and their order are selected in advance, as are the possible response categories—such as A, B, C, or D; agree–disagree; check from 1 to 10. The quantitative interview is useful when statistical analyses are to be performed and when large amounts of information are to be collected.

Interview Questions and Answers

Understanding the different types of interview questions may help you both to respond to questions more effectively—as in an employment interview—and to ask questions more effectively—as in an information-gathering interview. Questions may be analyzed in terms of at least the following dimensions: open–closed, neutral–biased, primary–follow-up, and direct–indirect.

Open–Closed

Openness in interview questions has to do with the degree of freedom you have to respond, both in content and format. At times a question will offer you almost unlimited latitude in responding; for example, "What are your goals?" "Why do you want to work at Peabody and Peabody?" At the opposite extreme, closed questions require only a yes or no; for example, "Are you willing to relocate to San Francisco?" "Can you use Lotus 1–2–3?" Between these extremes are short-answer questions, which are relatively closed and offer you only limited freedom in responding; for example, "What would you do as manager here?" "What computer skills do you have?" Part of the art of responding successfully in interviews is coming up with answers that are appropriate to questions' levels of openness. Thus, if you're asked a question like "Why do you want to work at Peabody and Peabody?" you're expected to speak at some length. If you're asked, "Are you willing to relocate to San Francisco?" then a simple yes or no (with or without a qualification) will suffice; for example, "Absolutely, though it would take me a few months to close my affairs here in Boston."

Neutral–Biased

Neutrality in an interview question—and its opposite, bias—relates to the extent to which the question provides the answer the interviewer wants from the interviewee. Some questions are neutral and don't specify any answer as more appropriate than any other. At the other extreme are questions that are biased, or loaded. These indicate quite clearly the particular answer the interviewer expects or wants. Compare the following questions:

- How did you feel about managing your own Web design firm?
- You must really enjoy managing your own Web design company, don't you?

The first question is neutral and allows you to respond in any way; it asks for no particular answer. The second question is biased; it specifies that the interviewer expects a yes. Between the neutrality of "How did you feel about your previous job?" and the bias of "You must have loved your previous job, didn't you?" there are questions that specify with

MEDIA WATCH

TELEVISION TALK SHOWS

Interviewing is a form of communication used widely in the media—in newspapers and magazines as well as on talk radio and on television. But it's the television talk show that has most captured the attention of the public, and TV talk shows are a media phenomenon that needs to be examined (Jacobs, 1995). In an article entitled "Talk Shows Are Good for You," frequent talk show psychologist Gilda Carle (1995) identifies some of the benefits of talk shows: They show us new communication techniques, teach us about new topics, break down myths, show us celebrities as real people, and make us laugh. Talk shows have also given a public platform to issues that were once hidden and to groups that have generally not had media exposure (Peck, 1995).

Talk shows are entertaining—but often they also present themselves as educational; as therapy for the masses; and as arbiters of how you, your parents, and your friends should live your lives. Especially in the monologue that closes many of the shows, talk show hosts with little or no professional training in the topic at hand dispense advice on a variety of issues. For instance, they regularly give communication advice with no basis in scientific research and foster myths about communication—perhaps the most prevalent being that communication will solve all problems, and that the more communication a couple has the better the relationship will be.

Many talk shows also give the impression that therapy takes one hour: The problem is introduced, the therapy is given, the catharsis takes place, and the cure emerges. "The programs," argued media theorist Janice Peck (1995), "discourage critical engagement with and reflection on those problems in favor of immediate identification and catharsis, and undermine the ability to take these problems seriously in the service of making them entertaining."

Talk shows also create an impression that every issue is divided into two extremes (Gamson, 1998). Polarizing guests—the gay activist and the fundamentalist preacher, the pro- and antiabortionist, the liberal and the conservative—makes for lively debate and generally holds viewer attention, although it also intensifies the animosities between groups. Despite the impression talk shows may convey, however, views that are opposite extremes don't accurately represent the attitudes of the majority of people in the world.

Follow-Up. *Do you watch talk shows? If so, what do you get out of them? What do you see as the main advantage of television talk shows? The main disadvantage? What can you learn about interviewing techniques from television talk show hosts?*

---

varying degrees of strength the answer the interviewer expects or prefers. For example:

- Did you like your previous job?
- Did you dislike your previous job very much?
- It seems like it would be an interesting job, no?

An interviewer who asks too many biased questions will learn less about the interviewee's talents or experiences than about the interviewee's ability to give the desired answer. As an interviewee, pay special attention to any biases in the question. Don't give the responses your interviewer expects if they're not what you believe to be correct or know to be true. This would be unethical. However, when your responses are not what the interviewer expects,

consider explaining why you're responding as you are. For example, to the biased question, "It seems like it would be an interesting job, no?" you might respond: "It was interesting most of the time, but it didn't allow for enough creativity."

Primary–Follow-Up

Primary questions introduce a topic; follow-up questions ask for elaboration on what was just said. Too many primary questions and not enough follow-up questions will often communicate a lack of interest and perhaps a failure to listen as effectively as possible. When we introduce a topic, we naturally expect people to ask follow-up questions. When they don't, we feel that they're not interested in what we're saying or aren't really listening.

The stereotypical psychiatric interviewer would ask a lot of follow-up questions, probing each and every thought the patient expresses. The stereotypical unresponsive partner would ask no follow-up questions. A balance between primary and follow-up questions, determined in large part by the situation and by your own communication goals, is desirable.

One way to judge whether you're achieving the appropriate balance is to mentally pause and ask yourself how you and your listener are enjoying the conversation or interview. If your listener seems not to be enjoying the interaction, try increasing your follow-up responses. Use the active listening responses discussed in Unit 5. If you're not finding the interview satisfactory, then probably your listener is not asking enough follow-up questions, not giving your statements enough attention. One helpful tactic to elicit more follow-up is to talk in specifics about yourself. Instead of "life is difficult," say "I'm going through a bad time." Also, clue your listener in a more obvious way to your desire to pursue this topic. Instead of just saying "I'm going through a bad time," continue with "and I'm not sure what I should do" and, even more directly, "and I need advice."

Direct–Indirect

The directness or indirectness of interview questions will vary greatly from one culture to another. In the United States, be prepared for rather direct questions, whether you're being interviewed for information or for a job. In Japan, on the other hand, the interviewee is expected to reveal himself or herself despite questions that are generally quite indirect.

Similarly, cultures vary in what they consider appropriate directness in, say, speaking of one's accomplishments in a job interview. In many Asian cultures the interviewee is expected to appear modest and unassuming and should allow his or her competencies to emerge indirectly during the interview. In the United States, on the other hand, you're expected to state your competencies without any significant modesty. In fact, many interviewers expect a certain amount of hyperbole and exaggeration.

Types of Interviews

Interviews can be classified on the basis of the goals the interviewer and interviewee want to achieve.

Here we'll look briefly at persuasive, appraisal, exit, and counseling interviews; the next two main sections will discuss information and employment interviews—probably the most important for college students—in detail.

The Persuasive Interview

In the **persuasive interview** the goal is to change an individual's attitudes, beliefs, or behaviors. The interviewer may ask questions that will lead the interviewee to the desired conclusion, or the interviewee may answer questions in a persuasive way. For example, if you go into a showroom to buy a new car, you interview the salesperson. The salesperson's goal is to get you to buy a particular car. He or she attempts to accomplish this by answering your questions persuasively. You ask about mileage, safety features, and finance terms. The salesperson discourses eloquently on the superiority of this car above all others.

All interviews contain elements of both information and persuasion. When, for example, a guest appears on *The Tonight Show* and talks about a new movie, information is communicated; but the performer is also trying to persuade the audience to see the movie. Informing and persuading usually go together in actual practice.

The Appraisal Interview

In the **appraisal interview**, an interviewee's performance is assessed by management or by more experienced colleagues. The general aim is to discover what the interviewee is doing well (and to praise this), and to find out what he or she is not doing well and why (and to correct this). These interviews are important because they help new members of an organization see how their performance matches up with the expectations of those making promotion and firing decisions.

The Exit Interview

The **exit interview** is used widely by organizations in the United States and throughout the world. All organizations compete in one way or another for superior workers. When an employee chooses to leave a company, it's important for the employer to know why so as to prevent other valuable workers from leaving as well. Another function of this interview is to provide a way of making the exit as pleasant and as efficient as possible for both employee and employer.

The Counseling Interview

Counseling interviews are conducted to provide guidance. The goal here is to help the interviewee deal more effectively with problems, work more effectively, get along better with friends or lovers, or cope more effectively with day-to-day living. For the interview to be of any value, the interviewer must learn a considerable amount about the person— habits, problems, self-perceptions, goals, and so on. With this information the counselor then tries to persuade the person to alter certain aspects of his or her thinking or behaving. The counselor may try to persuade you, for example, to listen more attentively when your spouse argues with you or to devote more time to your class work.

THE INFORMATION INTERVIEW

In the **information interview** the interviewer tries to learn something from the interviewee. In the information interview—unlike the employment interview—the person interviewed is usually a person of some reputation and accomplishment. The interviewer asks a series of questions designed to elicit the interviewee's views, beliefs, insights, perspectives, predictions, life history, and so on. Examples of the information interview include interviews published in popular magazines; the TV interviews conducted by David Letterman, Katie Couric, and Barbara Walters; and examinations conducted by a lawyer during a trial. All aim to elicit specific information from someone who supposedly knows something others don't know. In this discussion we'll concentrate on your role as the interviewer, as that is the role in which you're likely to find yourself now and in the near future.

Let's say that your interview is designed to get information about a particular field—for example, Web design. You want to know about the available job opportunities and the preparation you would need to get into this field. Here are a few guidelines for conducting such information-gathering interviews. These general guidelines will also prove useful in other types of interviews, and especially in the employment interview, which we will consider in the next section.

Select the Person You Wish to Interview

There are several ways to find a likely person to interview. Suppose you wish to learn something about Web publishing. Perhaps you look through your college catalog; there you find that a course on this general topic is offered by Professor Bernard Brommel. You think it might be worthwhile to interview him. Or you visit a variety of newsgroups and discover that one particular person has posted extremely well-reasoned articles; you'd like to interview her to get her opinion on Web design and advice on how you might break into this field. If you want to contact a book author, you can always write to the author in care of the publisher or editor (listed on the copyright page); also, many books give their authors' e-mail addresses. You can often find the address and phone number of a professional person by calling the appropriate professional association for a directory listing (the *Encyclopedia of Associations* lists just about every professional association in the country). Or you can write to the person via the association's website. Newsgroup and listserv writers are of course the easiest to contact, because their e-mail addresses are included with their posts. Last, you can often find experts through *The Yearbook of Experts, Authorities, and Spokespersons* and through a variety of websites; for example, http://www.experts.com and http://www.usc.edu/dept/news_service/experts_directory.html.

After you've selected an individual you hope to interview, but before you try to set up an appointment, try to learn something about this person. Consult an online library or a bookstore to see if this person has written a book, or go through a CD-ROM database to see if this person has written any research articles. Search through the databases covering computers, the Internet, and the World Wide Web. Search the Web and Usenet groups to see if the person has a Web page or posts to newsgroups. You may find that the person encourages people to correspond via e-mail.

Secure an Appointment

Phone the person or send a letter or e-mail requesting an interview. In your call or letter, identify the purpose of your request and that you would like a brief interview. For example, you might say: "I'm preparing for a career in Web design, and I would appreciate it if I could interview you to learn more about the subject. The interview would take about 15 minutes." (It's helpful to let the person know it will not take too long; he or she is more likely to agree to being interviewed.) Generally, it's best to be available at the interviewee's convenience. So indicate flexibility on your part; for example, "I can interview you any afternoon this week."

You may find it necessary to conduct the interview by phone. In this case, call to set up a time for a future interview call. For example, you might say, "I'm interested in a career in Web design, and I would like to interview you on the job opportunities in this field. If you agree, I can call you back at a time that's convenient for you." In this way, you don't run the risk of asking the person to hold still for an interview while eating lunch, talking with colleagues, or running to class.

Prepare Your Questions

Preparing questions ahead of time will ensure that you use the time available to your best advantage. Of course, as the interview progresses, other questions will come to mind and should be asked. But having a prepared list of questions will help you obtain the information you need most easily.

Establish Rapport with the Interviewee

Open the interview by thanking the person for making the time available to you. Many people receive lots of requests, so it helps if you also remind the person of your specific purpose. You might say something like this: "I really appreciate your making time for this interview. As I mentioned, I'm interested in learning about the job opportunities in Web design, and your expertise and experience in this area will help a great deal."

Ask Permission to Tape the Interview

Generally, it's a good idea to tape the interview. A tape will provide a complete record of the interview, which you'll be able to review as you need to. Taping will also free you to concentrate on the interview rather than on trying to write down the person's responses. But ask permission first. Some people prefer not to have informal interviews taped. Even if the interview is being conducted by phone, ask permission if you intend to tape the conversation.

Ask Open-Ended Questions

Use questions that provide the interviewee with room to discuss the issues you want to raise. Thus, instead of asking, "Do you have formal training in Web publishing?" (a question that requires a simple yes or no and will not be very informative), you might ask, "Can you tell me something about your background in this field?" (a question that is open-ended and allows the person greater freedom). You can then ask follow-up questions to pursue more specifically the topics that emerge in the interviewee's responses.

Close the Interview with an Expression of Appreciation

Thank the person for making the time available for the interview and for being informative, cooperative, helpful, or whatever. Showing your appreciation will make it a great deal easier if you want to return for a second interview.

Follow Up the Interview

Follow up the interview with a brief note of thanks—in which you might express your appreciation for the time given you, your enjoyment in speaking with the person, and your gratitude to the interviewee for providing the information you needed.

THE EMPLOYMENT INTERVIEW

Perhaps of most concern to college students is the **employment interview**. In this type of interview, a great deal of information and persuasion will be exchanged. The interviewer will learn about you, your interests, and your talents—and, if he or she is clever enough, about some of your weaknesses and liabilities. In turn, you'll be informed about the nature of the organization, its benefits, and its advantages—and, if you're clever enough, about some of its disadvantages and problems. For the purpose of this discussion, assume you're the interviewee.

Prepare Yourself

Before going into a job interview, do your homework. One interviewing counselor suggests that this homework should consist of researching four areas: the field, the position, the company, and current events (Taub, 1997).

First, research the career field you're considering and its current trends. With this information you'll be able to demonstrate that you're up to date and committed to the field.

Second, research the specific position you're applying for so you'll be able to show how your skills and talents mesh with the position. A good way to do this is to visit the organization's website. Most large corporations and, increasingly, many small firms maintain websites and frequently include detailed job descriptions. Be prepared to demonstrate your ability to perform each of the tasks noted in the job description. The Monster.com website shown in Going Online on page 234 will give you a good starting place to search the Web to learn about jobs and specific companies. An especially interesting website, http://www.salary.com/, provides a salary wizard to help you estimate potential salary and benefits.

Third, research the company or organization—its history, mission, and current directions. If it's a publishing company, familiarize yourself with its books and software products. If it's an advertising agency, familiarize yourself with its major clients and major advertising campaigns. A good way to do this is to call and ask the company to send you company brochures, newsletters, or perhaps a quarterly or annual report. And be sure to visit the company's website; not only will you learn lots of useful information about this company, but you will also show the interviewer that you make appropriate use of technology. With extensive knowledge of the company, you'll be able to show your interest in and focus on this specific company. Most company websites have similar address formats: www.nameofcompany.org.

Fourth, research what is going on in the world in general and in the business world in particular. This will increase your breadth of knowledge and allow you to demonstrate that you're a knowledgeable individual who continues to learn. Reading a good daily newspaper or weekly newsmagazine will help you master current events.

Through an employment interview both you and the organization are trying to fill a need. You want a job that will help build your career, and the organization wants an effective employee who will be a productive asset. View the interview as an opportunity to engage in a joint effort through which each can gain something beneficial. If you approach the interview in this cooperative frame of mind, you're less likely to become defensive; this, in turn, will make you a more appealing potential colleague.

The most important element you can prepare is your résumé. The résumé is a summary of essential information about your experience, education, and abilities. Often, a job applicant submits a résumé in response to a job listing, and if the potential employer thinks the applicant's résumé is promising, the candidate is invited for an interview. Because of the importance of the résumé and its close association with the interview, a sample one-page résumé and some guidelines to assist you in preparing your own are provided here. A variety of computer programs are available to help you in preparing your résumé; most offer an extensive array of templates that you fill in (or customize if you wish) with your specific data. The sample presented here was customized from a Corel Office Suite template. Lots of online websites also offer résumé advice; for example: www.jobstar.org/tools/resume, www.jobweb.org/catapult/guenov/restips.html, and www.dbm.com/jobguide/resprep.html. At www.10minuteresume.com you can enter the relevant information and the site will produce a résumé for you (and tell you something about the salary you might expect).

You can also post your résumé on the Internet through various websites. For example, www.careermosaic.com will post your résumé for four months. At Monster.com (www.monster.com) you can list your résumé and the type of job you're looking for, and the service will e-mail you when something appropriate comes up.

Another part of preparation is to analyze and manage the normal anxiety that accompanies em-

② For some people, employment objectives may be more general than indicated here; for example, "to secure a management trainee position with an international investment bank." If you have more specific objectives, put them down. Don't imply that you'll take just anything, but don't appear too specific or demanding, either.

③ List work experience in chronological order, beginning with your latest position and working back. Depending on your work experience, you may have to pare down what you write. Or, if you have little or nothing to write, you may have to search through your employment history for some relevant experience. Often, the dates of the various positions are included. If you have little or no paid work experience or large gaps in employment history due, say, to time off raising a family, include volunteer work or other unpaid work that requires skills important to the job; for example, coordinator of a little league team or treasurer of the PTA.

④ Provide more information than simply your educational degree. For example, include your major and your minor and perhaps sequences of courses in communication or management or some other field that will further establish your suitability for the job. List honors or awards if they're relevant to your education or job experience. If the awards are primarily educational (for example, Dean's List), list them under the Education heading; if job-related, list them under the Employment Experience heading.

⑤ Identify those activities that are relevant to the job skills you want to demonstrate (for example, debating) and also those that attest to the personal qualities you want to stress (for example, reliability and trustworthiness, as shown in being treasurer).

⑥ Highlight your special skills. Do you have some foreign language ability? Do you have experience with business or statistical software? If you do, put it down. Such competencies are relevant to many jobs.

① Your name, address, phone and fax number, and e-mail are generally centered at the top of the résumé.

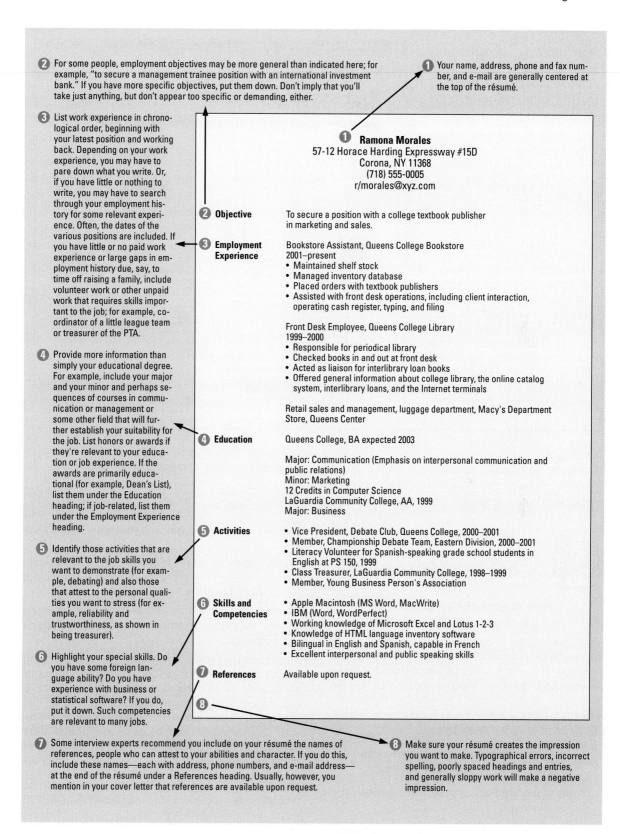

① **Ramona Morales**
57-12 Horace Harding Expressway #15D
Corona, NY 11368
(718) 555-0005
r/morales@xyz.com

② **Objective**

To secure a position with a college textbook publisher in marketing and sales.

③ **Employment Experience**

Bookstore Assistant, Queens College Bookstore
2001–present
- Maintained shelf stock
- Managed inventory database
- Placed orders with textbook publishers
- Assisted with front desk operations, including client interaction, operating cash register, typing, and filing

Front Desk Employee, Queens College Library
1999–2000
- Responsible for periodical library
- Checked books in and out at front desk
- Acted as liaison for interlibrary loan books
- Offered general information about college library, the online catalog system, interlibrary loans, and the Internet terminals

Retail sales and management, luggage department, Macy's Department Store, Queens Center

④ **Education**

Queens College, BA expected 2003

Major: Communication (Emphasis on interpersonal communication and public relations)
Minor: Marketing
12 Credits in Computer Science
LaGuardia Community College, AA, 1999
Major: Business

⑤ **Activities**

- Vice President, Debate Club, Queens College, 2000–2001
- Member, Championship Debate Team, Eastern Division, 2000–2001
- Literacy Volunteer for Spanish-speaking grade school students in English at PS 150, 1999
- Class Treasurer, LaGuardia Community College, 1998–1999
- Member, Young Business Person's Association

⑥ **Skills and Competencies**

- Apple Macintosh (MS Word, MacWrite)
- IBM (Word, WordPerfect)
- Working knowledge of Microsoft Excel and Lotus 1-2-3
- Knowledge of HTML language inventory software
- Bilingual in English and Spanish, capable in French
- Excellent interpersonal and public speaking skills

⑦ **References**

Available upon request.

⑧

⑦ Some interview experts recommend you include on your résumé the names of references, people who can attest to your abilities and character. If you do this, include these names—each with address, phone numbers, and e-mail address—at the end of the résumé under a References heading. Usually, however, you mention in your cover letter that references are available upon request.

⑧ Make sure your résumé creates the impression you want to make. Typographical errors, incorrect spelling, poorly spaced headings and entries, and generally sloppy work will make a negative impression.

GOING ONLINE

The Monster.com Website
http://www.monster.com

This screen presents the Monster.com home page. This website lists some 50,000 jobs you can access by keyword, location, or industry; it's just one of the many websites that are useful for finding jobs. Take a look at a few others, too. For example, www.flipdog.com/home.html identifies hundreds of thousands of job opportunities and allows you to post your résumé; www.careerpath.com organizes the classified ads from leading newspapers; and www.jobtrak.com is especially valuable for college students looking for their first job or for internships. What can you learn about the job opportunities in your field from these websites?

---

ployment interviews. You may wish to take the following self-test to assess your job interviewing apprehension before reading about this interview type.

TEST YOURSELF

How Apprehensive Are You in Employment Interviews?

This questionnaire is composed of five statements concerning feelings about communicating in the job interview setting. Indicate in the spaces provided the degree to which each statement adequately describes your feelings about the employment interview. Use the following scale: 1 = strongly agree; 2 = agree; 3 = undecided; 4 = disagree; or 5 = strongly disagree.

_____ **1.** While participating in a job interview with a potential employer, I am not nervous.

_____ **2.** Ordinarily, I am very tense and nervous in job interviews.

_____ **3.** I have no fear of speaking up in job interviews.

_____ **4.** I'm afraid to speak up in job interviews.

_____ **5.** Ordinarily, I am very calm and relaxed in job interviews.

How did you do? To compute your score, follow these steps:

1. Reverse your scores for items 2 and 4 as follows: 1 becomes 5, 2 becomes 4, 3 remains 3, 4 becomes 2, and 5 becomes 1.

2. Add the scores from all five items; be sure to use the reverse scores for items 2 and 4 and the original scores for 1, 3, and 5.

The higher your score, the greater your apprehension; for example, a score of 25 (the highest possible score) would indicate an extremely apprehensive individual, and a score of 5 (the lowest possible score) would indicate an extremely unapprehensive individual. How does your score compare with those of your peers? What score do you think would ensure optimum performance at the job interview?

What will you do? Your level of apprehension will probably differ somewhat depending on the type of job interview, your responsibilities, the need and desire you have for the job, and so on. What factors would make you especially apprehensive? Do the items in this questionnaire give you clues as to how to lessen your apprehension?

It has been found that people demonstrating apprehension during a job interview will be perceived less positively than would those demonstrating confidence and composure. How might you learn to better display confidence?

Source: From "A Progress Report on the Development of an Instrument to Measure Communication Apprehension in Employment Interviews," by Joe Ayres, Debbie M. Ayres, and Diane Sharp in *Communication Research Reports,* V. 10, 1993, pp. 87–94. Reprinted by permission. ✔

Establish Goals

All interviews have specific objectives. As part of your preparation, fix your goals firmly in your mind. Use them as guides to the remainder of your preparation and also to your behavior during and even after the interview. After establishing your

COMMUNICATION @ WORK

Confidence in Employment Interviews

Confidence is that feeling by which the mind embarks on great and honorable courses with a sure hope and trust in itself.

—Cicero

A special type of communication skill is that of communicating **confidence.** Make the interviewer see you as someone who can get the job done, who is confident. Here are some suggestions for communicating confidence—guidelines that are not limited in their application to interviewing but have relevance to all forms of communication. After reading these suggestions, try your hand at analyzing confidence in an interview; see "How Can You Display Confidence in an Interview?" at www.ablongman.com/devito. 🖱

▶ Take an active role in the interview. Initiate topics or questions when appropriate. Avoid appearing to be a passive participant waiting for some stimulus.

▶ Don't ask for agreement from the interviewer by using tag questions—for example, "That was appropriate, don't you think?"—or by saying normally declarative sentences with a rising intonation and thereby turning them into questions, as in "I'll arrive at nine?" By asking for agreement you communicate a lack of confidence in your own decision making or in your opinions.

▶ Admit mistakes. Attempting to cover up obvious mistakes communicates a lack of confidence. Only a confident person can openly admit her or his mistakes and not worry about what others will think.

▶ Avoid excessive movements, especially self-touching movements. Tapping a pencil on a desk, crossing and uncrossing your legs in rapid succession, or touching your face or hair all communicate an uneasiness, a lack of social confidence.

▶ Maintain eye contact with the interviewer. People who avoid eye contact often give the impression of being ill at ease, as if they're afraid to engage in meaningful interaction.

▶ Avoid vocalized pauses—the *ers* and *ahs* that frequently punctuate conversations and that communicate that you lack certainty and are hesitating, not quite sure what to say. Similarly, avoid the "like you know" or the "I mean" interjections.

Thinking about Your Communicating @ Work

What other kinds of confidence cues can you identify that would work in the employment interview? What kinds of verbal or nonverbal messages work against the communication of confidence?

objectives clearly in your own mind, relate your preparation to these goals. For example, in asking yourself how to dress, what to learn about the specific company, and what questions to pose during the interview, consider how your goals might offer answers to these questions.

Prepare Answers and Questions

If the interview is at all important to you, you'll probably think about it for some time. Use this time productively by rehearsing (by yourself or, if possible, with friends) the expected course of the interview.

Think about the questions that are likely to be asked and how you'll respond to them. Table 12.1 presents a list of questions commonly asked in employment interviews; drawn from a variety of interviewing experts, these are organized around

the major topics on the résumé (Seidman, 1991; Kennedy, 1996; Stewart & Cash, 1997). As you read down this list, visualize yourself at a job interview and try responding to the questions in the middle column. After you've formulated a specific response, look at the suggestions opposite each set of questions. Did your responses match the suggestions? Can you rephrase your responses for greater effectiveness? You may also find it helpful to rehearse with this list before going into the interview. Although not all of these questions will be asked in any one interview, be prepared to answer all of them. Realize that many interviewers form their impressions on the basis of your previous performance, which they take as an indication of your future performance. Keep this in mind when you discuss your previous position and work patterns.

Even though the interviewer will ask most of the questions, you too will want to ask questions. In addition to rehearsing some answers to anticipated

BUILDING COMMUNICATION SKILLS

How Can You Practice Interviewing Skills?

Form three-person groups, preferably consisting of persons who don't know one another well or who have had relatively little interaction. One person should be designated the interviewer, another the interviewee, and the third the interview analyst. The interview analyst should choose one of the following situations:

▶ An interview for the position of counselor at a camp for children with disabilities.

▶ An interview for a part in a new Broadway musical.

▶ An appraisal interview to focus on an employee's communication problems in relating to superiors.

▶ A teacher–student interview in which the teacher is trying to discover why the course he or she taught last semester was such a dismal failure.

▶ An interview between the chair of the Communication Department and a candidate for

the position of instructor of human communication.

After the situation is chosen, the interviewer should interview the interviewee for approximately 10 minutes. The analyst should observe but not interfere in any way. After the interview is over, the analyst should offer a detailed analysis, considering each of the following: (1) What happened during the interview (essentially a description of the interaction)? (2) What was well handled? (3) What went wrong? What aspects of the interview were not handled as effectively as they might have been? (4) What could have been done to make the interview more effective?

The interview analysts may then report their major findings to the class as a whole. A list of "common faults" or "suggestions for improving interviews" may then be developed by the group leader.

TABLE 12.1   Common Interview Questions

Question Areas	Examples	Suggestions
Objectives and Career Goals	What made you apply to Datacomm? Do you know much about Datacomm? What did you like most about Datacomm? If you took a job with us, where would you like to be in five years? What benefits do you want to get out of this job?	Be positive (and as specific as you can be) about the company. Demonstrate your knowledge of the company. Take a long-range view; no firm wants to hire someone who will be looking for another job in six months.
Education	What do you think of the education you got at Queens College? Why did you major in communication? What was majoring in communication at Queens like? What kinds of courses did you take? Did you do an internship? What were your responsibilities?	Be positive about your educational experience. Try to relate your educational experience to the specific job. Demonstrate competence but at the same time the willingness to continue your education (either formally or informally).
Previous Work Experience	Tell me about your previous work experience. What did you do exactly? Did you enjoy working at Happy Publications? Why did you leave? How does this previous experience relate to the work you'd be doing here at Datacomm? What kinds of problems did you encounter at your last position?	Again, be positive; never knock a previous job. If you do, the interviewer will think you may be criticizing them in the near future. Especially avoid criticizing specific people with whom you worked.
Special Competencies	I see here you have a speaking and writing knowledge of Spanish. Could you talk with someone on the phone in Spanish or write letters in Spanish to our customers? Do you know any other languages? How much do you know about computers? Accessing databases?	Before going into the interview, review your competencies. Explain your skills in as much detail as needed to establish their relevance to the job and your own specific competencies.
Personal	Tell me who you are. What do you like? What do you dislike? Are you willing to relocate? Are there places you would not consider relocating to? Do you think you'd have any trouble giving orders to others? Do you have difficulty working under deadlines?	Place yourself in the position of the interviewer and ask yourself what kind of person you would hire. Stress your ability to work independently but also as a member of a team. Stress your flexibility in adapting to new work situations.
References	Do the people you listed here know you personally or academically? Which of these people know you the best? Who would give you the best reference? Who else might know about your abilities that we might contact?	Be sure the people you list know you well and especially that they have special knowledge about you that is relevant to the job at hand.

questions, fix firmly in mind the questions you want to ask the interviewer.

After your preparations, you're ready for the interview proper. Several suggestions may guide you through this sometimes difficult procedure.

Make an Effective Presentation of Self

Making a good initial impression is probably the most important single part of the entire procedure.

If you fail here, it will be difficult to salvage the rest of the interview. So devote special care to the way in which you present yourself.

A great number of jobs are won or lost on the basis of physical appearance alone, so give attention to your physical presentation. Dress in a manner that shows that you care enough about the interview to make a good impression. At the same time, dress comfortably. To avoid extremes is perhaps the key guideline. When in doubt, it's probably best to err on the side of formality: Wear the tie, high heels, or dress.

Bring with you the appropriate materials, whatever they may be. At the very least bring a pen and paper; an extra copy or two of your résumé; and, if appropriate, a business card. If you're applying for a job in a field in which you've worked before, you might bring samples of your previous work.

An interesting perspective on self-presentation is provided by the theory of self-monitoring (see Unit 6), which argues that you regulate the way you present yourself to best achieve the effect you want. Self-monitoring, as you can appreciate, is especially prevalent in the employment interview, where so much depends on your making the right impression. If you haven't already done so, try taking the self-test "How much do you self-monitor?" to help you estimate your own tendency to self-monitor: **www.ablongman.com/devito**. ⌣🖰 As you'll see, self-monitoring has special application to the interview situation.

Arrive on Time

Arriving on time for a job interview means arriving 5 to 10 minutes early. This will allow you time to relax, to get accustomed to the general surroundings, and perhaps to fill out any forms that may be required. And it gives you a cushion should something delay you on the way.

Be sure you know the name of the organization, the job title, and the interviewer's name. Although you'll have much on your mind when you go into the interview, the interviewer's name is not one of the things you can afford to forget (or mispronounce).

In presenting yourself, don't err on the side of too much casualness or too much formality. When there's doubt, lean toward increased formality. Slouching back in the chair, smoking, and chewing gum or candy are obvious behaviors to avoid when you're trying to impress an interviewer.

Demonstrate Effective Interpersonal Communication

Throughout the interview, be certain that you demonstrate the skills of interpersonal communication that are spelled out in this book. The interview is the ideal place to put into practice all the skills you've learned. Here, for example, are the seven characteristics of conversational effectiveness considered in Unit 9 with special reference to the interview situation:

- *Openness.* Answer questions fully. Avoid one-word answers, which may signal a lack of interest or knowledge.
- *Empathy.* See the questions from the asker's point of view. Focus your eye contact and orient your body toward the interviewer. Lean forward as appropriate.
- *Positiveness.* Emphasize your positive qualities. Express positive interest in the position. Avoid statements critical of yourself and others.
- *Immediacy.* Connect yourself with the interviewer throughout the interview; for example, use the interviewer's name, focus clearly on the interviewer's remarks, and express responsibility for your thoughts and feelings.
- *Interaction management.* Ensure the interviewer's satisfaction by being positive, complimentary, and generally cooperative.
- *Expressiveness.* Let your nonverbal behaviors (especially facial expression and vocal variety) reflect your verbal messages and your general enthusiasm. Avoid fidgeting and excessive moving about. Vary your vocal rate, pitch, and pausing, for example, to best reflect your meanings (DeGroot & Motowidlo, 1999).
- *Other-orientation.* Focus on the interviewer and on the company. Express agreement and ask for clarification as appropriate.

In addition to demonstrating these qualities of effectiveness, avoid behaviors that create negative impressions during employment interviews. Here are a few mistakes people often make:

- They're unprepared; they forgot to bring their résumé, fail to show that they know anything about the company.
- They demonstrate poor communication skills; they avoid looking at the interviewer, slouch, slur their words, speak in an overly low or rapid

UNDERSTANDING THEORY AND RESEARCH

Talkaholism

A concept especially important in interviewing is *talkaholism*—the tendency to talk too much, to be a compulsive talker (McCroskey & Richmond, 1995). Not surprisingly, McCroskey and Richmond (1995) found talkaholics to be more assertive, more willing to communicate, and more positive about their own communication skills than people who were not talkaholics. Talkaholics were also more likely to be planning for careers demanding high communication skills (for example, public relations or advertising). A high number of talkaholics were majoring in journalism or communication. Persons who were low in talkaholism were likely to be more shy, introverted, and apprehensive than high talkaholics. In interviews with high talkaholics, the researchers found that talkaholics know they're compulsive talkers but that none of the 21 students studied in depth saw their talkaholism as a problem.

Working with Theories and Research. *On the basis of this study, what additional questions about this concept of compulsive communication might be worth researching? How might the concept of talkaholism and the conclusions reached in this study help you to understand better your own interviewing communication tendencies or those of others?*

voice, give one-word answers, fidget, dress inappropriately.

- They appear to have an unpleasant personality; they come across as defensive, cocky, lacking in assertiveness, extremely introverted, or overly aggressive.
- They show little initiative; they fail to pick up on ramifications of interviewer's questions, give one-word answers, don't ask questions as would be appropriate.
- They listen ineffectively; they're easily distracted, need to have questions repeated, fail to maintain appropriate eye contact.

Acknowledge Cultural Rules and Customs

Each culture has its own rules for communicating (Barna, 1985; Ruben, 1985; Spitzberg, 1991). These rules, whether in the interview situation or in friendly conversation, prescribe appropriate and inappropriate behavior, rewards and punishments, and what will help you get the job and what won't.

For example, earlier I gave general advice to emphasize your positive qualities, highlight your abilities and positive qualities, and minimize any negative characteristics or failings. But in some cultures—especially collectivist cultures such as those of China, Korea, and Japan—interviewees are expected to show modesty (Copeland & Griggs, 1985). In organizations that emphasize teamwork and cooperation, you may be seen as arrogant, brash, and unsuitable if you stress your own competencies too much. In collectivist cultures, too, great deference is to be shown to the interviewer who represents the company. If you don't treat the interviewer with great respect, you may appear to be disrespectful of the entire company. On the other hand, in individualistic cultures such as that of the United States, too much deference may make you appear unassertive, unsure of yourself, and unable to assume a position of authority.

And recall that (as mentioned earlier) cultures also vary greatly in attitudes toward directness. Too direct an approach may offend people of one culture, but too indirect an approach may offend people of another.

Mentally Review the Interview

Mentally review the interview afterwards so as to fix it firmly in your mind. What questions were asked? How did you answer them? Review and write down any important information the interviewer gave. Ask yourself what you could have done more effectively. Consider what you did effectively that you could repeat in other interviews. Ask yourself how you might correct your weaknesses and capitalize on your strengths.

Follow Up

In most cases, follow up an interview with a thank-you note to the interviewer. In this brief, professional letter, thank the interviewer for his or her time and consideration. Reiterate your interest in the organization, and perhaps add that you hope to hear from the interviewer soon. Even if you did not get the job, you might in a follow-up letter ask to be kept in mind for future openings.

This letter provides you with an opportunity to resell yourself—to mention again the qualities you possess and wish to emphasize but may have been too modest to expand upon at the time. The letter will help make you stand out in the mind of the interviewer, because not many interviewees write thank-you letters. It will help remind the interviewer of your interview. It will also tell the interviewer that you're still interested in the position. It's a kind of pat on the back to the interviewer that says, in effect, that the interview was an effective one.

THE LAWFULNESS OF QUESTIONS

Through the Equal Employment Opportunity Commission, the federal government has classified some employment interview questions as unlawful. Federal guidelines on unlawful questions apply in all 50 states; individual states also may have added further restrictions. You may find it interesting to take the following self-test (constructed with the good help of Stewart & Cash, 1997; Zincoff & Goyer, 1984; and Kirby, 2001) to see if you can identify which questions are lawful and which are unlawful (see Pullum, 1991).

TEST YOURSELF

Can You Identify Unlawful Questions?

For each question write L (Lawful) if you think the question is legal for an interviewer to ask in an employment interview or U (Unlawful) if you think the question is illegal. For each question you consider unlawful, indicate why you think it's so classified.

_____ 1. Are you married, Tom?

_____ 2. When did you graduate from high school, Mary?

_____ 3. Do you have a picture so I can attach it to your résumé?

_____ 4. Will you need to be near a mosque (church, synagogue)?

_____ 5. I see you taught courses in "gay and lesbian studies." Are you gay?

_____ 6. Is Chinese your native language?

_____ 7. Will you have difficulty getting a baby-sitter?

_____ 8. I notice that you walk with a limp. Is this a permanent injury?

_____ 9. Where were you born?

_____ 10. Have you ever been arrested for a crime?

_____ 11. How tall are you? What do you weigh?

_____ 12. I see you were in the army. Were you honorably discharged?

How did you do? All 12 questions are unlawful. The remaining discussion in this unit explains why each of these and similar questions are unlawful.

What will you do? In anticipation of being asked illegal questions, consider reviewing the questions in this self-test and try to develop the general principles that define illegality in employment interview questions. Also consider how you would respond to each question if you were asked this in an actual job interview. ✔

Unlawful Information Requests

Some of the more important areas about which unlawful questions are frequently asked concern age, marital status, race, religion, nationality, citizenship, physical condition, and arrest and criminal records. For example, it's legal to ask applicants whether they meet the legal age requirements for the job and can provide proof of that. But it's unlawful to ask their exact age—even in indirect ways, as illustrated in question 2 in the self-test. It's unlawful to ask about a person's marital status (question 1) or about family matters that are unrelated to the job (question 7). An interviewer may ask you,

Can you identify possible legitimate reasons for asking each of the questions given in the self-test on unlawful questions? Do you agree that certain requests for information should be considered illegal in a job interview? What types of questions do you think should be considered illegal?

however, to identify a close relative or guardian if you're a minor, or to name any relative who currently works for the company.

Questions concerning your race (questions 3 and 6), religion (4), national origin (9), affectional orientation (5), age (2), handicaps unrelated to job performance (8), or even arrest record (10) are unlawful, as are questions that attempt to get at this same information in oblique ways. Note, for example, that requiring a picture may be a way of discriminating against an applicant on the basis of gender, race, and/or age.

Thus, for example, the interviewer may ask you what languages you're fluent in but may not ask what your native language is (question 6), what language you speak at home, or what language your parents speak. The interviewer may ask you if you are in this country legally but may not ask if you were born in this country or naturalized (question 9). The interviewer may ask about the type of training you received in the military but not if you were honorably discharged (question 12).

The interviewer may inquire into your physical condition only insofar as your qualifications for the job are concerned. For example, the interviewer may ask, "Do you have any physical problems that might prevent you from fulfilling your responsibilities in this job?" But the interviewer may not ask about any physical disabilities (question 8) or about your height or weight (question 11). The interviewer may

BUILDING COMMUNICATION SKILLS

How Can You Respond to Unlawful Questions?

This exercise is designed to raise some of the unlawful questions that you don't have to answer, and to provide you with some practice in developing responses that protect your privacy while maintaining a positive relationship with the interviewer.

The self-test "Can you identify unlawful questions?" presented 12 unlawful questions. Assuming that you did not want to answer the questions, how would you respond to each of them? One useful procedure is to write your

responses and then compare them with those of other students, either in groups or with the class as a whole. Or form two-person groups and role-play the interviewer–interviewee situation. To make this realistic, the person playing the interviewer should press for an answer; the interviewee should continue to avoid answering, yet respond positively and cordially. You'll discover this is not always easy: Tempers often flare in this type of interaction.

ask you whether you've been convicted of a felony but not whether you've been arrested (question 10).

These are merely examples of some of the lawful and unlawful questions that may be asked during a job interview. Note that even the questions used as examples here might be lawful in certain specific situations. The test to apply is simple: Is the information related to your ability to perform the job? Such questions are referred to as BFOQ—bona fide occupational qualification—questions.

Once you understand what questions are unlawful, consider how to deal with them if they come up during an interview.

Strategies for Dealing with Unlawful Questions

Your first strategy should be to deal with unlawful questions by answering the part you don't object to and omitting any information you don't want to give. For example, if you're asked what language is spoken at home, you may respond with a statement such as "I have some language facility in Russian and Arabic" without giving a direct answer to the question. If asked to list all the organizations of which you're a member (an unlawful question in many states, because it's often a way of getting at political affiliation, religion, nationality, and various other areas), you might respond by saying something like "The only organizations I belong to that are relevant to this job are the International Communication Association and the National Communication Association."

This type of response is preferable to telling the interviewer that he or she is asking an unlawful question. In many cases the interviewer may not even be aware of the legality of various questions and may have no intention of trying to get at information you're not obliged to give. For example, the interviewer may recognize the national origin indicated by your last name and may simply want to mention that he or she is also from the same background. If you immediately take issue with the question, you may be creating problems where none really exist.

On the other hand, do recognize that in many employment interviews the unwritten intention is to keep certain people out, whether it's people who are older or those of a particular marital status, affectional orientation, nationality, religion, and so on. If you're confronted by questions that are unlawful and that you don't want to answer, and if the tactful method described above does not work and your interviewer persists—saying, for example, "Is Vietnamese the language spoken at home?" or "What other organizations have you belonged to?"—you might counter by saying that such information is irrelevant to the interview and to the position you're seeking. Again, be courteous but firm. Say something like "This position does not call for any particular language skill and so it does not matter what language is spoken in my home." Or you might say, "The organizations I mentioned are the only relevant ones; whatever other organizations I might belong to would certainly not interfere with my ability to perform in this company at this job."

If the interviewer still persists—and it's doubtful that many would after these rather clear and direct responses—you might explain that these questions are unlawful and that you're not going to answer them.

REFLECTIONS ON ETHICS IN HUMAN COMMUNICATION

Answering Questions

Another interesting issue with regard to questions is the ethical obligation you have when you respond to questions in all communication situations, not only in interviews. Here are a few such questions that others might ask of you; all are questions asking for information that you have. For each question there are extenuating circumstances that make your responding fully or truthfully extremely difficult. You consider these circumstances (noted under "Thought") as you think of what to say.

What would you do?

Question   [A 15-year-old asks] Was I adopted? Who are my real parents?

Thought   Yes, you were adopted, but I fear that you'll look for your biological parents and will be hurt when you find out that they're drug dealers.

Question   [A relationship partner of 20 years asks] Have you had any affairs since we've been together?

Thought   Yes, but I don't want to say anything, because the affairs were insignificant (none are ongoing) and will only create problems for the one important relationship in my life.

Question   [A potential romantic partner asks] What's your HIV status?

Thought   I've never been tested, but now is not the time to talk about this. I'll practice safe sex so as not to endanger my partner.

Question   [An interviewer says] You seem a bit old for this type of job. How old are you?

Thought   I am old for this job, but I need it anyway. Further, it's really illegal for the interviewer to ask my age. I don't want to turn the interviewer off by pointing this out, because I really need this job. Yet I don't want to reveal my age either.

SUMMARY

This unit introduced the process of interviewing, explored the nature of questions and answers, and identified the major forms of interviewing (focusing on information-gathering and employment interviews).

1. Interviewing is a form of interpersonal communication in which two persons interact largely through a question-and-answer format to achieve specific goals.
2. Six types of interviewing are the persuasive interview, the appraisal interview, the exit interview, the counseling interview, the information interview, and the employment interview.
3. Questions may be viewed as varying in their degree of openness, neutrality, primacy (or follow-up function), and directness.
4. In the information interview the following guidelines should prove useful: Select the person you wish to interview, secure an appointment, prepare your questions, establish rapport with the interviewee, ask permission to tape the interview, ask open-ended questions, and follow up the interview.
5. In the employment interviews the following guidelines should prove useful: Prepare yourself intellectually and physically for the interview, establish your goals, prepare answers to predicted questions, make an effective presentation of yourself, acknowledge cultural rules, mentally review the interview, and follow up the interview with a brief letter.
6. Interviewees should familiarize themselves with possible unlawful questions and develop strategies for dealing with these questions.

KEY TERMS

interviewing

informal interview

guided interview

standard open interview

quantitative interview

persuasive interview

appraisal interview	information interview	BFOQ questions
exit interview	employment interview	
counseling interview	unlawful questions	

 THINKING CRITICALLY ABOUT

Interviewing

1. How is a blind date like an interview? How is the first day of class like an interview?

2. How would you prepare a short interview guide to enable you to study one of the following questions: (1) Why do students select the elective courses they do? (2) Why do people become teachers (or law enforcement officers or health care workers)? (3) Why do people watch the television shows they watch?

3. Visit one of the websites noted in this chapter and locate a job that you think might be appropriate for yourself or for someone in the class. What do you see as the advantages and disadvantages of job searching on the Web?

4. Some positions ask for a list of references—people the employer could contact who could comment on your suitability for the position. Whom would you include on your reference list? Why would these individuals be appropriate for such a list? What (ideally) would each person say about you?

5. **Researching Interviewing.** How would you go about finding answers to such questions as these?
   - Are men and women equally effective in interviewing for information? Are men and women equally effective in job interview situations?
   - What questions do people ask about prospective blind dates? Do these questions change as people get older?
   - Who are the most credible television interviewers?
   - What characteristics do television talk show hosts have in common? How do hosts differ?
   - What résumé items will work against a candidate getting a job?

UNIT 13
Small Group Communication

Unit Contents

A great deal of your social and professional life will revolve around your participation in groups—groups for developing ideas, increasing self-awareness, learning, and solving problems. Understanding the nature and function of small groups and how you can use these groups effectively and efficiently will help you throughout your social and professional career. In this unit you'll learn

▶ how small groups operate and the rules the various types of groups follow

▶ how you can use groups to achieve a variety of personal, social, and professional goals

SMALL GROUPS

A **group** is a collection of individuals who are connected to one another by some common purpose and have some degree of organization among them. For *small groups* in particular, each of these characteristics needs to be explained a bit further.

A small group is, first, a collection of individuals few enough in number so that all members may communicate with relative ease as both senders and receivers. Generally, a small group consists of approximately 5 to 12 people. The important point to keep in mind is that each member should be able to function as both source and receiver with relative ease. If the group gets much larger than 12, this becomes difficult.

Second, the members of a group must be connected to one another through some common purpose. People on a bus normally do not constitute a group, because they're not working at some common purpose. If the bus gets stuck in a ditch, the riders may quickly become a group and work together to get the bus back on the road. In a small group the behavior of one member is significant for all other members. This does not mean that all members must have exactly the same purpose in being part of the group. But generally there must be some similarity in the individuals' reasons for interacting.

Third, the members must be connected by some organizing rules or structure. At times the structure is rigid—as in groups operating under parliamentary procedure, in which each comment must follow prescribed rules. At other times, as in a social gathering, the structure is very loose. Yet in both instances there's some organization and some structure: Two people don't speak at the same time, comments or questions by one member are

responded to by others rather than ignored, and so on.

Small Group Stages

The small group develops in much the same way that a conversation develops. As in conversation, there are five stages: opening, feedforward, business, feedback, closing. The *opening stage* is usually a getting-acquainted time in which members introduce themselves and engage in social small talk, or **phatic communication.** After this preliminary get-together, there's usually a *feedforward stage* in which members make some attempt to identify what needs to be done, who will do it, and so on. In formal business groups the meeting agenda (which is a perfect example of feedforward) may be reviewed and the tasks of the group identified. In informal social groups the feedforward may consist simply of introducing a topic of conversation or talking about what the group's members should do.

The *business stage* is the actual work on the tasks—the problem solving, the sharing of information, or whatever else the group needs to do. At the *feedback stage*, the group may reflect on what it has done and perhaps on what remains to be done. Some groups may even evaluate their performance at this stage. At the *closing stage*, the group members again return to their focus on individuals and will perhaps exchange closing comments—"Good seeing you again," and the like.

These stages are rarely separate from one another. Rather, they blend into one another. For example, the opening stage is not completely finished before the feedforward begins. Rather, as the opening comments are completed, the group begins to introduce feedforward; as the feedforward begins to end, the business starts.

Small Group Formats

Small groups serve their functions in a variety of formats. Among the most popular small group formats for relatively formal functions are the round table, the panel, the symposium, and the symposium–forum (Figure 13.1).

The Round Table.   In the **round table** format, group members arrange themselves in a circular or semicircular pattern. They share the information or solve the problem without any set pattern of who speaks when. Group interaction is informal, and members contribute as they see fit. A leader or moderator may be present; he or she may, for example, try to keep the discussion on the topic or encourage more reticent members to speak up.

The Panel.   In the **panel**, group members are "experts" but participate informally and without any set pattern of who speaks when, as in a round table. The difference is that there's an audience whose members may interject comments or ask questions. Many talk shows, such as the Jerry Springer and Oprah Winfrey shows, use this format.

A variation is the two-panel format, with an expert panel and a lay panel. The lay panel discusses the topic but may turn to the expert panel members when in need of technical information, additional data, or direction.

The Symposium.   In the **symposium,** each member delivers a prepared presentation much like a public speech. All speeches are addressed to different aspects of a single topic. A symposium leader introduces the speakers, provides transitions from one speaker to another, and may provide periodic summaries.

The Symposium–Forum.   The symposium–forum consists of two parts: a symposium, with prepared speeches, and a **forum,** with questions from the audience and responses by the speakers. The leader introduces the speakers and moderates the question-and-answer session.

Small Group Channels

Small groups use a wide variety of channels. Often, of course, they take place face-to-face; this is the channel that probably comes to mind when you think of group interaction. But today much small group interaction also takes place online. Online groups are proliferating and are becoming a part of people's experience throughout the world. They're important to many of us personally and socially as well as professionally. Two major types of online

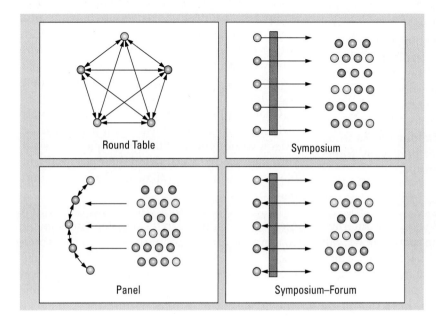

Figure 13.1

Small Group Formats

These four formats are general patterns that may describe a wide variety of groups. Within each type, there will naturally be considerable variation. For example, in the symposium–forum there's no set pattern for how much time will be spent on the symposium part and how much time will be spent on the forum part. Similarly, combinations may be used. Thus, for example, group members may each present a position paper (basically a symposium) and then participate in a round table discussion.

groups may be noted here: the mailing list group and the chat group. In conjunction with the following discussions, take a look at the "Credo for Free and Responsible Use of Electronic Communication Networks" at www.natcom.org. It's one attempt by a national communication association to articulate some of the ethical issues in electronic group communication.

Mailing List Groups

Mailing list groups are groups of people interested in particular topics who communicate with one another through e-mail. Generally, you subscribe to a list and communicate with all other members by addressing your mail to the group e-mail address. Any message you send to this address will be sent to all members who subscribe to the list at the same time; there are no asides to the person sitting next to you (as in face-to-face groups). A huge number of mailing lists categorized by topic are available at www.neosoft.com/internet/paml/bysubj.html. Another useful site is www.liszt.com, which contains a similarly large list. A list of frequently asked questions and mailing list addresses can be found at http://www.cis.ohio-state.edu/hypertext/faq/usenet/mail/mailing-lists/top.html. Of course you could also go to one of the search engines and search for mailing lists. To locate a mailing list on your next speech topic, you might e-mail your request to listserv@listserv.net. Send the message: "list public-speaking-topic"; for example, "list United Nations."

Communication through mailing lists does not take place in real time. It's like regular e-mail; you may send your message today, but it may not be read until next week and you may not get an answer for another week. Much of the spontaneity created by real-time communication is lost. For example, you may be very enthusiastic about a topic when you send your e-mail but may practically forget about it by the time someone responds.

Chat Groups

Chat groups have proliferated across the Internet. These groups enable members to communicate with one another in real time in discussion groups called channels. At any one time there may be perhaps 4,000 channels and 20,000 users online, so your chances of finding a topic you're interested in are fairly high. If you need help with chat group communication, take a look at the website for this text. If you want help with chat groups or Internet Relay Chat groups, check http://www.kei.com/irc.html, http://ftp.acsu.buffalo.edu/irc/www/ircdocs.html, or http://www.irchelp.org/.

Unlike mailing lists, chat group communication takes place in real time; you see and in many cases hear a member's message as it's being sent, with virtually no delay. As in mailing lists and face-to-face conversation, the purposes of chat groups vary from communication that simply maintains connection with others (what many would call "idle chatter" or phatic communication) to extremely significant interchanges of ideas.

Communication in a chat group resembles the conversation you would observe at a large party. The total number of guests divide up into small groups varying from two on up, and members of each group discuss their own topic or their own aspect of a general topic. For example, in a group about food, 10 people may be discussing food calories, 8 people may be discussing restaurant food preparation, and 2 people may be discussing the basic food groups, all on this one channel. So although you may be communicating in one primary group (say, dealing with restaurant food), you also have your eye trained to pick up something particularly interesting in another group, much as you do at a party. Chat groups also notify you when someone new comes into the group and when someone leaves the group. Like mailing lists, chat groups have the great advantage that they enable you to communicate with people you would never meet or interact with otherwise. Because such groups are international, they provide excellent exposure to other cultures, other ideas, and other ways of communicating.

Chat groups, unlike e-mail, also allow you to "whisper"—to communicate with just one other person without giving other participants access to your message. In this situation these groups resemble interpersonal rather than small group communication.

In face-to-face group communication, you're expected to contribute to the ongoing discussion. In chat groups you can simply observe; in fact, you're encouraged to lurk—to observe the group's interaction before you say anything yourself. In this way you'll be able to learn the customs of the group and not violate any of its rules or norms.

Small Group Culture

Many groups, especially those of long standing like work groups, develop small cultures with their own norms. **Group norms** are rules or standards of behavior identifying which behaviors are considered appropriate (for example, being willing to take on added tasks or directing conflict toward issues rather than toward people) and which are considered inappropriate (for example, coming in late or not contributing actively). Sometimes these rules for appropriate behavior are explicitly stated in a company contract or policy, such as "All members must attend department meetings." Sometimes the rules are implicit: "Members should be well groomed." Regardless of whether norms are spelled out or not, they're powerful regulators of members' behaviors.

Small group norms may apply to individual members as well as to the group as a whole and, of course, will differ from one society to another (Axtell, 1993). For example, in the United States men and women in business are expected to interact when making business decisions as well as when socializing. In Muslim and Buddhist societies, however, there are religious restrictions that prevent mixed-gender groups. In groups in societies such as those of the United States, Bangladesh, Australia, Germany, Finland, and Hong Kong, punctuality for business meetings is very important. But in Morocco, Italy, Brazil, Zambia, Ireland, and Panama, time is less highly regarded; and being late is no great insult and is even expected. In the United States and in much of Asia and Europe, meetings are typically held between two parties at a time. In many Persian Gulf states, however, the business executive is likely to conduct meetings with several different people—sometimes dealing with totally different issues—at the same time. In this situation you have to expect to share what in the United States would be "your time" with these other parties. In the United States very little interpersonal touching goes on during business meetings; in Arab countries, however, touching (for example, hand holding) is common and is a gesture of friendship.

Norms that regulate a particular group member's behavior, called **role** expectations, identify what each person in an organization is expected to do; for example, Pat has a great computer setup and so should play the role of secretary.

You're more likely to accept the norms of your group's culture when you feel your group membership is important and want to continue your membership in the group. You're also more likely to accept these norms when your group is cohesive: **Cohesiveness** means that you and the other members are closely connected, are attracted to one another, and depend on one another to meet your needs. Lastly, you're more apt to accept these norms if you'd be punished by negative reactions or exclusion from the group for violating them (Napier & Gershenfeld, 1992).

Small Group Apprehension

Just as you have apprehension in interpersonal conversations (see "How apprehensive are you in

Each culture has its own group norms. Can you identify the norms that your culture taught you about what's proper and what's improper in a business group?

conversations?" at **www.ablongman.com/devito**) and in interviewing (Unit 12), you probably experience apprehension to some degree in group discussions. Because small groups vary so widely, you're likely to experience different degrees of apprehension depending on the nature of the specific group. Work groups, for example, may cause greater apprehension than groups of friends. And interacting with superiors is likely to generate greater apprehension than meeting with peers or subordinates. Similarly, the degree of familiarity you have with the group members and the extent to which you see yourself as a part of the group (as opposed to an outsider) will also influence your apprehension. You may wish at this point to take the following apprehension self-test to measure your own apprehension in group discussions and meetings.

TEST YOURSELF

How Apprehensive Are You in Group Discussions and Meetings?

This questionnaire consists of 12 statements concerning feelings about communication in group discussions and meetings. Indicate in the space provided the degree to which each statement applies to you, using the following scale: 1 = strongly agree; 2 = agree; 3 = are undecided; 4 = disagree; or 5 = strongly disagree. There are no right or wrong answers. Some of the statements are similar to other statements, but don't be concerned about this. Work quickly; just record your first impression.

_____ 1. I dislike participating in group discussions.

_____ 2. Generally, I am comfortable while participating in group discussions.

_____ 3. I am tense and nervous while participating in group discussions.

_____ 4. I like to get involved in group discussions.

_____ 5. Engaging in a group discussion with new people makes me tense and nervous.

_____ 6. I am calm and relaxed while participating in group discussions.

_____ 7. Generally, I am nervous when I have to participate in a meeting.

_____ 8. Usually, I am calm and relaxed while participating in meetings.

_____ 9. I am very calm and relaxed when I am called upon to express an opinion at a meeting.

_____ 10. I am afraid to express myself at meetings.

_____ 11. Communicating at meetings usually makes me uncomfortable.

_____ 12. I am very relaxed when answering questions at a meeting.

How did you do?   This test will enable you to obtain two subscores, one for group discussions and one for meetings. For group discussions compute your score as follows:

1. Begin with the number 18; this is just used as a base so that you won't wind up with negative numbers.

2. To 18 add your scores for items 2, 4, and 6.

3. Subtract your scores for items 1, 3, and 5 from your step 2 total.

For meetings compute your score as follows:

1. Begin with the number 18; this is just used as a base so that you won't wind up with negative numbers.

2. To 18 add your scores for items 8, 9, and 12.

3. Subtract your scores for items 7, 10, and 11 from your step 2 total.

Scores above 18 show some degree of apprehension. Can you identify the specific aspects of small groups that influence your apprehension?

What will you do?   Think about the kinds of groups and meetings that generate the most apprehension for you. Can you identify the major characteristics of these high-apprehension groups? How do these differ from groups that generate little apprehension? What other factors might influence your small group apprehension? As you read the suggestions for reducing apprehension that are given in Unit 15, consider how these might be used in the various types of groups in which you participate.

Source: From James C. McCroskey, _An Introduction to Rhetorical Communication,_ 7th edition. Copyright © 1997. Reprinted by permission of Allyn & Bacon.   ✔

Power in the Small Group

Power permeates all small groups and in fact all relationships. It influences what you do, when, and with whom. It influences the employment you seek and the employment you get. It influences the friends you choose and don't choose and those who choose you and those who don't. It influences your

GOING ONLINE

Small Group Communication Website
http://www.abacon.com/commstudies/groups/group.html

Here is the home page of Allyn and Bacon's website for small group communication. Supplement your text reading with the material on this website. As you can see, it contains a wealth of material that's relevant to this unit—as well as to the next unit, on group membership and leadership.

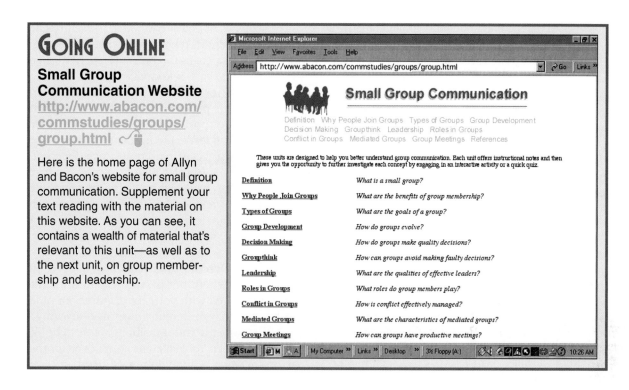

Small Group Communication

Definition   Why People Join Groups   Types of Groups   Group Development
Decision Making   Groupthink   Leadership   Roles in Groups
Conflict in Groups   Mediated Groups   Group Meetings   References

These units are designed to help you better understand group communication. Each unit offers instructional notes and then gives you the opportunity to further investigate each concept by engaging in an interactive activity or a quick quiz.

Definition	*What is a small group?*
Why People Join Groups	*What are the benefits of group membership?*
Types of Groups	*What are the goals of a group?*
Group Development	*How do groups evolve?*
Decision Making	*How do groups make quality decisions?*
Groupthink	*How can groups avoid making faulty decisions?*
Leadership	*What are the qualities of effective leaders?*
Roles in Groups	*What roles do group members play?*
Conflict in Groups	*How is conflict effectively managed?*
Mediated Groups	*What are the characteristics of mediated groups?*
Group Meetings	*How can groups have productive meetings?*

romantic and family relationships—their success, failure, and level of satisfaction or dissatisfaction.

Power is what enables one person (the one with power) to control the behaviors of others. Thus, if A has power over B and C, then A, by virtue of this power and through the exercise of this power (or the threat of exercising it), can control the behaviors of B and C. Differences in individuals' amounts and types of power influence who makes important decisions, who will prevail in an argument, and who will control the finances.

Although all relationships involve power, they differ in the types of power that the people use and to which they respond. The following self-test will help you identify the six major types of power.

TEST YOURSELF

How Powerful Are You?

For each statement, indicate which of the following descriptions is most appropriate, using the following scale: 1 = true of 20 percent or fewer of the people I know; 2 = true of about 21 to 40 percent of the people I know; 3 = true of about 41 to 60 percent of the people I know; 4 = true of about 61 to 80 percent of the people I know; and 5 = true of 81 percent or more of the people I know.

_____ **1.** My position is such that I often have to tell others what to do. For example, a mother's position demands that she tell her children what to do, a manager's position demands that he or she tell employees what to do, and so on.

_____ **2.** People wish to be like me or identified with me. For example, high school football players may admire the former professional football player who is now their coach and want to be like him.

_____ **3.** People see me as having the ability to give them what they want. For example, employers have the ability to give their employees increased pay, longer vacations, or improved working conditions.

_____ **4.** People see me as having the ability to administer punishment or to withhold things they want. For example, employers have the ability to reduce voluntary overtime, shorten vacation time, or fail to improve working conditions.

_____ **5.** Other people realize that I have expertise in certain areas of knowledge. For example, a doctor has expertise in medicine and so others turn to the doctor to tell them what to do.

Someone knowledgeable about computers similarly possesses expertise.

_____ **6.** Other people realize that I possess the communication ability to present an argument logically and persuasively.

How did you do?   These statements refer to the six major types of power, as described in the text following this self-test. Low scores (1s and 2s) indicate your belief that you possess little of these particular types of power, and high scores (4s and 5s) indicate your belief that you possess a great deal of these particular types of power.

What will you do?   How satisfied are you with your level of power? If you're not satisfied, what might you do about it? A good starting place, of course, is to learn the skills of communication—interpersonal, interviewing, small group, and public speaking—discussed in this text. Consider the kinds of communication patterns that would help you communicate power and exert influence in group situations.   ✔

The six types of power covered in the self-test are legitimate, referent, reward, coercive, expert, and information or persuasion power (French & Raven, 1968; Raven, Centers, & Rodrigues, 1975). You have **legitimate power** (self-test statement 1) over another when this person believes you have a right by virtue of your position (for example, you're the appointed group leader) to influence or control his or her behavior. Legitimate power usually comes from the leadership roles people occupy. Teachers are often seen to have legitimate power, and this is doubly true for religious teachers. Parents are seen as having legitimate power over their children. Employers, judges, managers, doctors, and police officers are others who may hold legitimate power.

You have **referent power** (statement 2) over another person when that person wishes to be like you or identified with you. For example, an older brother may have referent power over a younger brother because the younger sibling wants to be like his older brother. Your referent power over another person increases when you're well liked and well

UNDERSTANDING THEORY AND RESEARCH

Group Power

Unit 3 examined the theory of high- and low-power-distance cultures. Recall that in high-power-distance cultures power is concentrated in the hands of a few, and there's a great difference between the power of these people and that of the ordinary citizen (Hofstede, 1997). In low-power-distance cultures power is relatively evenly distributed throughout the citizenry. Groups may also be viewed in terms of high and low power distances. In high-power-distance groups the leader is far more powerful than the members. In low-power-distance groups the leaders and members differ much less in their power.

Consider the implications of this theory for your small group behavior. Of the groups in which you'll participate—as a member or as a leader—some will be high-power-distance groups and others will be low. The skill is to recognize which is which, to follow the rules

generally, and to break them only after you've thought through the consequences. For example, in low-power-distance groups (and cultures), you're expected to confront a group leader (or friend or supervisor) assertively; acting assertively denotes a general feeling of equality (Borden, 1991). In high-power-distance groups (and cultures), direct confrontation and assertiveness toward the leader (or toward any person in authority, such as a teacher or doctor) may be viewed negatively (Westwood, Tang, & Kirkbride, 1992; also see Bochner & Hesketh, 1994).

> **Working with Theories and Research.** *Do your attitudes and beliefs about power distance indicate that you come from a high- or a low-power-distance culture? Do you find the research conclusions consistent with your own experience?*

UNDERSTANDING THEORY AND RESEARCH

Group Polarization

Groups frequently make more extreme decisions than individuals—a tendency known as *group polarization* (Friedkin, 1999; Brauer, Judd, & Gliner, 1995). For example, a group will take greater risks if the members are already willing to take risks, and will become more cautious if the members are already cautious. What seems to happen is that as a group member you estimate how others in the group feel about risk taking. If you judge the group as one of high risk takers, you're likely to become more willing to take risks than you were before the group interaction. Similarly, if you judge the group members as cautious and as low risk takers, you'll become even more cautious than you were before the group interaction. In other words—and not surprisingly—your own attitudes toward risky decisions will be heavily influenced by the attitudes you think the group possesses, and you'll change your attitudes to more closely match those of the group. You'll become more risk prone if you think it's a high-risk group and less risk prone if you think it's a low-risk group.

> **Working with Theories and Research.** *Have you ever observed this group polarization tendency? What happened? What implications does this theory have for, say, gang members? For a professor joining a new faculty? For a stock investment analyst joining an investment firm?*

respected, when you're seen as attractive and prestigious, when you're of the same gender, and when you have attitudes and experiences similar to those of the other person. This is why role models are so important: Role models (sports figures are probably the best examples), by definition, possess referent power and exert great influence on those looking up to them.

You have **reward power** (statement 3) over a person if you have the ability to give that person rewards—either material (money, promotions, jewelry) or social (love, friendship, respect). Reward power increases attractiveness; we like those who have the power to reward us and who do in fact give us rewards.

Conversely, you have **coercive power** (statement 4) if you have the ability to remove rewards or to administer **punishments**. Usually, the two kinds of power go hand in hand; if you have reward power, you also have coercive power. For example, parents may grant as well as deny privileges to their children.

You possess **expert power** (statement 5) if group members regard you as having expertise or knowledge—whether or not you truly possess such expertise. Expert power increases when you are seen as being unbiased and having nothing to gain personally from influencing others. It decreases if you are seen as biased and as having something to gain from securing the compliance of others.

You have **information power,** or persuasion power (statement 6), if you're seen as someone who can communicate logically and persuasively. Generally, persuasion power is attributed to people who are seen as having significant information and the ability to use that information in presenting a well-reasoned argument.

IDEA-GENERATION GROUPS

Idea-generation groups are small groups that exist solely to generate ideas and often follow a formula called brainstorming (Osborn, 1957; Beebe & Masterson, 2000; DeVito, 1996). **Brainstorming** is a technique for bombarding a problem and generating as many ideas as possible. This technique involves two stages. The first is the brainstorming period proper; the second is the evaluation period.

The procedures are simple. A problem is selected that is amenable to many possible solutions or ideas. Group members are informed of the problem to be brainstormed before the actual session, so they can think about the topic. When the group meets, each person contributes as many ideas as he or she can think of. All ideas are recorded either in writing or on tape. During this idea-generating session, four general rules are followed.

Brainstorm Rule 1: Don't Criticize.

In a brainstorming session all ideas are recorded. They're not evaluated, nor are they even discussed. Any negative criticism—whether verbal or nonverbal—is itself criticized by the leader or the members. This is a good general rule to follow in all creative thinking: Allow your idea time to develop before you look for problems with it. At the same time, don't praise the ideas either. All evaluations should be suspended during the brainstorming session.

Brainstorm Rule 2: Strive for Quantity.

Linus Pauling, Nobel Prize winner for chemistry in 1954 and for peace in 1962, once said, "The best way to have a good idea is to have lots of ideas." This second rule of brainstorming embodies this concept. If you need an idea, you're more likely to find it in a group of many than in a group of few. Thus, in brainstorming, the more ideas the better.

Brainstorm Rule 3: Combine and Extend Ideas.

Although you may not criticize a particular idea, you may extend it or combine it in some way. The value of a particular idea may be the way it stimulates someone to combine or extend it. Even if your modification seems minor or obvious, say it. Don't censor yourself.

Brainstorm Rule 4: Develop the Wildest Ideas Possible.

The wilder the idea, the better. It's easier to tone an idea down than to build it up. A wild idea can easily be tempered, but it's not so easy to elaborate on a simple or conservative idea.

Sometimes a brainstorming session may break down, with members failing to contribute new ideas. At this point the moderator may prod the members with statements such as the following:

- Let's try to get a few more ideas before we close this session.
- Can we piggyback any other ideas or add extensions on the suggestion to. . . .
- Here's what we have so far. As I read the list of contributed suggestions, additional ideas may come to mind.

BUILDING COMMUNICATION SKILLS

How Can You Combat Idea Killers?

Think about how you can be on guard against negative criticism and how you can respond to such "idea killers" or "killer messages" as those listed below. These phrases aim to stop an idea from being developed, to kill it in its tracks before it can get off the ground. As you read down the list of these commonly heard killer messages, formulate at least one response you might use if someone used one of these on you. Also consider what you might say to yourself on occasions when you use these terms to censor your own creative thinking.

- We tried it before and it didn't work.
- It'll never work.

- No one would vote for it.
- It's too complex.
- It's too simple.
- It would take too long.
- It's too expensive.
- It's not logical.
- We don't have the facilities.
- It's a waste of time and money.
- What we have is good enough.
- It won't fly.
- It just doesn't fit us.
- It's impossible.

- Here's an aspect we haven't focused on. Does this stimulate any ideas?

After all the ideas are generated—a period lasting no longer than 15 or 20 minutes—the group evaluates the entire list of ideas, using the critical thinking skills developed throughout this text. The ideas that are unworkable are thrown out; those that show promise are retained and evaluated. During this stage negative criticism is allowed.

PERSONAL GROWTH GROUPS

Some personal growth groups, sometimes referred to as support groups, aim to help members cope with particular difficulties—such as drug addiction, having an alcoholic parent, being an ex-convict, or having a hyperactive child or a promiscuous spouse. Other groups are more clearly therapeutic and are designed to change significant aspects of an individual's personality or behavior.

Popular Personal Growth Groups

There are many varieties of support or personal growth groups. The encounter group, for example, tries to facilitate personal growth and the ability to deal effectively with other people (Rogers, 1970). One of its assumptions is that the members will be more effective psychologically and socially if they get to know and like themselves better. Consequently, the atmosphere of the encounter group is one of acceptance and support. Freedom to express one's inner thoughts, fears, and doubts is stressed.

The assertiveness training group aims to increase the willingness of its members to stand up for their rights and to act more assertively in a wide variety of situations (Adler, 1977).

The consciousness-raising group aims to help people cope with the problems society confronts them with. The members of a consciousness-raising group all have one characteristic in common (for example, they may all be women, unwed mothers, gay fathers, or recently unemployed executives). It's this commonality that leads the members to join together and help one another. In the consciousness-raising group the assumption is that similar people are best equipped to assist one another's personal growth. Structurally, the consciousness-raising group is leaderless. All members (usually numbering from 6 to 12) are equal in their control of the group and in their presumed knowledge.

Although all personal growth groups function somewhat differently, we can illustrate at least one possible pattern by looking at the steps and procedures that a sample consciousness-raising group might follow. These procedures are generally much more flexible than those followed in a problem-solving group, for example.

Some Rules and Procedures

Each group is likely to develop its own unique rules and procedures, yet you can get some idea of how such groups operate by looking at a fairly typical consciousness-raising group. The group may start each meeting by selecting a topic, usually by majority vote of the group. This topic may be drawn from a prepared list or suggested by one of the group members. But regardless of what topic is selected, it's always discussed from the point of view of the larger topic that brings these particular people together—let's say, sexual harassment. Whether the topic is men, employment, or family, it's pursued in light of the issues and problems of sexual harassment.

After a topic is selected, the first speaker is selected through some random procedure. That member speaks for about 10 minutes on his or her feelings, experiences, and thoughts. The focus is always on the individual. No interruptions are allowed. After the member has finished, the other group members may ask questions of clarification. The feedback from other members is to be totally supportive.

After questions of clarification have been answered, the next member speaks. The same procedure is followed until all members have spoken. After the last member has spoken, a general discussion follows. During this time members may relate different aspects of their experience to what the others have said. Or they may tell the group how they feel about some of the issues raised by others.

This procedure helps raise members' consciousness by giving them an opportunity to formulate and verbalize their thoughts on a particular topic, hear how others feel and think about the same topic, and formulate and answer questions of clarification.

INFORMATION-SHARING GROUPS

The purpose of information-sharing groups is to enable members to acquire new information or skills through a sharing of knowledge. In most information-sharing groups, all members have something to teach and something to learn. In some, however, the interaction takes place because some members have information and some don't.

Educational or Learning Groups

In educational or learning groups, the members pool their knowledge to the benefit of all. Members may follow a variety of discussion patterns. For example, a historical topic might be developed chronologically, with the discussion progressing from the past into the present and perhaps predicting the future. Issues in developmental psychology, such as physical maturity or language development in the child, might also be discussed chronologically. Some topics lend themselves to spatial development. For example, study of the development of the United States might take either a spatial pattern,

going from east to west, or a chronological pattern, going from 1776 to the present. Other suitable patterns, depending on the nature of the topic and the needs of the discussants, might be developed in terms of causes and effects, problems and solutions, or structures and functions.

Perhaps the most popular is the topical pattern. A group might discuss the challenges of raising a hyperactive child by itemizing and discussing each of the major problems. The structure of a corporation might also be considered in terms of its major divisions. As can be appreciated, topical approaches may be further systematized; for instance, a learning group might rank the problems of hyperactivity in terms of their importance or complexity or might order the major structures of the corporation in terms of decision-making power.

Focus Groups

A different type of learning group is the **focus group,** a small group assembled for a kind of in-depth interview. The aim here is to discover what people think about an issue or product; for exam-

---

BUILDING COMMUNICATION SKILLS

How Can You Listen to New Ideas?

A useful skill for listening to new ideas is PIP'N, a technique that derives from Carl Rogers's (1970) emphasis on paraphrasing as a means for ensuring understanding and Edward deBono's (1976) PMI (Plus, Minus, and Interesting) technique. PIP'N involves four steps:

P = *Paraphrase.* State in your own words what you think the other person is saying. This will ensure that you and the person proposing the idea are talking about the same thing. Your paraphrase will also provide the other person with the opportunity to elaborate or clarify his or her ideas.

I = *Interesting.* State something interesting that you find in the idea. Say why you think this idea might be interesting to you, to others, to the organization.

P = *Positive.* Say something positive about the idea. What is good about it? How might it solve a problem or make a situation better?

N = *Negative.* State any negatives that you think the idea might entail. Might it prove expensive? Difficult to implement? Is it directed at insignificant issues?

You may want to try using PIP'N the next time you hear about a new idea; say, in conversation or in a small group. For practice, try PIP'N on the PIP'N technique itself: (1) Paraphrase the PIP'N technique; (2) say why the technique is interesting; (3) say something positive about it; and (4) say something negative about it.

ple, what do men between 18 and 25 think of the new aftershave lotion and its packaging? What do young executives earning more than $100,000 think about buying a foreign luxury car?

In the focus group a leader tries to discover the beliefs, attitudes, thoughts, and feelings that members have so as to help an organization make decisions on changing the scent or redesigning the packaging or constructing advertisements for luxury cars. It is the leader's task to prod members to ana-lyze their thoughts and feelings on a deeper level and to use the thoughts of one member to stimulate the thoughts of others.

Generally, approximately 12 people are assembled. The leader explains the process, the time limits, and the general goal of the group—let's say, for example, to discover why these 12 individuals requested information on the XYZ health plan but purchased a plan from another company. The idea, of course, is that these 12 people are standing in

COMMUNICATION @ WORK

Networking

If I have seen further, it is by standing on the shoulders of giants.

—Sir Isaac Newton (1642–1727)

Networking is more than a technique for securing a job; it's a broad process of enlisting the aid of other people to help you solve a problem or to offer insights that bear on your problem—for example, how to publish your manuscript, where to go for low-cost auto insurance, how to find an apartment, or how to defrag your hard drive (Heenehan, 1997).

Start your networking with people you already know. You'll probably discover that you know a great number of people with specialized knowledge who can be of assistance (Rector & Neiva, 1996). You can also network with people who know the people you know. Thus, you may contact a friend's friend to find out if the firm he or she works for is hiring. Or you may contact people with whom you have no connection. Perhaps you've read something the person wrote or heard the person's name raised in connection with an area in which you're interested and you want to get more information. With e-mail addresses so readily available, it's now quite common to e-mail individuals who have particular expertise and ask them questions.

Try to establish relationships that are mutually beneficial. If you can provide others with helpful information, it's more likely that they'll provide helpful information for you. In this way, you establish a mutually satisfying and productive network.

Developing files and directories of potentially useful sources that you can contact for needed information may prove useful. For example, if you're a freelance artist, you might develop a list of persons who are in positions to offer you work or who can lead you to others who might offer such work. Authors, editors, art directors, administrative assistants, people in advertising, and a host of others might eventually provide useful leads. Creating a directory of such people and keeping in contact with them on a fairly regular basis can often simplify your obtaining freelance work.

Be proactive; initiate contacts rather than waiting for them to come to you. If you're also willing to help others, there's nothing wrong in asking these same people to help you. If you're respectful of their time and expertise, it's likely that they will respond favorably to your networking attempts. Following up your requests with thank-you notes, for example, will help you establish networks that can be ongoing relationships.

Thinking about Your Communicating @ Work

Have you ever networked to enlist the aid of someone who had information you needed? Have others ever enlisted your aid? How did these interactions work? Were they mutually productive?

for or representing a wider population. In this example, the leader, who is usually a professional facilitator rather than a member of the client organization itself, would ask a variety of questions such as: How did you hear about the XYZ health plan? What other health plans did you consider before making your actual purchase? What influenced you to buy the plan you eventually bought? Were any other people influential in helping you make your decision? Through the exploration of these and similar questions, the facilitator and the relevant members of the client organization (who may be seated behind a one-way mirror, watching the discussion) may put together a more effective health plan or more effective advertising strategies.

PROBLEM-SOLVING GROUPS

A **problem-solving group** is a collection of individuals who meet to solve a problem or to reach a decision. In one sense this is the most exacting kind of group to participate in. It requires not only a knowledge of small group communication techniques but also a thorough knowledge of the particular problem. And it usually demands faithful adherence to a somewhat rigid set of rules. We'll look at this group first in terms of the classic and still popular problem-solving approach whereby we identify the steps to go through in solving a problem. Next we'll survey several types of groups that are popular in organizations today: the nominal group, the Delphi method, quality circles, improvement groups, and task groups. Lastly, we'll consider the major decision-making methods.

The Problem-Solving Sequence

The approach developed by philosopher John Dewey (1910), the **problem-solving sequence,** is probably the one used most often. Six steps are identified (see Figure 13.2) and are designed to make problem solving more efficient and effective.

Figure 13.2
Steps in Problem-Solving Discussion

Although most small group theorists would advise you to follow the problem-solving pattern as presented here, others would alter it somewhat. For example, the pattern here advises you first to define the problem and then to establish criteria for identifying possible solutions. You would then keep these criteria in mind as you generated possible solutions (step 3). Another school of thought, however, would advise you to generate solutions first and to consider how they will be evaluated only after these solutions are proposed (Brilhart & Galanes, 1992). The advantage of this second approach is that you may generate more creative solutions if you're not restricted by standards of evaluation. The disadvantage is that you may spend a great deal of time generating very impractical solutions that would never meet the standards you'll eventually propose.

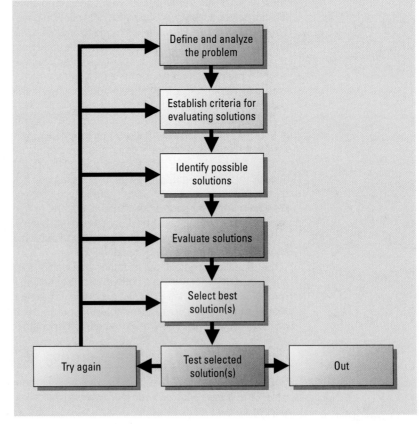

Define and Analyze the Problem

In many instances the nature of the problem is clearly specified. For example, a group of designers might discuss how to package a new soap project. In other instances, however, the problem may be vague, and it may remain for the group to define it in concrete terms. Thus, for example, the general problem may be poor campus communications. But such a vague and general topic is difficult to tackle in a problem-solving discussion, so it's helpful to specify the problem clearly.

Limit the problem so that it identifies a manageable area for discussion. A question such as "How can we improve our company?" is too broad and general. The group might limit the question by, for example, identifying one issue within the company on which to focus. You might, for example, choose among issues such as the company website, internal memos, management–worker relationships, qualifications for bonuses, flexible time schedules, and office furniture.

Define the problem as an open-ended question ("How can we improve the company website?") rather than as a statement ("The company website needs to be improved") or a yes/no question ("Does the website need improvement?"). The open-ended question allows for greater freedom of exploration. It doesn't restrict the ways in which the group may approach the problem.

Appropriate questions for most problems revolve around the following issues: (1) Duration: How long has the problem existed? Is it likely to continue in the future? What is the predicted course of the problem? For example, will it grow or lessen in impact? (2) Causes: What are the major causes of the problem? How certain can we be that these are the actual causes? (3) Effects: What are the effects of the problem? How significant are they? Who is affected by this problem? How significantly are they affected? Is this problem causing other problems? How important are these other problems?

Establish Criteria for Evaluating Solutions

Before any solutions are proposed, you need to decide how to evaluate them. At this stage you identify the standards or criteria that you'll use in evaluating solutions or in selecting one solution over another. Generally, two types of criteria need to be considered. First, there are the practical criteria. For example, you might decide that solutions to the website problem must not increase the budget, must lead to a higher volume of business, must be constructed in-house, must load almost immediately, and so on. Second, there are the value criteria. These are more difficult to identify. These might include, for example, requirements that the website reflect the culture of the company or that it represent the company's commitment to multiculturalism.

Identify Possible Solutions

At this stage identify as many solutions as possible. Focus on quantity rather than quality. Brainstorming may be particularly useful at this point (see the earlier discussion of idea-generation groups). Solutions to the website problem might include incorporating reviews of publications by company members, reviews of restaurants in the area, recruitment guidelines, and new employment opportunities within the company.

Evaluate Solutions

After all the solutions have been proposed, you go back and evaluate each according to the criteria you have established. For example, to what extent does incorporating reviews of area restaurants meet the evaluation criteria? Will it increase the budget? Each potential solution should be matched against the criteria.

An especially insightful technique for evaluating solutions (or gaining a different perspective on a problem) is offered by **critical thinking** pioneer Edward deBono (1987). The **critical thinking hats technique** involves thinking with six different "hats" and, in doing so, subjecting an issue to a six-part analysis.

- The *fact hat* focuses attention on the data—the facts and figures that bear on the problem. For example: What are the relevant data on the website? How can you get more information on the website's history? How much does it cost to establish and maintain a website? How much advertising revenue can you get?

- The *feeling hat* focuses attention on our feelings, emotions, and intuitions concerning the problem. How do you feel about the website and about making major changes?

- The *negative argument hat* asks that you become the devil's advocate. Why might this proposed solution fail? What is the worst-case scenario?

- The *positive benefits hat* asks that you look at the upside. What opportunities will a new format open up? What benefits will this website provide for employees? What would be the best thing that could happen?

- The *creative new idea hat* focuses attention on new ways of looking at the problem and can be easily combined with the techniques of brainstorming discussed earlier in this unit. What other ways can you look at this problem? What other functions can a website serve that have not been thought of? Can the website provide a service to the community as well?

- The *control of thinking hat* helps you analyze what you have done and are doing. It asks that you reflect on your own thinking processes and synthesize the results of your thinking. Have you adequately defined the problem? Are you focusing too much on insignificant issues? Have you given enough attention to possible negative effects?

Select the Best Solution(s)

At this stage the best solution or solutions are selected and put into operation. For instance, in the company website example, if "reviews of area restaurants" and "listings of new positions" best met the evaluation criteria, the group might then incorporate these two new items in the redesign of the website.

Groups may use different decision-making methods in deciding, for example, which criteria to use or which solutions to accept. Generally, groups use one of three methods: decision by authority, majority rule, or consensus.

Decision by Authority.   In decision by authority members voice their feelings and opinions but the leader, boss, or CEO makes the final decision. This is surely an efficient method; it gets things done quickly, and the amount of discussion can be limited as desired. Another advantage is that experienced and informed members (for example, those who have been with the company longest) will probably exert a greater influence on the final decision. The great disadvantage is that group members may not feel the need to contribute their insights and may become distanced from the power within the group or organization. Another disadvantage

is that this method may lead members to tell the decision maker what they feel she or he wants to hear, a condition that can easily lead to groupthink (Unit 14).

Majority Rule.   With this method the group agrees to abide by the majority decision and may vote on various issues as the group works toward solving its problem. Majority rule is efficient, as there's usually the option of calling for a vote when the majority is in agreement. This is a useful method for issues that are relatively unimportant (What company should service the water cooler?) and when member satisfaction and commitment are not essential. One disadvantage is that it can lead to factioning, in which various minorities align against the majority. The method may also lead to limiting discussion once a majority has agreed and a vote is called.

Consensus.   In some situations *consensus* means unanimous agreement; for example, a criminal jury must reach a unanimous decision to convict or acquit a defendant. In most business groups, however, consensus means that members agree that they can live with the solution; they agree that they can do whatever the solution requires (Kelly, 1994). Consensus is especially important when the group wants each member to be satisfied with and committed to the decision and the decision-making process as a whole (DeStephen & Hirokawa, 1988; Beebe & Masterson, 2000). The consensus method obviously takes the longest, and it can lead to a great deal of wasted time if members wish to prolong the discussion process needlessly or selfishly. This method may also put great pressure on the person who honestly disagrees but who doesn't want to prevent the group from making a decision.

Test Selected Solutions

After solutions are put into operation, test their effectiveness. The group might, for example, poll employees about the website changes or examine the number of hits. Or you might analyze the advertising revenue.

If the solutions you have adopted prove ineffective, you will need to go back to one of the previous stages and repeat part of the process. Often this takes the form of selecting other solutions to test. But it may also involve going farther back—to, for example, a reanalysis of the problem, an identifica-

MEDIA WATCH

WHO ARE THE GATEKEEPERS?

Gatekeepers are all around us, and the most important of these are the media.

The concept of *gatekeeping,* introduced by Kurt Lewin in his *Human Relations* (1947), involves two aspects:

▶ the process by which a message passes through various gates

▶ the people or groups that allow the message to pass (gatekeepers)

A gatekeeper's main function is to filter the messages an individual receives. As you were growing up, your parents gave you certain information and withheld other information. Depending on the culture in which you were raised, you may have been told about Santa Claus and the tooth fairy but not about cancer or mutual funds. Teachers are also gatekeepers. Teachers read books and journal articles, listen to papers at conferences, share information among themselves, and conduct their own research. After absorbing all this information, they pass some of it on to their students. Textbook authors serve a similar gatekeeping function (Robinson, 1993). Editors of newspapers, popular and scholarly periodicals, and publishing houses are also gatekeepers, as are those who regulate and monitor Internet messages (Lewis, 1995; Bodon, Powell, & Hickson, 1999).

The entertainment media, usually on the basis of their own codes and sometimes because of legal regulations, censor what gets through to viewers. For example, MTV serves as a gatekeeper and rejects some video clips because they violate some standard. Thus, for example, Madonna's "Justify My Love" was rejected because of its depiction of group sex, and David Bowie's "China Girl" was rejected because of a nude beach scene. Neil Young's "This Note's for You" and Seaweed's "Kid Candy" were rejected because they showed brand name products (Banks, 1995).

Follow-Up. *How do the following people function as gatekeepers in your ability to acquire information?*

▶ *The editor of your local or college newspaper*

▶ *Jerry Springer and Oprah Winfrey*

▶ *Your romantic partner (past or present)*

▶ *The president of the United States*

▶ *Network news shows*

▶ *The advertising department of a large corporation*

---

tion of other solutions, or a restatement of evaluation criteria.

Problem Solving at Work

The problem-solving sequence discussed here is used widely in business in a variety of different types of groups. Let's examine three group approaches popular in business that rely largely on the problem-solving techniques just discussed: the nominal group technique, the Delphi method, and quality circles.

The Nominal Group Technique

The **nominal group** technique is a method of problem solving that uses limited discussion and confidential voting to obtain a group decision. It's especially helpful when some members may be reluctant to voice their opinions in a regular problem-solving group or when the issue is controversial or sensitive. With this technique, each member contributes equally and each contribution is treated equally. Another advantage of the nominal group process is that it can be accomplished in a relatively short period of time. The nominal group approach can be divided into seven steps (Kelly, 1994):

1. The problem is defined and clarified for all members.
2. Each member writes down (without discussion or consultation with others) his or her ideas on or possible solutions to the problem.
3. Each member—in sequence—states one idea from his or her list, which is recorded on a board or flip chart so everyone can see it. This process is repeated until all suggestions are stated and recorded. Duplicates are then eliminated. Group

agreement is secured before overlapping ideas are combined.

4. Each suggestion is clarified (without debate). Ideally, each suggestion is given equal time.
5. Each member rank orders the suggestions in writing.
6. The rankings of the members are combined to get a group ranking, which is then written on the board.
7. Clarification, discussion, and possible reordering may follow.
8. The highest-ranking solution may then be selected to be tested, or perhaps several high-ranking solutions may be put into operation.

The Delphi Method

In the **Delphi method** a group of "experts" is established, but there's no interaction among them; instead, they communicate by repeatedly responding to questionnaires (Tersine & Riggs, 1980; Kelly, 1994). The Delphi method is especially useful when you want to involve people who are geographically distant from one another, when you want all members to become part of the solution and to uphold it, or when you want to minimize the effects of dominant members or even of peer pressure. The method is best explained as a series of steps (Kelly, 1994):

1. The problem is defined (for example, "We need to improve intradepartmental communication"). What each member is expected to do is specified (for example, each member should contribute five ideas on this specific question).
2. Each member then anonymously contributes five ideas in writing. This step used to be completed through questionnaires sent through traditional mail but is now more frequently done through e-mail, which greatly increases the speed with which this entire process can be accomplished.
3. The ideas of all members are combined, written up, and distributed to all members.
4. Members then select the three or four best ideas from this composite list and submit these.
5. From these responses another list is produced and distributed to all members.
6. Members then select the one or two best ideas from the new list and submit these.
7. From these responses another list is produced and distributed to all members. The process may

be repeated any number of times, but usually three rounds are sufficient for achieving a fair degree of agreement.

8. The "final" solutions are identified and are communicated to all members.

Quality Circles

A *quality circle* is a group of workers (usually about 6 to 12) whose task it is to investigate and make recommendations for improving the quality of some organizational function. The members are drawn from the workers whose area is being studied. Thus, for example, if the problem were to improve advertising on the Internet, then the quality circle membership would be drawn from the advertising and technology departments. Generally, the motivation for establishing quality circles is economic; the company's aim is to improve quality and profitability. Another related goal is to improve worker morale; because quality circles involve workers in decision making, workers may feel empowered and see themselves as more essential to the organization (Gorden & Nevins, 1993).

The basic idea is that people who work on similar tasks will be better able to improve their departments or jobs by pooling their insights and working through problems they share. The quality circle style of problem solving is often considered one of the major reasons for the success of many Japanese businesses, which use it extensively. Hundreds of U.S. organizations also use quality circles, but generally with less success than those in Japan (Gorden & Nevins, 1993).

Quality circle members investigate problems using any method they feel might be helpful; for example, they may form face-to-face problem-solving groups or use nominal groups or Delphi methods. The group then reports its findings and its suggestions to those who can do something about it. In some cases the quality circle members may implement their solutions without approval from upper management levels.

A somewhat similar type of group is the improvement or *kaizen* group, named for a Japanese term meaning "continual improvement" (Beebe & Masterson, 2000). Kaizen groups are based on the assumption that every process or product in any organization can be improved. Such groups may be set up for a certain amount of time or may be permanent.

REFLECTIONS ON ETHICS IN HUMAN COMMUNICATION

Telling Secrets

In groups of close friends, among family members, or in standing workplace committees, secrets are often exchanged on the implied assumption that they will not be revealed to outsiders. Revealing or not revealing such secrets often has ethical implications. In *Secrets* (1983), ethicist Sissela Bok identifies three types of situations in which she argues it would be unethical to reveal the secrets of another person. These conditions aren't always easy to identify in any given instance, but they do provide excellent starting points for asking whether or not it's ethical to reveal what we know about another person. And, of course, for any situation, there may be legitimate exceptions.

First, it's unethical to reveal information that you have promised to keep secret. When you make a promise to keep information hidden, you take on an ethical responsibility.

Second, it's unethical to say things about another person when you know the information to be false. When you try to deceive listeners by telling falsehoods about another, your communications are unethical.

Third, it's unethical to invade the privacy to which everyone is entitled: to reveal information that no one else has a right to know. This is especially unethical when such disclosures can hurt the individual involved.

There may be situations in which you have an obligation to reveal a secret. For example, Bok (1983) argues that you have an obligation to reveal a secret when keeping the information hidden will do more harm than good—a situation that is often not easy to determine.

What would you do?

▶ *A fellow student and close friend confides that he's secretly dating one of his professors, which violates college policy and your own value system.*

▶ *An instructor who supervises your study group confides that she is a confirmed racist and proud of it.*

▶ *A 16-year-old member of the wilderness group you're leading confides that she's having unprotected sex with her supervisor at work, a married man.*

▶ *A community religious leader confides that he's skimming a portion of the members' contributions to fund his retirement.*

▶ *An 18-year-old student whose internship you're supervising confides to you that he intends to commit suicide (an example offered by Bok).*

 ## SUMMARY

This unit introduced the nature of the small group and discussed four major types of groups and their functions.

1. A small group is a collection of individuals that is small enough for all members to communicate with relative ease as both senders and receivers. The members are related to one another by some common purpose and have some degree of organization or structure among them.

2. Small groups make use of four major formats: the round table, the panel, the symposium, and the symposium–forum.

3. Most small groups develop norms or rules that operate much like a culture's norms, identifying

what is considered appropriate behavior for the group members.

4. Power operates in all groups. Six types of power may be identified: legitimate, referent, reward, coercive, expert, and information or persuasion.

5. The idea-generation or brainstorming group attempts to generate as many ideas as possible.

6. The personal growth group helps members to deal with personal problems and to function more effectively. Popular types of personal growth groups are the encounter group, the assertiveness training group, and the consciousness-raising group.

7. The educational or learning group attempts to acquire new information or skill through a mutual sharing of knowledge or insight.

8. The focus group aims to discover what people think about an issue or product through a kind of in-depth group interview.

9. The problem-solving group attempts to solve a particular problem, or at least to reach a decision that may be a preface to the problem solving itself.

10. The six steps in the problem-solving sequence are: define and analyze the problem; establish criteria for evaluating solutions; identify possible solutions; evaluate solutions; select best solution(s); and test solution(s).

11. The six hats technique is especially useful in analyzing problems and consists of focusing on different aspects of the problem: facts, feelings, negative arguments, positive benefits, creative or new ways of viewing problems, and control of thinking processes.

12. Decision-making methods include authority, majority rule, and consensus.

13. Small groups that are widely used in business today include the nominal group, the Delphi method, and quality circles.

 # KEY TERMS

small group	small group norm	personal growth groups
small group stages	legitimate power	educational or learning group
small group formats	referent power	focus group
round table	reward power	problem-solving group
panel	coercive power	problem-solving sequence
symposium	expert power	nominal group technique
symposium–forum	information power	Delphi method
mailing list group	idea-generation group	quality circles
chat groups	brainstorming	

 # THINKING CRITICALLY ABOUT

Small Group Communication

1. Studies find that persons high in communication apprehension are generally less effective in idea-generation groups than are those low in apprehension (Jablin, 1981; Comadena, 1984; Cragan & Wright, 1990). Why do you think this is so?

2. What norms govern your class in human communication? What norms govern your family? Your place of work? Do you have any difficulty with any of these norms?

3. In research on chat groups, it was found that people were more likely to comment on another's message when that message was negative than when it was positive (Rollman, Krug, & Parente, 2000). Do you find this to be true? If so, why do you think this occurs?

4. Is the problem-solving sequence outlined in this unit also appropriate for resolving interpersonal conflicts? Can you trace an example through this sequence?

5. What type of criteria would an advertising agency use in evaluating a proposed campaign to sell soap? A university in evaluating ideas for a new

multicultural curriculum? Parents in evaluating a possible preschool for their children?

6. Visit the Creativity Web at http://members/ozemail.com.au-caveman/Creative/index2.html ⌒🖱 for a wealth of links to all aspects of creativity—quotations, affirmations, humor, discussions of the brain and the creative process, and more. What can you find here that might be of value in brainstorming and in idea generation generally?

7. Take the self-test, "How individualistic are you?" at www.ablongman.com/devito. ⌒🖱 How might an individualistic or collectivist orientation influence your group participation? As you read the next unit consider how individual–collective orientation influences group membership and group leadership.

8. **Researching Small Group Communication.** How might you go about finding answers to such questions as these?
   - Are group memberships more important to men or to women?
   - How effective is peer group instruction compared to instruction by lecture?
   - What personality or cultural factors are correlated with one's tendency to abide by the rules or norms of the group?
   - Is communication apprehension related to one's effectiveness in personal growth groups? In information-sharing groups? In problem-solving groups?
   - What decision-making methods work best for resolving family differences and problems?

UNIT 14
Members and Leaders

Unit Contents

Throughout your life you'll participate in a wide variety of groups—as a member of a work group, as a part of a social or neighborhood group, or as a player on a team. Probably you'll also lead some of these social or work groups, and your leadership responsibilities are likely to increase as you rise in the group hierarchy. In this unit you'll learn

▶ how membership and leadership work in groups

▶ how you can become a more effective member and a more responsive and influential leader

MEMBERS IN SMALL GROUP COMMUNICATION

You can view membership in small group communication situations from a variety of perspectives— in terms of the roles that members serve, the types of contributions they make, and the principles for more effective participation.

Member Roles

Group member roles fall into three general classes— group task roles, group building and maintenance roles, and individual roles—a classification introduced in early research (Benne & Sheats, 1948) and still widely used today (Lumsden & Lumsden, 1996; Beebe & Masterson, 2000). These roles are, of course, frequently served by leaders as well.

Think about your own behavior, your own membership style, as you read down the lists in the role descriptions that follow. Which of these do you regularly serve? Are there productive roles that you never or rarely serve? Are there destructive roles that you often serve?

Group Task Roles

Group task roles are those that help the group focus more specifically on achieving its goals. In serving any of these roles, you act not as an isolated individual but rather as a part of the larger whole. The needs and goals of the group dictate the task roles you serve. As an effective group member you would serve several of these functions.

Some people, however, lock into a few specific roles. For example, one person may almost always seek the opinions of others; another may concentrate on elaborating details; still another, on evaluating suggestions. Usually this kind of single focus is counterproductive. It's usually better for group task roles to be spread more evenly so that each member may serve many roles. The 12 specific group task roles are these:

- The *initiator–contributor* presents new ideas or new perspectives on old ideas, suggests new goals, or proposes new procedures or organizational strategies.

- The *information seeker* asks for facts and opinions and seeks clarification of the issues being discussed.

- The *opinion seeker* tries to discover the values underlying the group's task.

- The *information giver* presents facts and opinions to the group members.

- The *opinion giver* presents values and opinions and tries to spell out what the values of the group should be.

- The *elaborator* gives examples and tries to work out possible solutions, trying to build on what others have said.

- The *coordinator* spells out relationships among ideas and suggested solutions and coordinates the activities of the different members.

- The *orienter* summarizes what has been said and addresses the direction the group is taking.

- The *evaluator–critic* evaluates the group's decisions, questions the logic or practicality of the suggestions, and thus provides the group with both positive and negative feedback.

- The *energizer* stimulates the group to greater activity.

- The *procedural technician* takes care of various mechanical duties such as distributing group materials and arranging seating.

- The *recorder* writes down the group's activities, suggestions, and decisions; he or she serves as the memory of the group.

Group Building and Maintenance Roles

Most groups focus not only on the task to be performed but on interpersonal relationships among members. If the group is to function effectively, and if members are to be both satisfied and productive, these relationships must be nourished. When these needs are not met, group members may become irritable when the group process gets bogged down, may engage in frequent conflicts, or may find the small group process as a whole unsatisfying. The group and its members need the same kind of support that individuals need. The *group building and maintenance roles* serve this general function. Group building and maintenance functions are broken down into seven specific roles:

- The *encourager* supplies members with positive reinforcement in the form of social approval or praise for their ideas.

- The *harmonizer* mediates differences among group members.

- The *compromiser* offers compromises as a way to resolve conflicts between his or her ideas and those of others.

- The *gatekeeper–expediter* keeps the channels of communication open by reinforcing the efforts of others.

- The *standard setter* proposes standards for the functioning of the group or for its solutions.

- The *group observer and commentator* keeps a record of the proceedings and uses this in the group's evaluation of itself.

- The *follower* goes along with the members of the group, passively accepts the ideas of others, and functions more as an audience than as an active member.

Individual Roles

The group task and group building and maintenance roles just considered are productive roles; they aid the group in achieving its goals. *Individual roles,* on the other hand, are counterproductive; they hinder the group's productivity and member satisfaction largely because they focus on serving individual rather than group needs. Eight specific types are identified:

- The *aggressor* expresses negative evaluation of the actions or feelings of the group members; he or she attacks the group or the problem being considered.

- The *blocker* provides negative feedback, is disagreeable, and opposes other members or suggestions regardless of their merit.

- The *recognition seeker* tries to focus attention on himself or herself rather than on the task at hand, boasting about his or her own accomplishments.

- The *self-confessor* expresses his or her own feelings and personal perspectives rather than focusing on the group.

- The *playboy/playgirl* jokes around without any regard for the group process.

- The *dominator* tries to run the group or the group members by pulling rank, flattering members of the group, or acting the role of the boss.

- The *help seeker* expresses insecurity or confusion or deprecates himself or herself and thus tries to gain sympathy from the other members.

- The *special interest pleader* disregards the goals of the group and pleads the case of some special group.

As you might expect, your tendency to play group versus individual roles will be influenced by your culture—and especially your individualistic or collectivist orientation, as discussed in Unit 3. If you have not already done so, you may wish to explore your own tendency toward individualism or collectivism by taking the self-test "How individualistic are you?" at www.ablongman.com/devito. 🖱

Interaction Process Analysis

Another way of looking at the contributions group members make is through **interaction process analysis** (IPA), developed by Robert Bales (1950). In this system you analyze the contributions of members under four general categories: (1) social–emotional positive contributions, (2) social–emotional negative contributions, (3) attempted answers, and (4) questions. Each of these four areas contains three subdivisions, yielding a total of 12 categories into which you can classify group members' contributions (Table 14.1). Note that the categories under social–emotional positive are the natural opposites of those under social–emotional

TABLE 14.1 Interaction Process Analysis Form

The names of participants appear in the top spaces, as shown. In the column under each participant's name, you place a slash mark for each contribution in each of the 12 categories.

		Joe	Judy	Liz	Mike	Peg
Social–Emotional Positive Contributions	Shows solidarity					
	Shows tension release					
	Shows agreement					
Social–Emotional Negative Contributions	Shows disagreement					
	Shows tension					
	Shows antagonism					
Attempted Answers	Gives suggestions					
	Gives opinions					
	Gives information					
Questions	Asks for suggestions					
	Asks for opinions					
	Asks for information					

negative, and those under attempted answers are the natural opposites of those under questions. You may want to try out Bales's IPA system by listening to a small group discussion or a televised situation comedy or drama and recording the interactions using Table 14.1.

Both the three-part member role classification and the IPA categories are useful for analyzing the contributions members make in small group situations. When you look at member contributions through these systems, you can see, for example, if one member is locked into a particular role or if the group process is breaking down because too many people are serving individual rather than group goals or because social–emotional negative comments dominate the discussion. You should also be in a better position to offer improvement suggestions for individual members based on this analysis.

Member Participation

For another perspective on group membership, let's consider the recommendations for effective partic-ipation in small group communication. Look at these suggestions as an elaboration and extension of the characteristics of effective conversation enumerated in Unit 9.

Be Group or Team Oriented

In the small group you're a member of a team, a larger whole. As a group your task is to pool your talents, knowledge, and insights so as to arrive at a better solution than any one person could have developed. This call for group orientation is not to be taken as a suggestion that members abandon their individuality or give up their personal values or beliefs for the sake of the group, however. Individuality with a group orientation is what is advocated here.

Center Conflict on Issues

It's particularly important in the small group to center conflict on issues rather than on personalities. When you disagree, make it clear that your disagreement is with the solution suggested or with the ideas expressed, not with the person who expressed them. Similarly, when someone disagrees with what you say, don't take it as a personal attack. Instead, view this as an opportunity to discuss issues from an alternative point of view.

Be Critically Open-Minded

Come to the group with an open mind—equipped with information that will be useful to the discussion but not with your decision firmly made. Advance any solutions or conclusions tentatively rather than with certainty. Be willing to alter your suggestions and revise them in light of the discussion.

Ensure Understanding

Make sure that your ideas are understood by all participants. If something is worth saying, it's worth saying clearly. When in doubt, ask: "Is that clear?" "Did I explain that clearly?" Make sure, too, that you understand fully the contributions of other members, especially before you take issue with them. In fact, as explained in Unit 13, it's often wise to preface any extended disagreement with some kind of paraphrase to give the other person the opportunity to clarify, deny, or otherwise alter what was said. For example, you might say "As I understand it, you want to exclude freshmen from playing on the football team. Is that correct? I disagree with that idea and I'd like to explain why I think that would be a mistake."

Beware of Groupthink

Groupthink is a way of thinking that people use when agreement among members has become excessively important. Overemphasis on agreement among members tends to shut out realistic and logical analysis of a problem or of possible alternatives (Janis, 1983; Mullen, Tara, Salas, & Driskell, 1994). The term *groupthink* itself is meant to signal a "deterioration of mental efficiency, reality testing, and moral judgment that results from in-group pressures" (Janis, 1983, p. 9).

The following symptoms should help you recognize groupthink in groups you observe or participate in (Janis, 1983; Schafer & Crichlow, 1996):

- Group members think the group and its members are invulnerable.
- Members create rationalizations to avoid dealing with warnings or threats.
- Members believe their group is moral.
- Those opposed to the group are perceived in simplistic, stereotyped ways.

- Group pressure is applied to any member who expresses doubts or questions the group's arguments or proposals.
- Members censor their own doubts.
- Group members believe all are in unanimous agreement, whether this is stated or not.
- Group members emerge whose function it is to guard the information that gets to other members, especially when it may create diversity of opinion.

Here are three suggestions for combating groupthink. You may find it interesting to apply these suggestions to the situations described in the exercise "How Can You Combat Groupthink?" at www.ablongman.com/devito.

1. When too-simple solutions are offered to problems, try to illustrate (with specific examples, if possible) for the group members how the complexity of the problem is not going to yield to the solutions offered.
2. When you feel that members are not expressing their doubts about the group or its decisions, encourage members to voice disagreement. Ask members to play devil's advocate, to test the adequacy of the solution. Or, if members resist, do it yourself. Similarly, if you feel there is unexpressed disagreement, ask specifically if anyone disagrees. If you still get no response, it may be helpful to ask everyone to write his or her comments anonymously, then read them aloud to the group.
3. To combat the group pressure toward agreement, reward members who do voice disagreement or doubt. Say, for example, "That's a good argument; we need to hear more about the potential problems of this proposal. Does anyone else see any problems?"

LEADERS IN SMALL GROUP COMMUNICATION

A leader influences the thoughts and behaviors of others and establishes the direction that others follow. In many small groups one person serves as leader. In other groups leadership may be shared by several persons.

In some groups a person may be appointed the leader or may serve as leader because of her or his position within the company or hierarchy. In still other groups, the leader may emerge as the group proceeds in fulfilling its functions or may be elected leader by the group members. Two significant factors exert considerable influence on who emerges as group leader. One is the extent of active participation: The person who talks the most is more likely to emerge as leader (Mullen, Salas, & Driskell, 1989; Shaw & Gouran, 1990). The second factor is effective listening: Members who listen effectively will emerge as leaders more often than those who don't (Johnson & Bechler, 1998; Bechler & Johnson, 1995).

The emergent leader performs the duties of leadership, though not asked or expected to, and gradually becomes recognized by the members as the group's leader. And because this person has now proved herself or himself an effective leader, it's not surprising that this emergent leader often becomes the designated leader for future groups. Generally, the emergent leader serves as leader as long as the group members are satisfied. When they're not, they may encourage another member to emerge as leader. But as long as the emergent leader serves effectively, the group will probably not look to others.

In any case the role of the leader or leaders is vital to the well-being and effectiveness of the group. Even in leaderless groups in which all members are equal, leadership functions must still be served.

Approaches to Leadership

Not surprisingly, **leadership** has been the focus of considerable attention from theorists and researchers, who have used numerous approaches to understand this particular communication behavior. Before reading about these approaches, you may wish to take the self-test below to examine yourself as a leader.

TEST YOURSELF

Are You Leader Material?

This self-test is designed to stimulate you to think about yourself in the role of leader. Respond to the following statements in terms of how you perceive yourself and how you think others perceive you, using a 10-point scale ranging from 10 (extremely true) to 1 (extremely false).

Others see me as	I see myself as	Perceptions
____ 1.	____ 1.	Generally popular with group members
____ 2.	____ 2.	Knowledgeable about the topics and subjects discussed
____ 3.	____ 3.	Dependable
____ 4.	____ 4.	Effective in establishing group goals
____ 5.	____ 5.	Competent in giving directions
____ 6.	____ 6.	Capable of energizing group members
____ 7.	____ 7.	Charismatic (dynamic, engaging, powerful)
____ 8.	____ 8.	Empowering of group members
____ 9.	____ 9.	Moral and honest
____ 10.	____ 10.	Skilled in balancing the concerns of getting the task done and satisfying the group member's personal needs
____ 11.	____ 11.	Flexible in adjusting leadership style on the basis of the unique situation
____ 12.	____ 12.	Able to delegate responsibility

How did you do? This test was designed to encourage you to look at yourself in terms of the four approaches to leadership that will be discussed in the following text. Phrases 1–3 refer to the traits approach to leadership, which defines a leader as a person who possesses certain qualities. Phrases 4–6 refer to the functional approach, which defines a leader as a person who performs certain functions. Phrases 7–9 refer to the transformational approach, which defines a leader as a person who inspires the group members to become the best they can be. Phrases 10–12 refer to the situational approach, which defines a leader as someone who can adjust his or her style to balance the needs of the specific situation.

To compute your scores:

1. Add your scores for statements 1–3: _____.
   This will give you an idea of how you and others see you in terms of the leadership qualities identified by the traits approach.

2. Add your scores for statements 4–6: _____.
   This will give you an idea of how you and others see

you in relation to the varied leadership functions considered in the functional approach.

3. Add your scores for statements 7–9: _____. This will give you an idea of how you and others see you as a transformational leader.

4. Add your scores for statements 10–12: _____. This will give you an idea of how you and others see you as a situational leader.

What will you do? As you read the remainder of this unit and the rest of the book, try to identify specific skills and competencies you might learn that would enable you to increase your scores on all four approaches to leadership. Also, try searching the Web for information on "leadership" as well as, say, "business leadership" and "political leaders." ✔

The *traits approach to leadership* argues that leaders must possess certain qualities if they're to function effectively. Some of the traits found to be associated with leadership are intelligence, dominance, honesty, foresight, altruism, popularity, sociability, cooperativeness, knowledge, and dependability (Hackman & Johnson, 1991). The problem with the traits approach is that the specific qualities called for will vary with the situation, with the members, and with the culture in which the leader functions. Thus, for example, the leader's knowledge and personality are generally significant factors; but for some groups a knowledge of financial issues and a serious personality might be effective, whereas for other groups a knowledge of design and a more humorous personality might be effective.

The *functional approach to leadership* focuses on what the leader should do in a given situation. Some of these functions have already been examined in the discussion of group membership in which group roles were identified. Other functions found to be associated with leadership are setting group goals, giving direction to group members, and summarizing the group's progress (Schultz, 1996). Additional functions are identified in the section entitled "Functions of Leadership," later in this unit.

In the *transformational approach to leadership* the leader elevates the group's members, enabling them not only to accomplish the group task but to also emerge as more empowered individuals. At the center of the transformational approach is the concept of charisma, that quality of an individual that makes us believe in or want to follow him or

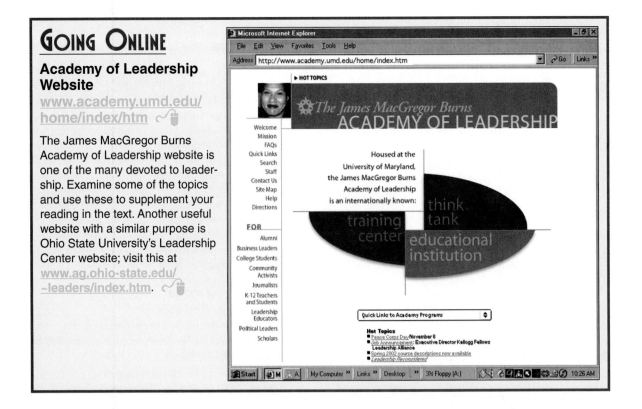

GOING ONLINE

Academy of Leadership Website

www.academy.umd.edu/home/index/htm

The James MacGregor Burns Academy of Leadership website is one of the many devoted to leadership. Examine some of the topics and use these to supplement your reading in the text. Another useful website with a similar purpose is Ohio State University's Leadership Center website; visit this at www.ag.ohio-state.edu/~leaders/index.htm.

UNDERSTANDING THEORY AND RESEARCH

Leadership Signals

Think about the types of cues you use to get group members to do certain things. Do you think you would get greater power by emphasizing your ability to do a task (task cues) or by making threats (dominance cues)? Consider the results of one interesting study (Driskell, Olmstead, & Salas, 1993). In this study task cues included maintaining eye contact, sitting at the head of the table, using a relatively rapid speech rate, speaking fluently, and gesturing appropriately. Dominance cues, on the other hand, included speaking in a loud and angry voice, pointing fingers, maintaining rigid posture, using forceful gestures, and lowering the eyebrows. Which leader would you be more apt to follow? Results showed that most people will be more influenced by speakers using task cues. They will also see such speakers as more competent and more likable. Persons using dominance cues, on the other hand, are perceived as less competent, less influential, less likable, and more self-oriented. The implication, at least from this one study, is that if you wish to gain influence in a group (and be liked), you should use task cues and avoid dominance cues.

> **Working with Theories and Research.** *Does your own experience support these findings? Might there be situations in which dominance cues would be more effective than task cues in gaining compliance from group members?*

her. Gandhi, Martin Luther King Jr., and John F. Kennedy may be cited as examples of transformational leaders. These leaders were seen as role models of what they asked of their members, were perceived as extremely competent and able leaders, and articulated moral goals (Northouse, 1997). We'll return to this concept of charisma in the discussion of credibility in Unit 19.

The *situational approach to leadership* focuses on the two major responsibilities of the leader—accomplishing the task at hand and ensuring the satisfaction of the members—and recognizes that the leader's style must vary on the basis of the specific situation. Just as you adjust your interpersonal style in conversation or your motivational appeals in public speaking on the basis of the particular situation, so you must adjust your leadership style. Leadership effectiveness, then, depends on combining the concerns for task and people according to the specifics of the situation. Some situations will call for high concentration on task issues but will need little in the way of people encouragement. For example, a group of scientists working on AIDS research would probably need a leader primarily to provide them with the needed information to accomplish their task. They would be self-motivating and would probably need little in the way of social and emotional encouragement. On the other hand, a group of recovering alcoholics might require leadership that stressed the social and emotional needs of the members.

If you'd like to explore your own orientation to this situational theory of leadership, take the self-test "What kind of leader are you?" at www.ablongman.com/devito. 🖱

Styles of Leadership

In addition to looking at the concerns of leadership with both task and people functions, as we did with the situational theory of leadership, we can also look at leadership in terms of its three major styles: laissez-faire, democratic, and authoritarian (Bennis & Nanus, 1985; Hackman & Johnson, 1991). Think about your own leadership style and the leadership styles of those you've worked with as you read the descriptions of these three styles. Which style are you likely to feel most comfortable using? Most comfortable working with as a group member?

As a **laissez-faire leader** you would take no initiative in directing or suggesting alternative courses of action. Rather, you would allow the group to develop and progress on its own, even allowing it to make its own mistakes. You would in effect give up or deny any real authority. As a laissez-faire leader you would answer questions or provide relevant information, but only when specifically asked. You would give little if any reinforcement to the group members. But you would not punish members, either; as a result you would be seen as nonthreatening. Generally, this type of leadership results in a satisfied but inefficient group.

As a **democratic leader** you would provide direction but allow the group to develop and progress the way its members wished. You would encourage group members to determine their own goals and procedures. You would stimulate self-direction and self-actualization on the part of the group members. Unlike the laissez-faire leader, a democratic leader would give members reinforcement and contribute suggestions for direction and alternative courses of action. Always, however, he or she would allow the group to make its own decisions. Generally, this form of leadership results in both satisfaction and efficiency.

As an **authoritarian leader** you would be the opposite of the laissez-faire leader. You would determine the group policies or make decisions without consulting or securing agreement from the members. You would be impersonal and would encourage communication to you and from you but not from member to member; you would seek to min-imize intragroup communication. In this way you would enhance your own importance and control.

As an authoritarian leader you would assume the greatest responsibility for the progress of the group and would not want interference from members. You would be concerned with getting the group to accept your decisions rather than making its own decisions. You might satisfy the group's psychological needs, in that you would reward and punish the group much as a parent does. If the authoritarian leader is competent, the group members may be highly efficient but are likely to be less personally satisfied.

The moderator of an Internet group, such as a mailing list or certain types of chat groups, is a kind of group leader. For example, a person usually sets up a mailing list, serves as leader for a time, then lets it operate as an automated system. Some chat groups also have "channel operators" who are like leaders; these too are usually the ones who established the group. The moderator (who may be a person or a computer program) may also serve as a filter or gatekeeper, allowing certain messages to go through and preventing others from going through. Much like a supervisor in an organization, the Internet group moderator may on occasion decide to exclude a particular member from further group participation, usually for violating the rules of the particular Internet group. Most Internet group mod-

With which leadership style are you most comfortable as a leader? As a member?

erators are laissez-faire leaders; they usually don't intrude in the group's ongoing interaction.

Each leadership style has its place; one style should not be considered superior to the others. Each is appropriate for a different purpose and for a different situation. In a social group at a friend's house, any leadership other than laissez-faire would be difficult to tolerate. When speed and efficiency are paramount, authoritarian leadership may be the most effective. Authoritarian leadership may also be more appropriate when group members continue to show lack of motivation toward the task despite democratic efforts to move them. When all members are approximately equal in their knowledge of the topic, or when the members are very concerned about their individual rights, the democratic leadership style seems more appropriate.

Functions of Leadership

In relatively formal small group situations, as when politicians plan a strategy, advertisers discuss a campaign, or teachers consider educational methods, the leader has several specific functions. Keep in mind that these functions are not the exclusive property of the leader. Nevertheless, when there is a specific leader, he or she is expected to perform them.

As you read about these functions, which include both task and people functions, keep in mind that an effective leader also needs knowledge of the topic of the discussion; the communication competence to make effective use of the group process and to use mindfulness, flexibility, and cultural sensitivity; and in addition the more specific skills of openness, empathy, positiveness, immediacy, interaction management, expressiveness, and other-orientation that were discussed in Unit 9.

Prepare for the Discussion

It often falls to the leader to provide members with necessary materials to read or view before the meeting. Preparations also may involve, for example, arranging a convenient meeting time and place; informing members of the purposes and goals of the meeting; and recommending that members come to the meeting with, for example, general ideas or specific proposals.

Similarly, groups form gradually and need to be eased into meaningful discussion. Diverse members should not be expected to sit down and discuss a problem without becoming familiar with one an-

other. Put more generally, the leader is responsible for any preparations and preliminaries necessary to ensure an orderly and productive group experience.

Activate the Group Agenda

Most groups have an **agenda**. An agenda is simply a list of the items the group wishes to complete—the tasks to which the group should devote its attention. Sometimes the agenda is prepared by a supervisor or a consultant or a CEO and is simply presented to the group. The group is then expected to follow the agenda item by item. At other times, the group will develop its own agenda, usually as its first or second item of business.

Generally, the more formal the group, the more important the agenda becomes. In informal groups the agenda may simply be general ideas in the minds of the members (for example, "We'll review the class assignment and then make plans for the weekend"). In formal business groups the agenda will be much more detailed and explicit. Some agendas specify not only the items that must be covered but also the order in which they should be covered and even the amount of time that should be devoted to each item.

Activate Group Interaction

Many groups need some prodding and stimulation to interact. Perhaps the group is newly formed and the members feel a bit uneasy with one another. As the group leader you would stimulate the members to interact. You would also serve this function if members began acting as individuals rather than as a group. In this case you would want to focus the members on their group task.

Maintain Effective Interaction

Even after the group was stimulated to group interaction, you would strive to see that members maintained effective interaction. If the discussion began to drag, you would prod the group to effective interaction: "Do we have any additional comments on the proposal to eliminate required courses?" "What do those of you who are members of the college curriculum committee think about the English Department's proposal to restructure required courses?" "Does anyone want to make any additional comments on eliminating the minor area of concentration?" As the leader you would want to ensure that all members had an opportunity to express themselves.

MEDIA WATCH

AGENDA-SETTING THEORY

In much the same way that a group leader sets an agenda, so do the media. In fact, agenda-setting theory argues that the media establish your agenda by focusing attention on certain people and events. The media tell you—by virtue of what they cover—who is important and what events are significant (McCombs & Shaw, 1972, 1993). The media don't tell you what to think; they tell you what to think about (Edelstein, 1993; McCombs, Lopez-Escobar, & Llamas, 2000).

Both salience and obtrusiveness influence the media's ability to establish your agenda (Folkerts & Lacy, 2001).

▶ The term *salience* refers to the importance of an issue to you. For example, if you live in a high-crime city, then news of crime, crime deterrents, and crime statistics are probably important to you. If the media cover such salient issues, then their ability to establish your agenda is enhanced. If they fail to cover such issues, then you're less likely to set your agenda on the basis of what the media say.

▶ *Obtrusiveness* describes the directness of your experience with an issue. If you have direct experience with an issue, then it's obtrusive; if you don't have direct experience, then it's unobtrusive. If tuition costs go up, then the tuition issue is obtrusive, because you (presumably) have direct experience with it. But if a volcano erupts on a faraway uninhabited island, it's unobtrusive. The media's agenda-setting influence is likely to be greater for unobtrusive issues, because you have no direct experience with these issues and hence have to rely on what the media tell you is or isn't important.

Follow-Up. *Although your interpersonal interactions are also influential in determining what is and what isn't important to you, the media probably set your agenda to some degree. At the very least, they lead you to focus attention on certain subjects and away from others. How and to what extent do the media establish your agenda? Can you identify specific examples?*

Empower Group Members

An important function of at least some leadership (though it is not limited to leadership) is to empower others—to help other group members (and also your relational partner, coworkers, employees, other students, or siblings) gain increased power over themselves and their environment. Some ways you might use to empower others include:

- Raise the person's self-esteem. Compliment, reinforce. Resist faultfinding; it doesn't benefit anyone and in fact disempowers.

- Share skills and decision-making power and authority.

- Offer constructive criticism. With friends or family, be willing to offer your perspective, to lend an ear to a first singing effort, or to listen to a new poem. With a group, be willing to react honestly to suggestions from all group members and not just to those from people in high positions.

- Encourage growth in all forms—academic, relational, and professional. The growth and em-

powerment of the other person enhances your own growth and power.

Manage Conflict

As in interpersonal relationships, conflict is a part of small group interaction. And it's a function of leadership to deal effectively with it. Small group communication researchers distinguish between procedural and people conflicts and offer a wide variety of conflict management strategies (Patton, Giffin, & Patton, 1989; Folger, Poole, & Stutman, 1997; Kindler, 1996).

Procedural conflicts involve disagreements over who is in charge (who is the leader or who should be the leader), what the agenda or task of the group should be, and how the group should conduct its business. The best way to deal with procedural problems is to prevent them from occurring in the first place by establishing early in the group's interaction who is to serve as leader and what the agenda should be. If procedural problems arise after these agreements are reached, members or the

BUILDING COMMUNICATION SKILLS

How Can You Empower Others?

What would you say, in each of the following situations, to help empower the individuals involved? After developing your responses, consider what you would stand to gain from your successful empowering of these individuals. How would your relationships with the individuals involved be different if you were successful in achieving your goal of empowering them? Can you identify any potential problems that might result from successful empowerment?

▶ You're a third-grade teacher. Most of your students are from the same ethnic–religious group; three, however, are from a very different group. The problem is that these three students are extremely reluctant to participate in class discussions; they stumble when they have to read in front of the class (although they read quite well in private) and they make all sorts of arithmetic mistakes when they do problems at the board. And, not surprisingly with third graders, many of the other students make fun of them and laugh at their mistakes. You want to empower these students, so as to help them realize their abilities and potential, and at the same time to increase intercultural understanding.

▶ You're managing four college interns at a local Web design firm, three women and one man. The women all know and are extremely supportive of one another, so they regularly contribute ideas and offer constructive criticism of one another's work. The man, however, seems left out. Although equally competent, he lacks confidence and so doesn't contribute ideas or offer suggestions for improving the work of others. In view of the fact that most of the online visitors to these particular websites are males, you really need his input.

▶ Your partner has been having lots of difficulties: Recently he lost his job, received poor grades in a night class he was taking, and started gaining lots of weight, something he was very careful to avoid in the past. At the same time, you're doing extremely well: You just got a promotion, got admitted to a great MBA program, and are looking your best. You want to give your partner back his confidence and want to empower him.

---

leader can refer the conflicting participants to the group's earlier decisions. When members disagree or become dissatisfied with these early decisions, they may become negative or antagonistic and may cease to participate in the discussion. When this happens (or if members want to change procedures), a brief discussion on the procedures can be held. The important point to realize is that procedural conflicts should be dealt with as procedural conflicts and should not be allowed to escalate into something else.

People conflicts can occur when one member dominates the group, when several members battle for control, or when some members refuse to participate. The leader should try to secure the com-

mitment of all members and to convince them that the progress of the group depends on everyone's contributions. At times it may be necessary to redirect the focus of the group to concentrate on people needs—on satisfying members' needs for group approval, for periodic rewards, or for encouragement. People conflicts are also created when people rather than ideas are attacked. The leader needs to ensure that attacks and disagreements are clearly focused on ideas, not people. And if a personal attack does get started, the leaders should step in to refocus the difference in opinion to the idea and away from the person.

The conflict management strategies presented in Unit 11 are also applicable to the small group situation. In addition, here are four principles that have special relevance to conflict management in small groups (Kindler, 1996):

• Preserve the dignity and respect of all members. Assume, for example, that each person's disagreement is legitimate and stems from a genuine concern for the good of the group. Therefore, treat disagreements kindly; even if someone attacks you personally, it's generally wise not to respond in kind but to redirect the criticism to the issues at hand.

• Listen empathically. Enter into the perspectives of the other members; try to feel what they're feeling without making any critical judgments. Try to ask yourself why these other people see the situation differently from the way you see it.

• Seek out and emphasize common ground. Even in the midst of disagreement, there are areas of common interest, common beliefs, and common aims. Find these and build on them.

• Value diversity and differences. Creative solutions often emerge from conflicting perspectives. So don't gloss over differences; instead, explore them for the valuable information they can give you.

Keep Members on Track

Many individuals are egocentric and will pursue only their own interests and concerns. As the leader it's your task to keep all members reasonably on track. Here are a few ways you might accomplish this:

• Ask questions that focus on the specific topic at hand; especially ask questions of those who seem to be wandering off into other directions.

• Interject internal summaries in which you briefly identify what has been accomplished and what the group needs to move on to next.

• Consider the value of setting a formal agenda and sticking to it.

BUILDING COMMUNICATION SKILLS

How Can You Deal with Small Group Complaints?

Assume that you're the leader of a work team consisting of members from each of the major departments in your company. For each of the following complaints explain (a) what you would say and (b) what objective your response would be designed to achieve.

In framing your responses try to follow these guidelines: (1) Let the person know that you're open to complaints and that you do view them as essential sources of information. (2) Show that you're following the suggestions for effective listening discussed in Unit 5; for example, that you listen supportively and with empathy. (3) Show that you understand both the thoughts and the feelings that go with the complaint. (4) Ask the other person what he or she would like you to do about the complaint.

▶ Reducing costs is an impossible task; we're wasting our time here. Costs have gone up;

there's no way we can reduce costs. Period. The end.

▶ Look, we've been at this for two hours and I still haven't heard anything about accounting, which is my department. I really don't know why I'm here. How can the accounting department help reduce costs?

▶ You're calling these meetings much too often and much too early to suit us. We'd like fewer meetings scheduled for later in the day.

▶ That's not fair. Why do I always have to take the minutes of these meetings? Can't we have a real secretary here?

▶ There's a good reason why I don't contribute to the discussion. I don't contribute because no one listens to what I say.

- Focus your own attention on the topics at hand; your own example will influence the behavior of the other members.

Ensure Member Satisfaction

Members have different psychological needs and wants, and many people enter groups to satisfy these personal concerns. Even though a group may, for example, deal with political issues, the members may have come together for reasons that are more psychological than political. If a group is to be effective, it must meet not only the surface purposes of the group but also the underlying or interpersonal purposes that motivated many of the members to come together in the first place.

Depending on the specific members, special adjustments may have to be made to accommodate people with disabilities. For example, often ignored in discussions of leadership functions are provisions for group members with hearing problems. Table 14.2 offers some suggestions.

Encourage Ongoing Evaluation and Improvement

Most groups encounter obstacles as they try to solve a problem, reach a decision, or generate ideas. Therefore, most could use some improvement. If the group is to improve, it must focus on itself. In other words, along with trying to solve some external problem, each group must try to solve its own internal problems as well; for example, it may need to deal with personal conflicts, failure of members to meet on time, or members who come unprepared. As the leader, try to identify any such difficulties and encourage and help the group to analyze and resolve them.

Follow Up on the Discussion

Just as with prediscussion functions, the leader is responsible for postdiscussion functions. Such functions might include summarizing the group's discussion, organizing future meetings, or presenting the group's decisions to some other group. Again,

---

TABLE 14.2   Facilitating Small Group Communications with Deaf People

- Seat the deaf person to his or her best advantage. This usually means a seat near the speaker so that the deaf person can see the speaker's lips.

- Provide new vocabulary in advance. If new vocabulary cannot be presented in advance, write the terms on paper, a chalkboard, or an overhead projector, if possible.

- Avoid unnecessary pacing and speaking when writing on a chalkboard. It is difficult to speech-read a person in motion, and impossible to speech-read one whose back is turned.

- Use visual aids if possible.

- Make sure the deaf person doesn't miss vital information. Write out any changes in meeting times, special assignments, additional instructions, and so on.

- Slow down the pace of communication slightly to facilitate understanding.

- Repeat questions and statements made from the back of the room and point to the person who's speaking.

- Allow full participation by the deaf person in the discussion. It is difficult for deaf persons to participate in group discussions because they are not sure when speakers have finished. The group leader or teacher should recognize the deaf person from time to time to allow full participation by that person.

- Use hands-on experience whenever possible in training situations.

- Use an interpreter in a large group setting.

- Use a note taker when possible to record information. It is difficult for many deaf persons to pay attention to a speaker and take notes simultaneously.

Source: From *Tips for Communicating with Deaf People.* Reprinted by permission of the Rochester Institute of Technology, National Technical Institute for the Deaf, 52 Lomb Memorial Drive, Rochester, NY 14623-0887.

UNDERSTANDING THEORY AND RESEARCH

Attila's Theory of Leadership

From a totally different perspective, consider these leadership qualities, paraphrased from Wes Roberts's *Leadership Secrets of Attila the Hun* (1987).

- *Empathy:* Leaders must develop an appreciation for and an understanding of other cultures and the values of their members.

- *Courage:* Leaders should be fearless and have the courage to complete their assignments; they must not complain about obstacles or be discouraged by adversity.

- *Accountability:* Leaders must hold themselves responsible for their own actions and for those of their group members.

- *Dependability:* Leaders must be reliable in carrying out their responsibilities; leaders must also depend on their members to accomplish matters they themselves can't oversee.

- *Credibility:* Leaders must be believable to both friends and enemies; they must possess the integrity and intelligence needed to secure and communicate accurate information.

- *Stewardship:* Leaders must be caretakers of their members' interests and well-being; they must guide and reward subordinates.

Working with Theories and Research. *In addition to these six, Attila also identified loyalty, desire, emotional stamina, physical stamina, decisiveness, anticipation, timing, competitiveness, self-confidence, responsibility, and tenacity. Review these 11 additional qualities and explain how you think they can contribute to effective group leadership.*

the leader is responsible for doing whatever needs to be done to ensure that the group's experience is a productive one.

MEMBERSHIP, LEADERSHIP, AND CULTURE

Most research on and theories about small group communication, membership, and leadership have emerged from universities in the United States and reflect U.S. culture. For example, in the United States—and in individualistic cultures generally—the individual group member is extremely important. But in collectivist cultures the individual is less important; it's the group that is the significant entity. In Japan, for example, group researchers find that "individual fulfillment of self is attained through finding and maintaining one's place within the group" (Cathcart & Cathcart, 1985, p. 191). In the United States, in contrast, individual fulfillment

of self is attained by the individual and through his or her own efforts, not by the group.

It's often thought that because group membership and group identity are so important in collectivist cultures, it's the group that makes important decisions. Actually, this does not seem to be the case. In fact, a study of 48 (highly collectivist) Japanese organizations found that participating in decision-making groups did not give the members decision-making power. Group members were encouraged to contribute ideas, but the decision-making power was reserved for the CEO or for managers higher up the organizational ladder (Brennan, 1991).

The discussion of member roles earlier in this unit devoted an entire category to individual roles, roles adopted by individuals to satisfy individual rather than group goals. In other cultures (notably collectivist cultures) these roles would probably not even be mentioned—simply because they wouldn't be acted out often enough to deserve such extended discussion. For example, in many collectivist cultures the group orientation is too pervasive for individuals to violate it by acting as the blocker, the recognition seeker, or the dominator.

One obvious consequence of this cultural difference can be seen when a group member commits a serious error. For example, let's say a team member submits the wrong advertising copy to the media. In a group governed by individualistic norms, that member is likely to be singled out, reprimanded, and perhaps fired. Further, the leader or supervisor is likely to distance himself or herself from this member for fear that blame for the error will "rub off." In a more collectivist culture, the error is more likely to be seen as a group mistake. The individual is unlikely to be singled out—especially not in public—and the leader is likely to shoulder part of the blame. The same is true when one member comes up with a great idea. In individualistic cul-

tures that person is likely to be rewarded, and the person's work group benefits only indirectly. In a collectivist culture it is the group that gets recognized and rewarded for the idea.

In a similar way, each culture's belief system influences group members' behavior. For example, members of many Asian cultures, influenced by Confucian principles, believe that "the protruding nail gets pounded down" and are therefore not likely to voice disagreement with the majority of the group. Americans, on the other hand, influenced by the belief that "the squeaky wheel gets the grease," are more likely to voice disagreement or to act in ways different from other group members in order to get what they want.

Also, each culture has its own rules of preferred and expected leadership style. In the United States the general and expected style for a group leader is

COMMUNICATION @ WORK

Mentoring as Leadership

True leadership must be for the benefit of the followers, not the enrichment of the leaders.

—Robert Townsend

A mentoring relationship is one in which an experienced individual helps to train someone who is less experienced. An accomplished teacher, for example, might mentor a young teacher who is newly arrived or who has never taught before. The mentor guides the new person through the ropes, teaches the strategies and techniques for success, and otherwise communicates his or her knowledge and experience to the "mentee."

The mentoring relationship is usually a one-on-one relationship between expert and novice, a relationship that is supportive and trusting. There's a mutual and open sharing of information and thoughts about the job. The relationship enables the novice to try out new skills under the guidance of an expert, to ask questions, and to obtain the feedback so necessary to the acquisition of complex skills.

In a study of middle-level managers, those who had mentors and participated in mentoring relationships were found to get more promotions and higher salaries than those who didn't (Scandura, 1992). And the mentoring relationship is one of the three primary paths to career achievement among African American men and women (Bridges, 1996).

At the same time that a mentor helps a newcomer, the mentor benefits from clarifying his or her thoughts, from seeing the job from the perspective of a newcomer, and from considering and formulating answers to a variety of questions. Much the way a teacher learns from teaching, a mentor learns from mentoring.

Thinking about Your Communicating @ Work

How might a mentor help you in your professional life? How might you go about finding a mentor?

democratic. Our political leaders are elected by a democratic process; similarly, boards of directors are elected by the shareholders of a corporation. In other situations, of course, leaders are chosen by those in authority. The directors choose the president of a company, and the president will normally decide who will supervise and who will be supervised within the organization. Even in this situation, however, we expect the supervisor to behave democratically—to listen to the ideas of employees, to take their views into consideration when decisions are to be made, to keep them informed of corporate developments, and to generally respect their interests. Also, we expect that leaders will be changed fairly regularly. We elect a president every four years, and company directors' elections are normally held each year.

In some other cultures, leaders are chosen by right of birth. They're not elected, nor are they expected to behave democratically. Similarly, their tenure as leaders is usually extremely long; they may hold their position their entire lives and then pass it on to their children. In other cases, leaders in a wide variety of roles may be named by a military dictator.

The important point to realize is that your membership and your leadership style are influenced by the culture in which you were raised. Consequently, when in a group with members of different cultures, consider the differences in both membership and leadership style that individuals bring with them. For example, a member who plays individual roles may be tolerated in many groups in the United States and in some cases may even be thought amusing and different. That same member playing the same roles in a group with a more collectivist orientation is likely to be evaluated much more negatively. Multicultural groups may find it helpful to discuss members' views of group membership and leadership and what constitutes comfortable interaction for them.

REFLECTIONS ON ETHICS IN HUMAN COMMUNICATION

The Leader's Ethical Responsibilities

Ethical qualities often figure prominently in the traits approach to leadership. Among those qualities is honesty: Leaders should be honest with group members, revealing agendas openly and presenting information fairly. Leaders should also be accountable, taking responsibility for their actions and decisions. Additionally, leaders should be concerned for the welfare of their members; a leader who was more concerned with his or her own personal interests than with the group task or the interpersonal needs of the members would clearly be acting unethically.

What would you do? *You're leading a discussion among a small group of high school freshmen,* whom you're mentoring. The discussion centers on marijuana use; your objective is to get the students to avoid trying it or, if they have tried it already, to stop smoking. During the discussion students ask you if you smoke pot. The truth is that on occasion you do—but it's a very controlled use, and you feel that it would only destroy your credibility and lead the students to experiment with or continue smoking pot if they knew about it. At the same time, you wonder if you can ethically lie to them and tell them that you have never smoked and do not now smoke. What would you do in this situation?*

SUMMARY

This unit examined the roles of members and leaders and the principles that govern effective group interaction.

1. A popular classification of small group member roles divides them into group task roles, group building and maintenance roles, and individual roles.

2. Twelve group task roles are: initiator–contributor, information seeker, opinion seeker, information giver, opinion giver, elaborator, coordinator, orienter, evaluator–critic, energizer, procedural technician, and recorder.

3. Seven group building and maintenance roles are: encourager, harmonizer, compromiser, gatekeeper–expediter, standard setter, group observer and commentator, and follower.

4. Eight individual roles are: aggressor, blocker, recognition seeker, self-confessor, playboy/playgirl, dominator, help seeker, and special interest pleader.

5. Interaction process analysis categorizes group members' contributions into four areas: social–emotional positive contributions, social–emotional negative contributions, attempted answers, and questions.

6. Member participation should be group-oriented, should center conflict on issues, should be critically open-minded, and should ensure understanding.

7. Groupthink is a way of thinking that develops when concurrence seeking in a cohesive group overrides realistic appraisal of alternative courses of action.

8. The traits approach to leadership focuses on personal characteristics that contribute to leadership; the functional approach centers on what the leader does (the functions the leader serves); and the transformational approach focuses on the leader's empowerment of the group members.

9. In the situational theory of leadership, leadership is seen as concerned with both accomplishing the task and serving the interpersonal needs of the members. The degree to which either concern is emphasized should depend on the specific group and the unique situation.

10. Three major leadership styles are: laissez-faire, democratic, and authoritarian. The laissez-faire leader avoids directing or suggesting what members should do. The democratic leader provides direction but allows members to do as they wish. The authoritarian leader makes the decisions for the group.

11. Among the leader's functions are: preparing members for the discussion, activating the group interaction, maintaining effective interaction, managing conflict, keeping members on track, ensuring member satisfaction, and encouraging ongoing evaluation and improvement.

12. The culture in which people are raised will greatly influence the ways in which members and leaders interact in small groups.

KEY TERMS

group task roles

group building and maintenance roles

individual roles

interaction process analysis

groupthink

leadership

traits approach to leadership

functional approach to leadership

transformational approach to leadership

situational approach to leadership

laissez-faire leader

democratic leader

authoritarian leader

agenda setting

THINKING CRITICALLY ABOUT

Members and Leaders in Group Communication

1. Can you identify roles that you habitually play in certain groups? Do you adopt these roles in your friendship, love, and family relationships as well?

2. Have you ever been in a group when groupthink was operating? If so, what were its symptoms? What effect did groupthink have on the process and conclusions of the group?

3. How would you characterize the leadership style of one of your local politicians, religious leaders, college instructors, or talk show hosts? How would you characterize your own leadership style? For example, are you usually more concerned with people or with tasks? Are you more likely to be a laissez-faire, democratic, or authoritarian leader?

4. It's been found that the person with the highest rate of participation in a group is the one most likely to be chosen leader (Mullen, Salas, & Driskell, 1989).

Do you find this to be true of the groups in which you have participated? Why do you suppose this relationship exists?

5. **Researching Members and Leaders** How would you go about finding answers to such questions as these?

- Do people who play individual roles in a group become unpopular with other group members?
- Can leadership styles be used to describe approaches to teaching? To parenting? To managing?
- Do women and men respond similarly to the different leadership styles? Do women and men exercise the different leadership styles with equal facility?
- How do members of individualistic and collectivist cultures view small group leadership?

UNIT 15
Public Speaking Topics, Audiences, and Research

Unit Contents

As you move up the hierarchy in your business and professional lives, you'll find an ever greater need for public speaking. In this unit you'll learn

◗ what public speaking is and the nature of the normal nervousness that most people feel

◗ how to control your anxiety and accomplish the first few steps in preparing a public speech—selecting and limiting your topic, analyzing your specific audience, and researching your topic

INTRODUCING PUBLIC SPEAKING

Fair questions to ask of a book or a course are "What will I get out of this?" and "How will the effort and time I put into this subject help me become more successful?" Here are just a few of the benefits you'll derive from this book's section on public speaking:

• Public speaking provides training in a variety of *personal and social competencies*. In the pages that follow you'll learn such skills as self-awareness, self-confidence, and ways to deal with the fear of communicating—skills that you'll apply in public speaking but that will also prove valuable in all of your social interactions.

• You'll also learn a wide variety of *academic and career skills*. For example, studying public speaking will teach you to conduct research; explain complex concepts; support an argument with logical, emotional, and ethical appeals; organize a variety of messages; and evaluate the validity of persuasive appeals.

• Speakers aren't born; they're made. It is through instruction, exposure to different speeches, feedback, and individual learning experiences that you become an effective speaker. Regardless of your present level of competence, you can improve through proper training. As you acquire the skills of public speaking, you'll also develop and refine your *general communication abilities;* you'll develop a more effective communication style, learn to give (and respond appropriately to) criticism, improve your listening skills, and refine your delivery skills.

In public speaking a speaker presents a relatively continuous message to a relatively large audience in a unique context. Like all forms of communication, public speaking is transactional (Watzlawick, Beavin, & Jackson, 1967; Watzlawick, 1978): Each element in the public speaking process depends on and interacts with all other elements. For example, the way in which you organize a speech will depend on such factors as the speech topic, the specific audience, the purpose you hope to achieve, and a host of other variables—all of which are examined in the remainder of this unit and in the units to follow.

Especially important is the mutual interaction and influence between speaker and listeners. True, when you give a speech, you do most of the speaking and the listeners do most of the listening. However, the listeners also send messages in the form of feedback—for example, applause, bored looks, nods of agreement or disagreement, and attentive glances. The audience also influences how you'll prepare and present your speech. It influences your arguments, your language, your method of organization, and, in fact, every choice you make. You would not, for example, present to men the same speech on "dressing for success" that you would give to women.

Public speaking is both a very old and a very new art. It's likely that public speaking principles were developed soon after our species began to talk. Much of contemporary public speaking, however, is based on the works of the ancient Greeks and Romans, who articulated an especially insightful system of rhetoric or public speaking. Contemporary public speaking builds on this classical heritage and also incorporates insights from the humanities, the social and behavioral sciences, and computer science and technology as well as contributions and perspectives from different cultures. You may wish to continue this look at public speaking as an area of study by examining "Historical Roots of Public Speaking" and "Growth and Development of Public Speaking" at www.ablongman.com/devito.

The preparation of a public speech involves 10 steps: (1) Select the topic and purpose; (2) analyze the audience; (3) research the topic; (4) formulate the thesis and identify the major problems; (5) support the major propositions; (6) organize the speech materials; (7) construct the conclusion, introduction, and transitions; (8) outline the speech; (9) word the speech; and (10) rehearse and deliver the speech. The first 3 of these steps are discussed in this unit; the remaining 7 are discussed in the next two units.

Apprehension in Public Speaking

Before beginning the actual speech preparation process, let's look first at what is probably your number one concern; stage fright, or what is now called **communication apprehension**. People experience apprehension in all forms of communication (as illustrated throughout this text), but public speaking apprehension is the most common and most severe (Richmond & McCroskey, 1998; Daly, McCroskey, Ayres, Hopf, & Ayres, 1997). Take the following apprehension test to measure your own fear of speaking in public.

TEST YOURSELF

How Apprehensive Are You in Public Speaking?

This questionnaire consists of six statements concerning your feelings about public speaking. Indicate the degree to which each statement applies to you, using the following scale: 1 = strongly agree; 2 = agree; 3 = are undecided; 4 = disagree; 5 = strongly disagree. There are no right or wrong answers. Don't be concerned that some of the statements are similar to others. Work quickly; just record your immediate response.

_____ **1.** I have no fear of giving a speech.

_____ **2.** Certain parts of my body feel very tense and rigid while giving a speech.

_____ **3.** I feel relaxed while giving a speech.

_____ **4.** My thoughts become confused and jumbled when I am giving a speech.

_____ **5.** I face the prospect of giving a speech with confidence.

_____ **6.** While giving a speech, I get so nervous that I forget facts I really know.

How did you do? To obtain your public speaking apprehension score, begin with the number 18 (selected so that you won't wind up with negative numbers) and add to it the scores for items 1, 3, and 5. Then, from this total, subtract the scores from items 2, 4, and 6. A score above 18 shows some degree of apprehension. Most people score above 18, so if you scored relatively high, you're among the vast majority of people. You may find it interesting to compare your score here with your other apprehension scores (from Unit 12 for job interviews and from Unit 13 for group discussions and meetings). Most people tend to score highest on public speaking and job interviews and relatively low on group discussion and meeting apprehension. Also, compare your apprehension in these situations with your apprehension in conversations by taking the self-test, "How apprehensive are you in conversations?" at www.ablongman.com/devito.

What will you do? As you read the suggestions for reducing apprehension in the text that follows, consider what you can do to incorporate these into your own public speaking experiences. Consider too how these suggestions might be useful in reducing apprehension more generally; for example, in social situations and in small groups and meetings. An extremely thorough discussion of communication apprehension may be found in Richmond and McCroskey's *Communication: Apprehension Avoidance and Effectiveness* (1998). Briefer discussions may be found at www.ablongman.com/devito; look for "Apprehension."

Source: From James C. McCroskey, *An Introduction to Rhetorical Communication*, 7th edition. Copyright © 1997. Reprinted by permission of Allyn & Bacon. ✔

There are several ways you can deal with your own public speaking anxiety: (1) reversing the factors that cause anxiety, (2) practicing performance visualization, and (3) systematically desensitizing yourself.

Reversing the Factors That Cause Apprehension

There are five factors that contribute to speaker apprehension; if you can reverse these factors or lessen their impact, you'll be able to reduce your anxiety. These five factors are new and different situations, subordinate status, conspicuousness, lack of similarity to the audience, and prior history (Beatty,

1988; Richmond & McCroskey, 1998; Watson & Dodd, 1984; Carducci & Zimbardo, 1995).

New and different situations will make you anxious; so gaining as much experience in public speaking as you can (making it less new and different) will lessen your anxiety. Learning to speak in public is similar to learning to drive a car or ski down a mountain. With experience the initial fears and anxieties give way to feelings of control, comfort, and pleasure. Experience will prove to you that a public speech can be effective despite your fears and anxieties. It will show you that the feeling of accomplishment you can derive from public speaking is rewarding and will outweigh any initial anxiety.

Try to reduce the newness of the situation by familiarizing yourself with the public speaking context. Try, for example, to rehearse in the room in which you will give your speech. Or stand at the front of the room before the actual presentation, as if you were giving your speech.

When you see yourself as having *subordinate status*—when, for example, you feel that others are better speakers or that they know more than you do—your anxiety increases. Thinking positively about yourself and being thorough in your preparation can help reduce this particular cause of anxiety. At the same time, put your apprehension in perspective. Fear increases when you feel that the audience's expectations are very high (Ayres, 1986). So maintain realistic expectations. Compete only with yourself; Your second speech does not have to be better than that of the previous speaker, but it should be better than your own first one. Remember that your audience does not expect perfection, either.

When you're the center of attention, as you normally are in public speaking, you feel *conspicuous* and your anxiety increases. Therefore, try thinking of public speaking as a type of conversation (some theorists call it "enlarged conversation"). Avoid the temptation to use chemicals as tension relievers; this will only make you feel more conspicuous and will thus increase your anxiety. Unless prescribed by a physician, avoid any chemical means for reducing apprehension—such as tranquilizers, marijuana, alcohol, or artificial stimulants. Chemicals also may impair other functions; for example, they may interfere with your ability to remember the parts of your speech, to accurately read audience feedback, or to regulate the timing of your speech.

When you feel you *lack similarity* with your audience, you may feel that your audience doesn't empathize with you and so may become anxious. Try emphasizing the commonalities you share with your listeners as you plan your speeches as well as during the actual presentation.

If you have a *prior history of apprehension*, you're more likely to dwell on such past experiences and become even more anxious. Positive public speaking experiences in this class will help reduce this cause of anxiety, however.

Performance Visualization

Performance visualization is designed both to reduce the outward signs of apprehension and to reduce the negative thinking that often creates anxiety (Ayres & Hopf, 1992, 1993; Ayres, Hopf, & Ayres, 1994).

First, develop a positive attitude and a positive self-perception. Visualize yourself in the role of the effective public speaker. Visualize yourself walking to the front of the room—fully and totally confident, fully in control of the situation. The audience listens in rapt attention and, as you finish, bursts into wild applause. Throughout this visualization, avoid all negative thoughts. As you visualize yourself as this effective speaker, take note of how you walk, look at your listeners, handle your notes, and respond to questions; think especially about how you feel about the public speaking experience.

Second, model your performance on that of an exceptionally effective speaker. View a particularly competent public speaker on video, for example, and make a mental "movie" of it. As you review the actual video and your mental movie, shift yourself into the role of speaker; become this speaker.

Systematically Desensitizing Yourself

Systematic desensitization is a technique for dealing with a variety of fears, including those involved in public speaking (Wolpe, 1957; Goss, Thompson, & Olds, 1978; Richmond & McCroskey, 1998). The general idea is to create a hierarchy of behaviors leading up to the desired but feared behavior (say, speaking before an audience). One specific hierarchy might look like this:

5. Giving a speech in class
4. Introducing another speaker to the class
3. Speaking in a group in front of the class
2. Answering a question in class
1. Asking a question in class

You begin at the bottom of this hierarchy and rehearse the step 1 behavior mentally over a period of days until you can clearly visualize asking a question in class without any uncomfortable anxiety. Once you can accomplish this, move to the second level. Here you visualize a somewhat more threatening behavior; say, answering a question. Once you can do this, move to the third level—and so on until you get to the desired behavior.

In creating your hierarchy, use small steps to help you get from one step to the next more easily. You might then go on to engage in the actual behaviors after you have comfortably visualized them: Ask a question, answer a question, and so on. Each success will make the next step easier.

As you gain control over your apprehension, your public speaking experiences will become more satisfying and you'll become a more confident speaker. Examine your own public speaking satisfaction now, and again at the end of the course, by taking the self-test "How satisfying is your public

COMMUNICATION @ WORK

Team Presentations

The achievements of an organization are the result of the combined efforts of each individual.

—Vince Lombardi

Team presentations are extremely popular in business settings. Generally, they follow the same rules and principles as do other public speeches. There are some differences, however.

Team presentations are given by two, three, four, or even more people to an audience. Each person on the team delivers a part of the speech. For example, in a presentation on the design of a planned new office space, one person may speak on the architectural layout, another on the furnishings, and still another on the temporary inconvenience that the change will necessitate. In a presentation on employee health plans, representatives from the health plans might each speak on their specific plan, identifying its provisions and advantages and handling audience questions. In an advertising company's presentation to a client, one team member might present the creative idea; another the media analysis, cost, and the audience they hope to address; and still another the anticipated sales results.

In using a team presentation, be sure that you allow time for the planning needed to coordinate the presentations; each person needs to know exactly what the others are going to talk about, so as not to repeat or contradict. Give special attention to the introduction and conclusion. The introduction should provide the audience with a clear unifying statement that links the speeches into one coherent presentation; the conclusion should wrap up the entire presentation, not just the last speech. Also, use transitions between the speeches so that the audience members know how the speech they just heard is connected to the speech they're going to hear. You want the audience to see these speeches, although delivered by different people, as parts of one unified and coordinated presentation. For example, a speaker who has just spoken on the proposed advertising campaign's creative concept might say: "Now that you know about the creative concept, Margaret is going to explain what audience this campaign is intended to reach and the media we intend to use."

Thinking about Your Communicating @ Work

What other advantages do you see to team presentations as compared with single-speaker presentations? What are some disadvantages?

speaking?" at www.ablongman.com/devito. For additional suggestions for developing confidence as a public speaker see "Developing Confidence" at www.ablongman.com/devito.

STEP 1: SELECT YOUR TOPIC AND PURPOSE

Your first step in preparing to give a speech is to select your topic and purpose (see Figure 15.1).

Your Topic

A suitable speech topic should (1) be worthwhile and deal with matters of substance; (2) be appropriate to you and your audience, and (3) be sensitive and appropriate to the culture in which the speech takes place.

The topic should be *worthwhile*; it should address an issue that has significant implications for the audience. Topics that are worthwhile have consequences—social, educational, political, and so on. The topic must be important enough to merit the time and attention of a group of intelligent and educated persons.

A suitable topic is *appropriate* to you as the speaker, to the audience you'll address, and to the occasion. When you select a topic you're interested in, you'll enjoy thinking and reading about it, and your interest and enjoyment will come through in your speech. Also look at your topic in terms of its appropriateness to the audience. What are they in-

Figure 15.1

The Steps in Preparing and Delivering a Public Speech

This figure presents the 10 steps of public speaking. Your own progress in constructing a public speech, however, doesn't always follow the logical and linear sequence shown here. That is, you'll probably not progress simply from Step 1 to 2 to 3 and so on. Instead, you might move from Step 1 to Step 2, back again to Step 1, ahead to Step 3, back again to Step 2, and so on throughout your preparation. For example, after selecting your subject and purpose (Step 1), you may progress to Step 2 and analyze your audience. On the basis of this analysis, however, you may wish to go back and modify your subject, your purpose, or both. Similarly, after you research your topic (Step 3), you may want more information on your audience. You may, therefore, return to Step 2. Use the order of these steps as general guides, but break the sequence when it seems logical to do so.

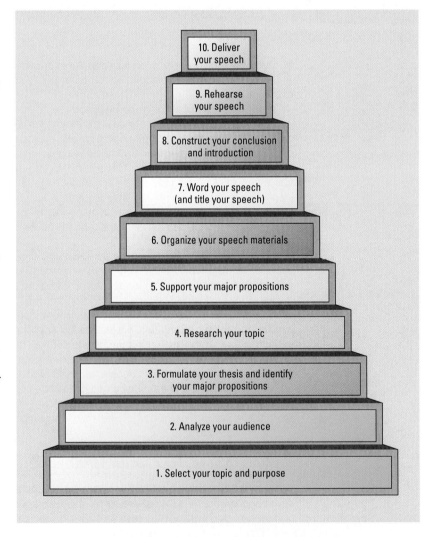

10. Deliver your speech

9. Rehearse your speech

8. Construct your conclusion and introduction

7. Word your speech (and title your speech)

6. Organize your speech materials

5. Support your major propositions

4. Research your topic

3. Formulate your thesis and identify your major propositions

2. Analyze your audience

1. Select your topic and purpose

terested in? What would they like to learn more about? What topics will make them feel that the time listening to your speech was well spent? It's a lot easier to please an audience when the topic interests them.

The topic should also be appropriate for the occasion. Some occasions call for humorous subjects or speeches of personal experience that would be out of place in other contexts. Similarly, time limitations will force you to exclude certain topics because they're too complex to cover in the time you have available.

Topics need to be *culture sensitive*. In many Arab, Asian, and African cultures, discussing sex in an audience of both men and women would be considered offensive. In other cultures (that of Scandinavia is a good example), sex is expected to be discussed openly and without embarrassment or discomfort. Each culture has its own **taboo** topics—subjects that should be avoided, especially by visitors from other cultures. For example, Roger Axtell in *Do's and Taboos around the World* (1993) recommends that visitors from the United States avoid discussing politics, language differences between French and Flemish, and religion in Belgium; family, religion, jobs, and negative comments on bullfighting in Spain; religion and Middle East politics in Iraq; World War II in Japan; politics, religion, corruption, and foreign aid in the Philippines; and race, local politics, and religion in the Caribbean.

Finding Topics

Having difficulty finding a topic is not uncommon; many, if not most, students of public speaking feel the same way. But do not despair. The objective of making classroom speeches is to learn not only the skills of public speaking but also the technique of finding topics—and there are literally thousands of subjects to talk about. Searching for speech topics is actually a relatively easy process. Here are four ways to find topics: topic lists, surveys, news items, and brainstorming.

Topic Lists.   Most public speaking textbooks contain suggestions for topics suitable for public speeches (DeVito, 2000; Osborn & Osborn, 2000; Verderber, 2000), as do books for writers (e.g., Lamm & Lamm, 1999). *The Speech Writer's Workshop Guide CD ROM, Version 2* (2000; see the preface to this book) contains a computerized list of hundreds of topics. An extensive list of suitable topics

may also be found at "The Dictionary of Topics" at www.ablongman.com/devito.

Topic lists may also be found on the Web. A useful list of more than 250 debate topics that can be modified for both informative and persuasive speeches can be found at the International Islamic University Malaysia's website at http://www.iiu.edu.my/stadd/spice/topics.html. Also, visit http://www.compassnet.com/~rdeneefe/topicgen.htm; it's a random topic generator that will suggest topics for conversation, writing, or public speaking.

Surveys.   Survey data are easier than ever to get now that many of the larger poll results are available on the Internet. For example, the Gallup organization website at http://www.gallup.com includes national and international surveys on political, social, consumer, and other issues speakers often talk about. The Polling Report website (www.pollingreport.com) will also prove useful; it provides a wealth of polling data on issues in political science, business, journalism, health, and social science. Another way is to go to the search directories such as Hotbot or Yahoo and examine the major directory topics and any subdivisions of those you'd care to pursue—a process that's explained later in this unit. Many search engines and browsers provide lists of "hot topics," which are often useful starting points. These lists pinpoint the subjects people are talking about and therefore often provide excellent speech topics.

Or you can conduct a survey yourself. Roam through the nonfiction section of your bookstore—online, if you prefer (for example, at Amazon, www.amazon.com; Barnes & Noble, www.bn.com; or Borders, www.borders.com)—and you'll quickly develop a list of the topics book buyers consider important. A glance at your newspaper's nonfiction best-seller list will give you an even quicker overview.

News Items.   Another useful starting point is a good newspaper or magazine. Here you'll find the important international and domestic issues, the financial issues, and the social issues all conveniently packaged in one place. The editorial page and the letters to the editor also help indicate what people are concerned about. Newsmagazines like *Time* and *Newsweek* and financial magazines such as *Forbes, Money,* and *Fortune* will provide a wealth of suggestions. Just about all major newspapers and newsmagazines now maintain websites that you can access without charge. Generally the newspaper or magazine will follow the pattern www.nameofpaper.com; for example, www.washingtonpost.com. The fastest-growing news sources are the news websites; for example, http://www.cnn.com/, http://www.sfgate.com/, http://www.usatoday.com/, www.nytimes.com, or www.newsworks.com, 🖱 which provides links to some 140 U.S. newspapers. If you want news on technology, there are lots of available websites. Take a look at Mercury Center (www.mercurycenter.com), CNETNews (www.news.com), NEWSBYTES News Network (www.newsbytes.com), Tech Web: The IT Network (www.techweb.com), and ZDNet (www.zdnet.com). 🖱 Similarly, news shows like 20/20, 60 Minutes, Meet the Press, and even the ubiquitous talk shows often identify the very issues that people are concerned with and on which there are conflicting points of view.

Brainstorming.   Another useful method is brainstorming, a technique discussed in Unit 13. Using brainstorming to help you generate topics is simple. You begin with your "problem," which in this

case is "What will I talk about?" You then record any idea that occurs to you. Allow your mind to free-associate. Don't censor yourself; instead, allow your ideas to flow as freely as possible. Record all your thoughts, regardless of how silly or inappropriate they may seem. Write them down or record them on tape. Try to generate as many ideas as possible. The more ideas you think of, the more chance there is that a suitable topic may emerge from the pile. After you've generated a sizable list—it should take no longer than five minutes—read over the list or replay the tape. Do any of the topics suggest other topics? If so, write these down as well. Can you combine or extend your ideas? Which ideas seem workable?

Limiting Topics

To be suitable for a public speech—or for any type of communication—a topic must be limited in scope; it must be narrowed down to fit the time constraints. Probably the most common problem for beginning speakers is that they attempt to cover a huge topic in too short a time. The inevitable result is that nothing specific is covered—everything is touched on, but only superficially. Narrowing your topic will also help you focus your collection

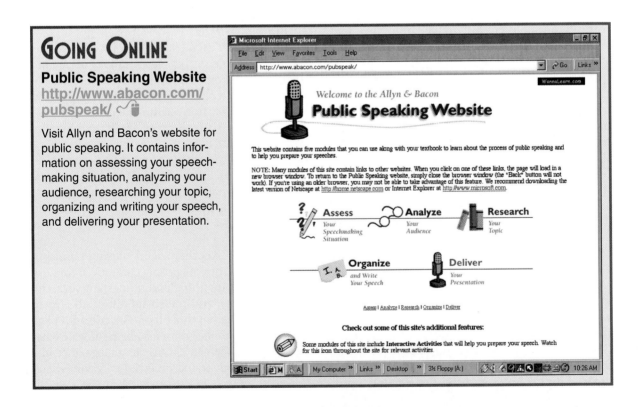

Going Online

Public Speaking Website
http://www.abacon.com/pubspeak/ 🖱

Visit Allyn and Bacon's website for public speaking. It contains information on assessing your speech-making situation, analyzing your audience, researching your topic, organizing and writing your speech, and delivering your presentation.

of research materials. If your topic is too broad, you'll be forced to review a lot more research material than you're going to need. Here are three methods for narrowing and limiting your topic.

Topoi: The System of Topics.   In the topoi technique, which comes to us from the classical rhetorics of ancient Greece and Rome, you ask a series of questions about your general subject. The process helps you see divisions or aspects of your general topic on which you might want to focus. For example, asking the typical reporter's questions (Who? What? Why? When? Where?) and a series of subquestions, you'll see different aspects of a topic. Let's say you want to give a speech on homelessness. Applying the system of topoi, you would ask such questions as:

- Who are the homeless?

- What does homelessness do to the people themselves and to society in general?

- Why are there so many homeless people?

- Where is homelessness most prevalent?

- How does someone become homeless?

- How can we help the homeless and prevent others from becoming homeless?

- Why must we be concerned with homelessness?

Tree Diagrams.   The construction of tree diagrams (actually, they resemble upside-down trees) can also help you narrow your topic. Let's say, for example, that you want to do a speech on mass communication. You might develop a tree diagram with branches for the various divisions, as shown in Figure 15.2. Thus, you can divide mass communication into film, television, radio, newspapers, and magazines. If television interested you most, then you'd develop branches from television; for example, comedy, news, soaps, sports, and quiz shows. Now let's say that it's the soaps that most interest you. In this case you'd create categories of soaps, perhaps prime-time and daytime. Keep dividing the topic until you get something that's significant, appropriate to you and your audience, and capable of being covered in some depth in the allotted time.

Search Directories.   A more technologically sophisticated way of both selecting and limiting your topic is to let a search directory, for example, do some of the work for you. A search directory is simply a nested list of topics. You go from the general to the increasingly more specific by selecting a

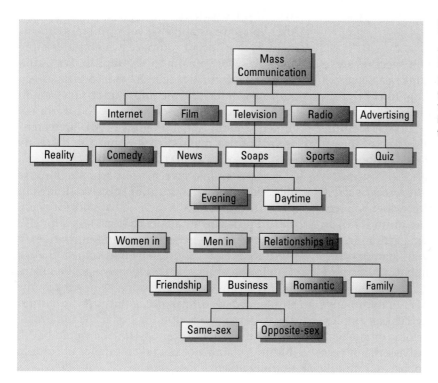

Figure 15.2

A Tree Diagram for Limiting Speech Topics

How would you draw a tree diagram for limiting topics beginning with such general subjects as immigration, education, sports, transportation, or politics?

BUILDING COMMUNICATION SKILLS

How Can You Limit a Topic?

Here are a few overly general topics. Using one of the methods discussed in this unit (or any other method you're familiar with), limit each of the following to a topic that would be reasonable for a 5- to 10-minute speech.

1. Dangerous sports
2. Race relations
3. Parole
4. Censorship on the Internet
5. Ecological problems
6. Problems faced by college students
7. Morality
8. Health and fitness
9. Ethical issues in politics
10. Urban violence

topic, and then a subdivision of that topic, and then a subdivision of that subdivision. Search directories are discussed in more detail under "Step 3" later in this unit.

Your Purpose

The purpose of your speech is the goal you hope to achieve by making your speech. It identifies the effect that you want your speech to have on your audience. In constructing your speech, identify first your general and second your specific purpose.

General Purposes

The two general purposes of public speeches are to inform and to persuade. In the *informative speech* you seek to create understanding: to clarify, enlighten, correct misunderstandings, demonstrate how to do something, describe how something works, or define a concept. In this type of speech you rely most heavily on materials that support—examples, illustrations, definitions, testimony, audiovisual aids, and the like. In the *persuasive speech* you try to influence attitudes or behaviors; you seek to strengthen or change existing attitudes or to prompt the audience to take some action. In this type of speech you rely heavily on materials that offer proof—on evidence, argument, and psychological appeals, for example.

Any persuasive speech is in part an informative speech and as such contains materials that amplify, illustrate, define, and so on. In its focus on strengthening or changing attitudes and behaviors, however, the persuasive speech must go beyond simply providing information. Logical, motivational, and credibility appeals (discussed in Unit 19) are essential.

Another type of speech—part informative and part persuasive—is the *special occasion speech*, a category that includes speeches of presentation and acceptance, toasts, eulogies, apologies, and speeches designed to secure goodwill. A complete unit on "The Special Occasion Speech" is available on the CD-ROM accompanying this book.

Specific Purposes

After you have established your general purpose, identify your specific purpose, which states more precisely what you aim to accomplish. For example, in an informative speech, your specific speech purpose will identify the information you want to convey to your audience, such as "to inform my audience about recent progress in AIDS research" or "to inform my audience about the currently used tests for HIV infection."

In a persuasive speech, your specific purpose identifies what you want your speech to lead your audience to believe, think, or perhaps do; for example, "to persuade my audience to get tested for HIV infection" or "to persuade my audience to learn more about how AIDS can be transmitted."

In formulating your specific purpose, be sure to limit it to what you can reasonably develop in the allotted time. For instance, a purpose "to inform my audience about clothing design" is too broad; a more limited and appropriate one would be "to inform my audience of the importance of color in clothing design."

Use an infinitive phrase. Begin the statement of your specific purpose with the word "to," as in "to persuade my audience to contribute a book to the library fund-raiser."

STEP 2: ANALYZE YOUR AUDIENCE

The characteristic that seems best to define an audience is common purpose: A public speaking audience is a group of individuals gathered together to hear a speech. If you're to be a successful speaker, then you must know your audience. This knowledge will help you in selecting your topic; phrasing your purpose; establishing a relationship between yourself and your audience; and choosing examples, illustrations, and logical and emotional appeals.

Your first step in audience analysis is to construct an audience profile in which you analyze audience members' sociological or demographic characteristics. These characteristics help you estimate the attitudes, beliefs, and values of your audience. If you want to effect changes in these attitudes, beliefs, and values, you have to know what they are.

Attitudes, Beliefs, and Values

An **attitude** is a tendency to act for or against a person, object, or position. If you have a positive attitude toward the death penalty, you're likely to argue or act in favor of the death penalty (for example, vote for a candidate who supports the death penalty). If you have a negative attitude toward the death penalty, then you're likely to argue or act against it. Attitudes toward the death penalty will influence how favorably or unfavorably listeners will respond to a speaker who supports or denounces capital punishment.

A **belief** is the confidence or conviction you have in the truth of some proposition. For example, you may believe that there is an afterlife, that education is the best way to rise from poverty, that democracy is the best form of government, or that all people are born equal. If your listeners believe that the death penalty is a deterrent to crime, for example, then they will be more likely to favor arguments for (and speakers who support) the death penalty than will listeners who don't believe in the connection between the death penalty and deterrence.

The term **value** refers to your perception of the worth or goodness (or worthlessness or badness) of some concept or idea. For example, you probably attribute positive values to financial success, education, and contributing to the common welfare. At the same time, you probably place negative values on chemical weapons, corrupt politicians, and selling drugs to children. Because the values an audience holds will influence how it responds to ideas related to those values, it's essential that you learn the values of your specific audience. For example, if the people in your audience place a high positive value on child welfare, then they are likely to vote for legislation that protects children or allocates money for breakfasts and lunches in school—and they might consider signing a petition, volunteering their time, or donating their money to advance the welfare of children. If you find that your audience places a negative value on big business, you may want to reconsider using the testimony of corporate leaders or the statistics compiled by corporations.

Analyzing the Sociology of the Audience

In analyzing an audience be careful not to assume that people covered by the same label are necessarily all alike. As soon as you begin to think about a sociological characteristic in terms of an expressed or implied "all," consider the possibility that you may be stereotyping. Don't assume that all women or all older people or all highly educated people think or believe the same things. They don't.

Nevertheless, there are characteristics that seem to be more common among one group than another, and it is these characteristics that you want to explore in your sociological analysis of your audience. Let's look at four major sociological or demographic variables: (1) cultural factors, (2) age, (3) gender, and (4) religion and religiousness.

Cultural Factors

Cultural factors such as nationality, race, and cultural identity are crucial in audience analysis. Largely because of different training and experiences, the interests, values, and goals of various cultural groups will differ. Further, cultural factors will influence each of the remaining sociological factors; for example, attitudes toward age and gender will differ greatly from one culture to another. Perhaps the primary question to ask is "Are the cultural beliefs and values of the audience relevant to your topic and purpose?" That is, might the cultural background(s) of your audience members influence the way they see your topic? If so, find out what these beliefs and values are and take these into consideration as you build your speech.

Age

Different age groups have different attitudes and beliefs, largely because they have had different experiences in different contexts. Take these differences into consideration in preparing your speeches. For example, let's say that you're an investment counselor and you want to persuade your listeners to invest their money to increase their earnings. Your speech to an audience of retired people (say in their 60s) would be very different from an address to an audience of young executives (say in their 30s). In considering the age of your audience, ask yourself if the age groups differ in goals, interests, and day-to-day concerns that may be related to your topic and purpose. Graduating from college, achieving corporate success, raising a family, and saving for retirement are concerns that differ greatly from one age group to another. Ask too if the groups differ in their ability to absorb and process information. Will they differ in their responses to visual cues? With a young audience, it may be best to keep up a steady, even swift pace. With older persons, you may wish to maintain a more moderate, measured pace.

Gender

Gender is one of the most difficult audience variables to analyze. In recent decades rapid social changes have made it difficult to pin down the effects of gender. As you analyze your audience in terms of gender, ask yourself if men and women differ in the values they consider important insofar as these values are related to your topic and purpose. For example, traditionally, men have been found to place greater importance on theoretical, economic, and political values. Traditionally, women have been found to place greater importance on aesthetic, social, and religious values. In framing appeals and in selecting examples, take into account the values your audience members consider most important.

Ask too if your topic will be seen as more interesting by one gender or the other. Will men and women have different attitudes toward the topic? Men and women do not, for example, respond in the same way to such topics as abortion, rape, and equal pay for equal work. Select your topics and supporting materials in light of the gender of your audience members. When your audience is mixed, make a special effort to relate "women's" topics to men and "men's" topics to women.

Religion and Religiousness

The religion and religiousness of your audience will often influence their responses to your speech. Religion permeates all topics and all issues. On a most obvious level, we know that such issues as attitudes toward birth control, abortion, and divorce are often connected to religion. Similarly, people's views on premarital sex, marriage, child rearing, money, cohabitation, responsibilities toward parents, and thousands of other issues are frequently influenced by religion. Religion is also important, however, in areas where its connection is not so obvious. For example, religion influences many people's ideas concerning such topics as obedience to authority; responsibility to government; and the usefulness of such qualities as honesty, guilt, and happiness.

Ask yourself if your topic or purpose might be seen as an attack on the religious beliefs of any segment of your audience. If so, then you might want to make adjustments—not necessarily to abandon your purpose, but to rephrase your arguments or incorporate different evidence. When arguing against any religious beliefs, recognize that you're going to meet stiff opposition. Proceed slowly and inductively; in other words, carefully present your evidence before expressing your argument.

Analyzing the Psychology of the Audience

In addition to looking at the sociological characteristics of audience members, it's often useful to consider their psychological characteristics—particularly their willingness to listen to you, their favorableness to your purpose, and their background knowledge. Suggestions for "Analyzing and Adapting to Your Audience during the Speech" are provided at www.ablongman.com/devito.

How Willing Is Your Audience?

Your immediate concern in a public speaking class, of course, is with audience willingness on the part

UNDERSTANDING THEORY AND RESEARCH

Secular and Sacred Cultures

In analyzing the cultural composition of your audience, consider whether members identify themselves as being a part of a secular or a sacred culture. *Secular cultures* are those in which religion does not dominate the attitudes and views of the people or greatly influence political or educational decisions (Hofstede, 1997, 1998; Dodd, 1995). Liberal Protestant cultures such as those of the Scandinavian countries clearly qualify as secular. *Sacred cultures,* on the other hand, are those in which religion and religious beliefs and values dominate personal lifestyles and influence politics, education, and just about every topic or issue imaginable. Many Islamic cultures are traditional examples of sacred cultures. Technically, the United States is a secular culture overall (the Constitution, for example, expressly separates church and state); but in some groups within the country, religion exerts powerful influence on schools (on issues ranging from prayers to condom distribution to sex education) and politics (from the selection of political leaders to concern for social welfare to gay rights legislation).

> **Working with Theories and Research.** *In which type of culture would you feel more comfortable? What advantages and disadvantages do you see in each type of culture?*

of your fellow students. Do they come to hear your speech because they have to, or do they come because they're interested in what you'll say? If they're a willing group, then you have few problems. And even if they're an unwilling group, all is not lost; you just have to work a little harder in preparing your speech. The unwilling audience demands special and delicate handling. Here are a few suggestions to help change your listeners from unwilling to willing:

- Secure their interest and attention as early in your speech as possible, and reinforce their interest throughout the speech by using little-known facts, quotations, startling statistics, examples, narratives, audiovisual aids, and the like.

- Reward the audience for their attendance and attention. Let the audience know you're aware they're making a sacrifice in coming to hear you speak. Tell them you appreciate it.

- Relate your topic and supporting materials directly to your audience's needs and wants. Show the audience how they can—for example—save time, make money, solve important problems, or become more popular. If you fail to do this, then your audience has good reason for not listening.

How Favorable Is Your Audience?

Audiences vary in the degree to which their ideas and attitudes will be favorable or unfavorable toward you, your topic, or your point of view. You may wish to examine your ability to predict audience favor toward various topics or beliefs by taking the self-test below.

TEST YOURSELF

How Well Do You Know Your Audience?

Here are some statements of beliefs that members of your class may agree or disagree with—and which you might want to use as basic theses (propositions) in your in-class speeches. Try predicting how favorable or unfavorable you think your class members would be to each of these beliefs. Use a 10-point scale ranging from 1 (extremely unfavorable) through 5 (relatively neutral) to 10 (extremely favorable).

_____ 1. The welfare of the family must come first, even before your own.

_____ 2. Sex outside of marriage is wrong and sinful.

_____ **3.** In a heterosexual relationship, a wife should submit graciously to the leadership of her husband.

_____ **4.** Individual states should be allowed to fly the Confederate flag if they wish.

_____ **5.** Intercultural relationships are okay in business but should be discouraged when it comes to intimate or romantic relationships; generally, the races should be kept "pure."

_____ **6.** Money is good; the quest for financial success is a perfectly respectable (even noble) one.

_____ **7.** Immigration into the United States should be curtailed, at least until current immigrants are assimilated.

_____ **8.** Parents who prevent their children from receiving the latest scientific cures because of a belief in faith healing should be prosecuted.

_____ **9.** Same-sex marriage should be legalized.

_____ **10.** Medicinal marijuana should be readily available.

_____ **11.** Physician-assisted suicide should be legalized.

_____ **12.** Male and female prostitution should be legalized and taxed like any other job that produces income.

How did you do? After you've indicated your predictions, discuss these with the class as a whole. How accurate were you in guessing your audience's beliefs?

What will you do? Practice adapting a thesis to both the favorable and the unfavorable audience. Select a thesis (one of those listed in this self-test or one of your own) toward which your audience would be highly favorable, and indicate how you'd adapt your speech to them. Then try the more difficult task: Select a thesis toward which your audience would be highly unfavorable, and indicate how you'd adapt to them. ✔

If, on analyzing the question, you conclude that your audience will be unfavorable to your chosen topic or viewpoint, the following suggestions should help.

- Clear up any possible misapprehensions that may be generating disagreement. For example, if the audience is hostile to your proposed team approach for a certain project because they wrongly think it will cause a reduction in their

autonomy, then tell them very directly that it won't, and perhaps explain why it won't.

- Build on commonalities; stress what you and the audience share as people, as interested citizens, as fellow students. When an audience sees similarity or common ground between itself and you, it becomes more favorable to both you and your speech.

- Organize your speech inductively. Try to build your speech from areas of agreement, through areas of slight disagreement, up to the major differences between the audience's attitudes and your position. Once areas of agreement are established, it's easier to bring up differences.

- Strive for small gains. Don't try, in a five-minute speech, to convince a pro-life group to contribute money for a new abortion clinic or to persuade a pro-choice group to vote against liberalizing abortion laws. Be content to get the audience to listen fairly and to see some validity in your position.

- Acknowledge the differences explicitly. If it's clear to the audience that they and you are at opposite ends of an issue, it may be helpful to acknowledge this directly. Show the audience that you understand and respect their position but that you'd like them to consider a different way of looking at things.

How Knowledgeable Is Your Audience?

Listeners differ greatly in the knowledge they have. Some listeners will be quite knowledgeable about a given topic; others will be almost totally ignorant. Mixed audiences are the most difficult ones. Treat audiences that lack knowledge of your topic very carefully. Never confuse a lack of audience knowledge with a lack of ability to understand.

- Don't talk down to your audience. No one wants to listen to a speaker putting them down.

- Don't confuse a lack of knowledge with a lack of intelligence. An audience may have no knowledge of your topic but be quite capable of following a clearly presented, logically developed argument. Try especially hard to use concrete examples, audiovisual aids, and simple language. Fill in background details as required. Avoid jargon and other specialized terminology that may not be clear to someone new to the subject. In short, never underestimate your audience's intelligence, but never overestimate their knowledge. Conversely, audiences with much knowledge also require special handling—because their response may well be "Why should I listen to this? I already know about this topic."

- Let the audience know that you're aware of their knowledge and expertise. Try to do this as early in the speech as possible. Emphasize that what you have to say will not be redundant. Tell them that you'll be presenting recent developments or new approaches. In short, let them know that they will not be wasting their time listening to your speech.

- Emphasize your credibility, especially your competence in this general subject area.

Your college or communication classroom very likely has its own cultural norms governing what would be seen as an appropriate topic. Consider, for example, whether the following speeches would be considered "appropriate" by members of your public speaking class or by the general college community: (1) a speech that seeks to convert listeners to a specific religious cult, (2) a speech supporting neo-Nazi values, (3) a speech supporting racial segregation, and (4) a speech that teaches listeners how to cheat on their income tax.

STEP 3: RESEARCH YOUR SPEECH TOPIC

In researching your speech you're likely to use traditional printed books, journals, magazines, newspapers, and pamphlets as well as online sources such as e-mail, newsgroups, the World Wide Web, and a vast array of computerized databases. Because the information available on just about any topic is so vast, it's understandably daunting for many people. So let's start with some general research principles and then examine specific sources of information. A self-test to help you assess your research competencies, "What do you know about research?" may be found at **www.ablongman. com/devito**.

General Principles of Research

After you've selected your topic, you'll need to find information on it. Here are some general principles to help you find the information you'll need (statistics, arguments for or against a proposition, examples, biographical data, or research findings, for example). These principles should also help make your search more effective and more efficient.

- Examine what you know, such as books or websites that are devoted to the topic or people who might know something about the topic. Consider also if you have personal experiences and observations that can be used.

- Work from the general to the specific. An encyclopedia article can get you started; or visit the Web and query a few search engines for a general overview. Many online articles contain references or links that will direct you to more specific and detailed information. A few especially good starting sites are LibrarySpot at **www.libraryspot.com**, which provides research and writing help useful for any topic; the Internet Public Library at **www.ipl.org.ref**, which helps you find research through a directory of topics; and the Reference Desk at **www. refdesk.com**, which contains links to a wide variety of reference works.

- Take accurate notes. Accuracy in the beginning will save you from wasting time returning to sources to check something or going to sources you've already consulted. If you want to collect

MEDIA WATCH

THE DIFFUSION OF INNOVATIONS

Mass media audiences are even more diverse and varied than public speaking audiences. One of the most interesting theories related to this diversity is the theory of the *diffusion of innovations.* This theory focuses on the way in which mass communications influence people's adoption of something new or different. The term *diffusion* refers to the passage of new information, innovations, or processes through society. The innovation may be of any type—soft contact lenses, laptop computers, PDAs, PowerPoint public speaking software. *Adoption* refers to people's positive reactions to and use of the innovation. Obviously, not all people adopt or reject any given innovation at the same time. Research in the area of information diffusion distinguishes five types of adopters (see Figure 15.3):

▶ The *innovators* (approximately 3 percent of the population) are the first to adopt the innovation. They are not necessarily the originators of the new idea, but they're the ones who introduce it on a reasonably broad scale.

▶ The *early adopters* (approximately 14 percent), sometimes called "the influentials," legitimize the idea and make it acceptable to people in general.

▶ The *early majority* (approximately 34 percent) follows the influentials and further legitimizes the innovation.

▶ The *late majority* (approximately 34 percent) adopts the innovation after about half the population has adopted it.

▶ The *laggards* (approximately 14 percent) are the last group to adopt the innovation and may take the lead from any of the preceding groups.

One last group, the *diehards,* never adopt the innovation. These include, for example, accountants who continue to do tax returns without the aid of computer software; teachers who never use multimedia in their classes; and lawyers and doctors who do their research solely through books, never availing themselves of computerized databases.

Not surprisingly, the innovators and the early adopters are usually younger than the late majority and the laggards and are of a higher socioeconomic status. They are more oriented toward change and make more use of available information.

Follow-Up. *Where would you position yourself on this diffusion of innovation curve when it comes to technology? Are you generally pleased with your positioning? If not, what might you do about it?*

Figure 15.3

The Five Types of Adopters

Source: Reprinted with the permission of The Free Press, a Division of Simon & Schuster, Inc. from *The Diffusion of Innovations,* Fourth Edition, by Everett M. Rogers. Copyright © 1995 by Everett M. Rogers. Copyright © 1962, 1971, 1983 by The Free Press.

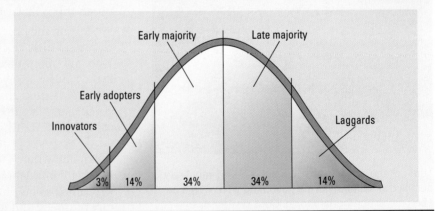

your material on paper, a looseleaf notebook works well to keep everything relating to a speech or article in the same place. If you want to file your material electronically, create a folder and title it something like PublicSpeakingSpeech1:Immigration. This will work especially well if you have a scanner and can scan into your folder material you find in print.

- Learn the available sources of information. Learn where the most useful materials are located or how they can be accessed. Learn the computer search facilities available at your college for accessing newspapers, research articles, corporate reports, magazines, or any type of media you may wish to use. Find out what databases are available. And—perhaps the most important suggestion of all—talk with your librarian. Librarians are experts in the very issues that may be giving you trouble and will be able to help you access just about any type of information you want.

General Internet Resources

There are three major categories of Internet resources you'll want to consider in researching your speeches: e-mail, newsgroups, and the World Wide Web.

E-Mail

Through e-mail you can write to specific people or to a group or listserv—an e-mail list of several to perhaps hundreds of people who exchange messages on a relatively specific topic. E-mail may prove useful in public speaking in several ways. For example, you can write to specific people who may be experts in the topic you're researching. Internet services are now making it quite easy to locate a person's e-mail address. Try, for example, the Netscape people page, which you can access from Netscape's home page or by going to http://guide.netscape.com/guide/people.html; or try Yahoo's directory (http://www.yahoo.com/search/people/) and its links to numerous other directories, among them Yahoo's own white pages (http://www.yahoo.com/Reference/White-Pages/). Another useful people search tool is http://www.procd.com/hl/direct.htm. Also try the sites that specialize in e-mail addresses, such as Four11 (http://www.four11.com), Who Where? (http://www.whowhere.com), and Switchboard (www.switchboard.com). ⌨ Four11 also provides a directory of regular telephone numbers as well as special directories for government personnel and celebrities.

You can join a mailing list or listserv that focuses on the topic you're researching and learn from the collective insights of all members. You can explore potentially useful listservs by using Liszt (www.liszt.com), ⌨ a directory of information about a wide variety of listservs that tells whether new members are welcomed. When joining a listserv, remember to lurk before contributing; get a feel for the group and for the types of messages its members send. Read the FAQs (frequently asked questions) to avoid asking questions that have already been answered. The types of questions listserv members seem to favor are those that ask for ideas and insights rather than those that ask for information readily available elsewhere.

In a class set up as a listserv, you'd be able to communicate with everyone else through e-mail. You'd be able, for example, to distribute an audience analysis questionnaire to find out what your audience knows about your topic or what their attitudes are about a variety of issues. For examples, see "Seeking Audience Information" at www.ablongman.com/devito. ⌨ You'd also be able to set up a critique group with a few accepting and supportive others in your class to get feedback on your speech or outline. Such a group would also be helpful for people who wanted to ask questions or to try out an idea before presenting it in the actual speech.

Newsgroups

Newsgroups are discussion forums for the exchange of ideas on a wide variety of topics. There are thousands of newsgroups on the Internet where you can post your messages (also called "articles" or "posts"), read the messages of others, and respond to the messages you read. Newsgroups are much like listservs in that they bring together a group of people interested in communicating about a common topic. Some newsgroups also include messages from news services such as the Associated Press or Reuters.

Newsgroups are useful sources of information; they contain news items, letters, and papers on just about any topic you can think of. Because there are so many newsgroups, you should have no problem finding several that deal with topics on which you'll be speaking. You can also save the news items you're particularly interested in to your own file. Search engines and directories will search the available newsgroups for the topics you request. You simply submit keywords that denote your research topic; the program will search its database of newsgroups and return a list of article titles and authors along with the date on which each was written and a relevance score for each article. You can then click on the titles that seem most closely related to what you're looking for.

Those newsgroups that get news feeds are especially useful, because the information is current and very likely presented in greater detail than you'd find in newspapers—which have to cut copy to fit space limitations. You're also likely to find a greater diversity of viewpoints than you'd find in, say, standard newsmagazines such as *Time* or *Newsweek*. Another advantage is that through newsgroups you can ask questions and get the opinions of others for your next speech; newsgroup members seem a generally receptive audience to whom you can communicate your thoughts and feelings. Reading through the FAQ file—see http://sunsite.unc.edu/usenet-i/info-center-faq.html ☞—will help you get the maximum benefit from newsgroup communication.

The World Wide Web

The World Wide Web, the most interesting and most valuable part of the Internet for research, is a vast collection of documents—some containing graphic, audio, and video components. Some documents appear in abstract; others, increasingly, in full-text form. Newspapers, newsmagazines, and numerous books are available in full text through a publisher or library. Some websites are available to the general public and others only by subscription.

In some instances you may know the Web address of the source you want to consult. In this case you can access the website by simply entering the address in your Web browser. Fortunately, Web addresses are becoming more standardized, making it easier for you to predict many relevant addresses. For example, the Web addresses of most corporations follow the same general format: www.NameOfCorporation.com—for example, www.Microsoft.com. ☞ You can access these websites for copies of speeches, annual reports, or other information you might need for your speech.

In most cases, however, searching the Web efficiently for speech topics requires the use of a search engine and some knowledge of how they operate. A search engine is a program that enables you to search a database or index of Internet sites for specific words you submit. These search engines are easily accessed through your Internet browser. And in fact the popular browsers—Netscape and Inter-

net Explorer, for example—have search functions as a part of their own home pages. They also provide convenient links to the most popular search engines and directories.

Most search engines operate similarly: You type in a word or phrase, and the program searches its databases and returns a list of sites, sometimes with an indication of how relevant the source will be to you and sometimes with a brief description of the site you can click on to visit.

A directory is a list of subjects or categories of Web links. You begin your search process by selecting the category you're most interested in, then go to a subcategory of that, then a subcategory of that until you reach the specific topic you're interested in. Many search engines also provide directories. Yahoo, Excite, and Infoseek (among others), for example, are both search engines and directories. Other popular directories include Magellan (http://www.mckinley.com/) and Point (http://www.pointcom.com/). ☞

Because each search engine or directory uses a somewhat different database and a different method for searching, no two search engines will yield the exact same results even when the exact same request is submitted to each. So when conducting research, be sure to use several of these search engines and directories. A good practice is to bookmark or list among your "favorites" each of the major search engines and directories.

If you know little about a topic and don't know any of the more specialized materials, try starting with a search engine that will locate other search engines and directories that are related to your topic. Three particularly useful engines are Beaucoup at www.beaucoup.com, Complete Planet at www.completeplanet.com, and Go Gettem at www.gogettem.com. ☞

Metasearch engines are also good starting points; these are the search engines that search the databases of a variety of search engines at the same time. These programs are especially useful if you want a broad search and you have the time to sift through lots of websites. Some of the more popular include: Ask Jeeves at www.aj.com, Google at http://www.google.com, Dog Pile at www.dogpile.com, and Northern Light at www.northernlight.com. ☞

Other, less extensive search engines (some of which also contain directories) include Yahoo! (www.yahoo.com), excite (www.excite.com), Alta-

Vista (http://altavista.digital.com), Go (www.go.com), and Lycos (www.lycos.com).

Because the databases these engines search are so vast and because they search for all occurrences of the words you submit, they invariably pull up lots of noise—documents that are totally unrelated to what you're looking for. Thus, it's important to learn to narrow your search and ask the search engine to look for specific rather than general topics. Further, despite their frequent updates, most of the search engines and directories will include a variety of expired links. Expect this; it's one of the inevitable problems created by a system that's so vast in size and changing so rapidly.

Databases

A database is an organized compilation of information contained in one place: in a printed book, in a computer, or on a CD-ROM. A dictionary, an encyclopedia, and an index to magazines are all examples of databases. Four types of databases will prove helpful: general reference sources, news sources, research and general interest articles and posts, and book sources.

General Reference Sources

General reference sources provide you with basic information that can help you think more clearly about your topic and offer you leads to more specialized sources. A few of the more useful are encyclopedias, biographical dictionaries, and almanacs.

Encyclopedias.   One of the best places to start researching your topic is a standard encyclopedia. It will give you a general overview of the subject and suggestions for additional reading. The most comprehensive and the most prestigious is the *Encyclopaedia Britannica,* available in print (32 volumes), on CD-ROM, and online. A variety of other encyclopedias are also available on CD-ROM or online; for example, *Compton's Multimedia Encyclopedia, Grolier's, Collier's,* and *Encarta.* CD-ROM and online encyclopedias have great advantages; for example, they allow you to locate articles, maps, diagrams, and even definitions of difficult terms (through the built-in dictionary) more easily and efficiently than hard-copy volumes—simply by typing in terms that describe the topic you want to

explore. Video illustrations and audio capabilities enable you to see and hear the exploding volcano, the heart pumping blood, the pronunciation of foreign terms, and the music of particular instruments. Hypertext capabilities enable you to get additional information by simply clicking on any term or phrase that is highlighted. You can then, of course, shift back and forth among these articles. Most of the CD-ROM encyclopedias have accompanying websites that provide periodic updates of the articles and additional materials, thus ensuring both recency and completeness. A useful place to start is with www.internetoracle.com/encyclop.htm, which provides hotlinks to a wide variety of online encyclopedias, both general and specific.

There are also many specialized encyclopedias. The *New Catholic Encyclopedia* (15 volumes) contains articles on such topics as philosophy, science, and art as these have been influenced by and have influenced the Catholic Church. The *Encyclopaedia Judaica* (16 volumes plus yearbooks) emphasizes Jewish life and includes biographies and detailed coverage of the Jewish contribution to world culture. The *Encyclopedia of Islam* and *Encyclopaedia of Buddhism* cover the development, beliefs, institutions, and personalities of Islam and Buddhism, respectively. Supplement these with appropriate websites devoted to specific religions; for example, http://www.utm.edu/martinarea/fbc/bfm.html (Southern Baptist), http://www.catholic.org/index.html (Catholic), http://www.geocities.com/RodeaDrive/1415/indexd.html (Hinduism), http://www.utexas.edu/students/amso (Islam), and http://jewishnet.net (Jewish-related sites).

For the physical, applied, and natural sciences there's the 20-volume *McGraw-Hill Encyclopedia of Science and Technology*. This is complemented by annual supplements. *Our Living World of Nature* is a 14-volume popular encyclopedia dealing with natural history from an ecological point of view (the online version is by subscription). *The International Encyclopedia of the Social Sciences* concentrates on the theory and methods of the social sciences in 17 well-researched volumes. Other widely used encyclopedias include the *Encyclopedia of Bioethics* (4 volumes), the *Encyclopedia of Religion* (16 volumes), and the *Encyclopedia of Philosophy* (4 volumes). Also check *The Internet Encyclopedia of Philosophy* at the University of Tennessee at Martin's site at www.utm.edu/research/iep.   The online

International Encyclopedia of the Social and Behavioral Sciences is available by subscription.

Biographical Material. As a speaker you'll often need information about particular individuals. For example, you may want to look up authors of books or articles you are consulting so as to find out something about their education, training, or other writings. Or you may wish to discover if there have been any critical evaluations of these authors' works in, say, book reviews or articles about them or their writings. Knowing something about your sources enhances your ability to evaluate their competence, present their credibility to the audience, and answer audience questions about your sources.

First, consult the *Biography and Genealogy Master Index*—in print, on CD-ROM, or online; it indexes more than 350 biographical indexes. This index will lead you to the best sources for the information you want. Or you may want to start with a more specific source. *The Dictionary of American Biography* (DAB) contains articles on famous deceased Americans from all areas of accomplishment. For living individuals, the best single source is *Current Biography,* issued monthly and in cumulative annual volumes. The essays in *Current Biography* are written by an editorial staff and therefore include both favorable and unfavorable comments. *Who's Who in America* also covers living individuals.

In addition, there are a host of other more specialized works, whose titles indicate their scope: *The Dictionary of Canadian Biography, The Dictionary of National Biography* (British), *Directory of American Scholars, International Who's Who, Who Was Who in America, Who's Who* (primarily British), *Dictionary of Scientific Biography, American Men and Women of Science, Great Lives from History* (25 volumes), *Notable American Women, National Cyclopedia of American Biography* (1888–1984), *Who's Who in the Arab World, Who's Who in the World, Who's Who in Finance and Industry, Who's Who in American Politics, Who's Who among Black Americans, Who's Who of American Women, Who's Who among Hispanic Americans,* the *Official Congressional Directory* (1809 to date), and the *Biographical Directory of the American Congress.*

Not surprisingly, there are lots of Internet sources for biographical information. For example, http://mgm.mit.edu:8080/pevzner/Nobel.html provides links to biographical information on all Nobel Prize winners. If you want information on members of the House of Representatives, try http://www.house.gov. And http://www.biography.com/ will provide you with brief biographies of some 15,000 famous people, living and dead. Other excellent sources include Lives, the Biography Resource at http://amillionlives.com and the Biographical Dictionary at http://s9.com/biography, which covers more than 28,000 men and women. Still another way to search for information on a person is simply to type the name of the person into one of the popular search engines.

Almanacs. Should you want information on the world's languages, household income, presidential elections, the countries of the world, national defense, sports, noted personalities, economics and employment, the environment, awards and prizes, science and technology, health and medicine, maps, world travel information, or postal rates, an almanac will prove extremely useful. Numerous inexpensive versions are published annually and are among the most up-to-date sources of information on many topics. The most popular are *The World Almanac and Book of Facts* (also available on CD-ROM), *The Universal Almanac,* and *The Canadian Almanac and Directory.* The *Information Please Almanac's* website provides access to a wide variety of almanacs (www.infoplease.com/almanacs.html). Another useful source is the Internet Public Library's list of almanac resources at www.ipl.org/ref/RR/static/ref05.00.00.html. You may find it helpful to begin with the accompanying website, which provides a wide variety of reference works (www.academicinfo.net).

The annual *Statistical Abstract of the United States* contains the most complete statistical data on population, vital statistics, health, education, law, geography and environment, elections, finances and employment, defense, insurance, labor, income, prices, banking and a wide variety of other topics. It's also available at www.census.gov. Other valuable statistical sources include *Vital Statistics of the United States* (especially useful for demographic statistics) and *Morbidity and Mortality Weekly Report* (useful for health-related issues). For international statistics see *United Nations Statistical Yearbook, World Statistics in Brief* and *UNESCO Statistical Yearbook.* Useful websites include http://cedr.1b1.gov/cdrom/doc/lookup_doc.html, for United States census data, and http://www.cs.cmu.edu/Web/references.

html, 🖱 which provides links to a wide variety of relevant reference materials.

News Sources

Often you'll want to read reports on accidents, political speeches, congressional actions, obituaries, financial news, international developments, United Nations actions, or any of a host of other topics. Or you may wish to locate the time of a particular event and learn something about what else was going on in the world at that particular time. For this type of information you may want to consult a reliable newspaper. Especially relevant are newspaper indexes and databases, newspaper and magazine websites, news wire services, and news networks online.

Newspaper Indexes and Databases.

One way to start a newspaper search is to consult one of the newspaper indexes—for example, the *National Newspaper Index*, which covers 27 newspapers, including the *Christian Science Monitor*, the *New York Times*, the *Wall Street Journal*, the *Los Angeles Times*, and the *Washington Post*. Each of these newspapers also has its own index. Many newspapers can be accessed online or through CD-ROM databases to which your college library probably subscribes. The *New York Times* database, for example, contains the complete editorial content of the paper, one of the world's most comprehensive newspapers. All aspects of news, sports, editorials, columns, obituaries, New York and regional news, and the *New York Times Book Review* and *Magazine* are included.

Newspaper and Newsmagazine Websites.

Most newspapers now maintain their own websites from which you can access current and past issues. Here are a few to get you started: www.latimes.com/ (*Los Angeles Times*), www.usatoday.com/ (*USA Today*), http://journal.link.wsj.com/ (*Wall Street Journal*), and www.nytimes.com (the *New York Times*). The *Washington Post* (www.washingtonpost.com) 🖱 maintains an especially extensive website; the accompanying Web page will give you an idea of the enormous amount of information it provides. Two particularly useful websites are http://www.newslink.org/menu.html, 🖱 which provides access to a variety of online newspapers and magazines, and Hotlinks to Newspapers Online, which provides links to more than 1,000 daily,

more than 400 weekly, and more than 100 international newspapers (www.naa.org/hotlinks/index.asp). 🖱

News Wire Services.

Three news wire services should prove helpful. The Associated Press can be accessed at http://www1.trib.com/NEWS/Apwire.html, Reuters at http://www.reuters.com/, and PR Newswire at http://www.prnewswire.com/. 🖱 The advantage of getting your information from a news wire service is that it's more complete than you'd find in a newspaper—which has to cut copy and, in some cases, may put a politically or socially motivated spin on the news.

News Networks Online.

All of the television news networks maintain extremely useful websites. Here are some of the most useful: Access CNN at http://www.cnn.com/, ESPN at http://espn.sportszone.com/, ABC News at http://www.abcnews.com/newsflash, CBS News at http://www.cbs.com/news/, and MSNBC News at http://www.msnbc.com/news. 🖱

Research and General Interest Articles and Posts

Academic and scientific research forms the core of what is known about people and the world; it is the most valid and the most reliable information you're likely to find. Research articles are reports of studies conducted by academicians and scientists around the world. For the most part these studies are conducted by unbiased researchers using the best research methods available. Further, this research is subjected to careful critical review by experts in the relevant field.

Each college library subscribes to a somewhat different package of CD-ROM and online databases. Each database contains information on the nature and scope of the database and user-friendly directions for searching, displaying, printing, and saving the retrieved information to disk. Here are just a few examples of databases that your college library is likely to have, either on CD-ROM or online.

America: History and Life.

This database contains citations and abstracts of the major scholarly literature in history. One of the useful features of this database (and various others) is that articles and the commentaries written in response to them are combined so that you can access all the relevant articles at the same time. This database also contains reviews from about 140 mainly U.S. and Canadian journals as well as reviews of works on microfilm, film, and video.

PsycINFO and Sociological Abstracts.
These two databases (in some systems these are referred to as PsycINFO and sociofile) are similar in format and so can be considered together. PsycINFO is a database of citations from approximately 1,300 journals in psychology and related fields in 27 languages, published in some 50 different countries. Sociological Abstracts is the sociological counterpart and contains citations from about 1,600 journals in sociology and related fields in 30 different languages, published in approximately 55 countries. Both databases also contain citations for books, book chapters, and dissertations of psychological and sociological relevance. Abstracts of around 250 words are provided for each article or book.

Medline.
The Medline database is the computerized version of *Index Medicus;* it's the National Library of Medicine's bibliographic database, the definitive source in the United States for biomedical literature. This database is enormous and contains citations from more than 3,700 journals "selected for inclusion because of their importance to health professions." The index is international in scope; 75 percent of the citations are published in English. Medline covers such categories as anatomy, diseases, chemicals, drugs, equipment, psychiatry, biological sciences, information science and communications, and health care. Articles since 1975 contain abstracts of about 250 words. The Web version of Medline is available free at the PubMed site: www.ncbi.nlm.nih.gov/medlineplus.

ERIC.
Should you be preparing a speech on some topic related to education—bilingualism, school violence, leadership training, teacher preparation, test anxiety, communication apprehension, and multiculturalism are a few examples—the Educational Resources Information Center (ERIC) database (available free on the Web at http://www.askeric.com) will prove useful. ERIC is a network of 16 contributing clearinghouses, each of which specializes in a separate subject area. Together they survey over 750 journals and provide complete citations and abstracts of 200 to 300 words. In addition, 850 ERIC document records

that contain the full text of the original work are also available. In addition to journal articles, ERIC also includes dissertations, convention papers, books, computer programs, nonprint media, and speeches.

The LEXIS/NEXIS system allows you to retrieve the complete text of articles from hundreds of newspapers, magazines, journals, and even newsletters in addition to a wide variety of legal and statutory records.

Other research sources often combine the academic with more popular articles. For example, the *Education Index,* published since 1929, indexes articles from about 330 journals and magazines relevant to education at all levels. It also indexes most of the speech communication journals and government periodicals. ERIC, discussed above, is a more comprehensive and efficient database to search. The *Social Sciences Index* covers periodicals in such areas as psychology, economics, sociology, and political science. Although more specialized indexes cover these subjects in greater depth, this one is useful for its cross-disciplinary coverage. Among the more specialized indexes that will prove useful to many speakers are the *Business Periodicals Index, Art Index, Applied Science and Technology Index, Biological and Agricultural Index, General Science Index, Index to Legal Periodicals,* and *Humanities Index.* All indexes noted in this paragraph are produced by the H. W. Wilson Company and are available for subscription databases. Check with your college library to see if these indexes are available to you. Another useful index is PAIS (Public Affairs Information Service); it provides citations and abstracts and is available at www.pais.inter.net.

The general interest articles appearing in popular magazines may prove useful for a variety of speech topics. Realize, however, that articles in magazines differ greatly from those in professional journals. For example, they're most often written by professional writers rather than by researchers. Magazine articles are often summaries of the research conducted by others, or they may be largely in the nature of opinion. Often they're simplified accounts of rather complex issues—written for the general public rather than for an audience of professional researchers. Further, they seldom undergo the rigorous review process that accompanies publication in a professional academic journal. As a result, articles appearing in popular magazines are much less reliable than those appearing in such professional research journals as, say, *Communication*

Monographs, Journal of Experimental Psychology, or *The New England Journal of Medicine.* Nevertheless, magazine articles and general posts are often very helpful for speakers. Here are a few suggestions for finding the information you want.

Indexes. Helpful in locating both scholarly research articles and popular magazine articles are the many available indexes. One of the most impressive indexes, *The Readers' Guide to Periodical Literature,* is available in print and electronic formats and covers magazine articles from 1900 to the present. This guide indexes by subject and by author (in one convenient alphabetical index) articles published in about 180 different magazines. *Readers' Guide* is valuable for its broad coverage, but it's limited in that it covers mostly general publications and only a few of the more specialized ones. The "First Search Help for Readers' Guide to Periodical Literature" at http://www.uni_stuttgart.de/ub/oclc/help/ReadersGuide_scope_help.htm ⌒🖱 will help you get the most from this valuable research tool.

The *Alternative Press Index* (also available on CD-ROM to which your library might subscribe) indexes approximately 250 "alternative, radical, and left publications." This index is valuable for speakers dealing with such issues as the Third World, minority rights, socialism, and the like. The National Institutes of Health maintain the National Library of Medicine at www.nlm.nih.gov/, which is essential for any topic dealing with health and medicine. A similar general index for legal issues from FindLaw is available at www.findlaw.com, and one for financial issues from Goinvest is at www.financialfind.com. ⌒🖱

Listservs, Usenet groups, and the World Wide Web. Listservs, newsgroups, and the World Wide Web, as explained earlier, contain a wide variety of articles, many more than you could possibly use in one or even many speeches. Explore relevant listservs through Liszt (www.liszt.com), newsgroups through Google (http://groups.google.com/); ⌒🖱 browse the vast array of World Wide

---

BUILDING COMMUNICATION SKILLS

How Can You Conduct Electronic Research?

This exercise is designed to illustrate the wide variety of information you can easily secure from computer searches and to focus attention on the process of conducting research rather than on research materials themselves. As you attempt to find one or more of the items below, try to focus on the processes you're following—take note, for example, of wrong turns and of how you might develop more efficient strategies for locating such information.

▸ an article on public speaking that appears in the ERIC database in the last five years

▸ an article on a psychological study on fear from the PsycINFO database

▸ an article on persuasion from the Sociofile database

▸ an article appearing in *The Quarterly Journal of Speech, Communication Monographs,* or

Communication Education that is of some interest to you

▸ an article from a business journal dealing with communication skills

▸ an article from any online newspaper dealing with college education

▸ an article on diabetes from Medline and one from the Web

▸ a list of listservs or Usenet groups concerned with ecological issues

▸ an article on divorce from any database, using any of the major search engines

▸ an article on immigration patterns during the last 20 years from the America: History and Life database

▸ a review of Jay Winik's book *April 1865*

Web documents with the help of the numerous search engines.

Book Sources

You can find books through a library and a bookstore. Each library catalogs its books, journals, and government documents in a slightly different way, depending on its size and the needs of its users. All, however, make use of some form of computerized catalog. These are uniformly easy and efficient to use. The catalog is the best place to find out what books are in your college library or in another library whose books you can secure on interlibrary loan, for example.

Generally, you'd access books and other printed material by looking up your major subject heading(s). A good way to do this is to make a list of the five or six major concepts that appear in your speech and look each of these up in the library catalog. Create a complete bibliography of available sources and examine each one. Sometimes you may want to locate works by or about a particular person. In this case, simply look up the author's name much as you would a concept.

Both general and specialized online libraries are available. The Library of Congress (http://www.loc.gov/) provides an online catalog of all its holdings as well as links to Internet search engines and a variety of useful indexes for researching a wide variety of topics. Useful directories to libraries, most in North America and Europe, can be found at http://www.llv.com/~msauers/libs/libs/html. And an especially rich source of links to reference cites can be found at http://www.state.wi.us/agencies/dpi/www/llb_res.html.

Browsing through any large brick-and-mortar bookstore is almost sure to give you insights into your topic. If you're talking about something that people are interested in today, there's likely to be a book dealing with it on the bookshelf of most bookstores. Visit too some of the online bookstores; for example, Amazon (www.amazon.com), Barnes & Noble (www.bn.com), or Borders (www.borders.com). Other useful sites include http://aaup.pupress.princeton.edu/ (Association of American University Presses), http://www.cs.cmu.edu/Web/People/spok/banned-books.html (links to texts of books that have been banned in the United States and elsewhere), and http://www.booksite.com/ (search tools for locating more than two million books).

Critically Evaluating Research

Collecting research materials—whether from traditional print sources, through listservs and the Web, or through interviews with experts—is only part of the process; the other part is critically evaluating them. Here are some questions to ask about research materials.

Is the Information Current?

Generally, the more current the material, the more useful it will be. With some topics—such as unemployment statistics, developments in AIDS research, or tuition costs—the recency of the information is crucial to its usefulness. Check important figures in a recent almanac, newspaper, or frequently updated Internet source.

The date of a newspaper, the copyright date of a book, or the date of a cited article or e-mail will help you identify the recency of the information. Unfortunately, not all Internet documents are dated, so at times you won't be able to tell when the document was written. You may, however, be able to write to the author and ask; many Internet writers include their e-mail address.

Is the Information Fair and Unbiased?

Bias is not easy to determine, but do try to examine any sources of potential bias. Obvious examples come quickly to mind: cigarette manufacturers' statements on health risks from smoking; newspaper and network editorials on the fairness of news reporting; the National Rifle Association's positions on gun control. Try checking the credibility of individual writers through a biographical dictionary or in relevant newspaper articles. Reviewing the research in the area will enable you to see how other experts view the author of a particular article. It will also enable you to see if the author's analysis of the situation takes into consideration all sides of the issue and represents these sides fairly and accurately. In some cases the author presents her or his credentials, and you can easily check if you wish to.

Distinguish between primary and secondary source material. Primary sources include, for example, an original research study as reported in an academic journal or a corporation's annual report. Secondary sources include, for example, summaries of scholarly research that appear in popular magazines or television news reports on a corporation's earnings. When using secondary sources, examine the information for any particular spin the writer may be giving the material. If possible, you may wish to check with the primary source to see what might have been left out or whether an article's conclusions are really warranted on the basis of the primary evidence.

Recognize that anyone can "publish" on the Internet. An article on the Internet can be written by world-renowned scientists or by elementary school students, by fair and objective reporters or by those who would slant the coverage to serve political or religious or social purposes. And it's not always easy to tell which is which. Again, find out what the author's qualifications are. Look carefully at any statistics or figures. Are these cited from reliable and recent sources? One useful technique used by many Web writers is to include in their document Internet links to the sources from which they derived, say, their statistics or predictions or arguments. If you

find these links, it's often worth checking them to see if the author did in fact fairly and accurately present the information.

Recognize also, however, that much information on the Internet is identical to the information you regularly read in print. Encyclopedias, newspapers and newsmagazines, and professional journals that appear on the Internet are often identical to the print copies, so there's no need to draw distinctions between print and Internet information when dealing with sites such as these.

Lots of assistance for evaluating Web materials is on the Web itself. For example, visit http://www.ala.org.acil/underwebev/html. ☞ This Web page, although addressed to librarians, provides five criteria for evaluating Internet materials. Other websites addressed to this issue include: the University of California at Santa Barbara website at www.library.ucsb.edu/untagle/jones/html,

UNDERSTANDING THEORY AND RESEARCH

Research Competencies

Indicate the research competencies you possess by responding to each of the following items, using the following scale: A = finding this would be simple; B = finding this would be possible, but would take some effort; and C = finding this would be impossible without asking someone for help.

_____ An article on India that appeared in the *New York Times* sometime in 1998

_____ Ten newsgroups dealing with the topic of computers

_____ Ten listservs dealing with topics relating to your professional goal

_____ The most recent price quotation for IBM stock

_____ Ten abstracts of articles dealing with hepatitis

_____ The communication courses (or pick another department) offered at Kansas State University (or pick another school)

_____ The population of Toronto and Tokyo

_____ The speeches given during the most recent session of Congress

_____ The biography of a state political figure

_____ Recent law cases dealing with sexual harassment

Working with Theories and Research. *One way to review this competencies test—and the topic of research generally—is to share your responses and your own research strengths and weaknesses in a small group with five or six others. As you discuss the various responses, also consider: Which avenues of research are the most efficient? Which are the most reliable? Which will prove the most credible with your peers?*

Lehigh University's www.lehigh.edu/~inref/guides/evaluating.web/html, Purdue University's webct.cc.purdue.edu:8900/web-ct/courses/LIB101/evalSrcs/evalweb.html, and New Mexico State's lib.nmsu.edu/instructor/evalcrit.html (suggested by Radford, Barnes, & Barr, 2002—itself a wonderful source for evaluating web materials).

Is the Evidence Reliable and the Reasoning Logical?

The most important question in evaluating research must focus on the evidence and reasoning an author uses in arriving at a conclusion. Ask yourself if the conclusions have been arrived at logically rather than, say, emotionally. Does the author offer clear evidence and sound arguments to support conclusions rather than, say, anecdotes or testimonials from like-minded people?

Another way to estimate reliability is to look at the publisher. Note especially if the publisher is a special interest group with a specific corporate, religious, political, or social agenda. If so, try to balance this publisher's perspective with information that represents the other sides of the issue.

In contrast, if an article appears in a journal sponsored by a respected professional organization such as the American Psychological Association or the National Communication Association (to mention just two), you can be pretty sure that the article has been carefully reviewed by experts before publication. If an article appears in the *New York Times*, the *Washington Post*, the *Wall Street Journal*, or any of the major newsmagazines or news networks, again, you can have reasonable confidence in the information. Major book publishers go to enormous effort to ensure the accuracy of what appears in print.

This claim of accuracy is, of course, a generalization that has on occasion been proved false. A few years ago, for example, a writer from the *Boston Globe* was found to have fabricated stories in her columns. The *Cincinnati Enquirer* paid the Chiquita Corporation more than $10 million for stories the newspaper later said were "untrue." And, in perhaps the most widely publicized example, both CNN and *Time* magazine apologized for claiming that the U.S. military had used lethal gas in Laos that was intended to kill American defectors (*New York Times*, July 5, 1998, Section 4, p.

2). So inaccuracies do creep into even the most respected sources.

Some Internet sources contain "about" files that will help you learn more about the author and perhaps about the author's sources. Sometimes you'll be able to contact the author via e-mail.

Integrating Research into the Speech

By integrating and acknowledging your sources of information in your speech, you'll give fair credit to those whose ideas and statements you're using—and at the same time you'll help establish your own reputation as a responsible researcher. Here are a few suggestions for integrating your research into your speech.

Mention the sources in your speech by citing at least the author and, if helpful, the publication and the date.

Provide smooth transitions between your words and the words of the author you're citing. Notice how, in this excerpt, Nancy Dickenson-Hazard (1998, p. 495) mentions the source and smoothly quotes from the book:

> David McNally, author of *Even Eagles Need a Push*, believes inspired persons know why they do what they do and why they want what they want. Furthermore, he says, "people perform at their best when contributing their talents to something they believe in."

Avoid useless expressions such as "I have a quote here" or "I want to quote an example." Let the audience know that you're quoting by pausing before the quote, taking a step forward, or referring to your notes to read the extended quotation. Marilyn Loden (1986, p. 473) does this effectively:

> Mary Kay Ash believes in feminine leadership. Recently she said: "A woman can no more duplicate the male style of leadership than an American businessman can exactly reproduce the Japanese style."

If you feel it's crucial that the audience know you're quoting and you want to state that this is a quotation, you might do it this way:

> Recently, Mary Kay Ash put this in perspective, and I quote: "A woman can no more duplicate the male style of leadership than an American businessman can exactly reproduce the Japanese style."

Use "signal verbs" to let the audience know your own evaluation of the material (Harnack & Kleppinger, 1997). Let's say, for example, that in an Internet article by Pat Doe you read the statement "Low self-esteem influences speaker apprehension." You can preface that information with any of a variety of signal verbs—such as *has proved that, says, argues that, speculates that, has found that, thinks,* or *wonders if.* For example, saying that "Pat Doe speculates that low self-esteem influences speaker appre-hension" is quite different from saying, "Pat Doe has proved that low self-esteem influences speaker apprehension." (You might then go on to explain briefly how this was proved.) Select the signal verb that best represents what Pat Doe said and meant and at the same time indicates the support or lack of support you're giving to Pat's statement. You may find it helpful to modify your verb in some way; for example, "convincingly argues" or "wildly speculates" will further indicate your support or lack of it.

REFLECTIONS ON ETHICS IN HUMAN COMMUNICATION

Plagiarizing (and How to Avoid It)

You commit plagiarism when you use material from another source without properly crediting it. Here are some forms plagiarism can take and some ways you can avoid it.

Using the exact words of another person. If you're using another person's exact words, cite the quotation exactly as it was written or spoken and credit the source. For example, in a speech on nonverbal communication, you might say something like: "According to Roger Axtell, in his *Gestures: The Do's and Taboos of Body Language around the World*, touching varies from one culture to another. Axtell says, 'In the Middle East, two Arab male friends may even be seen walking down the street hand-in-hand and all it signifies is friendship.'" Make it clear that you're using the person's exact words, as demonstrated in this example. In your speech outline, use quotation marks for any citation in which you use the person's exact words and give the full bibliographic reference just as you would in a history or sociology paper.

Using the ideas of another person. If you're using someone else's ideas, arguments, insights, or examples, even if you're not quoting them directly, you still have to acknowledge your source. Weave the sources into your speech without disturbing its natural flow and rhythm, saying, for example, "A recent article in *Time* magazine noted . . ." or "Professor Fox, in his lecture last week, argued that . . . ."

Using the organizational structure of another. If you're "only" using the organizational structure of another source, acknowledge your indebtedness. In these cases you can say something like "I'm here following the arguments given by Professor Marishu in her lecture on culture" or "This pattern for Web design comes from the work of Edward Almos in his book, *Designing Your Own Web Site.*"

What would you do? *You're really pressed to come up with a persuasive speech on a contemporary social issue and just don't have the time to research it. Fortunately, you can easily adapt a friend's term paper to this assignment. You figure that it's similar to using research you'd find yourself; and besides, you're writing the outline and delivering the speech. Would you use your friend's paper? If so, how would you acknowledge your sources?*

SUMMARY

This unit introduced the nature of public speaking and covered selecting and limiting the topic and purpose, analyzing and adapting to your audience, and researching your speech.

1. Public speaking also provides training to improve your personal and social competencies, academic and career skills, and general communication abilities.

2. Apprehension in public speaking is normal and can be managed by reversing the factors that cause anxiety, practicing performance visualization, and systematically desensitizing yourself.

3. The preparation of a public speech involves 10 steps: (1) select the topic and purpose; (2) analyze the audience; (3) research the topic; (4) formulate the thesis and identify the major problems; (5) support the major propositions; (6) organize the speech materials; (7) construct the conclusion, introduction, and transitions; (8) outline the speech; (9) word the speech; and (10) rehearse and deliver the speech. The first 3 of these steps were discussed in this unit; the remaining 7 are discussed in the next two units.

4. Speech topics should deal with significant issues that interest the audience. Subjects and purposes should be limited in scope.

5. In analyzing an audience, consider their attitudes, beliefs, and values. An attitude is a tendency to be-

have in a particular way. A belief is a conviction in the existence or nonexistence of some person, object, or event, for example, a belief in the existence of God or a belief in the usefulness of communication. A value is the measure of goodness or badness that you attribute to something, for example, you positively value democracy or you negatively value sexual discrimination.

6. In analyzing the audience, consider age, gender, cultural factors, religion and religiousness, the occasion, and the specific context.

7. Also analyze and adapt to your audience's willingness to hear your speech, how favorable the audience is to your point of view, and the knowledge that your audience has of your topic.

8. Research the topic, beginning with general sources and gradually exploring more specific and specialized sources.

9. Critically evaluate your research by asking if the research is current, if it is fair and unbiased, and if the evidence is reliable and the reasoning logical.

10. Integrate research into your speech by mentioning the sources, providing smooth transitions, avoiding useless expressions such as "I have a quote," and using signal verbs to communicate your own evaluation of the research.

KEY TERMS

public speaking	informative speech	audience knowledge
public speaking apprehension	persuasive speech	e-mail
performance visualization	special occasion speech	newsgroups
systematic desensitization	audience	World Wide Web
topic	audience analysis	search engine
taboo	attitude	directory
topoi	belief	database
tree diagrams	value	primary and secondary source material
search directories	sociological analysis	
general purpose	audience willingness	
specific purpose	audience favor	

THINKING CRITICALLY ABOUT

Public Speaking Topics, Audiences, and Research

1. Access the PsycINFO, Sociological Abstracts, or ERIC database and search for key terms and concepts discussed in this unit: for example, attitude, value, belief, and audience psychology. On the basis of this search, what might you add to this unit's discussions?

2. Using Liszt (www.liszt.com), explore the listservs that deal with topics related to your next speech. How many can you find? Using Google (http://groups.google.com/), investigate the available newsgroups dealing with topics related to your next speech. Try to find at least three.

3. A common belief is that religious people are more honest, more charitable, and more likely to reach out to those in need than are nonreligious people. A review of research, however, found that this seemingly logical connection was invalid (Kohn, 1989). For example, in a study of cheating among college students, religious beliefs bore little relationship to honesty; in fact, atheists were less likely to cheat than those who identified themselves as religious. Other studies have found that religious people were not any more likely to help those in need—for example, to work with retarded children or to comfort someone lying in the street. What assumptions about people's behavior can you make from knowing only that they are very religious?

4. Jack is scheduled to give a speech on careers in computer technology to a group of high school students who have been forced to attend career day on a Saturday and to listen to at least three speeches. The audience is definitely an unwilling one. What advice can you give Jack to help him deal with this type of audience?

5. Jill wants to give a speech on television talk shows and wants to include biographical information on some of the talk show hosts. What sources might Jill go to in order to get authoritative and current information on these hosts? What sources might she go to in order to get "fan" type information? What advice would you give Jill for distinguishing the two types of sources and information?

6. Prepare and deliver a two-minute speech in which you do one of the following:
   - evaluate the topics of recent talk shows against the criteria for a worthwhile and appropriate topic
   - explain the cultural factors operating in your class that need to be taken into consideration by the speaker selecting a topic and purpose
   - explain a particularly strong belief that you hold
   - describe members of your class in terms of how willing, favorable, and knowledgeable you see them to be about any specific topic or speaker
   - describe the audience of a popular magazine or television show or movie
   - explain the value of one reference book, website, database, listserv, or newsgroup for research in public speaking

UNIT 16
Supporting and Organizing Your Speech

ABC, Inc.

Unit Contents

Here the discussion of public speaking continues. In this unit you'll learn

▶ about speech theses and propositions, supporting materials, and organizational patterns and strategies

▶ how to develop your thesis and major propositions; support and organize them; and introduce, conclude, and tie the pieces of your speech together

STEP 4: FORMULATE YOUR THESIS AND MAJOR PROPOSITIONS

Your **thesis** is your main assertion; it's what you want the audience to absorb from your speech. The thesis of the *Rocky* movies was that the underdog can win; the thesis of the Martin Luther King Jr., "I Have a Dream" speech was that true equality must be granted to African Americans and to all people. From your thesis you'll be able to derive your major propositions, the main ideas that you will explore in order to prove or support your thesis.

Your Thesis

In an informative speech the thesis statement focuses on what you want your audience to learn. For example, a thesis for an informative speech on jealousy might be: "There are two main theories of jealousy." In a persuasive speech your thesis is what you want your audience to believe as a result of your speech. For example, a thesis for a persuasive speech against using animals for experimentation might be: "Animal experimentation should be banned." Notice that in informative speeches the thesis is relatively neutral and objective. In persua-

UNDERSTANDING THEORY AND RESEARCH

Primacy and Recency

Let's say that you have three propositions that you intend to arrange in topical order. How will you determine which to put first? The theory and research on primacy and recency offer help. As explained in Unit 4, the rule of primacy tells you that what an audience hears first will be remembered best and will have the greatest effect. The rule of recency argues that what the audience hears last (or most recently) will be remembered best and will have the greatest effect. Research findings on this controversy offer a few useful general suggestions.

▶ The middle is remembered least and has the least general effect. Thus, if you have a speech with three propositions, put the weakest one in the middle.

▶ If your listeners are favorable or neutral, lead with your strongest proposition. In this way you'll strengthen the conviction of those who

are already favorable—and get the neutrals on your side early.

▶ If your audience is hostile or holds views very different from yours, put your most powerful argument last and work up to it gradually, hoping that you can count on the listeners' staying with you until the end.

Research on memory tells us that the audience will remember very little of what you say. Interesting as your speech may be, listeners will forget most of it. Therefore, whether you put your main assertions first or last in your speech, repeat them in your conclusion.

Working with Theories and Research. *Examine your most recent speech or the speech you're currently working on in terms of the order of the propositions. What insights does primacy and recency give you for ordering your propositions?*

sive speeches, however, the thesis statement puts forth a point of view, an opinion; it's an arguable, debatable proposition.

Be sure to limit the thesis statement to one central idea. A statement such as "Animal experimentation should be banned, and companies engaging in it should be prosecuted" contains not one but two basic ideas.

Word your thesis as a simple declarative sentence: "Animal experimentation must be banned." This will help you focus your thinking, your collection of materials, and your organizational tasks.

Use the thesis statement to help you generate your main propositions. Each thesis contains within it an essential question, and it is this question that allows you to explore and subdivide the thesis. Your objective is to find this question and ask it of your thesis. For example, let's say your thesis is: "The Hart bill provides needed services for senior citizens." Stated in this form, the thesis suggests the obvious question "What are they?" The answers to this question suggest the main propositions of your speech; for example, healthcare, food, shelter, and recreational services. These four areas then become the four major propositions of your speech.

Use the thesis to help focus the audience's attention on your central idea. In some cases you may wish to state your thesis early in your speech. In other cases, such as situations in which your audience may be hostile to your thesis, it may be wise to give your evidence first and gradually move the audience into a more positive frame of mind before stating your thesis. Here are a few guidelines to help you make the right decision about when to introduce your thesis:

- In an informative speech, state your thesis early and state it clearly, and directly.

- In a persuasive speech before a neutral or positive audience, state your thesis explicitly and early in your speech.

- In a persuasive speech before an audience that is hostile to your position, delay revealing your thesis until you've moved your listeners closer to your point of view.

- Recognize that there are cultural differences in the way a thesis should be stated. In some Asian cultures, for example, making a point too directly or asking directly for audience compliance may be considered rude or insulting.

Major Propositions

The major propositions are the main points you marshal in support of your thesis. If your speech were a play, the propositions would be its acts. Let's look at how you can select and word your propositions and how you can logically arrange them.

In discussing the thesis, I mentioned that you can develop your main points or propositions by asking strategic questions. To see how this works in detail, imagine that you are giving a speech on the values of a college education to a group of high school students. Your thesis is: "A college education is valuable." You then ask, "Why is it valuable?" From this question you generate your major propositions. Your first step might be to brainstorm this question and generate as many answers as possible without evaluating them. You might come up with answers such as the following:

1. It helps you get a good job.
2. It increases your earning potential.
3. It gives you greater job mobility.
4. It helps you secure more creative work.
5. It helps you to appreciate the arts more fully.
6. It helps you to understand an extremely complex world.
7. It helps you understand different cultures.
8. It allows you to avoid taking a regular job for a few years.
9. It helps you meet lots of people and make new friends.
10. It helps you increase your personal effectiveness.

There are, of course, many other possibilities—but for purposes of illustration, these 10 possible main points will suffice. But not all 10 are equally valuable or relevant to your audience, so you should look over the list to see how to make it shorter and more meaningful. Try these suggestions:

1. Eliminate those points that seem least important to your thesis. On this basis you might want to eliminate number 8, as this seems least consistent with your intended emphasis on the positive values of college.
2. Combine those points that have a common focus. Notice, for example, that the first four points all center on the value of college in terms of jobs. You might, therefore, consider grouping these four items into one proposition: A college education helps you get a good job.

This point might be one of your major propositions, and you could develop it by defining what you mean by a "good job." This main point or proposition and its elaboration might look like this in your speech outline:

I. A college education helps you get a good job.
   A. College graduates earn higher salaries.
   B. College graduates enter more creative jobs.
   C. College graduates have greater job mobility.

Note that A, B, and C all relate to aspects or subdivisions of a "good job."

3. Select the points that are most relevant or interesting to your audience. You might decide that high school students would be interested in increasing personal effectiveness, so you might select point 10 for inclusion as a second major proposition.

4. In general, limit the number of main points. For your class speeches, which will generally range from 5 to 15 minutes, use two, three, or four main propositions. Too many main points will result in a speech that is confusing, contains too much information and too little amplification, and proves difficult to remember.

5. Word each of your major propositions in the same (parallel) style. When outlining, phrase points labeled with Roman numerals in a similar (parallel) style. Likewise, phrase points labeled with capital letters and subordinate to the same Roman numeral (for example, A, B, and C under point I or A, B, and C under point II) in a similar style. In item 2 above, parallel style was used in the example on college education and getting a good job. This parallel styling helps the audience follow and remember your speech.

6. Develop your main points so they are separate and discrete; don't allow them to overlap one another. Each section labeled with a Roman numeral should be a separate entity.

BUILDING COMMUNICATION SKILLS

How Can You Generate Major Propositions?

Try generating two or three major propositions (suitable for an informative or persuasive speech) from each of the following 10 thesis statements by asking strategic questions of each. Try following the general format illustrated in the text in the example of the values of a college education.

1. Tax (don't tax) property assets owned by religious organizations.

2. Require (don't require) adoption agencies to reveal the names of birth parents to all adopted children when they reach 18 years of age.

3. Permit (don't permit) condom advertisements in all media.

4. Make (don't make) the death penalty mandatory for those convicted of selling drugs to minors.

5. Elected political officials should (not) be allowed to serve as lobbyists at any time after their term of office has expired.

6. Courses on women's issues should (not) be required for all students at this college.

7. Legalize (don't legalize) soft drugs.

8. Build (don't build) houses for the homeless.

9. Support (don't support) mandatory instruction in AIDS prevention in all elementary and high schools.

10. Grant (don't grant) full equality to gay men and lesbians in the military.

STEP 5: SUPPORT YOUR PROPOSITIONS

Now that you've identified your major propositions—and having learned in Unit 15 how to search for information—you can devote attention to your next step: supporting your propositions. Among the most useful sources of support are examples, narratives, testimony, statistics, and presentation aids, all of which we'll cover in depth. In addition, however, there are a wide variety of other forms of support. A brief survey:

- *Quotations*, the exact words of another person, are useful for adding spice and wit as well as authority to your speeches. Make sure they're relatively short, easily understood, directly related to your point, and properly attributed.

- *Definitions*, statements of the meanings of terms, are helpful when complex terms are introduced or when you wish to provide a unique perspective on a subject. Don't overdo definitions; if too many definitions are needed, then your subject may be too complex for a short speech.

- *Comparisons and contrasts* are useful for highlighting similarities and differences between concepts; say, between two health care plans or between two cultures. A few major points of comparison and contrast may work better than an exhaustive list of similarities and differences, which listeners won't be able to remember.

- *Facts or series of facts*—verifiable truths—are useful to help you support a main idea. Don't allow individual facts to cloud your major propositions; make sure the facts are clearly linked to the proposition they support.

- *Repetition* means repeating your idea in the same words at strategic places throughout your speech; *restatement* means repeating your idea in different words. Both tactics are helpful for emphasizing a particular point, and both may be especially helpful when you are addressing listeners who learned your language as a second language and may not easily understand idioms and figures of speech. Repetition and restatement can be overdone and get boring, however; limit yourself to what is reasonable for increasing audience comprehension.

For suggestions on arranging supporting materials see "Adding and Arranging Supporting Materials" at **www.ablongman.com/devito**.

Examples

Examples are specific instances that are explained in varying degrees of detail. Examples are useful when you wish to make an abstract concept or idea concrete. It's easier for an audience to understand what you mean by, say, "love" or "friendship" if you provide a specific example along with your definition.

In using examples, keep in mind that their function is to make your ideas vivid and easily understood. Examples are useful for explaining a concept; they're not ends in themselves. Make them only as long as necessary to ensure that your purpose is achieved.

Also, use only enough examples to make your point. Make sure that the examples are sufficient to re-create your meaning in the minds of your listeners, but be careful not to use so many that the audience loses the very point you are making.

Make the relationship between your assertion and your example explicit. Show the audience exactly how your example relates to the assertion or concept you are explaining.

Narratives

Narratives, or stories, are often useful as supporting materials in a speech. Narratives give the audience what it wants: a good story. They help you maintain your audience's attention, because listeners automatically perk up when a story is told. The main value of narratives is that they allow you to bring an abstract concept down to specifics. Narratives may be of different types, and each serves a somewhat different purpose. Following Clella Jaffe (1998), we can distinguish three types of narrative: explanatory, exemplary, and persuasive.

- *Explanatory narratives* explain the way things are. The biblical book of Genesis, for example, explains the development of the world from a particular religious viewpoint. An eyewitness report might explain the events leading up to an accident.

- *Exemplary narratives* provide examples of excellence (or its opposite)—examples to follow or admire (or to avoid following). The stories of the lives of saints and martyrs are exemplary narratives, as are the Horatio Alger success stories. Similarly, many motivational speakers often include exemplary narratives in their speeches and will tell stories of what they were like when they were out of shape or on drugs or deep in debt.

- *Persuasive narratives* try to strengthen or change beliefs and attitudes. When Sally Struthers tells us of the plight of starving children, she's using a persuasive narrative. The parables in religious writings are persuasive in urging listeners to lead life in a particular way.

Keep your narratives relatively short and few in number. In most cases, one or possibly two narratives should be sufficient in a short five- to 15-minute speech. Make explicit the connection between your story and the point you are making. If the people in the audience don't get this connection, you lose not only the effectiveness of the story but also their attention (as they try to figure out why you told that story).

Testimony

The term *testimony* refers to the opinions of experts or the accounts of witnesses. Testimony helps to amplify your speech by adding a note of authority to your arguments. For example, you might want to use the testimony of a noted economist to support your predictions about inflation, or the testimony of someone who spent two years in a maximum-security prison to discourage young people from committing crimes.

When you cite testimony, stress first the competence of the person, whether that person is an expert or a witness. For example, citing the predictions of a world-famous economist of whom your audience has never heard will mean little unless you first explain the person's competence. You might say something like "This prediction comes from the world's leading economist, who has successfully predicted all major financial trends over the past 20 years." Now the audience will be prepared to lend credence to what this person says.

Second, stress the unbiased nature of the testimony. If the audience perceives the testimony to be biased—whether or not it really is—it will have little effect. You want to check out any possible biases

in a witness so that you can present accurate information. But you also want to make the audience see that the testimony is in fact unbiased.

Third, stress the recency of the testimony. If an audience has no way of knowing when the statement was made, it has no way of knowing how true this statement is today.

An exercise, "How Can You Critically Evaluate Testimony?" provides practice in using testimony as support; see **www.ablongman.com/devito**.

Statistics

Let's say you want to show that significant numbers of people are now getting their news from the Internet, that the cost of filmmaking has skyrocketed over the last 20 years, or that women buy significantly more books and magazines than men. To communicate these types of information, you'd use *statistics*—summary numbers that help you communicate the important characteristics of an otherwise complex set of numbers. Statistics help the audience see, for example, the percentage of people getting their news from the Internet, the average cost of films in 2002 versus previous years, or the difference between male and female book and magazine purchases. For a wealth of statistics see Going Online on page 320.

- *Make the statistics clear to your audience.* Remember, they'll hear the figures only once. Round off figures so they are easy to understand and retain.
- *Make the statistics meaningful.* When you are using statistics, it's often helpful to remind the audience of what the statistic itself means. For example, if you say, "The median price of a co-op apartment in San Francisco is $543,000," remind the audience that this means the middle price—that half of the co-ops are above $543,000 and half are below. Also, present numbers so that the audience can appreciate the meaning you want to convey. To say, for example, that the Sears Tower in Chicago is 1,559 feet tall doesn't help your hearers visualize its height. So consider saying something like "The Sears Tower is 1,559 feet tall. Just how tall is 1,559 feet? Well, it's as tall as the length of more than five football fields. It's as tall as 260 six-foot people standing on each other's heads."

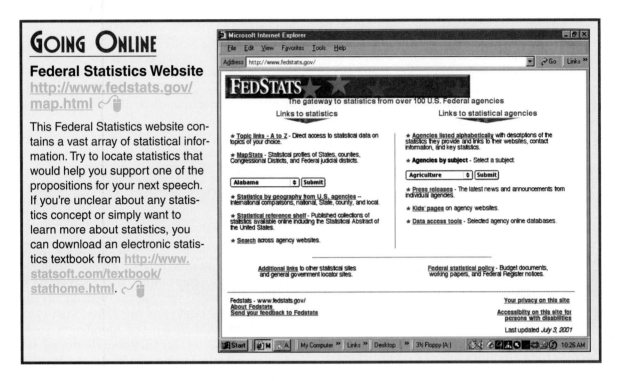

GOING ONLINE

Federal Statistics Website
http://www.fedstats.gov/
map.html

This Federal Statistics website contains a vast array of statistical information. Try to locate statistics that would help you support one of the propositions for your next speech. If you're unclear about any statistics concept or simply want to learn more about statistics, you can download an electronic statistics textbook from http://www.statsoft.com/textbook/stathome.html.

- *Connect the statistics with the proposition.* Make explicit the connection between the statistics and what they show. A statement, for example, that college professors make an average of $78,000 per year needs to be related specifically to the proposition that teachers' salaries should be raised—or lowered, depending on your point of view.

- *Use statistics in moderation.* Most listeners' capacity for numerical data presented in a speech is limited, so in most cases statistics should be used sparingly.

- *Visually (and verbally) reinforce the statistics.* Numbers are difficult to grasp and remember when they are presented without some kind of visual reinforcement, so it's often helpful to complement your oral presentation of statistics with some type of presentation aid—perhaps a graph or a chart.

Presentation Aids

When you're planning a speech, consider using some kind of presentation aid—a visual or auditory means for clarifying ideas. Ask yourself how you can visualize in your aid what you want your audience to remember. How can you reinforce your ideas

with additional media? If you want your audience to grasp increases in the sales tax, consider showing them a chart of rising sales taxes over the last 10 years. If you want them to see that Brand A is superior to Brand X, consider showing them a comparison chart identifying the superiority of Brand A.

Types of Presentation Aids

Among the presentation aids you have available are the actual object, models of the object, graphs, word charts, maps, people, photographs and illustrations, and tapes and CDs.

As a general rule (to which there are many exceptions), the best presentation aid is the object itself; bring it with you if you can. Notice that infomercials sell their product not only by talking about it but also by showing it to potential buyers. You see what George Foreman's Lean Mean Grilling Machine looks like and how it works. You see the jewelry, the clothing, and the new mop from a wide variety of angles and in varied settings. If you want to explain some tangible thing and you can show it to your audience, do so.

Models—replicas of actual objects—are useful for a variety of purposes. For example, if you wanted to explain complex structures such as the hearing or vocal mechanism, the brain, or the structure of DNA, you would almost have to use a model. You

BUILDING COMMUNICATION SKILLS

How Can You Liven Up Supporting Statements?

Here are some rather bland, uninteresting statements. Select one of them and amplify it by using at least three different types of supporting materials. For purposes of this exercise you may estimate, fabricate, or otherwise invent facts, figures, illustrations, examples, and the like. In fact, it may prove even more effective if you go to extremes in constructing these forms of support.

1. Bullfighting is morally wrong.
2. The Sears Tower in Chicago is tall.
3. Williams was my favorite instructor.
4. My grandparents left me a fortune in their will.
5. The college I just visited seems ideal.
6. The writer of this article is a real authority.
7. I knew I was marrying into money as soon as I walked into the house.
8. Considering what they did, punishment to the fullest extent of the law would be mild.
9. The psychic gave us good news.
10. The athlete lived an interesting life.

may remember from science classes that these models (and the pictures of them in the textbooks) make a lot more sense than verbal explanations alone. Models help to clarify relative size and position and how each part interacts with each other part. Large models can be used to help listeners visualize objects that are too small (or unavailable) to appreciate otherwise. In other cases, small models of large objects—objects that are too large to bring to your speech—are helpful. For example, in a speech on stretching exercises, one student used a 14-inch wooden artist's model.

Graphs are useful for showing differences over time, for showing how a whole is divided into parts, and for showing different amounts or sizes. Figure 16.1 on page 322 shows different types of graphs that can be drawn freehand or generated with the graphics capabilities of any word-processing or presentation software.

Word charts (which can also contain numbers and even graphics) are useful for lots of different types of information. For example, you might use a word chart to identify the key points that you cover in one of your propositions or in your entire speech—in the order in which you cover them, of course. Slide 5 in Figure 16.2 is a good example of a simple word chart listing the major topics discussed in the speech. Or you could use word charts to identify the steps in a process; for example, to summarize the steps in programming a VCR, dealing with sexual harassment, or installing a new computer

program. Another use of charts is for presenting information you want your audience to write down. Emergency phone numbers, addresses to write to, or titles of recommended books and websites are examples of the type of information that listeners will welcome in written form.

Maps are useful for illustrating a wide variety of concepts. If you want to show the locations of cities, lakes, rivers, or mountain ranges, maps will obviously prove useful as presentation aids. One speaker, for example, used a map to show the sizes and locations of rain forests. Maps are also helpful for illustrating population densities, immigration patterns, varied economic conditions, the spread of diseases, and hundreds of other issues you may wish to develop in your speeches. For example, in a talk on natural resources, one speaker used maps to illustrate the locations of large reserves of oil, gas, and precious metals. Another speaker used maps to illustrate concentrations of wealth; still another used maps to show worldwide differences in mortality rates.

You can also use maps to illustrate numerical differences. For example, you may want to use a map to show the wide variation in literacy rates throughout the world. For example, you might color the countries that have 90 to 100 percent literacy red, the countries having 80 to 89 percent literacy green, and so on. When you use maps in this way, it's often helpful to complement them with charts or graphs that, for example, give the specific literacy rates for

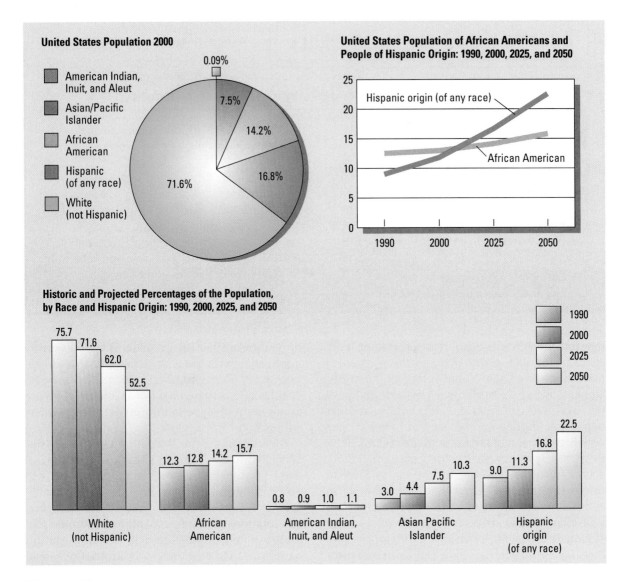

Figure 16.1

Assorted Graphs

Notice that each of the graphs serves a somewhat different purpose. The *pie chart* is especially useful if you want to show how some whole is divided into its parts and the relative sizes of the parts. From the pie chart you can easily see the relative percentages of the different groups in the U.S. population. Pie charts are especially helpful when you have three to five values to illustrate; any more than five creates a pie that is difficult to read at a glance. The *bar graph* presents the same information as the pie chart but for four different time periods. You might have used four pie charts—with each pie representing a different year—but comparisons would not have been as easy for an audience to make. The *line graph* shows how comparisons can be visualized with a very simple illustration. Notice that the graph is especially clear because it focuses on only two groups. Had it focused on eight or ten groups, it would have been difficult for an audience to understand.

the specific countries on which you want to concentrate. Although maps may seem complex to construct, computer programs now make the creation of such maps relatively simple. Further, a wide variety of maps may be downloaded from the Internet and then shown as slides or transparencies. Chances are you'll find a map on the Internet for exactly the purpose you need.

Oddly enough, *people* can function effectively as "presentation aids." For example, if you wanted to demonstrate the muscles of the body, you might use a bodybuilder. If you wanted to discuss different voice patterns, skin complexions, or hairstyles, you might use people as your aids. Aside from the obvious assistance they provide in demonstrating their muscles or voice qualities, people help to secure and maintain the attention and interest of the audience.

And don't overlook yourself as a (kind of) presentation aid. For example, if you are giving a speech on boxing strategies, exercise techniques, or sitting and standing postures that can lead to backaches, consider demonstrating them yourself. As an added plus, going through these demonstrations is likely to reduce your apprehension and make you more relaxed.

Photographs and illustrations are useful aids for a variety of purposes. Speeches on types of trees, styles of art or architecture, or types of exercise machines would profit greatly from a few well-chosen photographs or illustrations. If you want to show these but don't have the opportunity to put them onto slides, you may try simply holding them up as you refer to them. There are many hazards involved in using this type of aid, however, so pictures are recommended only with reservations. If the image is large enough for all members of the audience to see clearly (say, poster size); if it clearly illustrates what you want to illustrate; and if it's mounted on cardboard, then use it. Otherwise, don't. Fortunately, it's relatively easy to have photos enlarged or put onto slides.

Do not pass pictures around the room. This only draws attention away from what you are saying: Listeners will look for the pictures before the pictures circulate to them, will wonder what the pictures contain, and meanwhile will miss a great deal of your speech.

Tapes and CDs can be useful for many types of speeches as well. For a speech on advertising, for example, actual samples of commercials as played on radio or television would go a long way in helping the audience see exactly what you are talking about. These aids also provide variety by breaking up the oral presentation.

The Media of Presentation Aids

Once you've decided on the type of presentation aid you'll use, you need to decide on the medium you'll use to present it. Some of these media are low tech—for example, chalkboards, transparencies, and flip charts. These media are generally more effective in smaller, more informal situations, and especially for presentations that arise without prior notice, for which you simply don't have the time to prepare high-tech resources. Low-tech devices are also useful for highly interactive sessions; for example, the flip chart is still one of the best ways to record group members' contributions. More high-tech media such as slides and videotapes, are generally more effective with larger, more formal groups, in which you do most of the talking and the audience does most of the listening. High-tech materials may also be your only choice if the material you have to communicate is extremely complex or if the norms of your organization simply require that you use high-tech presentation formats.

The best strategy is to learn how to use both low- and high-tech resources. The decisions you make concerning which types of media to use should be based on the message you want to communicate and on the audience to whom you'll be speaking.

The *chalkboard* is the easiest to use, but not necessarily the most effective. All classrooms have such boards, and you have seen them used by teachers with greater or lesser effect; in some way, you've had "experience" with them. The chalkboard may be used effectively to present key terms or important definitions or even to outline the general structure of your speech. But don't use it if you can present the same information with a prepared chart or model. It takes too long to write out anything substantial. If you do write on the board, be careful not to turn your back to the audience. In this brief time you can easily lose their attention.

Chartboards are useful when you have just one or two relatively simple charts that you want to display during your speech. If you want to display your charts for several minutes, be sure you have a way of holding them up. For example, bring masking tape if you intend to secure them to the chalkboard, or enlist the aid of an audience member to hold them up. Use a light-colored board; white generally works best. Write in black; it provides the best contrast and is the easiest for people to read.

Flip charts, charts on large pads of paper (usually about 24 by 24 inches) mounted on a stand, can be used to record many types of information, which you reveal by flipping the pages as you deliver your speech. For example, if you were to discuss the various departments in an organization, you might have the key points relating to each department on a separate page of your flip chart. As you discussed the advertising department, you would show the advertising department chart. When you moved on to discuss the personnel department, you would flip to the chart dealing with personnel. You may find this device useful if you have a large number of word charts that you want to have easy control over. Make sure that the flip chart is positioned so that everyone in the audience can see it clearly and that the folding legs are positioned securely so it doesn't collapse when you flip the first page. Make sure you write large enough so that the people in the back can read your material without straining their eyes.

Flip charts also are especially useful for recording ideas at small group meetings. Unlike the chalkboard, the flip chart enables you to retain a written record of the meeting; should you need to, you can easily review the group's contributions.

Slides and transparency projections are helpful for showing a series of visuals that may be of very different types; for example, photographs, illustrations, charts, or tables. The slides can easily be created with many popular computer programs (see "Computer-Assisted Presentations" on page 326). To produce actual 35mm slides, you'll need considerable lead time; be sure to build this into your preparation time.

If you don't have access to a slide projector or don't have the lead time needed to construct slides, consider somewhat less sophisticated transparencies. You can create your visual in any of the word-processing or spreadsheet programs you normally use and probably can find a printer that will enable you to print transparencies. Another alternative is to use a copier that will produce transparencies.

When using any presentation aid, but especially with slides and transparencies, make sure that you have the proper equipment; for example, a projector, a table, a working outlet nearby, control over the lighting in the room, and whatever else you'll need to have the audience see your projections clearly.

An advantage of transparencies is that you can write on the transparencies (and on slides in computer presentations, as we discuss later) while you're speaking. You can circle important items, underline key terms, and draw lines connecting different terms.

Videotapes may serve a variety of purposes in public speaking. Basically, you have two options with videotapes. First, you can tape a scene from a film or television show with your VCR and show it at the appropriate time in your speech. Thus, for example, you might videotape examples of sexism in television sitcoms, violence on television talk shows, or types of transitions used in feature films and show these excerpts during your speech. As you can see, however, this type of video takes a great deal of time and preparation, so if you are going to use such excerpts you must plan well in advance. As a teacher, I use a variety of films and film excerpts to illustrate breakdowns in interpersonal communication, studies in which experimenters teach animals to communicate, aspects of nonverbal communication, and various other topics.

Second, you can create your own video with a simple camcorder. One student created a video of ethnic store signs to illustrate the "interculturalization" of the city. With the help (and agreement to be videotaped) of a few friends, another student created a three-minute video of religious holidays as celebrated by members of different religions and carefully coordinated each segment with her discussion of the relevant holiday.

In using videotapes do make sure that they don't occupy too much of your speaking time; after all, your main objective is to learn the principles of public speaking.

Handouts, or printed materials that you distribute to members of the audience, are especially helpful in explaining complex material and also in providing listeners with a permanent record of some aspect of your speech. Handouts are also useful for presenting information that you want your audience to refer to throughout the speech. Handouts encourage listeners to take notes, especially if you leave enough white space or even provide a specific place for notes—and this keeps them actively involved in your presentation. Handouts also reward the audience by giving them something for their attendance and attention. A variety of handouts can be easily prepared with many of the computer presentation packages that we'll consider in the last section of this unit.

You can distribute handouts at the beginning of, during, or after your speech; but realize that whichever system you use has both pros and cons. If you distribute materials before or during your speech, you run the risk of your listeners' reading the handout and not concentrating on your speech. On the other hand, if the listeners are getting the information you want to communicate—even if primarily from the handout—that isn't too bad. And, in a way, handouts allow listeners to process the information at their own pace.

You can encourage your audience to listen to you when you want them to and to look at the handout when you want them to by simply telling them: "Look at the graph on the top of page two of the handout; it summarizes recent census figures on immigration" or "We'll get back to the handout in a minute; now, however, I want to direct your attention to this next slide [or the second argument]."

If you distribute your handouts at the end of the speech, they will obviously not interfere with your presentation—but they may not be read at all. After all, listeners might reason, they heard the speech; why bother going through the handout? To counteract this very natural tendency, you might include additional material in the handout and mention this to your audience, saying something like "This handout contains all the slides shown here and three additional slides that provide economic data for Thailand, Cambodia, and Vietnam, which I didn't have time to cover. When you look at the data, you'll see that they mirror exactly the data provided in my talk on the other countries." When you provide additional information on your handout, it's more likely that it will get looked at and thus provide the reinforcement you want.

Preparing Presentation Aids

Once you have the idea of an aid you want to present and you know the medium you want to use, direct your attention to preparing your aid so it can best serve your purposes. Make sure that it adds clarity to your speech, that it's appealing to the listeners, and that it's culturally sensitive.

Clarity is the most important test of all. Make sure that the aid is clearly relevant—in the minds of your listeners—to your speech purpose. It may be attractive, well-designed, and easy to read, but if the listeners don't understand how it relates to your speech, leave it at home. Make sure your aid is large enough to be seen by everyone from all parts of the room. Use typefaces that are easy to see and easy to read. Use colors that will make

your message instantly clear; light colors on dark backgrounds or dark colors on light backgrounds provide the best contrast and seem to work best for most purposes. Be careful of using yellow, which is often difficult to see, especially if there's glare from the sun.

- Use direct phrases (not complete sentences); use bullets to highlight your points or your support (see Figure 16.2). Just as you phrase your propositions in parallel style, phrase your bullets in parallel style, usually by using the same part of speech (for example, all nouns or all infinitive phrases). And make sure that the meaning or relevance of any graphic is immediately clear. If it isn't, explain it.

- Use the aid to highlight a few essential points; don't clutter it with too much information. Four bullets on a slide or chart, for example, is about as much information as you should include. Make sure the aid is simple rather than complicated; like your verbal message, the aid should be instantly intelligible.

Presentation aids work best when they're *appealing*. Sloppy, poorly designed, or worn-out aids will detract from the purpose they are intended to serve. Presentation aids should be attractive enough to engage the attention of the audience—but not so attractive that they're distracting. The almost nude body draped across a car may be effective in selling underwear but will probably detract if your object is to explain the profit-and-loss statement of Intel Corporation.

Make sure your presentation aids are *culturally sensitive* and are easily interpreted by people from other cultures. For example, symbols that you may assume are universal may not be known by persons new to a culture. When speaking to international audiences, be sure to use universal symbols or explain those that are not universal. Be careful that your icons don't reveal an ethnocentric bias. For example, using the American dollar sign to symbolize "wealth" might be quite logical in your public speaking class but might be interpreted as ethnocentric if used with an audience of international visitors. Also, the meanings that different colors communicate vary greatly from one culture to another, as described in Unit 8. Revisit that unit, and particularly Table 8.3, to make sure that the colors you use don't send messages that you don't want to send. A self-test, "Can you distinguish universal from culture-specific icons?" at www.ablongman.com/devito, 🖱 will help you to explore this topic further.

Using Presentation Aids

Keep the following guidelines clearly in mind when using presentation aids.

- Know your aids intimately. Be sure you know in what order they are to be presented and how you plan to introduce them. Know exactly what goes where and when.

- Test the aids before using them. When testing the presentation aids ahead of time, be certain that they can be seen easily from all parts of the room.

- Rehearse your speech with the presentation aids incorporated into the presentation. Practice your actual movements with the aids you'll use. If you're going to use a chart, how will you use it? Will it stand by itself? Can you tape it somewhere? Do you have tape with you?

- Integrate your aids seamlessly into your speech. Just as a verbal example should flow naturally into the text and seem an integral part of the speech, so should the presentation aid. It should appear not as an afterthought but as an essential part of the speech.

- Don't talk to your aid. Both you and the aid should be focused on the audience. Know your aids so well that you can point to what you want without breaking eye contact with your audience. Or, at most, break audience eye contact for only a few seconds at a time.

- Use the aid when it's relevant: Show it when you want the audience to concentrate on it, then remove it. If you don't remove it, the audience's attention may remain focused on the visual when you want them to focus on your next point.

Computer-Assisted Presentations

There are a variety of presentation software packages available: PowerPoint, Corel Presentations, and Lotus Freelance are among the most popular and are very similar in what they do and how they do it. Figure 16.2 illustrates what a set of slides might look like; the slides are built around a speech outline that we'll discuss in Unit 17 and were constructed in PowerPoint, though a similar slide show could be produced with most presentation software programs. Also, realize that you can easily import photographs and have slides of these inserted into your slide show; or you can add video clips. As you review Figure 16.2, try to visualize how you would use a slide show in presenting your next speech.

Ways of Using Presentation Package Software.

Computer presentation software enables you to produce a variety of aids; the software will produce what you want. For example, you can construct slides on your computer, save them on a disk, and then have 35mm slides developed from the disk. To do this you need access to a slide printer—or you can send your files out (you can do this via modem) to a lab specializing in converting electronic files into 35mm slides. There may be a slide printer at your school, so check there first. Similarly, your local office supply store or copy shop, such as Staples, OfficeMax, or Kinko, may have exactly the services you need.

Or you can create your slides and then show them on your computer screen. If you are speaking to a very small group, it may be possible to have your listeners gather around your computer as you speak. With larger audiences, however, you'll need a computer projector or an LCD projection panel. Assuming that you have a properly equipped computer in the classroom, you can copy your entire presentation to a floppy disk and bring it with you on the day of the speech.

Computer presentation software also enables you to print out a variety of handouts:

- the slides shown during your speech as well as additional slides that you may not have time to include in the speech, but which you nevertheless want your listeners to look at when they read your handout

- the slides plus speaker's notes, the key points that you made as you showed each of the slides (the function that was used to produce Figure 16.2)

- the slides plus places for listeners to write notes next to each of them

- an outline of your talk

- any combination of the above

Overhead transparencies can also be created from your computer slides. To make overheads on many printers and most copiers, simply substitute

Slide 1

Speech title

This first slide introduces the topic with the title of the speech. Follow the general rules for titling your speech: Keep it short, provocative, and focused on your audience. If you put a graphic on this page, make sure that it doesn't detract from your title. What other graphics might work well here?

Slide 2

The thesis of the speech

You may or may not want to identify your thesis directly right at the beginning of your speech. Consider the arguments for and against identifying your thesis—both cultural and strategic—and the suggestions for when and how to state the thesis on page 315. As a listener, do you prefer it when speakers state their thesis right at the beginning? Or do you prefer it when the thesis is only implied and left for you to figure out?

Slide 3

Attention-getting device; corresponds to the Introduction's "I A"

This slide gains attention by relating the topic directly to the audience; it answers the listener's obvious question, "Why should I listen to this speech?"

Slide 4

S-A-T connection; corresponds to the Introduction's "II A–B"

This slide connects the speaker, the audience, and the topic. Because you talk about yourself in this part of your speech, some speakers may prefer to eliminate a verbal slide and use a graphic or a photo. Another alternative is to include your S-A-T connection with the previous attention-getting slide.

Slide 5

Orientation; corresponds to the Introduction's "III A–D"

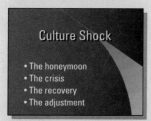

In this slide you give your orientation by identifying your major propositions. These four bullets will become your four major propositions.

Slide 6

First major proposition; corresponds to the Body's "I A"

This is your first major proposition and you'd introduce it, perhaps, by saying, "The honeymoon occurs first." If you want your audience to keep track of the stage number, you could use numbers in your slide; for example, "1. The Honeymoon" or "Stage 1, The Honeymoon." The graphic of the heart is meant to associate culture shock with good times and a romance-like experience. As a listener, would you prefer the speaker to explain this graphic or say nothing about it?

Figure 16.2

A Slide Show Speech

(continued)

Slide 7

Second major proposition; corresponds to the Body's "II A–B"

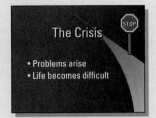

This is your second proposition and follows the previous slide in format. Again, a graphic is used. Can you think of a better graphic?

Slide 8

Third major proposition; corresponds to the Body's "III A–B"

This is your third major proposition and again follows the format of the previous two slides.

Slide 9

Fourth major proposition; corresponds to the Body's "IV A–B"

This is your fourth major proposition. As noted in the text, the sound of applause is programmed to come on with this slide, reinforcing the idea that we do adjust to this shock. Examine the sound effects you have available; what other sound effects would you use in this speech?

Slide 10

Summary; corresponds to the Conclusion's "I A–D"

This is your summary of your four major propositions; notice that it's the same as your orientation (Slide 5). This slide violates the general rule to use graphics in moderation. What do you think of the repetition of graphics? Do you think they add reinforcement? Do they detract from the verbal message?

Slide 11

Motivation; corresponds to the Conclusion's "II A–B"

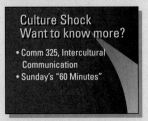

This part of the summary ideally motivates your listeners to pursue the topic in more detail.

Slide 12

Closure; corresponds to the Conclusion's "III"

This slide is intended to wrap up the speech—it contains the title and two graphics that will support the speaker's concluding statement: "By knowing about culture shock you'll be in a better position to deal with it at school and on the job." Notice that the conclusion is tied to the introduction by a similarity in font and text color; it helps signal that this is the last slide and the end of the speech.

Figure 16.2 *continued*

transparency paper for computer or copy paper. If you create your slides with a computer presentation package, you'll be able to produce professional-looking transparencies.

Suggestions for Using Presentation Software.

The templates and the suggestions of the program "Wizards" will parallel the suggestions offered here. Nevertheless, it's important to understand the qualities of effective slides in case you want to make changes in the suggested formats or even want to start from scratch.

In developing your slides, strive for clarity and consistency. For example, choose typeface styles, sizes, and colors that clearly distinguish the major propositions from the supporting materials. At the same time, use a consistent combination of fonts, colors, backgrounds, and graphics throughout your slides to give your presentation unity.

Use color (of type and background) and graphics sparingly. Remember that clarity is your goal; you want your audience to remember your ideas and not just the fact that all your slides were red, white, and blue. Likewise, too many graphics will distract your audience's attention from your verbal message. Also, be sure to choose graphics that support your tone. If your speech is on a serious topic, then the graphics (and photographs or illustrations) should contribute to this tone. Also, try to use graphics that are consistent with one another; generally it's better to use all shadow figures or all stick figures or all Victorian images than to mix them.

Generally, put one complete thought on a slide. Don't try to put too many words on one slide; use a few words on each slide, and expand on these during your speech. Try not to use more than two levels of thought in a slide—a major statement and two to four subordinate phrases (bulleted) are about all you can put on one slide. Avoid using subheads of subheads of subheads. Generally, use a sans-serif type (more attention-getting) for headings and a serif type (easier to read) for text (see Table 16.1 on page 330).

A good guideline to follow in designing your slides is to give all items in your outline that have the same level heads (for example, all the Roman numeral heads) the same typeface, size, and color throughout your presentation. Similarly, use the same font for all the A, B, C subheads, and so on. This will help your listeners follow the organization of your speech. Notice that this principle is followed

for the most part in the slides in Figure 16.2. It's broken in one case: The introduction and conclusion are set apart by being in a color and typeface different from the rest of the slides.

Consider using graphs, charts, and tables; you have a tremendous variety of graph and chart types (for example, pie and bar graphs and cumulative charts) and tables to choose from. If you are using presentation software that's part of a suite, then you'll find it especially easy to import files from your word processor or spreadsheet.

If there's a question-and-answer period following your speech, consider preparing a few extra slides to support responses to questions you anticipate being asked. Then when someone asks you a predicted question, you can say: "I anticipated that someone might ask that question; it raises an important issue. The data I've been able to find are presented in this chart." You then show the slide and explain it more fully. This is surely going the extra mile, but it can easily make your speech a real standout.

Use transitions wisely. Just as verbal transitions help you move from one part of your speech to another, presentational transitions help you move from one slide to the next with the desired effect—for example, blinds folding from left or right or top or bottom, or a quick fade.

Generally, consistency works best. Don't try to use too many different transitions in the same talk; it will detract attention from what you are saying. Generally, use the same transitions for all the slides in a single presentation. You might vary this a bit by, say, having the last slide introduced by a somewhat different transition; but any more variation is likely to work against the listeners' focusing on your message. In choosing transitions select one that's consistent with your speech purpose; don't use a frivolous black-and-yellow checkerboard transition in a speech on child abuse, for example.

Consider using sound effects with your transitions; but again, go easy. Overdoing it is sure to make your speech seem carelessly put together. In the slides in Figure 16.2, I programmed "applause" (one of the readily available sound effects) to come on as Slide 9—"The Adjustment"—comes on. As you read through Figure 16.2, you may find additional places where sound could be used effectively.

Build effects with bulleted items can help you focus your listeners' attention. For example, you can have each bulleted phrase fly from the top of the screen into its position; with the next mouse click,

TABLE 16.1 Some Typefaces

You have an enormous number of typefaces to choose from. Generally, select typefaces that are easy to read and that are consistent in tone to the message of your speech.

Typeface	Comments
Palatino Century Schoolbook Garamond Times	Serif typefaces retain some of the cursive strokes found in handwriting. The cursive stroke is illustrated especially in the *m* and *n*, which begin with a slight upsweep. Serif styles are easy to read and useful for blocks of text.
Helvetica Bauhaus Avant Garde Futura	Sans-serif typefaces (a style that is more bold and doesn't include the serif or upsweep) are useful for titles and headings but make reading long text difficult.
Serif Gothic Black **STENCIL** **Gill Sans Ultra Bold**	These extremely bold typefaces are tempting to use; but, as you can see, they're not easy to read. They're most appropriate for short titles.
Akzidenz Grotesk BETON COMPRESSED BOLD Franklin Gothic	These compressed typefaces are useful when you have to fit a lot of text into a small space. They are, however, difficult to read and so should generally be avoided (or at least used sparingly) in slides. It would be better to use an easier-to-read typeface and spread out the text over additional slides.
CASTELLAR ROSEWOOD JAZZ ASHLEY INLINE Linotext	Decorative styles like these, although difficult to read for extended text, make great headings or titles. Be careful, however, that the originality of your typefaces doesn't steal attention away from your message.
Mistral *Brush Script* *Freestyle Script* *Pepita*	Script typefaces are interesting and will give your presentation a personal look, as if you wrote it longhand. But they'll be difficult to read. If you're going to read the slides aloud word for word, then typefaces that are a bit more difficult to read may still be used with considerable effect.

the second bullet flies into position. Or you can have your bullets slide in from right to left or from left to right, and so on.

In listing four or five bulleted items, consider the value of hiding or dimming the previous bullet as you introduce the next one. Making the previous bullet disappear or fade into a lighter color when the next bullet appears further enables you to focus your listeners' attention on exactly the point you're discussing. Do be careful that you allow the audience time to read each bullet; otherwise they'll be frustrated when it disappears.

Use the spellchecker. You don't want to show professional-looking slides with misspellings; it can ruin your credibility and seriously damage the impact of your speech.

What other suggestions would you offer to a speaker giving a speech with a slide show?

STEP 6: ORGANIZE YOUR SPEECH

When you organize your ideas, you derive a variety of benefits. First, organization will help you prepare the speech. For example, as you organize your speech you'll be able to see if you have adequately and fairly supported each of your main points and if you are devoting approximately equal time to each of your main propositions. Organization also makes your speech easy to understand and remember. When you organize perhaps 30 pieces of specific information (such as statistics, statement of thesis, examples, illustrations, testimonials, transitions) into, say, three or four or five chunks, you're making it much easier for the audience to remember what you want them to remember. An added bonus here is that organization will also help you remember your speech. You'll be less likely to forget a carefully organized speech than you would a disorganized one. Organization will also contribute to your credibility. The audience is more likely to see the well-organized speaker as more competent, more knowledgeable, and more in control of the information in the speech.

Once you've identified the major propositions you wish to include in your speech, you need to devote attention to how you'll arrange these propositions in the body of your speech. When you follow a clearly identified organizational pattern, your listeners will be able to see your speech as a whole

and will be able to grasp the connections and relationships among your various pieces of information. Should they have a momentary lapse in attention—as they surely will at some point in just about every speech—you will be able to refocus their attention.

Consider each of the following organizational patterns in terms of the topics to which it's most applicable and the ways in which you can arrange your main points and supporting materials. The introduction, conclusion, and transitions are considered in depth under Step 7 in this unit. The mechanical aspects of outlining and additional guidance in preparing the outline are presented in Unit 17.

Temporal Pattern

Organization on the basis of some temporal (time) relationship is a pattern listeners will find easy to follow. Generally, when you use a *temporal pattern*, you organize your speech into two, three, or four major parts, beginning with the past and working up to the present or the future—or beginning with the present or the future and working back to the past.

The temporal (sometimes called "chronological") pattern is especially appropriate for informative speeches in which you wish to describe events or processes that occur over time. It's also useful when you wish to tell a story, demonstrate how something works, or examine the steps involved in some process. The events leading up to the Civil War, the steps toward a college education, or the history of writing would all be appropriate for temporal patterning. A speech on the development of language in the child might be organized in a temporal pattern and could be broken down something like this:

I. Babbling occurs around the 5th month.
II. Lallation occurs around the 6th month.
III. Echolalia occurs around the 9th month.
IV. "Communication" occurs around the 12th month.

Spatial Pattern

You can also organize your main points on the basis of space. The *spatial pattern* is especially useful when you wish to describe objects or places. Like the temporal pattern, it's an organizational pattern that listeners will find easy to follow as you progress—from top to bottom, from left to right, from inside to outside, or from east to west, for example. The structure of a place, an object, or even an animal is easily placed into a spatial pattern. You might describe the layout of a hospital, a school, or a skyscraper, or perhaps even the structure of a dinosaur, with a spatial pattern of organization.

Topical Pattern

When your topic conveniently divides itself into subdivisions, each of which is clear and approximately equal in importance, the *topical pattern* is most useful. A speech on important cities of the world might be organized into a topical pattern, as might be speeches on problems facing the college graduate, great works of literature, the world's major religions, and the like. The topical pattern would be an obvious one for organizing a speech on the powers of the government. The topic itself divides into three parts: legislative, executive, and judicial. A sample outline might look like this:

I. The legislative branch is controlled by Congress.
II. The executive branch is controlled by the president.
III. The judicial branch is controlled by the courts.

Problem–Solution Pattern

The *problem–solution pattern* is especially useful in persuasive speeches in which you want to convince the audience that a problem exists and that your solution would solve or lessen the problem. Let's say that you believe that jury awards for damages have gotten out of hand. You may want to persuade your audience, then, that jury awards for damages should be limited. A problem–solution pattern might be appropriate here. In the first part of your speech, you'd identify the problem(s) created by these large awards; in the second part, you'd propose the solution. A sample outline for such a speech might look something like this:

I. Jury awards for damages are out of control. [the general problem]
   A. These awards increase insurance rates. [a specific problem]
   B. These awards increase medical costs. [a second specific problem]
   C. These awards place unfair burdens on business. [a third specific problem]
II. Jury awards need to be limited. [the general solution]
   A. Greater evidence should be required before a case can be brought to trial. [a specific solution]
   B. Part of the award should be turned over to the state. [a second specific solution]
   C. Realistic estimates of financial damage must be used. [a third specific solution]

Cause–Effect/Effect–Cause Pattern

Similar to the problem–solution pattern is the cause–effect or effect–cause pattern. This pattern is useful in persuasive speeches in which you want to convince your audience of the causal connection existing between two events or elements. In the *cause–effect pattern* you divide the speech into two major sections: causes and effects. For example, a speech on the reasons for highway accidents or birth defects might lend itself to a cause–effect pattern. Here you might first consider, say, the causes of highway accidents or birth defects, then turn to some of the effects; for example, the number of deaths, the number of accidents, and so on.

Or suppose you wanted to demonstrate the causes for the increase in AIDS in your state. In this case you might use an effect–cause pattern that might look something like this:

I. AIDS is increasing. [general effect]
   A. AIDS is increasing among teenagers. [a specific effect]
   B. AIDS is increasing among IV drug users. [a second specific effect]
   C. AIDS is increasing among women. [a third specific effect]
II. Three factors contribute to this increase. [general causal statement]
   A. Teenagers are ignorant about how the HIV virus is transmitted. [a specific cause]
   B. IV drug users exchange tainted needles. [a second specific cause]
   C. Women are not practicing safe sex. [a third specific cause]

As you can see from this example, this type of speech is often combined with the problem–solution type. For example, after identifying the causes, the speaker might then treat the causes as problems and offer solutions for each problem/cause (for example: education for teens, free needle exchange programs, and education for men and women).

The Motivated Sequence

The **motivated sequence** is an organizational pattern in which you arrange your information so as to motivate your audience to respond positively to your purpose (McKerrow, Gronbeck, Ehninger, & Monroe, 2000). In contrast to the previous organizational patterns, which provided ways of organizing the main ideas in the body of the speech, the motivated sequence is a pattern for organizing the entire speech. Here the speech (introduction, body, and conclusion) is divided into five parts or steps: (1) attention, (2) need, (3) satisfaction, (4) visualization, and (5) action. An extended discussion of "The Motivated Sequence" along with a sample annotated outline may be found at **www.ablongman.com/devito**.

1. The attention step makes the audience give you their undivided *attention*. If you execute this step effectively, your audience should be anxious and ready to hear what you have to say. You can gain audience attention through a variety of means; for example, asking a question (rhetorical or actual) or making reference to audience members. These methods are presented in the "Introduction" discussion in the Step 7 section of this unit.

2. In the second part of your speech, you establish that a *need* exists for some kind of change. The audience should feel that something has to be learned or something has to be done because of this demonstrated need.

3. You satisfy the need by presenting the answer or the solution to the need you demonstrated in step 2 of the motivated sequence. On the basis of this *satisfaction* step, the audience should now believe that what you are informing them about or persuading them to do will satisfy the need.

4. *Visualization* intensifies the audience's feelings or beliefs. In this step you take the people in the audience beyond the present time and place and enable them to imagine the situation as it would be if the need were satisfied as you suggested in step 3. You might, for example, demonstrate the benefits that people would receive if your ideas were put into operation—or perhaps demonstrate the negative effects that people would suffer if your plan were not put into operation.

5. Tell the audience what *action* they should take to ensure that the need (step 2) is satisfied (step 3) as visualized (step 4). Here you want to move the audience in a particular direction—for example, to contribute free time to read to the blind. You can accomplish this step by stating what the audience members should do, using a variety of supporting materials and logical, emotional, and ethical appeals.

Additional Organizational Patterns

The six patterns just considered are the most common and the most useful for organizing most public speeches. But there are other patterns that might be appropriate for different topics:

Structure–Function.   The *structure–function pattern* is useful in informative speeches in which you want to discuss how something is constructed (its structural aspects) and what it does (its functional aspects). This pattern might be useful, for example, in a speech to explain what an organization is and what it does, the parts of a university and how they operate, or the sensory systems of the body and their various functions. This pattern might also be useful in a discussion of the nature of a living organism: its anatomy (that is, its structures) and its physiology (that is, its functions).

Comparison and Contrast. Arranging your material in a *comparison-and-contrast pattern* is useful in informative speeches in which you want to analyze, for example, two different theories, proposals, departments, or products in terms of their similarities and differences. In this type of speech you would be concerned not only with explaining each theory or proposal but also with how they're similar and how they're different.

Pro and Con, Advantages and Disadvantages. The *pro-and-con pattern*, sometimes called the advantages–disadvantages pattern, is useful in inform-

ative speeches in which you want to explain objectively the advantages (pros) and the disadvantages (cons) of, say, a plan, method, or product.

Claim and Proof. The *claim-and-proof pattern* is especially useful in a persuasive speech in which you want to prove the truth or usefulness of a particular proposition. It's the pattern that you see frequently in trials: The prosecution claims that the defendant is guilty and that the proof is the varied evidence—for example, evidence that the defendant had a motive, the defendant had the opportunity, and the defendant had no alibi. In this pattern your speech would consist of two major parts. In the first part you'd explain your claim (tuition must not be raised, library hours must be expanded, courses in Caribbean studies must be instituted). In the sec-

UNDERSTANDING THEORY AND RESEARCH

Culture and Speech Organization

Members of low-context cultures (see Unit 3) are usually direct in their reactions to others. Other low-context culture members generally appreciate this directness. But directness may seem insulting, insensitive, or unnecessary to the high-context cultural member. Conversely, to the low-context person, the high-context cultural member may appear vague, underhanded, or dishonest in his or her reluctance to be explicit or to engage in communication that a low-context person would consider open and direct.

High-context cultures prefer indirectness. Effective speakers seem to lead the audience in the general direction of the thesis but not explicitly and directly to it—at least, not as directly as would low-context culture members.

Speakers in Japan, to take one well-researched example, need to be careful lest they make their point too obvious or too direct and thereby insult the audience. Speakers in Japan are expected to lead their listeners to the conclusion through example, illustration, and various other indirect means (Lustig & Koester, 1999).

In the United States, in contrast, speakers are encouraged to be explicit and direct; to tell the audience, for example, exactly what the speaker wants them to do (see the discussion under Step 4 in this unit on focusing audience attention on the thesis).

Similarly, in the United States each major proposition of a speech or written composition should be developed by itself. Only when it's fully developed and finalized does the speaker or writer move on to the next point. Hindi culture, however, is less rigid and allows for many ideas' being considered in the same paragraph of an essay or in the same part of a speech (Lustig & Koester, 1999).

Working with Theories and Research. *As a listener, what type of organization do you prefer? For example, do you prefer a speaker who is direct or indirect? Do you prefer a speaker who clearly separates the major propositions or one who considers several propositions together?*

ond part you'd offer your evidence or proof as to why, for example, tuition must not be raised.

Multiple Definition. The *multiple-definition pattern* is often useful for explaining specific concepts: What is a born-again Christian? What is a scholar? What is multiculturalism? In this pattern each major heading consists of a different type of definition or way of looking at the concept. A variety of definition types is discussed in Unit 18.

Who? What? Why? Where? When? The *5W pattern* is the pattern of the journalist and is useful when you wish to report or explain an event such as a robbery, political coup, war, ceremony, or trial. In this pattern you'd have five major parts to the body of your speech, each dealing with the answers to one of these five questions.

STEP 7: CONSTRUCT YOUR INTRODUCTION, CONCLUSION, AND TRANSITIONS

Now that you have the body of your speech organized, devote your attention to the introduction, conclusion, and transitions that will hold the parts of your speech together.

Introduction

Begin collecting suitable material for your *introduction* as you prepare the entire speech, but wait until all the other parts are completed before you put the introduction together. In this way you'll be better able to determine which elements should be included and which should be eliminated.

Together with your general appearance and your nonverbal messages, the introduction gives your audience its first impression of you and your speech. Your introduction sets the tone for the rest of the speech; it tells your listeners what kind of a speech they'll hear.

Your introduction should serve three functions: It should gain attention, establish a speaker–audience–topic connection, and orient the audience as to what is to follow. Let's look at each of these functions and at the ways you can serve these functions.

Gain Attention

In your introduction, gain the attention of your audience and focus it on your speech topic. (Then, of course, maintain that attention throughout your speech). You can secure attention in numerous ways; here are just a few of them.

- Ask a question. Questions are effective because they are a change from declarative statements and call for an active response from listeners.

- Refer to audience members. Talking about the audience makes them perk up and pay attention, because you are involving them directly in your talk.

- Refer to recent happenings. Citing a previous speech, recent event, or prominent person currently making news helps you gain attention, because the audience is familiar with this current event and will pay attention to see how you are going to connect it to your speech topic.

- Use humor. A clever (and appropriate) anecdote is often useful in holding attention.

- Use an illustration or dramatic story. Much as we are drawn to soap operas, so are we drawn to illustrations and stories about people.

- Stress the importance of the topic. People pay attention to what they feel is important to them and ignore what seems unimportant or irrelevant. If your topic focuses on the interests of the audience, you might begin by referring directly to the audience.

- Use a presentation aid. Presentation aids are valuable because they are new and different. They engage our senses and thus our attention.

- Tell the audience to pay attention. A simple, "I want you to listen to this frightening statistic," or "I want you to pay particularly close attention to . . . ," used once or twice in a speech, will help gain audience attention.

- Use a quotation. Quotations are useful because the audience is likely to pay attention to the brief and clever remarks of someone they've heard of or read about. Do make sure, however, that the quotation relates directly to your topic.

- Cite a little-known fact or statistic. Little-known facts or statistics will help perk up an audience's attention. For example, headlines on unemployment statistics, crime in the schools, and political corruption sell newspapers because they gain attention.

Establish a Speaker–Audience–Topic Relationship

In addition to gaining attention, your introduction should establish connections among yourself as the speaker, the audience members, and your topic. Try to answer your listeners' inevitable question: Why should we listen to you speak on this topic? You can establish an effective speaker–audience–topic or S-A-T relationship in many different ways.

- Refer to others present. Not only will this help you to gain attention; it will also help you to establish a bond with the audience.

- Refer to the occasion. Often your speech will be connected directly with the occasion. By referring to the reason the audience has gathered, you can establish a connection between yourself, the audience, and the topic.

- Express your pleasure or interest in speaking.

- Establish your competence in the subject. Show the audience that you are really interested in and knowledgeable about the topic.

- Compliment the audience. Pay the people in the audience an honest and sincere compliment, and they will not only give you their attention but will also feel a part of your speech. In some cultures—those of Japan and Korea are good examples—the speaker is expected to compli-

MEDIA WATCH

PUBLIC RELATIONS

The field of public relations—communications designed to establish positive relationships between a corporation, agency, or similar group and the public—is very similar to advertising. Like advertising, public relations serves two major purposes: informing and persuading, with a clear emphasis on the latter (Folkerts & Lacy, 2001; Rodman, 2001). To accomplish these two purposes, public relations practitioners engage in a wide variety of activities:

▶ *Lobbying* to influence government officials or agencies to fund proposals, support nominees, or vote for or against upcoming bills.

▶ *Raising funds* for colleges, political candidates, charities, or public broadcasting stations.

▶ *Controlling crises* in an effort to repair potentially damaged images. For example, public relations people swing into action in cases of defective or problematic products—cars, dietary supplements, drugs—or when an organization is having financial problems.

▶ *Influencing public opinion,* to get voters to support a political candidate or initiative or to change their attitudes toward a variety of issues. Examples include abortion, campaign financing, gay rights, and a host of other issues you read about daily.

▶ *Establishing good relationships* between, say, a community and a company that wants to erect a mall in the neighborhood, between the commu-

nity and the police department, or between a company and the general public. Microsoft's donations to public education and to health organizations and the numerous corporate programs that support AIDS and cancer research, literacy efforts, college scholarships, and safe driving are good examples.

To get a better view of public relations, take a look at a variety of websites dealing with this area. Try, for example, **www.prsa.org** (the Public Relations Society of America, a professional accrediting agency), **www.prwatch.org** (the Center for Media and Democracy, an organization that monitors public relations efforts), and **www.bm.com** (Burson-Marsteller, currently the largest public relations firm in the United States). What can you learn about public relations from these websites?

Follow-Up. *Visualize yourself as a public relations professional whose job it is to raise funds for your college. What kinds of supporting materials would you use in, say, letters that you send to alumni? Or suppose you are in PR and your job is to reduce the mistrust that exists between the police department and a community. What kinds of supporting materials would you use in a speech to new police recruits? In a speech to community leaders?*

ment the audience. It's one of the essential parts of the introduction. Visitors from the United States who are speaking in a foreign country are often advised to compliment the country itself, its beauty, its culture.

- Express similarities with the audience. By stressing your own similarity with members of the audience, you create a relationship with them and become an "insider" instead of an "outsider."

Orient the Audience
The introduction should orient the audience in some way as to what is to follow in the body of the speech. Preview for the audience what you are going to say, as in "Tonight I'm going to discuss nuclear waste"; give a detailed preview, perhaps outlining your major propositions; or identify your goal by, for example, stating your thesis.

Conclusion

Your conclusion is especially important, because it's often the part of the speech that the audience remembers most clearly. It's your conclusion that in many cases determines what image of you is left in the minds of the audience. Devote special attention to this brief but crucial part of your speech. Let your conclusion serve three major functions: to summarize, motivate, and provide closure.

Summarize
The *summary* function is particularly important in an informative speech, less so in persuasive speeches or in speeches to entertain. You may summarize your speech in a variety of ways:

- Restate your thesis or purpose. In this type of brief summary, you restate the essential thrust of your speech, repeating your thesis or perhaps the goals you hoped to achieve.
- Restate the importance of the topic. Tell the audience again why your topic or thesis is so important.
- Restate your major propositions. Restate your thesis and the major propositions you used to support it.

Motivate
A second function of the conclusion—most appropriate in persuasive speeches—is to motivate the

people in the audience to do what you want them to do. In your conclusion you have the opportunity to give the audience one final push in the direction you wish them to take. Whether it's to buy stock, vote a particular way, or change an attitude, you can use the conclusion for a final *motivation*, a final appeal. Here are two excellent ways to motivate:

- Ask for a specific response. Specify what you want the audience to do after listening to your speech.
- Provide directions for future action. Spell out, most often in general terms, the direction you wish the audience to take.

Close
The third function of your conclusion is to provide *closure*. Often your summary will accomplish this, but in some instances it will prove insufficient. End your speech with a conclusion that is crisp and definite. Make the audience know that you have definitely and clearly ended. Some kind of wrap-up, some sort of final statement, is helpful in providing this feeling of closure. You may achieve closure through a variety of methods:

- Use a quotation. A quotation is often an effective means of providing closure.
- Refer to subsequent events. You may also achieve closure by referring to future events—events taking place either that day or soon afterwards.
- Refer back to the introduction. It's sometimes useful to connect your conclusion with your introduction.
- Pose a challenge or question. You may close your speech by leaving the audience with a provocative question to ponder or a challenge to consider. Or, you can pose a question and answer it by recapping your thesis and perhaps some of your major arguments or propositions.
- Thank the audience. Speakers frequently conclude their speeches by thanking the audience for their attention or for their invitation to address them.

Transitions

Transitions are words, phrases, or sentences that connect the various parts of your speech. They provide the audience with guideposts that help them

Mistakes in Introductions and Conclusions

I do not object to people looking at their watches when I am speaking. But I strongly object when they start shaking them to make sure they are still going.

—Lord William Norman Birkett

The introduction is perhaps the single most important part of every speech, so be especially careful to avoid the most common faults.

▶ In general, don't apologize. In much of the United States and western Europe, an apology is seen as an excuse for a lack of effectiveness. To apologize in your speech is therefore to encourage your audience to look for faults. In many other cultures (Japanese, Chinese, and Korean cultures are good examples), however, speakers are expected to begin with an apology. It's a way of complimenting the audience and placing them in a superior position. Speakers who don't apologize or act humbly may be seen as arrogant or as attempting to be superior to the audience.

▶ Avoid promising something that you will not in fact deliver. The speaker who promises to tell you how to solve your accounting problems, make a fortune in the stock market, or be the most popular person on campus, but who fails to deliver such insight, quickly loses credibility.

▶ Avoid gimmicks that gain attention but are irrelevant to the speech or inconsistent with your treatment of the topic. For example, slamming a book on the desk or telling a joke that bears no relation to your speech may accomplish the limited goal of gaining attention; but the audience will quickly see such behaviors as tricks designed to fool them into paying attention and will resent these tactics.

▶ Don't introduce your speech with such common but ineffective statements as "I'm really nervous, but here goes," "Before I begin my talk, I want to say . . . ," or "I hope I can remember everything I want to say." These statements will make your audience uncomfortable and will encourage them to focus on your delivery rather than on your message.

The conclusion, too, is an important part of your speech. Be careful to avoid its common problems:

▶ Don't introduce new material. You may, of course, give new expression to ideas covered in the body of the speech, but don't introduce new material. Instead, use your conclusion to reinforce what you've already said and to summarize.

▶ Don't dilute your position. Avoid being critical of your own material or your presentation. Saying, for example, "The information I presented is probably dated, but it was all I could find" or "I hope I wasn't too nervous" will detract from the credibility you've already established and may make the audience feel they've wasted their time listening to you.

▶ Don't drag out your conclusion. End crisply.

Thinking about Your Communicating @ Work

What other mistakes do you see speakers make when introducing and concluding their speeches? What advice would you give these speakers?

follow the development of your thoughts and arguments. Use transitions in at least the following places:

- between the introduction and the body of the speech
- between the body and the conclusion
- between the main points in the body of the speech

Here are the major transitional functions and some stylistic devices that you might use to serve these functions.

To announce the start of a major proposition or piece of evidence: First, . . ., A second argument . . ., A closely related problem . . ., If you want further evidence, look at . . ., Next . . ., Consider also . . ., An even more compelling argument . . ., My next point . . . .

To signal that you're drawing a conclusion from previously given evidence and argument: Thus, . . ., Therefore, . . ., So, as you can see . . ., It follows, then, that . . . .

To alert the audience to your introduction of a qualification or exception: But, . . ., However, also consider . . . .

To remind listeners of what has just been said and of its connection with another issue that will now be considered: In contrast to . . .; Consider also . . .; Not only . . . but also . . .; In addition to . . . we also need to look at . . .; Not only should we . . ., we should also . . . .

To signal the part of your speech you're approaching: By way of introduction . . .; In conclusion . . .; Now, let's discuss why we're here today . . .; So, what's the solution? What should we do?

To signal your organizational structure: I'll first explain the problems with jury awards and then propose a workable solution.

To summarize what you've already discussed. Consider using a special kind of transition: the internal summary. It's a statement that usually summarizes some major subdivision of your speech. Incorporate several internal summaries into your speech—perhaps working them into the transitions connecting, say, the major parts of your speech. An internal summary that also serves as a transition might look something like this:

> Inadequate recreational facilities, poor schooling, and a lack of adequate role models seem to be the major problems facing our youngsters. Each of these, however, can be remedied and even eliminated. Here's what we can do.

This brief passage reminds listeners of what they've just heard and previews what they'll hear next. The clear connection in their minds will fill in any gaps that may have been created through inattention, noise, and the like.

You can enhance your transitions by pausing between your transition and the next part of your speech. This will help the audience realize that a new part of your speech is coming. You might also take a step forward or to the side after saying your transition. This will also help to reinforce the movement from one part of your speech to another.

REFLECTIONS ON ETHICS IN HUMAN COMMUNICATION

Do the Ends Justify the Means?

A long-standing debate in ethics focuses on means and ends. Can worthy ends justify unsavory means? For example, would it be ethical for a public speaker to do things that would normally be considered unethical—say, making up statistics—if the end she or he hoped to achieve was a worthy one like keeping children from using drugs? Those taking an objective position would argue that ends cannot justify means; that a lie, for example, is always wrong, regardless of the specific situation. Those taking a subjective position would argue that at times the end does justify the means but that at other times it doesn't; it depends on the specific means and ends in question.

What would you do? *Here are several situations involving tensions between means and ends concerning the use of supporting materials. What would you do in each of these situations?*

1. *Would you make up statistics to support your point of view in a public speech if you knew that what you were advocating would benefit the audience?*

2. *Would you fabricate anecdotes and present these as having actually happened? In all likelihood, the incidents have happened; you just don't know that for sure. And they would make the speech really interesting.*

3. *You found a great quotation in a magazine and want to use it, but you don't know the qualifications of the author. Would it be acceptable to use a general qualification, like "a well-respected writer" or "an often quoted expert"?*

SUMMARY

This unit covered ways of supporting and organizing your main thoughts and introducing and concluding your speech.

1. Formulate the thesis of the speech. Develop your major propositions by asking relevant questions about this thesis.

2. Reinforce your major propositions with a variety of materials that support them. Suitable supporting materials include examples, narratives, testimony, statistics, and presentation aids as well as such devices as quotations, definitions, comparisons, statements of facts, and repetition and restatement.

3. Among the presentation aids you might consider are the actual object, models of the object, graphs, word charts, maps, people, photographs and illustrations, and tapes and CDs. These can be presented with a variety of media, for example, the chalkboard, chartboards, flip charts, slides and transparency projections, videotapes, and handouts. Presentation aids work best when they add clarity to your speech, are appealing to listeners, and are culturally sensitive.

4. Computer-assisted presentations such as PowerPoint, which have become extremely popular over the last few years, allow you to communicate lots of information in an interesting format, to print handouts to coordinate with your speech, and to create an outline and speaker's notes for your speech.

5. Organize the speech materials into a clear, easily identifiable thought pattern. Suitable organizing principles include temporal, spatial, topical, problem–solution, cause–effect/effect–cause, motivated sequence, structure–function, comparison-and-contrast, pro-and-con, claim-and-proof, multiple-definition, and who-what-why-where-when (5W) patterns.

6. Introductions should gain attention, establish a speaker–audience–topic (S-A-T) connection, and orient the audience as to what is to follow.

7. Conclusions should summarize the main ideas, provide a final motivation, and provide a crisp closing to the speech.

8. Transitions and internal summaries help connect and integrate the parts of the speech; they also help the listeners to better remember the speech.

KEY TERMS

thesis	narrative	presentation aid
proposition	testimony	temporal pattern
example	statistics	spatial pattern

topical pattern

problem–solution pattern

cause–effect pattern

motivated sequence

structure–function pattern

pro-and-con pattern

claim-and-proof pattern

comparison-and-contrast pattern

multiple-definition pattern

5W pattern

attention

speaker–audience–topic connection

orientation

summary

motivation

closure

transitions

THINKING CRITICALLY ABOUT

Supporting and Organizing Your Speech

1. What strategies of arrangement would you use if you were giving a pro-abortion rights speech to an antiabortion audience? What strategies would you use if you were giving a speech in favor of domestic partnership insurance to the assembled leaders of various gay rights organizations?

2. Jamie, a student at a community college in Texas, wants to give a speech on the cruelty of cockfighting. Most people in the predominantly Hispanic audience come from Mexico, where cockfighting is a legal and popular sport. Among the visuals Jamie's considering are extremely vivid photographs of cocks literally torn to shreds by their opponents, which have razor blades strapped to their feet. Would you advise Jamie to use these photographs if the audience were, say, moderately in favor of cockfighting? What if it were moderately against cockfighting? What general principle underlies your recommendations?

3. Visit one of the websites for quotations; for example, try **http://www.columbia.edu/acis/bartleby/ bartlett** (Barlett's Quotations), **http://us.imdb. com/** (a database of quotations from films), or **http://isleuth.com/quote.html** (a combined reference of different collections of quotations). Select a quotation suitable for use with the slide show of the speech on culture shock (Figure 16.2) and explain how you would use this on a new slide or on one of the 12 presented in the figure.

4. Shana wants to illustrate the rise and fall in the prices of 12 stocks over the last 10 years. She wants to argue that her investment club (an audience of 16 members who are active participants in the club's investments) should sell 3 of the stocks and keep the other 9. This is the first time Shana will be using visual aids, and she needs advice on what types of aids might best serve her purpose. What suggestions do you have for Shana?

5. Dave wants to set up a system of folders so he can conveniently store all the information he collects for his next three speeches, all of which will be built around the general topic of suicide. The first speech will deal with cultural views of suicide, the second will examine the current laws governing doctor-assisted suicides, and third will be a persuasive speech on doctor-assisted suicides. Dave wants to store all his outlines, research, speech critique forms, and anything else in a series of folders, which he's heard about but doesn't really know how to use. What advice can you give Dave to help him organize his speech folders? (The assumption here is that these are computer "folders," but physical folders would also work, though not as efficiently.)

6. Prepare an introduction and a conclusion to a hypothetical speech on one of the topics listed below, making sure that you gain attention, establish an S-A-T connection, and orient the audience in your introduction and that you review the speech's main points, motivate your audience, and provide closure in your conclusion. Be prepared to explain the methods you used to accomplish each of these functions.

   - Proficiency in a foreign language should be required of all college graduates.
   - All killing of wild animals should be declared illegal.
   - Properties owned by churches and charitable institutions should be taxed.
   - Suicide and its assistance by qualified medical personnel should be legalized.
   - Gambling should be legalized by all states.
   - College athletics should be abolished.
   - Tenure for college professors should be abolished.
   - Maximum sentences should be imposed even for first offenders of the drug laws.
   - Alcoholic beverages should be banned from campus.
   - Abortion should be declared illegal.

7. Prepare and deliver a two-minute speech in which you do one of the following:

- explain how you'd outline a speech on the geography of the United States, the structure of a table lamp, the need for improved sex education on campus, or the reasons why class members should contribute to UNICEF
- tell a personal story to illustrate a specific point, being sure to follow the suggestions offered in this unit
- explain a print ad that relies on statistics and show how the advertiser uses statistics to make a point
- select an advertisement and analyze it in terms of the motivated sequence
- describe the events portrayed in a recently seen television program, using a temporal pattern
- discuss a recent newspaper editorial or op-ed letter, using a problem–solution or cause–effect pattern
- explain how television commercials get your attention
- describe the introductions and conclusions used on television talk shows or on news programs
- explain a print ad that contains a visual and explain how the visual and the text complement each other

UNIT 17
Style and Delivery in Public Speaking

Unit Contents

Here the last three steps in public speaking are discussed. In this unit you'll learn

▶ the principles of outlining, style, and rehearsal and delivery

▶ how you can outline your speech so that an audience can easily follow it and remember it, word it for clarity and persuasiveness, and rehearse and deliver it for maximum impact

STEP 8: OUTLINE YOUR SPEECH

The outline is a blueprint for your speech; it lays out the elements of the speech and their relationship to one another. With this blueprint in front of you, you can see at a glance all the elements of organization—the functions of the introduction and conclusion, the transitions, the major propositions and their relationship to the thesis and purpose, and the adequacy of the supporting materials. And, like a blueprint for a building, the outline enables you to spot weaknesses that might otherwise go undetected.

Begin outlining when you first begin constructing your speech. In this way you'll take the best advantage of one of the major functions of an outline—to tell you where change is needed. Change and alter the outline as necessary at every stage of the speech construction process.

Outlines may be extremely detailed or extremely general. But because you're now in a learning environment whose objective is to make you a more proficient public speaker, a detailed full-sentence outline will serve best. The more detail you put into the outline, the easier it will be for you to examine the parts of the speech for all the qualities and characteristics that make a speech effective.

Constructing the Outline

After you've completed your research and mapped out an organizational plan for your speech, put this plan (this blueprint) on paper. Construct a "preparation outline" of your speech, using the following guidelines.

Preface the Outline with Identifying Data.
Before you begin the outline proper, identify the general and specific purposes as well as your thesis. This prefatory material should look something like this:

General Purpose: To inform.

Specific Purpose: To inform my audience of four major functions of the mass media.

Thesis: The mass media serve four major functions.

These identifying notes are not part of your speech proper. They're not, for example, mentioned in your oral presentation. Rather, they're guides to the preparation of the speech and the outline. They're like road signs to keep you going in the right direction and to signal when you've gone off course. One additional bit of identifying data should preface the preface: the title of your speech.

Outline the Introduction, Body, and Conclusion as Separate Units.
The introduction, body, and conclusion of the speech, although intimately connected, should be labeled separately and should be kept distinct in your outline. Like the preliminary identifying data, these labels are not spoken to the audience but are further guides to your preparation.

By keeping the introduction, body, and conclusion separate, you'll be able to see at a glance if they do in fact serve the functions you want them to serve. You'll be able to see where further amplification and support are needed. In short, you'll be able to see where there are problems and where repair is necessary.

At the same time, do make sure that you examine and see the speech as a whole—how the introduction leads to the body and the conclusion summarizes your propositions and brings your speech to a close.

Insert Transitions.
Insert [using square brackets, like these] transitions between the introduction and the body, the body and the conclusion, the major propositions of the body, and wherever else you think they might be useful.

Append a List of References.
Some instructors require that you append a list of references to your speeches. If this is requested, then do so at the end of the outline or on a separate page. Some instructors require that only sources cited in the speech be included in the list of references, whereas others

require that the full list of sources consulted be provided (those mentioned in the speech as well as those not mentioned).

Your research and references will prove most effective with your audience if you carefully integrate them into the speech. It will count for little if you consulted the latest works by the greatest authorities but never mention this to your audience. So, when appropriate, weave into your speech the source material you've consulted. In your outline, refer to the source material by author's name, date, and page in parentheses and then provide the complete citation in your list of references.

In your actual speech a source citation might be phrased something like this:

> According to John Naisbitt, author of the nationwide best-seller *Megatrends*, the bellwether states are California, Florida, Washington, Colorado, and Connecticut.

Regardless of what specific sourcing system is required (find out before you prepare your outline), make certain to include all sources of information, not just written materials. Personal interviews, information derived from course lectures, and data learned from television should all be included in your list of references.

Use a Consistent Set of Symbols. The following is the standard, accepted sequence of symbols for outlining:

    I.
        A.
            1.
                a.
                    (1)
                        (b)

Begin the introduction, the body, and the conclusion with Roman numeral I. Treat each of the three major parts as a complete unit.

Use Visual Aspects to Reflect the Organizational Pattern. Use proper and clear indentation. The outlining function of word-processing programs has many of these suggestions built into them.

Not this:

    I. Television caters to the lowest possible intelligence.
    II. Talk shows illustrate this.
    III. "General Hospital"

This:

    I. Television caters to the lowest possible intelligence.
        A. Talk shows illustrate this.
            1. *The Sally Jessy Raphael Show*
            2. *The Ricki Lake Show*
            3. *The Jerry Springer Show*
        B. Soap operas illustrate this.
            1. "As the World Turns"
            2. "General Hospital"
            3. "The Young and the Restless"

Use One Discrete Idea per Symbol. If your outline is to reflect the organizational pattern structuring the various items of information, use just one discrete idea per symbol. Compound sentences are sure giveaways that you have not limited each item to a single idea. Also, be sure that each item is discrete; that is, that it does not overlap with any other item. Instead of the overlapping "Education might be improved if teachers were better trained and if students were better motivated," break this statement into two propositions: "I. Education would be improved if teachers were better trained" and "II. Education would be improved if students were better motivated."

Use Complete Declarative Sentences. Phrase your ideas in the outline in complete declarative sentences rather than as questions or as phrases. This will further assist you in examining the essential relationships. It's much easier, for example, to see if one item of information supports another if both are phrased in the declarative mode. If one is a question and one is a statement, this will be more difficult.

Three Sample Outlines

Now that the principles of outlining are clear, here are some specific examples to illustrate how those principles are used in specific outlines. Presented here are a full-sentence preparation outline with annotations to guide you through the essential steps in outlining a speech; a skeletal outline that will provide a kind of template for a speech outline; and a delivery outline, which will illustrate the type of outline you might use in delivering your speech.

The Preparation Outline

Here's a relatively detailed *preparation outline* similar to the ones you might prepare in constructing your speech. The side notes should clarify both the content and the format of a full-sentence outline. This is the outline from which the PowerPoint slide show presented in Unit 16 (Figure 16.2) was designed.

Have You Ever Been Culture Shocked?

General Purpose:　To inform.

Specific Purpose:　To inform my audience of the four phases of culture shock.

Thesis:　Culture shock can be described in four stages.

Introduction

I. Many of you have experienced or will experience culture shock.
  A. Many people experience culture shock, that reaction to being in a culture very different from what you were used to.
  B. By understanding culture shock, you'll be in a better position to deal with it if and when it comes.
II. I've lived in four different cultures myself.
  A. I've always been interested in the way in which people adapt to different cultures.
  B. With our own campus becoming more culturally diverse every semester, the process of culture shock becomes important for us all.
III. Culture shock occurs in four stages (Oberg, 1960).
  A. The Honeymoon occurs first.
  B. The Crisis occurs second.
  C. The Recovery occurs third.
  D. The Adjustment occurs fourth.

Note the general format for the outline; note that the headings are clearly labeled and that the indenting helps you to see clearly the relationship that one item bears to the other. For example, in Introduction II, the outline format helps you to see that A and B are explanations (amplification, support) for II.

Generally the title, general and specific purposes, and thesis of the speech are prefaced to the outline. When the outline is an assignment that is to be handed in, additional information may be requested.

Note that the introduction, body, and conclusion are clearly labeled and separated visually.

The speaker assumes that the audience knows the general nature of culture shock and so does not go into detail as to its definition. But, just in case some audience members don't know and to refresh the memory of others, the speaker includes a brief definition.

Here the speaker attempts to connect the speaker, audience, and topic by stressing intercultural experiences and an abiding interest in the topic. Also, the speaker makes the topic important to the audience by referring to their everyday surroundings.

Note that references are integrated throughout the outline just as they would be in a term paper. In the actual speech, the speaker might say: "Anthropologist Kalervo Oberg, who coined the term *culture shock*, said it occurs in four stages."

The introduction serves the three functions noted: It gains attention (by involving the audience and by stressing the importance of the topic to the audience's desire to gain self-understanding); it connects the speaker, audience, and topic in a way that establishes the credibility of the speaker; and it orients the audience as to what is to follow. This particular orientation identifies both the number of stages and their names. If this speech were a much longer and more complex one, the orientation might also have included brief definitions of each stage.

[Let's follow the order in which these four stages occur and begin with the first stage, the Honeymoon.]

Body

   I. The Honeymoon occurs first.
      A. The honeymoon is the period of fascination with the new people and culture.
      B. You enjoy the people and the culture.
         1. You love the people.
            a. For example, the people in Zaire spend their time very differently from the way New Yorkers do.
            b. For example, my first 18 years living on a farm was very different from life in a college dorm.
         2. You love the culture.
            a. The great number of different religions in India fascinated me.
            b. Eating was an especially great experience.

[But, like many relationships, life is not all honeymoon; soon there comes a crisis.]

   II. The Crisis occurs second.
      A. The crisis is the period when you begin to experience problems.
         1. One-third of American workers abroad fail because of culture shock (Samovar & Porter, 1991, p. 232).
         2. The personal difficulties are also great.
      B. Life becomes difficult in the new culture.
         1. Communication is difficult.
         2. It's easy to offend people without realizing it.

[As you gain control over the crises, you began to recover.]

   III. The Recovery occurs third.
      A. The recovery is the period in which you learn how to cope.
      B. You begin to learn intercultural competence (Lustig & Koester, 1999).
         1. You learn how to communicate.
            a. Being able to go to the market and make my wants known was a great day for me.
            b. I was able to ask for a date.

This transition cues the audience into a four-part presentation. Also, the numbers repeated throughout the outline will further aid the audience in keeping track of where you are in the speech. Most important, it tells the audience that the speech will follow a temporal thought pattern.

Notice the parallel structure throughout the outline. For example, note that I, II, III, and IV in the body are all phrased in exactly the same way. Although this may seem unnecessarily redundant, it will help your audience follow your speech more closely and will also help you in logically structuring your thoughts.

Notice that there are lots of examples throughout this speech. These examples are identified only briefly in the outline and would naturally be elaborated on in the speech.

Notice too the internal organization of each major point. Each main assertion in the body contains a definition of the stage (IA, IIA, IIIA, and IVA) and examples (IB, IIB, IIIB, and IVB) to illustrate the stage.

Because this is a specific fact, some style manuals require that the page number be included in the reference citation.

Note that each statement in the outline is a complete sentence. You can easily convert this outline into a phrase or keyword outline for use in delivery. In the preparation outline, however, full sentences will help you see more clearly the relationships among items.

2. You learn the rules of the culture.
   a. The different religious ceremonies each have their own rules.
   b. Eating is a ritual experience in lots of places throughout Africa.

[Your recovery leads naturally into the next and final stage, the adjustment.]

IV. The Adjustment occurs fourth.
   A. The adjustment is the period when you come to enjoy the new culture.
   B. You come to appreciate the people and the culture.

[Let me summarize the stages you go through in experiencing culture shock.]

The transitions are inserted between all major parts of the speech. Although they may seem too numerous in this abbreviated outline, they will be appreciated by your audience, because the transitions will help them follow your speech.

Conclusion

I. Culture shock can be described in four stages.
   A. The Honeymoon is first.
   B. The Crisis is second.
   C. The Recovery is third.
   D. The Adjustment is fourth.
II. Culture shock is a fascinating process; you may want to explore it more fully.
   A. Lots of books on culture shock are on reserve for Communication 325: Culture and Communication.
   B. Sunday's *60 Minutes* is going to have a piece on culture shock.
III. By knowing the four stages, you can better understand the culture shock you may now be experiencing on the job, at school, or in your private life.

Notice that these four points correspond to I, II, III, and IV of the body and to III A, B, C, and D of the introduction. Notice how the similar wording adds clarity.

This step, in which the speaker motivates the listeners to continue learning about culture shock, is optional in informative speeches.

This step provides closure; it makes it clear that the speech is finished. It also serves to encourage reflection on the part of the audience as to their own experiences of culture shock.

REFERENCES

Lustig, Myron W., and Jolene Koester (1999). *Intercultural Competence: Interpersonal Communication across Cultures*, 3rd ed. Boston: Allyn and Bacon.

Oberg, Kalervo (1960). Culture Shock: Adjustment to New Cultural Environments. *Practical Anthropology* 7:177–182.

Samovar, Larry A., and Richard E. Porter (1995). *Communication between Cultures*, 2nd ed. Belmont, CA: Wadsworth.

This reference list includes just those sources that appear in the completed speech.

The Skeletal Outline

Here's a *skeletal outline*—a kind of template for structuring a speech. This particular outline would be appropriate for a speech using a temporal, spatial, or topical organization pattern. Note that in this skeletal outline there are three major propositions (I, II, and III in the body). These correspond to the III A, B, and C in the introduction (where you'd orient the audience) and to the I A, B, and C in the conclusion (where you'd summarize your major propositions). Once again, the transitions are signaled by square brackets. As you review this outline, the phrases printed in light ink will remind you of the functions of each outline item. Skeletal outlines for 13 different types of speeches may be found at **www.ablongman.com/devito**.

Title: _____.

General Purpose: your general aim (to inform, to persuade, to entertain) _____.

Specific Purpose: what you hope to achieve from this speech _____.

Thesis: your main assertion; the core of your speech _____.

Introduction

I. gain attention _____.

II. establish S-A-T connection _____.

III. orient audience _____.

   A. first major proposition; same as I in body _____.

   B. second major proposition; same as II in body _____.

   C. third major proposition; same as III in body _____.

[Transition: connect the introduction to the body _____]

Body

I. first major proposition _____.

   A. support for I (the first major proposition) _____.

   B. further support for I _____.

[Transition: connect the first major proposition to the second _____]

II. second major proposition _____.

   A. support for II (the second major proposition) _____.

   B. further support for II _____.

[Transition: connect the second major proposition to the third _____]

III. third major proposition _____.

   A. support for III _____.

   B. further support for III _____.

[Transition: connect the third major proposition (or all major propositions) to the conclusion _____]

Conclusion

I. summary _____.

   A. first major proposition; same as I in body _____.

   B. second major proposition; same as II in body _____.

   C. third major proposition; same as III in body _____.

II. motivation _____.

III. closure _____.

References

Alphabetical list of sources cited _____.

The Delivery Outline

Now that you've constructed a preparation outline, you need to construct a delivery outline. Resist the temptation to use your preparation outline to deliver the speech. If you use your preparation outline, you'll tend to read from the outline instead of presenting a seemingly extemporaneous speech in which you attend to and respond to audience feedback. Instead, construct a brief *delivery outline:* an outline that will assist rather than hinder your deliv-

ery of the speech. Here are some guidelines to follow in preparing this delivery outline.

- Be brief. Try to limit yourself to one side of one
  sheet of paper.

- Be clear. Be sure that you can see the outline
  while you're speaking. Use different colored inks,
  underlining, or whatever system will help you
  communicate your ideas.

- Be delivery minded. Include any guides to delivery that will help while you're speaking. Note in
  the outline when you'll use your presentation aid
  and when you'll remove it. A simple "show PA"
  or "remove PA" should suffice. You might also
  wish to note some speaking cues, such as "slow
  down" when reading a poetry excerpt, or perhaps
  a place where an extended pause might help.

- Rehearse with the delivery outline. In your rehearsals, use the delivery outline only. Remember, the objective is to make rehearsals as close to
  the real thing as possible.

The following is a sample delivery outline constructed from the preparation outline on culture
shock. Note that the outline is brief enough so that
you'll be able to use it effectively without losing eye
contact with the audience. It uses abbreviations
(for example, CS for culture shock) and phrases
rather than complete sentences. And yet it's detailed enough to include all essential parts of your
speech, including transitions. It contains delivery
notes specifically tailored to your own needs, such
as pause suggestions and guides to using visual
aids. Note also that it's clearly divided into introduction, body, and conclusion and uses the same
numbering system as the preparation outline.

PAUSE!

LOOK OVER THE AUDIENCE!

  I. Many experience CS
     A. CS: the reaction to being in a culture very
        different from your own
     B. By understanding CS, you'll be better able
        to deal with it

PAUSE SCAN AUDIENCE

 II. I've experienced CS
III. CS occurs in 4 stages (WRITE ON BOARD)
     A. Honeymoon

     B. Crisis
     C. Recovery
     D. Adjustment

[Let's examine these stages of CS]

PAUSE/STEP FORWARD

  I. Honeymoon
     A. fascination w/people and culture
     B. enjoyment of people and culture
        1. Zaire example
        2. farm to college dorm

[But, life is not all honeymoon—the crisis]

 II. Crisis
     A. problems arise
        1. 1/3 Am workers fail abroad
        2. personal difficulties
     B. life becomes difficult
        1. communication
        2. offend others

[As you gain control over the crises, you learn how
to cope]

PAUSE

III. Recovery
     A. period of learning to cope
     B. you learn intercultural competence
        1. communication becomes easier
        2. you learn the culture's rules

[As you recover, you adjust]

 IV. Adjustment
     A. learn to enjoy (again) the new culture
     B. appreciate people and culture

[These then are the four stages; let me summarize]

PAUSE BEFORE STARTING CONCLUSION

  I. CS occurs in 4 stages: honeymoon, crisis,
     recovery, & adjustment
 II. You can learn more about CS: books, *60 min-
     utes*
III. By knowing the 4 stages, you can better
     understand the culture shock you may now
     be experiencing on the job, at school, or in
     your private life.

PAUSE

ANY QUESTIONS?

STEP 9: WORD YOUR SPEECH

You're a successful public speaker when your listeners create in their minds the meanings you want them to create. You're successful when your listeners adopt the attitudes and behaviors you want them to adopt. The language choices you make—the words you select and the sentences you form—will greatly influence the meanings your listeners receive and, thus, how successful you are. Suggestions on how to "Make Your Speech Easy to Remember" may be found at www.ablongman.com/devito. 🖱

Oral Style

Oral style is the quality of spoken language that differentiates it from written language. You do not speak as you write (Akinnaso, 1982). The words and sentences you use differ. The major reason for this difference is that you compose speech instantly. You select your words and construct your sentences as you think your thoughts. There's very little time between the thought and the utterance. When you write, however, you compose your thoughts after considerable reflection. Even then you probably often rewrite and edit as you go along. Because of this, written language has a more formal tone. Spoken language is more informal, more colloquial. An extended example of the differences in "Oral and Written Style" may be found at www.ablongman.com/devito. 🖱

Generally, spoken language consists of shorter, simpler, and more familiar words than does written language. Also, there's more qualification in speech than in writing. For example, when speaking you probably make greater use of such expressions as *although, however, perhaps,* and the like. When writing, you probably edit these out.

Spoken language has a greater number of self-reference terms (terms that refer to the speaker herself or himself): *I, me, our, us,* and *you.* Spoken language also has a greater number of "allness" terms such as *all, none, every, always,* and *never.* When you write, you're probably more careful to edit out such allness terms, realizing that such terms often are not very descriptive of reality.

Spoken language has more pseudo-quantifying terms (for example, *many, much, very, lots*) and terms that include the speaker as part of the observation (for example, *It seems to me that* or *As I see it*). Fur-

ther, speech contains more verbs and adverbs; writing contains more nouns and adjectives.

Spoken and written language not only *do* differ, they *should* differ. The main reason why spoken and written language should differ is that the listener hears a speech only once; therefore, speech must be instantly intelligible. The reader, on the other hand, can reread an essay or look up an unfamiliar word. The reader can spend as much time as he or she wishes with the written page. The listener, in contrast, must move at the pace set by the speaker. The reader may reread a sentence or paragraph if there's a temporary attention lapse. The listener doesn't have this option.

For the most part, it's wise to use "oral style" in your public speeches. The public speech is composed much like a written essay, however. There's considerable thought and deliberation and much editing and restyling. Because of this, you'll need to devote special effort to retaining and polishing your oral style. In the rest of this section I'll present specific suggestions for achieving this goal.

Choosing Words

Choose carefully the words you use in your public speeches. Choose words to achieve clarity, vividness, appropriateness, a personal style, and forcefulness.

Clarity

Clarity in speaking style should be your primary goal. Here are some guidelines to help you make your speech clear.

Be Economical.   Don't waste words. Notice the wasted words in such expressions as "at nine A.M. *in the morning,*" "we *first* began the discussion," "I *myself personally,*" and "blue *in color.*" By withholding the italicized terms you eliminate unnecessary words and move closer to a more economical and clearer style.

Use Specific Terms and Numbers.   As we get more and more specific, we get a clearer and more detailed picture. Be specific. Don't say "dog" when you want your listeners to picture a St. Bernard. Don't say "car" when you want them to picture a limousine. The same is true of numbers. Don't say "earned a good salary" if you mean "earned $90,000 a year." Don't say "taxes will go up" when you mean "taxes will increase 7 percent."

Use Guide Phrases.   Use guide phrases to help listeners see that you're moving from one idea to another—phrases such as "now that we have seen how . . ., let us consider how . . .," and "my next argument. . . ." Terms such as *first, second, and also, although,* and *however* will help your audience follow your line of thinking.

Use Short, Familiar Terms.   Generally, favor the short word over the long one. Favor the familiar word over the unfamiliar word. Favor the more commonly used term over the rarely used term.

Carefully Assess Idioms.   Idioms are expressions that are unique to a specific language and whose meaning cannot be deduced from the individual words used. Expressions such as "kick the bucket," or "doesn't have a leg to stand on" are idioms; Either you know the meaning of the expression or you don't; you can't figure it out from only a knowledge of the individual words.

The positive side of idioms is that they give your speech a casual and informal air; they make your speech sound like a speech and not like a written essay. The negative side of idioms is that they create problems for listeners who are not native speakers of your language. Many non–native speakers will simply not understand the meaning of your idioms. This problem is especially important because audiences are becoming increasingly intercultural and because the number of idioms we use is extremely high.

Distinguish between Commonly Confused Words.   Many words, because they sound alike or are used in similar situations, are commonly confused. Try the self-test below, which covers 10 of the most frequently confused words.

TEST YOURSELF

Can You Distinguish between Commonly Confused Words?

Underline the word in parentheses that you would use in each sentence.

1. She (accepted, excepted) the award and thanked everyone (accept, except) the producer.
2. The teacher (affected, effected) his students greatly and will now (affect, effect) an entirely new curriculum.
3. Are you deciding (between, among) red and green or (between, among) red, green, and blue?
4. I've scaled higher mountains than this, so I'm sure I (can, may) scale this one; I and a few others know the hidden path, but I (can, may) not reveal this.
5. The table was (cheap, inexpensive) but has great style; the chairs cost a fortune but look (cheap, inexpensive).
6. We (discover, invent) uncharted lands but (discover, invent) computer programs.
7. He was direct and (explicit, implicit) in his denial of the crime but was vague and only (explicit, implicit) concerning his whereabouts.
8. She (implied, inferred) that she'd seek a divorce; we can only (imply, infer) her reasons.
9. The wedding was (tasteful, tasty) and the food (tasteful, tasty).
10. The student seemed (disinterested, uninterested) in the lecture. The teacher was (disinterested, uninterested) in who received what grades.

How did you do?   Here are the principles that govern correct usage: (1) Use *accept* to mean "receive" and *except* to mean with "the exclusion of." (2) Use *to affect* to mean "to have an effect on or to influence," and *to effect* to mean "to produce a result." (3) Use *between* when referring to two items and *among* when referring to more than two items. (4) Use *can* to refer to ability and *may* to refer to permission. (5) Use *cheap* to refer to something that is inferior and *inexpensive* to something that costs little. (6) Use *discover* to refer to the act of finding something out or learning something previously unknown, but use *invent* to refer to the act of originating something new. (7) Use *explicit* to mean "directly stated" and *implicit* to indicate the act of expressing something without actually stating it. (8) Use *imply* to mean "state indirectly" and *infer* to mean "draw a conclusion." (9) Use *tasteful* to refer to good taste, but use *tasty* to refer to something that tastes good. (10) Use *uninterested* to indicate a lack of interest and use *disinterested* to mean "objective" or "unbiased."

What will you do?   Your use of language can greatly enhance (or detract from) your persuasiveness. A word used incorrectly can lessen your credibility and general persuasiveness. Review your English handbook and identify other commonly confused words. Get into the habit of referring to a good dictionary whenever you have doubts about which word is preferred. ✔

Vividness

Select words to make your ideas vivid and to help your arguments come alive in the minds of your listeners: Use active verbs, strong verbs, figures of speech, and imagery.

Use Active Verbs.
Favor verbs that communicate activity rather than passivity. The verb to be, in all its forms—*is, are, was, were, will be*—is relatively inactive. Try using verbs of action instead. Rather than saying "The teacher was in the middle of the crowd," say "The teacher stood in the middle of the crowd." Instead of saying "The report was on the president's desk for three days," try "The report rested [or slept] on the president's desk for three days." Instead of saying "Management will be here tomorrow," consider "Management will descend on us tomorrow" or "Management jets in tomorrow."

Use Strong Verbs.
The verb is the strongest part of your sentence. Choose verbs carefully, and choose them so they accomplish a lot. Instead of saying "He walked through the forest," consider such terms as wandered, prowled, rambled, or roamed. Consider whether one of these might not better suit your intended meaning. Consult a thesaurus for any verb you suspect might be weak.

Use Figures of Speech.
Figures of speech help achieve vividness, in addition to making your speech more memorable and giving it a polished, well-crafted tone. Figures of speech are stylistic devices that have been a part of rhetoric since ancient times. Here are some of the major figures of speech; you may wish to incorporate a few of these into your next speech.

- *Alliteration* is the repetition of the same initial sound in two or more words, as in "fifty famous flavors" or the "cool, calculating leader."
- *Hyperbole* is the use of extreme exaggeration, as in "He cried like a faucet" or "I'm so hungry I could eat a whale."
- *Irony* is the use of a word or sentence whose literal meaning is the opposite of the message actually conveyed; for example, a teacher handing back failing examinations might say, "So pleased to see how many of you studied so hard."

- *Metaphor* compares two unlike things by stating that one thing "is" the other, as in "She's a lion when she wakes up" or "He's a real bulldozer."
- *Synecdoche* is the use of a part of an object to stand for the whole object, as in "All hands were on deck" (where "hands" stands for "sailor" or "crew member") or "green thumb" for "expert gardener."
- *Metonymy* is the substitution of a name for a title with which it's closely associated, as in "City Hall issued the following news release," in which "City Hall" stands for "the mayor" or "the city council."
- *Antithesis* is the presentation of contrary ideas in parallel form, as in "My loves are many, my enemies are few." Charles Dickens's opening words in *A Tale of Two Cities* are a famous antithesis: "It was the best of times; it was the worst of times."
- *Simile*, like metaphor, compares two unlike objects; but simile explicitly uses the words *like* or *as*; for example, "The manager is as gentle as an ox."
- *Personification* is the attribution of human characteristics to inanimate objects, as in "This room cries for activity" or "My car is tired and wants a drink."
- *Rhetorical questions* are questions used to make a statement or to produce a desired effect rather than to secure an answer, as in "Do you want to be popular?" "Do you want to get well?"

Use Imagery.
Appeal to the senses, especially our visual, auditory, and tactile senses. Make your audience see, hear, and feel what you're talking about.

In describing people or objects, create word "pictures" or *visual imagery*. When appropriate, describe such visual qualities as height, weight, color, size, shape, length, and contour. Let your audience see the sweat pouring down the faces of the coal miners; let them see the short, overweight, cigar-smoking executive in his pin-striped suit.

Use *auditory imagery* to describe sounds; let your listeners hear the car's tires screeching, the wind whistling, the bells chiming, the angry professor roaring.

Use terms referring to temperature, texture, and touch to create *tactile imagery*. Let your listeners feel the cool water running over their bodies or the punch of the prizefighter; let them feel the smooth skin of the newborn baby.

UNDERSTANDING THEORY AND RESEARCH

The Vividness of Imagery

This unit's suggestions for using imagery are offered as aids to making your speech more vivid than, say, normal conversation. However, there's evidence that overly vivid images can actually make your speech less memorable and less persuasive than it would be otehwise (Frey & Eagly, 1993). When a speaker's images are too vivid, they divert the listener's brain from following a logically presented series of thoughts or arguments. The brain focuses on these extremely vivid images and loses the speaker's train of thought. The advice, therefore, is to use vividness when it adds clarity to your ideas. When there's the possibility that your listeners may concentrate on the imagery rather than the idea, tone down the imagery.

> **Working with Theories and Research.** *What makes imagery too vivid? Can you find examples in advertisements or in public speeches of imagery that you consider too vivid?*

Still another way to make your speech vivid is to use humor; see "Humor in Public Speaking" at www.ablongman.com/devito.

Appropriateness

Use language that is appropriate to you as the speaker—and that is appropriate to your audience, the occasion, and the speech topic. Here are some general guidelines to help you achieve this quality.

Speak on the Appropriate Level of Formality.

The most effective public speaking style is less formal than the written essay but more formal than conversation. One way to achieve an informal style is to use contractions. Say *don't* instead of *do not, I'll* instead of *I shall,* and *wouldn't* instead of *would not.* Contractions give a public speech the sound and rhythm of conversation, a quality that most listeners react to favorably. Also, use personal pronouns rather than impersonal expressions. Say "I found" instead of "It has been found," or "I will present three arguments" instead of "Three arguments will be presented."

Avoid Unfamiliar Terms.

Avoid using terms the audience doesn't know. Avoid foreign and technical terms unless you're certain the audience is familiar with them. Similarly, avoid **jargon** (the technical vocabulary of a specialized field) unless you're sure the meanings are clear to your listeners. Some acronyms (such as NATO, UN, NOW, and CORE) are probably familiar to most audiences; many, however, are not. When you wish to use any specialized terms or abbreviations, explain their meaning fully to the audience.

Avoid Slang.

Avoid offending your audience with **slang,** which can embarrass your hearers or make them think you have little respect for them. Although your listeners may themselves use vulgar and offensive expressions, they often resent their use by public speakers.

Avoid Ethnic Expressions (Generally).

Ethnic expressions are words and phrases that are peculiar to a particular ethnic group. At times these expressions are known only by members of the ethnic group; at other times they may be known more widely but still recognized as ethnic expressions.

When you are speaking to a multicultural audience, it's generally best to avoid ethnic expressions unless they're integral to your speech and you explain them. Such expressions are often interpreted as exclusionist; they highlight the connection between the speaker and the members of that particular ethnic group and the lack of connection between the speaker and all others who are not members of that ethnic group. And, of course, ethnic expressions should never be used if you're not a member of the ethnic group.

If, on the other hand, you're speaking to people who all belong to one ethnic group and if you're

Talking Up and Talking Down

To me, the most important element in management is the human being. So the first essential is to treat people with consideration.

—Yoshiki Yamasaki

Talking up and talking down are two forms of communication that can present problems in workplace settings in the United States, where a kind of communication equality reigns.

When you talk up, you talk as a subordinate, as someone who is inferior to the person you're addressing. And although it's important to demonstrate respect for others and to acknowledge that in some situations others know more than you do, it's also important to show that you have power and information. Statements that put yourself down ("I'm really bad at writing reports"), that are unnecessarily and overly complimentary ("You're so great on the phone" or "If I only had your finesse"), or that are overly polite ("Thank you, Madam") may give the impression that you may not be up to the job at hand. Others may interpret your talking up as an indication that you are in fact inferior to others.

Talking down is probably the more common mistake. Here, you present yourself as superior or all-knowing. Examples include the doctor who speaks in medicalese to a sick patient—or who meets a new patient and says, "Hello, Pat, I'm Dr. Gonzalez." Or the lawyer who uses arcane legal terminology without any explanation and leaves it up to you to understand what he or she is saying. People also talk down when they tell others how they should act or feel: "You really shouldn't have said that" or "Don't be shy, speak your mind." Statements like these tell the other person that you know the right way to do things and that what they've been doing is wrong. So be especially careful of statements containing "should" and "ought"; they're often signals that you're talking down.

Thinking about Your Communicating @ Work

Can you provide examples of talking up or talking down that you've witnessed or been a party to recently? What effect did such messages have?

---

also a member, then such expressions are fine. In fact, they may well prove effective; being part of the common language of speaker and audience, they can help you stress your own similarities with the audience.

Personal Style

Audiences favor speakers who speak in a personal rather than an impersonal style, who speak with them rather than at them. You can achieve a more personal style by using personal pronouns, asking questions, and creating immediacy.

Use Personal Pronouns. Say *I, me, he, she,* and *you.* Avoid impersonal expressions such as *one* (as in "One is led to believe . . ."), *this speaker,* or *you, the*

listeners. These expressions distance the audience and create barriers rather than bridges.

Use Questions. Ask the audience questions to involve them. In a small audience, you might even briefly entertain responses. In larger audiences, you might ask the question, pause to allow the audience time to consider their responses, and then move on. When you direct questions to your listeners, they feel a part of the public speaking transaction.

Create Immediacy. Immediacy, as discussed in Unit 9, is a connectedness, a relatedness with one's listeners. Immediacy is the opposite of disconnectedness and separation. Here are some suggestions for creating immediacy through language:

- Use personal examples.
- Use terms that include both you and the audience; for example, *we* and *our*.
- Address the audience directly; say *you* rather than *students*; say "You'll enjoy reading" instead of "Everyone will enjoy reading"; say "I want you to see" instead of "I want people to see."
- Use specific names of audience members when appropriate.
- Express concern for the audience members.
- Reinforce or compliment the audience.
- Refer directly to commonalities between you and the audience; for example, "We are all children of immigrants" or "We all want to see our team in the playoffs."
- Refer to shared experiences and goals; for example, "We all want, we all need a more responsive PTA."
- Recognize audience feedback and refer to it in your speech. Say, for example, "I can see from your expressions that we're all anxious to get to our immediate problem."

Forcefulness/Power

Forceful or powerful language will help you achieve your purpose, whether it be informative or persuasive. Forceful language enables you to direct the audience's attention, thoughts, and feelings. To make your speech more forceful, eliminate weakeners, vary intensity, and avoid overused expressions.

Eliminate Weakeners.   Delete phrases that weaken your sentences. Among the major weakeners are uncertainty expressions and weak modifiers. Uncertainty expressions such as "I'm not sure of this, but"; "Perhaps it might"; or "Maybe it works this way" communicate a lack of commitment and conviction and will make your audience wonder if you're worth listening to. Weak modifiers such as "It works pretty well," "It's kind of like," or "It may be the one we want" make you seem unsure and indefinite about what you're saying.

Cut out any unnecessary verbiage that reduces the impact of your meaning. Instead of saying "There are lots of things we can do to help," say "We can do lots of things to help." Instead of saying "I'm sorry to be so graphic, but Senator Bingsley's proposal . . .," say "We need to be graphic. Senator

Bingsley's proposal . . . ." Instead of saying "It should be observed in this connection that, all things considered, money is not productive of happiness," say "Money doesn't bring happiness."

Here are a few additional suggestions—which, of course, are not limited in application to public speaking but relate as well to interpersonal and small group communication.

- Avoid hesitations ("I, er, want to say that, ah, this one is, er, the best, you know"); they make you sound unprepared and uncertain.
- Avoid using too many intensifiers ("Really, this was the greatest; it was truly phenomenal"); audiences will begin to doubt the speaker who goes overboard with the superlatives.
- Avoid tag questions ("I'll review the report now, okay?" "That is a great proposal, don't you think?"); they signal your need for approval and your own uncertainty and lack of conviction.
- Avoid self-critical statements ("I'm not very good at this," "This is my first speech"); they signal a lack of confidence and make public your sense of inadequacy.

In what ways is delivery in interpersonal communication similar to and different from delivery in public speaking?

- Avoid slang and vulgar expressions; they may signal low social class and hence little power; they may also communicate a lack of respect for your audience.

Vary Intensity as Appropriate. Just as you can vary your voice in intensity, you can also phrase your ideas with different degrees of stylistic intensity. You can, for example, refer to an action as "failing to support our position" or as "stabbing us in the back"; you can say that a new proposal will "endanger our goals" or will "destroy us completely"; you can refer to a child's behavior as "playful," "creative," or "destructive." Vary your language to express different degrees of intensity—from mild through neutral to extremely intense.

MEDIA WATCH

ADVERTISING

Like public speeches, advertising serves two major functions: to inform and to persuade. Advertising informs you in a variety of ways:

▶ Advertising makes you aware of a particular product or service, a function that's especially important with new products. Whether the advertising appears on television, the Internet, or billboards or in newspapers or magazines, it makes you aware that such a product or service exists.

▶ Advertising informs you about the product and perhaps its ingredients or its uses. Cereal commercials on television, for example, proudly tell you the fiber content (but seldom the sugar content). Aluminum foil ads tell you of foil's many uses, perhaps including some you hadn't thought of previously.

▶ Advertising tells you where to buy the product and perhaps how much it costs. Infomercials regularly give this information—the exact price of the product, the shipping and handling charges, and the phone number you need to call to get the bargain price.

▶ Advertising may correct erroneous claims made in previous ads. Thus, for example, Listerine was required to advertise that it doesn't kill germs that cause colds—as had been previously advertised.

Of course, advertising's real business is persuasion.

▶ Advertising seeks to establish a favorable image of a product—to make you think a certain way about the product or associate a particular feeling with it. Beer and soft drink advertisers regularly associate friendship and fun with their products; the idea is that when you see their products these positive associations will lead you to buy the advertised beverage. Automobile manufacturers want you to feel that their product is safe or sophisticated or sexy, and their advertisements are directed at giving you these impressions.

▶ Advertising may also work in the opposite direction and try to associate a product with negative feelings. The American Cancer Society's advertisements against smoking regularly attack the glamour image that cigarette manufacturers communicate, showing pictures of wrinkled and sick smokers.

▶ Advertisers may aim to convince you of the superiority of their product and the inferiority of the competition. This comparative advertising pits one detergent against another ("Ours has twice the cleaning power") or one car against another ("Ours is $2,000 less expensive and gives you greater mileage").

▶ Advertising often aims to get you to buy a product. Whether it's eyeglasses, furniture, perfume, or appliances, the advertiser wants to get you to the point where you'll go the store, make the phone call, or type in your credit card number and buy the product or service.

If you want to get an additional look at advertising, visit some of the websites dealing with it; for example, **www.aaaa.org** (the American Association of Advertising Agencies) and **www.AdAge.com** (Advertising Age, a major advertising magazine and a source for most major news on advertising and advertisers).

Follow-Up. *Keep a log for one full day of all the advertising with which you come into contact. Be prepared; it's going to be a very extensive log. Which of these advertisements informed or persuaded you? How would you describe the techniques the advertisers used to achieve their purpose?*

Avoid Bromides and Clichés. Bromides are trite sayings that are worn out because of constant usage. A few examples:

- Honesty is the best policy.
- If I can't do it well, I won't do it at all.
- I don't understand modern art, but I know what I like.

When we hear these hackneyed statements, we recognize them as unoriginal and uninspired.

Clichés are phrases that have lost their novelty and part of their meaning through overuse. Clichés call attention to themselves because of their overuse. Here are some examples of clichés to avoid:

- in this day and age
- tell it like it is
- free as a bird
- in the pink
- no sooner said than done
- it goes without saying
- few and far between
- over the hill
- no news is good news
- the life of the party
- keep your shirt on

Phrasing Sentences

Give the same careful consideration that you give to words to the sentences of your speech as well. Some guidelines follow.

Use Short Sentences

Short sentences are more forceful and economical. They are also easier for your audience to comprehend and remember. Listeners don't have the time or the inclination to unravel long and complex sentences. Help them to listen more efficiently. Use short rather than long sentences.

Use Direct Sentences

Direct sentences are easier to understand. They are also more forceful. Instead of saying "I want to tell you of the three main reasons why we should not adopt Program A," say "We should not adopt Program A. There are three main reasons."

Use Active Sentences

Active sentences—that is, sentences whose verbs are in the active voice—are easier to understand than passive ones. They also make your speech seem livelier and more vivid. Instead of saying "The lower court's decision was reversed by the Supreme Court," say "The Supreme Court reversed the lower court's decision." Instead of saying "The proposal was favored by management," say "Management favored the proposal."

Use Positive Sentences

Sentences phrased positively are easier to comprehend and remember than sentences phrased negatively. Notice how sentences *a* and *c* are easier to understand than sentences *b* and *d*:

a. The committee rejected the proposal.
b. The committee did not accept the proposal.
c. This committee works outside the normal company hierarchy.
d. This committee does not work within the normal company hierarchy.

Vary the Types of Sentences

The preceding advice to use short, direct, active, positive sentences is valid most of the time. Yet too many sentences of the same type or length will make your speech sound boring. So follow (generally) the preceding advice, but add variations as well.

STEP 10: REHEARSE AND DELIVER YOUR SPEECH

Your last step is to rehearse and deliver your speech. Let's look first at rehearsal.

Rehearsal

Use your rehearsal time effectively and efficiently for the following purposes:

- To develop a delivery that will help you achieve the objectives of your speech.
- To time your speech; if you time your rehearsals, you'll be able to see if you can add material or if you have to delete something.
- To see how the speech will flow as a whole and to make any changes and improvements you think necessary.

- To test the presentation aids, and to detect and resolve any technical problems.
- To learn the speech thoroughly.
- To reduce any feelings of apprehension and gain confidence.

The following procedures should assist you in achieving these goals.

Rehearse the Speech as a Whole
Rehearse the speech from beginning to end, not in parts. Rehearse it from getting out of your seat through the introduction, body, and conclusion, to returning to your seat. Be sure to rehearse the speech with all the examples and illustrations (and any audiovisual aids) included. This will enable you to connect the parts of the speech and see how they interact.

Time the Speech
Time the speech during each rehearsal. Make the necessary adjustments on the basis of this timing. If you're using computer presentation software, you'll be able to time your speech very precisely. It will also enable you to time the individual parts of your speech so you can achieve the balance you want—for example, you might want to spend twice as much time on the solutions as on the problems, or you might want to balance the introduction and conclusion so that each portion constitutes about 10 percent of your speech.

Approximate the Actual Speech Situation
Rehearse the speech under conditions as close as possible to those under which you'll deliver it. If possible, rehearse the speech in the same room in which you'll present it. If this is impossible, try to simulate the actual conditions as closely as you can—even in your living room or bathroom. If possible, rehearse the speech in front of a few supportive listeners. It's always helpful (and especially for your beginning speeches) that your listeners be supportive rather than too critical. Merely having listeners present during your rehearsal will further simulate the conditions under which you'll eventually speak. Get together with two or three other students in an empty classroom where you can take turns as speakers and listeners.

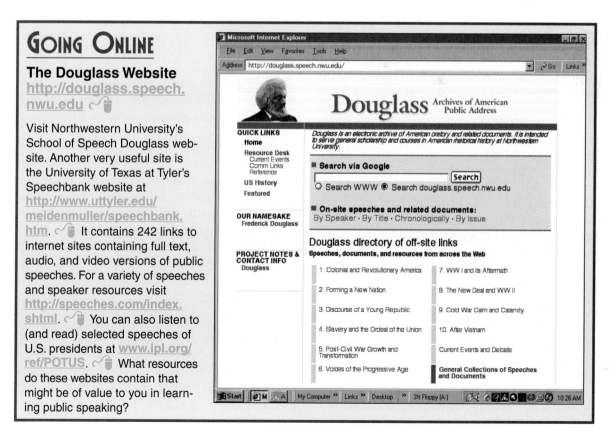

GOING ONLINE

The Douglass Website
http://douglass.speech.nwu.edu

Visit Northwestern University's School of Speech Douglass website. Another very useful site is the University of Texas at Tyler's Speechbank website at http://www.uttyler.edu/meidenmuller/speechbank.htm. It contains 242 links to internet sites containing full text, audio, and video versions of public speeches. For a variety of speeches and speaker resources visit http://speeches.com/index.shtml. You can also listen to (and read) selected speeches of U.S. presidents at www.ipl.org/ref/POTUS. What resources do these websites contain that might be of value to you in learning public speaking?

See Yourself as a Speaker

Rehearse the speech in front of a full-length mirror. This will enable you to see yourself and see how you'll appear to the audience. This may be extremely difficult at first, and you may have to force yourself to watch. After a few attempts, however, you'll begin to see the value of this experience. Practice your eye contact, your movements, and your gestures in front of the mirror.

Incorporate Changes and Make Delivery Notes

Make any needed changes in the speech between rehearsals. Do not interrupt your rehearsal to make notes or changes; if you do, you may never experience the entire speech from beginning to end. While making these changes note any words whose pronunciation you wish to check. Also, insert pause notations ("slow down" warnings, and other delivery suggestions) into your outline.

If possible, record your speech (ideally, on videotape) so you can hear exactly what your listeners will hear: your volume, rate, pitch, pronunciation, and pauses. You'll thus be in a better position to improve these qualities.

Rehearse Often

Rehearse the speech as often as seems necessary. Two useful guides are: (1) Rehearse the speech at least three or four times; less rehearsal than this is sure to be too little. (2) Rehearse the speech as long as your rehearsals continue to result in improvements in the speech or in your delivery. Some suggestions for a long-term delivery improvement program are presented next.

Undertake a Long-Term Delivery Improvement Program

To become a truly effective speaker, you may need to undertake a long-term delivery improvement program. Approach this project with a positive attitude: Tell yourself that you can do it and that you will do it.

1. First, seek feedback from someone whose opinion and insight you respect. Your public speaking instructor may be a logical choice, but someone majoring in communication or working in a communication field might also be appropriate. Get an honest and thorough appraisal of both your voice and your bodily action.

2. Learn to hear, see, and feel the differences between effective and ineffective patterns. For example, is your pitch too high or your volume too loud? A tape recorder will be very helpful. Learn to feel your rigid posture or your lack of arm and hand gestures. Once you've perceived these voice and/or body patterns, concentrate on learning more effective habits. Practice a few minutes each day. Avoid becoming too conscious of any source of ineffectiveness. Just try to increase your awareness and work on one problem at a time. Do not try to change all your patterns at once.

3. Seek additional feedback on the changes. Make certain that listeners agree that the new patterns you're practicing really are more effective. Remember that you hear yourself through bone conduction as well as through air transmission. Others hear you only through air transmission. So what you hear and what others hear will be different.

4. For voice improvement, consult a book on voice and diction for practice exercises and for additional information on the nature of volume, rate, pitch, and quality.

5. If difficulties persist, see a professional. For voice problems, see a speech clinician. Most campuses have a speech clinic, and you can easily avail yourself of its services. For bodily action difficulties, talk with your public speaking instructor.

6. Seek professional help if you're psychologically uncomfortable with any aspect of your voice or bodily action. It may be that all you have to do is to hear yourself or see yourself on a videotape—as others hear and see you—to convince yourself that you sound and look just fine. Regardless of what is causing this discomfort, however, if you're uncomfortable, do something about it. In a college community there's more assistance available to you at no cost than you'll ever be offered again. Make use of it.

Delivery

If you're like my own students, delivery creates more anxiety for you than any other aspect of public speaking. Few speakers worry about organization or audience analysis or style. Many worry about delivery, so you have lots of company. In this unit we'll examine general methods and principles of effectiveness in presentation that you can adapt to your own personality. Unit 18 offers specific suggestions for effectively presenting your speech.

Methods of Delivery

Speakers vary widely in their methods of delivery: Some speak "off-the-cuff," with no apparent preparation; others read their speeches from manuscript. Some memorize their speeches word for word; others construct a detailed outline, rehearse often, then speak extemporaneously.

Speaking Impromptu. In an **impromptu speech** you talk without any specific preparation. You and the topic meet for the first time and immediately the speech begins. On some occasions you will not be able to avoid speaking impromptu. In a classroom, after someone has spoken, you might give a brief impromptu speech of evaluation. In asking or answering questions in an interview situation you're giving impromptu speeches, albeit extremely short ones. At a meeting you may find yourself explaining a proposal or defending a plan of action; these too are impromptu speeches. Of course, impromptu speeches don't permit attention to the details of public speaking such as audience adaptation, research, and style.

Speaking from Manuscript. In a **manuscript speech** you read aloud the entire speech, which you've written out word for word. The manuscript speech allows you to control the timing precisely—a particularly important benefit when you are delivering a speech that will be recorded (on television, for example). Also, there's no risk of forgetting, no danger of being unable to find the right word. Another feature of the manuscript method is that it allows you to use the exact wording you (or a team of speechwriters) want. In the political arena this is often crucial. And, of course, because the speech is already written out, you can distribute copies and are therefore less likely to be misquoted.

Many audiences, however, don't like speakers to read their speeches, except perhaps with Tele-PrompTers on television. In face-to-face situations, audiences generally prefer speakers who interact with them. Reading a manuscript makes it difficult

BUILDING COMMUNICATION SKILLS

How Can You Speak Impromptu?

The following experience may prove useful as an exercise in delivery. Each student should take three index cards and write an impromptu speech topic on each card. The topics should be familiar but not clichés; they should be worthwhile and substantive, not trivial; and they should be neither too simplistic nor too complex. The cards should be collected and placed face down on a table. A speaker, chosen through some random process, should then select two cards, read the topics, choose one of them, and take approximately one or two minutes to prepare a two- to three-minute impromptu speech. A few guidelines:

1. Don't apologize. Everyone will have difficulty with this assignment, so there is no need to emphasize any problems you may have.
2. Don't express verbally or nonverbally any displeasure or any negative responses to the experience, the topic, the audience, or even yourself. Approach the entire task with a positive attitude and a positive appearance. It will help make the experience more enjoyable for both you and your audience.
3. When you select your topic, jot down two or three subtopics that you will cover and perhaps two or three bits of supporting material that you will use in amplifying these subtopics.
4. Develop your conclusion. It is probably best to use a simple summary conclusion in which you restate your main topic and the subordinate topics that you discussed.
5. Develop an introduction. Here it is probably best simply to identify your topic and orient the audience by telling them the two or three subtopics that you will cover.

to respond to listener feedback. You cannot easily make adjustments on the basis of feedback. And with the manuscript on a stationary lectern, as it most often is, it's impossible for you to move around.

Speaking from Memory.

In memorized delivery you write out the speech word for word (as in the manuscript method); but instead of reading it, you then commit the speech to memory and recite it or "act it out." Speaking from memory allows you freedom to move about and otherwise concentrate on delivery. It doesn't, however, allow easy adjusting to feedback, and you thus lose one of the main advantages of face-to-face contact.

One potential problem with this method is the risk of forgetting your speech. In a memorized speech each sentence cues the recall of the following sentence. Thus, when you forget one sentence, you may forget the rest of the speech. This danger, along with the natural nervousness that speakers feel, makes the memorizing method a poor choice in most situations.

Speaking Extemporaneously.

An **extemporaneous speech** involves thorough preparation but no commitment to the exact wording to be used during the speech. It often involves memorizing your opening lines (perhaps the first few sentences), your closing lines (perhaps the last few sentences), and your major propositions and the order in which you'll present them. You can also, if you wish, memorize selected phrases, sentences, or quotations. Memorizing the opening and closing lines will help you to focus your complete attention on the audience and will also put you more at ease. Once you know exactly what you'll say in opening and closing the speech, you'll feel more in control.

The extemporaneous method is useful in most speaking situations. Good college lecturers use the extemporaneous method. They prepare thoroughly and know what they want to say and in what order they want to say it, but they've made no commitment to exact wording. This method allows you to respond easily to feedback. Should a point need clarification, you can elaborate on it at the moment when it will be most effective. This method makes it easy to be natural, too, because you're being yourself. It's the method that comes closest to conversation. With the extemporaneous method, you can move about and interact with the audience.

Characteristics of Effective Delivery
Strive for delivery that is natural, reinforces the message, is varied, and has a conversational tone.

Effective Delivery Is Natural.

Listeners will enjoy and believe you more if you speak naturally, as if you were conversing with a small group of people. Don't allow your delivery to call attention to itself. Your ultimate aim should be to deliver the speech so naturally that the audience won't even notice your delivery. This will take some practice, but you can do it. When voice or bodily action is so prominent that it's distracting, the audience concentrates on the delivery and will fail to attend to your speech.

Effective Delivery Reinforces the Message.

Effective delivery should aid instant intelligibility. Your main objective is to make your ideas understandable to an audience. A voice that listeners have to strain to hear, a decrease in volume at the ends of sentences, or slurred diction will obviously hinder comprehension.

When you give a public speech, everything about you communicates. You cannot prevent yourself from sending messages to others. The way in which you dress is no exception. In fact, your attire will figure significantly in the way your audience assesses your credibility and even the extent to which they give you attention. In short, the way you present yourself physically will influence your effectiveness in all forms of persuasive and informative speaking. Unfortunately, there are no rules that will apply to all situations for all speakers. Thus, only general guidelines are offered here. Modify and tailor these for yourself and for each unique situation.

- Avoid extremes: Don't allow your clothes, hairstyle, and so on to detract attention from what you're saying.
- Dress comfortably: Be both physically and psychologically comfortable with your appearance so that you can concentrate your energies on what you're saying.
- Dress appropriately: Your appearance should be consistent with the specific public speaking occasion.

Effective Delivery Is Varied.

Listening to a speech is hard work for the audience. Flexible and varied delivery eases the listeners' task. Be especially careful to avoid monotonous patterns and predictable patterns.

Speakers who are monotonous keep their voices at the same pitch, volume, and rate throughout the speech. The monotonous speaker maintains a uniform level from the introduction to the conclusion. Like the drone of a motor, this easily puts the audience to sleep. Vary your pitch levels, your volume, and your rate of speaking. In a similar way, avoid monotony in bodily action. Avoid standing in exactly the same position throughout the speech. Use your body to express your ideas, to communicate to the audience what is going on in your head.

A predictable vocal pattern is a pattern in which, for example, the volume levels vary but always in the same sequence. Through repetition, the sequence soon becomes predictable. For example, each sentence may begin loud and then decline to a barely audible volume. In bodily action, the predictable speaker repeatedly uses the same movements or gestures. For example, a speaker may scan the audience from left to right to left to right throughout the entire speech. If the audience can predict the pattern of your voice or your bodily action, your speech will almost surely be ineffective. A patterned and predictable delivery will draw the audience's attention away from what you're saying.

Effective Delivery Is Conversational. Although more formal than conversation, delivery in public speaking should have some of the most important features of conversation. These qualities include immediacy, eye contact, expressiveness, and responsiveness to feedback.

Just as you can create a sense of immediacy through language, as discussed earlier, you can also create it with delivery. Make your listeners feel that you're talking directly and individually to each of them. You can communicate immediacy through delivery in a number of ways:

- Maintain appropriate eye contact with the audience members.
- Maintain a physical closeness that reinforces a psychological closeness; don't stand behind a desk or lectern.
- Smile.
- Move around a bit; avoid the appearance of being too scared to move.
- Stand with a direct and open body posture.

- Talk directly to your audience, not to your notes or to your visual aids.

When you maintain eye contact, you make the public speaking interaction more conversational (in addition to communicating immediacy). Look directly into your listeners' eyes. Lock eyes with different audience members for short periods.

When you're expressive, you communicate genuine involvement in the public speaking situation. You can communicate this quality of expressiveness, of involvement, in several ways:

- Express responsibility for your own thoughts and feelings.
- Vary your vocal rate, pitch, volume, and rhythm to communicate involvement and interest in the audience and in the topic.
- Allow your facial muscles and your entire body to reflect and echo this inner involvement.
- Use gestures appropriately; too few gestures may signal lack of interest, but too many can communicate uneasiness, awkwardness, or anxiety.

Read carefully the feedback signals sent by your audience. Then respond to these signals with verbal, vocal, and bodily adjustments. For example, respond to audience feedback signals communicating lack of comprehension or inability to hear with added explanation or increased volume.

Using Notes. For many speeches it may be helpful to use notes. A few simple guidelines may help you avoid some of the common errors made in using notes.

1. Keep notes to a minimum. The fewer notes you take with you, the better off you will be. The reason so many speakers bring notes with them is that they want to avoid the face-to-face interaction required. With experience, however, you should find this face-to-face interaction the best part of the public speaking experience.

2. Resist the normal temptation to bring with you the entire speech outline. You may rely on it too heavily and lose the direct contact with the audience. Instead, compose a delivery outline, as discussed earlier in this unit, using only key words. Bring this to the lectern with you—one side of an index card or at most an 8½-by-11-inch sheet should be sufficient. This will relieve any anxiety

BUILDING COMMUNICATION SKILLS

How Can You Respond Strategically and Ethically?

Consider the following situations that might arise in a public speaking situation. How would you respond to achieve your purpose and yet not violate any of your own ethical standards?

1. You've just given a speech to a racially diverse high school class on why they should attend your college. One audience member asks how racially diverse your faculty and students are. Your faculty is 94 percent European American, 4 percent Asian American, and 2 percent African American. You do know that the administration has been talking about making a major effort to recruit a more racially diverse faculty, but so far no action has been taken. Your student population is approximately 40 percent European American, 40 percent African American, 10 percent Hispanic, and 10 percent Asian American. What do you say?

2. You've just given a speech advocating banning alcohol on campus. In the speech you claimed that more than 70 percent of the

students favor banning alcohol. At the end of the speech, you realize that you made a mistake and that only 30 percent favor banning alcohol; because you were nervous, you mixed up the figures. There's a question-and-answer period, but no one asks about the figures. What do you say?

3. You represent the college newspaper and are asking the student government to increase the funding for the paper. The student government objects to giving extra money, because the paper has taken on lots of causes that are unpopular with the majority of students. You feel that it's essential for the paper to represent the disenfranchised and fully expect to continue to do just exactly as you have in the past. But if you say this, you won't get the added funding—and the paper won't be able to survive unless the funding is increased. You will get the funding if you say you'll give primary coverage to majority positions. What do you say?

over the possibility of forgetting your speech but will not be extensive enough to interfere with direct contact with your audience.

3. Don't make your notes more obvious than necessary, but at the same time don't try to hide them. For example, don't gesture with your notes—but don't turn away from the audience to steal glances at them, either. Use them openly and honestly but gracefully, with "open subtlety." To do this effectively, you'll have to know your notes intimately. Rehearse at least twice with the same notes that you will take with you to the speaker's stand.

4. When referring to your notes, pause to examine them; then regain eye contact with the audience and continue your speech. Don't read from your notes, just take cues from them. The one exception to this guideline is an extensive quotation or complex set of statistics that you have to read;

immediately after reading, however, resume direct eye contact with the audience.

Voice

Three dimensions of voice are significant to the public speaker: volume, rate, and pitch. Your manipulation of these elements will enable you to control your voice to maximum advantage.

Vocal volume is the relative intensity of the voice. (Loudness, on the other hand, refers to hearers' perception of that relative intensity). In an adequately controlled voice, volume will vary according to several factors. For example, the distance between speaker and listener, the competing noise, and the emphasis the speaker wishes to give an idea will all influence volume.

Problems with volume are easy to identify in others, though difficult to recognize in ourselves. One obvious problem is a voice that is too soft.

When speech is so soft that listeners have to strain to hear, they will soon tire of expending so much energy. A voice that is too loud can also prove disturbing, because it intrudes on our psychological space. However, it's interesting to note that a voice louder than normal communicates assertiveness (Page & Balloun, 1978) and will lead people to pay greater attention to you (Robinson & McArthur, 1982). On the other hand, it can also communicate aggressiveness and give others the impression that you'd be difficult to get along with.

The most common problem is too little volume variation. As mentioned earlier, a related problem is a volume pattern that, although varied, varies in an easily predictable pattern. If the audience can predict the pattern of volume changes, they will focus on that pattern and not on what you're saying.

A speaker who tends to fade away at the end of sentences is particularly disturbing to the audience. Here the speaker uses a volume that is largely appropriate but speaks the last few words of sentences at an extremely low volume. Be particularly careful when finishing sentences; make sure the audience is able to hear you without difficulty.

If you're using a microphone, test it first. Whether it's the kind that clips around your neck, the kind you hold in your hand, or the kind that is stationed at the podium, try it out first. Some speakers—talk show host Montel Williams is a good example—use the hand microphone as a prop and flip it in the air or from hand to hand as they emphasize a particular point. For your beginning speeches, it's probably best to avoid such techniques and to use the microphone as unobtrusively as you can.

Your *vocal rate* is the speed at which you speak. About 150 words per minute seems average for speaking as well as for reading aloud. Rate problems include speaking too fast, too slow, with too little variation, or with too predictable a pattern. If you talk too fast you deprive your listeners of time they need to understand and digest what you're saying. If the rate is extreme, the listeners will simply not be willing to expend the energy needed to understand your speech.

If your rate is too slow, it will encourage your listeners' thoughts to wander to matters unrelated to your speech. Be careful, therefore, neither to bore the audience by presenting information at too slow a rate, nor to set a pace that is too rapid for listeners to absorb. Strike a happy medium. Speak at a pace that engages the listeners and allows them time for reflection but without boring them.

UNDERSTANDING THEORY AND RESEARCH

Speech Rate

You've probably noticed that advertisers and salespeople generally talk at a rate faster than that of normal speech. But is a rapid **speech rate** effective? Are people who speak faster more persuasive? The answer is: It depends (Smith & Shaffer, 1991, 1995). The rapid speaker who speaks *against* your existing attitudes is generally more effective than the speaker who speaks at a normal rate. But the rapid speaker who speaks *in favor of* your existing attitudes (say, in an attempt to strengthen them) is actually less effective than the speaker who speaks at a normal rate. The reason for this is quite logical. In the case of the person who is speaking against your existing attitudes, the rapidity of speech doesn't give you the time

you need to think of counterarguments to rebut the speaker's position. So you're more likely to be influenced by the speaker's position, because you don't have the time to consider why the speaker may be incorrect. In the case of the person who is speaking in favor of your existing attitudes, the rapidity of speech doesn't give you time to mentally elaborate on the speaker's arguments, and consequently they don't carry as much persuasive force.

Working with Theories and Research. *Does your own experience support the findings from this research? How might you apply this research to increase your own persuasiveness?*

As with volume, rate variations may be under-used or totally absent. If you speak at the same rate throughout the entire speech, you're not making use of this important speech asset. Use variations in rate to call attention to certain points and to add variety. For example, if you describe the dull routine of an assembly line worker in a rapid and varied pace or evoke the wonder of a circus in a pace with absolutely no variation, you're surely misusing this important vocal dimension. Again, if you're interested in and conscious of what you're saying, your rate variations should flow naturally and effectively. Too predictable a pattern of rate variations is sometimes as bad as no variation at all. If the audience can predict—consciously or unconsciously—your rate pattern, you're in a vocal rut. You're not communicating ideas but reciting words you've memorized.

Vocal pitch is the relative highness or lowness of your voice as perceived by your listener. More technically, pitch results from the rate at which your vocal folds vibrate. If they vibrate rapidly, listeners will perceive your voice as having a high pitch. If they vibrate slowly, listeners will perceive your voice as having a low pitch.

Pitch changes often signal changes in the meanings of sentences. The most obvious is the difference between a statement and a question. Thus, vocal inflection or pitch makes the difference between the declarative sentence "So this is the proposal you want me to support" and the question "So this is the proposal you want me to support?"

The obvious problems that arise in relation to pitch are levels that are too high, too low, and too patterned. Neither of the first two problems is common in speakers with otherwise normal voices, and with practice you can correct a pitch pattern that is too predictable or monotonous. With increased speaking experience, pitch changes will come naturally from the sense of what you're saying. After all, each sentence is somewhat different from every other sentence, so there should be a normal variation—a variation that results not from some conscious or predetermined pattern but rather from the meanings you wish to convey to the audience.

Pauses

Pauses come in two basic types: filled and unfilled. Filled pauses are pauses in the stream of speech that we fill with vocalizations such as *er, um, ah,* and the like. Even expressions such as *well* and *you know,*

when used to fill up silence, are called filled pauses. These pauses are ineffective and weaken the strength of your message. They will make you appear hesitant, unprepared, and unsure of yourself.

Unfilled pauses, in contrast, are silences interjected into the normally fluent stream of speech. Unfilled pauses can be extremely effective if used correctly. Here are just a few examples of places where unfilled pauses—silences of a few seconds—should prove effective.

1. Pause at transitional points. This will signal that you're moving from one part of the speech to another or from one idea to another. It will help the listeners separate the main issues you're discussing.
2. Pause at the end of an important assertion. This will allow the audience time to think about the significance of what you're saying.
3. Pause after asking a rhetorical question. This will give your listeners time to think about how they would answer the question.
4. Pause before an important idea. This will help signal that what comes next is especially significant.

In addition, pauses are helpful both before you begin to speak and after you've concluded. Don't start speaking as soon as you get to the front of the room; rather, pause to scan the audience and gather your thoughts. Also, don't leave the podium as you speak your last word: Pause to allow your speech to sink in—and to avoid giving the audience the impression that you're anxious to leave them.

Bodily Action

Your body is a powerful instrument in your speech. You speak with your body as well as with your mouth. The total effect of the speech depends not only on what you say but also on the way you present it. It depends on your movements, gestures, and facial expressions as well as your words.

Six aspects of bodily action are especially important in public speaking: eye contact, facial expression, posture, gestures, movement, and proxemics.

Eye Contact. As I've emphasized so often before, the most important single aspect of bodily communication is eye contact. The two major problems with eye contact in public speaking are not enough eye contact and eye contact that does not cover the audience fairly. Speakers who do not maintain enough eye contact appear distant and uncon-cerned and may be seem as less trustworthy than speakers who look directly at their audience. And, of course, without eye contact, you will not be able to secure that all-important audience feedback.

Maintain eye contact with the entire audience. Involve all listeners in the public speaking transac-tion. Communicate equally with the members on the left and on the right, in both the back and the front.

Use eye contact to secure audience feedback. Are they interested? Bored? Puzzled? In agreement? In disagreement? Use your eyes to communicate your commitment to and interest in what you're saying. Communicate your confidence and commitment by making direct eye contact; avoid staring blankly through your audience or gazing over their heads, down at the floor, or out the window.

Facial Expression.

Facial expressions are espe-cially important in communicating **emotions**—your anger or fear, boredom or excitement, doubt or surprise. If you feel committed to and believe in your thesis, you'll probably display your emotional messages appropriately and effectively.

Nervousness and anxiety, however, can some-times prevent you from relaxing enough so that your emotions come through. Fortunately, time and practice will allow you to relax, and the emotions you feel will reveal themselves appropriately and automatically.

Generally, members of one culture will be able to recognize the emotions displayed facially by mem-bers of other cultures. But there are differences in what each culture considers appropriate to display. Each culture has its own "display rules" (Ekman, Friesen, & Ellsworth, 1972). For example, Japanese Americans watching a stress-inducing film sponta-neously displayed the same facial emotions as did other Americans when they thought they were un-observed. But when an observer was present, the Japanese masked (tried to hide) their emotional ex-pressions more than did the Americans (Gudykunst & Kim, 1992).

Posture.

When delivering your speech, stand straight but not stiff. Try to communicate a com-mand of the situation without communicating the discomfort that is actually quite common for begin-ning speakers.

Avoid the common posture mistakes: Avoid put-ting your hands in your pockets, and avoid leaning on the desk, the podium, or the chalkboard. With practice you'll come to feel more at ease and will communicate this by the way you stand before the audience.

Gestures.

Gestures in public speaking help illus-trate your verbal messages. We do this regularly in conversation. For example, when saying "Come here," you probably move your head, hands, arms, and perhaps your entire body to motion the listener in your direction. Your body and your verbal mes-sage say "Come here."

Avoid using your hands to preen; for example, restrain yourself from fixing your hair or adjusting your clothing. Avoid fidgeting with your watch, ring, or jewelry. Also avoid keeping your hands in your pockets or clasped in front of you or behind your back.

Effective gestures give the impression of being spontaneous and natural to you as the speaker, to your relationship with the audience, and to the sub-ject matter of your speech. If gestures seem planned or rehearsed, they'll appear phony and insincere. As a general rule, don't do anything with your hands that doesn't feel right for you; the audience will rec-ognize it as unnatural. If you feel relaxed and com-fortable with yourself and your audience, you'll gen-erate natural bodily action without conscious or studied attention.

Movement.

By *movement* here I am referring to your large bodily movements. It helps to move around a bit. It keeps both the audience and you more alert. Even when speaking behind a lectern, you can give the illusion of movement. You can step back or forward or flex your upper body so you ap-pear to be moving more than you are.

Avoid three potential problems of movement: too little, too much, and too patterned. Speakers who move too little often appear strapped to the podium, afraid of the audience, or too detached to involve themselves fully. At the other extreme, when there's too much movement, the audience begins to concentrate on the movement itself, wondering where the speaker will wind up next. With move-ment that is too patterned, the audience may be-come bored—too steady and predictable a rhythm quickly becomes tiring. The audience will often view the speaker as nonspontaneous and uninvolved.

Use gross movements to emphasize transitions or to emphasize the introduction of a new and important assertion. Thus, when making a transition, you might take a step forward to signal that something new is coming. Similarly, this type of movement might signal the introduction of an important assumption, a key piece of evidence, or a closely reasoned argument.

If you're using a lectern, you may wish to signal transitions by stepping to the side or in front of it and then behind it again as you move from one point to another. As always, it's best to avoid the extremes; too much movement around the lectern and no movement from the lectern are both to be avoided. You may wish to lean over the lectern when, say, posing a question to your listeners or advancing a particularly important argument. But never lean on the lectern; never use it as support.

Proxemics. Proxemics, as discussed in Unit 8, is the study of how you use space in communication. In public speaking the space between you and your listeners and among the listeners themselves is often a crucial factor. If you stand too close to the people in the audience, they may feel uncomfortable, as if their personal space is being violated. If you stand too far away from your audience, you may be perceived as uninvolved, uninterested, and uncomfortable. Watch where your instructor and other speakers stand, and adjust your own position accordingly.

REFLECTIONS ON ETHICS IN HUMAN COMMUNICATION

Criticizing Ethically

Throughout your public speaking training, you'll be called upon to critique the speeches of others. Just as you have ethical responsibilities as a speaker and as a listener, you also have such responsibilities as a critic. Here are a few guidelines you may want to consider.

First, ethical critics separate personal feelings about the speaker from their evaluations. A liking for the speaker should not lead you to give a positive evaluation to a speech, nor should disliking the speaker lead you to evaluate the speech negatively.

Second, ethical critics separate personal feelings about the issues from an evaluation of the validity of the arguments. The ethical critic recognizes the validity of an argument even if it contradicts a deeply held belief—and recognizes the fallaciousness of an argument even if it supports a deeply held belief.

Third, ethical critics are culturally sensitive; they are aware of their own ethnocentrism, and they don't negatively evaluate customs and forms of speech simply because they differ from their own. Conversely, ethical critics don't positively evaluate a speech just because it supports their own cultural beliefs and values. Ethical critics don't discriminate for or against speakers simply because they're of a particular gender, race, nationality, religion, age group, or affectional orientation.

What would you do? *You and your best friend, Pete, are taking this course together. Pete just gave a pretty terrible speech, and unfortunately, the instructor has asked you to offer a critique. The wrinkle here is that the instructor's grades for speeches seem to be heavily influenced by what student critics say. So in effect, your critique will largely determine Pete's grade. You'd like to give Pete a positive critique so he can earn a good grade—which he badly needs—and you figure you can always tell him the truth later and even work with him to help him improve. What would you do? Would you do anything differently if you would receive a grade for the critique itself based on how perceptive and accurate it was?*

SUMMARY

This unit focused on outlining, style, rehearsal, and delivery and offered suggestions for using preparation, skeletal, and delivery outlines; choosing words and phrasing sentences; and rehearsing and delivering your speech.

1. An outline is a blueprint that helps you organize and evaluate your speech. The preparation outline is extremely detailed and includes all of your main points, supporting materials, introduction, conclusion, transition, and references. The skeletal outline is a kind of template that can help you see where certain material can be placed. The delivery outline is a brief version of your preparation outline that you use as a guide when delivering your speech.

2. Compared with written style, oral style contains shorter, simpler, and more familiar words; greater qualification; and more self-referential terms.

3. Effective public speaking style is clear (be economical and specific; use guide phrases; and stick to short, familiar, and commonly used terms), vivid (use active verbs, strong verbs, figures of speech, and imagery), appropriate to your audience (speak on a suitable level of formality; avoid jargon and technical expressions; avoid slang, vulgarity, and offensive terms), personal (use personal pronouns, ask questions, and create immediacy), and forceful (eliminate weakeners, vary intensity, and avoid trite expressions).

4. In constructing sentences for public speeches, favor short, direct, active, and positively phrased sentences. Vary the type and length.

5. Use rehearsal to time your speech; perfect your volume, rate, and pitch; incorporate pauses and other delivery notes; and perfect your bodily action.

6. There are four basic methods of delivering a public speech. The impromptu method involves speaking without any specific preparation. The manuscript method involves writing out the entire speech and reading it to the audience. Memorized delivery involves writing out the speech, memorizing it, and reciting it. The extemporaneous method involves thorough preparation and memorizing of the main ideas and their order of appearance but no commitment to exact wording.

7. Effective delivery is natural, reinforces the message, is varied, and has a conversational quality. When you deliver your speech, regulate your voice for greatest effectiveness. Adjust your vocal volume, rate, and pitch as appropriate.

8. Use unfilled pauses to signal a transition between the major parts of the speech, to allow the audience time to think, to allow the audience to ponder a rhetorical question, or to signal the approach of a particularly important idea. Avoid filled pauses; they weaken your message.

9. Effective body action involves maintaining eye contact with your entire audience, allowing your facial expressions to convey your feelings, using your posture to communicate command of the public speaking interaction, gesturing naturally, and moving around a bit.

KEY TERMS

outline	slang	extemporaneous speech
preparation outline	personal style	monotonous patterns
skeletal outline	immediacy	predictable patterns
delivery outline	weakeners	vocal volume
oral style	clichés	vocal rate
clarity	impromptu speech	vocal pitch
vividness	manuscript speech	pauses
figures of speech	memorized delivery	

THINKING CRITICALLY ABOUT

Style and Delivery in Public Speaking

1. As part of her second employment interview, Shandra is asked to give a speech to the group of analysts she'd supervise (as well as to the management that will make the hiring decision). Shandra knows very little about the corporate culture; people working there describe it as "conservative," "professional but friendly," and "hardworking." What advice would you give Shandra concerning her speaking style? For example, should she strive for a personal style or an impersonal one? A powerful style? Should she strive for immediacy, or should she signal distance? Would your advice differ if Shandra were significantly older than the group she'd be supervising? Would your advice differ if Shandra were significantly younger than the group? Would you give different advice if the audience were all male? All female? Mixed?

2. Francisco is scheduled to give two speeches, one to a predominantly female audience of health professionals and one to a predominantly male audience of small business owners. His topic for both groups is the same: neighborhood violence. What advice—if any—would you give Francisco for tailoring his speech to the two different audiences? If you would not offer advice, why not?

3. John has this great joke that is only tangentially related to his speech topic. But the joke is so great that it will immediately get the audience actively involved in his speech; and this, John thinks, outweighs the fact that it isn't integrally related to the speech. John asks your advice; what do you suggest?

4. Michael has a very formal type of personality; he's very restrained in everything he does. But he wants to try to project a different image—the image of a much more personable, friendly, informal type of guy—in his speeches. What advice would you give Michael?

5. Whether or not you speak English as a second language, visit a website devoted to ESL; one such site is http://www.lang.uiuc.edu/r-li5/esl/). What can you learn from this website that could supplement the information covered in this unit?

6. Try rephrasing each of these clichés or idioms to make them—following the guidelines for language given in this unit—clear, vivid, appropriate, personal, and forceful.

- It's a blessing in disguise.
- He meant well, but he drove everyone up the wall.
- He just has to get his act together.
- She has a heart of gold.
- I talked and talked, but it was in one ear and out the other.
- Lighten up; keep your shirt on.
- He let it slip through his fingers.
- That Stephen King movie will make your hair stand on end.
- Well, it's easy being a Monday morning quarterback.
- It's water over the dam.
- It was fun, but it wasn't what it was cracked up to be.
- Wow, you're touchy. You get up on the wrong side of the bed?

7. Mary comes from a background very different from that of the other students in her class—Mary's family dressed for dinner, women were encouraged to be accepting rather than assertive, and politeness was emphasized above all else. If Mary communicates this image of herself, she thinks the class will see her as an outsider, not only as a speaker but also as a person. She wonders if there's anything she can do in her speeches to present herself in a light that others will respond to positively. What advice would you give Mary?

8. Prepare and deliver a two-minute speech in which you do one of the following:
- describe the language of a noted personality (in television, politics, arts, etc.)
- describe the delivery of a speaker you consider effective and the delivery of one you consider ineffective
- describe the delivery style of a prominent comedian or compare the delivery styles of any two comedians
- introduce an excerpt from literature and read the excerpt as you might a manuscript speech
- analyze an advertisement in terms of one or two of the characteristics of effective style: clarity, vividness, appropriateness, personal style, or forcefulness
- describe an object in the room using visual, auditory, and tactile imagery

UNIT 18
The Informative Speech

Unit Contents

Many of the speeches you'll deliver will be informative speeches, in which you'll explain to an audience how something works or how to do something. In this unit you'll learn

▶ the principles of informing listeners

▶ how you can develop speeches that describe objects, people, and events; define terms and theories; and demonstrate how something works or how to do something

GUIDELINES FOR INFORMATIVE SPEAKING

When you communicate "information," you tell your listeners something new, something they don't know. You may tell them about a new way of looking at old things or an old way of looking at new things. You may discuss a theory not previously heard of or a familiar theory not fully understood. You may discuss events that the audience may be unaware of or may have misconceptions about. Regardless of what type of informative speech you intend to give, the following guidelines should help.

Limit the Amount of Information

Resist the temptation to overload your listeners with information. Limit the breadth of information you communicate; instead, expand its depth. Limiting the amount of information lets you present a few items of information and explain these with examples, illustrations, and descriptions rather than presenting a wide array of items without this needed amplification. The speaker who attempts to discuss the physiological, psychological, social, and linguistic differences between men and women, for example, is clearly trying to cover too much and is going to be forced to cover these areas only superficially,

UNDERSTANDING THEORY AND RESEARCH

Information Theory

In the 1940s, mathematicians and engineers working at Bell Telephone Laboratories developed the mathematical theory of communication—which became known as *information theory* (Shannon & Weaver, 1949). This theory defined **information** as that which reduces uncertainty. For example, if I tell you my name and you already know it, then I haven't communicated information—because my message (my name) didn't reduce uncertainty; you already knew my name and so had no uncertainty in this connection. If, on the other hand, I tell you my salary or my educational background or my fears and dreams, that constitutes information, because these are things you presumably did not know. Although this theory doesn't explain the com-

plexities of human communication very well—for example, it views communication as a linear process (see Unit 2)—this view of information is especially helpful when you are thinking about the purpose of the informative speech: to communicate information, to tell the members of the audience something they didn't already know, or to send messages that reduce the uncertainty of your listeners about your speech topic.

Working with Theories and Research. *How much of your last telephone conversation do you think would qualify as "information"? What percentage of the content of the speeches you hear in class would be considered "information"?*

with the result that little new information will be communicated. Even covering one of these areas is likely to prove too broad. Instead, select one subdivision of one area—say, language development or differences in language problems—and develop that in depth.

Adjust the Level of Complexity

As you know from attending college classes, information can be presented in a very simplified form or in an extremely complex form. Adjusting the level of complexity on which you communicate is key and should be guided by a wide variety of factors we have already considered: the level of knowledge your audience has, the time you have available, the purpose you hope to achieve, the topic on which you're speaking, and so on. If you simplify a topic too much, you risk boring or, even worse, insulting your audience. If your talk is too complex, you risk confusing your audience and failing to communicate the desired information.

Generally, however, beginning speakers err on the side of being too complex and do not realize that a 5- or 10-minute speech does not allow much time to introduce sophisticated concepts or make an audience understand how a complicated process works. At least in your beginning speeches, try to keep it simple rather than complex. For example, make sure the words you use are familiar to your audience—or, if they're not, explain and define the terms as you use them. Remember too that jargon and technical vocabulary familiar to the computer hacker may not be familiar to the person who still uses a typewriter. Always see your topic from the point of view of the members of the audience; ask yourself how much they know about your topic and its unique language.

Stress Relevance and Usefulness

Listeners will remember your information best when they see it as useful and relevant to their own needs or goals. Notice that as a listener you regularly follow the principle of stressing relevance and usefulness. For example, in class you may attend to and remember the stages in the development of language in children simply because you know you'll be tested on the information and you want to earn a high grade. Or you may attend to the information because it will help you make a better impression in your job interview, make you a better parent, or enable you to deal with relationship problems. Like you, listeners attend to information that will prove useful to them.

If you want the audience to listen to your speech, relate your information to their needs, wants, or goals (Frymier & Shulman, 1995). Throughout your speech, but especially in the beginning, make sure your audience knows that the information you're presenting is relevant and useful to them now—or will be in the immediate future. For example, you might say something like:

> We all want financial security. We all want to be able to buy those luxuries we read so much about in magazines and see every evening on television. Wouldn't it be nice to be able to buy a car without worrying about where you're going to get the down payment or how you'll be able to make the monthly payments? Actually, that is not an unrealistic goal, as I'll demonstrate in this speech. In fact, I will show you several methods for investing your money that will enable you to increase your income by at least 20 percent.

Relate New Information to Old

Listeners will learn information more easily and retain it longer when you relate it to what they already know. In relating new information to old, link the unfamiliar to the familiar, the unseen to the seen, the untasted to the tasted. Here, for example, Teresa Jacob, a student at Ohio State University (Schnoor, 1997, p. 97), relates the problems of drug interactions (the new) to mixing chemicals in the school lab (the old or familiar):

> During our high school years, most of us learned in a chemistry class the danger of mixing harmless chemicals in lab. Add one drop of the wrong compound and suddenly you've created a stink bomb, or worse, an explosion. Millions of Americans run the same risk inside their bodies each day by combining drugs that are supposed to help restore or maintain good health.

Vary the Levels of Abstraction

You can talk about freedom of the press in **abstractions**—for example, by talking about the importance of getting information to the public, by referring to the Bill of Rights, and by relating a free press to the preservation of democracy. That is, you can talk about the topic on a relatively high **level of abstraction.** But you can also talk about freedom of

BUILDING COMMUNICATION SKILLS

How Can You Use the Abstraction Ladder?

The "abstraction ladder" is a device that illustrates the different levels of abstraction on which different ideas or entities exist. For example, as you go from "animal" to "dog" to "poodle" to "pampered white toy poodle," you're going down in terms of abstraction; You're getting more and more concrete and specific. As you get more specific, you more clearly communicate your own meanings and more easily direct the listener's attention to what you wish. For each of the terms listed below, indicate at least four possible terms of increasing specificity. The first example is done for you.

Level 1	Level 2 (more specific than 1)	Level 3 (more specific than 2)	Level 4 (more specific than 3)	Level 5 (more specific than 4)
house	mansion	brick mansion	large brick mansion	the governor's mansion
desire				
car				
toy				
magazine				
sports				

the press by citing specific examples: how a local newspaper was prevented from running a story critical of the town council or how Lucy Rinaldo was fired from the *Accord Sentinel* after she wrote a story critical of the mayor. In other words, you can talk about the topic on a relatively low level of abstraction, a level that is specific and concrete.

Varying the levels of abstraction—combining the abstract and the specific—seems to work best. Too many high abstractions without specifics or too many specifics without high abstractions will generally prove less effective than a combination of the two approaches.

Here, for example, is an excerpt from a speech on the issue of homelessness. Note that in the first paragraph we have a relatively abstract description of homelessness. In the second paragraph, we get into specifics. In the last paragraph the abstract and the concrete are connected.

Homelessness is a serious problem for all metropolitan areas throughout the country. It's currently estimated that there are more than 200,000 homeless people in New York City alone. But what is this really about? Let me tell you what it's about.

It's about a young man. He must be about 25 or 30, although he looks a lot older. He lives in a cardboard box on the side of my apartment house. We call him Tom, although we really don't know his name. All his possessions are stored in this huge box. I think it was a box from a refrigerator. Actually, he doesn't have very much, and what he has easily fits in this box. There's a blanket my neighbor threw out, some plastic bottles he puts water in, and some Styrofoam containers he picked up from the garbage from Burger King. He uses these to store whatever food he finds.

What is homelessness about? It's about Tom and 200,000 other "Toms" in New York and thousands of others throughout the rest of the country. And not all of them even have boxes to live in.

THE SPEECH OF DESCRIPTION

When you prepare a speech of description, you're concerned with explaining an object, person, event, or process. Here are a few examples:

Describing an Object or Person

- the structure of the brain
- the inventions of Thomas Edison
- the parts of a telephone
- the layout of the Alamo
- the hierarchy of a corporation
- the human body
- the components of a computer system

Describing an Event or Process

- the attack on the World Trade Center
- the events leading to World War II
- how to organize a body-building contest
- the breakdown of Russian communism
- how a newspaper is printed
- the process of buying a house
- purchasing stock online
- how a child acquires language
- how to read a textbook

Strategies for Describing

Here are some suggestions for describing objects, people, events, and processes.

Select an Appropriate Organizational Pattern

Choose the organizational pattern (see Unit 16) that best suits your topic. Consider using a spatial or a topical organization when describing objects and people, a temporal pattern for events and processes. For example, if you were to describe the layout of Philadelphia, you might start from the north and work down to the south (using a spatial pattern). If you were to describe the inventions of Thomas Edison, you might select the three or four major projects and discuss each of these equally (using a topical pattern).

If you were describing the events leading up to World War II, you might use a temporal pattern and start with the earliest and work up to the latest. A temporal pattern would also be appropriate for describing how a hurricane develops or how a parade is put together.

Use a Variety of Descriptive Categories

Describe the object or event with lots of descriptive categories. For example, for physical categories ask yourself questions such as these:

- What color is it?
- How big is it?
- What is it shaped like?
- How high is it?
- How much does it weigh?
- How long or short is it?
- What is its volume?
- How attractive/unattractive is it?

Also consider social, psychological, and economic categories, among others. In describing a person, for example, consider such categories as friendly/unfriendly, warm/cold, rich/poor, aggressive/meek, and pleasant/unpleasant.

Consider Using Presentation Aids

Presentation aids such as those described in Unit 16 will help you describe almost anything. Use them if you possibly can. In describing an object or person, show your listeners a picture of, for example, the brain, the inside of a telephone, or the human skeleton. In describing an event or process, show them a diagram or flowchart to illustrate the stages or steps; for example, show the steps involved in buying stock, publishing a newspaper, or putting a parade together.

Consider Who, What, Where, When, and Why

The 5 W categories (Unit 16) are especially useful when you want to describe an event or process. For example, if you're going to describe how to purchase a house, you might want to consider the people involved (who?), the steps you have to go through (what?), the places you'll have to go (where?), the time or sequence in which each of the steps has to take place (when?), and the advantages and disadvantages of buying the house (why?).

Developing the Speech of Description

Here are two sample outlines showing how you might go about constructing a speech of descrip-

```
┌─┤ UNDERSTANDING THEORY AND RESEARCH ├─┐
```

Signal-to-Noise Ratio

A useful way of looking at information is in terms of its **signal-to-noise ratio.** *Signal* in this context refers to information that is useful to you, information that you want. *Noise,* on the other hand, is what you find useless; it's what you do not want. So, for example, a mailing list or newsgroup that contained lots of useful information would be high in signal and low in noise; one that contains lots of useless information would be high in noise and

low in signal. Spam is high in noise and low in signal, as is static that interferes with radio, television, and telephone transmission.

> **Working with Theories and Research.** *Review your e-mail from the past week. What was signal and what was noise? Can you just as easily classify public speeches or advertisements or interpersonal conversations into signal and noise?*

tion. Each example includes both the thesis and the question asked of the thesis (which helps identify the major propositions of the speech). In this first example, the speaker describes four suggestions for increasing assertiveness (following a temporal sequence). Notice that the steps follow the order one would follow in becoming more assertive.

General Purpose: To inform.
Specific Purpose: To describe how we can become more assertive.
Thesis: Assertiveness can be increased. (How can assertiveness be increased?)

I. Analyze assertive behaviors.
II. Record your own assertive behaviors.
III. Rehearse assertive behaviors.
IV. Act assertively.

In this second example, the speaker describes the way in which fear works in intercultural communication.

General Purpose: To inform.
Specific Purpose: To describe the way fear works in intercultural communication.
Thesis: Fear influences intercultural communication. (How does fear influence intercultural communication?)

I. We fear disapproval.
II. We fear embarrassing ourselves.

III. We fear being harmed.

In delivering such a speech a speaker might begin by saying:

There are three major fears that interfere with intercultural communication. First, we fear disapproval—from members of our own group as well as from members of the other person's group. Second, we fear embarrassing ourselves, even making fools of ourselves, by saying the wrong thing or appearing insensitive. And third, we may fear being harmed—our stereotypes of the other group may lead us to see its members as dangerous or potentially harmful to us.

Let's look at each of these fears in more detail so as to see how they influence our own intercultural communication behavior.

Consider, first, the fear of disapproval.

THE SPEECH OF DEFINITION

What is leadership? What is a born-again Christian? What is the difference between sociology and psychology? What is a cultural anthropologist? What is safe sex? These are all topics for informative speeches of definition.

A definition is a statement of the meaning or significance of a concept or term. Use a speech of definition when you wish to explain a difficult or unfamiliar concept or when you wish to make a concept more vivid or forceful. You might wish to complement this discussion with a visit to one or more of the online dictionaries; for example, see the Hypertext Webster Interface at http://c.gp.cs.cmu.edu: 5103/prog/webster/ for an unusual dictionary that provides hypertext definitions so that you can get definitions of the words in the definition itself. Or visit Your Dictionary at www.yourdictionary. com/ for a wide variety of word books and materials.

In defining a particular term or in giving an entire speech of definition, you may focus on defining a term, elucidating a system or theory, or pinpointing the similarities and/or differences among terms or systems. It may be a subject new to the audience or one familiar to them but presented in a new and different way. Here are some examples of topics for speeches of definition:

Defining a Term

- What is multiculturalism?
- What is terrorism?
- What is a smart card?
- What is machismo?
- What is creativity?
- What is affirmative action?
- What is date rape?
- What is classism?
- What is political correctness?
- What is inflation?

Defining a System or Theory

- What is the classical theory of public speaking?
- What are the parts of a generative grammar?
- What are the major beliefs of Confucianism?
- What is expressionism?
- What is futurism?
- What is the "play theory" of mass communication?

Defining Similar and Dissimilar Terms or Systems

- Football and soccer: What's the difference?
- Communism and socialism: What are the similarities and differences?
- What do Christians and Muslims have in common?
- Oedipus and Electra: How do they differ?
- How do genetics and heredity relate to each other?

- What do ballet and square dancing have in common?
- What are the differences between critical and creative thinking?
- What do animal and human rights have in common?
- What are keyword and directory searches?
- How do freshwater and saltwater fishing differ?

Strategies for Defining

There are several approaches to defining your topic. Here are some suggestions.

Use a Variety of Definitions

When explaining a concept, it's helpful to define it in a number of different ways. Here are some of the most important ways to define a term.

Define by Etymology. The etymology or history of the development of a term can help clarify its meaning. If you look up the word *communication*, you may note that it comes from the Latin *communis*, meaning "common"; in communicating you seek to establish a commonness, a sameness, a similarity with another individual. And *woman* comes from the Anglo-Saxon *wifman*, which meant literally a "wife man," where the word *man* was applied to both sexes. Through phonetic change *wifman* became *woman*. Most larger dictionaries and, of course, etymological dictionaries will help you find useful etymological definitions.

Define by Authority. The words of expert authorities can also help with definition. You might, for example, define lateral thinking by authority and say that Edward deBono, who developed his conceptualization of lateral thinking in 1966, stated that "lateral thinking involves moving sideways to look at things in a different way. Instead of fixing on one particular approach and then working forward from that, the lateral thinker tries to find other approaches."

Or you define love and friendship by turning to the authority of cynic and satirist Ambrose Bierce, who defined love as nothing but "a temporary insanity curable by marriage" and friendship as "a ship big enough to carry two in fair weather, but only one in foul."

In what ways is the informative speech similar to and different from a stand-up comedy routine?

Define by Negation.   You might also define a term by negation—by noting what the term is not. "A wife," you might say, "is not a cook, a cleaning person, a baby-sitter, a seamstress, a sex partner. A wife is . . . ." Or "A teacher is not someone who tells you what you should know but rather one who . . . ." Here Michael Marien (1992, p. 340) defines futurists first negatively and then positively:

> Futurists do not use crystal balls. Indeed, they're generally loath to make firm predictions of what will happen. Rather, they make forecasts of what is probable, sketch scenarios of what is possible, and/or point to desirable futures—what is preferable and what strategies we should pursue to get there.

Define by Direct Symbolization.   You might also define a term by direct symbolization—by showing the actual thing or a picture or model of it. For example, a sales representative explaining a new computer keyboard would obviously use an actual keyboard in the speech. Similarly, a speech on magazine layout or on types of fabrics could include actual layout pages or fabric samples.

Use Definitions to Add Clarity

If the purpose of the definition is to clarify, then it must do just that. This might seem too obvious to mention—but in reality many speakers, perhaps for want of something to say, define terms that don't need extended definitions. Some speakers even use definitions that don't clarify but that actually complicate already complex concepts. Make sure your definitions define only what needs defining.

Use Credible Sources

When you quote an authority to define a term, make sure the person is in fact an authority. Tell the audience who the authority is and the basis for the individual's expertise. In the following excerpt, note how Russell Peterson (1985, p. 549) uses the expertise of Robert McNamara in his definition:

> When Robert McNamara was president of the World Bank, he coined the term "absolute poverty" to characterize a condition of life so degraded by malnutri-

---

BUILDING COMMUNICATION SKILLS

How Can You Define a Term?

Get some practice in defining terms—an essential skill in all forms of communication—by selecting one of the following terms and defining it, using at least three different types of definitions (etymology, authority, negation, or direct symbolization): *communication, love, friendship, conflict, leadership, audience.* If you have the opportunity, compare your definitions with those of others. You'll find it helpful to visit a few online dictionaries or thesauruses; try http://c.gp.cs.cmu.edu:5103/prog/webster/, http://www.m-w.com/netdict.htm, and/or http://humanities.uchicago.edu/forms_unrest/ROGET.html. A useful website containing links to varied types of dictionaries is http://www.bucknell.edu/~rbeard/diction.html.

tion, illiteracy, violence, disease and squalor, to be beneath any reasonable definition of human decency. In 1980, the World Bank estimated that 780 million persons in the developing countries lived in absolute poverty. That's about three times as many people as live in the entire United States.

Proceed from the Known to the Unknown

Start with what your audience knows and work up to what is new or unfamiliar. Let's say you want to explain the concept of phonemics, a topic with which your audience is totally unfamiliar. The specific idea you wish to get across is that each phoneme stands for a unique sound. You might proceed from the known to the unknown and begin your definition with something like this:

> We all know that in our written language each letter of the alphabet stands for a unit of the written language. Each letter is different from every other letter. A *t* is different from a *g* and a *g* is different from a *b* and so on. Each letter is called a grapheme. In English we know we have 26 such letters.
>
> We can look at the spoken language in much the same way. Each sound is different from every other sound. A *t* sound is different from a *d* and a *d* is different from a *k* and so on. Each individual sound is called a phoneme.

Now, let me explain in a little more detail what I mean by a phoneme.

Developing the Speech of Definition

Here are two examples of how you might go about constructing a speech of definition. In this first example, the speaker explains the symptoms of Alzheimer's disease, using a topical order to treat all symptoms equally.

General Purpose: To inform.
Specific Purpose: To define the major symptoms of Alzheimer's disease.
Thesis: There are four major symptoms of Alzheimer's. (What are these four symptoms?)

  I. Alzheimer's patients may experience memory impairment.
 II. Alzheimer's patients may experience speech difficulties.
III. Alzheimer's patients may experience a loss in abstract thinking.
 IV. Alzheimer's patients may experience personality changes.

GOING ONLINE

Gifts of Speech Website

http://gos.sbc.edu

Visit the Gifts of Speech website, a site devoted to women speakers, and read one of the speeches. In what specific ways does the speaker follow or not follow the suggestions for communicating information discussed in this unit?

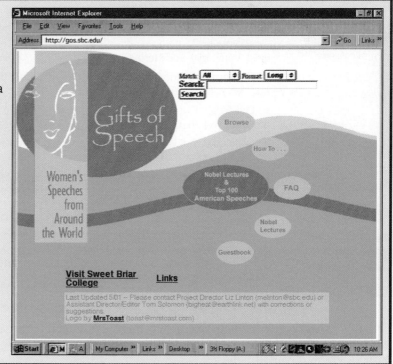

Information Overload

Everybody gets so much information all day long that they lose their common sense.

—Gertrude Stein

Information overload is one of the greatest obstacles to achieving efficiency in business and has even been linked to health problems in more than one-third of managers (Lee, 2000). Information is now generated at such a rapid rate that it's impossible to keep up with all that's relevant to your job. Today, for example, the American worker is exposed to more information in one year than a person living in 1900 was in his or her entire life. Invariably, you must select certain information to attend to and other information to omit. The junk mail and spam that seems to grow every day is a perfect example. The average employee today receives more than 50 e-mails daily. In one day the average manager sends and receives more than 100 documents.

One of the problems information overload creates is that it absorbs an enormous amount of time for workers at all levels of an organization. The more messages you have to deal with, the less time you have for those messages or tasks that are central to your functions. Similarly, errors become more likely under conditions of information overload, simply because you cannot devote the needed time to any one item. The more rushed you are, the more likely you are to make mistakes.

Another problem is that the overabundance of messages may make it difficult for a worker to prioritize—to determine efficiently which messages need immediate attention and which don't, which messages may be discarded and which must be retained.

Several suggestions should help you deal with information overload (Uris, 1986):

▶ Think before passing on messages. Not all messages must be passed on; not everyone needs to know everything.

▶ Use messages as they come to you, then throw them out; for example, write the date for a meeting on your calendar and then throw out the announcement. If it's a computer file, delete it. Or, if you're afraid you might need the information later, copy it to disk, label it carefully, and store it.

▶ Organize your messages. Create folders to help you store the information you need and retrieve it quickly.

▶ Get rid of extra copies. When you receive multiple copies, get rid of all but the one (if any) that you need.

▶ Distinguish between material that you should save and material that is only cluttering up your space.

▶ Throw out materials that can easily be located elsewhere. Data posted on nearby bulletin boards, for example, usually do not have to be on your desk as well.

Thinking about Your Communicating @ Work

How do you deal with information overload? Are you generally pleased with your handling of the information that comes your way? If not, what might you do to deal more effectively with the inevitable overload?

In this second example, the speaker selects three major types of lying for discussion and arranges these in a topical pattern.

General Purpose: To inform.
Specific Purpose: To define lying by explaining the major types of lying.

Thesis: There are three major kinds of lying. (What are the three major kinds of lying?)

I. Concealment is the process of hiding the truth.
II. Falsification is the process of presenting false information as if it were true.
III. Misdirection is the process of acknowledging a thought or feeling but misidentifying its cause.

In delivering such a speech, a speaker might begin the speech by saying:

A lie is a lie is a lie. True? Well, not exactly. Actually, there are three different ways we can lie. We can lie by concealing the truth. We can lie by falsification, by presenting false information as if it were true. And we can lie by misdirection, by acknowledging a thought or feeling but misidentifying its cause. Let's look at the first type of lie—the lie of concealment.

Most lies are lies of concealment. Most of the time when we lie we simply conceal the truth. We don't actually make any false statements. Rather, we simply don't reveal the truth. Let me give you some examples I overheard recently.

THE SPEECH OF DEMONSTRATION

In using demonstration (or in a speech devoted entirely to demonstration), you would explain how to do something or how something operates. Here are some examples of topics well adapted to the speech of demonstration:

Demonstrating How to Do Something

- how to give mouth-to-mouth resuscitation
- how to use PowerPoint
- how to balance a checkbook
- how to pilot a plane
- how to drive defensively
- how to mix colors
- how to say no
- how to prevent burnout
- how to ask for a raise
- how to burglar-proof your house
- how to develop your body

Demonstrating How Something Operates

- how the body maintains homeostasis
- how a thermostat operates
- how perception works
- how the Internet works
- how divorce laws work
- how e-mail works
- how probate works
- how a hurricane develops
- how a heart bypass operation is performed

Strategies for Demonstrating

In demonstrating how to do something or how something operates, consider the following guidelines.

Use Temporal Organization

In most cases a temporal pattern will work best in speeches of demonstration. Demonstrate each step in the order in which it's to be performed. In this way you'll avoid one of the major difficulties in demonstrating a process, backtracking. Don't skip steps, even if you think they're familiar to the audience; they may not be.

Connect each step to the next with appropriate transitions. For example, in explaining the Heimlich maneuver you might say:

Now that you have your arms around the choking victim's chest, your next step is to . . . ."

Assist your listeners by labeling the steps clearly; for example, say "the first step," "the second step," and so on.

Begin with an Overview

It's often helpful when demonstrating to give a broad general picture and then present each step in turn. For example, let's say you are talking about how to prepare a wall for painting. You might begin with a general overview:

In preparing the wall for painting, you want to make sure that the wall is smoothly sanded, free of dust, and dry. Sanding a wall is not like sanding a block of wood. So let's look at the proper way to sand a wall.

In this way, your listeners will have a general idea of how you'll go about demonstrating the process.

Consider the Value of Presentation Aids

Presentation aids are especially helpful in showing the sequential steps of a process. A good example of how aids work is the signs in all restaurants demonstrating the Heimlich maneuver. These signs demonstrate the steps with pictures as well as words. The combination of verbal and graphic information makes it easy to understand this lifesaving process. In a speech on the Heimlich maneuver, however, the best aid would be the pictures alone—so that the written words would not distract your audience from your oral explanation. Or, perhaps even better, you might enlist the aid of another person and demonstrate the actual movements.

Developing the Speech of Demonstration

Here are two examples of the speech of demonstration. In this first example, the speaker explains the proper way to argue by identifying the ways we should not argue. As you can see, these unproduc-

MEDIA WATCH

THE KNOWLEDGE GAP

The term *knowledge gap* refers to the difference in knowledge between one group and another; it's the division between those who have a great deal of knowledge and those who have significantly less. Researchers who have focused on the influence of mass media in widening this knowledge gap have generated what is known as the *knowledge gap hypothesis* (Tichenor, Donohue, & Olien, 1970; Severin & Tankard, 1988; Viswanath & Finnegan, 1995).

Information is valuable; it gives power and it can bring wealth. It gives you the means you need to get a high-paid job, to live a healthy life, to plan for retirement, or to accomplish just about any task you set for yourself (Mastin, 1998).

But information is also expensive, and not everyone has equal access to it. This is especially true as we live more of our lives in cyberspace. The new communication technologies—computers, CD-ROMs, the Internet, and satellite and cable television, for example—are major means for gaining information. Better-educated people have the money to own and the skills to master the new technologies and thus acquire more information. Less-educated people don't have the money to own or the skills to master the new technologies and thus cannot acquire much of the information that is out there. Thus, the educated have the means for becoming even better educated, and the gap widens. A particularly clear example of this pattern is seen in the educational level of Internet users (UCLA Internet Report, 2000):

▶ Of those with less than a high school education, 13 percent use the Internet

▶ Of high school graduates, 53 percent use the Internet

▶ Of those with some college education, 70 percent use the Internet

▶ Of college graduates and those with advanced degrees, 86 percent use the Internet

You can also witness the knowledge gap when you compare different cultures. Industrialized countries, for example, have the new technologies in their schools and offices, and many people can afford to buy their own computers and satellite systems. Access to the new technologies helps these countries develop even further. Developing countries, with little or no access to such technologies, cannot experience the same gains in knowledge and information as those with more technological access.

Even the language of a culture may influence the extent of the knowledge gap. For example, the English language dominates the Internet, so the Internet is more easily accessible to people in the United States and other English-speaking countries (and to educated people in other countries who speak English as a second language). Still another factor is that more than half the world's people do not use the Latin alphabet; Chinese, Japanese, Korean, and Arab peoples, for example, use alphabets that make software development and Internet access more difficult—at least at the present time.

Follow-Up. *Do you see the knowledge gap operating in your community or school? Can you see it in different cultures with which you're familiar?*

tive fight strategies are all about equal in value and are arranged in a topical order.

General Purpose: To inform.
Specific Purpose: To demonstrate how to fight fairly by identifying and demonstrating four unfair conflict strategies.
Thesis: Conflict can be made more productive. (How can conflict be made more productive?)

   I. Blame the other person.
  II. Unload all your previous grievances.
 III. Make light of the other person's displeasure.
 IV. Hit the other person with issues he or she cannot handle effectively.

In the next example, the speaker identifies and demonstrates how to listen actively.

General Purpose: To inform.
Specific Purpose: To demonstrate three techniques of active listening.
Thesis: We can learn active listening. (How can we learn active listening?)

   I. Paraphrase the speaker's meaning.
  II. Express understanding of the speaker's feelings.
 III. Ask questions.

In delivering the active listening speech, the speaker might begin by saying:

> Active listening is a special kind of listening. It's listening with total involvement, with a concern for the speaker. It's probably the most important type of listening you can engage in. Active listening consists of three steps: paraphrasing the speaker's meaning, expressing understanding of the speaker's feelings, and asking questions.
>
> Your first step in active listening is to paraphrase the speaker's meaning. What is a paraphrase? A paraphrase is a restatement in your own words of the speaker's meaning. That is, you express in your own words what you think the speaker meant. For example, let's say that the speaker said . . . .

A SAMPLE INFORMATIVE SPEECH

The speech that follows is presented as a kind of summary of this unit, as well as of Units 15, 16, and 17, which covered the 10 steps of preparing a public speech. Studying this speech will help you see how all 10 steps work together to produce a finished product; it will also help you identify the major parts of an informative speech and the way they fit together. First, carefully read the accompanying speech. For your first reading, ignore the critical thinking questions at the side. After you've read the entire speech, reread it, this time reading and responding to the critical thinking questions. These questions should help you analyze the speech and see the principles of public speaking in clear application. Another useful way to review the principles and strategies of informative speaking is by trying your hand at "Criticizing an Informative Speech" at www. ablongman.com/devito.

Pharmacogenomics

Jimmy Ficaro

In this speech Jimmy Ficaro, a student from the University of Texas, defines "pharmacogenomics" and shows that pharmacogenomics promises to alter health care as we now know it.

In 1998, a new drug for treating breast cancer, Herceptin, was hailed as the medical milestone of the twentieth century. This revolutionary drug shrank tumors and saved lives. In 1999, Cindy White, a 38-year-old mother of three, was prescribed Herceptin

Does this introduction gain your attention? If so, what specifically got your attention? If not, why not?

to treat a tumor on her left breast. Rather than curing her, the drug inflamed and enlarged the tumor, resulting in her death this past fall. Unfortunately, according to the January 2, 2001, edition of *Gene-Letter,* this is an all too common tale in the world of medicine. While the medical community understands that no one drug has the same impact on each of us, doctors continue to prescribe the same medications to each of us. Trial and error is the standard operating procedure, putting our health, our emotions, and our lives on the line. Until now. Enter pharmacogenomics, the science of how genes respond to medicine—in the form of a unique collaboration between pharmaceuticals and our individual genetic makeup—that will help physicians determine accurately and quickly how to best treat each of us for everything from the common cold to hypertension to Alzheimer's and AIDS.

Does the speaker make this topic relevant to you?

In a nation where 3.1 billion prescriptions are issued every year and over 2.1 million result in unexpected and potentially dangerous side effects, the September 2000 *Pharmacogenomics Journal* explains that adverse drug reactions are the fourth leading cause of death for Americans, trailing only heart disease, car accidents, and guns. Pharmacogenomics may be the medical miracle we've been waiting for.

In what ways does the speaker relate new information to what the audience presumably already knows?

So to better understand why the Centers for Disease Control Web page, last accessed March 24, 2001 and updated daily, predicts "that doctors will soon be treating diseases before they start," we must, first, examine what pharmacogenomics is; second, discuss how it works and its current aims; and, finally, address the potential challenges and future benefits of this prescription for pharmaceutical perfection.

How effective was the speaker's orientation?

At this point, do you think the speaker is attempting to cover too much material in this relatively short speech?

How effectively does the speaker use transitions? Can you identify two or three transitions?

As with all great advancements in medical technology, pharmacogenomics did not just appear; it is the result of the next logical step in medicine. The BioSpace Web page, last updated February 5, 2001, reports that nearly 40 years ago the field of pharmacogenetics started as scientists sought to study how genes affect the way drugs are metabolized. But until the mapping of the Human Genome Project was completed in winter of 2000, scientists were left without a means to apply what they were learning. According to the Human Genome Center Web page, last updated March 3, 2001, pharmacogenomics puts the map of the human genome to use.

What types of definitions has the speaker used? Might other kinds of definitions have been effective in helping listeners understand what *pharmacogenomics* means?

How would you evaluate the research sources the speaker used? Do the sources serve to support his assertions? Do they help establish his credibility?

Our individual, unique genetic makeup explains how quickly we absorb a drug, break it down, and whether or not its active ingredients will affect us—

and pharmacogenomics will tap into that genetic makeup to determine which drug treatments will lead to a cure, or which treatments will lead to a catastrophe. Because these treatments don't change the design of drugs but the way they are prescribed, they differ from the "designer drug" fad that swept medicine in the 1980s, which is not to be confused with the "designer jean" fad that swept high schools during that same decade, resulting in a different kind of adverse reaction altogether.

Understanding how we will react to drugs is the key to effective treatment, and as we explore how it works and its current aims, we will see that pharmacogenomics has the potential to radically change the world of medicine. The *Psychiatric Times* of November 2000 illustrates exactly how pharmacogenomics works. According to the National Center for Health Web page, last updated March 7, 2001, over 80 percent of us will suffer from hypertension, or high blood pressure. With over 50 treatment options available, pharmacogenomics will enable doctors to find the right treatment for each of us from the start. The procedure begins with a blood sample. From a small amount of your blood, your genetic makeup will be analyzed and then compared with blood samples from others successfully treated for hypertension. Proper treatments are then matched for those who share genetic similarities.

The association between certain genes and certain medicines is the primary aim of pharmacogenomics. Already, notes the spring 2000 Pharmacogenomics in Europe Conference, large databases for hypertension, Alzheimer's, breast cancer, and AIDS are being developed to give doctors the edge in the race to prescribe effective drugs. The January 3, 2000, issue of *Molecular Medicine* explains that enough of us are currently living with diseases like these that massive databases could be built within a year, at minimal costs.

Additionally, after the first blood analysis, a profile of your genetic makeup is saved for future comparisons. The February 12, 2001, *Workshop on Pharmacogenomics* explains that before a doctor will prescribe any medication, they will simply pull up your profile to determine what medications are least likely to produce side effects, virtually eliminating the potential for adverse drug reactions.

However, before pharmacogenomics can become the cure-all that it promises, it must overcome some significant obstacles. The three primary challenges

If you were giving this speech and wanted to use visual aids, what types of visuals would you use? What specific purpose might these visuals serve?

What do you think of this use of humor? Is it appropriate? Relevant? Effective?

What do you think of how the speaker integrates recent material from the Internet? Is it effectively done? Is there information that the speaker doesn't give, that you would like to hear?

How effectively does the speaker blend the abstract with the specific? Do you think the speech would have been improved with more generalizations? With more specifics?

How would you describe this speech in terms of level of complexity? Would this level have been effective if your class was the audience?

What are the major propositions that the speaker covers in this speech? Were they made sufficiently clear when first introduced?

come on a scientific, practical, and ethical level. Scientifically, the human genome is very complex, and it is difficult to pinpoint exactly which part of any gene is responsible for a given response to medication. *Time* magazine of February 12, 2001, explains that as many as seven genes could be responsible for how you respond to a drug. Just because two individuals have similar genetic profiles does not guarantee the same response every day.

On a practical level, creating the necessary databases may be easier said than done. While there would be enough samples to create the databases in less than a year for most diseases, the overall comparison of thousands of genetic makeups could take some time. The *Toronto Star* of January 2, 2001, contends that diseases with a low number of treatment options, like Alzheimer's, could have databases created within 14 months—yet other diseases, such as AIDS, could take as long as four years before the entire database is compiled.

Even more disconcerting are the ethical issues surrounding genetic information. The BioSpace Web page, last updated February 5, 2001, explains that the ethical questions are the most formidable issue facing pharmacogenomics. It will be difficult to convince us to donate the blood necessary to search for common genetic matches if we can't be assured that this information will remain confidential. Pharmaceutical companies need to determine demand for certain drugs, and your genetic makeup could be sold to the highest bidder. But that could be the least of our worries. Potentially, your genetic makeup could be used against you for everything from insurance approval to job opportunities.

While geneticists around the world realize these dangers, the benefits of pharmacogenomics go a long way in balancing the scale: emotionally healthy patients and better health care costs.

Scientific American of September 2000 warns that the psychological trauma of a failed treatment is often irreversible. Once a patient has tried a myriad of treatment plans without any positive results, the emotional strain increases. Reuters on March 10, 2001, explains that pharmacogenomics can alleviate this problem, since treatments will become more accurate; the psychological trauma endured by the patient is minimal.

Additionally, the cost of health care will be cut in half for most of us. Fewer adverse reactions, a smaller number of medications, and the ability to

Do you feel that the speaker explains the potential obstacles fairly?

How would you have titled the speech if this were to be given to your class?

detect disease quickly will all play major roles in the decreased costs for our own medical treatments. The February 13, 2001, *Financial Times* predicts that this new cost-effective treatment plan will provide millions who are uninsured and cannot afford treatment a chance at survival. There is no doubt that, as the challenges are overcome, the future for pharmacogenomics is as promising as penicillin.

Herceptin is still widely used to fight breast cancer—but thanks to pharmacogenomics, doctors are closer to knowing exactly when to prescribe it. Along with hypertension and breast cancer, a limitless number of diseases will be understood better as well. By looking at what pharmacogenomics is, how it works and its current aims, and the obstacles and benefits it faces, we know that the tragedy endured by Cindy White and her family does not have to be repeated. The medical milestone of this century will not be a drug at all, but rather—a new kind of prescription.

From "Pharmacogenics" speech by Jimmy Ficaro. Courtesy of Jimmy Ficaro, University of Texas.

Does the speaker effectively summarize the speech? Does he effectively bring the speech to a close? Is the technique of connecting the conclusion back to the introduction effective? What else might the speaker have said in his conclusion?

What do you remember most about this speech? What do you think you'll remember three or four months from now?

REFLECTIONS ON ETHICS IN HUMAN COMMUNICATION

Speaking Ethically

One interesting approach to ethics that has particular relevance to public speaking argues that speakers should be guided by four principles (Wallace, 1955; Johannesen, 1994):

1. You must have a thorough knowledge of the topic, an ability to answer relevant questions, and an awareness of the significant facts and opinions bearing on the issues you discuss.
2. You must present both facts and opinions fairly, without bending or spinning them to personal advantage. You must allow listeners to make the final judgment.
3. You must reveal the sources of these facts and opinions and must assist the listeners to evaluate any biases and prejudices in the sources.
4. You must acknowledge and respect opposing arguments and evidence. You must advocate

a tolerance for diversity. Any attempt to hide valid opposing arguments from the audience is unethical.

What would you do? *You're giving a persuasive speech arguing for condom machines in rest rooms on campus. You know, however, that the money to install these machines will have to come from an increase in student fees. You wonder if you can ethically give the speech without mentioning that student fees will have to be increased. After all, you don't have time to include all the important arguments and pieces of evidence—even those that support your position. You also figure that it's the listeners' responsibility to ask where the money is coming from and not your job to tell them. What would you do?*

SUMMARY

This unit focused on the informative speech, examining the guidelines to follow in informing others and the various types of informative speeches.

1. Informative speeches are more likely to be effective when they adhere to the following principles of informative speaking: Limit the amount of information you communicate, adjust the level of complexity, stress the relevance and the usefulness of the information to your audience, relate new information to old, and vary the levels of abstraction.

2. Speeches of description describe a process or procedure, an event, an object, or a person.
3. Speeches of definition define a term, system, or theory or explain similarities and/or differences among terms.
4. Speeches of demonstration show how to do something or how something operates.

KEY TERMS

informative speech

limiting the amount of information

adjusting the level of complexity

stressing relevance and usefulness

relating new information to old

varying the levels of abstraction

speech of description

speech of definition

speech of demonstration

THINKING CRITICALLY ABOUT

The Informative Speech

1. The three types of speeches discussed in this unit are among the most popular and can incorporate most informative speech topics and goals, but there are others. See www.ablongman.com/devito for "Other Classifications of Informative Speeches." Do these additional ways of looking at informative speaking help clarify the scope of the informative speech?

2. You want to give an informative speech on virtual reality simulation, but most of your audience members have never experienced it. How would you communicate this concept and this experience to your audience?

3. You're planning to give an informative speech on the history of doctor-assisted suicides and are considering the strategies that you might use. What organizational pattern would be appropriate? What types of presentation aids might you use? How would you define "doctor-assisted suicide"?

4. You're scheduled to be the third speaker in a series of six presentations. Unfortunately, the first speaker presented an excellent speech on your topic. What should you do?

5. Select an advertisement (television or print) and examine how closely it follows the principles of informative speaking identified here. In what ways does an advertisement differ from a speech?

6. Visit the website of the Society for Technical Communication at http://www.stc-va.org/ for guides for writing and speaking on technical matters.

7. Prepare and deliver a two-minute speech in which you do one of the following:
   - describe some common object in the classroom
   - define one of the following terms, using at least two different types of definitions: *love, friendship, power, pride, jealousy, truth, freedom, honesty,* or *faithfulness*
   - demonstrate—without the aid of the object—how to tie a shoelace, use a food processor, make a phone call, sew on a button, open a door with a credit card, move a block of text on a computer, print out a computer file, or use a template
   - explain one of the principles of informative speaking, using a variety of examples

UNIT 19
The Persuasive Speech

Unit Contents

In addition to informing others, you'll also be called upon to deliver speeches of persuasion—speeches that aim to influence the attitudes and beliefs and sometimes the behaviors of your listeners. In this unit you'll learn

▶ the guidelines to follow in your persuasive speaking

▶ how you can develop a wide variety of persuasive speeches

Most of the speeches you hear are persuasive. The speeches of politicians, advertisers, and religious leaders are clear examples. In many of your own speeches, you too will aim at **persuasion;** that is, you'll try to change your listeners' attitudes and beliefs or perhaps get them to do something. In school you might try to persuade others to (or not to) expand the core curriculum, use a plus–minus or a pass–fail grading system, disband the basketball team, allocate increased student funds for the school newspaper, establish competitive majors, or eliminate fraternity initiation rituals. On your job you may be called upon to speak in favor of (or against) a union, a wage increase proposal, a health benefit package, or the election of a new shop steward.

Recall from the discussion of the audience in Unit 15 that the attitudes, beliefs, and values of your listeners are important in persuasion—because people's behavior, which is what you ultimately want to influence, depends on their attitudes, beliefs, and values. So if you can change your listeners' beliefs about, say, abortion, you may get them to vote one way or another or to contribute to a group advocating a particular abortion position. If you can change the values that people place on animals and animal experimentation, you may get them to boycott (or not boycott) cosmetics companies that use animals in their testing.

Further, the audience members' attitudes, beliefs, and values will influence how they respond to your thesis, your propositions, your arguments, your evidence, and just about everything else you do in your speech. For example, if you were going to give a speech defending doctor-assisted suicide, it would be crucial for you to know the attitudes, beliefs, and values held by your audience before you framed and supported your propositions. You would have to prepare very different speeches for an audience that saw suicide of any kind as morally wrong as opposed to an audience whose concern centered on how doctor-assisted suicides should be monitored to prevent violations of the patients' wishes.

So, in constructing your persuasive speeches and in following the 10 guidelines for persuasive speaking discussed later in this unit, be sure to take into consideration the attitudes, beliefs, and values of the audience as these relate to anything you'll say in your speech—but particularly to your thesis, major propositions, and main supports. Additionally, as you read about the strategies of persuasion, keep in mind ethical considerations. A good way to begin this ethical focus is to take the self-test "[When] Is persuasion unethical?" at www.ablongman.com/devito. 🖱

FACTS, VALUES, AND POLICIES

A useful way to look at the issues you'll be dealing with in your persuasive speeches (whether as your thesis or as particular propositions) is to view them as questions of facts, values, or policies. A more detailed discussion of "Questions of Fact, Value, and Policy" is available at www.ablongman.com/devito. 🖱

Questions of Fact

A question of fact concerns what is or is not true, what does or does not exist, what did or did not happen. The questions of fact that we deal with in persuasive speeches have answers, but the answers are not that easy to find and in fact may never be found. Many questions concern controversial issues for which different people have different answers, as in these examples:

- Iraq is hiding chemical weapons.
- This company has a glass ceiling for women.
- Harry was slandered (or libeled or defamed).
- Marie's death was a case of doctor-assisted suicide.
- Marijuana leads to hard drugs.

UNDERSTANDING THEORY AND RESEARCH

Machiavellianism

Before reading about this fascinating concept, take the self-test below, "How machiavellian are you?" It focuses on your beliefs about how easily you think people can be manipulated.

TEST YOURSELF

How Machiavellian Are You?

For each statement record the number on the following scale that most closely represents your attitude: 1 = disagree a lot; 2 = disagree a little; 3 = neutral; 4 = agree a bit; and 5 = agree a lot.

_____ 1. The best way to handle people is to tell them what they want to hear.

_____ 2. When you ask someone to do something for you, it is best to give the real reasons rather than giving reasons that might carry more weight.

_____ 3. Anyone who completely trusts anyone else is asking for trouble.

_____ 4. It is hard to get ahead without cutting corners here and there.

_____ 5. It is safest to assume that all people have a vicious streak and it will come out when they are given a chance.

_____ 6. One should take action only when sure it is morally right.

_____ 7. Most people are basically good and kind.

_____ 8. There is no excuse for lying to someone.

_____ 9. Most people forget more easily the death of their parents than the loss of their property.

_____ 10. Generally speaking, people won't work hard unless they're forced to.

How did you do? To compute your "Mach score" follow these steps:

Reverse the scores on items 2, 6, 7, and 8 so that 5 becomes 1, 4 becomes 2, 3 remains 3, 2 becomes 4, and 1 becomes 5. Add all 10 scores, being sure to use the reversed numbers for 2, 6, 7, and 8. Your Machiavellianism score is a measure of the degree to which you believe that people in gen-

eral are manipulable, though not necessarily the degree to which you actually would or do manipulate others. If you scored somewhere between 35 and 50, you would be considered a high Mach; if you scored between 10 and 15, you would be considered a low Mach. Most of us score somewhere between these extremes.

What will you do? The concept of Machiavellianism is explained in more detail below. As you read the discussion, try to visualize what you would do in the various situations described. See if your score on this test is a generally accurate description of your own Machiavellianism.

Source: From "The Machiavellis Among Us," by Richard Christie in *Psychology Today*, V. 4, November 1970, pp. 82–86. Reprinted with permission from *Psychology Today* magazine, Copyright © 1970 Sussex Publishers, Inc. ✔

Research finds significant differences between those who score high and those who score low on the Machiavellianism scale. Low Machs are more easily susceptible to social influence; they're more easily persuaded. High Machs are more resistant to persuasion. Low Machs are more empathic; high Machs are more logical. Low Machs are more interpersonally oriented and involved with other people; high Machs, more assertive and more controlling. Business students (especially marketing students) score higher in Machiavellianism than do nonbusiness majors (McLean & Jones, 1992).

Machiavellianism seems at least in part to be culturally conditioned. An individualistic cultural orientation, which favors competition and being number one, seems more conducive to the development of Machiavellianism. A collectivist orientation, which favors cooperation and group membership, seems a less friendly environment for the development of Machiavellianism. Some evidence of this comes from research showing that Chinese students attending a traditional Chinese (Confucian) school rated lower in Machiavellianism than comparable Chinese students attending a Western-style school (Christie, 1970a and b).

continued

Understanding Theory and Research continued

Your own level of Machiavellianism will influence the communication choices you make. For example, high Machs are more strategic and manipulative in their self-disclosures than are low Machs; that is, high Machs will self-disclose in ways calculated to influence the attitudes and behaviors of listeners (Steinfatt, 1987).

Machiavellianism influences the way you seek to gain the compliance of others. High Machs

are more likely to be manipulative in their conflict-resolving behavior than are low Machs. High Machs are generally more effective individuals (they even earn higher grades in communication courses that involve face-to-face interaction; see Burgoon, 1971). Low-Mach women, however, are preferred as dating partners by both high- and low-Mach men (Steinfatt, 1987).

- Gay men and lesbians make competent military personnel.
- Television violence leads to violent behavior in viewers.

At other times, you may want to establish a question of fact as one of your major propositions. So, for example, let's say you're giving a speech arguing for a military policy in which gay men and lesbians are given full equality. In this case, in one of your propositions you might seek to establish as a matter of fact that gay men and lesbians make competent military personnel. With that fact established, you might then be in a better position to argue for equality in the military.

Questions of Value

A question of value concerns what a person considers good or bad, moral or immoral, just or unjust. Examples of theses devoted to questions of value might be:

- IQ tests are biased.
- Bullfighting is inhumane.
- Doctor-assisted suicide is a humane alternative for the terminally ill.
- Human cloning is morally justified.
- Abortion is wrong.
- Workplace discrimination on the basis of gender or race is wrong.
- The death penalty is morally unjustifiable.

You might also develop a specific proposition that turns on a question of value. For example, you might want to establish that IQ tests are biased as one of your propositions, with your thesis being that

IQ tests should be discontinued at your school. Or you might want to show that bullfighting is inhumane in a speech whose thesis is that bullfighting should be declared illegal throughout the world.

Questions of Policy

A question of policy concerns exactly what should be done: what policy should be adopted, what law should be changed, what practice should be followed, and so on. Persuasive speech theses often revolve around questions of policy, as in these examples:

- What should the college's sexual harassment policy be?
- What should this nation's drug policy be?
- What immigration policy should we adopt?
- What blood alcohol level should be used to define "drunk driving"?
- What should our laws say about doctor-assisted suicide?
- What should this university's position be on affirmative action?

Questions of policy are used more often as theses than as major propositions. Still, in some instances, you might phrase a major proposition around a policy issue. For example, in a speech designed to get your client off a driving-while-intoxicated charge, you might want to argue that the blood alcohol level that is used to establish drunk driving should be much higher than it currently is.

As noted previously, you can use questions from any of these categories to conceptualize a thesis statement or frame a major proposition. And a single speech may involve all three: questions of fact, value, and policy. For example, you might first point out that homelessness is growing (question of fact), then argue that everyone is responsible for the less fortunate (question of value), and finally conclude with your thesis that legislation must be enacted to reduce homelessness (question of policy).

GUIDELINES FOR PERSUASIVE SPEAKING

Your success in strengthening or changing attitudes or beliefs and in moving your listeners to action will depend on your use of the following guidelines, which are based on 10 essential principles of persuasion.

Anticipate Selective Exposure

Your listeners (in fact, all audiences) follow the **selective exposure principle.** As mentioned in Unit 4, the law of selective exposure has at least two parts:

1. Listeners actively seek out information that supports their existing opinions, beliefs, values, decisions, and behaviors.
2. Listeners actively avoid information that contradicts their existing opinions, beliefs, attitudes, values, and behaviors.

Of course, if we are very sure that our opinions and attitudes are logical and valid, then we may not bother to seek out supporting information or to avoid nonsupportive messages. We demonstrate selective exposure most often when our confidence in our opinions and beliefs is weak.

This principle of selective exposure suggests a number of implications. For example, if you want to persuade an audience that holds very different attitudes from your own, anticipate that selective exposure will be operating. If you present the audience with your thesis at the outset, they may tune you out without giving your position a fair hearing. So proceed inductively; that is, hold back on your thesis until you have presented your evidence and made your argument. Only then should you relate the evidence and argument to your initially contrary thesis. It's crucial to be thoroughly familiar with the attitudes of your audience if you want to succeed in making these necessary adjustments and adaptations.

Let's say you're giving a speech on the need to reduce spending on college athletic programs. If your audience were composed of listeners who agreed with you and wanted to cut athletic spending, you might lead with your thesis. Your introduction might go something like this:

> Our college athletic program is absorbing money that we can more profitably use for the library, science labs, and language labs. Let me explain how the money now going to unnecessary athletic programs could be better spent in these other areas.

On the other hand, if you were addressing alumni who strongly favored the existing athletic programs, you might want to lead with your evidence and hold off stating your thesis until the end of your speech.

Recognize Cultural Differences

Cultural differences, too, can strongly influence how audiences respond to persuasive attempts (Lustig & Koester, 1999; Dodd, 1995). In some cultures, for example, credibility is extremely influential in persuasion. If the religious leader says something, it's taken as true and therefore believed. In other cultures, religious leaders' credibility is assessed individually—not all religious leaders are seen as equally believable. In still other cultures, religious leaders' credibility is generally assessed negatively.

Most schools in the United States teach students to demand logical and reliable evidence before believing something. The emphasis on critical thinking throughout contemporary education (and in this text) is a good example of this concern with logic, argument, and evidence. Other cultures give much less importance to these forms of persuasion.

Some audiences favor a deductive pattern of reasoning: They expect to hear the general principle first and the evidence, examples, and argument second. Other audiences (Asian audiences are often cited as examples) favor a more inductive pattern, in which the speaker gives examples and illustrations first and presents the general principle or conclusion second.

Still other cultures expect a very clear statement of the speaker's conclusion. Low-context cultures (those of the United States, Germany, and Sweden, for example) generally expect an explicit statement of the speaker's position and an explicit statement of what he or she wants the audience to do. Low-

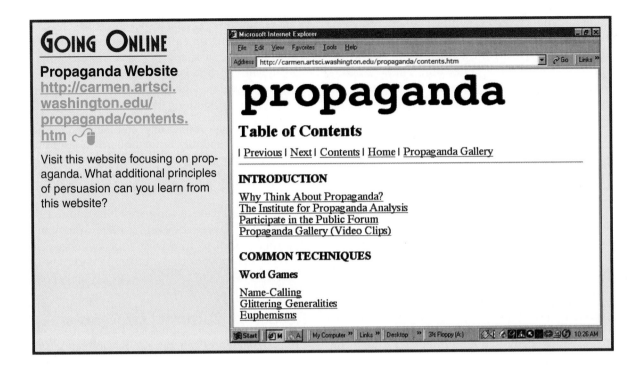

GOING ONLINE

Propaganda Website
http://carmen.artsci.
washington.edu/
propaganda/contents.
htm

Visit this website focusing on propaganda. What additional principles
of persuasion can you learn from
this website?

context cultures prefer to leave as little unspoken as possible. In contrast, people in high-context cultures (Japanese, Chinese, and Arabic groups, for example) prefer a less explicit statement and prefer to be led indirectly to the speaker's conclusion. An explicit statement ("Vote for Smith" or "Buy Viterall") may be perceived as too direct and even as insulting.

Encourage Audience Participation

The **audience participation principle** states that persuasion is greatest when the audience participates actively in your presentation. In experimental tests the same speech is delivered to different audiences. The attitudes of each audience are measured before and after the speech. The difference between their prespeech and postspeech attitudes is taken as a measure of the speech's effectiveness. For one audience the sequence consists of (1) pretest of attitudes, (2) presentation of the persuasive speech, and (3) posttest of attitudes. For another audience the sequence consists of (1) pretest of attitudes, (2) presentation of the persuasive speech, (3) audience's paraphrasing or summarizing of the speech, and (4) posttest of attitudes. Researchers consistently find that listeners who participate actively (as in paraphrasing or summarizing) are more per-

suaded than those who receive the message passively. Demagogues and propagandists who succeed in arousing huge crowds often have the crowds chant slogans, repeat catchphrases, and otherwise participate actively in the persuasive experience.

The implication here is simple: Persuasion is a transactional process. It involves both speaker and listeners. You will be more effective if you can get the audience to participate actively in the process.

Consider Prior Inoculation

The **inoculation principle** can be explained in terms of the biological analogy on which it's based (McGuire, 1964). Suppose that you lived in a germ-free environment. Upon leaving this germ-free environment and being exposed to germs, you would be particularly susceptible to infection, because your body would not have built up immunity—it would have no resistance. But resistance, the ability to fight off germs, can be achieved by the body, if not naturally, then through some form of inoculation. You can, for example, be injected with a weakened dose of an infectious microbe so that your body will begin building up antibodies that create "immunity" to this type of infection. Armed with these antibodies, your body will be able to fight off even powerful doses of this germ.

The situation in persuasion is similar to this biological process. Some of your attitudes and beliefs have existed in a "germ-free" environment; that is, they have never been attacked or challenged. For example, many of us have lived in an environment in which the values of a democratic form of government, the importance of education, and the traditional family structure have not been challenged. Consequently, we have not been "immunized" against attacks on these values and beliefs. We have no counterarguments (antibodies) prepared to fight off attacks on our beliefs, so if someone comes along with strong arguments against these beliefs, we can be easily persuaded.

Contrast these "germ-free" beliefs with issues that have been attacked and for which we have a ready arsenal of counterarguments. Our attitudes on the draft, nuclear weapons, college athletics, and thousands of other issues have been challenged in the press, on television, and in our interpersonal interactions. As a result of this exposure, we have counterarguments ready for any attacks on our beliefs concerning these issues. We have been inoculated and immunized against attempts to change these attitudes or beliefs.

If you're addressing an inoculated audience, take into consideration the fact that people in this audience have a ready arsenal of counterarguments to fight your persuasive assault. For example, if you're addressing heavy smokers on the need to stop smoking or alcoholics on the need to stop drinking, you can reasonably assume that these people have already heard your arguments and that they have already inoculated themselves against all the major arguments. In such situations, therefore, be prepared to achieve only small gains. Don't try to reverse totally the beliefs of a well-inoculated audience. For example, it would be asking too much to get the smokers or the alcoholics to quit their present behaviors as a result of one speech. But it might not be impossible to persuade them—at least some of them—to attend a meeting of a smoking clinic or Alcoholics Anonymous.

If you're trying to persuade an uninoculated audience, your task is often much simpler, because you do not have to penetrate a fully developed immunization shield. For example, it might be relatively easy to persuade a group of high school seniors about the values of a college core curriculum; they probably would not have thought much about the issue and probably would not have arguments against the core curriculum concept at their ready disposal.

Do recognize, however, that even when an audience has not immunized itself, audience members often take certain beliefs to be self-evident. As a result they may well tune out attacks on cherished beliefs or values. This might be the case, for example, if you tried to persuade an audience of communists to support capitalist policies. Although they might not have counterarguments ready, they might accept their communist beliefs as so fundamental that they simply would not listen to attacks on such beliefs. Again, proceed slowly and be content with small gains. A frontal attack on cherished beliefs generally creates impenetrable resistance. Instead, build your case by first presenting your arguments and evidence and then working up gradually to your conclusion.

Ask for Reasonable Amounts of Change

The **magnitude of change principle** states that the greater and more important the change you want to produce in your audience, the more difficult your task will be. The reason is simple: We normally demand a greater number of reasons and lots more evidence before we make important decisions—such as changing directions in our career, moving our family to another state, or investing our life savings in certain stocks.

On the other hand, we may be more easily persuaded (and demand less evidence) on relatively minor issues—whether to take a course in "Small Group Communication" rather than in "Persuasion" or to give to the United Heart Fund instead of the American Heart Fund.

People change gradually, in small degrees. And although there are cases of sudden conversions, this general principle holds true more often than not. Persuasion, therefore, is most effective when it strives for small changes and works over a considerable period of time. For example, a persuasive speech stands a better chance when it tries to get the alcoholic to attend just one AA meeting rather than to give up drinking for life. If you try to convince members of your audience to change their attitudes radically or to engage in behaviors to which they're initially opposed, your attempts may backfire. The audience may tune you out, closing its ears to even the best and most logical arguments.

When you have the opportunity to try to persuade your audience on several occasions (rather than simply delivering one speech), two **compliance-gaining strategies** will prove relevant: the foot-in-the-door and the door-in-the-face techniques.

Foot-in-the-Door Technique

As its name implies, the foot-in-the-door technique involves getting your foot in the door first. That is, you first request something small, something that your audience will easily comply with. Once this compliance has been achieved, you then make your real request (Freedman & Fraser, 1966; DeJong, 1979; Cialdini, 1984; Pratkanis & Aronson, 1991). Research shows that people are more apt to comply with a large request after they have complied with a similar but much smaller request. For example, in one study the objective was to get people to put a "Drive Carefully" sign on their lawn (a large request). When this large request was made first, only about 17 percent of the people were willing to comply. However, when this request was preceded by a much smaller request (to sign a petition), between 50 and 76 percent granted permission to install the sign. The smaller request and its compliance put the audience into an agreement mode and paved the way for the larger request.

In using this strategy, be sure that your first request is small enough to gain compliance. If it isn't, then you miss the chance ever to gain compliance with your desired and larger request.

Door-in-the-Face Technique

The door-in-the-face technique is the opposite of the foot-in-the-door strategy (Cialdini & Ascani, 1976; Cialdini, 1984). In this approach you first make a large request that you know will be refused; for example, "We're asking everyone to donate $100 for new school computers". Later, you make a more moderate request, the one you really want your listeners to comply with; for example, "Might you be willing to contribute $10?" In changing from the large to the more moderate request, you demonstrate your willingness to compromise and your sensitivity to your listeners. The general idea here is that your listeners will feel that because you have made a concession, they too will make a concession and at least contribute something. Listeners will probably also feel that $10 is actually quite little, considering the initial request, and, research shows, will be likely to comply and donate the $10.

In using this technique, be sure that your first request is significantly larger than your desired request but not so large as to seem absurd. If it's absurdly out of line, listeners are likely to reject the whole concept out of hand.

Stress Identification

If you can get your listeners to identify with you—if you can show your listeners that you and they share important attitudes, beliefs, and values—you'll clearly advance your persuasive goal. Other similarities are also important. For example, in some cases similarity of cultural, educational, or social background may help you identify yourself with your audience. Be aware, however, that insincere or dishonest identification is likely to backfire and create problems for the speaker. So avoid even implying similarities between yourself and your audience that don't exist.

Stress Consistency

People strive for consistency among their attitudes, beliefs, values, and behaviors. We expect there to be logical relationships among them, and when those relationships exist we feel comfortable. When we're conscious of inconsistencies, however, we feel uncomfortable and we seek change—usually just enough to restore balance and comfort.

You can probably see lots of examples of the principle of consistency in your own thoughts and behaviors. For example, if you have positive attitudes toward, say, animal rights, then you probably believe that animals do in fact have rights that have to be recognized; and if you were in a position to do something for animal rights, you might well do it.

Inconsistency or dissonance occurs when, say, attitudes contradict behavior. For example, if we have positive attitudes toward helping the homeless but don't actually do anything about it, we're probably in a state of dissonance or discomfort—not always, but when we think about the homeless and particularly when we bring to consciousness this discrepancy between attitude and behavior. And when a sense of dissonance occurs, we'll try to do something to reduce it. For example, if our dissonance becomes too uncomfortable, we may decide to give money to the homeless shelter or to buy coffee for the homeless man who sits by our apartment building.

As a persuasive speaker you should generally direct your propositions at increasing the audience's sense of consistency. Show them that by accepting your thesis they will bring their attitudes and behaviors into consistency and harmony. For example, you might remind your listeners of their positive attitude toward helping those less fortunate and then show them that when they do as you advise, their behavior will be consistent with their attitude. Salespeople use this technique regularly, saying, in essence, "You want status, you want performance, you want luxury; buy a BMW, it's your only choice." In this case, buying the BMW brings your behavior into consistency with your attitudes and values.

If the audience is experiencing dissonance, try to connect your thesis or your propositions to its reduction. For example, let's say you're giving a speech to persuade the neighborhood merchants to recycle more carefully. Although they believe in recycling, they aren't following the rules because, they say, it takes too much time. Here is a situation in which the audience is experiencing dissonance— their belief in the value of recycling is contradicted by their nonrecycling behavior. Your task as a speaker is to show the merchants how they can reduce dissonance by, for example, following a few simple procedures such as using color-coded trash cans. If you can show them how they can easily change their behavior to be consistent with their attitudes, you'll have a favorably disposed audience.

Use Logical Appeals

The application of **logic** in public communication consists basically of arguments, which in turn consist of evidence (for example, facts) and a conclusion. In other words, evidence together with a conclusion (that the evidence supports) equal an **argument.** Reasoning is the process you go through in forming conclusions on the basis of evidence. For example, you might reason that because college graduates earn more money than nongraduates (evidence), Jack and Jill should go to college if they wish to earn more money (conclusion). Although emotional and credibility appeals (to be discussed next) are also effective in persuading an audience, logical argument will prove most long lasting (Petty & Wegener, 1998). When you persuade listeners with logical arguments, they're more likely to remain persuaded over time and are more likely to resist counterarguments that may come up in the future.

The same principles of logic will prove useful to the speaker who constructs the speech, to the listener who receives and responds to the speech, and to the critic who evaluates the speech. The principles for evaluating logical evidence are the same principles that apply in evaluating research generally: currency, fairness, and reliability, as discussed in Unit 15. You may wish to review this discussion and at the same time to visit http://www.sjsu.edu/depts/itl/graphics/main.html for a wonderful website on critical and logical thinking.

Another way to look at logical support is to consider the kinds of thinking and arguing that should be *avoided* by the speaker and challenged by the listener and critic (Lee & Lee, 1972, 1995; Pratkanis & Aronson, 1991):

- In **name calling** the speaker gives an idea, a group of people, or a political philosophy a bad name ("atheist," "neo-Nazi") to try to get you to condemn the idea without analyzing the argument and evidence. The opposite of name calling is the **glittering generality** approach, in which the speaker tries to make you accept some idea by associating it with things you value highly ("democracy," "free speech," "academic freedom"). By using "virtue words" the speaker tries to get you to ignore the evidence and simply approve of the idea.

- The speaker using the **transfer** technique associates her or his idea with something you respect (to gain your approval) or with something you detest (to gain your rejection). For example, a speaker may characterize a proposal for condom distribution in schools as a means for "saving our children from AIDS" (to encourage acceptance) or as a means for "promoting sexual promiscuity" (to encourage disapproval). Sports car manufacturers try to get you to buy their cars by associating them with high status and sex appeal; marketing people for exercise clubs and diet plans endeavor to associate their programs with health, self-confidence, and interpersonal appeal.

- In the **testimonial** device the speaker evokes the image associated with some person to gain your approval (if you respect the person) or your rejection (if you don't respect the person). This is the technique of advertisers who use people dressed up to look like doctors or plumbers or chefs to sell their products. Sometimes this technique takes the form of allusions to vague and general "authorities," as in "experts agree," "scientists say," "good cooks know," or "dentists advise."

- The speaker using the **plain folks** approach identifies himself or herself with the audience. The speaker is good—the "reasoning" goes—because he or she is one of the people, just plain folks like everyone else.

- In **card stacking** the speaker selects only the evidence and arguments that support the case—and may even falsify evidence and distort the facts to better fit the case. Despite these misrepresentations, the speaker presents the supporting materials as "fair" and "impartial."

- Using the **bandwagon** method, the speaker persuades the audience to accept or reject an idea or proposal because "everybody's doing it" or because all the "right" people are doing it. The speaker persuades you to jump on this large and popular bandwagon. This is a familiar technique in political elections: Campaigns use results of

polls to get undecided voters to jump on the bandwagon with the leading candidate. After all, you don't want to vote for a loser.

- In **agenda setting** a speaker may argue that X is the issue and that all others are unimportant and insignificant. This kind of appeal is heard frequently: "Balancing the budget is the key to the city's survival." "There's only one issue confronting elementary education in our largest cities, and that is violence." In almost all situations, however, there are many issues and many sides to each issue. Often the person proclaiming that X is the issue really means, "I'll be able to persuade you if you focus solely on X and ignore the other issues."

- **Attack** involves accusing another person (usually an opponent) of some serious wrongdoing so that the issue under discussion never gets carefully examined. Arguments such as "How can we support a candidate who has been unfaithful (abused alcohol, avoided the military)?" are

COMMUNICATION @ WORK

Reward and Coercive Power

The perks of power work best in the corporate world when they're rewards for a job well done.

—John O. Whitney and Tina Packer

As explained in Unit 13, you have *reward power* over a person if you have the ability to give that person rewards, whether material (money, promotion, jewelry) or social (love, friendship, respect). Conversely, you have *coercive power* if you have the ability to deprive a person of rewards or to administer punishments. Usually, if you have reward power you also have coercive power. A manager can shower an employee with praise for a job well done and offer a nice year-end bonus (reward power), but can also criticize and deny that same employee a promotion (coercive power).

Reward power increases attractiveness; we like those who have the power to reward us and who do in fact give us rewards. Coercive power, on the other hand, decreases attractiveness; we dislike those who have the power to punish us and who threaten us with punishment, whether they actually follow through or not. Thus, as a manager, a teacher, or a group leader, you'll be better liked, more persuasive, and more powerful if you reward people for their desirable behaviors instead of punishing them for undesirable behaviors.

Thinking about Your Communicating @ Work

How do you respond to the reward and coercive power of others? How do you wield reward and coercive power over others? How might you exercise your power more effectively?

often heard in political discussions. When personal attack is used to draw attention away from other issues, it becomes unethical.

Use Emotional (Motivational) Appeals

When you use emotional (or motivational) appeals, you direct your appeals to your listeners' needs and desires. Although psychological appeals are never totally separate from logical appeals, we'll consider them separately here. We are concerned here with motives—with those forces that energize or move or motivate a person to develop, change, or strengthen particular attitudes or ways of behaving. For example, one motive might be the desire for status. This desire may motivate you to develop certain attitudes about what occupation to enter, the importance of saving and investing money, and so on. It may move some people to acquire certain objects—to buy Gucci shoes, a Rolex watch, or a Tiffany diamond. But appeals to status (or to any motive) may motivate different people in different ways. Thus, the status motive may lead one person to enter the poorly paid but respected occupation of social work. It may influence another to enter the well-paid but less respected used car business.

Motive Hierarchy

One of the most useful analyses of motives is Abraham Maslow's (1970) fivefold hierarchy of needs, reproduced in Figure 19.1. One of the assumptions of this classification is that you will seek to fulfill the need at the lowest level first and only then to meet the need at the next higher level. Thus, for example, you would not concern yourself with the need for security or freedom from fear if you were starving (that is, if your need for food had not been fulfilled). Similarly, you would not be concerned with friendship or affectional rela-

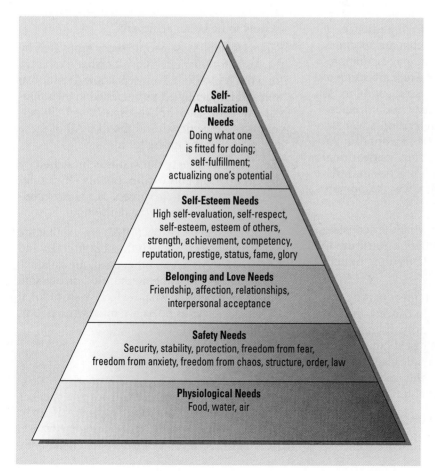

Figure 19.1

Maslow's Hierarchy of Needs

According to Maslow, satisfied needs do not motivate. For example, if the safety need of an individual is satisfied, that individual will not be motivated to seek further safety. Therefore, appeals to satisfied needs will not be persuasive for this listener. The insights of Maslow—as well as of various other theorists—underlie the principles of motivation discussed in this section.

Source: Data from Maslow (1970).

tionships if your need for protection and security had not been fulfilled.

According to Maslow's theory certain needs have to be satisfied before other needs can motivate behavior. Thus, you need to determine what needs of the audience members have been satisfied and, therefore, what needs you might use to motivate them. In most college classrooms, for example, you may assume that the two lowest levels—physiological needs and safety needs—have been reasonably fulfilled. For many students, however, needs at the third level (love needs) are not fulfilled, and propositions may be linked to these with great effectiveness. Thus, assuring your listeners that what you are saying will enable them to achieve more productive interpersonal relationships or greater peer acceptance will go a long way toward securing their attention and receptiveness. Additional "Motivational Principles" may be found at www.ablongman.com/devito.

Motive Appeals

Think about the ways in which appeals may be addressed to specific motives. Each audience, of course, is different, and motives that are appropriately appealed to in one situation may be inappropriate or ineffective in another. Here are some of the motives speakers (and advertisers) appeal to. As you read through the list, you may find it interesting to recall a recent print or television advertisement that used each of these motive appeals. An exercise, "How Can You Construct Motivational Appeals?" will provide you with practice in developing motivational appeals; see www.ablongman.com/devito.

- *Altruism.* People want to do what they consider the right thing—to help others, contribute to worthy causes, help the weak, feed the hungry, and cure the sick.

- *Fear.* People are motivated in great part by **fear appeals.** Common fears often concern the loss of things such as money, family, friends, love, attractiveness, health, job, or just about anything people possess and value. People also fear punishment, rejection, failure, the unknown, the uncertain, and the unpredictable.

- *Individuality and conformity.* People want to stand out from the crowd and may fear being lost in the crowd, indistinguishable from everyone else.

Yet many also want to conform, to be one of the crowd, to be "in."

- *Power, control, and influence.* People want power, control, and influence over themselves and over their own destinies. People also want control over other persons; they wish to be influential and to be opinion leaders.

- *Self-esteem and approval.* People want to be self-confident, to see themselves as worthy and contributing human beings. Because of this need, inspirational speeches of the "you are the greatest" type never seem to lack receptive—and suggestible—audiences.

- *Love and affiliation.* People are strongly motivated to affiliate, to love and be loved; they welcome assurances that someone (preferably lots of people) loves them and at the same time that they are capable of loving in return.

- *Achievement.* People want to achieve in whatever they do. We want to be successful as students, as friends, as parents, as lovers. This is why we read books and listen to speeches that purport to tell us how to be better achievers.

- *Financial gain.* Most people seem motivated by the desire for financial gain—for what it can buy, for what it can do. Advertisers know this motive well and frequently get us interested in their messages by using such keywords as "sale," "50 percent off," "save now," and the like. All of these are appeals to the desire for money.

- *Status.* In our society our status is measured by our occupation and wealth, but also by attainments such as athletic success, academic excellence, or superiority on the dance floor.

- *Self-actualization.* Maslow (1970) argued that the self-actualization motive influences attitudes and behaviors only after all other needs are satisfied. Yet we all have in some measure a desire to self-actualize, to become what we feel we are fit for. If we see ourselves as poets, we must write poetry, even in our garret.

Use Credibility Appeals

Think about how believable you are as a speaker. How believable are you in and of yourself, apart from any evidence or argument you might advance? What is there about you as a person that makes others believe or not believe you? These are questions of **credibility,** or believability.

On many occasions you have probably made judgments of speakers apart from any arguments, evidence, or motivational appeals they offered. Often you believe or disbelieve a speaker because of who the speaker is, not because of anything the speaker says. You may, for example, believe certain information or take certain action solely by virtue of Bill Gates's or Hillary Clinton's reputation, personality, or character. Alexander Pope put it more poetically in his "Essay on Criticism":

> Some judge of authors' names, not works, and then
> Nor praise nor blame the writings, but the men.

Credibility is not something the speaker has or does not have in any objective sense. Rather, it is a quality that a listener attributes to the speaker; it's a quality that the listener thinks the speaker possesses. In reality a speaker may be a stupid, immoral person. But if the audience perceives the speaker as intelligent and moral, then that speaker has high credibility. Further, research tells us, the audience will believe this speaker. The Understanding Theory and Research box on "Credibility Impressions" explains how credibility impressions are formed.

Everyone seems interested in credibility. Advertisers, for example, are interested in this factor because it relates directly to the effectiveness of their ad campaigns. Will Michael Jordan be an effective spokesperson for Hanes underwear? Bob Dole for Viagra? Jamie Lee Curtis for Sprint? Politicians are interested in credibility because it determines in great part how people vote. Educators are interested in it because students' perceptions of teacher credibility

UNDERSTANDING THEORY AND RESEARCH

Credibility Impressions

You form a credibility impression of a speaker on the basis of two sources of information. First, you assess the reputation of the speaker as you know it. This is initial—or what theorists call "extrinsic"—credibility. Second, you evaluate how that reputation is confirmed or refuted by what the speaker says and does during the speech. This is derived—or "intrinsic"—credibility. In other words, you combine what you know about the speaker's reputation with the more immediate information you get from present interactions and form a collective final assessment of credibility.

Working with Theories and Research. *Does this model adequately explain how you form credibility impressions of others? Can you derive from this model any practical advice for increasing your own credibility?*

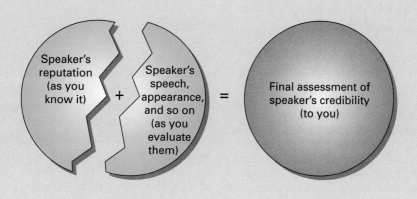

determine the degree of influence the teacher has on a class. There seems to be no communication situation that credibility does not influence.

The three major components that create an impression of credibility are competence, character, and charisma. Before reading about these specific components of credibility, you may wish to take the following self-test, "How Credible Are You?"

TEST YOURSELF

How Credible Are You?

Respond to each of the following phrases to indicate how you think members of this class (your audience) perceive you when you deliver a public speech. Use the following scale: 7 = very true; 6 = quite true; 5 = fairly true; 4 = neither true nor untrue; 3 = fairly untrue; 2 = quite untrue; and 1 = very untrue.

_____ **1.** Knowledgeable about the subject matter

_____ **2.** Experienced

_____ **3.** Confident

_____ **4.** Informed about the subject matter

_____ **5.** Fair in the presentation of material (evidence and argument)

_____ **6.** Concerned with the audience's needs

_____ **7.** Consistent over time on the issues addressed in the speech

_____ **8.** Similar to the audience in attitudes and values

_____ **9.** Positive rather than negative

_____ **10.** Assertive in personal style

_____ **11.** Enthusiastic about the topic and in general

_____ **12.** Active rather than passive

How did you do? This test focuses on the three qualities of credibility—competence, character, and charisma—and is based on a large body of research (e.g., McCroskey, 1997; Riggio, 1987). Items 1 through 4 refer to your perceived competence: How competent or capable does the audience consider you to be? Items 5 through 8 refer to your perceived character: Does the audience evaluate you as a person of good and moral character? Items 9 through 12 refer to your perceived charisma: Does the audience see you as dynamic and active rather than as static and passive?

What will you do? What specific steps can you take to change any audience perception that you feel is less than optimal? For example, how can you make yourself appear more competent? More moral or ethical? More charismatic?   ✔

Competence

The term **competence** refers to the knowledge and expertise a speaker is thought to have. The more knowledge and expertise the audience perceives the speaker as having, the more likely the audience will be to believe the speaker. For example, we believe a teacher to the extent that we think that teacher is knowledgeable on his or her subject.

Competence is logically subject-specific. Usually, it is limited to one specific field. That is, a person may be competent in one subject and totally incompetent in another. Your political science instructor may be quite competent in politics but quite incompetent in mathematics or economics.

Often, however, we do not distinguish carefully between areas of competence and incompetence. Thus, we may see a person whom we consider competent in politics as competent in general. We will, therefore, perceive this person as credible in many fields. This tendency is a version of the halo effect discussed in Unit 4: Listeners often generalize a perception of competence to all areas and see competence as a general trait of the individual.

This halo effect also has a counterpart, however—the reverse halo effect. Here a person seen as incompetent in, say, mathematics is perceived to be similarly incompetent in most other areas as well. As a critic of public communication, be particularly sensitive to the subject-specificity of competence. Be sensitive to both halo and reverse halo effects.

Character

We perceive a speaker as credible if we perceive that speaker as having high moral **character**. Here our concern is with the individual's honesty and basic nature. We want to know if we can trust the person, and we believe a speaker we can trust. Our perceptions of an individual's motives or intentions are particularly important when we judge character. When the audience sees your intentions as focused on their well-being (rather than on your own personal gain), they'll think you credible. And they'll believe you.

MEDIA WATCH

MEDIA CREDIBILITY

Among most Americans the media enjoy enormous credibility. Very likely you believe what you hear on television or read in the newspapers. In part you believe media because you believe media spokespersons such as Dan Rather, Ted Koppel, or Connie Chung. You may also believe what Oprah Winfrey says about interpersonal relationships, what Geraldo Rivera says about politics, and what Montel Williams says about dealing with problem teenagers—both because these personalities are so impressive and because they're on TV.

In a similar way, you are likely to believe what you read; you probably believe your newspapers and magazines. Unless it's marked "editorial" or "advertisement," you probably assume that what appears in a newspaper or newsmagazine is accurate and objective. The News Credibility Scale presented here provides an interesting way to look at the credibility of a newspaper. It's also an interesting way to think about the factors you take into consideration when you make any judgment of believability.

How Credible Is Your Newspaper?

Select a specific newspaper and circle the number for each dimension that best represents your feelings about this newspaper.

Is fair	5	4	3	2	1	Is unfair
Is unbiased	5	4	3	2	1	Is biased
Tells the whole story	5	4	3	2	1	Doesn't tell the whole story
Is accurate	5	4	3	2	1	Is inaccurate
Respects people's privacy	5	4	3	2	1	Invades people's privacy
Does watch after readers' interests	5	4	3	2	1	Does not watch after readers' interests
Is concerned about the community's well-being	5	4	3	2	1	Is not concerned about the community's well-being
Does separate fact and opinion	5	4	3	2	1	Does not separate fact and opinion
Can be trusted	5	4	3	2	1	Cannot be trusted
Is concerned about the public interest	5	4	3	2	1	Is concerned about making profits
Is factual	5	4	3	2	1	Is opinionated
Has well-trained reporters	5	4	3	2	1	Has poorly trained reporters

To compute your score, simply add up the circled numbers. The highest possible score would be 60, the lowest 12, and the midpoint 36. The higher the score, the greater the degree of credibility you perceive this newspaper to have and, more important, the more likely you are to believe this newspaper. This scale, although designed for newspapers, can easily be extended to all news media—television, magazines, radio, and the various computerized information sources—and across media. For example, how does the credibility of your local paper compare to CNN news?

Follow-Up. *You might try completing this scale for several different news media to see if the scores correspond to the degree with which you believe the different media. To what sources of news do you ascribe the highest credibility? To what specific newspapers or magazines and to which specific newscasters do you attribute most credibility? What reasons can you identify for your attribution of high credibility to some sources and less credibility to others?*

Source: Reprinted by permission of AEJMC publisher and copyright holder of "Measuring the Concept of Credibility," by C. Gaziano and K. McGrath, *Journalism Quarterly,* V. 36, 1986, pp. 451–462.

Generally, in the United States, speakers are advised to stress their credibility by communicating to their audience that they are competent, of good character, and dynamic or charismatic. In some cultures, however, to stress your own competence or that of your organization may be taken to suggest that your audience members are inferior or that their organizations are not as good as yours. As with any principle of communication, in establishing credibility it helps to know something of the culture of your listeners. How would most members of your culture weigh in on this question?

Charisma

Charisma is a combination of the speaker's personality and dynamism. We perceive as credible or believable speakers we like rather than speakers we do not like. We perceive speakers as credible if they are friendly and pleasant rather than aloof and reserved. Similarly, we favor the dynamic over the hesitant, nonassertive speaker. We perceive the shy, introverted, soft-spoken individual as less credible than the extroverted and forceful individual. The charismatic leaders in history have been dynamic people. Perhaps we feel that the dynamic speaker is open and honest in presenting herself or himself. The shy, introverted individual may be seen as hiding something. As speakers, there is much that we can do to increase our charisma and hence our perceived credibility.

THE SPEECH TO STRENGTHEN OR CHANGE ATTITUDES, BELIEFS, OR VALUES

Many speeches seek to strengthen existing attitudes, beliefs, or values. Much religious and political speak-

ing, for example, tries to strengthen beliefs and values that people already hold. In other words, the religious or political audience is often favorable to the speaker's purpose and willing to listen. Speeches designed to change attitudes or beliefs are more difficult to construct. Most people resist change—so when you try to get people to change their beliefs or attitudes you're fighting an uphill (though not impossible) battle.

Speeches designed to strengthen or change attitudes or beliefs come in many forms. Depending on the initial position of the audience, the following examples could be topics for speeches aimed at strengthening or changing attitudes or beliefs:

- Marijuana should be legalized.
- General education requirements should be abolished.
- College athletic programs should be expanded.
- History is a useless study.
- Television shows are mindless.
- CDs and tapes should be rated for excessive sex and violence.
- Puerto Rico should become the 51st state.

Strategies for Strengthening or Changing Attitudes, Beliefs, and Values

When you attempt to strengthen or change your listeners' attitudes, beliefs, and values, consider the following guidelines.

Estimate Listeners' Attitudes, Beliefs, and Values

Carefully estimate—as best you can—the current state of your listeners' attitudes, beliefs, and values. If your goal is to strengthen these, then you can state your thesis and your objectives as early in your speech as you wish. Because your listeners are in basic agreement with you, your statement of the thesis will help you create a bond of agreement between you. You might say, for example:

Like you, I am deeply committed to the fight against abortion. Tonight, I'd like to explain some new evidence that has recently come to light that we must know if we are to be effective in our fight against legalized abortion.

If, however, you're in basic disagreement with the audience and wish to change their attitudes, then reserve your statement of your thesis until you have provided them with your evidence and argument. Get listeners on your side first by stressing as many similarities between you and them as you can. Only after this should you try to change the audience's attitudes and beliefs. Continuing with the abortion example, but this time with an audience that is opposed to your antiabortion stance, you might say:

> We're all concerned with protecting the rights of the individual. No one wants to infringe on the rights of anyone. And it is from this point of view—from the point of view of the inalienable rights of the individual—that I want to examine the abortion issue.

In this way, you stress your similarity with the audience before you state your antiabortion position.

Seek Small Changes

When you are addressing an audience that is opposed to your position and your goal is to change their attitudes and beliefs, seek change in small increments. Let's say, for example, that your ultimate goal is to get an antiabortion group to favor abortion on demand. Obviously, this goal is too great to achieve in one speech. Therefore, strive for small changes. Here, for example, is an excerpt in which the speaker attempts to get an antiabortion audience to agree that some abortions should be legalized. The speaker begins as follows:

> One of the great lessons I learned in college was that most extreme positions are wrong. Most of the important truths lie somewhere between the extreme opposites. And today I want to talk with you about one of these truths. I want to talk with you about rape and the problems faced by the mother carrying a child conceived in this most violent of all the violent crimes we can imagine.

Notice that the speaker does not state a totally pro–abortion rights position but instead focuses on one area of the abortion debate and attempts to get the audience to agree that in some cases abortion should be legalized.

Demonstrate Your Credibility

To demonstrate credibility, as explained earlier, manifest competence, character, and charisma: Show your listeners that you are knowledgeable about the topic, have their best interests at heart, and are willing and ready to speak out in favor of these important concerns.

Give Listeners Good Reasons

Give the members of your audience good reasons for believing what you want them to believe. Give them hard evidence and logical arguments. Show them how the attitudes and beliefs you are promoting relate directly to their goals, their motives.

Developing the Speech to Strengthen or Change Attitudes, Beliefs, and Values

Here are some examples of speech outlines to clarify the nature of this type of persuasive speech. As in the examples offered in Unit 18, these examples present the purposes, the thesis, and the question asked of the thesis to help identify the major propositions of the speech.

This first example deals with birth control and uses a topical organizational pattern.

General Purpose: To persuade (to strengthen or change attitudes, beliefs, and values).

Specific Purpose: To persuade my audience that advertisements for birth control devices should be allowed in all media.

Thesis: Media advertising of birth control devices is desirable. (Why is media advertising desirable?)

I. Birth control information is needed.
   A. Birth control information is needed to prevent disease.
   B. Birth control information is needed to prevent unwanted pregnancies.
II. Birth control information is not available to the very people who need it most.
III. Birth control information can best be disseminated through the media.

In this second example, the speaker uses a problem–solution organizational pattern, first presenting the problems created by cigarette smoking, then proposing the solution.

General Purpose: To persuade (to strengthen or change attitudes, beliefs, and values).

Specific Purpose: To persuade my audience that cigarette advertising should be banned from all media.

Thesis: Cigarette advertising should be abolished. (Why should cigarette advertising be abolished?)

I. Cigarette smoking is a national problem.
   A. Cigarette smoking causes lung cancer.
   B. Cigarette smoking pollutes the air.
   C. Cigarette smoking raises the cost of health care.
II. Cigarette smoking would be lessened if advertisements were prohibited.

III. Fewer people would start to smoke.
IV. Smokers would smoke less.

In delivering such a speech a speaker might begin like this:

I think we all realize that cigarette smoking is a national problem that affects each and every one of us. No one escapes the problems caused by cigarette smoking—not the smoker and not the nonsmoker. Cigarette smoking causes lung cancer. Cigarette smoking pollutes the air. And cigarette smoking raises the cost of health care for everyone.

Let's look first at the most publicized of all smoking problems: lung cancer. There can be no doubt—

BUILDING COMMUNICATION SKILLS

How Can You Identify the Available Means of Persuasion?

The objective of this exercise is to stimulate you to identify the available means of persuasion that might be used in speeches on a variety of contemporary cultural issues. What persuasive strategies would you use to convince your class of the validity of either point of view on any of these issues? For example, what persuasive strategies would you use to persuade members of your class that interracial adoption should be encouraged? What strategies would you use to persuade your audience that interracial adoption should be discouraged? Do realize that the points of view presented here are simplified for purposes of this exercise; they are by no means complete analyses of these complex issues.

Point of View: Interracial Adoption. Those in favor of interracial adoption argue that the welfare of the child—who might not get adopted if not by someone of another race—must be considered first. Adoption, regardless of race, is good for the child and therefore is a positive social process. Those opposed to interracial adoption argue that every child needs to be raised in a family of the same race if the child is to develop self-esteem and become a functioning member of his or her own race. Interracial adoption is therefore a negative social process.

Point of View: Gay Men and Lesbians in the Military. Regardless of the status of the current law, many people within the U.S. military are opposed to the presence of gay men and lesbians in the armed forces. The gay and lesbian communities argue that gay men and lesbians should be given exactly the same rights and responsibilities as heterosexuals— no more, no less. Those opposed argue that gay men and lesbians will undermine the image of the military and will make heterosexuals uncomfortable.

Point of View: Affirmative Action. Those in favor of affirmative action argue that because of injustices experienced for many generations by certain groups (racial, national, gender), those groups should now be given preferential treatment—to correct the imbalance caused by past discrimination. Those opposed to affirmative action argue that merit must be the sole criterion for promotion, jobs, entrance to graduate schools, and so on, and that affirmative action is just reverse discrimination; one form of injustice cannot correct another form of injustice.

the scientific evidence is overwhelming—that cigarette smoking is a direct cause of lung cancer. Research studies conducted by the American Cancer Society and by research institutes throughout the world all come to the same conclusion: Cigarette smoking causes lung cancer. Consider some of the specific evidence. A recent study—reported in the November 2001 issue of . . . .

THE SPEECH TO STIMULATE ACTION

Speeches designed to stimulate the audience to take some action or to engage in some specific behavior are referred to as speeches to actuate. The persuasive speech that seeks to motivate a specific behavior may focus on just about any behavior imaginable. For example:

- Vote in the next election.
- Vote for Smith.
- Do not vote for Smith.
- Give money to the American Cancer Society.
- Buy a ticket to the football game.
- Watch *20/20*.
- Major in economics.
- Take a course in computer science.
- Buy a Pontiac.

Strategies for Stimulating Listeners to Action

When designing a speech to get listeners to do something, keep the following guidelines in mind.

Be Realistic
Set reasonable goals for what you want the audience to do. Remember you have only 5 or 15 minutes, and in that time you cannot move the proverbial mountain. So ask for small, easily performed behaviors—signing a petition, voting in the next election, donating a small amount of money.

Demonstrate Your Own Compliance
As a general rule, never ask the audience to do what you have not done yourself. So demonstrate your own willingness to do what you want the audience to do. If you don't, your listeners will rightfully ask, "Why haven't you done it?" In addition to making it clear that you have done what you want them to do, show them that you're pleased to have done so. Tell them of the satisfaction you derive from donating blood or from reading to blind students.

Stress Specific Advantages
Stress the specific advantages of the desired behaviors. Don't ask your audience to engage in behaviors solely for abstract reasons. Give them concrete, specific reasons why they will benefit from the actions you want them to engage in. Instead of telling your listeners that they should devote time to reading to blind students because it's the right thing to do, show them how much they will enjoy the experience and how much they will personally benefit from it.

Developing the Speech to Stimulate Action

Here are a few examples of the speech to actuate. First is a speech on devoting time to helping people with disabilities. Here the speaker asks for a change in the way most people spend their leisure time. The speech utilizes a topical organizational pattern; that is, each of the subtopics is treated about equally.

General Purpose: To persuade (to stimulate action).

Specific Purpose: To persuade members of my audience to devote some of their leisure time to helping people with disabilities.

Thesis: Leisure time can be well used to help people with disabilities (How can we use leisure time to help people with disabilities? or What can we do to help people with disabilities?)

  I. Read for the blind.
    A. Read to a blind student.
    B. Make a recording of a textbook for blind students.
 II. Run errands for students confined to wheelchairs.
III. Type for students who can't use their hands.

BUILDING COMMUNICATION SKILLS

How Can You Construct Logical, Motivational, and Credibility Appeals?

Below are statements suitable as theses for a variety of persuasive speeches. Select one of these statements and construct (1) a logical appeal, (2) a specific motivational appeal, and (3) a credibility appeal that would prove effective in persuading your class.

▶ Condoms should (not) be distributed to students in both junior and senior high school.

▶ Sports involving cruelty to animals, such as bullfighting, cockfighting, and foxhunting, should (not) be universally condemned and declared illegal.

▶ Tenure for college teachers should (not) be abolished.

▶ Marijuana should (not) be legalized for medical purposes in all states.

▶ Gay and lesbian marriages should (not) be declared legal.

▶ Immigration from Mexico and Latin America should be expanded (restricted).

▶ Affirmative action is (not) morally warranted.

▶ Retirement should (not) be mandatory at age 65 for all government employees.

▶ The death penalty is (not) morally wrong.

▶ Too little (too much) government and corporate money is spent on accommodating people with handicaps.

In this second example the speaker tries to persuade an audience of parents and teachers to approve a new multicultural curriculum for the town's high school; the speech stresses two major issues.

General Purpose: To persuade (to stimulate action)

Specific Purpose: To persuade my audience to approve the adoption of the multicultural curriculum.

Thesis: The multicultural curriculum is beneficial. (Why is the multicultural curriculum beneficial?)

I. The multicultural curriculum will teach tolerance.

II. The multicultural curriculum will raise all students' self-esteem.

In opening the speech, the speaker might say:

We've all heard about the new multicultural curriculum proposed for the high schools in our county. After years of research I can tell you what we know about the effects of multicultural education on students. And what we know is that multicultural education—such as the approach embodied in the curriculum before you—teaches tolerance for all people and all groups and, equally important, raises the self-esteem of all our sons and daughters. Let me explain how this curriculum teaches tolerance.

A SAMPLE PERSUASIVE SPEECH

This speech and its annotations are presented as a summary of our discussion of the persuasive speech. As with the informative speech in Unit 18, read the speech without looking at the critical thinking questions at the side. Then reread the speech, this time responding to the questions. Another useful way to summarize the principles and strategies of persuasive speaking is to try your hand at "Criticizing a Persuasive Speech," a speech specifically written as an exercise in persuasive speaking criticism (www.ablongman.com/devito).

The Perils of Philanthropy

Upendri Gunasekera

In this persuasive speech Upendri Gunasekera argues that Americans should think twice about making charitable donations to fraudulent or mismanaged organizations.

"Save the Children has touched the lives of millions of children and their families around the world with the help of caring people like you! You can help stop the suffering and give deserving children in need a better life today and hope for the future. Sponsor a child like this girl, Korotoumou Kone, a nine-year old Malian, for $20 a month, just 67 cents a day, to provide for some of her basic needs."

But what if I were to tell you that only three months after your sponsorship began, the girl died? In fact, *The Chronicle of Philanthropy*, March 26, 1998, reported that the *Chicago Tribune* journalist who sponsored this child through Save the Children went to Mali to check up on the girl and found she had died nearly two years earlier. Save the Children never bothered to inform the reporter that the intended recipient of her generosity was dead. Oops.

The Chronicle of Philanthropy goes on to state that as of January 14, 1999, 400,000 Americans were child supporters, donating $400 million each year through these programs. Was the money they sent to those charities received by the hunger-stricken children we see on TV? All too often, the answer is a resounding NO. The truth is that in the last year alone, the *Chicago Tribune* found 24 other children sponsored by Save the Children who died a year before their sponsor ever learned the devastating truth. In most cases, the money becomes a part of the bureaucracy or is given to the oppressive government. In order to fight the fraud, but still help the needy, the American public needs to realize the extent of international charity fraud and be made aware of the few trustworthy international relief charities that do exist.

To do this, we must first understand how the media skews our perspective of the situation through news reports and advertisements. Second, we will focus on international relief charities, and who is really benefiting from your money. And finally, we will see how the situation can really be ameliorated with your help. First, let's do a little investigative journalism of our own.

Journalists and human rights investigators realize that human rights reporting is made more effec-

What do you think of the opening "attention getter"? Did it gain your attention? Did it make you want to hear or read more?

How effective is the speaker's orientation? Does the orientation make it clear what the major parts of the speech will be?

tive by graphic visual images, according to Frederic A. Moritz in *US Human Rights Report*, September, 1998. "The concentration of refugees in camps supervised by international bodies such as the United Nations High Commission for Refugees provides relatively easy access for journalists who need to interview and photograph victims of war and repression . . . ." People send money because that's what the media feeds them.

George Alagiah of BBC Television was quoted in Alex de Waal's 1997 book *Famine Crimes:* "Relief agencies depend upon us for publicity and we need them to tell us where the stories are. We try not to ask the questions too bluntly: "'Where will we find the most starving babies?' And they never answer explicity. We get the pictures just the same." Even James Gibson, the director of the Childreach program in Haiti, quite frankly stated in 1998, "The American public is more inclined to respond to emotional rather than intellectual appeals." But Michael Maren, in his 1997 book *The Road to Hell*, states: "There is perhaps nothing more wretched than the exploitation of children for fund-raising, yet nothing more common." Exploitation like this picture. And this picture. And even this picture.

These children and communities need our assistance, but the exploitative journalism that captures our attention and calls us to action is causing us to throw money at a flawed system. Unfortunately, the good-hearted Americans who sent their money to this child would be grieved to know that their money actually went into this man's pocket: Mobutu Sese Seko, the recently fallen dictator of Zaire, here pictured in his villa on the French Riviera, where the architecture and menu look nothing like the relief camps of his people.

The media squeezes out our every last teardrop, while the charity organizations get to cash in. This money is harming those we intend to help the most. The harm is delivered in the form of international relief charities like Save the Children, AmeriCares, the UN, and various religious agencies.

A November 10, 1998, *Fortune* magazine report found that this $50 billion-a-year industry was providing for six-figure salaries and first-class plane tickets. Kerby Anderson, in a 1998 *Probe Ministries International* report, also found that most of the money benefits political leaders and businessmen. And if it's not being pocketed, organizations like AmeriCares are using it to ship 10,000 cases of Gatorade to Zaire, for AmeriCares believed that the supposed

Do you agree that the American public is persuaded more by emotional than by intellectual appeals? Are you?

The visual aids the speaker used were not included in the printed speech text, so we can't evaluate them. But if you were giving the speech, what types of visuals would you have shown at this point?

This visual of Mobuto's villa (not seen) would seem to provide an extremely vivid contrast to the pictures of starving children. Why do you think this technique of vivid contrast is generally so effective?

Here the speaker moves from the first major proposition (the way the media appeals to our emotions) to the second proposition (the misdeeds of some relief charities). Is this transition clear? What other ways might the speaker have moved from the first to the second issue?

energy nourishment one recieves from Gatorade would be sufficient to protect an individual from the life-threatening disease cholera. However, Dr. Michael Toole from the Centers for Disease Control states, "While Gatorade might be good for athletes, it is not good for cholera victims." But let's not forget the biggest charity organization of them all, the UN.

The *New Republic*, December 1994, reveals that many third world countries see the United Nations, the world-renowned foreign aid organization, as inherently corrupt, "and UN bureaucrats are in Somalia only to enrich themselves." In fact, that same year, $4 million in cash disappeared from a UN compound. It could have been stolen, given to high-ranking government officials, pocketed by some locals, or carried off by fire ants—they just don't know. Even Sergio de Mello, the UN's Under-secretary General for Humanitarian Affairs and Emergency Relief, states in *London Mail Guardian*, April 8, 1998, that the UN has made mistakes and needs to be "more aware of the consequences." More aware of a $4 million loss? Here's a tip—when you put $4 million in a room, write down the room number. But unfortunately, the UN didn't take my advice, as was indicated in their recent charitable mission to Kosovo. *The Chronicle of Philanthropy*, April 22, 1998, reported that the disorganization of the UN High Commission for Refugees actually hindered relief efforts, resulting in the loss of medical supplies worth $500,000.

Or what about the March 15, 1998, *Chicago Tribune* report of how Children International raised $25,000 in sponsorships to provide a Filipino village with a number of doctors and 20 to 30 toilets. From the $25,000, the children only received one sporadic doctor and one toilet. Now, unless they contracted NASA to build one of those high-tech toilets, I don't think it could have cost $25,000. What happened to all the money? Your guess is as good as mine. And all those letters you receive from your child? Well, they're fabricated. At least that's what the director of the Christian Children's Fund said in the *Chicago Tribune*, March 22, 1998.

All of this paints a very bad picture for those people who need help. When donors don't know where their money is going and then find out it is being squandered, they're not likely to give additional money to charities. Legitimate charities are hurt by exploitative nonlegitimate charities, unless you know who the legitimate international relief charities are.

How effective are these examples in making you realize that much of the money given to help the children is wasted?

Does the speaker convince you that relief organizations have misused the money given to them? If so, what specifically convinced you? If not, what additional proof would you want?

Here is the second transition, moving from the second major proposition (waste by the relief charities) to the third proposition (what we can do to help the needy and yet not contribute to organizations that waste our money). Is this transition effective? In what other ways might you move from the second issue to the third?

There are two international relief charities, Oxfam and the French group Doctors without Borders, who have topped the list of charities that are morally and financially smart and effective in their originally intended purpose. The same cholera victims AmeriCares tried to help with Gatorade, Doctors without Borders treated effectively and efficiently. In fact, in 1997, the National Charities Information Bureau found that 80 percent of the revenues generated for Doctors without Borders was used for emergency and medical purposes. *The Chronicle of Philanthropy* also compiles an annual Philanthropy 400 list of the top charities based upon financial statements, annual reports, and a questionnaire response. The top five international relief charities issued November 25, 1998, are the American Red Cross, Gift in Kind International, World Vision, Goodwill Industries International, and Campus Crusade International.

There are other international relief organizations worthy of your money, but it would be wise to follow the *Chronicle*'s tips for safe giving so as not to fall prey to con artists. Beware of high-emotion, no-substance ads and phone solicitations, and never pay by cash or credit card—always pay by check, payable to the full name of the charity, so only the specified charity may cash in on your money, thus ensuring yourself as well as the charity.

Next time you see those ads on TV of starving children waiting for you to send them money, remember that they are suffering at the hands of those very charities. Today, we have seen how exploitative the media has become and how nonlegitimate charities have misused our money, and identified the truly legitimate charities, those worthy of your donations. The sponsorship agent in charge of Korotoumou Kone told the sponsoring journalist that Korotoumou was healthy and continuing in her studies, but it had been exactly two years after her death. We cannot allow our ignorance to act as a partner in the exploitation of these people. As the journalist then responded, "She's dead. She did not live beyond her 12th birthday."

This speech was delivered by Upendri Gunasekera of Ohio University at the 127th Annual Interstate Oratorical Association contest held at Georgetown College in Lexington, Kentucky (April 23–24, 1999). Reprinted by permission.

Are you convinced that the charities named by the speaker are the best ones to contribute to? If not, what additional information would you want?

What do you think of the suggestions for ensuring that your money goes where you want it to go? What, if any, additional information might the speaker have included?

How effective is the summary statement of the three major points made in the speech?

What do you think of the speaker's technique of tying the conclusion back to the introduction (with the story of Korotoumou)?

 **REFLECTIONS ON ETHICS IN HUMAN COMMUNICATION**

Appealing to Emotions Ethically

Emotional appeals are all around. Persons who want to censor the Internet may appeal to your fear of children's accessing pornographic materials; those who want to restrict the media's portrayal of violence may appeal to your fear of increased violence in your community. Other examples include the real estate broker's appeals to your desire for status, the favor-seeking friend's appeals to your desire for social approval, and the salesperson's appeals to your desire for sexual rewards. Here are some situations in which emotional appeals may figure into your own persuasive efforts.

What would you do in the following situations?

▶ *You're a parent of two young teenagers and want to dissuade them from becoming sexually active. Would it be ethical for you to use emotional appeals to scare them so that they'll avoid sexual relationships? Would it be ethical to use the same appeals if your goal was to dissuade your teenagers from associating with teens of other races?*

▶ *You're working for an advertising agency that wants to use fear appeals in a campaign designed to prevent the spread of sexually transmitted diseases. Would it be ethical for you to participate in this work? Would it be ethical to use the same appeals if the motive was to sell SUVs?*

▶ *You've been hired by a religious organization that wants you to write speeches using fear appeals to persuade people to live their lives as this religion advocates. For example, the group wants you to vividly depict the horrors of hell that will befall anyone who does not follow their beliefs. Would it be ethical for you to write such speeches?*

 ◆◆ SUMMARY ◆◆

This unit focused on persuasive speeches, examining the principles of persuasion and the ways to develop the speeches to strengthen or change attitude and belief and to motivate to action.

1. Persuasive speeches can often be classified as revolving around three types of questions: (1) Questions of fact focus on what is or is not; (2) questions of value focus on what is good or bad; and (3) questions of policy focus on what should be done.

2. Among the principles of persuasion are selective exposure, cultural differences, audience participation, inoculation, magnitude of change, identification, consistency and dissonance, logic, emotional/motivational appeals, and credibility.

3. In seeking to strengthen or change an audience's attitudes, beliefs, or values, follow these general principles: Estimate the current status of your listeners' attitudes, beliefs, and values; seek change in small increments; demonstrate your credibility; and give your listeners logical and motivational reasons.

4. In endeavoring to move an audience to action, consider these general guidelines: Be realistic in what you ask listeners to do, asking for small, easily performed behaviors; demonstrate your own willingness to do what you're asking your listeners to do; and stress specific benefits to be gained from compliance.

KEY TERMS

question of fact

question of value

question of policy

selective exposure principle

cultural differences principle

audience participation principle

inoculation principle

magnitude of change principle

foot-in-the-door technique

door-in-the-face technique

identification

consistency

logic

emotional (motivational) appeals

credibility

speeches to strengthen or change attitudes or beliefs

speeches to stimulate action

THINKING CRITICALLY ABOUT

The Persuasive Speech

1. You're planning to give a speech urging more conscientiousness recycling to two very different audiences. One audience is composed solely of women and the other audience solely of men. Otherwise the audience members are similar: They are all college-educated professionals, around 30 years old. In what ways would the two speeches differ? What general principles or assumptions about gender would you be making as you differentiated these two speeches?

2. You want to get your listeners to contribute one hour a week to the college's program of helping high school students prepare for college. You're considering using the foot-in-the-door or the door-in-the-face technique. How would you develop each of these strategies? Which would you eventually use?

3. Read a persuasive speech, focusing on the principles of persuasion noted in this unit. Does the speaker make use of any of these principles? What persuasive principles can you identify from reading the speech?

4. Examine a speech for questions of fact, value, and policy. How are these issues used in the speech?

5. Visit the National Press Club website at **http://npc. press.org/** for complete texts of speeches presented at the club's luncheons. Read one of the speeches and evaluate it in terms of the principles of persuasion discussed in this unit. This is also an excellent research website; it provides guides that will prove useful for just about any topic.

6. Visit the "Speaker's Companion" website at **http:// www.lm.com/~chipp/spkrhome.htm**. How would you compare the principles discussed in this unit with the principles used in this program?

7. Prepare and deliver a two-minute speech in which you do one of the following:
   - explain an interesting attitude, belief, or value that you have come across
   - explain how a speech strengthened or changed one of your attitudes or beliefs
   - explain an advertisement in terms of the principles of persuasion
   - explain cultural differences in popularly held beliefs regarding such concepts as God, life, death, family, happiness, education, law, or men and women

GLOSSARY OF HUMAN COMMUNICATION CONCEPTS AND SKILLS

A word is dead
When it is said,
Some say.
I say it just
Begins to live
That day.
—*Emily Dickinson*

Listed here are definitions of the technical terms of human communication—the words that are peculiar or unique to this discipline—and, where appropriate, the corresponding skills. These definitions and statements of skills should make new or difficult terms a bit easier to understand and should help to place the skill in context. The statements of skills appear in italics. All boldface terms within the definitions appear as separate entries in the glossary.

abstraction A general concept derived from a class of objects; a part representation of some whole.

abstraction process The process by which a general concept is derived from specifics; the process by which some (never all) characteristics of an object, person, or event are perceived by the senses or included in some term, phrase, or sentence.

accent The stress or emphasis placed on a syllable when pronounced.

acculturation The processes by which a person's culture is modified or changed through contact with or exposure to another culture.

active listening A process of putting together into some meaningful whole the listener's understanding of the speaker's total message—the verbal and the nonverbal, the content and the feelings. *Listen actively by paraphrasing the speaker's meanings, expressing an understanding of the speaker's feelings, and asking questions to check the accuracy of your understanding of the speaker.*

adaptors Nonverbal behaviors that satisfy some personal need and usually occur without awareness; for example, scratching to relieve an itch or moistening your lips to relieve the dry feeling. Three types of adaptors are often distinguished: **self-adaptors**, **alter-adaptors**, and **object-adaptors**. *Generally, avoid adaptors (especially self-adaptors); they interfere with effective communication and may be taken as a sign of your discomfort or anxiety.*

adjustment (principle of) The principle of verbal interaction that claims that communication takes place only to the extent that the parties communicating share the same system of signals. *Expand the common areas between you and significant others; learn one another's system of communication signals and meanings in order to increase understanding and interpersonal communication effectiveness.*

affect displays Movements of the facial area that convey emotional meaning—for example, anger, fear, and surprise.

affinity-seeking strategies Behaviors designed to increase our interpersonal attractiveness. *Use the various affinity-seeking strategies (for example, listening, openness, and dynamism), as appropriate to the interpersonal relationship and the situation, to increase your own interpersonal attractiveness.*

affirmation The communication of support and approval. *Use affirmation to express your supportiveness and to raise esteem.*

agenda A list of the items that a small group must deal with in the order in which they should be covered.

agenda setting A persuasive technique in which the speaker argues that XYZ is the issue and that all others are unimportant.

aggressiveness See **verbal aggressiveness**.

allness The assumption that all can be known or is known about a given person, issue, object, or event. *End statements with an implicit "et cetera" ("etc.") to indicate that more could be known and said; avoid allness terms and statements.*

alter-adaptors Body movements you make in response to your current interactions; for example, crossing your arms over your chest when someone unpleasant approaches or moving closer to someone you like.

altercasting Placing the listener in a specific role for a specific purpose and asking that the listener approach the question or problem from the perspective of this specific role.

ambiguity The condition in which a message may be interpreted as having more than one meaning.

analogy, reasoning from Reasoning in which you compare like things and conclude that because they are alike in so many respects, they are also alike in some previously unknown respect.

apology A type of excuse in which you acknowledge responsibility for your behavior, generally ask forgiveness, and claim that the behavior will not happen again.

appraisal interview A type of **interview** in which the interviewee's performance is assessed by management or by more experienced colleagues.

apprehension See **communication apprehension**.

argument Evidence (for example, facts or statistics) and a conclusion drawn from the evidence.

argumentativeness A willingness to argue for a point of view, to speak your mind. *Cultivate your argumentativeness, your willingness to argue for what you believe, by, for example, treating disagreements as objectively as possible, reaffirming the other, stressing equality, expressing interest in the other's position, and allowing the other person to save face.* Distinguished from **verbal aggressiveness**.

artifactual communication Communication that takes place through the wearing and arrangement of various artifacts—for example, clothing, jewelry, buttons, or the furniture in your house and its arrangement.

assertiveness A willingness to stand up for one's rights but with a respect for the rights of others. *Increase your level of assertiveness (if desired) by analyzing the assertive and nonassertive behaviors of others, analyzing your own behaviors in terms of assertiveness, recording your behaviors, rehearsing assertive behaviors, and acting assertively in appropriate situations. Secure feedback from others for further guidance in increasing assertiveness.*

assimilation A process of message distortion in which we rework messages to conform to our own attitudes, prejudices, needs, and values.

attack A persuasive technique that involves accusing another person (usually an opponent) of some serious wrongdoing so that the issue under discussion never gets examined.

attention The process of responding to a stimulus or stimuli; usually some consciousness of responding is implied.

attitude A predisposition to respond for or against an object, person, or position.

attraction The state or process by which one individual is drawn to another by having a highly positive evaluation of that other person.

attraction theory A theory holding that we form relationships on the basis of our attraction to another person.

attractiveness The degree to which a person is perceived to possess a pleasing physical appearance and an appealing personality.

attribution A process through which we attempt to understand the behaviors of others (as well as our own), particularly the reasons or motivations for these behaviors.

attribution theory A theory concerned with the processes involved in our attributions of causation or motivation to others' behavior. *In attempting to identify the motivation for behaviors, examine consensus, consistency, distinctiveness, and controllability. Generally, low consensus, high consistency, low distinctiveness, and high controllability identify internally motivated behavior; high consensus, low consistency, high distinctiveness, and low controllability identify externally motivated behavior.*

audience participation principle A principle of persuasion stating that persuasion is achieved more effectively when the audience participates actively.

authoritarian leader A group leader who determines the group policies or makes decisions without consulting or securing agreement from group members.

avoidance An unproductive **conflict** strategy in which a person takes mental or physical flight from the actual conflict.

backchanneling cues Listener responses to a speaker that do not ask for the speaking role. *Respond to backchanneling cues as appropriate to the conversation. Use backchanneling cues to let the speaker know you are listening.*

bandwagon A persuasive technique through which the speaker tries to gain compliance by saying that "everyone is doing it" and urging you to jump on the bandwagon.

barrier to communication Any factor (physical or psychological) that prevents or hinders effective communication. *Applying the skills of human communication covered throughout this text will help reduce existing barriers and prevent others from arising.*

belief Confidence in the existence or truth of something; conviction. *Weigh both verbal and nonverbal messages before making believability judgments. Increase your own sensitivity to nonverbal (and verbal) deception cues—for example, too little movement, long pauses, slow speech, increased speech errors, mouth guard, nose touching, eye rubbing, or the use of few words, especially monosyllabic answers. But use such cues only to formulate hypotheses, not to draw conclusions, concerning deception.*

beltlining An unproductive **conflict** strategy in which one person hits at the level at which the other person cannot withstand the blow. *Avoid it.*

blame An unproductive **conflict** strategy in which we attribute the cause of the conflict to the other person or devote our energies to discovering who is the cause and avoid talking about the issues causing the conflict. *Avoid using blame to win an argument, especially with those with whom you're in close relationships.*

boundary marker A marker that demarcates the borderline between one person's territory and another's—for example, a fence.

brainstorming A technique for generating ideas either alone or, more usually, in a small group. *In brainstorming avoid evaluating contributions, strive for quantity, combine and extend your own ideas or the ideas of others, and try really wild ideas.*

breadth The number of topics about which individuals in a relationship communicate.

card stacking A persuasive technique in which the speaker selects only the evidence and arguments that build his or her case and omits or distorts any contradictory evidence.

causes and effects, reasoning from A form of reasoning in which you reason that certain effects are due to specific causes or that specific causes produce certain effects.

censorship Deliberate restriction imposed on a person's (or a population's) right to produce, distribute, or receive various communications.

central marker A marker or item that is placed in a territory to reserve it for a specific person—for example, a sweater thrown over a library chair to signal that the chair is taken.

certainty An attitude of **closed-mindedness** that creates defensiveness among communication participants; opposed to **provisionalism.**

channel The vehicle or medium through which signals are sent.

character One of the components of **credibility:** an individual's honesty, basic nature, and moral qualities. *In establishing character stress your fairness, your concern for enduring values, and your similarity with the audience.*

charisma One of the components of **credibility:** an individual's dynamism or forcefulness. *In establishing charisma demonstrate positiveness, act assertively, and express enthusiasm.*

cherishing behaviors Small behaviors we enjoy receiving from others, especially from our relational partner—for example, a kiss, a smile, or a gift of flowers.

chronemics The study of the communicative nature of time—the way you treat time and use it to convey messages. Two general areas of chronemics are **cultural time** and **psychological time.**

civil inattention Polite ignoring of others so as not to invade their privacy.

cliché An overused expression that has lost its novelty and part of its meaning and that calls attention to itself because of its overuse; "tall, dark, and handsome" as a description of a man is a cliché. *Avoid clichés in all forms of communication.*

closed-mindedness An unwillingness to receive certain communication messages.

code A set of symbols used to translate a message from one form to another.

coercive power Power dependent on a person's ability to punish or to remove rewards from others.

cognitive restructuring A therapeutic process of substituting logical and realistic beliefs for unrealistic beliefs; used in reducing communication apprehension and in raising self-esteem.

cohesiveness The property of togetherness. Applied to group communication situations, cohesiveness has to do with the level of mutual attraction among members; it is a measure of the extent to which individual members of a group work together as a group.

collectivist culture A culture in which the group's goals are given greater importance than the individual's and where, for example, benevolence, tradition, and conformity are given special emphasis. Opposed to **individualistic culture.**

color communication The meanings that different cultures communicate. *Use colors (in clothing and in room décor, for example) to convey desired meanings. Recognize the different cultural meanings that colors have.*

communication (1) The process or act of communicating; (2) the actual message or messages sent and received; (3) the study of the processes involved in the sending and receiving of messages. (The term *communicology* is suggested for the third definition.)

communication accommodation theory Theory holding that speakers adjust their speaking style to their listeners to gain social approval and achieve greater communication effectiveness.

communication apprehension Fear or anxiety over communicating. May be "trait apprehension"—a fear of communication generally, regardless of the specific situation—or state apprehension, a fear that is specific to a given communication situation. *Manage your own communication apprehension by reversing the potential causes of apprehension, trying performance visualization, systematically desensitizing yourself, and using the skills and techniques for dealing with apprehension.*

communicative competence A knowledge of the rules and skills of communication; often refers to the qualities that make for effectiveness in communication.

communication networks The pathways of messages; the organizational structures through which messages are sent and received.

communicology The study of communication, particularly the subsection concerned with human communication.

competence One of the qualities of **credibility** which encompasses a person's ability and knowledge. *In establishing your competence tell your listeners of your special experience or training, cite a variety of research sources, and stress the particular competencies of your sources.*

complementarity A principle of **attraction** holding that one is attracted by qualities one does not possess or one wishes to possess and to people who are opposite or different from oneself; opposed to **similarity.** *Identify the characteristics that you do not find in yourself but admire in others and that therefore might be important in influencing your perception of another person.*

complementary relationship A relationship in which the behavior of one person serves as the stimulus for the complementary behavior of the other; in complementary relationships, behavioral differences are maximized.

compliance-gaining strategies Behaviors that are directed toward gaining the agreement of others; behaviors designed to persuade others to do as we wish. *Use the various compliance-gaining strategies to increase your own persuasive power.*

compliance-resisting strategies Behaviors directed at resisting the persuasive attempts of others. *Use such strategies as identity management, nonnegotiation, negotiation, and justification as appropriate in resisting compliance.*

confidence A quality of interpersonal effectiveness; a comfortable, at-ease feeling in interpersonal communication situations. *Communicate a feeling of being comfortable and at ease with the interaction through appropriate verbal and nonverbal signals.*

confirmation A communication pattern that acknowledges another person's presence and also indicates an acceptance of this person, this person's definition of self, and the relationship as defined or viewed by this other person; opposed to **disconfirmation**. *Avoid those verbal and nonverbal behaviors that disconfirm another person. Substitute confirming behaviors, behaviors that acknowledge the presence and the contributions of the other person.*

conflict An extreme form of competition in which a person attempts to bring a rival to surrender; a situation in which one person's behaviors are directed at preventing something or at interfering with or harming another individual. *See also* **interpersonal conflict.**

congruence A condition in which both verbal and nonverbal behaviors reinforce each other.

connotation The feeling or emotional aspect of meaning, generally viewed as consisting of the evaluative (for example, good–bad), potency (strong–weak), and activity (fast–slow) dimensions; the associations of a term. *See also* **denotation.**

consensus A principle of attribution through which we attempt to establish whether other people react or behave in the same way as the person on whom we are now focusing. If the person is acting in accordance with the general consensus, then we seek reasons for the behavior outside the individual; if the person is not acting in accordance with the general consensus, then we seek reasons that are internal to the individual.

consistency A perceptual process that influences us to maintain harmony among our perceptions; to see what we expect to see and to be uncomfortable when our perceptions run contrary to our expectations. *Recognize the human tendency to seek and to see consistency even where it does not exist—to see our friends as all positive and our enemies as all negative, for example.*

contact The first stage of an interpersonal relationship, in which an initial perceptual and interactional encounter occurs.

content and relationship dimensions A principle of communication that suggests that messages refer both to content (the world external to both speaker and listener) and to the relationship existing between the individuals who are interacting.

context The physical, psychological, social, and temporal environment in which communication takes place. *Assess the context in which messages are communicated and interpret communication behavior accordingly; avoid seeing messages as independent of context.*

controllability One of the factors we consider in judging whether or not a person is responsible for his or her behavior. If the person was in control, then we judge that he or she was responsible. See **attribution theory.**

conversation Two-person communication usually possessing an opening, feedforward, a business stage, feedback, and a closing.

conversational management The ways in which a conversation is conducted. *Respond to conversational turn cues from the other person, and use conversational cues to signal your own desire to exchange (or maintain) speaker or listener roles.*

conversational turns The process of exchanging the speaker and listener roles during conversation. *Become sensitive to and respond appropriately to conversational turn cues, such as turn-maintaining, turn-yielding, turn-requesting, and turn-denying cues.*

counseling interview A type of **interview** in which the interviewer tries to learn about the interviewee in an attempt to provide some form of guidance, advice, or insight.

credibility The degree to which a speaker is perceived to be believable; **competence, character,** and **charisma** (dynamism) are the major dimensions of credibility.

critical thinking The process of logically evaluating reasons and evidence and reaching a judgment on the basis of this analysis.

critical thinking hats technique A technique developed by Edward deBono in which a problem or issue is viewed from six distinct perspectives.

criticism The reasoned judgment of some work; although often equated with faultfinding, criticism can involve both positive and negative evaluations.

cultural display Outward artifacts that communicate one's cultural identification; for example, clothing or religious jewelry.

cultural rules Rules that are specific to a given cultural group. *Respond to messages according to the cultural rules of the sender; in order to prevent misinterpretation of intended meanings, avoid interpreting the messages of others exclusively through the perspective of your own culture.*

cultural time The meanings given to time communication by a particular culture.

culture The relatively specialized lifestyle of a group of people—consisting of their values, beliefs, artifacts, ways of behaving, and ways of communicating—that is passed on from one generation to the next.

culture shock The psychological reaction we experience at being placed in a culture very different from our own or from what we are used to.

date An **extensional device** used to emphasize the notion of constant change and symbolized by a subscript: for example, John Smith$_{1994}$ is not John Smith$_{2002}$.

deception cues Verbal or nonverbal cues that reveal that a person may be lying.

decoder Something that takes a message in one form (for example, sound waves) and translates it into another form (for example, nerve impulses) from which meaning can be formulated (for example, in vocal–auditory communication). In face-to-face human communication, the decoder is the auditory mechanism; in electronic communication, the decoder is, for example, the telephone earpiece.

decoding The process of extracting a message from a code—for example, translating speech sounds into nerve impulses. *See also* **encoding.**

defensiveness An attitude of an individual or an atmosphere in a group characterized by threats, fear, and domination. Messages evidencing evaluation, control, strategy, neutrality, superiority, and certainty are assumed to lead to defensiveness. Opposed to **supportiveness.**

Delphi method A type of problem-solving procedure in which questionnaires are used to poll group members (who don't interact among themselves) on several occasions so as to arrive at a group decision on, say, the most important problems a company faces or activities a group might undertake.

democratic leader A group leader who stimulates self-direction and self-actualization by the group members.

denial One of the obstacles to the expression of emotion; the process by which we deny our emotions to ourselves or to others.

denotation Referential meaning; the objective or descriptive meaning of a word. *See also* **connotation.**

depenetration A reversal of penetration; a condition in which the **breadth** and **depth** of a relationship decrease. See **social penetration theory.**

depth The degree to which the inner personality—the inner core of an individual—is penetrated in interpersonal interaction.

deterioration A stage in an interpersonal relationship in which the bonds holding the individuals together are weakened.

direct speech Speech in which the speaker's intentions are stated clearly and directly. *Use direct speech, for example, in making requests or in responding to others (1) to encourage compromise; (2) to acknowledge responsibility for your own feelings and desires; and (3) to state your own desires honestly so as to encourage honesty, openness, and supportiveness in others.*

disclaimer Statement that asks the listener to receive what the speaker says as intended without its reflecting negatively on the image of the speaker. *Avoid using disclaimers that may not be accepted by your listeners; they may raise the very doubts you wish to put to rest. But consider using disclaimers when you think your future messages might offend your listeners.*

disconfirmation The process by which a person ignores or denies the right of another individual even to define himself or herself; opposed to **confirmation.**

dissolution The breaking of the bonds holding an interpersonal relationship together. *In dealing with the end of a relationship, consider: (1) breaking the loneliness–depression cycle, (2) taking time out to get to know yourself as an individual, (3) bolstering your self-esteem, (4) removing or avoiding*

uncomfortable symbols that may remind you of your past relationship and may make you uncomfortable, (5) seeking the support of friends and relatives, and (6) avoiding the repetition of negative patterns.*

dyadic communication Two-person communication.

dyadic consciousness An awareness of an interpersonal relationship or pairing of two individuals; distinguished from situations in which two individuals are together but do not perceive themselves as being a unit or twosome.

dyadic effect The process by which one person in a dyad imitates the behavior of the other person; usually refers to the tendency of one person's self-disclosures to prompt the other to self-disclose also. *Be responsive to the dyadic effect; if it is not operating, consider why.*

earmarker A marker that identifies an item as belonging to a specific person—for example, a nameplate on a desk or initials on an attaché case.

effect The outcome or consequence of an action or behavior; communication is always assumed to have some effect.

emblems Nonverbal behaviors or gestures that directly translate words or phrases—for example, the signs for "OK" and "peace."

emotions The feelings we have—for example, our feelings of guilt, anger, or sorrow.

empathy Feeling another person's feeling; feeling or perceiving something as does another person. *Increase empathic understanding by sharing experiences, role-playing, and seeing the world from others' perspective. Express this empathic understanding verbally and nonverbally.*

employment interview A type of **interview** in which the interviewee is questioned to ascertain his or her suitability for a particular job. *In interviewing for a job: Prepare yourself, prepare answers and questions, make an effective presentation of self, acknowledge cultural rules and customs, demonstrate effective interpersonal communication, and follow up the interview.*

encoder Something that takes a message in one form (for example, nerve impulses) and translates it into another form (for example, sound waves). In face-to-face human communication, the encoder is the speaking mechanism; in electronic communication, the encoder is, for example, the telephone mouthpiece.

encoding The process of putting a message into a code—for example, translating nerve impulses into speech sounds. *See also* **decoding.**

enculturation The process by which culture is transmitted from one generation to another.

E-prime A form of the language that omits the verb "to be" except when it is used as an auxiliary or in statements of existence. Designed to eliminate the tendency toward **projection.**

equilibrium theory A theory of proxemics holding that intimacy and physical closeness are positively related; as relationship becomes more intimate, the individuals will use shorter distances between them.

equity theory A theory claiming that we experience relational satisfaction when there is an equal distribution of rewards and costs between the two persons in the relationship.

et cetera (etc.) An **extensional device** used to emphasize the notion of infinite complexity; because one can never know all about anything, any statement about the world or an event must end with an explicit or implicit "et cetera." *Use the implicit or explicit "et cetera" to remind yourself and others that there is more to be known, more to be said.*

ethics The branch of philosophy that deals with the rightness or wrongness of actions; the study of moral values.

ethnocentrism The tendency to see others and their behaviors through our own cultural filters, often as distortions of our own behaviors; the tendency to evaluate the values and beliefs of our own culture more positively than those of another culture.

excuse An explanation designed to lessen the negative consequences of something done or said. *Avoid excessive excuse making. Too many excuses may backfire and create image problems for the excuse maker.*

exit interview A type of **interview** in which employee and management discuss the reasons for the employee's leaving the organization.

expectancy violations theory A theory of proxemics holding that people have a certain expectancy for space relationships. When that is violated (say, a person stands too close to you or a romantic partner maintains abnormally large distances from you), the relationship comes into clearer focus and you wonder why this "normal distance" is being violated.

expert power Power based on a person's expertise or knowledge; knowledge gives an individual expert power.

expressiveness A quality of interpersonal effectiveness; genuine involvement in speaking and listening, conveyed verbally and nonverbally. *Communicate involvement and interest by providing appropriate feedback, assuming responsibility for your thoughts and feelings and your role as speaker and listener, and using variety and flexibility in voice and bodily action.*

extemporaneous speech A speech that is thoroughly prepared and organized in detail and in which certain aspects of style are predetermined, but which is not memorized or read aloud from a written script.

extensional devices Linguistic devices proposed by Alfred Korzybski to make language a more accurate means for talking about the world. The extensional devices include **et cetera, date,** and **index.**

extensional orientation A point of view in which the primary consideration is given to the world of experience and only secondary consideration is given to labels. Opposed to **intensional orientation.**

face-saving Maintaining a positive public self-image in the minds of others.

facial feedback hypothesis The hypothesis or theory that your facial expressions can produce physiological and emotional effects.

facial management techniques Techniques used to mask certain emotions and to emphasize others; for example,

intensifying your expression of happiness to make a friend feel good about a promotion.

fact–inference confusion A misevaluation in which one makes an inference, regards it as a fact, and acts upon it as if it were a fact. *Distinguish facts from inferences; respond to inferences as inferences and not as facts.*

factual statement A statement made by the observer after observation and limited to what is observed. *See also* **inferential statement.**

family A group of people who consider themselves related and connected to one another and among whom the actions of one person have consequences for others.

fear appeal Effort to persuade people to believe or to act in a certain way by encouraging or creating fears among them.

feedback Information that is given back to the source. Feedback may come from the source's own messages (as when we hear what we are saying) or from the receiver(s) in the form of applause, yawns, puzzled looks, questions, letters to the editor of a newspaper, increased or decreased subscriptions to a magazine, and so forth. *To increase communication efficiency and satisfaction, give clear feedback to others, and respond to others' feedback, either through corrective measures or by continuing current performance. See also* **negative feedback, positive feedback.**

feedforward Information that is sent in advance of a message telling the listener something about what is to follow. *When appropriate, preface your messages in order to open the channels of communication, to preview the messages to be sent, to disclaim, and to altercast. In your use of feedforward, be brief, use feedforward sparingly, and follow through on your feedforward promises. Also, be sure to respond to the feedforward as well as the content messages of others.*

field of experience The sum total of an individual's experiences, which influences his or her ability to communicate. In some views of communication, two people can communicate only to the extent that their fields of experience overlap.

flexibility The ability to adjust communication strategies on the basis of the unique situation. *Apply the principles of interpersonal communication with flexibility; remember that each situation calls for somewhat different skills.*

focus group A group designed to explore the feelings and attitudes of its individual members and which usually follows a question-and-answer format.

force An unproductive **conflict** strategy in which someone attempts to win an argument by physical force or threats of force. *Avoid it.*

forum A small group format in which members of the group answer questions from the audience; often follows a **symposium.**

friendship An interpersonal relationship between two persons that is mutually productive, established and maintained through perceived mutual free choice, and characterized by mutual positive regard. *Adjust your verbal and nonverbal communication as appropriate to the stages of your various friendships. Learn the rules that govern each friendship; follow them or risk damaging the relationship.*

fundamental attribution error The tendency to attribute a person's behavior to the kind of person he or she is (to the person's personality, say) and to not give sufficient importance to the situation the person is in.

general semantics The study of the relationships among language, thought, and behavior.

glittering generality Comment in which a speaker tries to gain your acceptance of an idea by associating it with things you value highly; the opposite of **name calling.**

gossip Communication about someone not present, some third party, usually about matters that are private to this third party. *Avoid gossip that breaches confidentiality, is known to be false, and/or is unnecessarily invasive.*

grapevine The informal lines through which messages in an organization may travel; these informal lines resemble a physical grapevine, with its unpredictable pattern of branches.

group A collection of individuals related to one another with some common purpose and with some structure among them.

group norm Rule or expectation of appropriate behavior for a member of a group.

groupthink A tendency observed in some groups in which agreement among members becomes more important than the exploration of the issues at hand.

gunnysacking An unproductive **conflict** strategy of storing up grievances—as if in a gunnysack—and holding them in readiness to dump on the person with whom one is in conflict. *Avoid it.*

halo effect The tendency to generalize an individual's virtue or expertise from one area to another.

haptics The study of touch communication.

heterosexist language Language that assumes that all people are heterosexual and thereby denigrates lesbians and gay men. *Avoid it.*

high-context culture A culture in which much of the information in communication is in the context or in the person rather than explicitly coded in the verbal messages. **Collectivist cultures** are generally high context. Opposed to **low-context culture.**

home field advantage The increased power that comes from being in your own territory.

home territories Territories with which individuals have a sense of intimacy and over which they exercise control—for example, a professor's office.

idea-generation group A group whose purpose is to generate ideas; see **brainstorming.**

illustrators Nonverbal behaviors that accompany and literally illustrate verbal messages—for example, an upward gesture that accompanies the verbalization "It's up there."

I-messages Messages in which the speaker accepts responsibility for personal thoughts and behaviors; messages in which the speaker's point of view is stated explicitly. Opposed to **you-messages.** *Use I-messages to take responsibility for your thoughts and behaviors.*

immediacy A quality of interpersonal effectiveness; a sense of contact and togetherness; a feeling of interest and liking for the other person. *Communicate immediacy through appropriate word choice, feedback, eye contact, body posture, and physical closeness.*

implicit personality theory A theory of personality that each individual maintains, complete with rules or systems, and through which the individual perceives others. *Be conscious of your implicit personality theories; avoid drawing firm conclusions about other people on the basis of these theories.*

impromptu speech A speech given without any explicit prior preparation.

index An **extensional device** used to emphasize the notion of nonidentity (the concept that no two things are the same) and symbolized by a subscript—for example, politician$_1$ is not politician$_2$. *See also* **indiscrimination.**

indirect speech Speech that may hide the speaker's true intentions or that the speaker may use to make requests and observations indirectly. *Use indirect speech, for example, (1) to express a desire without insulting or offending anyone, (2) to ask for compliments in a socially acceptable manner, or (3) to disagree without being disagreeable.*

indiscrimination A misevaluation caused by categorizing people, events, or objects into a particular class and responding to them only as members of the class; a failure to recognize that each individual is unique; a failure to apply the **index.** *Index your terms and statements to emphasize that each person and event is unique; avoid treating groups of individuals the same way because they are covered by the same label or term.*

individualistic culture A culture in which the individual's goals and preferences are given greater importance than the group's. Opposed to **collectivist culture.**

inevitability A principle of communication holding that communication cannot be avoided; all behavior in an interactional setting is communication. *Because all behavior in an interactional situation communicates, seek out nonobvious messages and meanings.*

inferential statement A statement that can be made by anyone, is not limited to what is observed, and can be made at any time. *See also* **factual statement.**

informal time terms Terms that describe approximate rather than exact time; for example, "soon," "early," and "in a while." *Recognize that informal time terms are often the cause of interpersonal difficulties. When misunderstanding is likely, use more precise terms.*

information That which reduces uncertainty.

information overload A condition in which the amount of information is too great to be dealt with effectively or the number or complexity of messages is so great that the individual or organization is not able to deal with them.

information power Power based on a person's information and ability to communicate logically and persuasively. Also called "persuasion power."

informative interview A type of **interview** in which the interviewer asks the interviewee, usually a person of some reputation and accomplishment, questions designed to elicit his or her views, predictions, and perspectives on specific topics. *In interviewing for information, secure an* appointment, prepare your questions, establish rapport with the interviewer, ask permission to tape the interview, and close and follow up the interview.

inoculation principle A principle of persuasion stating that persuasion will be more difficult to achieve when beliefs and attitudes that have already been challenged are attacked, because the individual has built up defenses against such attacks in a manner similar to inoculation. *In persuading an audience inoculated against your position, be content with small gains; trying to reverse an inoculated audience in one speech is probably unrealistic.*

intensional orientation A point of view in which primary consideration is given to the way things are labeled and only secondary consideration (if any) to the world of experience. *Avoid this orientation: Respond first to things, and avoid responding to labels as if they were things. Do not let labels distort your perception of the world.* Opposed to **extensional orientation.**

interaction management A quality of interpersonal effectiveness; the control of interactions through management of conversational turns, fluency, and message consistency. *Manage the interaction to the satisfaction of both parties by sharing the roles of speaker and listener, avoiding long and awkward silences, and being consistent in your verbal and nonverbal messages.*

interaction process analysis A content analysis method that classifies messages into four general categories: social–emotional positive, social–emotional negative, attempted answers, and questions.

intercultural communication Communication that takes place between persons of different cultures or persons who have different cultural beliefs, values, or ways of behaving.

interpersonal communication Communication between two persons or among a small group of persons and distinguished from public or mass communication; communication of a personal nature and distinguished from impersonal communication; communication between or among intimates or those involved in a close relationship; often, intrapersonal, dyadic, and small group communication in general.

interpersonal conflict A type of disagreement between two people who are interdependent (what one person does has an effect on the other person), who perceive their goals to be incompatible (if one person's goal is achieved the other's cannot be), and who may see each other as interfering with the achievement of a goal. *To fight more productively, look for win–win strategies, fight actively, use talk instead of force, focus on the present rather than gunnysacking, use face-enhancing instead of face-detracting strategies, express acceptance instead of attacking the other person, and use your skills in argumentation, not in verbal aggressiveness.*

interpersonal perception Our perceptions of people; the processes through which we interpret and evaluate people and their behavior. *Increase the accuracy of your interpersonal perceptions by checking your perceptions, subjecting your perceptions to critical thinking, reducing uncertainty,* and becoming aware of cultural differences and influences on perception.

interview A particular form of interpersonal communication in which two persons interact largely through a question-and-answer format for the purpose of achieving specific goals. Also see the specific types of interviews: **appraisal interview, counseling interview, employment interview, exit interview, information interview,** and **persuasive interview.**

intimacy The closest interpersonal relationship; usually a close primary relationship.

intimate distance The closest proxemic distance, ranging from touching to 18 inches. *See also* **proxemics.**

intrapersonal communication Communication with oneself.

invasion Unwarranted entrance into another's territory that changes the meaning of the territory.

involvement The stage in an interpersonal relationship that normally follows contact. In this stage the individuals get to know each other better and explore the potential for greater intimacy.

irreversibility A principle of communication holding that communication cannot be reversed; once something has been communicated, it cannot be uncommunicated. *In order to prevent resentment and ill feeling, avoid saying things (for example, in anger) or making commitments that you may wish to retract (but will not be able to).*

jargon The technical language of any specialized group, often a professional class, which is unintelligible to individuals not belonging to the group; "shop talk."

Johari window A diagram of the four selves (open, blind, hidden, and **unknown**) that illustrates the different kinds of information in each self.

kinesics The study of the communicative dimensions of facial and bodily movements.

laissez-faire leader A group leader who allows the group to develop and progress or make mistakes on its own.

leadership The quality by which one individual directs or influences the thoughts and/or the behaviors of others. *See* **laissez-faire leader, democratic leader,** and **authoritarian leader.**

leave-taking cues Verbal and nonverbal cues that indicate a desire to terminate a conversation. *Increase your sensitivity to leave-taking cues; pick up on the leave-taking cues of others, and communicate such cues tactfully so as not to insult or offend others.*

legitimate power Power based on people's belief that an individual has a right, by virtue of position, to influence or control others' behavior.

leveling A process of message distortion in which a message is repeated but the number of details is reduced, some details are omitted entirely, and some details lose their complexity.

level of abstraction The relative distance of a term or statement from the actual perception. A low-order abstraction would be a description of the perception, whereas a high-order abstraction would consist of inferences about inferences about descriptions of a perception.

listening An active process of receiving messages sent orally; this process consists of five stages: receiving, understanding, remembering, evaluating, and responding. *Adjust your listening perspective, as the situation warrants, between judgmental and nonjudgmental, surface and depth, and empathic and objective listening. Listen actively when appropriate.*

logic The science of reasoning; the study of the principles governing the analysis of inference making.

looking-glass self The self-concept that results from the image of yourself that others reveal to you.

low-context culture A culture in which most of the information in communication is explicitly stated in the verbal messages. **Individualistic cultures** are usually low-context cultures. Opposed to **high-context culture**.

magnitude of change principle A principle of persuasion stating that the greater and more important the change desired by the speaker, the more difficult achieving this change will be.

maintenance A stage of relationship stability at which the relationship does not progress or deteriorate significantly; a continuation as opposed to a dissolution of a relationship.

maintenance strategies Specific behaviors designed to preserve an interpersonal relationship. *Use appropriate maintenance strategies (for example, openness, sharing joint activities, and acting positively) to preserve a valued relationship. See also* **relationship repair.**

manipulation An unproductive **conflict** strategy that avoids open conflict; instead, a person makes attempts to divert the conflict by being especially charming and getting the other person into a noncombative frame of mind. *Avoid it.*

manuscript speech A speech designed to be read verbatim from a script.

markers Devices that signify that a certain territory belongs to a particular person. *Become sensitive to the markers of others, and learn to use these markers to define your own territories and to communicate the desired impression. See also* **boundary marker, central marker,** and **earmarker.**

mass communication Communication addressed to an extremely large audience, mediated by audio and/or visual transmitters, and processed by gatekeepers before transmission.

matching hypothesis Theory stating that we date and mate with people who are similar to ourselves—who match us—in physical attractiveness.

message Any signal or combination of signals that serves as a **stimulus** for a **receiver.**

metacommunication Communication about communication. *Metacommunicate to ensure that you understand the other person's thoughts and feelings; give clear feedforward, explain feelings as well as thoughts, paraphrase your own complex thoughts, and ask questions.*

metalanguage Language used to talk about language.

metamessage A message that makes reference to another message; for example, the statements "Did I make myself clear?" or "That's a lie" refer to other messages and are therefore considered metamessages. *Use metamessages to clarify your understanding of what another thinks and feels.*

metaskills Skills for regulating more specific skills; for example, the skills of interpersonal communication, such as openness and empathy, must be regulated by the metaskills of flexibility, mindfulness, and metacommunication.

mindfulness and mindlessness States of relative awareness. In a mindful state, we are aware of the logic and rationality of our behaviors and the logical connections existing among elements. In a mindless state, we are unaware of this logic and rationality. *Apply the principles of interpersonal communication mindfully rather than mindlessly. Increase mindfulness by creating and re-creating categories, being open to new information and points of view, and being careful of relying too heavily on first impressions.*

mixed message A message that contradicts itself; a message that asks for two different (often incompatible) responses. *Avoid emitting mixed messages by focusing clearly on your purposes when communicating and by increasing conscious control over your verbal and nonverbal behaviors. Detect mixed messages in other people's communications and respond to them as appropriate. Avoid sending mixed messages; they make you appear unsure and unfocused.*

models Representations of objects or processes.

monochronic time orientation A view of time in which things are done sequentially; one thing is scheduled at a time. Opposed to **polychronic time orientation**.

motivated sequence An organizational pattern for arranging the information in a discourse to motivate an audience to respond positively to one's purpose.

name calling A persuasive technique in which the speaker gives an idea a derogatory name.

negative feedback Feedback that serves a corrective function by informing the source that his or her message is not being received in the way intended. Negative feedback serves to redirect the source's behavior. Looks of boredom, shouts of disagreement, letters critical of newspaper policy, and teachers' instructions on how better to approach a problem are examples of negative feedback. *See also* **positive feedback.**

neutrality A response pattern lacking in personal involvement; opposed to **empathy.**

noise Anything that interferes with a person's receiving a message as the source intended the message to be received. Noise is present in a communication system to the extent that the message received is not the message sent. *Combat the effects of physical, semantic, and psychological noise by eliminating or lessening the sources of physical noise, securing agreement on meanings, and interacting with an open mind in order to increase communication accuracy.*

nominal group A collection of individuals who record their thoughts and opinions, which are then distributed to others. Without direct interaction, the thoughts and opinions are gradually pared down until a manageable list (of solutions or decisions) is produced. When this occurs, the nominal group (a group in name only) may restructure itself into a **problem-solving group** that analyzes the final list.

nonnegotiation An unproductive **conflict** strategy in which the individual refuses to discuss the conflict or to listen to the other person.

nonverbal communication Communication without words; communication by means of space, gestures, facial expressions, touching, vocal variation, and silence, for example.

nonverbal dominance Nonverbal behavior that allows one person to achieve psychological dominance over another. *Resist (as sender and receiver) nonverbal expressions of dominance when they are inappropriate—for example, when they are sexist.*

norms *See* **group norms.**

object-adaptors Movements that involve your manipulation of some object; for example, punching holes in or drawing on a Styrofoam coffee cup, clicking a ballpoint pen, or chewing on a pencil. *Avoid object-adaptors; they generally communicate discomfort and a lack of control over the communication situation.*

olfactory communication Communication by smell.

openness A quality of interpersonal effectiveness encompassing (1) a willingness to interact openly with others, to self-disclose as appropriate; (2) a willingness to react honestly to incoming stimuli; and (3) a willingness to own one's feelings and thoughts.

oral style The style of spoken discourse. When compared with written style, oral style consists of shorter, simpler, and more familiar words; more qualification, self-reference terms, allness terms, verbs, and adverbs; and more concrete terms and terms indicative of consciousness of projection—for example, "as I see it."

other-orientation A quality of interpersonal effectiveness involving attentiveness, interest, and concern for the other person. *Convey concern for and interest in the other person by means of empathic responses, appropriate feedback, and attentive listening responses.*

owning feelings The process by which you take responsibility for your own feelings instead of attributing them to others. *Use I-messages to express ownership and to acknowledge responsibility for your own thoughts and feelings.*

panel A small group format in which "expert" participants speak without any set pattern and an audience is present.

paralanguage The vocal (but nonverbal) aspect of speech. Paralanguage consists of voice qualities (for example, pitch range, resonance, tempo); vocal characterizers (laughing or crying, yelling or whispering); vocal qualifiers (intensity, pitch height); and vocal segregates ("uh-uh," meaning "no," or "sh" meaning "silence"). *Vary paralinguistic elements, such as rate, volume, and stress, to add variety and emphasis to your communications; and be responsive to the meanings communicated by others' paralanguage.*

parasocial relationships Relationships between real and imagined or fictional characters; usually relationships between a viewer and a fictional character in a television show.

pauses Silent periods in the normally fluent stream of speech. Pauses are of two major types: filled pauses (interruptions in speech that are filled with such vocalizations as "er" or "um") and unfilled pauses (silences of unusually long duration).

perception The process of becoming aware of objects and events from the senses. *See* **interpersonal perception**.

perception checking The process of verifying your understanding of some message or situation or feeling to reduce uncertainty. *Use perception checking to get more information about your impressions: (1) Describe what you see or hear and what you think is happening, and (2) ask whether this is correct or in error.*

perceptual accentuation A process that leads you to see what you expect to see and what you want to see—for example, seeing people you like as better looking and smarter than people you do not like. *Be aware of the influence your own needs, wants, and expectations have on your perceptions. Recognize that what you perceive is a function both of what exists in reality and what is going on inside your own head.*

personal distance The second-closest **proxemic distance,** ranging from 18 inches to 4 feet. *See also* **proxemics.**

personal rejection An unproductive conflict strategy in which an individual withholds love and affection and seeks to win the argument by getting the other person to break down under this withdrawal.

persuasion The process of influencing attitudes and behavior.

persuasive interview A type of **interview** in which the interviewer attempts to change the interviewee's attitudes or behavior.

phatic communication Communication that is primarily social; communication designed to open the channels of communication rather than to communicate something about the external world; "Hello" and "How are you?" in everyday interaction are examples.

pitch The highness or lowness of the vocal tone.

plain folks A persuasive strategy in which the speaker identifies himself or herself and the proposal with the audience.

polarization A form of fallacious reasoning in which only two extremes are considered; also referred to as "black-or-white" and "either–or" thinking or two-valued orientation. *In order to describe reality more accurately, use middle terms and qualifiers when describing the world; avoid talking in terms of polar opposites (black and white, good and bad).*

polychronic time orientation A view of time in which several things may be scheduled or engaged in at the same time. Opposed to **monochronic time orientation**.

positive feedback Feedback that supports or reinforces the continuation of behavior along the same lines in which it is already proceeding—for example, applause during a speech.

positiveness A characteristic of effective communication involving positive attitudes toward oneself and toward the interpersonal interaction. Can also mean complimenting another and expressing acceptance and approval. *Verbally and nonverbally communicate a positive attitude toward yourself, others, and the situation with smiles, positive facial expressions, attentive gestures, positive verbal expressions, and the elimination or reduction of negative appraisals.*

power The ability to control the behaviors of others.

power communication Behaviors such as forceful speech; avoidance of weak modifiers and excessive body movement; and demonstration of knowledge, preparation, and organization in the matters at hand, all of which convey a sense of authority.

power play A consistent pattern of behavior in which one person tries to control the behavior of another. *Identify the power plays people use on you and respond to these power plays so as to stop them. Use an effective management strategy such as "cooperation"—in which you express your feelings, describe the behavior you object to, and state a cooperative response.*

premature self-disclosures Disclosures that are made before a relationship has developed sufficiently. *Resist too intimate or too negative self-disclosures early in the development of a relationship.*

primacy effect Condition in which what comes first exerts greater influence than what comes later. *See also* **recency effect.**

primacy–recency Perceptual distortion pattern: In primacy we give more credence to that which occurs first; in recency we give more credence to that which occurs last (that is, most recently). *Resist the normal tendency to form lasting impressions from first impressions, which can color both what we see later and the conclusions we draw. Take the time and effort to revise your impressions of others on the basis of new information. Be at your very best in first encounters, because others may well be operating with a primacy bias.*

primary relationship The relationship between two people that they consider their most (or one of their most) important; for example, the relationship between spouses or domestic partners.

primary territory Areas that we can consider our exclusive preserve—for example, our own room or office.

problem-solving group A group whose primary task is to solve a problem or, more often, to reach a decision.

problem-solving sequence A logical step-by-step process for solving a problem. This sequence, frequently used by groups, consists of defining and analyzing the problem, establishing criteria for evaluating solutions, identifying possible solutions, evaluating solutions, selecting the best solution, and testing the selected solutions.

process Ongoing activity; communication is referred to as a process because it is always changing, always in motion.

projection A psychological process whereby we attribute characteristics or feelings of our own to others; often, the process whereby we attribute our own faults to others.

pronunciation The production of syllables or words according to some accepted standard—for example, as presented in a dictionary.

protection theory A theory of proxemics holding that people establish a body-buffer zone to protect themselves from unwanted closeness, touching, or attack.

provisionalism An attitude of open-mindedness that leads to the creation of supportiveness; opposed to **certainty.**

proxemic distances The spatial distances that are maintained in communication and social interaction. *Adjust spatial (proxemic) distances as appropriate to the specific interaction; avoid distances that are too far, too close, or otherwise inappropriate, as they might falsely convey, for example, aloofness or aggression.*

proxemics The study of the communicative function of space; the study of how people unconsciously structure their space—the distances between people in their interactions, the organization of spaces in homes and offices, and even the design of cities.

proximity As a principle of perception, the tendency to perceive people or events that are physically close as belonging together or representing some unit; physical closeness; one of the qualities influencing interpersonal **attraction.** *Use physical proximity to increase interpersonal attractiveness.*

psychological time The importance you place on past, present, or future time. *Recognize the significance of your own time orientation to your ultimate success, and make whatever adjustments you think desirable.*

public communication Communication in which the source is one person and the receiver is an audience of many persons.

public distance The longest **proxemic distance,** ranging from 12 to over 25 feet.

public territories Areas that are open to all people—for example, restaurants or parks.

punctuation of communication The breaking up of continuous communication sequences into short sequences with identifiable beginnings and endings or stimuli and responses. *To increase empathy and mutual understanding, see the sequence of events punctuated from perspectives other than your own.*

punishment Noxious or aversive stimulation.

pupillometrics The study of communication through changes in the size of the pupils of the eyes. *Detect pupil dilation and constriction, and formulate hypotheses (not conclusions) concerning their possible meanings.*

purr words Highly positive words that express the speaker's feelings rather than refer to any objective reality; opposed to **snarl words.**

racist language Language that is derogatory toward members of a particular race. *Avoid racist language so as not to offend or alienate others or reinforce stereotypes.*

rate The speed with which you speak, generally measured in words per minute.

receiver Any person or thing that takes in messages. Receivers may be individuals listening to or reading a message, a group of persons hearing a speech, a scattered television audience, or machines that store information.

recency effect Condition in which what comes last (that is, most recently) exerts greater influence than what comes first. *See also* **primacy effect.**

referent power Power dependent on one's desire to identify with or be like another person.

regulators Nonverbal behaviors that monitor or control the communications of another person.

reinforcement theory A theory of behavior that when applied to relationships would hold (essentially) that relationships develop because they are rewarding and end because they are punishing. *Reinforce others as a way to increase interpersonal attractiveness and general interpersonal satisfaction.*

rejection A response to an individual that spurns or denies the validity of that individual's self-view.

relational communication Communication between or among intimates or those in close relationships; used by some theorists as synonymous with **interpersonal communication.**

relationship deterioration The stage of a relationship during which the connecting bonds between the partners weaken and the partners begin drifting apart.

relationship development The stages of relationships during which you move closer to intimacy; in the model of relationships presented here, relationship development includes the contact and involvement stages.

relationship dialectics theory A theory that describes relationships in terms of the dynamics between competing opposite desires or motivations, such as the desire for autonomy and the desire to belong to someone, desires for novelty and for predictability, and desires for closedness and for openness.

relationship maintenance The processes by which you attempt to keep a relationship stable.

relationship messages Messages that comment on the relationship between the speakers rather than on matters external to them. *In order to ensure a more complete understanding of the messages intended, recognize and respond to relationship as well as content messages.*

relationship repair Attempts to reverse the process of relationship deterioration. *To repair a relationship, recognize the problem, engage in productive conflict resolution, pose possible solutions, affirm each other, integrate solutions into normal behavior, and take risks.*

response Any bit of overt or covert behavior.

reward power Power based on a person's ability to reward (or punish) others.

rigid complementarity The inability to break away from the complementary type of relationship that was once appropriate and now is no longer.

role The part an individual plays in a group; an individual's function or expected behavior.

round table A small group format in which participants are seated in a circular arrangement and interact informally, with or without a leader or moderator.

rules theory A theory that describes relationships as interactions governed by a series of rules that a couple agrees to follow. When the rules are followed, the relationship is maintained; when they are broken, the relationship experiences difficulty.

secondary territories Areas that do not belong to a particular person but have been occupied by that person and are therefore associated with her or him—for example, the seat you normally take in class.

selective exposure principle A principle of perception and persuasion that states that listeners actively seek out information that supports their opinions and actively avoid information that contradicts their existing opinions, beliefs, attitudes, and values.

self-acceptance A sense of comfort or satisfaction with ourselves, our virtues and vices, and our abilities and limitations.

self-adaptors Movements that usually satisfy a physical need, especially to make you more comfortable; for example, scratching your head to relieve an itch, moistening your lips because they feel dry, or pushing your hair out of your eyes. *Because these often communicate nervousness or discomfort, they are best avoided.*

self-attribution A process through which we seek to account for and understand the reasons and motivations for our own behaviors.

self-awareness The degree to which a person knows himself or herself. *Increase self-awareness by asking yourself about yourself and listening to others; actively seek information about yourself from others by carefully observing their interactions with you and by asking relevant questions. See yourself from different perspectives (see your different selves), and increase your "open self" (see* **Johari window***).*

self-concept An individual's self-evaluation; an individual's self-appraisal.

self-disclosure The process of revealing something about ourselves to another, usually information that would normally be kept hidden. *Self-disclose when the motivation is to improve the relationship, when the context and the relationship are appropriate for the self-disclosure, when there is an opportunity for open and honest responses, when the self-disclosures will be clear and direct, when there are appropriate reciprocal disclosures, and when you have examined and are willing to take on the possible risks that self-disclosure might entail. To secure the maximum advantage and reduce the possibility of negative effects, self-disclose selectively; regulate your self-disclosures as appropriate to the context, topic, audience, and potential rewards and risks. In responding to the disclosures of others, demonstrate the skills of effective listening, express support for the discloser (but resist evaluation), reinforce the disclosing behavior, keep the disclosures confidential, and avoid using the disclosures against the person.*

self-esteem The value you place on yourself; your self-evaluation. Usually refers to the positive value we place on ourselves. *Increase your self-esteem by attacking self-destructive statements and engage in self-affirmation.*

self-fulfilling prophecy The situation in which we make a prediction and by making it cause it to come true—as when we expect a class to be boring and then fulfill this expectation by perceiving it as boring. *Avoid fulfilling your own negative prophecies and seeing only what you want to see. Be especially careful to examine your perceptions when they conform too closely to your expectations; check to make sure that you are seeing what exists in real life, not just in your expectations or predictions.*

self-monitoring Manipulating the image we present to others in interpersonal interactions so as to create a favorable impression. *Monitor your verbal and nonverbal behavior as appropriate to communicate the desired impression.*

self-serving bias A bias that operates in the **self-attribution** process and leads us to take credit for the positive consequences and to deny responsibility for the negative consequences of our behaviors. *In examining the causes of your own behavior, beware of the tendency to attribute negative behaviors to external factors and positive behaviors to internal factors. Ask yourself whether and how the self-serving bias might be operating.*

sexist language Language derogatory to one gender, usually women. *Whether man or woman, avoid sexist language—for example, terms that presume maleness as the norm ("policeman" or "mailman") or terms that may be considered insulting or demeaning.*

sexual harassment Unsolicited and unwanted sexual messages. *If confronted with workplace sexual harassment, consider talking to the harasser, collecting evidence, using appropriate channels within the organization, or filing a complaint. To avoid any risk of being accused of sexual harassment, begin with the assumption that others at work are not interested in sexual advances and stories. Listen for negative reactions to any sexually explicit discussions, and avoid behaviors you think might prove offensive.*

shyness A condition of discomfort and uneasiness in interpersonal situations.

silence The absence of vocal communication; often misunderstood to refer to the absence of any and all communication. Silence is often used to communicate feelings or to prevent communication about certain topics. *Interpret silences of others through their culturally determined rules rather than your own.*

similarity A principle of **attraction** holding that one is attracted to qualities similar to those possessed by oneself and to people who are similar to oneself; opposed to **complementarity.**

slang Language used by special groups that often is not considered proper by the general society.

small group communication Communication among a collection of individuals small enough in number that all members may interact with relative ease as both senders and receivers, the members being related to each other by some common purpose and with some degree of organization or structure.

snarl words Highly negative words that express the feelings of the speaker rather than refer to any objective reality; opposite to **purr words.**

social comparison processes The processes by which you compare yourself (for example, your abilities, opinions, and values) with others and then assess and evaluate yourself; one of the sources of **self-concept.**

social distance The third **proxemic distance,** ranging from 4 to 12 feet; the distance at which business is usually conducted.

social exchange theory A theory hypothesizing that we seek and maintain relationships in which our rewards or profits are greater than our costs and that we avoid or terminate relationships in which the costs exceed the rewards.

social penetration theory A theory focusing on how relationships develop from superficial to intimate and from few to many areas of interpersonal interaction.

source Any person or thing that creates messages. A source may be anything from an individual speaking, writing, or gesturing to a computer sending an error message.

spatial distance Physical distance that signals the type of relationship you are in: intimate, personal, social, or public. *Let your spatial relationships reflect your interpersonal relationships.*

speech rate Variations in rate used to increase communication efficiency and persuasiveness as appropriate.

spontaneity The communication pattern in which one verbalizes what one is thinking without attempting to develop strategies for control; encourages **supportiveness.**

static evaluation An orientation that fails to recognize that the world is characterized by constant change; an attitude that sees people and events as fixed rather than as constantly changing. *Date your statements to emphasize constant change; avoid the tendency to think of and describe things as static and unchanging.*

status The relative level a person occupies in a hierarchy. Status always involves a comparison, and thus one individual's status is only relative to the status of another.

stereotype In communication, a fixed impression of a group of people through which we then perceive specific individuals; stereotypes are most often negative but may also be positive. *Avoid stereotyping others; instead, see and respond to each person as a unique individual.*

stimulus Any external or internal change that impinges on or arouses an organism.

stimulus–response models of communication Models of communication that assume that the process of communication is linear, beginning with a stimulus that then leads to a response.

subjectivity Principle of perception stating that our perceptions are not objective but are influenced by our wants and needs and our expectations and predictions.

supportiveness An attitude of an individual or an atmosphere in a group that is characterized by openness, absence of fear, and a genuine feeling of equality. *Exhibit supportiveness to others by being descriptive rather than evaluative, spontaneous rather than strategic, and provisional rather than certain.*

symmetrical relationship A relation between two or more persons in which one person's behavior serves as a stimulus for the same type of behavior in the other person(s). Examples of such relationships include those in which anger in one person encourages or serves as a stimulus for anger in another person or in which a critical comment by the person leads the other person to respond in a like manner.

symposium A small group format in which each member of the group delivers a relatively prepared talk on some aspect of the topic. Often combined with a **forum**.

systematic desensitization A theory and technique for dealing with fears (such as communication apprehension) in which you gradually expose yourself to, and develop a comfort level with, fear-producing stimuli.

taboo Forbidden; culturally censored. Taboo language is language that is frowned upon by "polite society." Topics and specific words may be considered taboo—for example, death, sex, certain forms of illness, and various words denoting sexual activities and excretory functions. *Avoid taboo expressions; substitute more socially acceptable expressions or euphemisms where and when appropriate.*

territoriality A possessive or ownership reaction to an area of space or to particular objects. *Establish and maintain territory nonverbally by marking or otherwise indicating temporary or permanent ownership. Become sensitive to the territorial behavior of others.*

testimonial A persuasive technique in which the speaker uses the authority or image of some positively evaluated person to gain your approval or of some negatively evaluated person to gain your rejection.

theory A general statement or principle applicable to a number of related phenomena.

thesis The main assertion of a message—for example, the theme of a public speech.

temporal communication The messages communicated by a person's time orientation and treatment of time.

touch avoidance The tendency to avoid touching and being touched by others. *Recognize that some people may prefer to avoid touching and being touched. Avoid drawing too many conclusions about people from the way they treat interpersonal touching.*

touch communication Communication through tactile means. *Use touch when appropriate to express positive affect, playfulness, control, and ritualistic meanings and to serve task-related functions. Avoid touching that is unwelcome or that may be considered inappropriate.*

transactional Characterized by mutual influence among elements; communication is a transactional process because no element is independent of any other element.

transfer A persuasive technique in which a speaker associates an idea with something you respect to gain your approval or with something you dislike to gain your rejection.

uncertainty reduction strategies Passive, active, and interactive ways of increasing your accuracy in interpersonal perception. *Use all three strategies as ways of reducing your uncertainty about others.*

uncertainty reduction theory Theory holding that as relationships develop, uncertainty is reduced; relationship development is seen as a process of reducing uncertainty about one another.

universal of interpersonal communication A feature of communication common to all interpersonal communication acts.

unknown self That part of the self that contains information about the self that is unknown to oneself and to others, but that is inferred to exist on the basis of various projective tests, slips of the tongue, dream analyses, and the like.

upward communication Communication in which the messages originate from the lower levels of an organization or hierarchy and are sent to upper levels—for example, line worker to management.

value Relative worth of an object; a quality that makes something desirable or undesirable; ideals or customs about which we have emotional responses, whether positive or negative.

verbal aggressiveness A method of winning an argument by attacking the other person's **self-concept.** *Avoid inflicting psychological pain on the other person to win an argument.* Often considered opposed to **argumentativeness**.

visual dominance The use of your eyes to maintain a superior or dominant position; for example, when making an especially important point, you might look intently at the other person. *Use visual dominance behavior when you wish to emphasize certain messages.*

voice qualities Aspects of **paralanguage**—specifically, pitch range, vocal lip control, glottis control, pitch control, articulation control, rhythm control, resonance, and tempo.

volume The relative loudness of the voice.

withdrawal (1) A reaction to territorial encroachment in which we leave the territory. (2) A tendency to close oneself off from conflicts rather than confront the issues.

you-messages Messages in which the speaker denies responsibility for his or her own thoughts and behaviors; messages that attribute the speaker's perception to another person; messages of blame. Opposed to **I-messages.**

BIBLIOGRAPHY

Entries in blue are cited in the CD-ROM units.

Adler, R. B. (1977). *Confidence in communication: A guide to assertive and social skills.* New York: Holt, Rinehart & Winston.

Aiex, N. K., & Aiex, P. (1992). *Health communication in the 90s.* ERIC Clearing House on Reading, English, and Communication Digest #76 (EDO-CS-92-09 October 1992).

Akert, R. M., & Panter, A. T. (1988). Extraversion and the ability to decode nonverbal communication. *Personality & Individual Differences, 9,* 965–972.

Akinnaso, F. N. (1982). On the differences between spoken and written language. *Language and Speech, 25* (Part 2), 97–125.

Albas, D. C., McCluskey, K. W., & Albas, C. A. (1976). Perception of the emotional content of speech: A comparison of two Canadian groups. *Journal of Cross-Cultural Psychology, 7* (December), 481–490.

Alessandra, T. (1986). *How to listen effectively, speaking of success* (Video Tape Series). San Diego, CA: Levitz Sommer Productions.

Al-Simadi, F. A. (2000). Detection of deception behavior: A cross-cultural test. *Social Behavior & Personality, 28,* 455–461.

Altman, I. (1975). *The environment and social behavior.* Monterey, CA: Brooks/Cole.

Altman, I., & Taylor, D. (1973). *Social penetration: The development of interpersonal relationships.* New York: Holt, Rinehart & Winston.

Andersen, P. (1991). Explaining intercultural differences in nonverbal communication. In L. A. Samovar & R. E. Porter, eds., *Intercultural communication: A reader* (6th ed., pp. 286–296). Belmont, CA: Wadsworth.

Andersen, P. A., & Leibowitz, K. (1978). The development and nature of the construct touch avoidance. *Environmental Psychology and Nonverbal Behavior, 3,* 89–106.

Angier, N. (1995, May 9). Scientists mull role of empathy in man and beast. *New York Times,* pp. C1, C6.

Argyle, M. (1986). Rules for social relationships in four cultures. *Australian Journal of Psychology, 38* (December), 309–318.

Argyle, M. (1988). *Bodily communication* (2nd ed.). New York: Methuen.

Argyle, M., & Henderson, M. (1984). The rules of friendship. *Journal of Social and Personal Relationships, 1* (June), 211–237.

Argyle, M., & Ingham, R. (1972). Gaze, mutual gaze, and distance. *Semiotica, 1,* 32–49.

Arliss, L. P. (1991). *Gender communication.* Englewood Cliffs, NJ: Prentice-Hall.

Armstrong, C. B., & Rubin, A. M. (1989). Talk radio as interpersonal communication. *Journal of Communication, 39* (Spring), 84–94.

Aronson, E., Wilson, T. D., & Akert, R. M. (1999). *Social psychology: The heart and the mind* (3rd ed.). New York: Longman.

Asch, S. (1946). Forming impressions of personality. *Journal of Abnormal and Social Psychology, 41,* 258–290.

Aspinwall, L. G., & Taylor, S. E. (1993). Effects of social comparison direction, threat, and self-esteem on affect, evaluation, and expected success. *Journal of Personality and Social Psychology, 64,* 708–722.

Aune, K.-S., Buller, D. B., & Aune, R. K. (1996). Display rule development in romantic relationships: Emotion management and perceived appropriateness of emotions across relationship stages. *Human Communication Research, 23* (September), 115–145.

Aune, R. K., & Kikuchi, T. (1993). Effects of language intensity similarity on perceptions of credibility, relational attributions, and persuasion. *Journal of Language and Social Psychology, 12* (September), 224–238.

Axtell, R. E. (1990). *Do's and taboos of hosting international visitors.* New York: Wiley.

Axtell, R. E. (1992). *Do's and taboos of public speaking: How to get those butterflies flying in formation.* New York: Wiley.

Axtell, R. E. (1993). *Do's and taboos around the world* (3rd ed.). New York: Wiley.

Ayres, J. (1983). Strategies to maintain relationships: Their identification and perceived usage. *Communication Quarterly, 31,* 62–67.

Ayres, J. (1986). Perceptions of speaking ability: An explanation for stage fright. *Communication Education, 35,* 275–287.

Ayres, J., Ayres, D. M., & Sharp, D. (1993). A progress report on the development of an instrument to measure communication apprehension in employment interviews. *Communication Research Reports, 10,* 87–94.

Ayres, J., & Hopf, T. S. (1992). Visualization: Reducing speech anxiety and enhancing performance. *Communication Reports, 5,* 1–10.

Ayres, J., & Hopf, T. S. (1993). *Coping with speech anxiety.* Norwood, NJ: Ablex.

Ayres, J., Hopf, T. S., & Ayres, D. M. (1994). An examination of whether imaging ability enhances the effectiveness of an intervention designed to reduce speech anxiety. *Communication Education, 43* (July), 252–258.

Ayres, J., Hopf, T., & Ayres, D. M. (1997). Visualization and performance visualization: Applications, evidence, and speculation. In J. A. Daly, J. C. McCroskey, J. Ayres, T. S. Hopf, & D. M. Ayres, *Avoiding communication: Shyness, reticence, and communication apprehension* (2nd ed., pp. 401–419). Cresskill, NJ: Hampton Press.

Bach, G. R., & Wyden, P. (1968). *The intimate enemy.* New York: Avon.

Bailey, B. (1997). Communication of respect in interethnic service encounters. *Language in Society, 26* (September), 327–356.

Bales, R. F. (1950). *Interaction process analysis: A method for the study of small groups.* Cambridge, MA: Addison-Wesley.

Balswick, J. O., & Peck, C. (1971). The inexpressive male: A tragedy of American society? *The Family Coordinator, 20,* 363–368.

B-1

Banks, J. (1995, April). *MTV as gatekeeper and censor: A survey of the program service's attempts to impose its standards on U.S. popular music.* Paper presented at the Eastern Communication Association Convention, Pittsburgh, PA.

Barbato, C. A., & Perse, E. M. (1992). Interpersonal communication motives and the life position of elders. *Communication Research, 19,* 516–531.

Barge, J. K. (1994). *Leadership: Communication skills for organizations and groups.* New York: St. Martin's.

Barker, D. C. (1998). The talk radio community: Nontraditional social networks and political participation. *Social Science Quarterly, 79* (June), 261–272.

Barker, L. L., Edwards, R., Gaines, C., Gladney, K., & Holley, F. (1980). An investigation of proportional time spent in various communication activities by college students. *Journal of Applied Communication Research, 8,* 101–109.

Barker, L. L., & Gaut, D. (2002). *Communication* (8th ed.). Boston: Allyn & Bacon.

Barna, L. M. (1985). Stumbling blocks in intercultural communication. In L. A. Samovar & R. E. Porter (Eds.), *Intercultural communication: A reader* (4th ed., pp. 330–338). Belmont, CA: Wadsworth.

Barnlund, D. C. (1970). A transactional model of communication. In J. Akin, A. Goldberg, G. Myers, & J. Stewart (Eds.), *Language behavior: A book of readings in communication.* The Hague: Mouton.

Barnlund, D. C. (1989). *Communicative styles of Japanese and Americans: Images and realities.* Belmont, CA: Wadsworth.

Baron, R. A. (1990). Countering the effects of destructive criticism: The relative efficacy of four interventions. *Journal of Applied Psychology, 75* (June), 235–245.

Baron, R. A., & Byrne, D. (1984). *Social psychology: Understanding human interaction* (4th ed.). Boston: Allyn & Bacon.

Barrett, L., & Godfrey, T. (1988). Listening. *Person-Centered Review, 3* (November), 410–425.

Barron, J. (1995, January 11). It's time to mind your e-manners. *New York Times,* p. C1.

Basso, K. H. (1972). To give up on words: Silence in Apache culture. In P. P. Giglioli (Ed.), *Language and social context.* New York: Penguin.

Baxter, L. A. (1983). Relationship disengagement: An examination of the reversal hypothesis. *Western Journal of Speech Communication, 47,* 85–98.

Baxter, L. A. (1986). Gender differences in the heterosexual relationship rules embedded in break-up accounts. *Journal of Social and Personal Relationships, 3,* 289–306.

Baxter, L. A. (1988). A dialectical perspective on communication strategies in relationship development. In S. Duck (Ed.), *Handbook of Personal Relationships.* New York: Wiley.

Baxter, L. A. (1990). Dialectical contradictions in relationship development. *Journal of Social and Personal Relationships, 7* (February), 69–88.

Baxter, L. A., & Simon, E. P. (1993). Relationship maintenance strategies and dialectical contradictions in personal relationships. *Journal of Social and Personal Relationships, 10* (May), 225–242.

Beach, W. A. (1990–91). Avoiding ownership for alleged wrongdoings. *Research on Language and Social Interaction, 24,* 1–36.

Beatty, M. J. (1988). Situational and predispositional correlates of public speaking anxiety. *Communication Education, 37,* 28–39.

Bechler, C., & Johnson, S. D. (1995). Leadership and listening: A study of member perceptions. *Small Group Research, 26,* 77–85.

Becker, S. L., & Roberts, C. L. (1992). *Discovering mass communication* (3rd ed.). New York: HarperCollins.

Beebe, S. A., & Masterson, J. T. (2000). *Communicating in small groups: Principles and practices* (6th ed.). Boston: Allyn & Bacon.

Behzadi, K. G. (1994). Interpersonal conflict and emotions in an Iranian cultural practice: QAHR and ASHTI. *Culture, Medicine, and Psychiatry, 18* (September), 321–359.

Beier, E. (1974). How we send emotional messages. *Psychology Today, 8* (October), 53–56.

Bell, R. A., & Daly, J. A. (1984). The affinity-seeking function of communication. *Communication Monographs, 51,* 91–115.

Bell, S. T., Kuriloff, P. J., & Lottes, I. (1994). Understanding attributions of blame in stranger rape and date rape situations: An examination of gender, race, identification, and students' social perceptions of rape victims. *Journal of Applied Social Psychology, 24* (October), 1719–1734.

Benne, K. D., & Sheats, P. (1948). Functional roles of group members. *Journal of Social Issues, 4,* 41–49.

Bennett, M. (1990). Children's understanding of the mitigating function of disclaimers. *Journal of Social Psychology, 130* (February), 29–37.

Bennis, W., & Nanus, B. (1985). *Leaders: The strategies for taking charge.* New York: Harper & Row.

Berg, J. H., & Archer, R. L. (1983). The disclosure–liking relationship. *Human Communication Research, 10,* 269–281.

Berger, C. R., & Bradac, J. J. (1982). *Language and social knowledge: Uncertainty in interpersonal relations.* London: Edward Arnold.

Bernstein, W. M., Stephan, W. G., & Davis, M. H. (1979). Explaining attributions for achievement: A path analytic approach. *Journal of Personality and Social Psychology, 37,* 1810–1821.

Berry, J. W., Poortinga, Y. H., Segall, M. H., & Dasen, P. R. (1992). *Cross-cultural psychology: Research and applications.* NY: Cambridge University Press.

Blieszner, R., & Adams, R. G. (1992). *Adult friendship.* Thousand Oaks, CA: Sage.

Blumstein, P., & Schwartz, P. (1983). *American couples: Money, work, sex.* New York: Morrow.

Bochner, A. (1984). The functions of human communication in interpersonal bonding. In C. C. Arnold & J. W. Bowers (Eds.), *Handbook of rhetorical and communication theory* (pp. 544–621). Boston: Allyn & Bacon.

Bochner, A., & Kelly, C. (1974). Interpersonal competence: Rationale, philosophy, and implementation of a conceptual framework. *Communication Education, 23,* 279–301.

Bochner, A. P., & Yerby, J. (1977). Factors affecting instruction in interpersonal competence. *Communication Education, 26,* 91–103.

Bochner, S., & Hesketh, B. (1994). Power, distance, individualism/collectivism, and job-related attitudes in a culturally diverse work group. *Journal of Cross-Cultural Psychology, 25* (June), 233–257.

Bodon, J., Powell, L., & Hickson, M., III. (1999). Critiques of gatekeeping in scholarly journals: An analysis of perceptions and data. *Journal of the Association for Communication Administration, 28* (May), 60–70.

Bok, S. (1978). *Lying: Moral choice in public and private life.* New York: Pantheon.

Bok, S. (1983). *Secrets.* New York: Vintage.

Bok, S. (1998). *Mayhem: Violence as public entertainment.* Reading, MA: Perseus Books.

Bond, Jr., C. F., & Atoum, A. O. (2000). International deception. *Personality & Social Psychology Bulletin, 26* (March), 385–395.

Borden, G. (1991). *Cultural orientation: An approach to understanding intercultural communication.* Englewood Cliffs, NJ: Prentice-Hall.

Bosmajian, H. (1974). *The language of oppression.* Washington, D.C.: Public Affairs Press.

Bourland, D. D., Jr. (1965–66). A linguistic note: Writing in E-prime. *General Semantics Bulletin, 32–33,* 111–114.

Brauer, M., Judd, C. M., & Gliner, M. D. (1995). The effects of repeated expressions on attitude polarization during group discussions. *Journal of Personality and Social Psychology, 68* (June), 1014–1029.

Bravo, E., & Cassedy, E. (1992). *The 9 to 5 guide to combating sexual harassment.* New York: Wiley.

Brennan, M. (1991). Mismanagement and quality circles: How middle managers influence direct participation. *Employee Relations, 13,* 22–32.

Bridges, C. R. (1996). The characteristics of career achievement perceived by African American college administrators. *Journal of Black Studies, 26* (July), 748–767.

Brilhart, J., & Galanes, G. (1992). *Effective group discussion* (7th ed.). Dubuque, IA: Brown & Benchmark.

Brody, J. E. (1991, April 28). How to foster self-esteem. *New York Times Magazine,* pp. 26–27.

Brody, J. E. (1994, March 21). Notions of beauty transcend culture, new study suggests. *New York Times,* p. A14.

Brody, L. R. (1985). Gender differences in emotional development: A review of theories and research. *Journal of Personality, 53* (June), 102–149.

Brown, J. D., & Schulze, L. (1990). The effects of race, gender, and fandom on audience interpretations of Madonna's music videos. *Journal of Communication, 40* (Spring), 88–102.

Brown, P., & Levinson, S. C. (1988). *Politeness: Some universals of language usage.* NY: Cambridge University Press.

Brown, P. (1980). How and why are women more polite: Some evidence from a Mayan community. In S. McConnell-Ginet, R. Borker, & M. Furman (Eds.), *Women and language in literature and society* (pp. 111–136). New York: Praeger.

Brownell, J. (1987). Listening: The toughest management skill. *Cornell Hotel and Restaurant Administration Quarterly, 27,* 64–71.

Bruneau, T. (1985). The time dimension in intercultural communication. In L. A. Samovar & R. E. Porter (Eds.), *Intercultural communication: A reader* (4th ed., pp. 280–289). Belmont, CA: Wadsworth.

Bruneau, T. (1990). Chronemics: The study of time in human interaction. In J. A. Devito & M. L. Hecht (Eds.), *The nonverbal communication reader* (pp. 301–311). Prospect Heights, IL: Waveland Press.

Bugental, J., & Zelen, S. (1950). Investigations into the "self-concept": I. The W-A-Y technique. *Journal of Personality, 18,* 483–498.

Bull, R., & Rumsey, N. (1988). *The social psychology of facial appearance.* New York: Springer-Verlag.

Buller, D. B., & Aune, R. K. (1992). The effects of speech rate similarity on compliance: Application of communication accommodation theory. *Western Journal of Communication, 56* (Winter), 37–53.

Buller, D. B., LePoire, B. A., Aune, K., & Eloy, S. (1992). Social perceptions as mediators of the effect of speech rate similarity on compliance. *Human Communication Research, 19* (December), 286–311.

Burgoon, J. K. (1978). A communication model of personal space violations: Explication and an initial test. *Human Communication Research, 4,* 129–142.

Burgoon, J. K. (1991). Relational message interpretations of touch, conversational distance, and posture. *Journal of Nonverbal Behavior, 15* (Winter), 233–259.

Burgoon, J. K., Berger, C. R., & Waldron, V. R. (2000). Mindfulness and interpersonal communication. *Journal of Social Issues, 56,* 105–127.

Burgoon, J. K., Buller, D. B., & Woodall, W. G. (1996). *Nonverbal communication: The unspoken dialogue* (2nd ed.). New York: McGraw-Hill.

Burgoon, M. (1971). The relationship between willingness to manipulate others and success in two different types of basic speech communication courses. *Communication Education, 20,* 178–183.

Burke, N. D. (1993). Restricting gang clothing in the public schools. *West's Education Law Quarterly, 2* (July), 391–404.

Burleson, B. R., Kunkel, A. W., & Birch, J. D. (1994). Thoughts about talk in romantic relationships: Similarity makes for attraction (and happiness, too). *Communication Quarterly, 42* (Summer), 259–273.

Burleson, B. R., Samter, W., & Luccetti, A. E. (1992). Similarity in communication values as a predictor of friendship choices: Studies of friends and best friends. *Southern Communication Journal, 57,* 260–276.

Busse, W. M., & Birk, J. M. (1993). The effects of self-disclosure and competitiveness on friendship for male graduate students over 35. *Journal of College Student Development, 34* (May), 169–174.

Butler, P. E. (1981). *Talking to yourself: Learning the language of self-support.* New York: Harper & Row.

Callan, V. J. (1993). Subordinate-manager communication in different sex dyads: Consequences for job satisfaction. *Journal of Occupational & Organizational Psychology, 66* (March), 1–15.

Canary, D. J., Cupach, W. R., & Messman, S. J. (1995). *Relationship conflict.* Thousand Oaks, CA: Sage.

Canary, D. J., & Hause, K. S. (1993). Is there any reason to research sex differences in communication? *Communication Quarterly, 41* (Spring), 129–144.

Canary, D. J., & Stafford, L. (1994a). *Communication and relational maintenance.* San Diego, CA: Academic Press.

Canary, D. J., & Stafford, L. (1994b). Maintaining relationships through strategic and routine interaction. In D. J. Canary & L. Stafford (Eds.), *Communication and relational maintenance.* San Diego, CA: Academic Press.

Canary, D. J., Stafford, L., Hause, K. S., & Wallace, L. A. (1993). An inductive analysis of relational maintenance strategies: Comparisons among lovers, relatives, friends, and others. *Communication Research Reports, 10* (June), 5–14.

Cappella, J. N. (1993). The facial feedback hypothesis in human interaction: Review and speculation. *Journal of Language and Social Psychology, 12* (March–June), 13–29.

Carducci, B. J., with P. G. Zimbardo (1995). Are you shy? *Psychology Today, 28* (November–December), pp. 34–41, 64–70, 78–82.

Carle, G. (1995, Spring). 10 reasons why talk shows are good for you. *All Talk,* p. 27.

Cassell, M. M., Jackson, C., & Cheuvront, B. (1998). Health communication in the Internet: An effective channel for health behavior change? *Journal of Health Communication, 3* (January–March), 71–79.

Castleberry, S. B., & Shepherd, D. D. (1993). Effective interpersonal listening and personal selling. *Journal of Personal Selling and Sales Management, 13,* 35–49.

Cate, R., Henton, J., Koval, J., Christopher, R., & Lloyd, S. (1982). Premarital abuse: A social psychological perspective. *Journal of Family Issues, 3,* 79–90.

Cathcart, D., & Cathcart, R. (1985). Japanese social experience and concept of groups. In L. A. Samovar & R. E. Porter (Eds.), *Intercultural communication: A reader* (4th ed., pp. 190–197). Belmont, CA: Wadsworth.

Cegala, D. J., Savage, G. T., Brunner, C. C., & Conrad, A. B. (1982). An elaboration of the meaning of interaction involvement. *Communication Monographs, 49,* 229–248.

Chadwick-Jones, J. K. (1976). *Social exchange theory: Its structure and influence in social psychology.* New York: Academic Press.

Chaney, R. H., Givens, C. A., Aoki, M. F., & Gombiner, M. L. (1989). Pupillary responses in recognizing awareness in persons with profound mental retardation. *Perceptual and Motor Skills, 69* (October), 523–528.

Chang, H.-C., & Holt, G. R. (1996). The changing Chinese interpersonal world: Popular themes in interpersonal communication books in modern Taiwan. *Communication Quarterly, 44* (Winter), 85–106.

Chanowitz, B., & Langer, E. (1981). Premature cognitive commitment. *Journal of Personality and Social Psychology, 41,* 1051–1063.

Chen, G.-M. (1990). Intercultural communication competence: Some perspectives of research. *The Howard Journal of Communication, 2* (Summer), 243–261.

Chen, G.-M. (1992). *Differences in self-disclosure patterns among Americans versus Chinese: A comparative study.* Paper presented at the annual meeting of the Eastern Communication Association, Portland, ME.

Cheney, G. & Tompkins, P. K. (1987). Coming to terms with organizational identification and commitment. *Central States Speech Journal, 38* (Spring), 1–15.

Cherulnik, P. D. (1979). Sex differences in the expression of emotion in a structured social encounter. *Sex Roles, 5* (August), 413–424.

Christie, R. (1970a). The Machiavellis among us. *Psychology Today, 4* (November), pp. 82–86.

Christie, R. (1970b). Scale construction. In R. Christie & F. L. Geis (Eds.), *Studies in Machiavellianism* (pp. 35–52). New York: Academic Press.

Cialdini, R. T. (1984). *Influence: How and why people agree to things.* New York: Morrow.

Cialdini, R. T., & Ascani, K. (1976). Test of a concession procedure for inducing verbal, behavioral, and further compliance with a request to give blood. *Journal of Applied Psychology, 61,* 295–300.

Coates, E. J., & Feldman, R. S. (1996). Gender differences in nonverbal correlates of social status. *Personality and Social Psychology Bulletin, 22* (October), 1014–1022.

Coates, J. (1986). *Women, men and language.* New York: Longman.

Cohen, C. E. (1983). Inferring the characteristics of other people: Categories and attribute accessibility. *Journal of Personality and Social Psychology, 44,* 34–44.

Cohen, J. (2001, January 18). On the Internet, love really is blind. *New York Times,* pp. G1, G9.

Cole, T., & Leets, L. (1999). Attachment styles and intimate television viewing: Insecurely forming relationships in a parasocial way. *Journal of Social and Personal Relationships, 16* (August), 495–511.

Collier, M. J. (1991). Conflict competence within African, Mexican, and Anglo-American friendships. In S. Ting-Toomey & F. Korzenny (Eds.), *Cross-cultural interpersonal communication* (pp. 132–154). Thousand Oaks, CA: Sage.

Collins, C. L., & Gould, O. N. (1994). Getting to know you: How own age and other's age relate to self-disclosure. *International Journal of Aging and Human Development, 39,* 55–66.

Comadena, M. E. (1984). Brainstorming groups: Ambiguity tolerance, communication apprehension, task attraction, and individual productivity. *Small Group Behavior, 15,* 251–254.

Cook, M. (1971). *Interpersonal perception.* Baltimore, MD: Penguin.

Cooley, C. H. (1922). *Human nature and the social order* (Rev. ed.). New York: Scribners.

Copeland, L., & Griggs, L. (1985). *Going international: How to make friends and deal effectively in the global marketplace.* New York: Random House.

Coupland, N., Coupland, J., Giles, H., Henwood, K., et al. (1988). Elderly self-disclosure: Interactional and intergroup issues. *Language & Communication, 8,* 109–133.

Cragan, J. F., & Wright, D. W. (1990). Small group communication research of the 1980s: A synthesis and critique. *Communication Studies, 41* (Fall), 212–236.

Crohn, J. (1995). *Mixed matches.* New York: Fawcett.

Crown, C. L., & Cummins, D. A. (1998). Objective versus perceived vocal interruptions in the dialogues of unacquainted pairs, friends, and couples. *Journal of Language and Social Psychology, 17* (September), 372–389.

Dainton, M., & Stafford, L. (1993). Routine maintenance behaviors: A comparison of relationship type, partner similarity, and sex differences. *Journal of Social and Personal Relationships, 10,* 255–272.

Daly, J. A., McCroskey, J. C., Ayres, J., Hopf, T., & Ayres, D. M. (1997). *Avoiding communication: Shyness, reticence, and communication apprehension* (2nd ed.). Cresskill, NJ: Hampton Press.

Darley, J. M., & Oleson, K. C. (1993). Introduction to research on interpersonal expectations. In P. D. Blanck (Ed.), *Interpersonal expectations: Theory, research, and applications. Studies in emotion and social interaction* (pp. 45–63). New York: Cambridge University Press.

Davis, K. (1977). The care and cultivation of the corporate grapevine. In R. Huseman, C. Logue, & D. Freshley (Eds.), *Readings in interpersonal and organizational communication* (3rd ed., pp. 131–136). Boston: Holbrook.

Davis, K. (1980). Management communication and the grapevine. In S. Ferguson & S. D. Ferguson (Eds.), *Intercom: Readings in organizational communication* (pp. 55–66). Rochelle Park, NJ: Hayden Books.

Davis, M. S. (1973). *Intimate relations*. New York: Free Press.

Davison, W. P. (1983). The third-person effects and the differential impact in negative political advertising. *Journalism Quarterly, 68*, 680–688.

Davitz, J. R. (Ed.). (1964). *The communication of emotional meaning*. New York: McGraw-Hill.

Deal, J. E., & Wampler, K. S. (1986). Dating violence: The primacy of previous experience. *Journal of Social and Personal Relationships, 3*, 457–471.

deBono, E. (1976). *Teaching thinking*. New York: Penguin.

deBono, E. (1987). *The six thinking hats*. New York: Penguin.

DeFrancisco, V. (1991). The sound of silence: How men silence women in marital relations. *Discourse and Society, 2*, 413–423.

DeGroot, T., & Motowidlo, S. J. (1999). Why visual and vocal interview cues can affect interviewers' judgments and predict job performance. *Journal of Applied Psychology, 84* (December), 986–993.

DeJong, W. (1979). An examination of self-perception mediation of the foot-in-the-door effect. *Journal of Personality and Social Psychology, 37*, 2221–2239.

DePaulo, B. M. (1992). Nonverbal behavior and self-presentation. *Psychological Bulletin, 111*, 203–212.

Derlega, V. J., Winstead, B. A., Wong, P. T. P., & Greenspan, M. (1987). Self-disclosure and relationship development: An attributional analysis. In M. E. Roloff & G. R. Miller (Eds.), *Interpersonal processes: New directions in communication research* (pp. 172–187). Thousand Oaks, CA: Sage.

Derlega, V. J., Winstead, B. A., Wong, P. T. P., & Hunter, S. (1985). Gender effects in an initial encounter: A case where men exceed women in disclosure. *Journal of Social and Personal Relationships, 2*, 25–44.

Derne, S. (1999). Making sex violent: Love as force in recent Hindi films. *Violence against Women, 5* (May), 548–575.

DeStephen, R., & Hirokawa, R. (1988). Small group consensus: Stability of group support of the decision, task process, and group relationships. *Small Group Behavior 19*, 227–239.

DeTurck, M. A. (1987). When communication fails: Physical aggression as a compliance-gaining strategy. *Communication Monographs, 54*, 106–112.

DeVito, J. A. (1974). *General semantics: Guide and workbook* (Rev. ed.). DeLand, FL: Everett/Edwards.

DeVito, J. A. (1996). *Brainstorms: How to think more creatively about communication (or about anything else)*. New York: Longman.

DeVito, J. A. (2000). *The elements of public speaking* (7th ed.). New York: Longman.

Dewey, J. (1910). *How we think*. Boston: Heath.

Dickenson-Hazard, N. (1998, June 1). Nursing: The next millennium. *Vital Speeches of the Day*, 493–495.

Dietz, T. L. (1998). An examination of violence and gender role portrayals in video games: Implications for gender socialization and aggressive behavior. *Sex Roles, 38* (March), 425–442.

Dindia, K., & Baxter, L. A. (1987). Strategies for maintaining and repairing marital relationships. *Journal of Social and Personal Relationships, 4*, 143–158.

Dindia, K., & Fitzpatrick, M. A. (1985). Marital communication: Three approaches compared. In S. Duck & D. Perlman (Eds.), *Understanding personal relationships: An interdisciplinary approach* (pp. 137–158). Thousand Oaks, CA: Sage.

Dodd, C. H. (1995). *Dynamics of intercultural communication* (4th ed.). Dubuque, IA: William C. Brown.

Dolgin, K. G., Meyer, L., & Schwartz, J. (1991). Effects of gender, target's gender, topic, and self-esteem on disclosure to best and middling friends. *Sex Roles, 25*, 311–329.

Dominick, J. R. (2000). *The dynamics of mass communication* (6th ed.). New York: McGraw-Hill.

Donaldson, S. (1992). Gender and discourse: The case of interruptions. *Carleton Papers in Applied Language Studies, 9*, 47–66.

Donohue, W. A., with Kolt, R. (1992). *Managing interpersonal conflict*. Thousand Oaks, CA: Sage.

Dresser, N. (1996). *Multicultural manners: New rules of etiquette for a changing society*. New York: Wiley.

Dreyfuss, H. (1971). *Symbol sourcebook*. New York: McGraw-Hill.

Driskell, J., Olmstead, B., & Salas, E. (1993). Task cues, dominance cues, and influence in task groups. *Journal of Applied Psychology, 78* (February), 51–60.

Drucker, S. J., & Gumpert, G. (1991). Public space and communication: The zoning of public interaction. *Communication Theory, 1* (November), 294–310.

Dsilva, M. U., & Whyte, L. O. (1998). Cultural differences in conflict styles: Vietnamese refugees and established residents. *The Howard Journal of Communications, 9* (January–March), 57–68.

Duncan, S. D., Jr. (1972). Some signals and rules for taking speaking turns in conversation. *Journal of Personality and Social Psychology, 23*, 283–292.

Duran, R. L., & Kelly, L. (1988). The influence of communicative competence on perceived task, social, and physical attractiveness. *Communication Quarterly, 36*, 41–49.

Eagly, A. H., & Crowley, M. (1986). Gender and helping behavior: A meta-analytic review of the social psychological literature. *Psychological Bulletin, 100* (November), 283–308.

Eakins, B., & Eakins, R. G. (1978). *Sex differences in communication*. Boston: Houghton Mifflin.

Edelstein, A. S. (1993). Thinking about the criterion variable in agenda-setting research. *Journal of Communication, 43*, 85–99.

Eden, D. (1992). Leadership and expectations: Pygmalion effects and other self-fulfilling prophecies in organizations. *Leadership Quarterly, 3* (Winter), 271–305.

Eder, D., & Enke, J. L. (1991). The structure of gossip: Opportunities and constraints on collective expression among adolescents. *American Sociological Review, 56*, 494–508.

Ehrenhaus, P. (1988). Silence and symbolic expression. *Communication Monographs, 55* (March), 41–57.

Einstein, E. (1995). Success or sabotage: Which self-fulfilling prophecy will the stepfamily create? In D. K. Huntley (Ed.), *Understanding stepfamilies: Implications for assessment and treatment*. Alexandria, VA: American Counseling Association.

Ekman, P. (1985). *Telling lies: Clues to deceit in the marketplace, politics, and marriage*. New York: Norton.

Ekman, P., & Friesen, W. V. (1969). The repertoire of nonverbal behavior: Categories, origins, usage, and coding. *Semiotica, 1*, 49–98.

Ekman, P., Friesen, W. V., & Ellsworth, P. (1972). *Emotion in the human face: Guidelines for research and an integration of findings*. New York: Pergamon Press.

Ellis, A. (1988). *How to stubbornly refuse to make yourself miserable about anything, yes anything.* Secaucus, NJ: Lyle Stuart.

Ellis, A., & Harper, R. A. (1975). *A new guide to rational living.* Hollywood, CA: Wilshire Books.

Emmers-Sommer, T. M., & Allen, M. (1999). Surveying the effect of media effects: A meta-analytic summary of the media effects research in *Human Communication Research*. *Human Communication Research, 25* (June), 478–497.

Epley, N., & Dunning, D. (2000). Feeling "holier than thou": Are self-serving assessments produced by errors in self- or social prediction? *Journal of Personality and Social Psychology, 79* (December), 861–875.

Esten, G., & Willmott, L. (1993). Double-bind messages: The effects of attitude towards disability on therapy. *Women and Therapy, 14,* 29–41.

Exline, R. V., Ellyson, S. L., & Long, B. (1975). Visual behavior as an aspect of power role relationships. In P. Pliner, L. Krames, & T. Alloway (Eds.), *Nonverbal communication of aggression.* New York: Plenum Press.

Festinger, L. (1954). A theory of social comparison processes. *Human Relations, 7,* 117–140.

Field, R. H. G. (1989). The self-fulfilling prophecy leader: Achieving the Metharme Effect. *Journal of Management Studies, 26* (March), 151–175.

Fischer, A. H. (1993). Sex differences in emotionality: Fact or stereotype? *Feminism & Psychology, 3,* 303–318.

Fiske, S. T., & Taylor, S. E. (1984). *Social cognition.* Reading, MA: Addison-Wesley.

Fitzpatrick, M. A. (1983). Predicting couples' communication from couples' self-reports. In R. N. Bostrom (Ed.), *Communication Yearbook 7* (pp. 49–82). Thousand Oaks, CA: Sage.

Fitzpatrick, M. A. (1988). *Between husbands and wives: Communication in marriage.* Thousand Oaks, CA: Sage.

Fitzpatrick, M. A. (1991). Sex differences in marital conflict: Social psychophysiological versus cognitive explanations. *Text, 11,* 341–364.

Foddy, M., & Crundall, I. (1993). A field study of social comparison processes in ability evaluation. *British Journal of Social Psychology, 32* (December), 287–305.

Folger, J. P., Poole, M. S., & Stutman, R. K. (1997). *Working through conflict: A communication perspective* (3rd ed.). New York: Longman.

Folkerts, J., & Lacy, S. (2001). *The media in your life: An introduction to mass communication* (2nd ed.). Boston: Allyn & Bacon.

Fraser, B. (1990). Perspectives on politeness. *Journal of Pragmatics, 14* (April), 219–236.

Fraser, Christopher O. (2000). The social goals of excuses: Self-serving attributions or politeness strategies. *Journal of Applied Social Psychology, 30* (March), 599–611.

Frederikse, M. E., Lu, A., Aylward, E., Barta, P., & Pearlson, G. (1999). Sex differences in the inferior parietal lobule. *Cerebral Cortex, 9,* 869–901.

Freedman, J., & Fraser, S. (1966). Compliance without pressure: The foot-in-the-door technique. *Journal of Personality and Social Psychology, 4,* 195–202.

French, J. R. P., Jr., & Raven, B. (1968). The bases of social power. In D. Cartwright & A. Zander (Eds.), *Group dynamics: Research and theory* (3rd ed., pp. 259–269). New York: Harper & Row.

Frentz, T. (1976). *A general approach to episodic structure.* Paper presented at the Western Speech Association Convention, San Francisco, CA. Cited in Reardon (1987).

Frey, K. J., & Eagly, A. H. (1993). Vividness can undermine the persuasiveness of messages. *Journal of Personality and Social Psychology, 65* (July), 32–44.

Friedkin, N. E. (1999). Choice shift and group polarization. *American Sociological Review, 64* (December), 856–875.

Frymier, A. B., & Schulman, G. M. (1995). "What's in it for me?": Increasing content relevance to enhance students' motivation. *Communication Education, 44* (January), 40–50.

Frymier, A. B., & Thompson, C. A. (1992). Perceived teacher affinity-seeking in relation to perceived teacher credibility. *Communication Education, 41* (October), 388–399.

Furlow, F. B. (1996). The smell of love. *Psychology Today* (March/April), 38–45.

Furnham, A., & Bitar, N. (1993). The stereotyped portrayal of men and women in British television advertisements. *Sex Roles, 29* (August), 297–310.

Furnham, A., & Bochner, S. (1986). *Culture shock: Psychological reactions to unfamiliar environments.* New York: Methuen.

Gabriel, Y. (1998). An introduction to the social psychology of insults in organizations. *Human Relations, 51* (November), 1329–1354.

Gabrielides, C., Stephan, W. G., Ybarra, O., Pearson, V. M. D. S., & Villareal, L. (1997). Preferred styles of conflict resolution: Mexico and the United States. *Journal of Cross-Cultural Psychology, 28* (November), 661–677.

Gamson, J. (1998). Publicity traps: Television talk shows and lesbian, gay, bisexual, and transgender visibility. *Sexualities, 1* (February), 11–41.

Gao, G. (1991). Stability of romantic relationships in China and the United States. In S. Ting-Toomey & F. Korzenny (Eds.), *Cross-cultural interpersonal communication* (pp. 99–115). Thousand Oaks, CA: Sage.

Gaziano, C., & McGrath, K. (1986). Measuring the concept of credibility. *Journalism Quarterly, 63,* 451–462.

Gelles, R., & Coarnell, C. (1985). *Intimate violence in families.* Thousand Oaks, CA: Sage.

Gerbner, G., Cross, L. P., Morgan, M., & Signorielli, N. (1980). The "mainstreaming" of America: Violence profile no. 11. *Journal of Communication, 30,* 10–29.

Gergen, K. J., Greenberg, M. S., & Willis, R. H. (1980). *Social exchange: Advances in theory and research.* New York: Plenum Press.

Giles, H., Mulac, A., Bradac, J. J., & Johnson, P. (1987). Speech accommodation theory: The first decade and beyond. In M. L. McLaughlin (Ed.), *Communication yearbook 10* (pp. 13–48). Thousand Oaks, CA: Sage.

Giordano, J. (1989). *Telecommuting and organizational culture: A study of corporate consciousness and identification.* Unpublished doctoral dissertation, University of Massachusetts, Amherst.

Glucksberg, S., & Danks, J. H. (1975). *Experimental psycholinguistics: An introduction.* Hillsdale, NJ: Erlbaum.

Goffman, E. (1971). *Relations in public: Microstudies of the public order.* New York: HarperCollins.

Goleman, D. (1995, February 14). For man and beast, language of love shares many traits. *New York Times,* pp. C1, C9.

Gonzalez, A., & Zimbardo, P. G. (1985). Time in perspective. *Psychology Today, 19,* 20–26.

Gonzenbach, W. J., King, C., & Jablonski, P. (1999). Homosexuals and the military: An analysis of the spiral of silence. *Howard Journal of Communication, 10* (October–December), 281–296.

Goode, E. (2000, August 8). How culture molds habits of thought. *New York Times,* pp. F1, F8.

Gorden, W. I., & Nevins, R. J. (1993). *We mean business: Building communication competence in business and professions.* New York: Longman.

Gordon, T. (1975). *P.E.T.: Parent effectiveness training.* New York: New American Library.

Gorham, B. W. (1999). Stereotypes and the media: So what? *Howard Journal of Communications, 10* (October–December), 229–247.

Goss, B., Thompson, M., & Olds, S. (1978). Behavioral support for systematic desensitization for communication apprehension. *Human Communication Research, 4,* 158–163.

Gottman, J. M., & Carrere, S. (1994). Why can't men and women get along? Developmental roots and marital inequities. In D. J. Canary & L. Stafford (Eds.), *Communication and relational maintenance* (pp. 203–229). San Diego, CA: Academic Press.

Gottman, J. M., & Levenson, R. W. (1999). Dysfunctional marital conflict: Women are being unfairly blamed. *Journal of Divorce and Remarriage, 31,* 1–17.

Gould, S. J. (1995, June 7). No more "wretched refuse." *New York Times,* p. A27.

Gouran, D. S., & Hirokawa, R. Y. (1986). Counteractive functions of communication in effective group decision-making. In R. Y. Hirokawa & M. S. Poole (Eds.), *Communication and group decision-making* (pp. 81–90). Thousand Oaks, CA: Sage.

Graham, E. E. (1994). Interpersonal communication motives scale. In R. B. Rubin, P. Palmgreen, & H. E. Sypher (Eds.), *Communication research measures: A sourcebook* (pp. 211–216). New York: Guilford.

Graham, E. E., Barbato, C. A., & Perse, E. M. (1993). The interpersonal communication motives model. *Communication Quarterly, 41,* 172–186.

Graham, J. A., & Argyle, M. (1975). The effects of different patterns of gaze, combined with different facial expressions, on impression formation. *Journal of Human Movement Studies, 1* (December), 178–182.

Graham, J. A., Bitti, P. R., & Argyle, M. (1975). A Cross-cultural study of the communication of emotion by facial and gestural cues. *Journal of Human Movement Studies, 1* (June), 68–77.

Grandey, A. A. (2000). Emotion regulation in the workplace: A new way to conceptualize emotional labor. *Journal of Occupational Health and Psychology, 5* (January), 95–110.

Grant, A. E., Guthrie, K. K., & Ball-Rokeach, S. J. (1991). Television shopping: A media system dependency perspective. *Communication Research, 18* (December), 773–798.

Grice, H. P. (1975). Logic and conversation. In P. Cole and J. L. Morgan (Eds.), *Syntax and semantics: Vol. 3. Speech Acts* (pp. 41–58). New York: Seminar Press.

Griffin, E. (1991). *A first look at communication theory.* New York: McGraw-Hill.

Gross, L. (1991). The contested closet: The ethics and politics of outing. *Critical Studies in Mass Communication, 8* (September), 352–388.

Grossin, W. (1987). Monochronic time, polychronic time and policies for development. *Studi di Sociologia, 25* (January–March),18–25.

Gudykunst, W. B. (1994). *Bridging differences: Effective intergroup communication* (2nd ed.). Thousand Oaks, CA: Sage.

Gudykunst, W. B., & Kim, Y. Y. (1992). *Communicating with strangers: An approach to intercultural communication* (2nd ed.). New York: Random House.

Gudykunst, W. B., & Ting-Toomey, S., with Chua, E. (1988). *Culture and interpersonal communication.* Thousand Oaks, CA: Sage.

Gudykunst, W. B. (Ed.). (1983). *Intercultural communication theory: Current perspectives.* Thousand Oaks, CA: Sage.

Guerrero, L. K., Eloy, S. V., & Wabnik, A. I. (1993). Linking maintenance strategies to relationship development and disengagement: A reconceptualization. *Journal of Social and Personal Relationships, 10,* 273–282.

Guerrero, L. K., & Andersen, P. A. (1994). Patterns of matching and initiation: Touch behavior and touch avoidance across romantic relationship stages. *Journal of Nonverbal Behavior, 18* (Summer), 137–153.

Guerrero, L. K., DeVito, J. A., & Hecht, M. L. (Eds.). (1999). *The nonverbal communication reader: Class and contemporary readings* (2nd ed.). Prospect Heights, IL: Waveland Press.

Gumpert, G., & Drucker, S. J. (1995). Place as medium: Exegesis of the cafe drinking coffee, the art of watching others, civil conversation—with excursions into the effects of architecture and interior design. *The Speech Communication Annual, 9* (Spring), 7–32.

Guo-Ming, C., & Starosta, W. J. (1995). Intercultural communication competence: A synthesis. In B. R. Burleson (Ed.), *Communication Yearbook 19.* Thousand Oaks, CA: Sage.

Haar, B. F., & Krahe, B. (1999). Strategies for resolving interpersonal conflicts in adolescence: A German-Indonesian comparison. *Journal of Cross-Cultural Psychology, 30* (November), 667–683.

Hackman, M. Z., & Johnson, C. E. (1991). *Leadership: A communication perspective.* Prospect Heights, IL: Waveland Press.

Haferkamp, C. J. (1991–92). Orientations to conflict: Gender, attributions, resolution strategies, and self-monitoring. *Current Psychology Research and Reviews, 10* (Winter), 227–240.

Hall, E. T. (1959). *The silent language.* Garden City, NY: Doubleday.

Hall, E. T. (1963). A system for the notation of proxemic behavior. *American Anthropologist, 65,* 1003–1026.

Hall, E. T. (1976). *Beyond culture.* Garden City, NY: Doubleday.

Hall, E. T., & Hall, M. R. (1987). *Hidden differences: Doing business with the Japanese.* New York: Doubleday.

Hall, J. K. (1993). Tengo una bomba: The paralinguistic and linguistic conventions of the oral practice Chismeando. *Research on Language and Social Interaction, 26,* 55–83.

Halmari, H. (1995). The organization of episode structure in Finnish/Finnish and Finish/Anglo-American business telephone conversations: An intercultural perspective. ERIC Clearinghouse: FL022794 (Accession No. ED386914).

Hambrick, R. S. (1991). *The management skills builder: Self-directed learning strategies for career development.* New York: Praeger.

Haney, W. (1973). *Communication and organizational behavior: Text and cases* (3rd ed.). Homewood, IL: Irwin.

Harnack, A., & Kleppinger, E. (1997). *Online! The Internet guide for students and writers*. New York: St. Martin's.

Hatfield, E., & Rapson, R. L. (1996). *Love and sex: Cross-cultural perspectives*. Boston: Allyn & Bacon.

Havlena, W. J., Holbrook, M. B., & Lehmann, D. R. (1989). Assessing the validity of emotional typologies. *Psychology and Marketing, 6* (Summer), 97–112.

Hayakawa, S. I., & Hayakawa, A. R. (1990) *Language in thought and action* (5th ed.). New York: Harcourt Brace Jovanovich.

Hays, R. B. (1989). The day-to-day functioning of close versus casual friendships. *Journal of Social and Personal Relationships, 6*, 21–37.

Heap, J. L. (1992). Seeing snubs: An introduction to sequential analysis of classroom interaction. *Journal of Classroom Interaction, 27*, 23–28.

Heasley, J. B., Babbitt, C. E., & Burbach, H. J. (1995). Gender differences in college students' perceptions of "fighting words." *Sociological Viewpoints, 11* (Fall), 30–40.

Hecht, M. L. (1978a). The conceptualization and measurement of interpersonal communication satisfaction. *Human Communication Research, 4*, 253–264.

Hecht, M. L. (1978b). Toward a conceptualization of communication satisfaction. *Quarterly Journal of Speech, 64*, 47–62.

Hecht, M. L., Collier, M. J., & Ribeau, S. (1993). *African American communication: Ethnic identity and cultural interpretation*. Thousand Oaks, CA: Sage.

Heenehan, M. (1997). *Networking*. New York: Random House.

Heiskell, T. L., & Rychiak, J. F. (1986). The therapeutic relationship: Inexperienced therapists' affective preference and empathic communication. *Journal of Social and Personal Relationships, 3*, 267–274.

Hellweg, S. A. (1992). Organizational grapevines. In K. L. Hutchinson (Ed.), *Readings in organizational communication* (pp. 159–172). Dubuque, IA: William. C. Brown.

Hendrick, C., & Hendrick, S. (1990). A relationship-specific version of the love attitudes scale. In J. W. Heulip (Ed.), *Handbook of replication research in the behavioral and social sciences* [Special issue]. *Journal of Social Behavior and Personality, 5*, 239–254.

Henley, N. M. (1977). *Body politics: Power, sex, and nonverbal communication*. Englewood Cliffs, NJ: Prentice-Hall.

Hess, E. H. (1975). *The tell-tale eye*. New York: Van Nostrand Reinhold.

Hess, E. H., Seltzer, A. L., & Schlien, J. M. (1965). Pupil response of hetero- and homosexual males to pictures of men and women: A pilot study. *Journal of Abnormal Psychology, 70*, 165–168.

Hess, U., Kappas, A., McHugo, G. J., Lanzetta, J. T., et al. (1992). The facilitative effect of facial expression on the self-generation of emotion. *International Journal of Psychophysiology, 12* (May), 251–265.

Hewitt, J., & Stokes, R. (1975). Disclaimers. *American Sociological Review, 40*, 1–11.

Hilton, L. (2000). They heard it through the grapevine. *South Florida Business Journal, 21* (August), 53.

Hocker, J. L., & Wilmot, W. W. (1985). *Interpersonal conflict* (2nd ed.). Dubuque, IA: William C. Brown.

Hoffner, C., et al. (2001). The third-person effect in perceptions of the influence of television violence. *Journal of Communication, 51* (June), 283–299.

Hofstede, G. (1984). *Culture's consequences: International differences in work-related values*. Thousand Oaks, CA: Sage.

Hofstede, G. (1997). *Cultures and organizations: Software of the mind*. New York: McGraw-Hill.

Hofstede, G. (Ed.). (1998). *Masculinity and femininity: The taboo dimension of national cultures*. Thousand Oaks, CA: Sage.

Hofstetter, C. R., & Gianos, C. L. (1997). Political talk radio: Actions speak louder than words. *Journal of Broadcasting and Electronic Media, 41* (Fall), 501–515.

Hoft, N. L. (1995). *International technical communication: How to export information about high technology*. New York: Wiley.

Holden, J. M. (1991). The most frequent personality priority pairings in marriage and marriage counseling. *Individual Psychology Journal of Adlerian Theory, Research, and Practice, 47* (September), 392–398.

Holmes, J. (1986). Compliments and compliment responses in New Zealand English. *Anthropological Linguistics, 28*, 485–508.

Holmes, J. (1995). *Women, men and politeness*. New York: Longman.

Hosman, L. A. (1989). The evaluative consequences of hedges, hesitations, and intensifiers: Powerful and powerless speech styles. *Human Communication Research, 15*, 383–406.

Hunt, M. O. (2000). Status, religion, and the "belief in a just world": Comparing African Americans, Latinos, and whites. *Social Science Quarterly, 81* (March), 325–343.

Iizuka, Y. (1993). Regulators in Japanese conversation. *Psychological Reports, 72* (February), 203–209.

Imahori, T. T., & Cupach, W. R. (1994). A cross-cultural comparison of the interpretation and management of face: U.S. American and Japanese responses to embarrassing predicaments. *International Journal of Intercultural Relations, 18* (Spring), 193–219.

Infante, D. A. (1988). *Arguing constructively*. Prospect Heights, IL: Waveland Press.

Infante, D. A., & Rancer, A. S. (1982). A conceptualization and measure of argumentativeness. *Journal of Personality Assessment, 46*, 72–80.

Infante, D. A., & Rancer, A. S. (1995). Argumentativeness and verbal aggressiveness: A review of recent theory and research. In B. R. Burleson (Ed.), *Communication Yearbook 19*. Thousand Oaks, CA: Sage.

Infante, D. A., & Wigley, C. J. (1986). Verbal aggressiveness: An interpersonal model and measure. *Communication Monographs, 53*, 61–69.

Insel, P. M., & Jacobson, L. F. (Eds.). (1975). *What do you expect? An inquiry into self-fulfilling prophecies*. Menlo Park, CA: Cummings.

Jablin, F. M. (1981). Cultivating imagination: Factors that enhance and inhibit creativity in brainstorming groups. *Human Communication Research, 7*, 245–258.

Jacobs, A. J. (1995, December 8). Talkin' trash. *Entertainment Weekly*, pp. 42–43.

Jaffe, C. (1998). *Public speaking: Concepts and skills for a diverse society* (2nd ed.). Belmont, CA: Wadsworth.

Jaksa, J. A., & Pritchard, M. S. (1994). *Communication ethics: Methods of analysis* (2nd ed.). Belmont, CA: Wadsworth.

James, D. L. (1995). *The executive guide to Asia-Pacific communications*. New York: Kodansha International.

James, P., & Weingarten, J. (1995). *Internet guide for windows 95*. Research Triangle Park, NC: Ventana.

James-Catalano, C. N. (1996). *Researching on the World Wide Web*. Rocklin, CA: Prima.

Jamieson, K. H., & Campbell, K. K. (1992). *The interplay of influence* (3rd ed.). Belmont, CA: Wadsworth.

Jandt, F. E. (2000). *Intercultural communication* (3rd ed.). Thousand Oaks, CA: Sage.

Janis, I. (1983). *Victims of group thinking: A psychological study of foreign policy decisions and fiascoes* (2nd ed.). Boston: Houghton Mifflin.

Jaworski, A. (1993). *The power of silence: Social and pragmatic perspectives.* Thousand Oaks, CA: Sage.

Jecker, J., & Landy, D. (1969). Liking a person as a function of doing him a favor. *Human Relations, 22,* 371–378.

Johannesen, R. L. (1974). The functions of silence: A plea for communication research. *Western Speech, 38* (Winter), 25–35.

Johannesen, R. L. (1994). *Ethics in human communication* (5th ed.). Prospect Heights, IL: Waveland Press.

Johansson, W., & Percy, W. A. (1994). *Outing: Shattering the conspiracy of silence.* New York: Harrington Park Press.

Johnson, K. (1998, May 5). Self-image is suffering from lack of esteem. *New York Times,* p. F7.

Johnson, M. P. (1973). Commitment: A conceptual structure and empirical application. *Sociological Quarterly, 14,* 395–406.

Johnson, M. P. (1982). Social and cognitive features of the dissolution of commitment to relationships. In S. Duck (Ed.), *Personal Relationships: 4. Dissolving personal relationships* (pp. 51–73). New York: Academic Press.

Johnson, M. P. (1991). Commitment to personal relationships. In W. H. Jones & D. Perlman (Eds.), *Advances in personal relationships* (Vol. 3, pp. 117–143). London: Jessica Kingsley.

Johnson, S. A. (1993). *When "I love you" turns violent: Emotional and physical abuse in dating relationships.* Far Hills, NJ: New Horizon Press.

Johnson, S. D., & Bechler, C. (1998). Examining the relationships between listening effectiveness and leadership emergence: Perceptions, behaviors, and recall. *Small Group Research, 29* (August), 452–471.

Joiner, T. E. (1994). Contagious depression: Existence, specificity to depressed symptoms, and the role of reassurance seeking. *Journal of Personality and Social Psychology, 67,* 287–296.

Joinson, A. N. (2001). Self-disclosure in computer-mediated communication. The role of self-awareness and visual anonymity. *European Journal of Social Psychology, 31* (March–April), 177–192.

Jones, E. E., et al. (1984). *Social stigma: The psychology of marked relationships.* New York: W. H. Freeman.

Jones, E. E., & Davis, K. E. (1965). From acts to dispositions: The attribution process in person perception. In L. Berkowitz (Ed.), *Advances in experimental social psychology* (Vol. 2, pp. 219–266). New York: Academic Press.

Jones, S. (1986). Sex differences in touch communication. *Western Journal of Speech Communication, 50,* 227–241.

Jones, S., & Yarbrough, A. E. (1985). A naturalistic study of the meanings of touch. *Communication Monographs, 52,* 19–56. A version of this paper appears in DeVito and Hecht (1990).

Jourard, S. M. (1968). *Disclosing man to himself.* New York: Van Nostrand Reinhold.

Jourard, S. M. (1971a). *Self-disclosure.* New York: Wiley.

Jourard, S. M. (1971b). *The transparent self* (Rev. ed.). New York: Van Nostrand Reinhold.

Joyner, R. (1993). An auto-interview on the need for E-prime. *Etc.: A Review of General Semantics, 50* (Fall), 317–325.

Kanner, B. (1989, April 3). Color schemes. *New York Magazine,* pp. 22–23.

Kanter, A. B. (1995). *The essential book of interviewing: Everything you need to know from both sides of the table.* New York: Random House.

Kapoor, S., Wolfe, A., & Blue, J. (1995). Universal values structure and individualism–collectivism: A U.S. test. *Communication Research Reports, 12* (Spring), 112–123.

Kealey, D. J., & Ruben, B. D. (1983). Cross-cultural personnel selection criteria, issues, and methods. In D. Landis & R. W. Brislin (Eds.), *Handbook of intercultural training. Vol. 1: Issues in theory and design* (pp. 155–175). NY: Pergamon.

Kearney, P., Plax, T. G., Richmond, V. P., & McCroskey, J. C. (1984). Power in the classroom IV: Alternatives to discipline. In R. B. Bostrom (Ed.), *Communication Yearbook* (8th ed., pp. 724–746). Thousand Oaks, CA: Sage.

Kelley, H. H. (1979). *Personal relationships: Their structures and processes.* Hillsdale, NJ: Erlbaum.

Kelly, P. K. (1994). *Team decision-making techniques.* Irvine, CA: Richard Chang Associates.

Kennedy, C. W., & Camden, C. T. (1988). A new look at interruptions. *Western Journal of Speech Communication, 47,* 45–58.

Kennedy, J. L. (1996). *Job interviews for dummies.* NY: Hungry Minds.

Ketcham, H. (1958). *Color planning for business and industry.* New York: Harper.

Keyes, R. (1980). *The height of your life.* New York: Warner Books.

Kim, H. J. (1991). Influence of language and similarity on initial intercultural attraction. In S. Ting-Toomey & F. Korzenny (Eds.), *Cross-cultural interpersonal communication* (pp. 213–229). Thousand Oaks, CA: Sage.

Kim, M.-S., & Sharkey, W. F. (1995). Independent and interdependent construals of self: Explaining cultural patterns of interpersonal communication in multi-cultural organizational settings. *Communication Quarterly, 43* (Winter), 20–38.

Kim, S. H., & Smith, R. H. (1993). Revenge and conflict escalation. *Negotiation Journal, 9* (January), 37–43.

Kim, Y. Y. (1988). Communication and acculturation. In L. A. Samovar & R. E. Porter (Eds.), *Intercultural communication: A reader* (4th ed., pp. 344–354). Belmont, CA: Wadsworth.

Kindler, H. S. (1996). *Managing disagreement constructively* (Rev. ed.). Menlo Park, CA: Crisp Publications.

Kiraly, Z. (2000). The relationship between emotional self-disclosure of male and female adolescents' friendship. *Dissertation abstracts international: Section B. The Sciences and Engineering, 60* (February), 3619.

Kirby, D. (2001, January 30). Finessing interviews: Don't ask, do tell. *New York Times,* p. G2.

Klein, J. (Ed.). (1992). The E-prime controversy: A symposium [Special issue]. *Etc.: A Review of General Semantics, 49*(2).

Kleinfeld, N. R. (1992, October 25). The smell of money. *New York Times,* Section 9, pp. 1, 8.

Kleinke, C. L. (1986). *Meeting and understanding people.* New York: W. H. Freeman.

Kleinke, C. L., & Dean, G. O. (1990). Evaluation of men and women receiving positive and negative responses with various acquaintance strategies. *Journal of Social Behavior and Personality, 5,* 369–377.

Klineberg, O., & Hull, W. F. (1979). *At a foreign university: An international study of adaptation and coping.* New York: Praeger.

Knapp, M. L., & Hall, J. (1997). *Nonverbal behavior in human interaction* (4th ed.). New York: Holt, Rinehart & Winston.

Knapp, M. L., Hart, R. P., Friedrich, G. W., & Shulman, G. M. (1973). The rhetoric of goodbye: Verbal and nonverbal correlates of human leave-taking. *Communication Monographs, 40,* 182–198.

Knapp, M. L., & Taylor, E. H. (1995). Commitment and its communication in romantic relationships. In A. L. Weber & J. H. Harvey (Eds.), *Perspectives on close relationships* (pp. 153–175). Boston: Allyn & Bacon.

Knapp, M. L., & Vangelisti, A. L. (2000). *Interpersonal communication and human relationships* (4th ed.). Boston: Allyn & Bacon.

Kochman, T. (1981). *Black and white: Styles in conflict.* Chicago, IL: University of Chicago Press.

Kohn, A. (1989). Do religious people help more? Not so you'd notice. *Psychology Today* (December), 66–68.

Korzybski, A. (1933). *Science and sanity.* Lakeville, CT: International Non-Aristotelian Library.

Kposowa, A. J. (2000). Marital status and suicide in the National Longitudinal Mortality Study. *Journal of Epidemiology and Community Health, 54* (April), 254–261.

Kramarae, C. (1981). *Women and men speaking.* Rowley, MA: Newbury House.

Kramarae, C. (1999). The language and nature of the Internet: The meaning of Global English. *New Media & Society, 1* (April), 47–53.

Kramer, R. (1997). Leading by listening: An empirical test of Carl Rogers's theory of human relationship using interpersonal assessments of leaders by followers. *Dissertation Abstracts International: Section A. Humanities and Social Sciences, 58* (August), 0514.

Krebs, G. L. (1990). *Organizational communication* (2nd ed.). Boston: Allyn & Bacon, 1990.

Krivonos, P. D., & Knapp, M. L. (1975). Initiating communication: What do you say when you say hello? *Central States Speech Journal, 26,* 115–125.

Kurdek, L. A. (1994). Areas of conflict for gay, lesbian, and heterosexual couples: What couples argue about influences relationship satisfaction. *Journal of Marriage and the Family, 56* (November), 923–934.

Kurdek, L. A. (1995). Developmental changes in relationship quality in gay and lesbian cohabiting couples. *Developmental Psychology, 31* (January), 86–93.

Labott, S. M., Martin, R. B., Eason, P. S., & Berkey, E. Y. (1991). Social reactions to the expression of emotion. *Cognition and Emotion, 5* (September–November), 397–417.

Laing, M. (1993). Gossip: Does it play a role in the socialization of nurses? *Journal of Nursing Scholarship, 25* (Spring), 37–43.

Laing, R. D., Phillipson, H., & Lee, A. R. (1966). *Interpersonal perception.* New York: Springer.

Lamm, K., & Lamm, K. (1999). *10,000 ideas for term papers, projects, reports, and speeches* (5th ed.). New York: Arco.

Langer, E. J. (1989). *Mindfulness.* Reading, MA: Addison-Wesley.

Lanzetta, J. T., Cartwright-Smith, J., & Kleck, R. E. (1976). Effects of nonverbal dissimulations on emotional experience and autonomic arousal. *Journal of Personality and Social Psychology, 33,* 354–370.

Larsen, R. J., Kasimatis, M., & Frey, K. (1992). Facilitating the furrowed brow: An unobtrusive test of the facial feedback hypothesis applied to unpleasant affect. *Cognition and Emotion, 6* (September), 321–338.

Lawlor, J. (1998, August 27). Videoconferencing: From stage fright to stage presence. *New York Times,* p. G6.

Lazarsfeld, P. F., & Merton, R. K. (1951). Mass communication, popular taste, and organized social action. In L. Bryson (Ed.), *The communication of ideas* (pp. 95–118). NY: Harper & Row.

Lea, M., & Spears, R. (1995). Love at first byte? Building personal relationships over computer networks. In J. T. Wood & S. Duck (Eds.), *Under-studied relationships: Off the beaten track* (pp. 197–233). Thousand Oaks, CA: Sage.

Leaper, C., & Holliday, H. (1995). Gossip in same-gender and cross-gender friends' conversations. *Personal Relationships, 2* (September), 237–246.

Leathers, D. G. (1997). *Successful nonverbal communication: Principles and applications* (3rd ed.). New York: Macmillan.

Lebow, J. (1998). Not just talk, maybe some risk: The therapeutic potentials and pitfalls of computer-mediated conversation. *Journal of Marital and Family Therapy, 24* (April), 203–206.

Lederer, W. J. (1984). *Creating a good relationship.* New York: Norton.

Lee, A. M., & Lee, E. B. (1972). *The fine art of propaganda.* San Francisco: International Society for General Semantics.

Lee, A. M., & Lee, E. B. (1995). The iconography of propaganda analysis. *ETC.: A Review of General Semantics, 52* (Spring), 13–17.

Lee, J. A. (1976). *The colors of love.* New York: Bantam.

Lee, K. (2000, November 1). Information overload threatens employee productivity. *Employee Benefit News* (Securities Data Publishing, Inc.), p. 1.

Lee, R. L. M. (1984). Malaysian queue culture: An ethnography of urban public behavior. *Southeast Asian Journal of Social Science, 12,* 36–50.

Leung, K. (1987). Some determinants of reactions to procedural models for conflict resolution: A cross-national study. *Journal of Personality and Social Psychology, 53,* 898–908.

Leung, K. (1988). Some determinants of conflict avoidance. *Journal of Cross-Cultural Psychology, 19* (March), 125–136.

Lever, J. (1995, August 22). The 1995 *Advocate* survey of sexuality and relationships: The women, lesbian sex survey. *The Advocate,* 687/688, pp. 22–30.

Levesque, M. J. (1995). Excuses as a method of impression management: Toward an understanding of the determinants of excuse effectiveness. *Dissertation Abstractions International Section B: The Sciences and Engineering, 56* (August), 1150.

Levin, D. (2000). Virtual attraction: What rocks your boat. *CyberPsychology & Behavior, 3* (August), 565–573.

Lewin, K. (1947). *Human relations.* New York: Harper & Row.

Lewis, D. (1989). *The secret language of success.* New York: Carroll & Graf.

Lewis, M. (2001, July 15). Faking it. *The New York Times Magazine,* pp. 32–37, 44, 61–63.

Lewis, P. H. (1995, November 13). The new Internet gatekeepers. *New York Times,* pp. D1, D6.

Lindeman, M., Harakka, T., & Keltikangas-Jarvinen, L. (1997). Age and gender differences in adolescents' reactions to conflict situations: Aggression, prosociality, and withdrawal. *Journal of Youth and Adolescence, 26* (June), 339–351.

Loden, M. (1986, May 15). Feminine leadership. *Vital Speeches of the Day,* 472–475.

Lu, S. (1998, October 9). *Critical reflections on phatic communication research: schematizations, limitations and alternatives.* Paper delivered at the New York State Speech Communication Association, Monticello, New York.

Luft, J. (1969). *Of human interaction* (3rd ed.). Palo Alto, CA: Mayfield.

Luft, J. (1984). *Group processes: An introduction to group dynamics* (3rd ed.). Palo Alto, CA: Mayfield.

Lukens, J. (1978). Ethnocentric speech. *Ethnic Groups, 2,* 35–53.

Lumsden, G., & Lumsden, D. (1996). *Communicating in groups and teams* (2nd ed.). Belmont, CA: Wadsworth.

Lustig, M. W., & Koester, J. (1999). *Intercultural competence: Interpersonal communication across cultures* (3rd ed.). New York: Longman.

Ma, K. (1996). *The modern Madame Butterfly: Fantasy and reality in Japanese cross-cultural relationships.* Rutland, VT: Charles E. Tuttle.

Ma, R. (1992). The role of unofficial intermediaries in interpersonal conflicts in the Chinese culture. *Communication Quarterly, 40* (Summer), 269–278.

MacLachlan, J. (1979). What people really think of fast talkers. *Psychology Today, 13* (November), 113–117.

Maggio, R. (1997). *Talking about people: A guide to fair and accurate language.* Phoenix, AZ: Oryx Press.

Main, F., & Oliver, R. (1988). Complementary, symmetrical, and parallel personality priorities as indicators of marital adjustment. *Individual Psychology Journal of Adlerian Theory, Research, and Practice, 44* (September), 324–332.

Malandro, L. A., Barker, L., & Barker, D. A. (1989). *Nonverbal communication* (2nd ed.). New York: Random House.

Malinowski, B. (1923). The problem of meaning in primitive languages. In C. K. Ogden & I. A. Richards, *The meaning of meaning* (pp. 296–336). New York: Harcourt Brace Jovanovich.

Manes, J., & Wolfson, N. (1981). The compliment formula. In F. Coulmas (Ed.), *Conversational routines* (pp. 115–132). The Hague: Mouton.

Mao, L. R. (1994). Beyond politeness theory: "Face" revisited and renewed. *Journal of Pragmatics, 21* (May), 451–486.

Marien, M. (1992). *Vital Speeches of the Day* (March 15), 340–344.

Markman, H. J., Silvern, L., Clements, M., & Kraft-Hanak, S. (1993). Men and women dealing with conflict in heterosexual relationships. *Journal of Social Issues, 49* (Fall), 107–125.

Marsh, P. (1988). *Eye to eye: How people interact.* Topfield, MA: Salem House.

Marshall, E. (1983). *Eye language: Understanding the eloquent eye.* New York: New Trend.

Marshall, L. L., & Rose, P. (1987). Gender, stress, and violence in the adult relationships of a sample of college students. *Journal of Social and Personal Relationships, 4,* 299–316.

Martin, M. M., & Anderson, C. M. (1995). Roommate similarity: Are roommates who are similar in their communication traits more satisfied? *Communication Research Reports, 12* (Spring), 46–52.

Martin, M. M., & Rubin, R. B. (1994). Development of a communication flexibility measure. *The Southern Communication Journal, 59* (Winter), 171–178.

Martin, S. L., & Klimoski, R. J. (1990). Use of verbal protocols to trace cognitions associated with self- and supervisor evaluations of performance. *Organizational Behavior and Human Decision Processes, 46,* 135–154.

Maslow, A. (1970). *Motivation and personality.* NY: HarperCollins.

Mastin, T. (1998). Employees' understanding of employer-sponsored retirement plans: A knowledge gap perspective. *Public Relations Review, 24* (Winter), 521–534.

Matsumoto, D. (1991). Cultural influences on facial expressions of emotion. *Southern Communication Journal, 56* (Winter), 128–137.

Matsumoto, D. (1994). *People: Psychology from a cultural perspective.* Pacific Grove, CA: Brooks/Cole.

Matsumoto, D. (1996). *Culture and psychology.* Pacific Grove, CA: Brooks/Cole.

Matsumoto, D., & Kudoh, T. (1993). American-Japanese cultural differences in attributions of personality based on smiles. *Journal of Nonverbal Behavior, 17,* 231–243.

May, R. A. B. (1999). Tavern culture and television viewing: The influence of local viewing culture on patron's reception of television programs. *Journal of Contemporary Ethnography, 28* (February), 69–99.

McAuley, E., Blissmer, B., Katula, J., Duncan, T. E., & Mihalko, S. L. (2000). Physical activity, self-esteem, and self-efficacy relationships in older adults: A randomized controlled trial. *Annals of Behavioral Medicine, 22* (Spring), 131–139.

McCall, D. L., & Green, R. G. (1991). Symmetricality and complementarity and their relationship to marital stability. *Journal of Divorce and Remarriage, 15,* 23–32.

McCombs, M. E., Lopez-Escobar, E., & Llamas, J. P. (2000). Setting the agenda of attributes in the 1996 Spanish general election. *Journal of Communication, 50* (Spring), 77–92.

McCombs, M. E., & Shaw, D. L. (1972). The agenda-setting function of mass media. *Public Opinion Quarterly, 36,* 176–185.

McCombs, M. E., & Shaw, D. L. (1993). The evolution of agenda-setting research: Twenty-five years in the marketplace of ideas. *Journal of Communication, 43,* 58–67.

McCroskey, J. C. (1997). *Introduction to rhetorical communication* (7th ed.). Englewood Cliffs, NJ: Prentice-Hall.

McCroskey, J. C., & Richmond, V. P. (1995). Correlates of compulsive communication: Quantitative and qualitative characteristics. *Communication Quarterly, 43* (Winter), 39–52.

McCroskey, J., & Wheeless, L. (1976). *Introduction to human communication.* Boston: Allyn & Bacon.

McGill, M. E. (1985). *The McGill report on male intimacy.* New York: Harper & Row.

McGuire, W. J. (1964). Inducing resistance to persuasion: Some contemporary approaches. In L. Berkowitz (Ed.), *Advances in experimental social psychology* (Vol. 1, pp. 191–229). New York: Academic Press.

McKerrow, R. E., Gronbeck, B. E., Ehninger, D., & Monroe, A. H. (2000). *Principles and types of speech communication* (14th ed.). Boston: Allyn & Bacon.

McLaughlin, M. L. (1984). *Conversation: How talk is organized.* Thousand Oaks, CA: Sage.

McLean, P. A., & Jones, B. D. (1992). Machiavellianism and business education. *Psychological Reports, 71* (August), 57–58.

McLoyd, V., & Wilson, L. (1992). Telling them like it is: The role of economic and environmental factors in single mothers' discussions with their children. *American Journal of Community Psychology, 20* (August), 419–444.

Mehrabian, A. (1976). *Public places and private spaces*. New York: Basic Books.

Merton, R. K. (1957). *Social theory and social structure*. New York: Free Press.

Messick, R. M., & Cook, K. S. (Eds.). (1983). *Equity theory: Psychological and sociological perspectives*. New York: Praeger.

Metts, S. (1989). An exploratory investigation of deception in close relationships. *Journal of Social and Personal Relationships, 6* (May), 159–179.

Meyer, J. R. (1994). Effect of situational features on the likelihood of addressing face needs in requests. *Southern Communication Journal, 59* (Spring), 240–254.

Midooka, K. (1990). Characteristics of Japanese style communication. *Media, Culture and Society, 12* (October), 477–89.

Miller, D. T., Turnbull, W., & McFarland, C. (1988). Particularistic and universalistic evaluation in the social comparison process. *Journal of Personality and Social Psychology, 55* (December), 908–917.

Miller, G. R. (1978). The current state of theory and research in interpersonal communication. *Human Communication Research, 4*, 164–178.

Miller, G. R., & Burgoon, J. (1990). Factors affecting assessments of witness credibility. In J. A. DeVito & M. L. Hecht (Eds.), *The nonverbal communication reader* (pp. 340–357). Prospect Heights, IL: Waveland Press.

Miller, G. R., & Parks, M. R. (1982). Communication in dissolving relationships. In S. Duck (Ed.), *Personal relationships. 4: Dissolving personal relationships*. New York: Academic Press.

Miller, J. G. (1984). Culture and the development of everyday social explanation. *Journal of Personality and Social Psychology, 46*, 961–978.

Miller, M. J., & Wilcox, C. T. (1986). Measuring perceived hassles and uplifts among the elderly. *Journal of Human Behavior and Learning, 3*, 38–46.

Mok, T. A. (1998a). Asian Americans and standards of attractiveness: What's in the eye of the beholder? *Cultural Diversity & Mental Health, 4*, 1–18.

Mok, T. A. (1998b). Getting the message: Media images and stereotypes and their effect on Asian Americans. *Cultural Diversity and Ethnic Minority Psychology, 4*, 185–202.

Molloy, J. (1975). *Dress for success*. New York: P. H. Wyden.

Molloy, J. (1977). *The woman's dress for success book*. NY: Warner Books.

Molloy, J. (1981). *Molloy's live for success*. New York: Bantam.

Montagu, A. (1971). *Touching: The human significance of the skin*. New York: Harper & Row.

Moon, D. G. (1966). Concepts of "culture": Implications for intercultural communication research. *Communication Quarterly, 44* (Winter), 70–84.

Morales, J. (1995, May 2). London: Death by outing. *The Advocate, 680*, pp. 20–22.

Morgan, M., & Shanahan, J. (1991). Television and the cultivation of political attitudes in Argentina. *Journal of Communication, 41*, (Winter), 88–103.

Morreale, S. P., Osborn, M. M., & Pearson, J. C. (2000). Why communication is important: A rationale for the centrality of the study of communication. *Journal of the Association for Communication Administration, 29* (January), 1–25.

Morris, D. (1977). *Manwatching: A field guide to human behavior*. New York: Abrams.

Mullen, B., Tara, A., Salas, E., & Driskell, J. E. (1994). Group cohesiveness and quality of decision making: An integration of tests of the groupthink hypothesis. *Small Group Research, 25* 189–204.

Muller, B., Salas, E., & Driskell, J. (1989). Salience, motivation, and artifact as contributions to the relation between participation rate and leadership. *Journal of Experimental Social Psychology, 25* (November), 545–559.

Murata, K. (1994). Intrusive or co-operative? A cross-cultural study of interruption. *Journal of Pragmatics, 21* (April), 385–400.

Murphy, R. (1958). The speech as literary genre. *Quarterly Journal of Speech, 44* (April), 117–27.

Naifeh, S., & Smith, G. W. (1984). *Why can't men open up? Overcoming men's fear of intimacy*. New York: Clarkson N. Potter.

Naisbitt, J. (1984). *Megatrends: Ten new directions transforming our lives*. New York: Warner.

Nakanishi, M. (1986). Perceptions of self-disclosure in initial interaction: A Japanese sample. *Human Communication Research, 13* (Winter), 167–190.

Napier, R. W., & Gershenfeld, M. K. (1992). *Groups: Theory and experience* (5th ed.). Boston: Houghton Mifflin.

National Institute of Mental Health. (1982). *Television and behavior: Ten years of scientific progress and implications for the eighties*. Rockville, MD: National Institute of Mental Health.

Neugarten, B. (1979). Time, age, and the life cycle. *American Journal of Psychiatry, 136*, 887–894.

Ng, S. H., Loong, C. S. F., He, A. P., Liu, J. H., & Weatherall, A. (2000). Communication correlates of individualism and collectivism: Talk directed at one or more addressees in family conversations. *Journal of Language and Social Psychology, 19* (March), 26–45.

Nice, M. L., & Katzev, R. (1998). Internet romantics: The frequency and nature of romantic on-line relationships. *CyberPsychology and Behavior, 1* (Fall), 217–223.

Nicotera, A. M., & Rancer, A. S. (1994). The influence of sex on self-perceptions and social stereotyping of aggressive communication predispositions. *Western Journal of Communication, 58* (Fall), 283–307.

Noble, B. P. (1994, August 14). The gender wars: Talking peace. *New York Times*, p. 21.

Noelle-Neumann, E. (1973). Return to the concept of powerful mass media. In H. Eguchi & K. Sata (Eds.), *Studies in broadcasting: An international annual of broadcasting science* (pp. 67–112). Tokyo: Nippon Hoso Kyokai.

Noelle-Neumann, E. (1980). Mass media and social change in developed societies. In G. C. Wilhoit & H. de Bock (Eds.), *Mass communication review yearbook* (Vol. 1, pp. 657–678). Thousand Oaks, CA: Sage.

Noelle-Neumann, E. (1991). The theory of public opinion: The concept of the spiral of silence. In J. A. Anderson (Ed.), *Communication yearbook 14* (pp. 256–287). Thousand Oaks, CA: Sage.

Noller, P. (1993). Gender and emotional communication in marriage: Different cultures or differential social power? In *Emotional communication, culture, and power* [Special issue]. *Journal of Language and Social Psychology, 12* (March–June), 132–152.

Noller, P., & Fitzpatrick, M. A. (1993). *Communication in family relationships*. Englewood Cliffs, NJ: Prentice-Hall.

Northouse, P. G. (1997). *Leadership: Theory and practice*. Thousand Oaks, CA: Sage.

Oatley, K., & Duncan, E. (1994). The experience of emotions in everyday life. *Cognition and Emotion, 8*, 369–381.

Oberg, K. (1960). Culture shock: Adjustment to new cultural environments. *Practical Anthropology, 7*, 177–182.

Offerman, L. R., & Hellman, P. S. (1997). Culture's consequences for leadership behavior: National values in action. *Journal of Cross-Cultural Psychology, 28* (May), 342–351.

Oggins, J., Veroff, J., & Leber, D. (1993). Perceptions of marital interaction among black and white newlyweds. *Journal of Personality and Social Psychology, 65* (September), 494–511.

O'Hair, D., Cody, M. J., Goss, B., & Krayer, K. J. (1988). The effect of gender, deceit orientation and communicator style on macro-assessments of honesty. *Communication Quarterly, 36*, 77–93.

O'Hair, D., Cody, M. J., & McLaughlin, M. L. (1981). Prepared lies, spontaneous lies, Machiavellianism, and nonverbal communication. *Human Communication Research, 7*, 325–339.

Olday, D., & Wesley, B. (1990). Intimate relationship violence among divorcees. *Free Inquiry in Creative Sociology, 18* (May), 63–71.

Osborn, A. (1957). *Applied imagination* (Rev. ed.). New York: Scribners.

Osborn, M., & Osborn, S. (2000). *Speaking in public* (5th ed.). Boston: Houghton Mifflin.

Oswald, R. F. (2000). A member of the wedding? Heterosexism and family ritual. *Journal of Social and Personal Relationships, 17* (June), 349–368.

Page, R. A., & Balloun, J. L. (1978). The effect of voice volume on the perception of personality. *Journal of Social Psychology, 105*, 65–72.

Parks, M. R. (1995). Webs of influence in interpersonal relationships. In C. R. Berger & M. E. Burgoon (Eds.), *Communication and social influence processes* (pp. 155–178). East Lansing: Michigan State University Press.

Parks, M. R., & Floyd, K. (1996). Making friends in cyberspace. *Journal of Communication, 46* (Winter): 80–97.

Parsons, C. K., Liden, R. C., & Bauer, T. N. (2001). Personal perception in employment interviews. In M. London (Ed.), *How people evaluate others in organizations* (pp. 67–90). Mahwah, NJ: Lawrence Erlbaum.

Patton, B. R., Giffin, K., & Patton, E. N. (1989). *Decision-making group interaction* (3rd ed.). New York: HarperCollins.

Pearson, J. C. (1980). Sex roles and self-disclosure. *Psychological Reports, 47*, 640.

Pearson, J. C., & Spitzberg, B. H. (1990). *Interpersonal communication: Concepts, components, and contexts* (2nd ed.). Dubuque, IA: William C. Brown.

Pearson, J. C., West, R., & Turner, L. H. (1995). *Gender and communication* (3rd. ed.). Dubuque, IA: William C. Brown.

Peck, J. (1995). TV talk shows as therapeutic discourse: The ideological labor of the televised talking cure. *Communication Theory, 5* (February), 58–81.

Penfield, J. (Ed.). (1987). *Women and language in transition.* Albany, NY: State University of New York Press.

Pennebaker, J. W. (1991). *Opening up: The healing power of confiding in others.* New York: Avon.

Peplau, L. A., & Perlman, D. (Eds.). (1982). *Loneliness: A sourcebook of current theory, research, and therapy.* New York: Wiley/Interscience.

Perlman, D., & Peplau, L. A. (1981). Toward a social psychology of loneliness. In S. Duck & R. Gilmour (Eds.), *Personal Relationships. 3: Personal Relationships in Disorder* (pp. 31–56). New York: Academic Press.

Perse, E. M., & Rubin, R. B. (1989). Attribution in social and parasocial relationhips. *Communication Research, 16* (February), 59–77.

Peters, R. (1987). *Practical intelligence: Working smarter in business and the professions.* New York: HarperCollins.

Peterson, C. C. (1996). The ticking of the social clock: Adults' beliefs about the timing of transition events. *International Journal of Aging and Human Development, 42*, 189–203.

Peterson, R. W. (1985). *Vital speeches of the day* (July), 549.

Petrocelli, W., & Repa, B. K. (1992). *Sexual harassment on the job.* Berkeley, CA: Nolo Press.

Petronio, S. (Ed.). (2000). *Balancing the secrets of private disclosures.* Mahwah, NJ: Erlbaum.

Petronio, S., & Bantz, C. (1991). Controlling the ramifications of disclosure: "Don't tell anybody but. . . ." *Journal of Language and Social Psychology, 10*, 263–269.

Petty, R. E., & Wegener, D. T. (1998). Attitude change: Multiple roles for persuasion variables. In D. T. Gilbert, S. T. Fiske, & G. Lindzey (Eds.), *The handbook of social psychology* (4th ed., Vol. 1, pp. 323–390). New York: McGraw-Hill.

Piot, C. D. (1993). Secrecy, ambiguity, and the everyday in Kabre culture. *American Anthropologist, 95* (June), 353–370.

Pittenger, R. E., Hockett, C. F., & Danehy, J. J. (1960). *The first five minutes.* Ithaca, NY: Paul Martineau.

Place, K. S., & Becker, J. A. (1991). The influence of pragmatic competence on the likeability of grade school children. *Discourse Processes, 14* (April–June), 227–241.

Plutchik, R. (1980). *Emotion: A psycho-evolutionary synthesis.* New York: Harper & Row.

Pollack, A. (1995, August 7). A cyberspace front in a multicultural war. *New York Times,* pp. D1, D4.

Porter, J. R., & Washington, R. E. (1993). Minority identity and self-esteem. *Annual Review of Sociology, 19*, 139–161.

Porter, R. H., & Moore, J. D. (1981). Human kin recognition by olfactory cues. *Physiology and Behavior, 27*, 493–495.

Porter, S., Brit, A. R., Yuille, J. C., & Lehman, D. R. (2000). Negotiating false memories: Interviewer and rememberer characteristics relate to memory distortion. *Psychological Science, 11* (November), 507–510.

Postman, N., & Powers, S. (1992). *How to watch TV news.* New York: Penguin.

Potter, W. J. (1986). Perceived reality and the cultivation hypothesis. *Journal of Broadcasting and Electronic Media, 30*, 159–174.

Potter, W. J., & Chang, I. C. (1990). Television exposure measures and the cultivation hypothesis. *Journal of Broadcasting and Electronic Media, 34*, 313–333.

Pratkanis, A. R. (2000). Altercasting as an influence tactic. In D. J. Terry & M. A. Hogg (Eds.), *Attitudes, behavior, and social context: The role of norms and group membership* (pp. 201–226). Mahwah, NJ: Erlbaum.

Pratkanis, A. R., & Aronson, E. (1991). *Age of propaganda: The everyday use and abuse of persuasion.* New York: W. H. Freeman.

Prisbell, M. (1994). Students' perceptions of teachers' use of affinity-seeking and its relationship to teachers' competence. *Perceptual and Motor Skills, 78* (April), 641–642.

Proctor, R. F. (1991). *An exploratory analysis of responses to owned messages in interpersonal communication.* Unpublished doctoral dissertation, Bowling Green University.

Prosky, P. S. (1992). Complementary and symmetrical couples. *Family Therapy, 19*, 215–221.

Prusank, D. T., Duran, R. L., & DeLillo, D. A. (1993). Interpersonal relationships in women's magazines: Dating and relating in the 1970s and 1980s. *Journal of Social and Personal Relationships, 10* (August), 307–320.

Pullum, Stephen J. (1991). Illegal questions in the selection interview: Going beyond contemporary business and professional communication textbooks. *Bulletin of the Association for Business Communication, 54* (September), 36–43.

Rabinowitz, F. E. (1991). The male-to-male embrace: Breaking the touch taboo in a men's therapy group. *Journal of Counseling and Development, 69* (July–August), 574–576.

Radford, M. L. (1998). Approach or avoidance? The role of nonverbal communication in the academic library user's decision to initiate a reference encounter. *Library Trends, 46* (Spring), 699–717.

Radford, M. L., Barnes, S. B., & Barr, L. R. (2002). *Web research: Selecting, evaluating and citing.* Boston: Allyn & Bacon.

Ramsey, S. J. (1981). The kinesics of femininity in Japanese women. *Language Sciences, 3,* 104–123.

Rancer, A. S. (1998). Argumentativeness. In J. C. McCroskey, J. A. Daly, M. M. Martin, & M. J. Beatty (Eds.), *Communication and personality: Trait perspectives* (pp. 149–170). Cresskill, NJ: Hampton Press.

Rancer, A. S., Kosberg, R. L., & Baukus, R. A. (1992). Beliefs about arguing as predictors of trait argumentativeness: Implications for training in argument and conflict management. *Communication Education, 41* (October), 375–387.

Raney, R. F. (2000, May 11). Study finds Internet of social benefit to users. *New York Times,* p. G7.

Rankin, P. (1929). Listening ability. *Proceedings of the Ohio State Educational Conference's Ninth Annual Session.*

Raven, R., Centers, C., & Rodrigues, A. (1975). The bases of conjugal power. In R. E. Cromwell & D. H. Olson (Eds.), *Power in families* (pp. 217–234). New York: Halsted Press.

Rawlins, W. K. (1989). A dialectical analysis of the tensions, functions, and strategic challenges of communication in young adult friendships. In J. A. Andersen (Ed.), *Communication yearbook 12* (pp. 157–189). Thousand Oaks, CA: Sage.

Rawlins, W. K. (1992). *Friendship matters: Communication, dialectics, and the life course.* Hawthorne, NY: Aldine DeGruyter.

Reardon, K. K. (1987). *Where minds meet: Interpersonal communication.* Belmont, CA.: Wadsworth.

Rector, M., & Neiva, E. (1996). Communication and personal relationships in Brazil. In W. B. Gudykunst, S. Ting-Toomey, & T. Nishida, *Communication in personal relationships across cultures* (pp. 156–173). Thousand Oaks, CA: Sage.

Reisman, J. M. (1979). *Anatomy of friendship.* Lexington, MA: Lewis.

Reisman, J. M. (1981). Adult friendships. In S. Duck & R. Gilmour (Eds.), *Personal relationships. 2: Developing personal relationships* (pp. 205–230). New York: Academic Press.

Reynolds, C. L., & Schnoor, L. G. (Eds.). (1991). *1989 championship debates and speeches.* Normal, IL: American Forensic Association.

Rich, A. L. (1974). *Interracial communication.* New York: Harper & Row.

Richards, I. A. (1951). Communication between men: The meaning of language. In H. von Foerster (Ed.), *Cybernetics, transactions of the eighth conference.*

Richmond, V. P., & McCroskey, J. C. (1998). *Communication: Apprehension, avoidance, and effectiveness* (5th ed.). Boston: Allyn & Bacon.

Riggio, R. E. (1987). *The charisma quotient.* New York: Dodd, Mead.

Roach, D. K. (1991). The influence and effects of gender and status on university instructor affinity-seeking behavior. *Southern Communication Journal, 57* (Fall), 73–80.

Roberts, W. (1987). *Leadership secrets of Attila the Hun.* New York: Warner.

Robinson, J., & McArthur, L. Z. (1982). Impact of salient vocal qualities on casual attribution for a speaker's behavior. *Journal of Personality and Social Psychology, 43,* 236–247.

Robinson, W. P. (1993). Lying in the public domain. *American Behavioral Scientist, 36* (January), 359–382.

Rodman, G. (2001). *Making sense of media: An introduction to mass communication.* Boston: Allyn & Bacon.

Rodriguez, M. (1988). Do Blacks and Hispanics evaluate assertive male and female characters differently? *Howard Journal of Communication, 1,* 101–107.

Rogers, C. (1970). *Carl Rogers on encounter groups.* New York: Harrow Books.

Rogers, C., & Farson, R. (1981). Active listening. In J. A. DeVito (Ed.), *Communication: Concepts and processes* (3rd ed., pp. 137–147). Englewood Cliffs, NJ: Prentice-Hall.

Rogers-Millar, E., & Millar, F. E. (1979). Domineeringness and dominance: A transactional view. *Human Communication Research* (Spring), 238–246.

Rollman, J. B., Krug, K., & Parente, F. (2000). The chat room phenomenon: Reciprocal communication in cyberspace. *CyberPsychology and Behavior, 3* (April), 161–166.

Rosenbaum, M. E. (1986). The repulsion hypothesis: On the nondevelopment of relationships. *Journal of Personality and Social Psychology, 51,* 1156–1166.

Rosenfeld, L. B. (1979). Self-disclosure avoidance: Why I am afraid to tell you who I am. *Communication Monographs, 46* (1979), 63–74.

Rosenfeld, L. B., & Bowen, G. L. (1991). Marital disclosure and marital satisfaction: Direct-effect versus interaction-effect Models. *Western Journal of Speech Communication, 55* (Winter), 69–84.

Rosenthal, R., & DePaulo, B. M. (1979). Sex differences in accommodation in nonverbal communication. In R. Rosenthal (Ed.), *Skill in nonverbal communication: Individual differences* (pp. 68–103). Cambridge, MA: Oelgeschlager, Gunn & Hain.

Rosenthal, R., & Jacobson, L. (1992). *Pygmalion in the classroom.* New York: Holt, Rinehart & Winston.

Rosnow, R. L. (1977). Gossip and marketplace psychology. *Journal of Communication, 27* (Winter), 158–163.

Rotello, G. (1995, April 18). The inning of outing. *The Advocate, 679,* p. 80.

Rothwell, J. D. (1992). *In mixed company: Small group communication.* Fort Worth, TX: Harcourt Brace Jovanovich.

Ruben, B. D. (1985). Human communication and cross-cultural effectiveness. In L. A. Samovar & R. E. Porter (Eds.), *Intercultural communication: A reader* (4th ed., pp. 338–356). Belmont, CA: Wadsworth.

Rubenstein, C. (1993, June 10). Fighting sexual harassment in schools. *New York Times,* p. C8.

Rubenstein, C., & Shaver, P. (1982). *In search of intimacy*. New York: Delacorte.

Rubin, A. M. (1994). News credibility scale. In R. B. Rubin, P. Palmgreen, & H. E. Sypher (Eds.), *Communication research measures: A source book*. New York: Guilford.

Rubin, A. M., Perse, E., & Powell, R. (1985). Loneliness, parasocial interaction, and local television news viewing. *Human Communication Research, 12*, 155–180.

Rubin, R. B. (1982). Assessing speaking and listening competence at the college level: The communication competency assessment instrument. *Communication Education, 31* (January), 19–32.

Rubin, R. B. (1985). The validity of the communication competency assessment instrument. *Communication Monographs, 52*, 173–185.

Rubin, R. B., Fernandez-Collado, C., & Hernandez-Sampieri, R. (1992). A cross-cultural examination of interpersonal communication motives in Mexico and the United States. *International Journal of Intercultural Relations, 16*, 145–157.

Rubin, R. B., & Martin, M. M. (1994). Development of a measure of interpersonal communication competence. *Communication Research Reports, 11*, 33–44.

Rubin, R. B., & Martin, M. M. (1998). Interpersonal communication motives. In J. C. McCroskey, J. A. Daly, M. M. Martin, & M. J. Beatty (Eds.), *Communication and personality: Trait perspectives* (pp. 287–307). Cresskill, NJ: Hampton Press.

Rubin, R. B., & McHugh, M. (1987). Development of parasocial interaction relationships. *Journal of Broadcasting and Electronic Media, 31*, 279–292.

Rubin, R. B., Perse, E. M., & Barbato, C. A. (1988). Conceptualization and measurement of interpersonal communication motives. *Human Communication Research, 14*, 602–628.

Rubin, R. B., & Rubin, A. M. (1992). Antecedents of interpersonal communication motivation. *Communication Quarterly, 40*, 315–317.

Rubin, Z. (1973). *Liking and loving: An invitation to social psychology*. New York: Holt.

Rubin, Z., & McNeil, E. B. (1985). *Psychology: Being human* (4th ed.). New York: Harper & Row.

Ruggiero, T. E. (2000). Uses and gratifications theory in the 21st century. *Mass Communication & Society, 3* (Winter), 3–37.

Rundquist, S. (1992). Indirectness: A gender study of Fluting Grice's maxims. *Journal of Pragmatics, 18* (November), 431–449.

Rusbult, C. E., & Buunk, B. P. (1993). Commitment processes in close relationships: An interdependence analysis. *Journal of Social and Personal Relationships, 10* (May), 175–204.

Ruscher, J. B. (2001). *Prejudiced communication: A social psychological perspective*. New York: Guilford.

Rutledge, T., & Linden, W. (2000). Self-deception predicts the development of hypertension. *Journal of Hypertension, 16*, 1–7.

Sabatelli, R. M., & Pearce, J. (1986). Exploring marital expectations. *Journal of Social and Personal Relationships, 3*, 307–321.

Salekin, R. T., Ogloff, J. R. P., McGarland, C., & Rogers, R. (1995). Influencing jurors' perceptions of guilt: Expression of emotionality during testimony. *Behavioral Sciences and the Law, 13* (Spring), 293–305.

Samovar, L. A., & Porter, R. E. (1995). *Communication between cultures* (2nd ed.). Belmont, CA: Wadsworth.

Sayre, S. (1992). T-shirt messages: Fortune or folly for advertisers? In S. R. Danna (Ed.), *Advertising and popular culture* (pp. 73–82). Bowling Green, OH: Bowling Green State University Popular Press.

Scandura, T. (1992). Mentorship and career mobility: An empirical investigation. *Journal of Organizational Behavior, 13*, 169–174.

Schaap, C., Buunk, B., & Kerkstra, A. (1988). Marital conflict resolution. In P. Noller & M. A. Fitzpatrick (Eds.), *Perspectives on marital interaction* (pp. 203–244). Philadelphia: Multilingual Matters.

Schachter, S. (1964). The interaction of cognitive and physiological determinants of emotional state. In L. Berkowitz (Ed.), *Advances in experimental social psychology*, Vol. 1. New York: Academic Press.

Schafer, M., & Crichlow, S. (1996). Antecedents of groupthink. *Journal of Conflict Resolution, 40* (September), 415–435.

Scherer, K. R. (1986). Vocal affect expression. *Psychological Bulletin, 99*, 143–165.

Scheufele, D. A., & Moy, P. (2000). Twenty-five years of the spiral of silence: A conceptual review and empirical outlook. *International Journal of Public Opinion Research, 12* (Spring), 3–28.

Schlenker, B. R., Pontari, B. A., & Christopher, A. N. (2001). Excuses and character: Personal and social implications of excuses. *Personality and Social Psychology Review, 5*, 15–32.

Schnoor, L. G. (Ed.). (1997). *Winning orations of the interstate oratorical association*. Mankato, MN: Interstate Oratorical Association.

Schnoor, L. G. (Ed.). (1999). *Winning orations of the interstate oratorical association*. Mankato, MN: Interstate Oratorical Association.

Schott, G., & Selwyn, N. (2000). Examining the "male, antisocial" stereotype of high computer users. *Journal of Educational Computing Research, 23*, 291–303.

Schramm, W., & Porter, W. E. (1982). *Men, women, messages and media: Understanding human communication*. NY: Harper & Row.

Schultz, B. G. (1996). *Communicating in the small group: Theory and practice* (2nd ed.). New York: HarperCollins.

Schwartz, M., and the Task Force on Bias-Free Language of the Association of American University Presses. (1995). *Guidelines for bias-free writing*. Bloomington, IN: Indiana University Press.

Seidman, I. E. (1991). *Interviewing as qualitative research: A guide for researchers in education and the social sciences*. New York: Teachers College, Columbia University.

Severin, W. J., with Tankard, J. W., Jr. (1988). *Communication theories* (2nd ed.). New York: Longman.

Shaffer, D. R., Pegalis, L. J., & Cornell, D. P. (1991). Interactive effects of social context and sex role identity on female self-disclosure during the acquaintance process. *Sex Roles, 24* (January), 1–19.

Shaffer, D. R., Pegalis, L. J., & Cornell, D. P. (1992). Gender and self-disclosure revisited: Personal and contextual variations in self-disclosure to same-sex acquaintants. *Journal of Social Psychology, 132* (June), 307–315.

Shannon, C. E., & Weaver, W. (1949). *The mathematical theory of communication*. Urbana, IL: University of Illinois Press.

Shannon, J. (1987). Don't smile when you say that. *Executive Female, 10*, 33, 43.

Shaw, M. E., & Gouran, D. S. (1990). Group dynamics and communication. In G. Dahnke & G. W. Clatterbuck (Eds.), *Human communication: Theory and research.* Belmont, CA: Wadsworth.

Shea, V. (1994). *Netiquette.* San Rafael, CA: Albion Books.

Shimanoff, S. B. (1985). Rules governing the verbal expression of emotions between married couples. *Western Journal of Speech Communication, 49* (Summer), 147–165.

Shimanoff, S. (1980). *Communication rules: Theory and research.* Thousand Oaks, CA: Sage.

Siegert, J. R., & Stamp, G. H. (1994). "Our first big fight" as a milestone in the development of close relationships. *Communication Monographs, 61* (December), 345–360.

Signorile, M. (1993). *Queer in America: Sex, the media, and the closets of power.* New York: Random House.

Signorielli, N., & Lears, M. (1992). Children, television, and concepts about chores: Attitudes and behaviors. *Sex Roles, 27* (August), 157–170.

Slade, M. (1995, February 19). We forgot to write a headline. But it's not our fault. *New York Times,* p. 5.

Smith, B. (1996). Care and feeding of the office grapevine. *Management Review, 85* (February), 6.

Smith, P. B., Dugan, S., Peterson, M. F., & Leung, K. (1998). Individualism: Collectivism and the handling of disagreement. *International Journal of Intercultural Relations, 22* (August), 351–367.

Smith, S. M., & Shaffer, D. R. (1991). Celerity and cajolery: Rapid speech may promote or inhibit persuasion through its impact on message elaboration. *Personality and Social Psychology Bulletin, 17* (December), 663–669.

Smith, S. M., & Shaffer, D. R. (1995). Speed of speech and persuasion: Evidence for multiple effects. *Personality and Social Psychology Bulletin, 21* (October), 1051–1060.

Smith-Lovin, L., & Brody, C. (1989). Interruptions in group discussions: The effects of gender and group composition. *American Sociological Review, 54* (June), 424–435.

Snyder, C. R. (1984). Excuses, excuses. *Psychology Today, 18,* 50–55.

Snyder, C. R., Higgins, R. L., & Stucky, R. J. (1983). *Excuses: Masquerades in search of grace.* New York: Wiley.

Snyder, M. (1987). *Public appearances, private realities.* New York: W. H. Freeman.

Snyder, M. (1992). A gender-informed model of couple and family therapy: Relationship enhancement therapy. *Contemporary Family Therapy: An International Journal, 14* (February), 15–31.

Solomon, G. B., et al. (1996). The self-fulfilling prophecy in college basketball: Implications for effective coaching. *Journal of Applied Sport Psychology, 8* (March), 44–59.

Sommer, R. (1969). *Personal space: The behavioral basis of design.* Englewood Cliffs, NJ: Prentice-Hall.

Sorenson, P. S., Hawkins, K., & Sorenson, R. L. (1995). Gender, psychological type and conflict style preferences. *Management Communication Quarterly, 9* (August), 115–126.

Spiers, C. J. (1998). Commitment and stability in lesbian relationships. *Dissertation Abstracts International Section B: The Sciences and Engineering, 59,* 3076.

Spitzberg, B. H. (1991). Intercultural communication competence. In L. A. Samovar & R. E. Porter (Eds.), *Intercultural communication: A reader* (pp. 353–365). Belmont, CA: Wadsworth.

Spitzberg, B. H., & Cupach, W. R. (1984). *Interpersonal communication competence.* Beverly Hills, CA: Sage.

Spitzberg, B. H., & Cupach, W. R. (1989). *Handbook of interpersonal competence research.* New York: Springer.

Spitzberg, B. H., & Hecht, M. L. (1984). A component model of relational competence. *Human Communication Research, 10,* 575–599.

Sprecher, S., & Metts, S. (1989). Development of the "romantic beliefs scale" and examination of the effects of gender and gender-role orientation. *Journal of Social and Personal Relationships, 6,* 387–411.

Staines, G. L., Pottick, K. J., & Fudge, D. A. (1986). Wives' employment and husbands' attitudes toward work and life. *Journal of Applied Psychology, 71,* 118–128.

Steil, L. K., Barker, L. L., & Watson, K. W. (1983). *Effective listening: Key to your success.* Reading, MA: Addison-Wesley.

Steinfatt, T. M. (1987). Personality and communication: Classic approaches. In J. C. McCroskey & J. A. Daly (Eds.), *Personality and interpersonal communication* (pp. 42–126). Thousand Oaks, CA: Sage.

Stephan, W. G., & Stephan, C. W. (1985). Intergroup anxiety. *Journal of Social Issues, 41,* 157–175.

Stephan, W. G., Stephan, C. W., Wenzel, B., & Cornelius, J. (1991). Intergroup interaction and self-disclosure. *Journal of Applied Social Psychology, 21* (August), 1370–1378.

Stewart, C. J., & Cash, W. B., Jr. (1997). *Interviewing: Principles and practices* (8th ed.). Dubuque, IA: William C. Brown.

Stratford, J. (1998). Women and men in conversation: A consideration of therapists' interruptions in therapeutic discourse. *Journal of Family Therapy, 20* (November), 383–394.

Strecker, I. (1993). Cultural variations in the concept of "face." *Multilingua 12,* 119–141.

Swim, J. K., & Hyers, L. L. (1999). Excuse me—what did you say?!: Women's public and private responses to sexist remarks. *Journal of Experimental Social Psychology, 35* (January), 68–88.

Tanaka, K. (1999). Judgments of fairness by just world believers. *Journal of Social Psychology, 139* (October), 631–638.

Tang, S., & Zuo, J. (2000). Dating attitudes and behaviors of American and Chinese college students. *The Social Science Journal, 37* (January), 67–78.

Tannen, D. (1990). *You just don't understand: Women and men in conversation.* New York: Morrow.

Tannen, D. (1994a). *Gender and discourse.* New York: Oxford University Press.

Tannen, D. (1994b). *Talking from 9 to 5: How women's and men's conversational styles affect who gets heard, who gets credit, and what gets done at work.* New York: Morrow.

Tannen, D. (2001). *I only say this because I love you: How the way we talk can make or break family relationships throughout our lives.* New York: Random House.

Taub, M. (1997). *Interviews.* Princeton, NJ: Princeton Review.

Tersine, R. J., & Riggs, W. E. (1980). The Delphi technique: A long-range planning tool. In S. Ferguson & S. D. Ferguson (Eds.), *Intercom: Readings in organizational communication* (pp. 366–373). Rochelle Park, NJ: Hayden Books.

Thibaut, J. W., & Kelley, H. H. (1986). *The social psychology of groups.* New Brunswick, NJ: Transaction.

Thorne, B., Kramarae, C., & Henley, N. (Eds.). (1983). *Language, gender and society.* Rowley, MA: Newbury House.

Tichenor, P. J., Donohue, G. A., & Olien, C. N. (1970). Mass media flow and differential growth in knowledge. *Public Opinion Quarterly, 34,* 159–170.

Ting-Toomey, S. (1985). Toward a theory of conflict and culture. *International and Intercultural Communication Annual, 9,* 71–86.

Ting-Toomey, S. (1986). Conflict communication styles in black and white subjective cultures. In Y. Y. Kim (Ed.), *Interethnic communication: Current research* (pp. 75–88). Thousand Oaks, CA: Sage.

Torbiorn, I. (1982). *Living abroad.* New York: Wiley.

Trager, G. L. (1958). Paralanguage: A first approximation. *Studies in Linguistics, 13,* 1–12.

Trager, G. L. (1961). The typology of paralanguage. *Anthropological Linguistics, 3,* 17–21.

Trower, P. (1981). Social skill disorder. In S. Duck & R. Gilmour (Eds.), *Personal relationships 3* (pp. 97–110). New York: Academic Press.

UCLA Internet report: Surveying the digital future (2000). Los Angeles: UCLA Center for Communication Policy.

Ueleke, W., et al. (1983). Inequity resolving behavior as a response to inequity in a hypothetical marital relationship. *A Quarterly Journal of Human Behavior, 20,* 4–8.

Ulfelder, S. (1997, July 14). Lies, damn lies and the Internet. *Computerworld, 31,* pp. 75ff.

UNESCO [United Nations Educational, Scientific, and Cultural Organization]. (1993). *World education report.* Paris: UNESCO Publishing.

Uris, A. (1986). *101 of the greatest ideas in management.* NY: Wiley.

Valenti, J. (1982). *Speaking up with confidence: How to prepare, learn, and deliver effective speeches.* New York: Morrow.

Verderber, R. (2000). *The challenge of effective speaking* (11th ed.). Belmont, CA: Wadsworth.

Vergeer, M., Lubbers, M., & Scheepers, P. (2000). Exposure to newspapers and attitudes toward ethnic minorities: A longitudinal analysis. *Howard Journal of Communication, 11* (April–June), 127–143.

Vernon, J. A., Williams, J. A., Phillips, T., & Wilson, J. (1990). Media stereotyping: A comparison of the way elderly women and men are portrayed on prime-time television. *Journal of Women and Aging, 4,* 55–68.

Victor, D. (1992). *International business communication.* New York: HarperCollins.

Viswanath, K., & Finnegan, J. R., Jr. (1995). The knowledge-gap hypothesis: Twenty-five years later. In B. R. Burleson (Ed.), *Communication yearbook 19.* Thousand Oaks, CA: Sage.

Vrij, A., & Mann, S. (2001). Telling and detecting lies in a high-stake situation: The case of a convicted murderer. *Applied Cognitive Psychology, 15* (March–April), 187–203.

Wade, Carole & Tavris, Carol (1998). *Psychology* (5th ed.). New York: Longman.

Wallace, K. (1955). An ethical basis of communication. *Communication Education, 4* (January), 1–9.

Walster, E., & Walster, G. W. (1978). *A new look at love.* Reading, MA: Addison-Wesley.

Walster, E., Walter, G. W., & Berscheid, E. (1978). *Equity: Theory and research.* Boston: Allyn & Bacon.

Walters, A. S., & Curran, M. C. (1996). "Excuse me, sir? May I help you and your boyfriend?": Salespersons' differential treatment of homosexual and straight customers. *Journal of Homosexuality, 31,* 135–152.

Watson, A. K., & Cadey H. D. (1984). Alleviating communication apprehension through rational emotive therapy: A comparative evaluation. *Communication Education, 33,* 257–266.

Watzlawick, P. (1977). *How real is real? Confusion, disinformation, communication: An anecdotal introduction to communications theory.* New York: Vintage.

Watzlawick, P. (1978). *The language of change: Elements of therapeutic communication.* New York: Basic Books.

Watzlawick, P., Beavin, J. H., & Jackson, D. D. (1967). *Pragmatics of human communication: A study of interactional patterns, pathologies, and paradoxes.* New York: Norton.

Weinberg, H. L. (1958). *Levels of knowing and existence.* New York: Harper & Row.

Weiner, B., Russell, D., & Lerman, D. (1979). "Affective consequences of causal ascriptions." In J. H. Harvey, W. J. Ickes, & R. F. Kidd (Eds.), *New directions in attribution research,* Vol. 2. Hillsdale, NJ: Erlbaum.

Weinstein, E. A., & Deutschberger, P. (1963). Some dimensions of altercasting. *Sociometry, 26,* 454–466.

Weinstein, F. (1995, April). Professionally speaking. *Profiles: The Magazine of Continental Airlines,* pp. 50–55.

Werner, E. K. (1975). *A study of communication time.* Unpublished master's thesis, University of Maryland, College Park. Cited in Wolvin and Coakley (1982).

Werrbach, G. B., Grotevant, H. D., & Cooper, C. R. (1990). Gender differences in adolescents' identity development in the domain of sex role concepts. *Sex Roles, 23* (October), 349–362.

Westwood, R. I., Tang, F. F., & Kirkbride, P. S. (1992). Chinese conflict behavior: Cultural antecedents and behavioral consequences. *Organizational Development Journal, 10* (Summer), 13–19.

Wetzel, P. J. (1988). Are "powerless" communication strategies the Japanese norm? *Language in Society, 17,* 555–564.

Wheeless, L. R., & Grotz, J. (1977). The measurement of trust and its relationship to self-disclosure. *Human Communication Research, 3,* 250–257.

Wigley, C. J., III. (1998). Verbal aggressiveness. In J. C. McCroskey, J. A. Daly, M. M. Martin, & M. J. Beatty (Eds.), *Communication and personality: Trait perspectives* (pp. 191–214). Cresskill, NJ: Hampton Press.

Wilkins, B. M., & Andersen, P. A. (1991). Gender differences and similarities in management communication: A meta-analysis. *Management Communication Quarterly, 5* (August), 6–35.

Wilmot, W. W. (1987). *Dyadic communication* (3rd ed.). New York: Random House.

Wilson, A. P., & Bishard, T. G. (1994). Here's the dirt on gossip. *American School Board Journal, 181* (December), 27–29.

Wilson, K. G., & Hayes, S. C. (2000). Why it is crucial to understand thinking and feeling: An analysis and application to drug abuse. *Behavior Analyst, 23* (Spring), 25–43.

Wilson, R. A. (1989). Toward understanding E-prime. *Etc.: A review of General Semantics, 46,* 316–319.

Windahl, S., & Signitzer, B., with Olson, J. T. (1992). *Using communication theory: An introduction to planned communication.* Thousand Oaks, CA: Sage.

Winquist, L. A., Mohr, C. D., & Kenny, D. A. (1998). The female positivity effect in the perception of others. *Journal of Research in Personality, 32* (September), 370–388.

Wispé, L. G., & Drambarean, N. C. (1953). Physiological need, word frequency, and visual duration thresholds. *Journal of Experimental Psychology, 46,* 25–31.

Withecomb, J. L. (1997). Causes of violence in children. *Journal of mental health, 5* (October), 433–442.

Wolfson, N. (1988). The bulge: A theory of speech behaviour and social distance. In J. Fine (Ed.), *Second language discourse: A textbook of current research* (pp. 21–38). Norwood, NJ: Ablex.

Wolfson, S. (2000). Students' estimates of the prevalence of drug use: Evidence for a false consensus effect. *Psychology of Addictive Behaviors, 14* (September), 295–298.

Wolpe, J. (1957). *Psychotherapy by reciprocal inhibition.* Stanford, CA: Stanford University Press.

Wolvin, A. D., & Coakley, C. G. (1982). *Listening.* Dubuque, IA: William C. Brown.

Won-Doornink, M.-J. (1985). Self-disclosure and reciprocity in conversation: A cross-national study. *Social Psychology Quarterly, 48,* 97–107.

Woodward, K. L. (1998, June 22). Religion: Using the bully pulpit? *Time,* p. 69.

Wright, J. W., & Hosman, L. W. (1983). Language style and sex bias in the courtroom: The effects of male and female use of hedges and intensifiers on impression formation. *Southern Speech Communication Journal, 48,* 137–152.

Young, K. S., et al. (2000). Online infidelity: A new dimension in couple relationships with implications for evaluation and treatment. *Sexual Addiction and Compulsivity, 7,* 59–74.

Zimmerman, A. (2000, November 10). If boys just want to have fun, this may bring them down. *Wall Street Journal,* pp. A1, A12.

Zincoff, M. Z., & Goyer, R. S. (1984). *Interviewing.* New York: Macmillan.

Zuckerman, M., Klorman, R., Larrance, D. T., & Spiegel, N. H. (1981). Facial, autonomic, and subjective components of emotion: The facial feedback hypothesis versus the externalizer–internalizer distinction. *Journal of Personality and Social Psychology, 41,* 929–944.

INDEX

The letters b, f, and t following page numbers indicate boxes, figures, and tables, respectively. G indicates a glossary entry. Entries in blue appear in the CD-ROM units.